FRIEDRICH ENGELS AND MARXIAN POLITICAL ECONOMY

This book rejects the commonly encountered perception of Friedrich Engels as perpetuator of a "tragic deception" of Marx, and the equally persistent body of opinion treating him as "his master's voice." Engels's claim to recognition is reinforced by an exceptional contribution in the 1840s to the very foundations of the Marxian enterprise, a contribution entailing not only the "vision" but some of the building blocks in the working out of that vision. Subsequently, he proved himself to be a sophisticated interpreter of the doctrine of historical materialism and an important contributor in his own right. This volume serves as a companion to Samuel Hollander's *The Economics of Karl Marx* (Cambridge University Press, 2008).

Samuel Hollander is University Professor Emeritus at the University of Toronto, Canada, where he served on the faculty from 1963 to 1998. An Officer of the Order of Canada and a Fellow of the Royal Society of Canada, Professor Hollander holds an honorary Doctorate of Law from McMaster University, Ontario, Canada, and was a Research Director at the Centre National de la Recherche Scientifique of France from 1999 to 2000. His major books have been devoted to studies of Adam Smith, David Ricardo, John Stuart Mill, Thomas Robert Malthus, Jean-Baptiste Say, and Karl Marx.

HISTORICAL PERSPECTIVES ON MODERN ECONOMICS

General Editor: Craufurd D. Goodwin, Duke University

This series contains original works that challenge and enlighten historians of economics. For the profession as a whole, it promotes better understanding of the origin and content of modern economics.

Other Books in the Series

Arie Arnon, *Monetary Theory and Policy from Hume and Smith to Wicksell: Money, Credit, and the Economy*

William J. Barber, *Designs within Disorder: Franklin D. Roosevelt, the Economists, and the Shaping of American Economic Policy, 1933–1945*

William J. Barber, *From New Era to New Deal: Herbert Hoover, the Economists, and American Economic Policy, 1921–1933*

Fillipo Cesarano, *Monetary Theory and Bretton Woods: The Construction of an International Monetary Order*

Timothy Davis, *Ricardo's Macroeconomics: Money, Trade Cycles, and Growth*

Jerry Evensky, *Adam Smith's Moral Philosophy: A Historical and Contemporary Perspective on Markets, Law, Ethics, and Culture*

M. June Flanders, *International Monetary Economics, 1870–1960: Between the Classical and the New Classical*

J. Daniel Hammond, *Theory and Measurement: Causality Issues in Milton Friedman's Monetary Economics*

Samuel Hollander, *The Economics of Karl Marx: Analysis and Application*

Lars Jonung (ed.), *The Stockholm School of Economics Revisited*

Kyun Kim, *Equilibrium Business Cycle Theory in Historical Perspective*

Gerald M. Koot, *English Historical Economics, 1870–1926: The Rise of Economic History and Mercantilism*

David Laidler, *Fabricating the Keynesian Revolution: Studies of the Inter-War Literature on Money, the Cycle, and Unemployment*

Odd Langholm, *The Legacy of Scholasticism in Economic Thought: Antecedents of Choice and Power*

Robert Leonard, *Von Neumann, Morgenstern, and the Creation of Game Theory*

Harro Maas, *William Stanley Jevons and the Making of Modern Economics*

Series list continues after the Index.

Friedrich Engels and Marxian Political Economy

SAMUEL HOLLANDER
University of Toronto, Canada

CAMBRIDGE
UNIVERSITY PRESS

CAMBRIDGE UNIVERSITY PRESS
Cambridge, New York, Melbourne, Madrid, Cape Town,
Singapore, São Paulo, Delhi, Mexico City

Cambridge University Press
32 Avenue of the Americas, New York, NY 10013-2473, USA

www.cambridge.org
Information on this title: www.cambridge.org/9780521761635

First published 2011
Reprinted 2012

A catalog record for this publication is available from the British Library.

Library of Congress Cataloging in Publication Data

Hollander, Samuel, 1937–
Friedrich Engels and Marxian Political Economy / Samuel Hollander.
   p.   cm. – (Historical Perspectives onModern Economics)
Includes bibliographical references and index.
ISBN 978-0-521-76163-5
1. Engels, Friedrich, 1820–1895 – Contributions in economics.
2. Marxian economics.   3. Historical materialism.   I. Title.
HX274.7.E5243H65 2011
335.4´12–dc22   2010046597

ISBN 978-0-521-76163-5 Hardback

To the memory of
Laurence S. Moss
1944–2009

"Without you, I would never had been able to bring the work to a conclusion, and I can assure you it always weighed like a nightmare on my conscience that you were allowing your fine energies to be squandered and to rust in commerce, chiefly for my sake, and, into the bargain, that you had to share all my *petites misères*."

(Marx to Engels, 7 May 1867; MECW *42*: 371)

"Even Engels was not right about everything. It wouldn't be a bad thing if we could implicate Engels somewhere in Bukharin's writing."

(Stalin, cited in Bullock 1993: 402)

Contents

Preface

This book is a companion to my *The Economics of Karl Marx* (*EKM*) published by Cambridge University Press in 2008. My objective is to contribute toward the better appreciation of the contribution to Marxian political economy made by Friedrich Engels. His positions on history and on the natural sciences are taken into account, but only insofar as they pertain to the primary theme. No consideration is accorded Engels as journalist or student of anthropology, law, literature, religion, sociology, linguistics, and military affairs. In Chapter Six I touch on matters of personality when I review Engels's relationship with Marx; in other contexts his business experience proves pertinent. Biography is certainly important, but I shall not provide a detailed account of Engels's life, because we are well served already, as by Carver, Henderson, Hunley, McLellan, Mayer, Riazanov, and, most recently, Hunt. Nonetheless, a brief chronology of select events pertaining to Engels to which I refer in the text and notes may prove helpful to readers, more helpful I think than a nominal potted life. This I provide in an Appendix to the Prolegomena.

Chapter One is devoted to Engels's early contributions to economics, before Marx had assembled his technical apparatus. Here I fulfill a promise made at the close of *EKM* to justify the contention that Engels provided the "vision" and entered into several of the processes at play in the working out of that vision (Hollander 2008: 488).

Two chapters deal with the complex issue of "revisionism." The first, on constitutional reform (Chapter Four), allows equal billing to Marx because this theme was left in abeyance in *EKM*. The second, on welfare reform within capitalism (Chapter Five), elaborates the account in *EKM*, taking particular notice of Engels's recognition in the last decade of his life – after Marx had passed from the scene – of ongoing structural changes in the British economy, and the implications to be drawn for the transition to communism.

I take this opportunity to thank attendees at several recent conference presentations for helpful comments on aspects of my Engels research: "Making the Most of Anomaly in the History of Economic Thought: Smith, Marx–Engels, and Keynes," Thomas Guggenheim Program in the History of Economic Thought, First

Bi-annual Symposium, Ben-Gurion University, Beer Sheba, Israel, 14 July 2009; "Engels and Marx on Economic Organization, Income Distribution, and the Price Mechanism," Halsworth Foundation Lecture, 41st Annual History of Economic Thought Conference (U.K.), University of Manchester, 2 September 2009; and "Understanding Engels (and Marx) and Adam Smith on Economic Organization and the Price Mechanism," The Heritage Foundation (Washington) and the Center for Political and Economic Thought, Saint Vincent College, La Trobe, Pennsylvania, USA, 2 November 2009.

I am greatly obliged to Professor John King and Professor Michael Perelman. This book has without question been much improved as a result of their advice and criticism, but I insist on taking full responsibility for the final outcome. A paper by Dr. Alain Alcouffe and Dr. Julian Wells entitled "Marx, Mathematics, and Mega 2," read at the aforementioned Manchester conference, proved most helpful to me when I composed Chapter Seven. It is a pleasure to acknowledge a profound debt to Haim Chertok – to my good fortune newly resident in Arad – for his efforts to improve the style of my manuscript and, more generally, for providing a little humor with which to confront the permanently (so it seems to me) unhappy state of this part of the world. Once again, I am pleased to express my appreciation to the Inter-Library Loan Department of the Aranne Library, Ben-Gurion University of the Negev, Beer Sheba, for its efficient and obliging service and to the Department of Economics for financial support in this regard. Thanks are also due to my granddaughter Jasmine Adi Hollander for library and computer assistance.

For permission to draw in Chapters Three and Seven on my article of 2004 "Economic Organization, Distribution and the Equality Issue: The Marx–Engels Perspective," *Review of Austrian Economics 17*: 5–39, I am obliged to Springer Publishing. A version of Chapter Four, entitled "Marx and Engels on Constitutional Reform vs. Revolution," appears in *Theoria: A Journal of Social and Political Theory*, Issue 122, 2010. I thank Berghahn Books New York for permission to make use of this article in the present work, and Professor David Reisman for his comments on that article.

I have been concerned in working on Engels with the "big" issues. However, there is much pleasure and benefit to be derived, I have found, from his wise observations regarding events of the day that often have immediate relevance for our own problems. Two favorites come to mind, one regarding a plan to sell the shares of insolvent banks to the state (1880, "The Socialism of Mr. Bismarck"; MECW *24*: 277–80), and a second regarding problems of parliamentary democracy (1891, "Introduction to Karl Marx, *The Civil War in France*"; MECW *27*: 189).

Arad, Israel
28 February 2011

Prolegomena

A. Some Ground Clearing

Gareth Stedman Jones refers to the "one-sidedness of most modern treatments of Engels.... For, from at least the end of World War I, assessment of Engels's particular contribution to Marxism had become a highly charged political question. After a period of unrivalled prestige, between the 1880s and 1914, Engels's reputation suffered first in the revolutionary leftish critique of the failings of the Second International and subsequently in the non-communist or anti-communist critique of the excesses of the Third" (1982: 290–1). Kircz and Löwy have phrased the state of affairs with felicity:

Too often we have seen attempts to create a kind of Holy Duality with semi-religious connotations. This type of hagiography, typical of the tradition of the Second and especially the Third International, not only hampers the proper understanding of the dynamics and historical role of the two friends, but also blocks the continuation and expansion of the program they started. As a reaction to this attitude we also encounter numerous attempts to artificially separate the two men, mostly with the objective of promoting Marx to the position of universal (and therefore politically neutralized) thinker and to degrade Engels to the position of an operationalist schema-builder and moral founder of social-democratic degeneration and the Stalinist nightmare. (1998: 5)

Hunt laments that "in certain ideological circles [Engels] has been landed with responsibility for the terrible excesses of twentieth-century Marxism-Leninism. For as Marx's stock has risen, so Engels's has fallen. Increasingly, the trend has been to separate off an ethical, humanist Karl Marx from a mechanical, scientistic Engels, and blame the latter for sanctifying the state crimes of communist Russia, China and south-east Asia" (2009: 5).

Beyond all this there is the frequently encountered condemnation of Engels as "revisionist" traitor to the cause, and also the suggestion that Engels (in the terms of Steger and Carver in their account of the state of play) "in his later writings – either mistakenly or intentionally – embarke[d] on a substantial reinterpretation of Marx's work, thereby significantly departing from the latter's intellectual

1

venture" (1999: 6). Publication of the original manuscripts relating to *Capital* in the *Karl Marx–Friedrich Engels Gesamtausgabe* (MEGA) edition has exacerbated matters by suggesting to some that Engels's editorial work on the last two volumes is unreliable (see Chapter Six, p. 308), which charge – if proven justified – would render the present work, based as it is on the *Marx–Engels Collected Works* (MECW), correspondingly suspect.[1] Further muddying the waters is what has been termed "the current fashion of Engels-baiting, which normally rests upon an exaggeration of Marx's Hegelian background, and vulgarization of Engels" (Duncan 1973: ix).

Against the assertion of a divorce between Marx and Engels, for one reason or another, stands an equally persistent body of opinion treating Engels merely as His Master's Voice (see below, p. 22). It will be a main objective of this work to seek a path between these extremes. Before proceeding to a review of the essays, though, let us briefly survey the first contacts between Engels and Marx and the course of their respective transformations into "communists."

Engels first mentions Marx in print in November 1843. In his article "Progress of Social Reform on the Continent" for *The New Moral World*, he writes that "[a]s early as autumn, 1842, some of the party" – referring to the so-called Young or New Hegelians, and apparently including himself in the number – "contended for the insufficiency of political change, and declared their opinion to be, that a *Social* revolution based upon common, property, was the only state of mankind agreeing with their abstract principles . . . " (MECW 3: 406). Although this trend did not yet include the party leaders (Bauer, Feuerbach, and Ruge), nonetheless "[c]ommunism . . . was such a *necessary* consequence of New Hegelian philosophy, that no opposition could keep it down, and, in the course of this present year [1843], the originators of it had the satisfaction of seeing one republican after the other join their ranks. Besides Dr. [Moses] Hess, one of the editors of the now suppressed *Rhenish Gazette* [*Rheinische Zeitung*], and who was, in fact, the first Communist of the party, there are now a great many others" – including "Dr. Marx, another of the editors of the *Rhenish Gazette*".[2] As for Hegel himself, he had been

---

[1] The charge goes back a long way, Kautsky alluding in 1926 to "[c]onjectures" that "Engels had not always completely caught Marx's train of thought and had not always arranged and edited the manuscript in accordance with the this train of thought," though adding that had he undertaken the "gigantic" editorial task, as some had advised, "and that I came to another result than Engels on one or another point," there would be "no guarantee that my version was truer to Marx's train of thought than was Engels'" (cited in Vollgraf and Jungnickel 2002 [1994]: 39).

[2] On the Young Hegelians, see Mayer (1969 [1936]: 18–24), McLellan (1973: 30–3, 34–40), Stedman Jones (2002: 74–98), and Hunt (2009: 54–60). What Engels intended by the New Hegelian philosophy is not here spelled out, but presumably it includes the principle – said to reflect an evolution from Hegel's philosophy – that "[a]ll the basic principles of Christianity, and even of what has hitherto been called religion itself, have fallen before the inexorable criticism of reason" (1842; "Schelling and Revelation," MECW 2: 197).

On the significance of Engels's first encounter with Hess, in summer 1844, see Stedman Jones (2002: 55–7).

"so much occupied with abstract questions, that he neglected to free himself from the prejudices of his age – an age of restoration for old systems of government and religion" (404), while adding that "the philosophical efforts of the German nation, from Kant to Hegel . . . must end in Communism" (406).[3]

Hobsbawm makes the point that Marx and Engels "were relative late-comers to communism," considering that "by the early 1840s a flourishing socialist and communist movement, both theoretical and practical, had existed for some time in France, Britain and the USA" (1982a: 1). The impression we have from Engels's account is that Marx turned to communism, independently of (and a little later than) Engels himself, sometime in 1843, possibly – this, however, is not stated explicitly – in consequence of Young Hegelian influence.[4] Now, according to Engels's retrospect half a century later, the first encounter between Engels and Marx – in the Cologne offices of the *Rheinische Zeitung*, in November 1842 – was a "chilly" one, for Marx had very recently "taken a stand against the Bauers, i.e., he had said he was opposed not only to the *Rheinische Zeitung* becoming predominantly a vehicle for *theological* propaganda, atheism, etc., rather than for political discussion and

---

[3] What is implied here is not properly explained, but most pertinent is a retrospective account provided decades later "of the true significance and revolutionary character of Hegelian philosophy . . . the termination of the whole movement since Kant," namely "that it once and for all dealt the death blow to the final products of human thought and action"; for

all successive historical states are only transitory stages in the endless course of development of human society from the lower to the higher. Each stage is necessary, and therefore justified for the time and conditions to which it owes its origin. But in the face of new, higher conditions which gradually develop in its own womb, it loses its validity and justification. It must give way to a higher stage, which will also in its turn decay and perish. Just as the bourgeoisie by large-scale industry, competition and the world market dissolves in practice all stable time-honoured institutions, so this dialectical philosophy dissolves all conceptions of final, absolute truth and of absolute states of humanity corresponding to it. Against it [dialectical philosophy] nothing is final, absolute, sacred. It reveals the transitory character of everything and in everything; nothing can endure against it except the uninterrupted process of becoming and passing away, of ascending without end from the lower to the higher. (1888; *Ludwig Feuerbach and the End of Classical German Philosophy*, MECW 26: 359–60)

Similarly, in *Socialism: Utopian and Scientific* (1892 [1880]: MECW 24: 302).

In the manuscript *Dialectics of Nature* (1873–82), Engels reduces to three the laws of dialectics, all traced to Hegel: "The law of the transformation of quantity into quality, and vice versa; The law of the interpenetration of opposites; The law of the negation of the negation" (MECW 25: 356). The objection to Hegel is that "these laws are foisted on nature and history as laws of thought, and not deduced from them. This is the source of the whole forced and often outrageous treatment; the universe, willy-nilly, has to conform to a system of thought which itself is only the product of a definite stage of development of human thought. If we turn the thing around, then everything becomes simple, and the dialectical laws that look so extremely mysterious in idealist philosophy at once become simple and clear as noonday."

[4] Marx's original commitment to the proletarian cause is reflected in "Contribution to the Critique of Hegel's *Philosophy of Law*," written late 1843 to January 1844 and published in the *Deutsch-Französiche Jahrbücher* in 1844. That his new position was ultimately based on Hegel's philosophy has been denied, "however much his language may be that of Young Hegelian journalism" (McLellan 1973: 96–7).

action, but also to Edgar Bauer's hot air brand of communism, which was based on a sheer love of 'going to extremes' and was soon replaced by Edgar with other kinds of extremist hot air. Since I corresponded with the Bauers, I was regarded as their ally, whereas they caused me to view Marx with suspicion" (to Mehring, April 1895; see "Correspondence," MECW *50*: 503). One is given to understand that the difference between Engels and Marx had been based on a misunderstanding, because Engels had already abandoned what has been termed "the bohemian anti-Christian excesses" characterizing the club known as the *Freien* (the free) and had turned away from Edgar Bauer's "frequent denunciations of the politics of a *juste milieu*" or liberal political compromise (Stedman Jones 1982: 302; 2002: 55, 140; also McLellan 1973: 51; Hunt 2009: 57–60).

As for Marx's actual position on communism at this time, Engels says only that he opposed the "hot air" brand and sought to discuss practical politics. In fact, Marx, partly under the influence of German immigrant workers living in Paris, where he had arrived in October 1843, was himself in the process of converting to communism (McLellan 1973: 86–7; Hobsbawm 1982a; Stedman Jones 2002: 145–76). Thus, though as late as October to November 1843, when Engels composed the *Outlines*, he still belonged in Marx's eyes to "la gauche hégélienne," from which he had broken away on ideological grounds (Bottigelli 1969: xx), he would have become aware of Engels's actual position from the manuscript that he published in his new (short-lived) journal, the *Deutsch-Französische Jahrbücher* early in 1844. When in September Marx and Engels met again, there was ample common ground for the commencement of their collaboration (see Hunt 2009: 120).

The notion of a Marx imbued with Hegelianism to a greater degree than Engels does not ring true. We have seen, in the first place, that at the outset in 1842–3 Engels traced his own adoption of the communist option to Young Hegelian influence – and possibly attributed the same transition process to Marx. Now the following year, it is true, Engels focuses on aspects of Hegelianism that he had come to oppose, insisting that "'Man' will always remain a wraith so long as his basis is not empirical man. In short we must take our departure from empiricism and materialism if our concepts, and notably our 'man,' are to be something real; we must deduce the general from the particular, not from itself, or *à la* Hegel, from thin air" (to Marx, 19 November 1844; see "Correspondence," MECW *38*: 12).[5] This letter to Marx suggests that the initiative derived from Engels; in any event, that Marx did not dispute this critical perspective is apparent from the joint critique of Hegel's idealist philosophy in *The Holy Family* – written September to November 1844 – with its striking reference to "the cage of the Hegelian way of viewing things," and applause for Feuerbach's recognition that "*History* does *nothing*, it 'possesses *no* immense wealth,' it 'wages *no* battles.' It is *man*, real, living man who does all that,

---

[5] See also "A Fragment of Fourier's on Trade" (written in the second half of 1845), referring with approval to Fourier's "great hatred of philosophy," and criticizing Hegel's theory that "arranges past history according to its liking," and (yet more strongly) the Post-Hegelian "speculative constructions . . . [that] no longer make any sense at all" (MECW *4*: 641–2).

who possesses and fights; 'history' is not, as it were, a person apart, using man as a means to achieve *its own* aims; history is *nothing but* the activity of man pursuing his aims" (1845; MECW *4*: 92–3). In the same vein, the joint *The German Ideology*, in spelling out the premises of the materialist conception of history, refers to "real individuals, their activity and the material conditions of their life ... premises [which] can thus be verified in a purely empirical way" (1845–6; MECW *5*: 31). Furthermore, Marx himself refers to Proudhon's inability "to follow the real course of history," and his creation of a "dialectical phantasmagoria ... [a]nebulous realm of the imagination [which] soars above time and place. In a word, it is Hegelian trash, it is not history" (28 December 1846; see " Correspondence," MECW *38*: 97).

Engels, in the final resort, found an honorable place for Hegel's historical perspective in general, as will be apparent from the extract given in note 3 from *Ludwig Feuerbach*. Indicative too is the defense made in *Anti-Dühring* (1894) of the most celebrated of propositions in *Capital*, whereby the "monopoly of capital becomes a fetter upon the mode of production, which has sprung up and flourished along with, and under it. Centralisation of the means of production and socialisation of labour at last reach a point where they become incompatible with their capitalist integument. This integument is burst asunder. The knell of capitalist private property sounds. The expropriators are expropriated" (MECW *35*: 750, cited in MECW *25*: 123–4). To be noted, in particular, is Engels's insistence that Marx does not actually base himself directly on dialectical reasoning as Dühring mistakenly believed, but rather "shows from history ... that just as formerly petty industry by its very development necessarily created the conditions of its own annihilation, i.e., of the expropriation of the small proprietors, so now the capitalist mode of production has likewise created the material conditions from which it must perish" (124). The process as such is thus a historical one. But it is "at the same time a dialectical process ... ," for "after Marx has completed his proof on the basis of historical and economic facts," he proceeds to restate the process in Hegelian or dialectic terms: "The capitalist mode of appropriation, the result of the capitalist mode of production, produces capitalist private property. This is the first negation of individual private property, as founded on the labour of the proprietor. But capitalist production begets, with the inexorability of a law of Nature, its own negation. It is the negation of negation. This does not re-establish private property for the producer [laborer], but gives him individual property based on the acquisitions of the capitalist era: i.e., on co-operation and the possession in common of the land and the means of production" (MECW *35*: 751).

That Engels accurately represented Marx's position is confirmed by Marx himself when protesting a review of *Capital* by Dühring: "he practises deception. ... He knows full well that my method of exposition is *not* Hegelian, since I am a materialist, and Hegel an idealist. Hegel's dialectic is the basic form of all dialectic, but only *after* being stripped of its mystical form, and it is precisely this which distinguishes *my* method" (to Kugelmann, 6 March 1868; see "Correspondence," MECW *42*: 544).

The substantive objections to Hegel of the 1840s are thus by no means erased. When reviewing Marx's *A Contribution to the Critique of Political Economy*, Engels explains retrospectively that it had been "essential to subject the Hegelian method to thoroughgoing criticism," but once that was achieved the merits of Hegel's mode of thinking emerged: "However abstract and idealist the form employed, the development of his ideas runs always parallel to the development of world history, and the latter is indeed supposed to be only the proof of the former. Although this reversed the actual relation and stood it on its head, yet the real content was invariably incorporated in his philosophy" (1859; MECW *16*: 474). Similarly, in the Preface to the second (1885) edition of *Anti-Dühring*, Engels writes of "the laws which Hegel first developed in all-embracing but mystic form, and which we made it one of our aims to strip of this mystic form and to bring clearly before the mind in their complete simplicity and universality" (MECW *25*: 11–12).[6]

It must be pointed out that the break from the radicalism of the Young Hegelians, and the subsequent objections to Hegelian "idealism," did not prevent Engels from reliance on the dialectical development of the concept of private property (see Stedman Jones 1982: 305–6; Claeys 1984: 224; Hunt 2009: 103). Indeed, later, in the discussion of historical materialism, Engels represents what amounts to causal interdependence as Hegelian "dialectics" (see Chapter Seven, pp. 330, 332–3). In any event, as far as concerns technical economics, and even (as we have seen from *Anti-Dühring*) evolutionary tendencies, what Schumpeter said of Marx applies equally to Engels: "He enjoyed certain formal analogies which may be found between his and Hegel's argument. He liked to testify to his Hegelianism and to use Hegelian phraseology. But this is all. Nowhere did he betray positive science to metaphysics" (Schumpeter 1950: 9–10; also Aarons 2009: 61–4).

A second supposed contrast, between a "humanistic" Marx vis-à-vis a "positivist" Engels concerned only with socialism as means to enhancing productivity, has been effectively contested by Rigby (1992: 5, 81, 207). Two almost identical citations from the early *Principles of Communism* and the later *Anti-Dühring* must suffice here to make the point with regard to Engels: "large-scale industry and the unlimited expansion of production which it makes possible can bring into being a social order in which so much of all the necessaries of life will be produced that every member of society will thereby be enabled to develop and exercise all his powers and abilities in perfect freedom" (1847; MECW *6*: 347); "the colossal productive forces created within the capitalist mode of production which the latter can no longer master, are only waiting to be taken possession of by a society organized for co-operative work on a planned basis to ensure to all members of society the

---

[6] By "universality" Engels intends the relevance of dialectical laws to nature, though "there could be no question of building the laws of dialectics into nature, but of discovering them in it and evolving them from it" (MECW: *25*: 12–13). See also note 3 on this matter. I have been unable to corroborate Hunt's affirmation that "Marx had been drawn back to the work of Hegel in the 1870s and was the first to make the claim that the dialectical law applied to both nature and society" (2009: 302).

means of existence and of the free development of their capacities, and indeed in constantly increasing measure" (1878; MECW 25: 139).

B. The Essays

The first essay sets out by examining, from the perspective of its specifically economic content, Engels's first major work, the *Outlines of a Critique of Political Economy* (the *Umrisse*), written October to November 1843 and first published in Marx's *Deutsch-Französische Jahrbücher* in 1844. The purpose of the exercise is to evaluate the extent of Engels's contribution to Marxian theory in the early years, and of Marx's recognition of that contribution.

Engels's early *general* influence on Marx is often enough asserted. Here is one example: "Engels's remarkable article *Outlines* . . . was in fact the starting point of Marx's economic studies" (Meek 1971: 53); the document "preceded all of Marx's writings . . . play[ing] a vital part in turning Marx's interests from philosophy to political economy" (Hutchison 1981: 3); Engels "made a very promising start in the early 1840s, when his *Outlines* . . . exerted a major influence on Marx" (Howard and King 1989: 8). More specifically, Stedman Jones maintains not only that Engels "was the first of the German philosophical left to shift the discussion towards political economy and to highlight the connections between private property, political economy and modern social conditions in the transition to communism," but also that his essay "strongly influenced Marx's own first reflections on Political Economy in the 1844 manuscripts" (1982: 305; see also 2002: 123). Moreover, Oakley maintains that the *Outlines* "gave Marx his first explicit insights into the nature of capitalism and stimulated his interest in political economy as the source of a critical comprehension of the contemporary human situations" (1984: 27).

Needless to say, the character of any influence will depend upon the character of the work in question. A word first on some modern reactions by historians. Schumpeter dismissed the *Outlines* as a "distinctly weak performance" (1954: 386), and Bottigelli writes that Engels "ne voit encore que l'aspect extérieur des choses et, sur ce plan, sa critique relève plus de l'indignation morale que de la science" (1969: xxi). Further, although Rubel recognizes Engels's contribution to "les grands thèmes de la future" (1968: lvi), he also minimizes its analytical content and represents it as the work of a moralizing pamphleteer: "Cet essai n'a rien d'une analyse objective; il se signale par la violence du moraliste pamphlétaire plutôt que par la rigueur du critique disséquant d'un système de production et d'échange" (lv). Berg represents the *Outlines* as "a loose compilation of the criticisms of political economy and the analysis of industrialization long popularized in the Owenite and unstamped press" (1980: 320). Oakley, at one stage, found that the *Outlines* "lacked sophistication" and that Engels's "observations were largely polemical and impressionistic" (1983: 25). Even Claeys – to whom we owe a debt for tracing Engels's probable sources – maintains that Engels was "ill-acquainted with political economy" (1984: 208). Sowell dismisses the work as "an obscure essay" (2006: 166).

In line with his emphasis on Engels's predominantly "non-scientific" orientation, Bottigelli says of the *Outlines* that it was "sans doute pour Marx la première critique socialiste approfondie de l'économie politique.... [S]i [elle] a eu une si profonde influence sur [Marx] ... c'est qu'ils parlaient tous deux le même langage et qu'ils avaient les mêmes préoccupations" (Bottigelli 1969: xxi). Similarly, Rubel maintains that "le ton" of the *Notebooks* – referring to notes taken by Marx in 1844 – "rappelle parfois celui de l'*Esquisse* [*Outlines*], dont Marx adopte certaines idées"; he describes Marx's later approval, in his *Contribution to a Critique of Political Economy* (1859) and in *Capital 1* (1867), as reflecting "l'hommage au premier auteur qui avait su sinon lui révéler une nouvelle vérité théorique, du moins partager avec lui la haine d'une morale déguisée en science pour justifier le scandale de la misère des masses et de la déchéance humaine" (Rubel 1968: lvi–lvii).

There is, in contrast, a large body of opinion that takes the work rather more seriously for its specifically analytical contribution (see, e.g., Mayer 1934 *I*: 158–9, 1969 [1936]: 55–6, 158–9; McLellan 1977: 67–8, 69; Hutchison 1981: 3–6; Stedman Jones 1982: 296; Carver 1983: 155; Oakley 1984: 27, 30–6; Hobsbawm 1998: 24–5; Steger and Carver 1999: 3–4; Hunt 2009: 117). There is indeed merit to this position. Admittedly, it is impossible to deny a pervasive "moralistic" or "humanist" flavor to the *Outlines*; the terms describing capitalistic private-property relations – egoism, cupidity, envy, greed, theft, pillage, violence, trickery, cheating, blackmail, terror, barbarity, crime, mistrust, sordid traffic, hypocrisy – make this clear. The discussion of the classical literature, particularly the representation of Malthusian doctrine as vile, infamous, hideous, blasphemous, and odious, further reinforces the polemical flavor of his contribution. But none of this should be allowed to disguise a serious and impressive analytical contribution – more extensive than is usually appreciated even in the literature sympathetic to Engels's achievements, which tends to focus on the cyclical component – and also a surprisingly sophisticated appreciation of the Ricardian and Sayian analyses of pricing. These contentions I shall support by a close scrutiny of the text with respect to value and distribution, demographics, the role of science, and macroeconomic instability. Thus my position is consistent with, but goes further and is more specific than, Hutchison's evaluation that the *Umrisse* "announced ... what were to become two or three of the most interesting and least invalid themes of Marxist political economy (recognized even by Schumpeter [1950: 40–2])," alluding to Engels's perception of cyclical movements, business concentration, and an emphasis on technological change (Hutchison 1981: 3–5); or that of Hobsbawm, whereby Engels "brought to Marx the elements of a model which demonstrated the fluctuating and self-destabilizing nature of the operations of the capitalist economy – notably the outlines of a theory of economic crises" (1998: 24).

It will, therefore, be one of my tasks to specify with precision Marx's early "debt" to Engels, a debt extending beyond the implications of the private-property axiom (which Marx properly recognized) to conspicuous features of what was to make up Marxist theory more narrowly conceived – concentration of capital, the reserve army of unemployed in relation to the cycle, inflows into the work force of various kinds, and falling living standards – and also to the Marxist vision of capitalist evolution. These latter contributions, I shall further maintain, Marx failed properly to acknowledge. Such neglect might well account for the "invisibility" of "the considerable independent contribution that Engels made to the development of Marxist theory" (Stedman Jones 1982: 296; see also Oakley 1984: 27).

I shall also address aspects of Engels's own obligations in the *Outlines* to earlier and contemporary works, particularly to the classical authors and the English socialists. The treatment here is carried further in Chapter Three, with particular reference to Owen, Gray, and Bray on economic organization and planning.

In Engels's more famous work, *The Condition of the Working Class in England*, written between September 1844 and March 1845, will be found a wide range of "Marxian" theoretical issues, several of which make an earlier appearance in the *Outlines*, including the character of the industrialization process; the labor market, with particular reference to subsistence wages and the contrast between slave and "free" labor; the consequences of technical change; the reserve army of unemployed; worsening crises; the downward trend of the real wage; and inevitable revolution. Certainly – and here I corroborate the position expressed in Henderson (1976: 72) and Hunt (2009: 104) – much more is involved than a descriptive account of living conditions. As in the case of the *Outlines* I shall give a detailed account of the analyses, but I also take into consideration the objections in Hobsbawm (1964) to the celebrated critique of Engels by the "cheerful historians" Henderson and Chaloner in their 1958 edition of *The Condition of the Working Class in England*, as well as the fair editorial evaluations by, inter alia, Hobsbawm (1998) and McLellan (1998) in their editions of the work. Again, the question of Engels's sources arises. Particularly interesting is the still-disputed question of his possible familiarity with Eugène Buret (1840).

Several of the major themes in *The Condition* will be found briefly summarized in the catechism *Principles of Communism*, composed by Engels in 1847 under the auspices of the League of Communists, and expanding on a Draft of a "Communist Confession of Faith" written earlier that year.[7] Although *The Condition* is a far richer work than the *Principles*, the latter is of the highest significance as providing the blueprint for the *Communist Manifesto*; see, for example, Laski (1967 [1948]: 19–20), Rubel (1963: 159), and Carver (1983, Chapter 3; 1998: 57). Mehring wrote more generally that "[a]s far as the style permits us to judge, it would appear that Marx had a greater hand in shaping its final form, but, as his own draft shows, Engels was not behind Marx in his understanding of the problems at issue and he ranks side by side with Marx as the author of it" (Mehring 1935 [1933]: 175). *Par contre* the linkage is minimized by Ryazanoff in his Introduction to the *Manifesto*: "When we compare the Manifesto with the sketch by Engels . . . we

---

[7]   On the League of Communists and its predecessor the League of the Just, see Stedman Jones (2002: 39–49, 51).

realize how right Engels was when, writing after Marx's death, he declared . . . that 'the fundamental proposition which forms its nucleus belongs to Marx'" (Ryazanoff 1930 [1922]: 21). The editors of the MECW version allow no more than that "[i]n writing the *Manifesto* the founders of Marxism used some of the propositions formulated in the *Principles of Communism*" (MECW 6: 684). Further, the importance of the document is insufficiently allowed by Oakley when he opines that the *Manifesto* was "written with some contributions from Engels" (1985: 284; see also 1984: 14). At all events, Beamish is right that the relationship between the *Manifesto* and the *Principles of Communism* "needs to be better understood than it has tended to be in the past" (1998: 219–20).

* * *

In his Preface to *Capital 2* Engels refers, rightly I believe, to the theory of surplus value as "the pith and marrow" of Marxian political economy (1885; MECW 36: 6). In his Introduction to *Anti-Dühring* in 1878, and in the extract published as *Socialism: Utopian and Scientific* in 1880, Engels refers to Marx's "two great discoveries, the materialistic conception of history and the revelation of the secret of capitalistic production through surplus-value. . . . With these discoveries Socialism became a science" (MECW 24: 305; MECW 25: 27; see also "Karl Marx," 1877, MECW 24: 191–5). As for the second "discovery,"

It was shown that the appropriation of unpaid labour is the basis of the capitalist mode of production and of the exploitation of the worker that occurs under it; that even if the capitalist buys the labour-power of his labourers at its full value as a commodity on the market, he yet extracts more value from it than he paid for; and that in the ultimate analysis this surplus-value forms those sums of value from which are heaped up the constantly increasing masses of capital in the hands of the possessing classes. The genesis of capitalist production and the production of capital were both explained.

The supreme importance of the surplus-value doctrine to Engels – on which see also Thompson (1984: 104–5) and Hunt (2009: 237–8, 299, 304–5) – justifies close examination of the precise sense of the attribution to Marx of "discoverer." This will occupy us in the second essay. There is a related issue, namely Engels's rejection of two charges by Karl Rodbertus-Jagetzow that Marx had plagiarized his work.[8] Because the theory of surplus value, with its foundation in the labor-power concept, lies at the heart of the entire Marxian enterprise, Rodbertus's accusation of plagiarism on Marx's part, if valid, would be devastatingly damaging. Rodbertus is an unfamiliar figure to many modern readers, troublesome thorn in the flesh though he was for Engels. The classic positions by Böhm-Bawerk, Marshall, Knight,

---

[8]   The first complaint, which relates to *Zur Erkenntniss* 1842, is made in a letter to J. Zeller dated 14 March 1875, printed in *Zeitschrift für die gesammte Staatswissenschaft*, Vol. 35, 1879, p. 219. The second complaint relates to *Sociale Briefe an von Kirchmann. Dritter Brief* 1851, and it appears in a letter to R. Meyer dated 29 November 1871 (Rodbertus-Jagetzow 1881: 111). Engels takes for granted that the more specific second charge was also intended by the first, general charge.

and Schumpeter on the importance of Rodbertus will therefore be briefly reviewed at this point.

Eugen von Böhm-Bawerk's famous survey of exploitation theory represents Marxian doctrine as "founded in many respects on the pioneering work of Rodbertus," though "built up with some originality and a considerable degree of acute logical power into an organic whole" (1890: 323). Similarly, after a review of Marx's discussion of surplus value as unpaid labor time, Böhm-Bawerk points out that we find "all the essential propositions combined by Rodbertus in his theory of interest: the doctrine that the value of goods is measured by quantity of labour; that labour alone creates all value; that in the loan contract the worker receives less value than he creates, and that necessity compels him to acquiesce in this; that the capitalist appropriates the surplus to himself; and that consequently the profit so obtained has the character of plunder from the produce of the labour of others" (374).

Alfred Marshall did not go so far, but he did identify the two doctrines of surplus. He subjects them to the same criticism:

This practical conclusion [that it would be for the general happiness and therefore right, that no private person should be allowed to own any of the means of production, nor any direct means of enjoyment, save such as he needs for his own use] has been supported by other arguments which will claim our attention; but at present we are only concerned with the doctrine that has been used by William Thompson, Rodbertus, Karl Marx, and others in support of it. They argued that labour always produces a "Surplus" [Note: This is Marx's phrase. Rodbertus had called it a "Plus"] above its wages and the wear-and-tear of capital used in aiding it: and that the wrong done to labour lies in the exploitation of this surplus by others. But this assumption that the whole of this Surplus is the produce of labour, already takes for granted what they ultimately profess to prove by it; they make no attempt to prove it; and it is not true. (Marshall 1920 [1890]: 586–7)

Again, both Rodbertus and Marx based themselves on the (erroneous) interpretation of Ricardo that "interest does not enter into that cost of production which governs (or rather takes part in governing) value" (817).

Frank Knight described the German socialist approach to profit – including Rodbertus and Lassalle as well as Marx and Engels – as entailing "a simple classification of income in which all that is not wages is a profit which represents exploitation of the working classes. Capital is equivalent to property.... It is analogous to a robber baron's crag, a toll-gate on a natural highway, or a political franchise to exploit" (Knight 1964 [1921]: 27–8). There is no place here for "profit" as a return to one or more productive activities.

Joseph Schumpeter writes of authors "to whom Marx was unkind in inverse proportion to their distance from him and whose work ran in many points parallel to his (Sismondi, Rodbertus, John Stuart Mill)" (1950: 22); again: "in the theory of surplus value and also in other matters, the affinity of Marx's teachings with that of Sismondi and Rodbertus is obvious" (39). Nonetheless, this does not quite amount to Böhm-Bawerk's positive assertion of debt. Indeed, Schumpeter accepted Engels's defense of Marx against the charge that he had "borrowed" from Rodbertus:

Fundamentally, and in the same sense as Marx, [Rodbertus] was a Ricardian. His analytic effort was an effort to develop Ricardian doctrine in a certain direction and was in essentials parallel to, though different from, Marx's effort. According to dates of publication, Marx could have derived inspiration from Rodbertus, particularly as regards the unitary conception of all non-wage incomes – Marx's surplus value and Rodbertus' "rent" – which is a feature of both schemata. In the main, however, Rodbertus taught Marx how not to go about his task and how to avoid the grossest errors. Therefore, and also because Marx's theoretical developments seem to follow naturally from Ricardo's formulations – given the directions in which those developments were to aim – I do not think that there any cogent reason for challenging Engels' repudiation of the idea that Marx had "borrowed" from Rodbertus. (Schumpeter 1954: 506)

Evaluating Engels's refutation of the charge that Marx had "borrowed" from Rodbertus will be my primary concern. The defense occurs in two conspicuous locations of 1885. In the first – the Preface to the first German edition of *Poverty of Philosophy* where notice is given of a prospective broader treatment – Engels charges Rodbertus with "an act of slander" reflecting jealousy and ignorance:

This is not the place to deal with relations between Marx and Rodbertus; an opportunity for that is sure to present itself to me very soon. Suffice it to note here that when Rodbertus accuses Marx of having "plundered" him and of having "freely used in his *Capital* without quoting him" his work *Zur Erkenntniss* [1842], he allows himself to indulge in an act of slander which is only explicable by the irksomeness of unrecognised genius and by his remarkable ignorance of things taking place outside Prussia, and especially of socialist and economic literature. Neither these charges, nor the above-mentioned work by Rodbertus ever came to Marx's sight; all he knew of Rodbertus was the three *Sociale Briefe* and even these certainly not before 1858 or 1859. (MECW 26: 279)

The elaboration of the defense turns entirely on Rodbertus's *Zur Erkenntniss*, Engels insisting on the high relevance of Marx's original attack on Proudhon in 1847 for the undermining of Rodbertus: "How could [Marx] have known that, in trouncing Proudhon, he was hitting Rodbertus, the idol of the careerists of today, who was unknown to him even by name at that time?" (278); for Rodbertus's 1842 work "brings forth anticipations of Proudhon as well as the communism of Weitling likewise (again unconsciously) contained in it" (279).

In the second formulation of his defense of Marx against Rodbertus, the Preface to the second volume of *Capital* (1885), Engels provides a fuller statement of his conception of Marx's primary theoretical innovations. These are the analysis of surplus value, based on the concept of "labor power" and its breakdown into its different forms – profit, interest, and rent; and the solution to the value–price conundrum – the Transformation. The context is the rebuttal of Rodbertus's charge that his *Zur Erkenntniss* had "been very nicely used . . . by Marx, without, however, giving me credit for it," and also that "[i]n my third social letter I have shown *virtually in the same way* as Marx, only more briefly and clearly, whence the *surplus-value* of the capitalist *originates*" (MECW *36*: 10). Engels protested that "[i]t was only around 1859, through Lassalle, that Marx learned of the existence of an economist named Rodbertus and thereupon Marx looked up the 'third social letter' in the British Museum" (11).[9] However, by this juncture "his own critique of political economy had been completed, not only in its fundamental outlines, but also in its more important details"; for he had known "very well . . . without the help of Rodbertus, not only whence but also *how* 'the surplus value of the capitalist' originated [as] proved by his *Poverty of Philosophy*, 1847, and by his lectures on wage-labour and capital," delivered in December 1847 and published in April 1849. Marx had indeed himself pointed out in 1880 that his *Poverty of Philosophy* "contains the seeds of the theory developed after twenty years' work in *Capital*" (MECW *24*: 326), and in *Capital* itself that his *Wage Labour and Capital* – referred to with some justice by Rubel as Marx's "premier texte proprement théorique" (Rubel 1963: 1595) – already contained the essentials of the mature surplus-value doctrine (MECW *35*: 577).

The theory of surplus value Engels described as the first of two issues on which the Ricardo school suffered "shipwreck" about 1830 (MECW *36*: 22). The second relates to the apparent conundrum that profit-rate uniformity is inconsistent with the labor theory of value and the theory of surplus value based upon it:

According to the Ricardian law of value, two capitals employing equal quantities of equally paid living labour, all other conditions being equal, produce products of equal value, and likewise surplus value, or profit, of equal quantity, in equal periods of time. But if they employ unequal quantities of living labour, they cannot produce equal amounts of surplus value, or, as the Ricardians say, equal amounts of profit. Now in reality the opposite takes place. In actual fact, equal capitals, regardless of how much or how little living labour they employ, produce equal average profits in equal times. Here there is therefore a contradiction of the law of value which had been noticed by Ricardo himself, but which his school also was unable to resolve. (23)[10]

At this point, to be sure, Rodbertus's name again appears but it is to deny that he had resolved the conundrum: "Rodbertus likewise could not but note this contradiction. But instead of resolving it, he made it one of the starting-points of his utopia (*Zur Erkenntniss*, p. 131)," whereas Marx "had resolved this contradiction already" in the manuscript of his *Zur Kritik* – referring to what is today known as *Theories of Surplus Value* 1862–3. This solution would presently be revealed to the

---

[9] At some later period a copy of the *Third Social Letter* was lent to Marx by Lassalle, who wrote asking for its return on 9 June 1862, prompting Marx to make a serious study of the book (see editorial note MECW *31*: 593 n. 99).

[10] Ricardo's notice of the contradiction presumably refers to his analysis of deviations of prices from values.

public, thus providing an opportunity to test the alleged superiority of Rodbertus's economics:

According to the plan of *Capital*, this solution will be provided in Book III. Months will pass before that will be published. Hence those economists who claim to have discovered in Rodbertus the secret source and a superior predecessor of Marx have now an opportunity to demonstrate what Rodbertus's political economy can accomplish. If they can show how an equal average rate of profit can and must come about, not only without a violation of the law of value, but rather on the very basis of it, we are willing to discuss the matter further with them. In the meantime they had better make haste. (MECW *36*: 23)[11]

Now it is essential to determine whether or not Engels was justified in his defense of Marx against the accusation of plagiarism. Much depends on his claim that Marx first encountered Rodbertus's work around 1859, for by then Marx had already published his "Wage Labour and Capital" and, yet more significant, had composed his *Grundrisse*, the first spelling out the surplus-value concept and the second expounding a quite sophisticated version of the Transformation. However, even if Marx can be exonerated of the accusation – and this seems to be the case – it would still remain true that Rodbertus's *Zur Ekenntniss* accomplished a major advance in "Marxian" theory well ahead of Marx. How Marx could have been wholly unaware of the 1842 volume until late in the day is a mystery.

I also record Engels's effort to escape the dilemma created by his insistence on the unoriginality of Rodbertus on surplus value in the light of earlier contributions by an anonymous pamphleteer of 1821 and other writers during the 1820s and 1830s, for, should this be the case, Marx too must have been equally culpable. It appears furthermore that Engels misrepresented Rodbertus's socialist scheme for the future in the attempt to distinguish it from that of Marx and himself.

This chapter continues with Engels's famous challenge to readers in 1885 – the "Prize Essay Competition" – to solve the apparent conflict between uniformity of rates of profit throughout the system and the "law of value," before the publication of *Capital 3*, a challenge partly designed to enhance Marx's status in the light of Rodbertus's charge of unoriginality.

I close this segment by attending to Engels's extension of the Transformation solution to the historical dimension, namely his attempt to construct a sort of theory of economic history.

* * *

In an influential review of W. O. Henderson's *Life of Friedrich Engels*, the late T. W. Hutchison wrote angrily that it "would be . . . quite erroneous to suppose, because Engels and Marx for decades on end believed that the demise of capitalism, which

[11] The third book only appeared in Autumn 1894. In a note to the press, Engels describes the contents of this book in relation to the first two and to a "fourth and final book, which will contain a critical historical survey of the theories of surplus value" (MECW *27*: 434). A second note further elaborates the contents of the third volume (MECW *27*: 435–6).

they so desired, was only months away, that they therefore felt any intellectual or moral obligation to give some thought to the kind of economic organization which would, or could, follow. The Utopian vacuities blurted out by Engels are as far as they got" (Hutchison 1981: 14). The charge is yet stronger. Engels, in the Preface to his first German edition (1885) of Marx's *The Poverty of Philosophy*, "has the effrontery to attack, for Utopian naiveté, some of the socialist rivals of himself and Marx, such as Proudhon, John Gray and Rodbertus, especially the last named," for neglecting the functioning of the competitive price mechanism when elaborating his socialist scheme for the future. "What," Hutchison goes on, "is most extraordinary is the combination of penetrating critical insight regarding the vital function of the competitive price mechanism as applied to the Utopian notions of Rodbertus together with the totally uncritical, purblind complacency regarding his own and Marx's Utopian assumptions (as he himself had earlier revealed them in his 'Principles of Communism') in such irresponsible vacuities as 'the joint and planned exploitation of the forces of production by society as a whole'" (1981: 15–16).

Hutchison, following Henderson, did well to bring to our attention Engels's appreciation of the rationing and information-yielding role of the competitive pricing mechanism as revealed in his critique of Rodbertus; in fact, the evidence for such appreciation is far more extensive than Hutchison apparently realized, extending, for example, to a detailed analysis of the working-class housing shortage, to credit control, and to protection.[12] The problem that arises, and that urgently requires resolution, is much more serious to that extent. In fact, Hutchison might well have directed his indictment of "purblind complacency" equally at Marx, who applied precisely the same market-based case against Proudhon as that which Engels applied against Rodbertus, and made a variety of other applications of the market principle to the analysis of various reform and interventionist proposals.

Hutchison did not attempt to deal with the perceived anomaly. In fact, he presumed that the founding fathers had little to say regarding the features of their desired system of communist organization beyond the loose notion of "joint and planned exploitation of the forces of production by society as a whole." In taking this line, Hutchison was following what seems to be received doctrine, for there is a paucity of detailed discussion of Marx's perception of communism, and even less that of Engels. This generalization applies even to admirers of Marx. Thus Hobsbawm asserts that Marx and Engels "refused to speculate about the details of the coming socialist society and its arrangements . . . [T]hey provided no concrete guidance of practical use on such problems as the nature of the socialization of the economy or the arrangements for planning it" (1982b: 257). Further, Dobb simply

---

[12] In Chapter Seven I take up these illustrations as revelatory of Engels's methodology of political economy. Much of this discussion turns on *The Housing Question* (1872–3), a rather neglected item.

alludes to "Marx's reference to 'common ownership of the means of production' as characteristic of the socialist mode of production in his *Critique of the Gotha Programme*" (1969: 124n.); and though he allows "that ownership *per se* does not exhaust Marx's category of social relations of production," nonetheless "ownership does constitute their fulcrum." Now to say that productive capital should be in the hands of the state tells us too little: Is it strictly central control that Marx envisaged, or did he allow decentralized decision making? What, in particular, of socialist production as cooperation? Were there no other features worth mentioning? A brief statement by Brewer sums up what seems to be the standard position: "The organization of a future society would be determined by its people as they went along, and could not be forecast in detail" (Brewer 1984: 3).

Foley has stated the presumed lacuna as a "puzzle": "One of the most puzzling things about the study of Marx's economics is that his writings overwhelmingly consist of a detailed critique of capitalism even though his motivation is to promote the cause of socialism. This puzzle is compounded by the fact that Marx never wrote a systematic and detailed description of what he meant by socialism, although scattered through his writings are passing comments and references to socialist economic practice and substantial critiques of other writers' conceptions of socialism" (Foley 1986: 158). But Foley does, to his credit, seek to define Marx's vision of "socialism" by following up some of these references. So does Pokorni (1993: 26–31). I shall take this path with respect to Engels as well as Marx.

Now it is indisputable that both Marx and Engels frequently denied any intention of dictating to future generations the precise organizational arrangements that would be most appropriate at each and every moment and under all circumstances. We shall encounter a rich sampling of such disclaimers. All the more important it is, therefore, that I bring to light the materials that reveal the future system they had in mind, albeit that such a system would emerge in different economies at different times and under a variety of local circumstances. Their system, I show, excludes money and markets, allows no place for consumer sovereignty, entails centralized decisions regarding investment and resource allocation – even statements supporting cooperation as a temporary form presume an overall central plan – and justifies pay differentials on grounds of the "natural inequality" of labor. What was envisaged may be described as a sort of autarkic "war economy" entailing the production of consumption goods as well as capital goods selected by the planners, the former category allocated according to workers' claims based on their labor contributions – perhaps rights to a bundle of goods is what was envisaged – account taken of natural (as distinct from learned) skill differentials.

Sowell in his account writes simply, "Although it may be empirically true that different ideologies generally regard central planning in different ways, it is not ultimately in principle an ideological question. Marx and Engels were unsparing in their criticisms of their fellow socialists and fellow communists who wanted to replace price competition with central planning" (1980: 218). Nevertheless, I see a problem requiring resolution – the apparent anomaly that Marx and Engels supported central control notwithstanding their profound appreciation of the positive functions of the competitive pricing mechanism. The resolution, I suggest, lies in the very character of the Marx–Engels vision of communism as a form of organization simplified to the point that there would be no need for a price mechanism. In sharp contrast, Rodbertus's scheme – at least as interpreted by Engels – retained features of an exploitative private-property system, including in particular the circulation of money. Such is my hypothesis, without which we are left with Hutchison's attribution to Engels of utter irresponsibility, even dishonesty. (The broader implications of my demonstration for the character of Marxian political economy will be explored in Chapter Seven).

Finally, I shall also be concerned with the accuracy of Engels's interpretation of Rodbertus. We show that Rodbertus, in his early writings of 1842 and 1851 on which Engels based his objections, had himself spelled out a "simplified" system of central control rid of capitalistic residuals. In his effort to protect Marx's reputation, Engels exaggerated the perceived differences between the Marx–Engels and Rodbertus schemes.

* * *

In 1895, the year of his death, Engels reissued Marx's *The Class Struggles in France 1848–1850* – first published in 1850 in Marx's short-lived journal *Neue Rheinische Zeitung* – with an Introduction endorsing peaceful political tactics and commending the progress made by Social Democracy in Germany through the electoral process. One commentator finds that this Introduction shows Engels – not Eduard Bernstein in his *The Preconditions of Socialism* of 1899 – to have been the "first Revisionist" or the "first Social Democrat," in proposing "that an entirely new mode of the class struggle was necessary, one which utilized universal suffrage and parliamentarianism," a position "which he and Marx had denounced over the course of many years" (Elliott 1967: 73–5). Indeed, Bernstein's line of reasoning – "In all developed countries, we are seeing the privileges of the capitalist bourgeoisie gradually giving way to democratic institutions" (Bernstein 1993 [1899]: 2) – "seemed to be a continuation of Engels's 1895 'Preface'" (76). Robert Tucker, too, leaves the impression that Engels introduced a *new* dimension: "the Introduction is notable for its hearty approval of the tactics that had evolved in Social Democratic practice in the late nineteenth century" (Tucker 1972: 406). There is even a book entitled *The Tragic Deception* to convey "the process by which a disciple revises the teachings of a teacher" and represent Engels as "the first revisionist," who "was directly responsible for the evolutionism and accommodationism of the Second International" (Levine 1975: xv, 182–3). Finally, Howard and King write, though rather hesitantly, of the 1895 Introduction that it "is still open to interpretation (as it was read by Bernstein himself) as the first major revisionist text" (1989: 73).

These accounts apparently take for granted that, in contrast with Engels, Marx himself was no "heretic," though Bernstein himself pointed out that in the joint 1872 edition of the *Communist Manifesto* Marx had allowed – with the experience of the Paris Commune in mind – that violent revolution might not always be appropriate (Bernstein 1993 [1899]: 3). As Levine puts it, there was "a continuity of Marx's thought on the question of revolution" from his early writings in 1844 until the Paris Commune of 1871: "Structural changes in society, total transformations of social relationships were impossible without the use of political violence. Ruling classes did not voluntarily surrender their power" (Levine 1975: 57). This perspective is expressed similarly in yet another account, this one by Harding, whereby the failure of the French revolutions of 1789 and 1848 led Marx to conclude that "[t]he search for a peaceful transformation of capitalism was ... characteristic of utopian socialism" (Harding 1983: 514); only occasionally – Harding cites a single speech of September 1872 – did Marx acknowledge that "the workers may attain their goal by peaceful means," for "in most continental countries the lever of the revolution will have to be force."

There are yet other evaluations. Carver represents Engels as "a democrat" who "wholeheartedly supported, in theory and in practice, national and international movements for representative and responsible government, which I take here as a working definition of democracy" (1996: 2). The same applies to Marx (1, 26–7); and, for both, not just late in the day.[13] With respect to a postrevolutionary regime, Sowell also maintains that both Marx and Engels "saw the desirable features of such a government as including universal suffrage and civil liberties – what people today loosely call democracy, and what at the time represented a wide area of agreement with nineteenth-century laissez-faire liberals" (Sowell 2006: 192; see also 1985: 143–51).

According to Lichtheim, "as time went on" both Marx and Engels "adapted themselves to the trend" of modern social democracy, with Engels going somewhat further: "by the 1890s it had become the conviction of Engels – Marx was no longer there – that political power resided in the vote, and that a duly elected legislature with a Socialist majority was both an attainable goal and the surest guarantee of victory" (Lichtheim 1964: 223, 230). Indeed, by 1895 "he had fully accepted the democratic viewpoint" (230n.). Avineri points to Marx's allowances from early days for the achievement of proletarian control by means of universal suffrage; certainly, "he never envisaged a violent revolution in England even in his earlier writings" (Avineri 1968: 217). However, he apparently shares Lichtheim's view that Engels took his revisionism further than had Marx: "In his late years Engels tended to adopt a wholly evolutionary attitude. In his 1891 remarks to the Erfurt Programme he envisages the possibility of peaceful evolution in "democratic republics like France and the U.S.A. and monarchies like England" – but not in Germany.... In his 1895 Introduction to *The Class Struggles in France* Engels is so overwhelmed by the SPD's success at the polls that he bases all his hopes on universal suffrage and even

[13] Nimtz charges Carver with performing "contortions" to create a divorce between Marx and Engels (Nimtz 2000: 281–2; and note 125). This, however, is certainly not the case in the present context.

explains the military hopelessness of barricade war under modern technology and communication" (217n.). A similar view is expressed in Przeworski (1985: 12).

More recently, however, Hunley has written of Engels's "alleged reformism," rejecting social-democratic attributions; he makes this conclusion with respect to Marx as well as Engels:

At different times both placed different emphases on the value and need for revolutionary or parliamentary tactics. Engels lived twelve years longer than Marx and adapted his position to the changed circumstances of the late 1880s and early to middle 1890s – as Marx surely would have done had he lived that long. None of the positions Engels took after Marx's death, however, were fundamentally at variance with those Marx had supported in the 1870s. Neither man ever abandoned the idea of revolution; both, in the years after 1848, simply redefined the conditions under which it would take place. (1991: 111)

Nimtz commends Hunley (Nimtz 2000: 353n.) and expands the latter's argument that no social-democratic orientation can be ascribed to Engels by insisting that he envisaged the parliamentary route as nothing more than "a 'gauge' ... to determine when to resort to armed struggle" – citing a passage from *The Origin of the Family* (1884) – totally unconcerned was he with "winning a majority through ... elections" (261, 263; also Nimtz 1999: 224–5). Violence and force – as Nimtz sees it – were, for Engels, the sole means of achieving proletarian victory.

In my fourth chapter I review the primary texts in an attempt to bring some order to the rather confusing picture that has emerged and to account in the process for the extraordinarily wide range of opinion regarding Engels's position.[14] To pin Engels down is no easy undertaking, because his statements vary with ruling circumstances and specific objective, rhetorical intent, and indeed mood of the moment, so that a broad range of formulation rather than select citation is necessary to an unusual degree. Accuracy of interpretation requires that one be alert to the contrast between prescriptive statements – as in many cases his support for universal suffrage appear to be – and descriptive statements, as in many cases his observations on revolution appear to be.

The 1895 Introduction to "The Class Struggles in France" does not, I finally conclude, signify a major change in Engels's attitude considering his recognition, not belatedly but over several decades, of political concessions by the British ruling class in particular, in effect its surrender to the proletariat by extension of the franchise. And since from the 1840s Marx recognized and applauded the potential of the social-democratic route, at least under the appropriate conditions – including national character – Engels was scarcely deviating from Marx and certainly not belatedly. Indeed, some of Marx's affirmations are quite as strong as those of Engels in 1895. There was, then, ample opportunity for any serious deviations to emerge between the partners during Marx's lifetime; given their absence, we

---

[14] The range of opinion is, in fact, even greater than I have indicated. See the excellent account in Rigby (1992: 206–7).

may be confident that he would have approved of Engels's Introduction, especially had he been able to take account of the impressive electoral reforms of 1884–5 in Britain and Germany.

Although we must take full account of allowances (especially but not only in the British case) for a "proletarian dictatorship" achieved by means of the polls in a peaceful and constitutional manner, it is no less important to reject the view whereby in 1895 Engels "fully accepted the democratic viewpoint" or "based all his hopes on universal suffrage." I refer to what I shall call "limits" to Engels's revisionism. The parliamentary route was only the most effective means, at least under certain conditions, of creating a "dictatorship of the proletariat" with the ultimate goal of achieving a classless communist system. Accordingly, Engels would have found unacceptable a parliamentary system generating a working-class majority unwilling to carry out the communist program – toeing the Party line was an axiom of his support for universal suffrage – or a working-class electorate choosing to replace the Party at the polls. (Here lies a primary difference with Eduard Bernstein, as we shall see in the Epilogue.) My position is in line with that of Kolakowski (2005: 296–7), and also that of Levin, who has expressed the matter succinctly thus: "Marx and Engels were less dismissive of parliamentarism [sic] than often assumed. The more extended the franchise, the more the new possibilities that could be turned to advantage. In some countries universal suffrage might even provide a framework for moving towards communism. Liberal democracy, and the participatory possibilities it offered, were actually not accorded much intrinsic value, but welcomed merely as a means of moving beyond it. It was just one more way in which the bourgeoisie produced its own gravediggers" (1989: 141).

Beyond this, Engels (like Marx) made allowance for the use of force to protect the "dictatorship" from counter-revolution by making a "stern example" of "traitors." (Here the contribution by Collier 1996: 34–5 is particularly helpful.) There is, then, some consolation for those like Nimtz – but going back in fact to the "anarchist" Michael Bakunin (1973 [1872]) – who view the founders as red in tooth and claw. Nonetheless, there is no call here to the barricades, such as Nimtz imagines; what one encounters, rather, is a justification for defensive violence in the event of a reactionary attempt to reverse proletarian parliamentary gains once achieved by the proletariat.

* * *

This overview of the literature on Engels as "revisionist" has thus far been limited to constitutional matters. The prospect of economic and social reform within capitalist arrangement requires equally close attention; this exercise is undertaken in Chapter Five, where I demonstrate the prospect, as envisaged by both Engels and Marx, of improving working-class living conditions in the light of empirical evidence. A separation of the two themes adds to clarity, as may be seen from the circumstance that major welfare advances were recognized in the British case long before universal male suffrage was legislated, and more generally because our authors themselves insisted on the contrast between "social" and "political" reforms, while at the same time perceiving that agitation for trade-union legitimacy and factory legislation provided a first-rate political training for the working classes.

To reject the perception of Engels as "reformer" – as does Nimtz (2000: 254, 258, 269, and 281) – is to neglect an entire range of welfare reforms undertaken by the capitalist state recognized and applauded by Engels. The same applies to Marx. This neglect undermines the position of Fernbach, who maintains, on the basis of a letter to Bolte of 1871, that Marx engaged in a "steadfast attack on all visible reformist manifestations. . . . No more than in the [Communist] Manifesto does Marx leave a theoretical space for the possibility of a workers' movement that is organized politically as a class yet struggles for reforms within the capitalist system" (Fernbach 1974: 58–9). This assertion is then taken up by Saville to justify the position that "Marx gave no emphasis to the influence, or possible influence of bourgeois ideas upon the working classes (1987: 281 and note 81). The evidence, however, points away from this perspective not only with regard to Marx, but also with regard to Engels, our main concern.

Unacceptable too is Ludwig von Mises's particularly misleading position that "Marx and the school of orthodox Marxism" grew increasingly more opposed to social reform measures within capitalist organization in later years – viewing them as "reactionary" – than they had been earlier: "From the point of view of this later doctrine Marx and the school of orthodox Marxism reject all policies that pretend to restrain, to regulate and to improve capitalism. Such policies, they declare, are not only futile, but outright harmful. For they rather delay the coming of age of capitalism, its maturity, and thereby also its collapse. They are therefore not progressive, but reactionary" (1980 [1950]: 29). The evidence points rather to increasing appreciation on the part of Marx and Engels, as time passed, of the potential for, and desirability of, welfare reform within capitalist organiza-tion. Indeed, social reform comes to be represented as a necessary characteristic of advanced capitalism, reflecting in large part for Marx the fear of increasing proletarian power, and supplemented by Engels by the positive implications of concentration for unionization (intended by the great corporations as a barrier to entry) and for factory legislation.

As with constitutional reform, so with welfare reform, Marx and Engels thus emerge as the "first revisionists," the latter actually lagging somewhat behind the former insofar as concerns welfare programs. However, there are "limits" to Engels's revisionism regarding welfare improvement, though of a different order to those encountered in the constitutional context. Engels had there expressed a concern with the prospect of counter-revolution– "concern" may be a misnomer because he seems at times to relish the prospect – whereas, to the contrary, he expressed an equal concern with the prospect, indeed the actuality, of major reform by the capitalist state with respect to social and welfare matters. Now (as I show in Chapter Four), at no time was the ultimate objective, namely the replacement of capitalist institutions, abandoned. Nevertheless, secularly rising real wages and improving living conditions, albeit limited to the unionized factories and (from the late 1880s) specific instances of unskilled workers, threatened to compromise the desired outcome by rendering the capitalist option attractive to workers. Engels discerned a twofold resolution of this dilemma: First, the perceived onset of secular decline with the end of Britain's industrial monopoly in consequence of American and German competition, boding ill for further social and economic advances favorable to labor; second, the perceived threat to living standards, applying also to Germany and the United States, emanating from massive Chinese immigration. Indeed, these prospects reinforced the necessity for a central-control system.

* * *

A main theme of Chapter Six, devoted to aspects of the Marx–Engels relationship and serving as a preliminary overview of the study as a whole, relates to the widely held view of Engels as His Master's Voice, well expressed in Isaiah Berlin's biographical sketch:

[Engels] possessed a quality essential for permanent intercourse with a man of Marx's temperament, a total uncompetitiveness in relation to him, absence of all desire to resist the impact of that powerful personality, to preserve and retain a protected position of his own; on the contrary, he was only too eager to receive his whole intellectual sustenance from Marx unquestioningly, like a devoted pupil, and he repaid him by his sanity, his enthusiasm, his vitality, his gaiety, and finally, in the most literal sense, by supplying him with means of livelihood at moments of desperate poverty. Marx, who, like many dedicated intellectuals, was himself haunted by a perpetual feeling of insecurity, and was morbidly thin-skinned and jealously suspicious of the least signs of antagonism to his person or his doctrines, required at least one person who understood his outlook, in whom he could confide completely, on whom he could lean as heavily and as often as he wished. In Engels he found a devoted friend and intellectual, whose very pedestrianism restored his sense of perspective and his belief in himself and his purpose. (Berlin 1963: 103–4)

Schumpeter goes somewhat further: "His self-effacing loyalty cannot but command our highest respect. Throughout he aspired only to be the faithful henchman and mouthpiece of the Lord Marx. It is therefore only from necessity that I point out – for it is necessary to do so to enable the reader to understand our situation with respect to the Marxist manuscripts that Engels edited – that he was not Marx's intellectual equal, and that . . . he was particularly deficient in technical economics" (Schumpeter 1954: 386n.). A note in *Capitalism, Socialism and Democracy* expresses the same negative view: "I observe that the few comments on Engels that are contained in this sketch ["Marx the Economist"] are of a derogatory nature. This is unfortunate and not due to any intention to belittle the merits of that eminent man. I do think however that it should be frankly admitted that intellectually and especially as a theorist he stood far below Marx. We cannot even be sure that he always got the latter's meaning. His interpretations must therefore be used with care" (Schumpeter 1950: 39n.).[15]

Mention should also be made of an important discussion paper by Maximilien Rubel – "The Marx Legend, or Engels the Founder of Marxism" – prepared for the 150th-anniversary celebrations in 1970 of Engels's birth held in Wuppertal, East Germany, but that Rubel was not allowed to present by the scientific committee in charge (Rubel 1981: 15–16). The paper does not take a stance at the other extreme to that of Berlin or Schumpeter, as the title suggests. It turns rather on Marx's famous declaration: "What is certain is that I am not a Marxist," reported by Engels in a letter to Bernstein, 3 November 1882 (MECW 46: 356); and later to Carl Schmidt, 5 August 1890 and Paul Lafargue, 27 August 1890 (MECW 49: 7, 22).[16] Rubel speaks of Engels "glorifying Marx's name" – notwithstanding Marx's opposition to use of the terms "Marxist" or "Marxian" – in an attempt to counter the damage caused by widespread misuse of a "mystifying catchword," though "[m]ore than anyone else, he was aware that it risked corrupting the essential meaning of Marx's writings, which Marx himself considered to be the theoretical expression of an actual social movement and in no sense as a doctrine invented by an individual for the use of a political and intellectual elite" (Rubel 1981: 19–22; see also Rubel 1968: cxxviii). Especially because of French – and also German – doctrinal clashes, Engels felt obliged, however regretfully, to give his sanction to use of the objectionable terms "marxists" and "marxism." This account implies that Engels's "glorification" of Marx reflects nothing more than a perceived strategic necessity.[17] However, in the same paper, Rubel insists that "he left no doubt whatsoever about the authorship of the great 'scientific discoveries,' that he attributed to Marx alone" (20n.) – Rubel, however, excludes the principles of historical materialism and surplus value from his list of Marx's discoveries – and he accepts at face value Engels's frequent minimizations of his own contributions to the "theory" (20), much in the manner of Berlin or Schumpeter.

It is this perspective that I challenge. In so doing I follow Gareth Stedman Jones when he blames Engels's "own very modest assessments of his contribution" as an obstacle to recognition of his contribution to Marxist theory (1982: 296),

[15] Howard and King write simply of Engels's "lack of capacity as a political economist," and they refer to an informally agreed upon division of labor, with Marx responsible for political economy (1989: 6–7).
[16] Marx actually complained to Engels from Paris that "[t]he 'Marxistes' and the 'Anti-Marxistes'" – referring to the French congresses organized by the reformist Possibilists and the collectivists – had "*both* done their damnedest to ruin my stay in France" (30 September 1882; MECW 46: 339). The French "Possibilists" advocated the transformation of capitalism into socialism by gradual reform through a policy of "pursuing the possible" (MECW 49: 567 n. 3).
[17] Marx himself condemned the "cult of personality." Neither he nor Engels, he declared, "cares a straw for popularity. . . . When Engels and I first joined the secret communist society, we did so on condition that anything conducive to a superstitious belief in authority be eliminated from the Rules" (to W. Blos, 10 November 1877; MECW 45: 288).

and Hunt, who insists likewise that "if Marx's voice is being heard again today, then it is also time we stripped away Engels's modesty and allowed his richly iconoclastic ideas to be explored beyond the memory of Marx" (2009: 7). Some readers have been too ready to take him at his word when he deprecates himself, failing to discount a natural modesty not confined to his relationship with Marx. In any event, as we shall see, Engels in fact frequently did express pride in his contributions and insisted on due recognition. His position regarding the doctrine of historical materialism – one of the planks of scientific socialism – will prove of particular interest.

Finally, I examine in this chapter Engels's role as editor of the Marx manuscripts, particularly those relating to *Capital 3*, in approaching the perennial charge that Engels distorted Marx's intentions. This issue has taken on new importance in the light of the publication of the original Marx documents in the MEGA series. My considered opinion is that the charge has not been proven.

* * *

The concluding chapter is devoted to a methodological overview of Engels's Marxian political economy, drawing on the preceding six essays but also taking account of Engels's late statements relating to historical materialism, and introducing (in an Appendix) the issue of an alternative Russian road to communism. The secondary literature in the case of this chapter will be discussed in situ.

A brief Epilogue takes account of Engels's immediate intellectual heritage, with particular reference to his protégés Eduard Bernstein and Karl Kautsky. This exercise provides the opportunity to recapitulate our reading of Engels on economic organization and "revisionism."

ONE

Engels's Early Contribution

A. Introduction

There is some excuse for the tendency to play down Engels's *Outlines of a Critique of Political Economy* (1844) as a contribution to Marxian economic theory. Its polemical tone, particularly its sharp condemnation of the classical literature with regard to the private-property axiom with which I commence this chapter, encourages this tendency. Nevertheless, the *Outlines* in fact provides a sophisticated evaluation of classical value theory and emerges as the founding document in the Marxian theoretical tradition, especially its macroeconomic dimension.

Rather than merely a descriptive account of working and living conditions, *The Condition of the Working Class in England* (1845) is then shown to provide significant elaborations of the main theoretical themes of the *Outlines*. Furthermore, the wholly bleak perception of contemporary working-class conditions usually attributed to Engels proves to be an exaggeration of his actual position, although it is valid concerning his evaluation of future prospects.

Again largely from the theoretical perspective, I next emphasize the status of the *Principles of Communism* (1847) – much of it drawn from the two earlier documents – as a template for the *Communist Manifesto* (1848). Finally, I briefly consider Engels's sources in composing the *Outlines* and *The Condition of the Working Class*.

B. *Outlines of a Critique of Political Economy* I: On the Classical Literature

According to Engels's account, the eighteenth century saw revolutionary developments in economics, namely the rejection of mercantilism – but with one major restriction: "It did not occur to economics to question the *validity of private property*" (MECW 3: 419). In fact, "the only *positive* advance which liberal economics has made is the elaboration of the laws of private property" (421). Furthermore, especially with respect to commercial policy, the economists drew illogical and inconsequential conclusions reflecting "the humane spirit of the century" from a private-property axiom that could not bear the weight placed upon it; for in point of fact, the "humane" conclusions were independent of the science itself, a conflict generating contradictions hidden by "sophistry and hypocrisy":

Therefore, the new economics was only half an advance. It was obliged to betray and to disavow its own premises, to have recourse to sophistry and hypocrisy so as to cover up the contradictions in which it became entangled, so as to reach the conclusions to which it was driven not by its premises but by the humane spirit of the century. Thus economics took on a philanthropic character. It withdrew its favour from the producers and bestowed it on the consumers. It affected a solemn abhorrence of the bloody terror of the mercantile system, and proclaimed trade to be a bond of friendship and union among nations as among individuals (419).

That the private-property premise reasserted itself soon enough was manifest in the Malthusian population and Smithian free-trade doctrines (420).

But Engels is optimistic. For the economist "does not know that with all his egotistical reasoning he nevertheless forms but a link in the chain of mankind's universal progress. He does not know that by his dissolution of all sectional interests he merely paves the way for the great transformation to which the century is moving – the reconciliation of mankind with nature and with itself" (MECW 3: 424). Smith's system thus represented "necessary advance . . . by overthrow[ing] the mercantile system with its monopolies and hindrances to trade, so that the true consequences of private property could come to light" (420). A corresponding allowance is made with regard to Malthus.

Moreover, whereas Smith (and Malthus) had some excuse for retaining the standard axioms, Ricardo and, even less, McCulloch and James Mill had none. For "the modern economists had the whole system complete before them: the consequences had all been drawn; the contradictions came clearly enough to light; yet they did not come to examining the premises. . . . The nearer the economists come to the present time, the further they depart from honesty" (MECW 3: 420). Only a perspective that abandons the premises common to both the mercantile and "modern" systems could get at the truth:

Even the mercantile system cannot be correctly judged by modern economics since the latter is itself one-sided and as yet burdened with that very system's premises. Only that view which rises above the opposition of the two systems, which criticizes the premises common to both and proceeds from a purely human, universal basis, can assign to both their proper position. It will become evident that the protagonists of free trade are more inveterate monopolists than the old mercantilists themselves. It will become evident that the sham humanity of the modern economists hides a barbarism of which their predecessors knew nothing; that the older economists' conceptual confusion is simple and consistent compared with the double-tongued logic of their attackers, and that neither of the two factions can reproach the other with anything which would not recoil upon themselves (420–1).[1]

---

[1] Engels adds that from this perspective the reemergence of mercantilist-style protectionism in Germany could be appreciated: "This is why modern liberal economics cannot comprehend

At the same time, regarding matters "strictly economic," it is allowed that the free-traders had a stronger hand than the "monopolists," though not relative to the English Socialists: "on all points where it is a question of deciding which is the shortest road to wealth – i.e., in all strictly economic controversies – the protagonists of free trade have right on their side. That is, needless to say, in controversies with the monopolists – not with the opponents of private property, for the English Socialists have long since proved both practically and theoretically that the latter are in a position to settle economic questions more correctly even from an economic point of view" (MECW 3: 421). However, despite his commendation of the free-traders relative to the Mercantilists, Engels proceeds to a position on trade wholly at odds with that of Smith – "*the economic Luther*" – and the Classics: "In every purchase and sale . . . two men with diametrically opposed interests confront each other. . . . Thus, the first maxim in trade is secretiveness – the concealment of everything which might reduce the value of the article in question. The result is that in trade it is permitted to take the utmost advantage of the ignorance, the trust, of the opposing party, and likewise to impute qualities to one's commodity which it does not possess. In a word, trade is legalised fraud" (422). Now this perspective on trade extends to the international level and the family itself (423–4), although the perceived superiority of the Classics over the Mercantilists obviously relates to their efficiency case for free trade. For all that, a pervasive Smithian influence on several of the components of Engels's account, including labor-market analysis, will become apparent.

Notwithstanding the polemical character of his account, Engels scarcely distorted Smith's position when he charged economics with "affect[ing] a solemn abhorrence of the bloody terror of the mercantile system." For Smith had indeed protested that "the cruelest of our revenue laws, I will venture to affirm, are mild and gentle, in comparison of some of those which the clamour of our merchants and manufacturers has extorted from the legislature, for the support of their own absurd and oppressive [wool] monopolies. Like the laws of Draco, these laws may be said to be written in blood" (Smith 1976 [1776]: 647–8). Engels's charge of "hypocrisy" addressed against orthodoxy also cannot be dismissed as wholly groundless. After all, the *Wealth of Nations* contains a severe indictment of the market system yet fails to carry the case further than to allow for some modest correctives. Consider the matter of equity. Smith made no proposals for meaningful institutional reform although he recognized the severe biases against labor endemic to the market system. Now it might be said that any such complaint is anachronistic; yet his was also the age of Godwin and Condorcet, and only a generation later the famously misnamed "Ricardian Socialists" actually drew their inspiration

the restoration of the mercantile system by List [1841], whilst for us the matter is quite simple. The inconsistency and ambiguity of liberal economics must of necessity dissolve again into its basic components. Just as theology must either regress to blind faith or progress towards free philosophy, free trade must produce the restoration of monopolies on the one hand and the abolition of private property on the other" (MECW 3: 421).

from Smith (Hollander 1980). Smith, it is true, looked on rapid accumulation as tending to weaken monopsonistic pressures to labor's advantage (Hollander 1973: 319–20); however, accumulation – and efficient resource allocation as a means of maximizing the surplus available for accumulation – is made to depend upon the thoroughly untrustworthy class of merchants and manufacturers, always prone to monopoly and antisocial conspiracy. One might have expected from Smith a more serious treatment of the dilemma, and to that extent Engels's objections have merit.

Engels opined that social conditions were sufficiently grim for Smith's social-ist successors to have questioned the ruling institutional arrangements. It would doubtless have surprised him to learn that even Ricardo had actually expressed himself in terms suggesting that he too was in some doubt as to "what is to be done?" To James Mill he had written, "I . . . have looked with some interest at a work on Polit. Econ. by Mr. Piercy Ravenstone which though full of the greatest errors has some good things to say in it – he is a strenuous and able advocate for Reform" (28 August 1821; Ricardo 1951–73 *9*: 45); and to Malthus he had similarly observed, "Have you seen a work on Population and Polit. Econ. by Mr. Ravenstone? I have read it. I think it is full of errors and shews that the author has a very limited know-ledge of the subject, yet I felt a great interest in perusing it. The cause of the distress of the labouring class is well stated, but he appears not to be aware of the difficulty of providing a remedy" (10 September 1821; Ricardo 1951–73 *9*: 62–3). Now, as Jacob Viner phrased the matter, "since Ravenstone's explanation of the causes of the distress of the working-classes consisted essentially of the claim that the landlord, the capitalist, and the tax-gatherer deprived labour of the product of its effort, and used their booty to maintain the privileged classes in idleness or in unproductive activities, Ricardo's partially laudatory comments should be especially surprising to the many economists who have regarded him as primarily an apologist for the moneyed classes" (Viner 1933: 117). Engels, it will be clear, falls into this category.

C. *Outlines of a Critique* II: Value and Distribution

We turn now to technical matters. Controversy over the "value" issue, Engels asserted, was a "modern" affair because the mercantilists had taken no position (MECW *3*: 424). He had largely in mind the Ricardo–Say debates, though he makes no specific mention of Ricardo's labor theory of value, and nowhere seriously explores the source of profits, though what little he had to say suggests that he found it in production rather than in circulation (430–1, cited below, pp. 33–4).

As for *real* value, Engels ascribes to Ricardo and McCulloch a cost-based pos-ition unrelated to the competitive adjustment process – an alleged weakness that he found incomprehensible: "The English . . . assert that the abstract value of a thing is determined by the costs of production. *Nota bene* the abstract value, not the exchange-value. . . . Why are the costs of production the measure of value? Because . . . no one in ordinary conditions and leaving aside the circumstance of competition would sell an object for less than it costs him to produce it.... [D]oes the economist never stop to think that as soon as competition is left out of account there is no guarantee at all that the producer will sell his commodity just at the cost of production?" (MECW 3: 424–5). The word "determined" in the first sentence of this passage might better be rendered "defined," as indeed Engels has it in the immediately preceding paragraph: "There was a protracted quarrel over the nature of real value between the English, who defined the costs of production as the expression of real value, and the Frenchman Say, who claimed to measure this value by the utility of an object" (424).

Engels then proceeds to his main positive contribution. To make sense of the doctrine, the English economists found themselves obliged, despite themselves, to allow a role to demand or "Say's much decried utility" coupled with "competition"; for "abstract value" and its alleged "determination" by cost were, by themselves, meaningless "abstractions": "Supposing someone were to make with tremendous exertion and at enormous cost something utterly useless, something which no one desires – is that also worth its production costs? Certainly not, says the economist: Who will want to buy it? So we suddenly have not only Say's much decried utility but alongside it – with 'buying' – the circumstance of competition.... Abstract value and its determination by the costs of production are, after all, only abstractions, nonentities" (MECW 3: 425). Similarly, Say's objectionable "abstraction" had to be corrected by allowing for costs of production and therefore also competition, which Say – like Ricardo – allegedly omitted: "If we turn to Say, we find the same abstraction.... According to this theory, the necessities of life ought to possess more value than luxury articles. The only possible way to arrive at a more or less objective, *apparently* general decision on the greater or lesser utility of an object is, under the dominion of private property, by competition.... But if competition is admitted production costs come in as well; for no one will sell for less than what he has himself invested in production. Thus, here, too, the one side of the opposition passes over involuntarily into the other" (425–6).

Engels concludes by insisting on both the cost and utility blades of the scissors in the exchange process: "The value of an object includes both factors, which the contending parties arbitrarily separate – and, as we have seen, unsuccessfully. Value is the relation of production costs to utility. The first application of value is the decision as to whether a thing ought to be produced at all; i.e., as to whether utility counterbalances production costs. Only then can one talk of the application of value to exchange" (MECW 3: 426). Engels did well to recognize that orthodoxy – in either the Ricardo or Say version – required both utility and costs to make any sense at all of its own doctrine. To this day there are those who do not wholly appreciate this feature of Classical economics.

Engels might be understood thus far as championing standard allocation doctrine such that relative prices will be equal where production costs are equal, and this by way of the market demand–supply mechanism. However, we shall now see that this is not Engels's own conclusion.

The argument continues thus: "The production costs of two objects being equal, the deciding factor determining their comparative value will be utility." In all likelihood Engels was here digressing from the private-property state to an *ideal* communal state, for he proceeds to just such a discussion: "This basis is the only just basis of exchange. But if one proceeds from this basis, who is to decide the utility of the object? . . . The contradiction between the real inherent utility of the thing and the determination of that utility, between the determination of utility and the freedom of those who exchange, cannot be superseded without superseding private property; and once this is superseded, there can no longer be any question of exchange as it exists at present" (MECW 3: 426). "The practical application of the concept of value," he concludes, will in the ideal state "be increasingly confined to the decision about production, and that is its proper sphere." There is no place for a pricing mechanism in the ideal state, a matter to be elaborated in Chapter Three.

As for our main concern, private-property organization, Engels once more reverts to the necessity of introducing "competition" into the picture, allowance made for both costs and utility. Here, however, he introduces a fundamental qualification – the characteristic *instability* of the variables: "But what kind of utility, what kind of production costs, does [orthodox theory] introduce? Its utility depends on chance, on fashion, on the whim of the rich; its production costs fluctuate with the fortuitous relationship of demand and supply" (MECW 3: 426–7).

Before considering the full significance of this remark, note the assertion that "[t]he difference between real value and exchange value is based on [the] fact that the value of a thing differs from the so-called equivalent given for it in trade; i.e., that the equivalent is not an equivalent" (MECW 3: 427). Price (Engels insists on the term "price" as more honest than "exchange value," which disguises the "immorality of trade") is represented more specifically as determined "by the reciprocal action of production costs and competition" – a "purely empirical law" and the "first to be discovered by the economist" – such that "in a state of equilibrium, when demand and supply cover each other . . . what remains over are the costs of production and it is these which the economist proceeds to call 'real value,' whereas it is merely a definite aspect of price. Thus everything in economics stands on its head. Value, the primary factor, the source of price, is made dependent on price, its own product." Drawing on Feuerbach – presumably Feuerbach 1841 – Engels concluded that "[a]s is well known, this inversion is the essence of abstraction," the latter a term directed subsequently by Marx against Ricardian economics (see Hollander 2008: 169–71).

The priority here accorded the market determination of cost price, and the relegation of "real value" to a special case only of market price, is a fair enough representation of orthodoxy, capturing the equilibrating role accorded "competition." (The formulation dilutes the immediately preceding criticism of Ricardo and Say.) However, although Engels declared the "empirical law" of costs to be "quite correct," he in fact goes on to emphasize the *instability* mentioned above, attributing it to ignorance on the part of the market players, as a result of which a state of equilibrium is never achieved: "The law of competition is that demand and supply always strive to complement each other, and therefore never do so.... Supply ... is either too big or too small, never corresponding to demand; because in this unconscious condition of mankind no one knows how big supply or demand is.... So it goes on unendingly – a permanently unhealthy state of affairs – a constant alternation of over-stimulation and flagging which precludes all advance – a state of perpetual fluctuation without ever reaching its goal" (MECW 3: 433). Engels did not, therefore, himself subscribe to a cost theory of competitive price, with even the notion of a tendency to costs being suspect. This position is expressed very clearly in a passage that undermines the very concept of stable value: "In this continuous up-and-down, everyone *must* seek to hit upon the most favourable moment for purchase and sale; everyone must become a speculator ... must enrich himself at the expense of others, must calculate on the misfortune of others, or let chance win for him.... [T]he honest 'respectable' merchant ... is as bad as the speculators in stocks and shares. He speculates just as much as they do. He has to: competition compels him to. And his trading activity therefore implies the same immorality as theirs" (434–5).[2]

The *Outlines* reverts also to an inherent "contradiction of competition," conveying the general message that "the contradictions of capitalist economy could not be resolved on the basis of that economy" (Kolakowski 2005: 119). Competition must inevitably generate monopoly, albeit only temporarily: "Competition is based on self-interest, and self-interest in turn breeds monopoly. In short, competition passes over into monopoly. On the other hand, monopoly cannot stem the tide of competition – indeed, it itself breeds competition; just as a prohibition of imports, for instance, or high tariffs positively breed the competition of smuggling" (MECW 3: 432). As has been pointed out, there is no clear suggestion here of the "decline of the market" (Howard and King 2008: 221–2). Engels cuts short the sequence envisaged by concluding that because "[m]onopoly produces free competition, and the latter, in turn, produces monopoly ... both must fall, and these difficulties must be resolved through the transcendence of the principle which gives rise to them," namely through a social transformation (MECW 3: 442). Furthermore, only in a "rational" or communally organized system can a rational allocation be achieved: "The truth of the relation of competition is the relation of consumption to productivity. In a world worthy of mankind there will be no other competition than this. The community will have to calculate what it can produce with the means at its disposal; and in accordance with the relationship of this productive power to the mass of consumers it will determine how far it has to

---

[2] Despite his denying here an efficient equilibrating or allocative role to the demand–supply or "competitive" mechanism under capitalist organization, Engels appeals to that sort of analysis in interpreting crime and demographics (MECW 3: 442).

raise or lower production, how far it has to give way to, or curtail, luxury" (435).[3] One again notes the implicit absence of a pricing mechanism under appropriate communal arrangement; nonetheless, that a sort of "competition" would then manifest itself is allowed: "Subjective competition – the contest of capital against capital, of labour against labour, etc. – will under these conditions be reduced to the spirit of emulation grounded in human nature (a concept tolerably set forth so far only by Fourier [1829]) which after the transcendence of opposing interests will be confined to its proper and rational sphere."[4]

* * *

We return to Engels's allowance that "competition" was implied by the orthodox version of cost-price determination (above, p. 29). Competition enters by a second route – again, it is alleged, silently – in the determination of each of the distributive elements constituting costs: "But let us suppose once more for a moment that the economist is correct – how then will he determine the costs of production without taking account of competition? When examining the costs of production we shall see that this category too is based on competition, and here once more it becomes evident how little the economist is able to substantiate his claims" (MECW 3: 425).

The issue turns formally on the determinants of the specific elements comprising costs: "According to the economists, the production costs of a commodity consist of three elements: the rent for the piece of land required to produce the raw material; the capital with its profit, and the wages for the labour required for production and manufacture" (MECW 3: 427). However, although rent is said to enter into cost price, Engels focuses in what follows entirely on Ricardian differential rent. He remarks, correctly, that the payment of rent depends on land scarcity (he uses the term "monopoly" but this was standard procedure), but then he errs by supposing that classical differential rent rejected this property, failing to realize that for Ricardo differential rent is a special case of the genus scarcity rent: "After this enlightenment about the origin of the value of land it is, however, very strange to have to hear from the economist that the rent of land is the difference between the yield from the land for which rent is paid and from the worst land worth cultivating at all" (428).[5] The Ricardian doctrine did not, in brief, "cover the causation of rent," an objection reminiscent of Say, who had complained that Ricardo isolated the cause of rent not in the general scarcity principle but in the existence of differentials as such (Hollander 2005: 131).[6] Engels also objected – an incomprehensible objection – that the doctrine required "in practice" the "instantaneous" contraction of the

---

[3] See Engels's retrospective remark of 1877 in *Anti-Dühring* regarding the "balancing of useful effects and expenditure of labour on making decisions concerning production ... in a communist society" (MECW 25: 295n.).

[4] For helpful discussions of Fourier, see Cole (1962: 62–74); and Hunt (2009: 71–2).

[5] Engels was unaware of Ricardo's allowance for diminishing returns at the *intensive* margin. See his letter to Marx, 29 January 1851 (MECW 38: 271).

[6] On this issue, see Mill (1963–91 [1828] 4: 174; 1963–91 [1848a] 3: 428).

margin upon a fall in demand: "This definition is indeed correct in practice if one presupposes that a fall in demand reacts *instantaneously* on rent, and at once puts a corresponding amount of the worst cultivated land out of cultivation. This, however, is not the case, and the definition is therefore inadequate" (MECW 3: 428).

For all that, Engels himself gave qualified approval to the differential-rent principle. Explicit reference is made to T. P. Thompson (1826), "the champion of the Anti-Corn law league, [who] revived Adam Smith's definition, and substantiated it," whereby "rent is the relation between the competition of those striving for the use of the land and the limited quantity of available land" (MECW 3: 428–9). In contrast, the principle of "competition," which properly accounted for "the origin of rent," did not – so Engels believed – take into account "the varying fertility of the soil, just as the previous explanation leaves out competition" (429). The way out, "[a]s in the case of the concept of value," was "to combine these two definitions so as to find the correct definition which follows from the development of the thing itself and thus embraces all practice. Rent is the relation between the productivity of the land, the natural side (which in turn consists of *natural* fertility and *human* cultivation – labour applied to effect improvement), and the human side, competition."[7] Now all this is in fact standard doctrine; it is strange that although Engels rejected classical cost-price analysis based on "competition" on grounds of instability of the variables, he yet adopted the standard rent doctrine though similarly based.

Engels turns next to capital. He emphasizes that the economists regarded capital as a factor apart (albeit formally representing it as "stored-up labour") without realizing that the rift resulted from the private-property institution (MECW 3: 430).[8] This separation of capital and labor is followed by further subdivisions: "capital is divided once more into the original capital and profit – the increment of capital, which it receives in the process of production; although in practice profit is immediately lumped together with capital and set into motion with it. Indeed,

---

[7] Engels proceeds to the charge that, on one hand, the landlord "practises robbery in exploiting for his own benefit the increase in population which that increases competition and thus the value of his estate" (MECW 3: 429). On the other hand, he ruled out other standard charges against the landlord: "The axioms which qualify as robbery the landowner's method of deriving an income – namely, that each has a right to the product of his labour, or that no one shall reap where he has not sown – are not advanced by us. The first excludes the duty of feeding children; the second deprives each generation of the right to live, since each generation starts with what it inherits from the preceding generation."

At a more general level, trading in land was seen as wholly immoral, on a par almost with "self-alienation" – an allusion to slavery (MECW 3: 429–30).

[8] That capital and labor are originally united presumably refers to some early period in history when labor owned the capital it worked with. Relevant here is a reference – in the discussion of land – to "the original act of appropriation itself... justified by the assertion of the still earlier existence of *common* property rights" (MECW 3: 429), which to Engels demonstrated how "private property leads us into contradictions."

even profit is in its turn split into interest and profit proper." Furthermore, "[a]ll these subtle splits and divisions stem from the original separation of capital from labour and from the culmination of this separation – the division of mankind into capitalists and workers – a division which daily becomes ever more acute, and which, as we shall see, is bound to deepen."

Although in the case of rent, and to a lesser extent that of interest, some allowance is made for the productivity dimension, Engels insists on the incommensurability of the factor shares in the product as one analytical consequence of the splits and subsplits arising from private property: "What share land, capital and labour each have in any particular product cannot be determined. The three magnitudes are incommensurable. The land produces the raw material, but not without capital and labour. Capital presupposes land and labour. And labour presupposes *at least* land, and usually also capital" (MECW 3: 431). It was a problem resolved in practice only by an "alien" and "fortuitous" standard: "[W]hen it comes to dividing the proceeds among the three elements under existing conditions, there is no inherent standard; it is an entirely alien and with regard to them fortuitous standard that decides – competition, the cunning right of the stronger."

The abolition of private property in land would allegedly resolve the problem, but the specifics of communal allocative arrangement are not explored in any detail: "If here again we abandon private property, rent is reduced to its truth, to the rational notion which essentially lies at its root. The value of the land divorced from it as rent then reverts to the land itself. This value, to be measured by the productivity of equal areas of land subjected to equal applications of labour, is indeed taken into account as part of the production costs when determining the value of products; and like rent, it is the relation of productivity to competition – but to true competition, such as will be developed when its time comes" (MECW 3: 430). Similarly, with respect to capital, "[i]f we abandon private property, then all these unnatural divisions disappear. The difference between interest and profit disappears; capital is nothing without labour, without movement. The significance of profit is reduced to the weight which capital carries in the determination of the costs of production; and profit thus remains inherent in capital, in the same way as capital itself reverts to its original unity with labour" (431). The same is said of labor, "the main factor in production, the 'source of wealth'": "Just as capital has already been separated from labour, so labour is now in turn split for a second time: the product of labour confronts labour as wages, is separated from it, and is in its turn as usual determined by competition – there being, as we have seen, no firm standard determining labour's share in production. If we do away with private property, this unnatural separation also disappears. Labour becomes its own reward, and the true significance of the wages of labour, hitherto alienated, comes to light – namely, the significance of labour for the determination of the production costs of a thing." A rationally organized economy would thus take into account – apart from labor – the (shadow) returns to land and capital in determining relative values, an impressive insight indeed.

We return to private-property organization. The outcome of the competitive process in labor's case is a "subsistence" minimum – "only the very barest necessities, the mere means of subsistence, fall to the lot of labour" – considering labor's disadvantages in the bargaining process: "labour is weaker than either landed property or capital, for the worker must work to live, whilst the landowner can live on his rent, and the capitalist on his interest, or, if the need arises, on his capital or on capitalised property in land" (MECW 3: 441). Beyond this, "the stronger worker drives the weaker out of the market, just as "large capital and large landed property swallow small capital and small landed property," alluding to business concentration or "centralisation."

D. *Outlines of a Critique* III: On Malthus, Science, and Macroeconomic Instability

To better appreciate Engels's position on labor, we turn to his attitude toward Malthus, who is represented as the "originator" of the population doctrine. The account of Malthus is scarcely well considered. It sets out by asserting that, according to Malthus, "population is always pressing on the means of subsistence;... as soon as production increases, population increases in the same proportion" (MECW 3: 437). Engels, though, goes further, ascribing to Malthus the position "that the inherent tendency of the population to multiply in excess of the available means of subsistence is the root of all misery and all vice. For, when there are too many people, they have to be disposed of in one way or another: either they must be killed by violence or they must starve. But when this has happened, there is once more a gap which other multipliers of the population immediately start to fill up once more: and so the old misery begins all over again." The pattern allegedly applied universally, "not only in civilised, but also in primitive conditions. In New Holland, with a population density of *one* per square mile, the savages suffer just as much from over-population as England." Moreover, this "vile, infamous theory, this hideous, blasphemy against nature and mankind" implied that "since it is precisely the poor who are the surplus, nothing should be done for them except to make their dying of starvation as easy as possible, and to convince them that it cannot be helped and that there is no other salvation for their whole class than keeping propagation down to the absolute minimum."

Engels diluted somewhat his harsh evaluation of Malthus. The Malthusian theory had at least "shown us how in the last instance private property had turned man into a commodity whose production and destruction also depend solely on demand" (MECW 3: 439–40). Rather more positively, "the production of labour-power has been regulated so far by the law of competition and is therefore also exposed to periodic crises and fluctuations – this is a fact whose establishment constitutes Malthus' merit" (438).

A weakness of Malthus's principle, brought to light by Archibald Alison (1840), was its neglect of "the fact that each adult can produce more than he himself needs – a fact without which mankind could not multiply, indeed could not even exist; if it were not so how could those still growing up live?" (MECW 3: 438). On the basis of this proposition Engels concluded – apparently drawing upon Watts (1842: 14, cited in Claeys 1984: 220) – that a large population is actually a public good:

> For the economist, only that person really demands, only that person is a real consumer, who has an equivalent to offer for what he receives. But if it is a fact that every adult produces more than he himself can consume, that children are like trees which give superabundant returns on the outlays invested in them – and these certainly are facts, are they not? – then it must be assumed that each worker ought to be able to produce far more than he needs and that the community, therefore, ought to be very glad to provide him with everything he needs; one must consider a large family to be a very welcome gift for the community. But the economist, with his crude outlook, knows no other equivalent than that which is paid to him in tangible ready cash. (MECW 3: 438–9)

A further feature of Alison's account is that "[t]he productive power at mankind's disposal is immeasurable. The productivity of the soil can be increased *ad infinitum* by the application of capital, labour and science" (MECW 3: 436). Here Engels contrasts some sort of rational communal approach extending to "science" with the actual, irrational, approach: "This immeasurable productive capacity, handled consciously and in the interest of all, would soon reduce to a minimum the labour falling to the share of mankind. Left to competition, it does the same, but within a context of antitheses," alluding to those "mad" (cyclical) features of the system that economists found inexplicable. A little earlier in his text Engels had actually rejected the orthodox threefold categorization of factors, in favor of his own – land, labor, (which includes capital), and "the mental element of invention, of thought" (427). "What," he asks (427–8), "has the economist to do with inventiveness? Have not all inventions fallen into his lap without any effort on his part? Has *one* of them cost him anything? Why then should he bother about them in the calculation of production costs? ... Science is no concern of his. What does it matter to him that he has received its gifts through Berthollet, Davy, Liebig, Watt, Cartwright, etc. – gifts which have benefited him and his production immeasurably?"

That scientific effort is unpaid in going conditions seems to be implied in all this. By contrast, "in a rational order ... the mental element certainly belongs among the elements of production and will find its place, too, in economics among the costs of production" (MECW 3: 428). And apparently alluding to prospects were capitalists only to fund science properly, Engels continues: "it is certainly gratifying to know that the promotion of science also brings its material reward"; indeed, "a single achievement of science like James Watt's steam-engine has brought in more for the world in the first fifty years of its existence than the world has spent on the promotion of science since the beginning of time." However, even with respect to the going system, entailing at best the underfunding of science, Engels felt able to declare that "science increases at least as much as population. The latter increases in proportion to the size of the previous generation, science advances in proportion to the knowledge bequeathed to it by the previous generation, and thus under the most ordinary conditions also in a geometrical progression. And what is impossible to science?" (440).[9]

We recall Engels's ascription to Malthus of a universal principle of excess population relative to food supply. This he denied on Alison's grounds – but even Alison, Engels added, "does not go to the root of the matter, and therefore in the end reaches the same conclusion as Malthus" (MECW 3: 438). It is allowed that "surplus population, or labour power," did in actuality characterize advanced capitalist societies; for "[t]he population is only too large where the productive power as a whole is too large. The condition of every over-populated country, particularly England, since the time when Malthus wrote, makes this abundantly clear." Nevertheless, such "over-population" was to be understood – Engels here silently follows Watts (see Claeys 1984: 220) – relative to "means of employment," Malthus's error being "to confuse means of subsistence with [means of] employment," although expansion of the latter was the more constraining of the two: "Only in their end-result" – we would say in the long run – "are the means of employment increased by the increase in machine power and capital. The means of subsistence increase as soon as productive power increases even slightly."

Although the term "Reserve Army of Unemployed" had not yet been coined, it is evidently a Reserve Army that is intended by "surplus population" relative to means of employment as characterizing advanced capitalist systems. Moreover, that "the population is too large where the productive power as a whole is too large" intimates that the unemployment in question is related to the technological maturity of operations, reflecting knowledge creation. However, notwithstanding the supposed "permanent" character of such unemployment, it is still the case that, as the means of employment expand over time, so too, in consequence, does population. For "the number of people produced depends on the number of people who can be employed," and the means of employment are assumed to increase, albeit slowly, with "increase in machine power and capital," as we have seen. This brief formulation, which would not perhaps alone suffice to establish the proposition in question, is reinforced by the affirmation in *The Condition of the Working Class* the following year that "machinery and the expansion of industry which it produced" are responsible for growth of population (below, p. 49). The existence of a permanent

---

[9] One did not have to go so far considering current potential: "It is absurd to talk of over-population so long as 'there is enough waste land in the valley of the Mississippi for the whole population of Europe to be transplanted there' [Alison 1840: 548]; so long as no more than one-third of the earth can be considered cultivated, and so long as the production of this third itself can be raised sixfold and more by the application of improvements already known" (MECW 3: 440).

labor excess relative to means of employment does not preclude long-run expansion of labor supply.

* * *

In addition to Malthus's "merit" in recognizing treatment of labor within private-property organization as a commodity subject to the rules of competition (above, p. 35), there was the negative merit that "the Malthusian theory has certainly been a necessary point of transition which has taken us an immense step further. Thanks to this theory, as to economics as a whole, our attention has been drawn to the productive power of the earth and of mankind; and after overcoming this economic despair we have been made for ever secure against the fear of over-population" (MECW 3: 439). A complexity of the first order, however, is created by Engels's insistence on moral restraint even in a "transformed" society that alone could provide the education required to instill an appropriate sense of responsibility: "We derive from [the Malthusian theory] the most powerful economic arguments for a social transformation. For even if Malthus were completely right, this transformation would have to be undertaken straight away; for only this transformation, only the education of the masses which it provides, makes possible that moral restraint of the propagative instinct which Malthus himself presents as the most effective and easiest remedy for over-population."[10] Now though the significance of moral restraint is said to hold good only if Malthus is supposed to be right, Engels must surely have presumed this to be the case; why else claim that the Malthusian theory based on "the fear of over-population" – the context relates to "the productive power of the earth," that is, to means of subsistence, not means of employment – provided "the most powerful economic arguments for a social transformation"? Why too bother to mention the efficacy of education under communal arrangement? Furthermore, if there is a possibility of Malthusian overpopulation even under communism (to be resolved by moral restraint), what can possibly be its source? Engels, after all, had earlier asserted, following Alison, that "each worker ought to be able to produce far more than he needs . . . [so that] one must consider a large family to be a very welcome gift for the community." All in all, acceptance of the need for moral restraint suggests recognition of a "Malthusian" population problem – excess population relative to "means of subsistence" – an actual problem in existing society (with no hope of solution), and a potential problem in a reformed system (with a solution at hand in education) wholly in conflict with the criticism of Malthus based on Alison. I can offer no resolution.

The affirmation of 1844 that "even if Malthus were completely right," only communism could ensure moral restraint, is reiterated nearly forty years later in

---

[10] Although, for Engels, Malthus's proposal for population control had no hope of success in a system based on self-interested calculation, he does not spell out the rationale for his evaluation. Marx was to make out a case based on free-riding (Hollander 2008: 221).

a letter of 1 February 1881 to Karl Kautsky. This letter takes us a step further, though our problem remains unresolved. Here Engels refers to "the problem of how to avoid what looks like imminent over-population and the threat of collapse" (MECW 46: 56), though he refuses to come to the aid of reformist socialists – the "armchair socialists" such as Schmoller, Wagner, and Brentano – with proposals for a solution. It is most unlikely that "the problem" was one envisaged only by the reformers and not by Engels himself, because were that the case he would surely have taken the opportunity to say so. In any event – precisely as in 1844 – he goes on to raise "the abstract possibility that mankind will increase numerically to such an extent that its propagation will have to be kept within bounds," insisting that a solution could only be achieved by a communist régime:

The abstract possibility that mankind will increase numerically to such an extent that its propagation will have to be kept within bounds does, of course, exist. But should communist society ever find itself compelled to regulate the production of humans in the same way as it has already regulated the production of things, then it, and it alone, will be able to effect this without difficulty. In such a society it would not, or so it seems to me, be particularly difficult to obtain deliberately a result which has already come about naturally and haphazardly in France and Lower Austria. (57)

Though Engels had in mind some form or other of "moral restraint" encouraged by a state education program – because he cites the 1844 formulation – he refrains to go into detail: "At all events, it's for those chaps to decide whether, when and how, it's to be done and what means they wish to use. I don't consider myself qualified to supply them with suggestions and advice about this" (57–8).[11]

* * *

We return to the emphasis in 1844 on science. The private-property system is apparently at no great disadvantage relative to communal arrangement in knowledge creation (above, pp. 36–7). However, expanding productive capacity by means of increase in capital and labor coupled with application of science generates severe instability in a private-property system, as we shall presently see. Moreover, the flow of invention takes the form with private property of labor-saving devices in reaction to labor scarcity and rising wages: "in present conditions science . . . is directed against labour. Almost all mechanical inventions, for instance, have been occasioned by the lack of labour-power; in particular Hargreaves,' Crompton's and Arkwright's cotton-spinning machines. . . . The last great invention in cotton-spinning, the self-acting mule, was occasioned solely by the demand for labour, and rising wages" (MECW 3: 442–3). The latter invention "doubled machine-labour, and thereby cut down hand-labour by half; it threw half the workers out of employment, and thereby reduced the wages of the others by half; it crushed

---

[11] J. S. Mill in 1851 was no more prepared to elaborate (Mill 1963–91 [1851] 5: 449). Engels's position is similar to Mill's except in his insistence that only communist society could provide a solution.

a plot of the workers against the factory owners, and destroyed the last vestige of strength with which labour had still held out in the struggle against capital" (443). Engels is drawing here on Ure (1835).

Engels's response to the orthodox "reemployment" case, whereby machinery embodying new technology favors employment by lowering cost price and extending the market, is problematic. Engels did not reject the case out of hand, but although he agreed that "the workers put out of work" are ultimately reemployed, he goes on to ask this rhetorical question: "But is the economist forgetting, then, that the production of labour-power is regulated by competition; that labour-power is always pressing on the means of employment, and that, therefore, when these advantages are due to become operative, a surplus of competitors for work is already waiting for them, and will thus render these advantages illusory; whilst the disadvantages – the sudden withdrawal of the means of subsistence from one half of the workers and the fall in wages for the other half – are not illusory?" (443). But whence the supposed "surplus of competitors for work" or a surplus of unemployed apart from those originally dismissed? A rephrasing of the question in terms of ongoing technical change provides the apparent answer: "Is the economist forgetting that the progress of invention never stands still, and that these [labor-displacing] disadvantages therefore perpetuate themselves?"[12] The problem is that to argue thus is inconsistent with the initial attribution of the bias toward labor-saving technology to labor scarcity.

* * *

In the course of his refutation of the equilibrating function of the demand–supply mechanism on grounds of an inherent instability of both the cost and utility elements, Engels takes up a corresponding macroeconomic instability – throwing further light on the observations already touched on in the critique of Malthus – reflected in regular five- to seven-year cycles: "The economist comes along with his lovely theory of demand and supply, proves to you that 'one can never produce too much,' and practice replies with trade crises, which reappear as regularly as the comets, and of which we have now on the average one every five to seven years," and this since the last third of the eighteenth century (MECW 3: 433). (Engels here cites Wade 1833: 211.)[13] This "natural law" of competition would

---

[12] Engels asks further, "Is [the economist] forgetting that with the division of labour, developed to such a high degree by our civilisation, a worker can only live if he can be used at this particular machine for this particular detailed operation; that the change-over from one type of employment to another, newer type is almost invariably an absolute impossibility for the adult worker?" (MECW 3: 443).

[13] Besomi (2008: 625) maintains that Wade's 1833 account is less satisfactory than an earlier analysis in 1826. There generalization to the economy as a whole was recognized, whereas the later work advises that workers be trained in several occupations because "[i]t never happens that all branches of industry are simultaneously depressed" (1833: 264). This feature, however, should not be exaggerated. The 1833 account of a five- to seven-year cycle itself certainly implies an aggregate movement, and it is this that attracted Engels: "The commercial cycle is ordinarily completed in five or seven years, within which terms it will be found,

not apply in a rationally organized society: "What are we to think of a law which can only assert itself through periodic upheavals? It is certainly a natural law based on the unconsciousness of the participants. If the producers as such knew how much the consumers required, if they were to organise production, if they were to share it out amongst themselves, then the fluctuations of competition and its tendency to crisis would be impossible" (433–4). Engels in fact envisaged an increasing "universalization" and hence worsening of cycles – culminating in a "social revolution" – bringing into the picture an inflow of small capitalists into the working class:

But as long as you continue to produce in the present unconscious, thoughtless manner, at the mercy of chance – for just so long trade crises will remain; and each successive crisis is bound to become more universal and therefore worse than the preceding one; is bound to impoverish a larger body of small capitalists, and to augment in increasing proportion the numbers of the class who live by labour alone, thus considerably enlarging the mass of labour to be employed (the major problem of our economists) and finally causing a social revolution such as has never been dreamt of in the philosophy of the economists. (434)

The "worsening" of crises thus reflects the expanding range of activities affected by cyclical forces.

Engels then proceeds to relate cycles to secular expansion, with such expansion occurring during quiescent periods: "When the fluctuation of competition is small, when demand and supply, consumption and production, are almost equal, a stage must be reached in the development of production where there is so much superfluous productive power that the great mass of the nation has nothing to live on, that the people starve from sheer abundance. For some considerable time England has found herself in this crazy position, in this living absurdity" (MECW 3: 435). Why it follows that "the great mass... has nothing to live on" is left unexplained, but some form of underconsumption may have been intended. In any event, the situation then ruling is said to be the inevitable prelude to cyclical instability: "When production is subject to greater fluctuations, as it is bound to be in consequence of such a situation, then the alternation of boom and crisis, over-production and slump, sets in" (436). This "mad situation," of "coexisting wealth and poverty," the economist could not understand. Above all, "he could not afford to admit that this contradiction is a simple consequence of competition; for in that case his entire system would have fallen to bits." He accordingly invented the Malthusian population theory: "I shall not accept as competent" – Engels

by reference to our commercial history during the last seventy years, alternate periods of prosperity and depression have been experienced.... It is the nature of great and precipitous changes to involve the innocent with the guilty; and this was one of the most fatal results of the late reaction: it not only swept away the delusive projects of the unprincipled adventurer, but paralyzed the operations of real business and commendable enterprise" (211–12). So too does a striking conclusion: "Fluctuations in employment are the great bane of communities. A nation had better be stationary in riches than be carried transiently forward by a sudden impulse of prosperity to be followed by equal or deeper depression" (268).

protested – "any defence of the Malthusian theory which does not explain to me on the basis of its own principles how a people can starve from sheer plenty and bring this into harmony with reason and fact" (439).

A further feature of Engels's account will be recalled, namely the process of business concentration: "[L]arge property increas[es] much more rapidly than small property, since a much smaller portion is deducted from its proceeds as property-expenses" (441). This process, which is exacerbated by crises, is represented as a "law . . . immanent in private property as all the others. The middle classes must increasingly disappear until the world is divided into millionaires and paupers, into large landowners and poor farm labourers. All the laws, all the dividing of landed property, all the possible splitting-up of capital, are of no avail: this result must and will come, unless it is anticipated by a total transformation of social conditions, a fusion of opposed interests, an abolition of private property" (441). In this context we encounter a clash of perspectives. For the foregoing formulation implies a permanent decline in the significance of competitive markets – a feature of the later Marx–Engels evolutionary orientation (see Chapter Three, Section H). By contrast, we have also encountered (above, p. 31) the notion of a temporary monopoly that carries no such implication.

E. *The Holy Family*: Some Brief Observations

A variety of interesting observations pertaining to the labor market are found in Engels's contribution to the jointly published work *The Holy Family* (1845), written over the period September to November 1844.[14] There is insistence upon a wage scale in the industrial sector: "In reality all *grades of wages* exist in English factories, from 1s 6d to 40s and more," rather than a single rate of 11s, as some supposed (MECW 4: 13). He refers to agricultural wages at or close to the subsistence minimum: "With the repeal of the English Corn Laws agricultural labourers will have to put up with a lowering of wages, in regard to which, however, we must most submissively remark that that destitute class cannot be deprived of another penny without being reduced to absolute starvation." Now this conclusion scarcely follows, because the lowering of money wages reflects a lower corn price; for Engels insisted – pace the "Critical Critics" (the Bauer brothers and other young Hegelians) – that the Anti-Corn-Law Leaguers knew very well that "*ceteris paribus,*

---

[14] *The Holy Family* – a title suggested by the German editor – was published under the names of Engels and Marx (in that order). "Doubtless Marx intended, by this friendly gesture, a commitment that he hoped would be permanent" (Rubel 1982: 422). The work was directed against the so-called Young Hegelians, the "Critical Critics – Bruno Bauer and Company." Engels was unaware of Marx's full contribution until he saw the volume in print: "The fact that you enlarged the *Critical Criticism* to twenty sheets surprised me not a little. But it is all to the good, for it means that much can now be disseminated which would otherwise have lain for heaven knows how long in your escritoire" (20 January 1845; MECW 38: 18). He was, though, embarrassed to find his name listed first on the title page: "I can see from the announcement that you have put my name first. Why? I contributed practically nothing to it and anyone can identify your style" (7 March; 25).

a drop in the price of bread must be followed by a drop in wages, so that all would remain as it was" (16). Furthermore, "these people expect that, granted there is a drop in wages and a consequent lowering of production costs, the result will be an expansion of the market. This, they expect, would lead to a reduction of competition among the workers, and consequently wages would still be kept a little higher in comparison with the price of bread than they are now." If Engels actually accepts the logic attributed here to the Anti-Corn-Law-League – formally he is neutral – he would be adopting the position that a general wage cut reduces costs, which is the Smithian rather than the Ricardian view.

Brief remarks are also directed against "Critical Criticism" on the question of Britain's international competitiveness: "It decrees that England is to become a huge workshop for the world, although the un-Critical mass of Americans, Germans and Belgians are ruining one market after another for the English by their competition" (MECW 4: 14). This issue was to take on high significance some forty years later (see Chapter Six, p. 296). We find, too, insistence on the Ten Hours' Bill as a threat to the factory system: "Criticism decrees that Lord *Ashley's Ten Hour Bill* is a half-hearted *juste-milieu* measure . . . while the factory-owners, the Chartists, the landowners – in short, all that makes up the mass nature of England – have so far considered this measure as an expression, the mildest possible one admittedly, of a downright radical principle, since it would lay the axe at the root of foreign trade and thereby at the root of the factory system."[15]

Finally, there is an interesting evaluation of British industrial history: "In real history the *cotton industry* was founded mainly on *Hargreaves' jenny* and *Arkwright's throstle, Crompton's mule* being only an improvement of the spinning jenny according to the new principle discovered by Arkwright. . . . In reality, the invention of the steam-engine *preceded* all the above-mentioned inventions; according to Criticism it is the crown of them all and the *last*" (MECW 4: 12–13).

F. *The Condition of the Working Class in England* I: The Industrialization Process

Our next port of call is Engels's best known work, *The Condition of the Working Class in England*, composed over the period September 1844 to March 1845 (MECW 4: 296, 701–2).[16] The starting point relates to the major changes in industrial organization since the mid-eighteenth century, rather than to private property and its implications as in the *Outlines* (on this contrast, see Stedman Jones 1982: 309–14). Before considering the analytical conceptions relating to the labor market

---

[15] Engels cited a Parliamentary speech of 15 March 1844 by the Home Secretary, Sir James Graham, to the effect that a machine working fewer hours per day would *not* remain usable longer: "the time when it would be worn out would be the same – twelve years" (citing Hansard Parliamentary Debates; MECW 4: 15), charging the "Critical Critics" with distorting Graham's position.

[16] Several editions were later authorized: the American 1887 (actually edited by Engels), the second German (1892), and the English (1892), with the title reading *The Condition of the Working Class in England in 1844*.

that emerge in this work, let us attend first to descriptive matters involving the industrialization process and emergence of the proletariat, having in mind a helpful summary of the main theme that had already appeared in "The Condition of England. The Eighteenth Century" (1844):

The most important effect of the eighteenth century for England was the creation of the proletariat by the industrial revolution. The new industry demanded a constantly available mass of workers for the countless new branches of production, and moreover workers such as had previously not existed. Up to 1780 England had few proletarians, a fact which emerges inevitably from the social condition of the nation as described above. Industry concentrated work in factories and towns; it became impossible to combine manufacturing and agricultural activity, and the new working class was reduced to complete dependence on its labour. What had hitherto been the exception became the rule and spread gradually outside the towns too. Small-scale farming was ousted by the large tenant farmers and thus a new class of agricultural labourers was created. The population of the towns trebled and quadrupled and almost the whole of this increase consisted solely of workers. The expansion of mining likewise required a large number of new workers, and those too lived solely from their daily wage. (MECW 3: 487)

The fuller version of 1845 describes domestic spinning and weaving under conditions of "constant increase in the demand for the home market, keeping pace with the slow increase of population" (MECW 4: 308). The "victory of machine-work over hand-work" – reflecting the competitive advantage of the new technologies – entailed "a rapid fall in price of all manufactured commodities, prosperity of commerce and manufacture, the conquest of nearly all the unprotected foreign markets, the sudden multiplication of capital and national wealth"; and also "a still more rapid multiplication of the proletariat" and "the destruction of all property-holding and of all security of employment for the working-class" (312).[17] The labor-supply increase alluded to is represented as reflecting not only an inflow from the agricultural districts in response to wage increases but also natural population growth: "the proletariat was called into existence by the introduction of machinery. The rapid extension of manufacture demanded hands, wages rose, and troops of workmen migrated from the agricultural districts to the towns. Population multiplied enormously, and nearly all the increase took place in the proletariat" (321).[18] To this is added Irish immigration, which was also in response to rising labor demand.

[17] On the essential contribution of the document as pertaining to the creation of the proletariat, see Hobsbawm (1969: 9), Berg (1980: 323–6), Himmelfarb (1984: 282–5), Dennehy (1996: 104), and McLellan (1998: xix).

[18] The following passage may possibly also allude to population increase in response to increased labor demand: "But as soon as the immeasurable importance of mechanical power was practically demonstrated, every energy was concentrated in the effort to exploit this power in all directions, and to exploit it in the interest of individual inventors and manufacturers; and the demand for machinery, fuel, and materials called a mass of workers and a number of trades into redoubled activity" (MECW 4: 316–17).

Engels describes the working man who belonged to the new propertyless class as having no hope of rising into the middle class, contrasting with a degree of upward mobility under hand-work organization (MECW 4: 321). However, the middle class itself was threatened, the modern arrangement characterized by social bifurcation: "Manufacture, on a small scale, created the middle-class; on a large scale, it created the working-class, and raised the elect of the middle-class to the throne, but only to overthrow them the more surely when the time comes. Meanwhile, it is an undenied and easily explained fact that the numerous petty middle-class of the 'good old times' has been annihilated by manufacture, and resolved into rich capitalists on the one hand and poor workers on the other" (325). Engels himself notes (325n.) that much of this is to be found already in the *Outlines*, as we have seen, for example, in the context of business concentration.

G. *The Condition of the Working Class in England* II: Earnings, Employment, and Population Growth

We turn now to wage-rate determination under the new industrial conditions. The key is provided by "competition," a battle "fought not between the different classes of society only, but also between the individual members of these classes" (MECW 4: 375). This intraclass competition between workers is "the sharpest weapon against the proletariat in the hands of the bourgeoisie," which explains "the effort of the workers to nullify this competition by associations (376)." In the absence of union counterpressure, the advantage is with the employing class, which "has gained a monopoly of all means of existence," and "which is protected in its monopoly by the power of the state." The bourgeoisie "offers [the proletarian] the means of living, but only for an 'equivalent,' for his work," and it "even lets him have the appearance of acting from free choice, of making a contract with free, unconstrained consent, as a responsible agent who has attained his majority," though he is "in law and in fact, the slave of the bourgeoisie." Lacking is the formal notion of "labor power" as the object of purchase by employers, though the term itself is sometimes encountered (e.g., above, pp. 35, 37), and the technical concept may be implied in the elaboration that "the worker of today seems to be free because he is not sold once for all, but piecemeal by the day, the week, the year, and because no one owner sells him to another, but he is forced to sell himself in this way instead, being the slave of no particular person, but of the whole property-holding class" (379).

In this context we encounter the "subsistence" wage as the worker's reservation price: "To . . . competition of the workers there is but one limit; no worker will work for less than he needs to subsist. If he must starve, he will prefer to starve in idleness than in toil" (376). This limit is socially determined; "the Englishman, who is still somewhat civilised, needs more than the Irishman, who goes in rags, eats potatoes, and sleeps in a pig-sty." Furthermore, a gradual degradation of standards is recognized: "But that does not hinder the Irishman's competing with the

Englishman, and gradually forcing the rate of wages, and with it the Englishman's level of civilisation, down to the Irishman's level" (MECW 4: 376–7).

Several further qualifications must be noted. By the foregoing description Engels intended unskilled labor, because he goes on to point out that "[c]ertain kinds of work require a certain grade of civilisation, and to these belong almost all forms of industrial occupation; hence the interest of the bourgeoisie requires in this case that wages should be high enough to enable the workman to keep himself upon the required plane" (MECW 4: 377). This formulation implies a sort of one-sided diktat by the employer who takes into account what is perceived to be "required," as does a passage identifying the employer's interest in financing the laborer's ability to raise up an efficient replacement: "The newly immigrated Irishman, encamped in the first stable that offers... would be a poor mill-hand. The mill-hand must, therefore, have wages enough to enable him to bring up his children to regular work; but no more, lest he should be able to get on without the wages of his children, and so make something else of them than mere working-men." An important detail should be noted. The wage rate allowed by the employer is the wage per (average) family rather than per individual: "When every member of the family works, the individual worker can get on with proportionately less, and the bourgeoisie has made the most of the opportunity of employing and making profitable the labour of women and children afforded by machine-work.... [T]he usual wages form an average according to which a fully employed family gets on pretty well, and one which embraces few members able to work, pretty badly."

The matter is not left here, for Engels explores the process of wage determination in terms of pressures generated by "competition" between laborers in falling markets and between capitalists in rising markets, generating deviations of the wage from "subsistence." Thus under adverse market conditions the wage might fall below subsistence: "But in the worst case, every working-man... contents himself with half-pay and the hope of better times" (MECW 4: 377).[19] In the case of above-subsistence wages engendered by rising demand for labor – reflecting the rising demand for commodities – "the competition among the workers falls away" while employers "compete among themselves" (378). More specifically, Engels says this: "The capitalist in search of workmen knows very well that his profits increase as prices rise in consequence of the increased demand for his goods, and pays a trifle higher wages rather than let the whole profit escape him.... So one capitalist after another goes in chase of workers, and wages rise; but only as high as the increasing demand permits. If the capitalist, who willingly sacrificed a part of his extraordinary profit, runs into danger of sacrificing any part of his ordinary average profit, he takes very good care not to pay more than average wages."

The subsistence wage itself Engels then restates as simply the "average" wage ruling in the absence of "competition" between capitalists and between workers,

---

[19] The below-subsistence case apparently reflects short-run situations rather than the depression of "standards."

an average that exceeds the minimum physiologically conceivable to allow for customary living conditions: "From this we can determine the average rate of wages. Under average circumstances, when neither workers nor capitalists have reason to compete, especially among themselves, when there are just as many workers at hand as can be employed in producing precisely the goods that are demanded, wages stand a little above the minimum. How far they rise above the minimum will depend upon the average needs and the grade of civilisation of the workers" (MECW 4: 378).[20] Although we have seen that Engels seemed at one point to represent the subsistence wage as imposed by diktat, in this particular instance employers "must reconcile themselves" to pay a wage appropriate to the standard, "not less, because the workers are not competing among themselves, and have no occasion to content themselves with less; not more, because the capitalists, in the absence of competition among themselves, have no occasion to attract working-men by extraordinary favours" (378–9). Again, with respect to skill acquisition, it is less a matter of employers' diktat as one of "induc[ing] the worker to acquire such skill" as is appropriate: "Most industrial occupations demand a certain skill and regularity, and for these qualities, which involve a certain grade of civilisation, the average [1887: the rate of] wages must be such as to induce the worker to acquire such skill and subject himself to such regularity" (379). Hence there emerged a wage scale, "the average wages of industrial workers [being] higher than those of mere porters, day-labourers, etc., higher especially than those of agricultural labourers."

* * *

Engels's account of temporary wage movements above and below subsistence under pressure of "competition," between capitalists in the one case and between workers in the other, immediately brings to mind the competitive process elaborated in Chapter Seven of the *Wealth of Nations*, "On Market and Natural Prices," with "competition" entailing a race between buyers to obtain what is in short supply. It is precisely this analysis that Smith himself applied to the labor market. For example, in the case of an initial excess labor demand, "masters . . . who want more workmen, bid against one another, in order to get them [scarce labor], which sometimes raises both the real and the money price of their labour"; and in the case of excess labor supply "[a] considerable number of people are thrown out of employment, who bid against one another in order to get it, which sometimes lowers both the real and the money price of labour" (Smith 1937 [1776]: 86).

Engels himself favorably cited passages from the *Wealth of Nations* relating the long-run real wage to the economy's growth rate (MECW 4: 380), namely that "[t]he wages paid to journeymen and servants of every kind, must be such as may

---

[20] That an equilibrium state entails the absence of "competition" is a position maintained both by Marx and the early Austrian economists (see Hollander 2008: 36–7).

enable them, one with another, to continue the race of journeymen and servants, according as the increasing, diminishing, or stationary demand of the society may happen to require" (Smith 1937 [1776]: 80), and "[t]hat the demand for men, like that for any *other commodity*, necessarily regulates the production of men, quickens it when it goes on too slowly, and stops it when it advances too fast" (Engels's emphasis). When elaborating Smith's treatment of labor as commodity, Engels also makes explicit the operation of a population mechanism involving marriage, birth, and mortality rates: "*Just as in the case of any other commodity!* If there are too few labourers on hand, prices, i.e., wages, rise, the workers are more prosperous, marriages multiply, more children are born and more live to grow up, until a sufficient number of labourers has been secured. If there are too many on hand, prices fall, want of work, poverty, and starvation, and consequent diseases arise, and the 'surplus population' is put out of the way."

Supplementing some of the more moderate comments in the *Outlines* is a surprisingly respectful, albeit always critical, attitude toward Malthus. I have in mind the methodologically sophisticated observation that Malthus's notion of inadequacy of food supplies – excess population relative to "available means of subsistence" rather than means of employment – implies a faulty causal sequence. Any apparent inadequacy should be interpreted not as reflecting scarce natural resources, but reduced demand for wage goods when the market turns unfavorable as a consequence of technical progress. Inadequacy of food supplies must be understood as a consequence, not a cause:

And Malthus, who carried the foregoing proposition of Smith farther, was also right, in his way, in asserting that there is always a surplus population; that there are always too many people in the world; he is wrong only when he asserts that there are more people on hand than can be maintained from the available means of subsistence.... The productiveness of each hand raised to the highest pitch by the competition of the workers among themselves, the division of labour, the introduction of machinery, the subjugation of the forces of Nature, deprive a multitude of workers of bread. These starving workers are then removed from the market, they can buy nothing, and the quantity of articles of consumption previously required by them is no longer in demand, need no longer be produced. (MECW 4: 380–1)[21]

Engels subsequently asserts that the Malthus position regarding a "surplus population" – "that it is the lot, the eternal destiny of mankind, to exist in too great numbers" – "is now the pet theory of all genuine English bourgeois, and very naturally, since it is the most specious excuse for them, and has, moreover, *a good deal of truth in it under existing conditions*" (570; emphasis added). This statement of

---

[21] The first sentence cited reads as follows in the 1887 American and 1892 English editions: "And Malthus, who carried the foregoing proposition of Smith farther, was also right, in his way, in asserting that there are always more people on hand than can be maintained from the available means of subsistence" (MECW 4: 380n.). The original version, which remains unchanged in the 1892 German edition, is much clearer.

accord is inexplicable unless read subject to the qualification regarding the proper direction of causation.[22]

* * *

To the proposition that labor-saving technical change reduces the demand by labor for wage goods, Engels attaches a remark on the multiplier effects affecting workers in the wage-goods sectors: "the workers previously employed in producing them are therefore driven out of work, and are also removed from the market, and so it goes on, always the same old round" (MECW 4: 381). However, this is only the case "if other circumstances did not intervene," whereas Engels (with recent British experience in mind) posits net secular growth in aggregate demand for labor, the "other circumstances" at play including reemployment generated by the reduced costs resulting from new technology: "The introduction of the industrial forces already referred to for increasing production leads, in the course of time, to a reduction of prices of the articles produced and to consequent increased consumption, so that a large part of the displaced workers finally, after long suffering, find work again in new branches of labour." Expanded exports, which one supposes are also enhanced by reduced costs, also play a part: "If, in addition to this, the conquest of foreign markets constantly and rapidly increases the demand for manufactured goods, as has been the case in England during the past sixty years, the demand for hands increases, and, in proportion to it, the population. Thus, instead of diminishing, the population of the British Empire has increased with extraordinary rapidity, and is still increasing."

Population growth, be it noted, is represented as a response to growing employment opportunities. The same estimate of a positive employment effect of machinery, with a population increase reacting to an increasing demand for labor induced by technical progress, is confirmed in a later text: "The bourgeois forgets, in fighting the working-man, the most ordinary principles of his own Political Economy. He who at other times swears by Malthus, cries out in his anxiety before the workers: 'Where could the millions by which the population of England has increased find work, without the improvements in machinery?' [Symons 1839] As though the bourgeois did not know well enough that without machinery and the expansion of industry which it produced, these 'millions' would never have been brought into the world and grown up!" (MECW 4: 432–3).[23] This perspective is wholly in line with the *Outlines*.

The problem we must now face is that in this same context Engels also elaborates the negative employment effects of machinery on factory hands in the textile sectors,[24] distinguishing between "well-ordered" systems where so-called improvement "could only be a source of rejoicing," and competitively organized systems

---

[22] Engels neglected Malthus's own investigation into the order of precedence, on which see Hollander (1997: 209).

[23] In the German editions of 1845 and 1892, Symons's question is followed by "Nonsense!"

[24] Engels cites Ure (1836) and Baines (1835) on the history of cotton manufacture.

where "[e]very improvement in machinery throws workers out of employment, and the greater the advance, the more numerous the unemployed" (MECW 4: 429). It is allowed that "[t]he bourgeoisie is so far correct that under certain conditions favourable for the general development of manufacture, every reduction in price of goods *in which the raw material is cheap*, greatly increases consumption, and gives rise to the building of new factories" (Engels's emphasis), but the reemployment argument neglected the lag between expansion of final demand and capital construction – "the fact that it takes years for these results of the decrease in price to follow and for new factories to be built"; the replacement of adult male labor by female and child labor; and the necessity for retraining, because "whole branches of industry fall away, or are so changed that they must be learned afresh" (431).[25] The apologists also forgot that "improvement" is not a once-and-for-all event – a theme encountered in the *Outlines* (above, p. 40) – but "goes steadily on, and that as soon as the operative has succeeded in making himself at home in a new branch, if he actually does succeed in so doing, this, too, is taken from him, and with it the last remnant of security which remained to him for winning his bread."

All in all, Engels concluded, "[t]he consequences of improvement in machinery under our present social conditions are, for the working-man, solely injurious, and often in the highest degree oppressive. Every new advance brings with it loss of employment, want, and suffering" (MECW 4: 433). He points out that loss of employment in consequence of "[e]very new advance" is a disaster for the discharged laborers "in a country like England, where, without that, there is usually a 'surplus population,'" referring presumably to sources of excess labor supply such as Irish immigration (above, p. 45). He adds this: "And what a dispiriting, unnerving influence this uncertainty of his position in life, consequent upon the unceasing progress of machinery and the unemployment resulting from it, must exercise upon the worker, whose lot is precarious enough without it!"[26]

Engels misleads on his own terms by declaring that "the consequences of improvement of machinery" are "solely injurious" to labor, considering his equally strong insistence on the positive employment effects of machinery. Nevertheless, the contrasting evaluations can be reconciled. The negative effects may be understood as pertinent to the short-run situation only, as is implied by the references to time lags between final-demand expansion and capital construction and the necessity for retraining; the positive effects are of a secular order as reflected in the affirmation that the introduction of new technology "leads, *in the course of time*,"

---

[25] Engels complains that the bourgeoisie "takes good care not to confess what it usually harps upon, whenever the question of forbidding the work of children is broached, that factory-work must be learned in earliest youth [1845 and 1892 versions also include "and indeed before the age of ten"] in order to be learned properly" (MECW 4: 431). He cites Lord Ashley's evidence before the House of Commons on the Ten Hours' Bill (15 March 1844) "to prove the crowding out of adult males" (436).

[26] The phrase "and the unemployment resulting from it" is removed in the 1887 edition, which is consistent with the view long expressed that machinery raises the *long-run* demand for labor, but suggesting a weakening of the reserve army category. For a confirmation, see Chapter Five on the New Unionism.

to reduced prices and consequently increased consumption, "so that a large part of the displaced workers finally, after long suffering find work again" (emphasis added), and in the further affirmation that "machinery and the expansion of industry which it produced" is responsible for population growth.

The same problem also arises with regard to the related matter of the effect of improved machinery on wages, and perhaps the same solution applies: "The bourgeoisie insists that although the price of piece-work has been reduced, yet the total of wages for the week's work has rather risen than fallen, and the condition of the operatives rather improved than deteriorated. It is hard to get to the bottom of the matter, for the operatives usually dwell upon the price of piece-work. But it is certain that the weekly wage, also, has in many branches of work, been reduced by the improvement of machinery" (MECW 4: 431–2).[27] A contrast between sectors further complicates the picture or the positive effect of machinery on wages is said to pertain only in sectors requiring high skill and subject to union protection: "The so-called fine spinners . . . do receive high wages, thirty to forty shillings a week, because they have a powerful association for keeping wages up, and their craft requires long training; but the coarse spinners who have to compete against self-actors (which are not as yet adapted for fine spinning), and whose association was broken down by the introduction of these machines, receive very low wages" (432). Even regarding the general wage, however, Engels proceeds with surprising caution when he asserts merely that wage reduction was the opinion of workers: "That wages in general have been reduced by the improvement of machinery is the unanimous testimony of the operatives. The bourgeois assertion that the condition of the working-class has been improved by machinery is most vigorously proclaimed a falsehood in every meeting of working-men in the factory districts." He adds that labor's position relative to capital would have deteriorated even were the "absolute" or weekly wage unchanged, "the operatives [having] had quietly to look on while the manufacturers filled their purses from every improvement without giving the hands the smallest share in the gain."[28]

The foregoing discussion modifies the picture commonly given of Engels as portraying an unmitigated and unambiguous deterioration in working-class living standards in consequence of industrialization and mechanization. To his credit, his evaluation is rather more balanced.[29]

---

[27] The "worst situation," characterized by handloom weaving, entailed labor still employed but obliged to compete against new technology (MECW 4: 433–4).

[28] Engels here is on uncertain grounds, because he himself insisted that innovating capitalists benefit only from the immediate effects: "But the bourgeoisie gets the benefit of the improvements in machinery; it has a capital opportunity for piling up money during the first years while many old machines are still in use, and the improvement not yet universally introduced; and it would be too much to ask that it should have an open eye for the disadvantages inseparable from these improvements" (MECW 4: 431).

[29] See Hobsbawm (1964: 105–19) for objections to the "cheerful historians" Chaloner and Henderson in their 1958 edition of *The Condition of the Working Class*; also see the critical comments by McLellan whereby "Engels emerged rather better than his editors" (1993: xvii).

    In their second edition in 1971, Chaloner and Henderson fail to respond to Hobsbawm. The grand divide should not be exaggerated, though, because Hobsbawm did not maintain that

H. *The Condition of the Working Class in England* III: The Cyclical Dimension, and the Industrial Reserve Army

Notwithstanding the long-term expansion in aggregate labor demand reflecting the use of machinery, Engels underscored a "permanent surplus" of population: "in spite of the extension of industry, in spite of the demand for working-men which, in general, has increased, there is, according to the confession of all the official political parties (Tory, Whig, and Radical), permanent surplus, superfluous population; the competition among the workers is constantly greater than the competition to secure workers" (MECW 4: 381). This pattern cannot be attributed to population growth, which is envisaged as occurring in appropriate response to rising labor demand (above, p. 49). Part of the explanation may be found in ongoing technological change, though if innovation is ongoing then so too are the related cost reductions and demand expansions. Nonetheless, there is also a cyclical dimension to take under consideration.

Elaborating the account in the *Outlines*, Engels attributes recurring crises to limited knowledge by firms of market conditions, especially foreign markets: "although the manufacturer may know how much of each article is consumed in each country annually, he cannot know how much is on hand at every given moment, much less can he know how much his competitors export thither. He can only draw most uncertain inferences from the perpetual fluctuations in prices, as to the quantities on hand and the needs of the moment" (MECW 4: 381–2). Accordingly, "[u]pon the slightest favourable report, each one exports what he can, and before long such a market is glutted, sales stop, capital remains inactive, prices fall, and English manufacture has no further employment for its hands" (382). The coincidence of cyclical movement across industries is attributed to "the centralising tendency of competition, which drives the hands thrown out of one branch into such other branches as are most easily accessible, and transfers the goods which cannot be disposed of in one market to other markets," a tendency that "has gradually brought the single minor crises nearer together and united them into one periodically recurring crisis. Such a crisis usually recurs once in five years after a brief period of activity and general prosperity; the home market, like all foreign ones, is glutted with English goods, which it can only slowly absorb."[30]

there exists firm evidence for an actual deterioration of living conditions. For a summary of research findings relating to the living-standard debate during the first half of the century, see Boyer (1998). The broad outcome is that real wages tended upward in general from 1818–20 through 1849–50, though with deterioration in the 1830s and early 1840s, with handloom work an exception.

A complexity is created by the character of Manchester, Engels's special focus of attention, as supposedly representative of British industry as a whole with respect to industry structure, cyclical instability, levels of unemployment, and the rate of adoption of new technology. See, on this issue, Boyer (1998: 157) and Hunt (2009: Chapter 3).

[30] On the coincidence of cycles across industries, see also Besomi (2008: 630).

In the Appendix to the 1887 American edition, and also in the Prefaces to the English edition and the Second German edition of 1892, Engels referred to "[t]he recurring period

There follows a graphic description of depression entailing general glut, bankruptcies, plant shutdowns, part-time work and layoffs, depletion of accumulated savings, falling wages, and pressure on poor relief. "The most depressed period," Engels adds, "is brief, lasting, at worst, but one, two, or two and a half years" (388).

Recovery is attributed to the exhaustion of stocks and signs of short supply, which is then reinforced by renewed speculative pressures, always with an emphasis on foreign markets:

Gradually the state of things improves; the accumulations of goods are consumed, the general depression among the men of commerce and manufacture prevents a too hasty replenishing of the markets, and at last rising prices and favourable reports from all directions restore activity. Most of the markets are distant ones; demand increases and prices rise constantly while the first exports are arriving; people struggle for the first goods, the first sales enliven trade still more, the prospective ones promise still higher prices; expecting a further rise, merchants begin to buy upon speculation, and so withdraw from consumption the articles intended for it, just when they are most needed. Speculation forces prices still higher, by inspiring others to purchase, and appropriating new importations at once. (MECW 4: 382–3)

An extension to domestic capital construction follows: "All this is reported to England, manufacturers begin to produce with a will, new mills are built, every means is employed to make the most of the favourable moment" (383). In addition "speculation arises here, too, exerting the same influence as upon foreign markets, raising prices, withdrawing goods from consumption, spurring manufacture in both ways to the highest pitch of effort."

Here Engels returns to the forces responsible for a collapse, not though in terms of the ignorance of distant export markets outlined earlier – though doubtless this remains a factor – but rather as resulting from essentially unjustified speculation in the home market: "Then come the daring speculators working with fictitious capital, living upon credit, ruined if they cannot speedily sell; they hurl themselves into this universal, disorderly race for profits, multiply the disorder and haste by their unbridled passion, which drives prices and production to madness. It is a frantic struggle, which carries away even the most experienced and phlegmatic; goods are spun, woven, hammered, as if all mankind were to be newly equipped, as though two thousand million new consumers had been discovered in the moon."

At this point in the cycle the speculative mood alters, initially abroad, the downward sequence thereby set in motion accelerating with credit contraction: "All at once the shaky speculators abroad, who must have money, begin to sell, below market price of course, for their need is urgent; one sale is followed by others, prices fluctuate, speculators throw their goods upon the market in terror,

of the great industrial crisis . . . stated in the text as five years. This was the period apparently indicated by the course of events from 1825 to 1842. But the industrial history from 1842 to 1868 has shown that the real period is one of ten years; that the intermediate revolutions were secondary, and tended more and more to disappear" (MECW 26: 404; 27: 314). See also *Anti-Dühring* for an account of the ten-year cycle written in 1877 (MECW 25: 263).

the market is disordered, credit shaken, one house after another stops payments, bankruptcy follows bankruptcy, and the discovery is made that three times more goods are on hand or under way than can be consumed." Once news of glutted markets reaches England, "where production has been going on at full speed meanwhile, panic seizes all hands, failures abroad cause others in England, the panic crushes a number of firms, all reserves are thrown upon the market here, too, in the moment of anxiety, and the alarm is still further exaggerated. This is the beginning of the crisis, which then takes precisely the same course as its predecessor, and gives place in turn to a season of prosperity."

* * *

We can now return to the main theme. In the account of the cycle we find explicit reference to "an unemployed reserve army of workers." Whether the term was initially coined by Engels is unclear, but it is the substance that matters. The principle point is the indispensability of a labor force adequate to satisfy requirements at peak levels of activity, but only partially used at other periods:

From this it is clear that English manufacture must have, at all times save the brief periods of highest prosperity, an unemployed reserve army of workers, in order to be able to produce the masses of goods required by the market in the liveliest months. This reserve army is larger or smaller, according as the state of the market occasions the employment of a larger or smaller proportion of its members.... This reserve army ... is the "surplus population" of England, which keeps body and soul together by begging, stealing, street-sweeping, collecting manure, pushing hand-carts, driving donkeys, peddling, or performing occasional small jobs. (MECW 4: 384)

I understand this cyclical pattern to be superimposed on a secular trend (described above, pp. 41, 49) entailing expansion of capital, employment opportunities, and, accordingly, population and labor supply.[31] Population growth, not the reserve army, fuels the secular expansion of the work force, which is fully employed at cyclical peaks – references to a "permanently" superfluous population (above, p. 52) mislead – and in excess supply to a greater or lesser extent at other periods of the cycle.

---

[31] My identification of changes in population with changes in the industrial work force is justified, at least as a first approximation, because Engels treats inflows from agriculture and from Ireland as secondary responses to the primary, industrial, forces at play; moreover, female and child labor is treated as relevant only in the less-advanced sectors of industry (MECW 4: 386).

Engels makes explicit his primary concern with the *advanced industrial sector* in a statistical comment on the order of magnitude of the unemployed: "Of this surplus population there are, according to the reports of the Poor Law commissioners, on an average, a million and a half in England and Wales.... Moreover, this million and a half includes only those who actually apply to the parish for relief; the great multitude who struggle on without recourse to this most hated expedient, it does not embrace. On the other hand, a good part of the number belongs to the agricultural districts, and does not enter into the present discussion" (386).

This pattern implies that real wages suffice – on average, over the cycle – to generate the appropriate growth of the population; the expansionary forces during upturns, acting on accumulation and accordingly population, outweigh the depressive pressures at other periods. On Engels's Smithian grounds, the fact that "the population of the British Empire has increased with extraordinary rapidity, and is still increasing" (above, p. 49) implies a real wage that exceeds subsistence, when the population is merely maintained. When a degeneration of standards is introduced, however, as from English to Irish levels, population growth continues even when wages have fallen to the original (English) subsistence rate and ceases only at the new (Irish) rate.

We come next to a statement regarding worsening industrial crises: "During a crisis this number [surplus population] naturally increases markedly, and want reaches its highest pitch. Take, for instance, the crisis of 1842, which, being the latest, was the most violent; for the intensity of the crisis increases with each repetition, and the next, which may be expected not later than 1847 [Engels notes "And it came in 1847" in the 1887 American version] will probably be still more violent and lasting" (MECW 4: 386).[32] Now a worsening of crises implies a secular fall in the real wage, notwithstanding that – according to Engels's own evaluation – population growth induced by rapid capital accumulation was proceeding apace. Secularly falling real wages are in part attributed to Irish immigration, "another cause of abasement" – in addition to the cyclical pattern – to which the English worker is exposed, "a cause permanently active in forcing the whole class downwards" (388); for "the Irish have, as Dr. Kay says, discovered the minimum of the necessities of life, and are now making the English workers acquainted with it" (390–1). However, the account of a secular fall in real wages, primarily affecting unskilled occupations but carried over somewhat to the laboring class as a whole (392), concludes by perceiving Irish immigration as a contributing cause only of deterioration: "it is easy to understand how the degrading position of the English workers, engendered by our modern industry [the 1887 version uses "history"], and its immediate consequences, has been still more degraded by the presence of Irish competition." A reliance on this text alone would confirm a picture of deteriorating earnings independent of immigration.

A later discussion of the likely effects of Corn Law repeal is relevant for us here. Here Engels provides an orthodox analysis of the prospective reduction in the money wages following a fall in the corn price, coupled with the by-then standard theme that reduced cost prices, by expanding the international market,

---

[32] Engels suggests that the worst was over in Manchester: "When I came to Manchester in November, 1842, there were crowds of unemployed working-men at every street corner, and many mills were still standing idle. In the following months these unwilling corner loafers gradually vanished, and the factories came into activity once more" (MECW 4: 387). Subsequently, Engels refers to the "next [crisis], in 1846 or 1847," followed by one "which, according to the analogy of its predecessors, must break out in 1852 or 1853," though subject to the absence of major changes in political and commercial conditions.

would raise the demand for labor: "The manufacturer can compete more readily, the demand for English goods increases, and, with it, the demand for labour" (MECW 4: 566). Now one consequence of an increase in labor demand, Engels proceeds, would be absorption of unemployed labor – a pool of available labor is taken for granted – and a rise of wages. Why wages should rise at all in these circumstances is unclear, but in any event any such rise would be temporary in consequence of Irish immigration and also population growth: "In consequence of this increased demand wages would actually rise somewhat, and the unemployed workers be re-employed; but for how long? The 'surplus population' of England, and especially of Ireland, is sufficient to supply English manufacture with the necessary operatives, even if it were doubled; and, in a few years, the small advantage of the repeal of the Corn Laws would be balanced, a new crisis would follow, and we should be back at the point from which we started, while the first stimulus to manufacture would have increased population meanwhile" (566).[33] We find once again that immigration and population growth, rather than the pool of unemployed, constitute the main sources of labor supply for industrial expansion of a secular order, which is consistent with the weight placed earlier in the text on population growth in response to rapid capital accumulation induced by new technology.

An important contrast between "permanent" agricultural and "periodic" industrial unemployment confirms the cyclical significance of the industrial reserve. The context is the transformation of farming:

It became . . . the interest of the farmers to . . . drive the farm-hand from the farm, and transform him into a day-labourer. This took place pretty generally towards the end of the twenties of the present century [the 1887 version uses "towards the year 1830"] and the consequence was that the hitherto latent to use an expression from physics [the 1887 version omits "to . . . physics"] over-population was set free, the rate of wages forced down, and the poor-rate enormously increased. From this time the agricultural districts became the main seats [1887 uses "the headquarters"] of *permanent*, as the manufacturing districts [1887, "had long been"] of *periodic pauperism*: and the modification of the Poor Law was the first measure which the State was obliged to apply to the daily increasing impoverishment of the country parishes. (MECW 4: 549–50)

Thus the problem of "permanent" agricultural unemployment had its source in the transition to large-scale farming, the adoption of threshing and other machinery, and the employment of female and child labor, or the fact that the "system of industrial production ha[d] made its entrance" (550). There is, however, an outstanding

---

[33] Engels implies Ricardo's position that a fall in the money wages will raise the profit rate. However, he also predicts, on Smithian grounds, that increased competition between capitals will bring the profit rate down once again: "the manufacturers have in view solely the immediate advantage which the repeal of the Corn Laws would bring them. They are too narrow-minded to see that, even for themselves, no permanent advantage can arise from this measure, because their competition with each other would soon force the profit of the individual back to its old level" (MECW 4: 566).

contrast with industry – the fact of land scarcity, for "[t]he 'over-population' came to light all at once, and could not, as in the manufacturing districts, be absorbed by the needs of an increasing production. New factories could always be built, if there were consumers for their products, but new land could not be created."[34] Nevertheless, although Engels's playing down of secular industrial unemployment – a "surplus population" in industry – confirms the assumption of expanding secular employment, it is unlikely that he had abandoned the usual assumption of a "permanent" industrial reserve. A pool of unemployed people, supplied by those displaced by the innovative process and the various sources noted above, and available for temporary reabsorption in the active labor force upon increase in cyclical demand, is consistent with a secular expansion of demand for labor.

I. *The Condition of the Working Class in England* IV:
Longer-Term Forecasts

Engels's longer-term prognostications put paid to any doubts he may have entertained regarding the course of real wages. Taking issue with McCulloch (1837a), he raises the threat of American industrial preeminence: "If any country is adapted to holding a monopoly of manufacture, it is America. Should English manufacture be thus vanquished – and in the course of the next twenty years, if the present conditions remain unchanged, this is inevitable – the majority of the proletariat must become forever superfluous, and has no other choice than to starve or to rebel" (MECW 4: 580). However, the prospect of worsening cycles remained even were England to retain its industrial preeminence, Engels expatiating on an inevitable inflow into the work force from the middle classes as a result of rising industrial "concentration," and relating the increasing severity of crises to the growing quantitative significance of the "industrial system" based on a capital–labor relation: "But assuming that England retained the monopoly of manufactures, that its factories perpetually multiply, what must be the result? The commercial crises would continue, and grow more violent, more terrible, with the extension of industry and the multiplication of the proletariat. The proletariat would increase in geometrical proportion, in consequence of the progressive ruin of the lower middle-class and the giant strides with which capital is concentrating itself in the hands of the few; and the proletariat would soon embrace the whole nation, with the exception of a few millionaires." (See also "Speeches in Elberfeld," 1845; MECW 4: 257.) The dire prediction also provided the key to prospective revolution: "But in this development there comes a stage at which the proletariat perceives how easily the existing power

---

[34] As for the matter of land scarcity, Engels explains that "[t]he cultivation of waste common land was too risky a speculation for big capital to be invested in it following the conclusion of peace [1815]" [the 1887 version states: "The cultivation of waste common land was too daring a speculation for the bad times following the conclusion of peace"] (MECW 4: 550). The outcome was a wage reduced to "the minimum" – exacerbated by the Old Poor Law – and a "surplus population that could not be got rid of."

may be overthrown, and then follows a revolution.... The commercial crises, the mightiest levers for all independent development of the proletariat, will probably shorten the process, acting in concert with foreign competition and the deepening ruin of the lower middle-class. I think the people will not endure more than one more crisis" (580–1).[35] This matter will be further explored in Chapter Four.

J. The *Principles of Communism* and the *Communist Manifesto*

Several of the major themes in *The Condition of the Working Class* are summarized in the *Principles of Communism* – the blueprint for the *Manifesto of the Communist Party* – composed in 1847.[36] Question 4 of the document describes the origins of the proletariat in "the industrial revolution which took place in England in the latter half of the last century and which has repeated itself since then in all the civilized countries of the world" (MECW 6: 341). The "industrial revolution" itself in manufacturing was "brought about by the invention of the steam-engine, of various spinning machines, of the power-loom, and of a great number of other mechanical devices. These machines which were very expensive and, consequentially, could only be purchased by big capitalists, changed the entire hitherto existing mode of production and supplanted the former workers because machines produced cheaper and better commodities than could the workers with their imperfect spinning-wheels and hand-looms" (341–2). The new processes entailed increased division of labor, "so that the worker who formerly had made a whole article now produced only a part of it" (342), which in turn encouraged further mechanization (a Smithian theme). The same transition occurred in the handicrafts, which "likewise fell increasingly under the domination of the factory system, for here also the big capitalists more and more supplanted the small craftsmen by the establishment of large workshops, in which many savings on costs can be made and there can be a very high division of labour." The outcome was the ruination of "the smaller master handicraftsmen," and a transformation in the position of the workers, leaving in place "two new classes" – the bourgeoisie and the proletariat: "I. The class of big capitalists who already now in all civilised countries almost exclusively own all the means of subsistence and the raw materials and instruments (machinery, factories, etc.), needed for the production of these means of subsistence.... II. The class of the completely propertyless, who are compelled therefore to sell their labour to the bourgeois in order to obtain the necessary means of subsistence in exchange" (342–3).

Question 5 treating "the sale of the labour of the proletarians" – no mention here of labor power – envisages labor as "a commodity like any other [whose]

---

[35] See also Hobsbawm (1964: 125) for the interpretation of Engels whereby it is "[i]ntolerable periodic unemployment," rather than a downward trend in the real wage, that would spur proletarian revolution.

[36] This document, discovered only in 1968 (by Bert Andréas), in turns expands on an earlier "Draft of a Communist Confession of Faith" of June 1847 (MECW 6: 96–103).

price is determined by the same laws as that of any other commodity... under the domination of large-scale industry or of free competition" (MECW 6: 343).[37] More specifically, we find reference to "the cost of production of labour" in terms of "the means of subsistence required for the worker to maintain himself in a condition in which he is capable of working and to prevent the working class from dying out." The subsistence wage is represented as an "average" around which the market wage fluctuates, and the subsistence cost of labor as an "economic law of wages" that "will come to be more stringently applied the more all branches of labour are taken over by large-scale industry." As I have frequently noted, population growth is precluded by a wage rate reduced to "subsistence," unless the minimum standard itself is deteriorating. This complexity is not always spelled out in accounts for public consumption.

Question 7 contrasts slave and proletarian (MECW 6: 343–4). Question 11 deals with "the immediate results" of the industrial revolution considering the political and economic power both of the bourgeoisie and the proletariat, the latter in terms of its growth and concentration (346). Here we encounter the notion of falling real wages – increasing absolute misery – and consequently an enhanced prospect of revolution: "Further, the more it develops, the more machines are invented which displace manual labour, the more large-scale industry... depresses wages to their minimum, and thereby makes the condition of the proletariat more and more unbearable. Thus, through the growing discontent of the proletariat, on the one hand, and through its growing power, on the other, the industrial revolution prepares a social revolution by the proletariat."

The pattern of five- to seven-year cycles is taken up in Question 12, with the crisis described in terms of periodic overproduction – this too a result of the industrial revolution: "In the steam-engine and the other machines large-scale industry created the means of increasing industrial production in a short time and at slight expense to an unlimited extent.... The result was that the goods manufactured could not be sold, and a so-called trade crisis ensued. Factories had to stand idle, factory owners went bankrupt, and the workers lost their bread.... After a while the surplus products were sold, the factories started working again, wages went up, and gradually business was more brisk than ever" (MECW 6: 346–7). This

---

[37] A little later, one encounters an instance of circular reasoning with respect to "free competition" and its relation to large-scale industry. Engels sets out by explaining that in place of the aristocracy and build-burghers, the industrial revolution "put free competition, that is, a state of society in which everyone has the right to engage in any branch of industry he likes, and where nothing can hinder him in carrying it on except lack of the necessary capital. The introduction of free competition is therefore the public declaration that henceforward the members of society are only unequal in so far as their capital is unequal, that capital has become the decisive power and therefore the capitalists, the bourgeois, have become the first class in society" (MECW 6: 346). Apparently, then, "free competition" results from large-scale industry – but Engels concludes by asserting that "free competition is necessary for the beginning of large-scale industry since it is the only state of society in which large-scale industry can grow."

too presaged "revolution": "Thus since the beginning of this century the state of industry has continually fluctuated between periods of prosperity and periods of crisis, and almost regularly every five to seven years a similar crisis has occurred, and every time it has entailed the greatest misery for the workers, general revolutionary ferment, and the greatest danger to the entire existing system" (347).

The phenomenon of "regularly recurring trade crises" is said in Question 13 to reflect the fact that large-scale industry, which had "created free competition," had "nevertheless outgrown free competition; that competition and in general the carrying on of industrial production by individuals have become a fetter upon large-scale industry which it [large-scale industry] must and will break." Large-scale industry on capitalistic lines could "only survive through a general confusion repeating itself every seven years . . . ; therefore . . . either large-scale industry itself must be given up, which is utterly impossible, or . . . it absolutely necessitates a completely new organisation of society, in which industrial production is no longer directed by individual factory owners, competing one against the other, but by the whole of society according to a fixed plan and according to the needs of all."[38] Precisely what Engels may have intended by his forecast of "revolution" and reconstruction of society will be explored in Chapter Four.

We come now to an impressive account of what today would be described as a globalization process in a developmental context.[39] The account constitutes part of Engels's response to Question 11: "What were the immediate results of the industrial revolution . . . ":

[O]wing to the continual cheapening of the price of industrial products as a result of machine labour, the old system of manufacture or industry founded upon manual labour was completely destroyed in all countries of the world. All semi-barbarian countries, which until now had been more or less outside historical development and whose industry had until now been based on manufacture, were thus forcibly torn out of their isolation. They bought the cheaper commodities of the English and let their own manufactory workers go to ruin. Thus countries that for thousands of years had made no progress, for example India, were revolutionized through and through, and even China is now marching towards a revolution. It has reached the point that a new machine invented today in England, throws millions of workers in China out of work within a year. Large-scale industry has thus brought all the peoples of the earth into relationship with one another, thrown all the small local markets into the world market, prepared the way everywhere for civilization and progress, and brought it about that everything that happens in the civilized countries must have its repercussions on all other countries. (345)

[38] There is here, perhaps, an implication of "the decline of the market," contrasting with the position in the *Outlines*.

[39] This account elaborates a brief statement in the joint *The German Ideology* whereby "history becomes world history. Thus, for instance, if in England a machine is invented which deprives countless workers of bread in India and China, and overturns the whole form of existence of these empires, this invention becomes a world-historical fact" (1845; MECW 5: 51).

Engels concludes, rather too readily perhaps, that the globalization process ensured a revolutionary outcome in all countries: "So if now in England or France the workers liberate themselves, this must lead to revolutions in all other countries, which sooner or later will also bring about the liberation of the workers in those countries."

* * *

The *Communist Manifesto*, published in February 1848, was written at the behest of the Communist League meeting in London, from November 29 to December 8, 1847. Engels and Marx worked together during December, but Marx worked alone throughout January and was responsible for writing up the document: "La redaction définitive du *Manifeste* incombait... au seul Marx" (Rubel 1963: 159; also Andréas 1963: 1; Hobsbawm 1998: 4; McLellan 1998: xii).[40] The theoretical observations – already found in the *Principles of Communism*[41] – include the following. (1) Worsening overproduction crises presaging the collapse of capitalism (MECW 6: 489–90). (2) Treatment of labor as "commodity" subject to "all the fluctuations of the market," but on an average equal to its "cost of production" (490–1), or the subsistence level: "The average price of wage-labour is the minimum wage, *i.e.*, that quantum of the means of subsistence, which is absolutely requisite to keep the labourer in bare existence as a labourer. What, therefore, the wage-labourer appropriates by means of his labour, merely suffices to prolong and reproduce a bare existence" (499).[42] (3) Downward pressure on the subsistence minimum itself as a result of deskilling (490–1), and consequential replacement of men by women and children: "the more modern industry becomes developed, the more is the labour of men superseded by that of women and children [the 1888 version uses "of women"]. Differences of age and sex have no longer any distinctive social validity for the working class. All are instruments of labour, more or less expensive to use, according to their age and sex" (491).[43] (4) Pressure on the real wage resulting from the use of machinery and division of labor, and from downward mobility into the work force in consequence of concentration of capital: "The former lower strata [the 1888 version uses "the lower strata"] of the middle

---

[40] See also McLellan (1973: 180), and MECW 6 (697–9) for relevant data. Engels wrote prefaces for the German editions of 1883 and 1890 and for the English edition of 1888.

[41] For the reliance of the *Communist Manifesto* on the *Principles*, see, e.g., Laski (1967 [1948]: 19), Andréas (1963: 3), Rubel (1963: 159), Carver (1983, Chapter 3), McLellan (1993), Beamish (1998: 232), Boyer (1998: 154–5), and Carver (1998: 57). But see the rather weak editorial comment in MECW 6: 684: "In writing the *Manifesto* the founders of Marxism used some propositions formulated in the *Principles of Communism*." Ryazanoff also plays down the linkage (1930 [1922]: 21); he points out that "[t]he program put forward proposals which had already been put forward by communists in the past, and which had evoked the minimum dissent" (190–1).

[42] Rubel recognizes that in the relevant passage in the text, Marx "simply adopts as his own the 'iron law of wages'" (Rubel 1963: 1578). The term itself is from Lassalle (1571).

[43] The 1888 insertion is by Engels. His deletion of the reference to child labor presumably reflects reformist legislation.

class – the small tradespeople, shopkeepers, and rentiers [the 1888 version uses "retired tradesmen generally"], the handicraftsmen and peasants – all these sink gradually into the proletariat, partly because their diminutive capital does not suffice for the scale on which Modern Industry is carried on, and is swamped in the competition with the large capitalists, partly because their specialized skill is rendered worthless by new methods of production" (491–2).

There is, too, elaboration of the effect of industrial "concentration" on the proletariat, particularly the major political consequences favoring labor. This is one of the themes of the *Principles*, as we have seen: "This organisation of the proletarians into a class, and consequently into a political party, is continually being upset again by the competition between the workers themselves. But it ever rises up again, stronger, firmer, and mightier. It compels legislative recognition of particular interests of the workers, by taking advantage of the divisions among the bourgeoisie itself. Thus the ten-hours' bill in England was carried" (MECW 6: 493).[44] Nonetheless, the forces at play generating "pauperism . . . more rapidly than population and wealth" – this is merely asserted – play the key role in determining the final, revolutionary, outcome:

The modern labourer . . . instead of rising with the progress of industry, sinks deeper and deeper below the conditions of existence of his own class. He becomes a pauper, and pauperism develops more rapidly than population and wealth. And here it becomes evident, that the bourgeoisie is unfit any longer to be the ruling class in society. . . . It is unfit to rule because it is incompetent to assure an existence to its slave within his slavery, because it cannot help letting him into such a state, that it has to feed him instead of being fed by him. Society can no longer live under this bourgeoisie, in other words, its existence is no longer compatible with society. (495–6)

More specifically, the celebrated dramatic conclusion has it that the proletariat – the matter of "pauperism" seems to be set aside or at least is not intended to be taken literally – organized in "revolutionary combination, due to association," alluding to unionization, brings about a transformation:

The essential condition for the existence, and for the sway of the bourgeois class, is the formation and augmentation of capital; the condition for capital is wage-labour. Wage-labour rests exclusively on competition between the labourers. The advance of industry, whose involuntary promoter is the bourgeoisie, replaces the isolation of the labourers, due to competition, by their revolutionary combination, due to association. The development of Modern Industry, therefore, cuts from under its feet the very foundation on which the bourgeoisie produces and appropriates products. What the bourgeoisie, therefore, produces, above all, is its own grave-diggers. Its fall and the victory of the proletariat are equally inevitable. (MECW 6: 496)

---

[44] Cf. Rubel (1963: 1579), where Engels's *Principles of Communism* is cited: "At the same time, the
     industrial revolution masses together the bourgeoisie and the proletarians in the great towns
     where industry is most advantageously undertaken; by this concentration of great masses in a
     single area, the proletarians acquire a consciousness of their power."

Marx, in fact, added nothing to this some twenty years later in *Capital* in his Chapter 32, "Historical Tendency of Capitalist Accumulation" (MECW 35: 750; cited above, p. 5).

The dependence of the *Communist Manifesto* on the *Principles of Communism* is apparent also in its recommended measures 7, 8, and 9. As for 7, "Extension of factories and instruments of production owned by the State; the bringing into cultivation of waste-lands, and the improvement of the soil generally in accordance with a common plan" (MECW 6: 505), we have encountered the planning recommendation in the *Principles* (above, p. 60; see Sanderson 1969: 80–1 on this particular dependency). Recommendation 8, "Equal liability of all to labour. Establishment of industrial armies, especially for agriculture," and 9, "Combination of agriculture and manufacturing industries, gradual abolition of the distinction between town and country, by a more equable distribution of the population over the country," reproduce the texts of the *Principles* almost word for word (cf. MECW 6: 351).

The "globalization" theme in the *Communist Manifesto* (MECW 6: 487–8) has attracted much attention (e.g., Hobsbawm 1998: 16–18; Hollander 2008: 489; Howard and King 2008: 220). But this theme too, we have seen, is already conspicuous in the *Principles of Communism* (above, pp. 60–1).

McLellan maintains that though the *Principles of Communism* "was drawn on quite extensively" in the *Communist Manifesto*, "greater emphasis [was] given by Marx to politics," as illustrated by his description of the modern state as merely "a committee for managing the common affairs of the whole bourgeoisie" seeing in it a reflection of contemporary France in particular (1973: 180–1, regarding MECW 6: 486). I find this assertion problematic, for the substance of Marx's celebrated phrase regarding the modern state is already very well expressed by Engels:

The bourgeoisie having . . . annihilated the social power of the nobility and the guild burghers, annihilated their political power as well. Having become the first class in society, the bourgeoisie proclaimed itself also the first class in the political sphere. It did this by establishing the representative system, which rests upon bourgeois equality before the law and the legal recognition of free competition, and which in European countries was introduced in the form of constitutional monarchy. Under these constitutional monarchies those only are electors who possess a certain amount of capital, that is to say, the bourgeois; these bourgeois electors elect the deputies, and these bourgeois deputies, by means of the right to refuse taxes, elect a bourgeois government. (MECW 6: 346)

Marx's celebrated representation of "the history of all hitherto existing society [as] the history of class struggles" (MECW 6: 482) and his prediction of the "inevitable" victory of the proletariat over the bourgeoisie (496) are already central to the Engels document (348–9). In that document too we find an account of the extraordinary accomplishments of the bourgeoisie, namely its creation of "capital and productive forces on a scale hitherto unheard of," and also of the "means . . . to increase these productive forces in a short time to an infinite extent" (349) – an idea encapsulated so vividly in the *Communist Manifesto* by the famous statement regarding the achievement of "wonders far surpassing Egyptian pyramids, Roman aqueducts, and Gothic cathedrals" (487). On these broad issues Engels has temporal priority. The same applies to Marx's criticisms of various contemporary types of socialism (compare the *Communist Manifesto*, Section III, MECW 6: 507–17, and Engels's response to Question 24, MECW 6: 355–6).

There are, however, differences to note regarding the communist party program. Thus, whereas Marx called for the "abolition of all rights of inheritance" (MECW 6: 505), Engels recommended "[e]qual rights of inheritance to be enjoyed by illegitimate and legitimate children," limiting himself to "abolition of inheritance by collateral lines (brothers, nephews, etc.)" and the imposition of "high inheritance taxes" (replies to Questions 1, 11; 350–1). Possony has pointed to Engels's greater moderation in a variety of other respects: "The two documents set forth roughly the same concrete program, except that Engels spoke of *limiting* private property, the *gradual* expropriation of landed property, the paying of indemnities for expropriated property, the competition of state-owned and privately owned enterprises" (1954: xvii–xviii).[45] For all that, there can be no gainsaying that Marx was using Engels's draft of the program in designing his own – that the section in question "was very largely inspired" thereby (McLellan 1973: 184). More generally, Carver properly recognizes the reliance of the *Communist Manifesto* on the *Principles of Communism* (1998: 57).

K. On Marx's Reception of the *Outlines*

Let us return to the *Outlines*. A direct impact of this early work on Marx is frequently taken for granted in the literature, as I pointed out in the Prolegomena. The numerous close parallels between the Engels document and Marx's own early contribution, which I shall carefully enumerate, certainly introduce the strong likelihood of actual "influence," although I shall also take note of divergences. And how are we to account for Marx's failure to accord the document appropriate recognition, in the light of his readiness to specify intellectual obligations to other sources?

Marx in his Preface to the *Economic and Philosophic Manuscripts* of 1844 noted Engels's contribution in the *Outlines*: "besides the French and English socialists I have also used German socialist works. The only *original* German works of substance in this science, however – other than Weitling's writings – are the essays by *Hess*... and *Umrisse zu einer Kritik der Nationalökonomie* by *Engels* in the *Deutsch-Französische Jahrbücher*" (MECW 3: 232).[46] In his contribution to the joint *The Holy Family* (1845) Marx recognized the *Outlines* more specifically as an advance over Proudhon, who, in criticizing orthodoxy, retained entities only

---

[45] Engels in the 1888 edition of the *Communist Manifesto* plays down the details of the program.

[46] On Marx's *Manuscripts* of 1844, and also his *Notebooks* of 1843–5, see Hollander (2008: 6, 165).

appropriate assuming private property: "Proudhon does not consider the further creations of private property, e.g., wages, trade, value, price, money, etc., as forms of private property in themselves, as they are considered, for example, in the *Deutsch-Französische Jahrbücher* (see *Outlines of a Critique of Political Economy* by F. Engels), but uses these economic premises in arguing against the political economists" (MECW 4: 32).[47] The irrelevance for Marx of the concept "value" within communist organization (see Hollander 2008: 399) confirms the lasting significance of Engels's contribution. Nonetheless, our concern is largely with the reaction to the details of Engels's contribution, and to this matter let us turn.

Marx composed a précis of the *Outlines* in the first half of 1844 as part of his note-taking enterprise (MECW 3: 375–6; see also 596, 610). The summary does not convey precisely what Engels actually wrote. Thus it is not meaningful to say that for Ricardo and James Mill – Engels actually has Ricardo and McCulloch – "competition as against the cost of production represents utility," whereas for J. B. Say "it is the cost of production." What Engels wrote in fact is that Ricardo and McCulloch, despite themselves, brought in "Say's much decried utility [and] alongside it... 'buying' – the circumstance of competition"; and that to make any sense of Say's position on value as utility, it was essential to bring into the picture competition, though once it is introduced "production costs come in as well" (above, p. 29). The following sentences regarding "value" are also unhelpful: "*Value* is the ratio of the *production costs* to *utility*. Its immediate application: the *decision* whether to produce at all, whether utility outweighs the cost of production. The practical application of the concept of value is limited to the decision about production." What Engels in fact wrote is that "[v]alue is the relation of production costs to utility," intending the *mutual* determination of value by costs and utility such that any decision to produce requires that utility "counterbalances" costs (above, p. 29); most important, the *précis* does not clarify that Engels assumes away private property, that is, refers to a reformed society, when he writes that "[t]he practical application of the concept of value will... be increasingly confined to the decision about production, and that is its proper sphere" (above, p. 30). This same proviso should be applied to two other propositions (above, p. 34) as paraphrased by Marx: (1) that "the *value of land* is to be measured by the productiveness of equal areas using equal amounts of labour," and (2) that profit "remains inherent in capital, and the latter reverts to labour."

In his précis, however, Marx does not firmly commit himself one way or another. We must look to the more considered material in the *Notes de lecture* or *Notebooks* and the body of the *Economic and Philosophic Manuscripts*, both composed in 1844, to discern the common ground with Engels.

---

[47] Cf. Rubel: "In calling Engels to the rescue, Marx acknowledges himself to be a disciple of his friend whom, fifteen years later, he would praise for his 'brilliant outline' ('*l'esquisse géniale*') of 1844" (Rubel 1982: 1597).
   Lenin later focused on Engels's examination of "the principal phenomena of the contemporary economic order from a socialist standpoint, regarding them as necessary consequences of the rule of private property" (Lenin 1960 [1896]: 24).

Both Engels and Marx – Engels always ahead of Marx – recognize that Ricardian cost theory requires the demand–supply apparatus; and both complain of an alleged failure by Ricardo and his followers to make such formal allowance, though paradoxically both occasionally defend Ricardo and his school by conceding that the apparatus is admitted "sous l'aspect de la concurrence" ("as an adjunct of competition"), as Marx put it (see Hollander 2008: 171 regarding the *Notebooks*, Marx 1968: 35; for Engels, see above, pp. 29–30). At the same time, both deny the alleged "tendency" of market to cost price (or "real value"), appealing to an inherent instability of the cost and utility components that generates volatile market prices and render "competition" incapable of achieving "equilibrium" (Hollander 2008: 171 regarding Marx 1968: 35; for Engels, above, pp. 30–1). Now in this regard Marx refers favorably not to Engels, but to J. B. Say's assertion that the "natural price" is an "illusion," with only "current prices" pertaining: "le prix naturel . . . paraît être chimérique. Il n'y a que des prix courants en économie politique" (Hollander 2008: 169, regarding Marx 1968: 10). Here let us also note Marx's reference to Say on "utility" – identified by Marx in this context with "competition" – according to which utility-competition is merely a matter of "mode" or "caprice" (Hollander 2008: 169n. 8, regarding Marx 1968: 8), although Engels too had earlier asserted of Say's utility that it depended on "chance," "fashion," or "whim" (MECW 3: 426) – or what Engels called "subjective utility" because "no other kind of utility can exist at present."

Mandel refers to what he calls Marx's "polémique" against the labor theory of value in the *Notebooks*, asserting that it follows "step by step the same polemic already developed by Engels on the same subject in the *Outlines*" (Mandel 1967: 40). Intended here in part is Marx's acceptance at this time of Proudhon's notion of the source of surplus value: "Ricardo proves that labor ('le travail') accounts for the entire price, since capital too is composed of labor; Say shows [Say 1819 1: 28–9] that Ricardo neglected profits and rent, since capital and land are not provided freely. Proudhon *rightly* concluded from this that, where private property exists, a commodity costs more than its value; it is precisely this tribute that is paid to the property owner" ("Proudhon en conclut *à juste titre* que là où existe la propriété privée un objet coûte plus cher qu'il ne vaut; c'est précisément ce tribut-là qui est payé au propriétaire privé") (Hollander 2008: 168, regarding Marx 1968: 8–9; emphasis added). For my part, I see no dependency here on Engels, who alludes neither to Ricardo's labor theory – he identifies Ricardo's "real value" merely with "costs" – nor to the problem of surplus and its origin, apart from an inconclusive generalization regarding labor as "source of wealth" (above, p. 34).[48] However, as Mandel recognizes (1967: 41), there is a strong Engels connection in the objection that orthodox theory does not deal adequately with the workings of competition, to which we now turn.

---

[48] Mandel also maintains that Marx, following Engels, identified "value" and "price." This is indeed the case at times, as in Comments on James Mill in 1844, but surely not in the present context.

We may justifiably talk of a polemic on the part both of Engels and Marx against abstraction and abstract laws and in favor of theory that directly mirrors the real world of markets. Thus Engels against Ricardo: "Abstract value and its determination by the costs of production are, after all, only abstractions, nonentities" (above, p. 29). Engels found "quite correct" the empirical proposition that "price" – read here "market price" – is "determined by the reciprocal action of costs and competition" and, indeed, that price in "a state of equilibrium, when demand and supply cover each other," reflects "real value" or costs (p. 30). However, such "equilibrium" was at best only momentary and it was objectionable to base oneself on such abstractions (pp. 30–1). Similar terms are used by Marx in his reference to the error of the Ricardo school of representing as the "abstract law," a situation where in reality only "momentarily" and "accidentally" are supply and demand in equilibrium (Hollander 2008: 169, regarding Marx 1968: 10); and in his complaint that by their use of "averages," which "removed all accidental circumstances... that might impede their generalizations," the Ricardians increasingly distanced themselves from "real life"(Hollander 2008: 170–1, regarding Marx 1968: 35).

Recall now Engels's position that rent reflects both "the relation between the productivity of land, the natural side" and "the human side, competition," suggesting a market solution based on supply (cost) and demand considerations (above, p. 33). Notwithstanding, in examining the composition of production costs he steps back: "What share land, capital and labour each have in any particular product cannot be determined," for "[t]he three magnitudes are incommensurable." This requires sales proceeds to be allocated by means of "competition," intending here "the cunning right of the stronger" (above, p. 34). Productivity considerations are after all, so it seems, irrelevant when it comes to distribution. For Marx, too, "production costs are themselves determined by competition rather than by production," by which he intends to divorce the returns to capital and land in a private-property environment from their contributions to production (Hollander 2008: 169, regarding Marx 1968: 10).[49] Here we have the origin of the position to the same effect in *Capital*.

* * *

Engels's denial that the factor returns relate simply to their productivity contribution applies specifically to private-property arrangement. It is "under existing conditions" that appeal must be made to "the cunning right of the stronger." In a rationally organized society the matter is quite different (above, p. 34). Now this perspective was clearly acceptable to Marx. Abstracting from private property, "natural price amounts to costs of production... the object is worth the labor and capital expended" ("le prix naturel, c'est les frais de production.... La chose vaut-elle le travail dépensé et le capital dépensé"), implying that communal

---

[49] This is the context of Marx's praise for Proudhon's position on exploitation, discussed above.

arrangement would ensure rational resource allocation: "Henceforth, in the _community_ the relevant question is whether a particulier land area should be devoted to this rather than that product." ("Dès lors, dans _la communauté_, la question peut-elle se poser de savoir si telle terre produira tel produit plutôt que tel autre?" (see Marx 1968: 10). Marx makes no mention of Engels having drawn this conclusion in the _Outlines_.

When, in the _Manuscripts_ Marx formulated the "ordinary wage" in physiological minimum-of-subsistence terms, he drew on Smith (Hollander 2008: 172, regarding MECW 3: 235); he is silent on Engels here and with respect to labor's bargaining disadvantages, though both themes are conspicuous in the _Outlines_ (above, p. 35).[50] "Concentration" or "centralization" of capitals is important for both (for Marx, see Hollander 2008: 173, 174, regarding MECW 3: 238, 252; for Engels, see above, pp. 35, 42), though Marx mentions not Engels but Schulz and Pecqueur. The same is true of the demise of the middle class with its implications for increasing labor supply and falling wages (Hollander 2008: 173, regarding MECW 3: 238; for Engels, see above, p. 42). Marx neglected to refer to Engels on labor as "commodity," citing rather Smith and Ricardo (Hollander 2008: 166, regarding MECW 3: 235; for Engels, see above, pp. 35, 38); or on social conflict as the product of private property as such (Hollander 2008: 181, regarding Marx 1968: 36–7; for Engels, see above, p. 34); or on cyclical instability (Hollander 2008: 183, regarding Marx 1968: 11–12; for Engels, see above, pp. 40–2). As for the latter, Marx again cites Schulz and Pecqueur although, as Rubel recognizes, "Marx follows pretty closely" Engels's _Outlines_ (Rubel 1968: 1601).

Even on the matter of "alienation" – with which we have not been directly concerned – where there is so much in common, Marx in the _Manuscripts_ cites Engels's _Outlines_ but once, namely the description of Adam Smith as "the Luther of Political Economy" (MECW 3: 290).[51] In fact, apart from the Preface, this is the sole mention made of Engels.

The neglect of the _Outlines_ in 1844 is surprising, if we consider that Marx was not miserly with respect to other authors, including at this time Proudhon.[52] However, I am not suggesting that the Marx documents duplicate Engels.[53] He went further in the _Manuscripts_ regarding the inverse wage–profit relation (Hollander 2008:

---

[50] However, unlike Marx, Engels defines the subsistence wage in physical, not value, terms (above, p. 35).

[51] For his part, Engels had just referred to "a certain artless Catholic candour" on the part of mercantilist writers (MECW 3: 422). Marx contrasts the adherents of the mercantile system, who viewed private property "as an _objective_ substance confronting men," with Smith, who brought man "within the orbit of private property" (290–1).

[52] In _The Holy Family_, written in Autumn 1844, Marx pays tribute to Proudhon, though on basic methodological issues rather than the specific technical matters that have preoccupied us (Hollander 2008: 184–5).

[53] Note that Marx, independent of Engels, had "identified the proletariat as the key agent in the creation of significant social change" (Beamish 1998: 224, regarding the "Contribution to the Critique of Hegel's Philosophy of Law" 1844; MECW 3: 186).

167, regarding MECW 3: 284–5), and in his initial exploration of the source of surplus value (above, p. 66).

Claeys also points out that on two matters Marx offered "a somewhat more detailed theoretical analysis of individual doctrines in political economy than Engels" (Claeys 1984: 230). First is his "more detailed exposition of the various advantages which bigger capitals have over smaller," which is a valid remark in my opinion. Second is his "more detailed discussion of why the landlord's interest is not that of society as a whole, and how the progressive capitalisation of agriculture takes place, such that eventually only two social classes are left, capitalists and workers." It is certainly true that Marx expatiated in the *Manuscripts* on the "abolition of the distinction between capitalist and landowner" as land ownership became subject to capitalist calculation (Hollander 2008: 168, regarding MECW 3: 266), whereas for Engels the consequence of "centralisation" is that "[t]he middle classes must increasingly disappear until the world is divided into [industrial] millionaires and paupers, into large landowners and poor farm labourers" (above, p. 42). However, there is more in common here than appears, because Marx too emphasizes the ruination of the small capitalist; landownership does not disappear for him – its character alone changes.

There is also Marx's proposition that the return on capital varies positively with labor intensity (Hollander 2008: 175, regarding MECW 3: 249). This is the key issue "resolved" much later by the Transformation, an intellectual process requiring, of course, abandonment of the objection that, under private property, there was no meaningful tendency of market price to cost price. Already in "Wage Labour and Capital" (1849), Marx made out a strong case for the processes involving supply adjustment ensuring a tendency to cost price, thus reinforcing the regulative rather than the chaotic character of markets (MECW 9: 206–8).

Conversely, in one important respect, Marx falls short of Engels. He has scarcely anything to say on Malthusian population theory (Hollander 2008: 184, regarding the *Notebooks*, Marx 1968: 42), whereas Engels's objections proceeded at an impressive level, incorporating both the role of science in eliminating the problem of excess population relative to subsistence and replacing it by one of excess population – a permanent labor surplus or reserve army of unemployed – relative to means of employment considering the labor-saving bias of new technology (above, p. 37). All this, of course, is found in the later Marx.

Also present in the *Outlines* is the proposition that the existence of a reserve army, with its source in ongoing mechanization, does not conflict with the expansion over time of population and the work force in response to secular increase in the "means of employment" and thus demand for labor (above, pp. 37–8). There may be some excuse for a neglect of this proposition because it is formulated all too briefly, and little is said of the details of population growth. However, *The Condition of the Working Class* provides impressive elaborations. The outstanding feature of the mechanization process is net secular growth in aggregate labor demand – any displacement more than compensated for – and consequently rapid population growth (above, pp. 49, 52, 54). Here the reserve army emerges as a force sufficient to service capitalists' exceptional requirements at peak levels of cyclical activity, whereas the requisite labor supply to meet long-term industrial growth derives not from the pool of unemployed but, apart from immigration, from population growth. This perspective implies a dual labor force, though the duality is not watertight; those in the pool of unemployed do depress somewhat the wages of those employed (on which matter, see Chapter Five, p. 256).

We unfortunately lack information regarding Marx's immediate reaction to *The Condition* on its appearance (Oakley 1984: 73–4). However, the foregoing perspective on industrial development is in nearly all respects that elaborated by Marx in the late 1840s (see Hollander 2008: 216–18, 218–22, 230),[54] whereas the numerous references in *Capital 1* to the work relate rather to its descriptive contribution "from the beginning of modern industry in England to 1845" (MECW *35*: 248n.). Indeed, Marx commended its "zest and passion . . . boldness of vision, and absence of all learned or scientific reservations" (to Engels, 9 April 1863; MECW *41*: 469).

Several other propositions in Marx's documents composed in the late 1840s – *The Poverty of Philosophy* (1847), "Wages" (1847), and "Wage Labour and Capital" (1849) – may have drawn upon Engels's *Outlines*. This holds good of the proposition in *The Poverty of Philosophy* that in a rationally organized society – free of capital–labor and individual exchange relations – there would occur "an actual agreement based upon the relation between the sum of productive forces and the sum of existing needs" (MECW *6*: 143; for the similar proposition in the *Outlines*, see above, pp. 31–2). There is also tacit approval of Engels's position regarding the status that would be accorded "the real inherent utility of [a] thing" in reaching the "decision about production" (above, p. 30), assuming the abolition of the private-property exchange system. Thus: "In a future society, in which class antagonism will have ceased, in which there will no longer be any classes, use will no longer be determined by the *minimum* time of production; but the time of production devoted to an article will be determined by the degree of its social utility" (134).[55] Furthermore, much of Marx's discussion in the late 1840s regarding concentration of capital, the reserve army in relation to trade cycles, inflows into the labor force from the middle classes, and the use of female and child labor leading to

---

[54] Note, however, one difference. For Engels the reemployment effects of machinery extend to "a large part of the displaced workers" (above, p. 49) – similarly in 1844 it is the "workers put out of work" who are ultimately reemployed (above, p. 40) – whereas for Marx it is specifically the contingent of "*remplaçants*" entering the work force for the first time who benefit from the net expansion of demand for labor induced by machinery, those actually displaced remaining in the pool of unemployed except possibly near cyclical peaks (Hollander 2008: 216, regarding *Wage Labour and Capital* 1849; MECW *9*: 226).

[55] The rejection of minimum cost is Marx's contribution. That Engels did not go so far is suggested by his remarks in the *Outlines* regarding "rational" calculation (above, pp. 31–2 and note 3).

absolute immizeration rehearse his informal formulations of 1844 with their prior appearance in the *Outlines*.

* * *

We must now take account of Marx's description of the *Outlines* in *A Contribution to the Critique of Political Economy* as a "brilliant essay on the critique of economic categories" (1859; MECW *29*: 264). Does this not alter the picture of apparent neglect that has emerged so far? The full passage, of high importance as a recognition of a shared change in orientation in 1845, runs as follows:

Frederick Engels, with whom I maintained a constant exchange of ideas by correspondence since the publication of his brilliant essay on the critique of economic categories (printed in the *Deutsch-Französische Jahrbücher*), arrived by another road (compare his *Condition of the Working-Class in England*) at the same result as I, and when in the spring of 1845 he too came to live in Brussels, we decided to set forth together our conception as opposed to the ideological one of German philosophy, in fact to settle accounts with our former philosophical conscience.

Now, by his reference to Engels's "critique of economic categories," Marx intended a more general methodological advance over Proudhon, not the detailed analyses of technical matters that have concerned us. This is also the case in his contribution to the joint *The Holy Family* from 1845, which recognizes Engels's advance over Proudhon in "consider[ing] the further creations of private property, e.g., wages, trade, value, price, money, etc., as forms of private property in themselves" (above, p. 65). Furthermore, the tribute is an aside from our present perspective, because Marx's main concern was to establish shared credit for the conception of historical materialism – in contrast with an earlier grounding in German philosophy – having in mind more specifically *The Condition of the Working Class in England* (as we shall see in Chapter Six). We are thus still left with the fact that Marx neglected to acknowledge the near identity between the *Outlines* and his own position on a wide variety of specific theoretical matters.

Recall that, in the *Outlines*, Engels approved in principle of Ricardian differential-rent theory – provided that the scarcity property is recognized – but objected in practice on the grounds that there is no instantaneous withdrawal of marginal units upon a fall in demand, such as he believed Ricardo envisaged (above, pp. 32–3). In his early précis of the *Outlines*, Marx notes this objection without comment (MECW *3*: 375). He is silent regarding the matter in the 1844 documents. However, in later correspondence he is more forthcoming: "Ricardo invariably supposes – which is theoretically false – that under all conditions in the market, it is the commodity produced in the *most unfavourable* circumstances which determines the market value. You yourself had already put forward the correct argument in the *Deutsch-Französische Jahrbücher*," referring to the *Outlines* (9 August 1862;

MECW 41: 404). Marx presumably intended by his commendation the aforementioned objection by Engels, and the letter suggests that Marx learned more on economic theory from the *Outlines* than his public stance seems to indicate.

Be that as it may, there are but three specific references to the *Outlines* in *Capital 1*, all touched on in the note-taking of 1844: (1) "What are we to think of a law [of 'competition'] which can only assert itself through periodic upheavals? It is certainly a natural law based on the unconsciousness of the participants" (Engels, MECW 3: 433–4, above p. 44; cited in MECW 35: 86n.). (2) "[C]apital is divided . . . into the original capital and profit – the increment of capital . . . although in practice profit is immediately lumped together with capital and set into motion with it" (Engels, MECW 3: 430, above p. 33; cited MECW 35: 162n.). (3) "The difference between real value and exchange value is based on the fact that the value of a thing differs from the so-called equivalent given for it in trade, i.e., that the equivalent is not an equivalent" (MECW 3: 427, above p. 30; cited MECW 35: 174n.). However, these are matters of detail where Engels appears among several references.

A late estimate of Engels in Marx's Introduction to the French edition of *Socialism: Utopian and Scientific* (1880) calls for comment: "Frederick Engels, one of the foremost representatives of contemporary socialism, distinguished himself in 1844 with his *Outlines of a Critique of Political Economy.* . . . The *Outlines* already formulates certain general principles of scientific socialism. Engels was then living in Manchester, where he wrote (in German) *The Condition of the Working Class* (1845), an important work to which Marx did full justice in *Capital*" (MECW 24: 335). Marx seems to imply here that he had not treated the *Outlines* in *Capital* with quite the same consideration as *The Condition*. Again, though, by referring to certain unspecified "general principles of scientific socialism," Marx indicates that he does not have in mind the more specific contributions that have concerned us.

Marx's response to Engels's contribution to several of the building blocks of Marxian technical economics remains, I conclude, muted to the end. Is a qualification in order once we allow for informal recognition? Rubel refers to Marx's "admitted admiration for his friend's talents," adding that he "even considered himself to be Engels's disciple" (Rubel 1981: 23). In support, he cites Marx's comment to Engels: "As you know, 1. I'm always late off the mark with everything, and 2. I invariably follow in your footsteps" (4 July 1864; MECW 41: 546).[56] The context, however, which relates to Engels's casual explorations into physiology and Marx's plan to follow suit, does not affect my conclusion.

A letter to Engels dated 8 January 1868 regarding a review of *Capital* by Dühring does seem to indicate a warming of attitude:

---

[56] Rubel refers to Marx's "admitted admiration for his friend's talents," adding that he "even considered himself to be Engels's disciple" (1981: 23). In support, he cites this letter of 4 July.

As for Mr. Dühring's modest objection to the determination of value, he will be astonished when he sees in Volume II how little the determination of value [labor values] counts for "directly" in bourgeois society. Actually, no form of society can prevent the labour time at the disposal of society from regulating production one way or another. But so long as this regulation is not effected through the direct and conscious control of society over its labour time – which is only possible under common ownership – but through the movement of commodity prices, then things will remain as you so aptly described them already in the *Deutsch-Französische Jahrbücher*. (MECW 42: 515)

Marx had in mind at the outset of the extract the Transformation as it applies in a private-property system. But what did he intend by the commendation? That he had in mind Engels's focus on the unstable character of the price mechanism in a market system (above, p. 31) seems to me unlikely because the Transformation requires stability, and it will be recalled that Marx had in 1849 argued strongly for supply adjustment ensuring a tendency to cost price, reinforcing the regulative character of markets (above, p. 69). It is therefore more likely that he intended Engels's elucidation of macroeconomic instability.[57]

L. A Note on Sources

The *Outlines* refers to Fourier (1829) on the "spirit of emulation" under communist organization, which would replace the faulty operation of "competition" under private-property arrangement (above, p. 32); to T. P. Thompson (1826) on Ricardian rent theory (p. 32); to Alison (1840) – extensively – on the role of science and the implications for Malthusian population doctrine (pp. 35–7); to Ure (1835) on the damaging effects of machinery on labor (p. 40); to Ure (1836) and also Baines (1835) on the history of cotton manufacture; and to Wade (1833) on a five- to seven-year endogenous trade cycle (p. 40). There is also favorable reference to unspecified "English Socialists" (above, p. 27). There are no specific allusions to contemporary socialist and working-class radical hostility to Malthus as expressed, for example, by the so-called Ricardian Socialists, namely W. Thompson, Hodgskin, Gray, and Bray (see King 1983: 360–1).

With one exception, the extensive discussion of Smith, Malthus, Ricardo, McCulloch, James Mill, and Say lacks specific citations, raising the possibility that Engels drew upon these classics second hand. The exception is a citation from the *Wealth of Nations* to the effect that "commerce must become 'among nations, as among individuals, a bond of union and friendship' instead of being 'the most fertile source of discord and animosity'" (MECW 3: 423, citing Smith 1976 [1776]: 493).[58] However, this single citation does not necessarily conflict with Claeys's evaluation that only in 1844 or 1845, after composition of the *Outlines*, did Engels come to study the *Wealth of Nations* carefully (Claeys 1984: 225), or even that he was unfamiliar with the original in November 1843 (208). When discussing

---

[57] The formulation regarding Engels in Hollander (2008: 228) requires qualification.
[58] The reference to the *Wealth of Nations* provided in MECW (3: 423) is inaccurate.

technological unemployment (above, pp. 39–40)[59] Engels makes no mention of Ricardo's chapter "Of Machinery" in the 1821 edition of the *Principles*. Again, although Engels's observations regarding volatile market prices (above, pp. 30–1) and also Ricardo on rent (p. 32) seem to have derived from Say, he may have been familiar with Say at one remove, possibly via Proudhon (below, p. 75).

John Watts is one writer on the private-property institution and its implications much admired by Engels at the time he composed the *Outlines*. In "Letters from London" for a Swiss paper (9 June 1843), he refers to Watts as an "outstanding" representative of the "English Socialists" – a group founded by Robert Owen, he later adds – "who has written some very talented pamphlets on the existence of God and on political economy" (MECW 3: 385). The characteristic feature of this group of lecturers and writers was the founding "their communist propositions" on "proof based on facts, in accepting which they are indeed careful." Engels goes on to maintain that "[t]he assertion that half of the working classes of Manchester share their views on property is no exaggeration" (386).

Proudhon at this time is also accorded high praise with regard to the rise of communist sentiment against private property: "The most important writer . . . in this line is Proudhon, a young man, who published two or three years ago his work: *What is Property? (Qu'est ce que la Propriété?)* where he gave the answer: '*La propriété c'est le vol.*' Property is robbery. . . . The right of private property, the consequences of this institution, competition, immorality, misery, are here developed with a power of intellect, and real scientific research, which I never since found united in a single volume" ("Progress of Social Reform on the Continent," January 1844; MECW 3: 399).

These commendations justify Claeys's identification of both Watts and Proudhon as prime sources for the *Outlines* (see also Stedman Jones 1987: 144–5). Thus Claeys argues, with Watts in mind, that "Engels' political economy in 1843 was chiefly indebted to Owenism, though aspects of his argument were also inspired by some of Proudhon's formulations" (Claeys 1984: 225; also 209). He intends in particular Watts's *The Facts and Fictions of Political Economists* (1842) for the "essential characteristic of competition" as irreconcilable "separation of interests" (221, 222n.);[60] for increasing centralization of property (223–4);[61] for "the inability of the market to assimilate the real demand of all existing consumers, to expand such demand to meet an ever increasing capacity to produce" (220);[62]

---

[59] Marx in his Paris notebooks uses the second (1835) edition of Constancio's French translation of Ricardo's *Principles*, namely the 1817 edition containing Say's notes. Possibly Engels was familiar with this edition.

[60] This feature is also attributed to Owen, Gray, Thompson, and Bray.

[61] There are, though, significant methodological differences between Engels and Watts, the former representing the centralization process as a "law," "more rigorous" than Watts's mere "tendency" (Claeys 1984: 224). On this general feature, see Chapter Seven, Section E.

[62] See also the reference to John Gray (1825, 1831). Engels in *Anti-Dühring* attributes under-consumption cycles to Fourier 1829: "[T]he character of these crises is so clearly defined that Fourier hit all of them off when he described the first as *crise pléthorique*, a crisis from plethora" (1878; MECW 25: 263).

and for the faster growth of population relative to "means of employment" rather than "means of subsistence" (220n.).[63] As for the Proudhon linkage, Claeys points out that Engels's discussion of Say parallels that by Proudhon almost exactly; moreover, like Engels, Proudhon "juxtaposes an essentially public, *political* conception of 'objective' social utility to the arbitrariness of Say's subjective utility, a conception which is in other words based on social need (presumably assessed through democratic consultation) rather than market demand" (215). However, Engels may also have owed to Watts the "idea of social utility that he found helpful in balancing Proudhon's 'cost in time and expense'" (216).

Claeys further suggests that on the inseparability of the factor contributions and their incommensurability (above, p. 34), Engels "probably" followed Proudhon (Claeys 1984: 219).[64] The idea of labor as "source of wealth" "remains a latent assumption in the *Umrisse*'s critique [see above, p. 34], as it does for Proudhon," whereas "it is the fundamental concept" for Watts (218; also 222). Claeys (217–19) also considers possible links to Watts and Proudhon on the matter of rent as the relation of productivity and competition (above, pp. 33, 34). On the "mental element of invention" (above, pp. 36), Claeys points to Thomas Hodgskin, "whose work Engels may have known" (219n.).

It is frequently noted that, decades earlier, Owen had written of the negative effects of "manufacturing" on "the health and morals" of the people unless this tendency is counteracted by legislative interference (Owen 1817). Sismondi had recognized the class of propertyless proletarians and the damaging impact of competition on labor: "My objections are not to machines, not to inventions, not to civilisation, but only to the modern organisation of society, which deprives the working man of any property other than his hands, and gives him no guarantee against competition, of which he will inevitably become a victim. Suppose that all people share equally in the product of the labour in which they have participated, then every technical invention will in all possible cases be a blessing for all of them" (1827 2: 433). There is no mention of these works.

Apart from technological unemployment, Sismondi had also taken note of the increasing concentration of capital and recurring trade cycles (Sowell 1987: 350; also Schumpeter 1954: 493ff.). Engels, though, specifically expressed his indebtedness to John Wade regarding the periodicity of cycles as integral to the capitalist process (above, pp. 40, 73). The *worsening* of the endogenous cycle with an expansion of the range of activities subject to cyclical pressures does not, however, derive from Wade. Nevertheless, Wade does write regarding "commercial depression and prosperity" that "[b]anking and the introduction of paper currency, may have increased their intensity, and caused them to alternate in shorter periods" (Wade 1833: 254).

---

[63] Regarding the impact of "the Owenite lecturer" John Wade, particularly his perspective on trade as "evil," and to which "more than to aught else, we owe what we have of natural depravity," see Hunt (2009: 93–4).

[64] Engels also refers to William Thompson (1824) on "the impracticability of estimating the whole produce of the labour of individuals."

Moses Hess (1842) has been proposed as a source for the *Outlines* concerning concentration (Hutchison 1981: 7). However, shortly thereafter, in *The Holy Family*, Engels himself credits Gaskell (1833), Carlyle (1840, 1843), and Alison (1840) with recognition of centralization and its consequences for labor (1845; MECW 4: 14).[65]

It has been claimed that the English socialists – inter alia Hodgskin, Bray, Gray, and Thompson – tended to identify the source of "exploitation" income in the exchange rather than the production process, which is the Marxian perspective (see Thompson 1984: 106n.; 1998: 128).[66] However, I will show in Chapter Two that Bray, for one, perceived of exploitation in terms of unpaid labor hours.[67] It will also be recalled that Engels commended the "English Socialists" (above, p. 27), and what little he had to say regarding profit in 1844 does suggest a source in the production process (MECW 3: 430, cited above, p. 33). Whether he drew this perception from this source, however, is another matter.[68]

* * *

Most intriguing is the possible influence of Eugène Buret's *De la Misère des Classes Laborieuses en Angleterre et en France* (1840). When this work is mentioned in modern literature, it is invariably in discussion of sources for *The Condition of the Working Class*, and this is not surprising if we consider the account Buret provides of working-class living conditions in London, Manchester, Liverpool, Leeds, Glasgow, Edinburgh, and other British cities (1840 *I*: 315–40). However, there is, in fact, a great deal that corresponds to the more technical analysis in the *Outlines* – and the further elaborations in *The Condition* – and a summary of

---

[65] On the influence of Hess (the "Red Rabbi") regarding prospective revolution, see Mayer (1969 [1936]: 25–30), Stedman Jones (1982: 306–8, 2002: 55–9), Claeys (1984: 209), McLellan (1993: xi–xii), and Hunt (2009: 76–7).

[66] I avoid the misleading designation "Ricardian socialists" in favor of the neutral "English socialists," the term favored by Engels. (For an excellent account of the writers in question, see King 1983.) The former term should preferably be restricted to designate writers who, Marx believed, made socialist applications of Ricardian theory, inter alia Hodgskin, Thompson, Edmonds, Bray, and Gray (see Chapter Three, p. 172).

[67] The essential requirement for identification of exploitation in the exchange process is reliance on market imperfection, particularly monopsonistic pressure. Here we must beware of word-mindedness. It is true that Bray refers to the "system of unequal exchanges" (1839: 48–50), but by this term it is not market imperfection that is intended as is sometimes presumed (see, e.g., King 1983: 346–8; Thompson 1984: 106n.); but King 1983: 352–3 on Gray, and several others, offers a more accurate interpretation. Hodgskin likewise does not base his view on market imperfection (Hollander 1980).

[68] See Oakley (1984: 34) for a similar interpretation; Stedman Jones (1982: 305) offers a different reading of the text.

  Whether, when composing the *Outlines*, Engels had a profound knowledge of the group has been questioned (Thompson 1984: 80; also Laski 1967 [1948]: 28–9, Saville 1987: 216). Nonetheless, it is indicative of some degree of sophistication that Engels should, at about this time, have lamented the Socialists' lack of theory, with Owen among others in mind (see Chapter Three, p. 152).

Buret's contribution is in order, especially because this material is rarely discussed in the English literature.[69]

Buret touches inter alia on poverty as a "un phénomène de la civilisation," namely of industrialization (1840 *I*: 118–23); on labor nominally "free" – the nominal freedom of labor supported by reference to de Tocqueville (*II*: 208) – but in fact a commodity ("travail merchandise") subject to downward wage pressure in consequence of capitalists' superior bargaining power, which reflects the inability of labor to wait out disputes in the face of tacit combinations of masters (*I*: 43–4, 49–51; *II*: 73, 138–9, 200, 204–5). He represents industrial activity as perpetual class war, the object of one party being personal wealth rather than people's welfare ("la possession de la richesse, et non le bonheur des hommes") (*I*: 20), and of the other the defensive strategies of Chartism and union activity (*I*: 62; *II*: 50–7, 208, 417). The inability of unions to reverse a downward wage trend he describes as "une loi économique" that is aggravated by "competition between workers" for employment (*II*: 138–9, 201), with only the small number of skilled workers able to protect themselves against competition from capitalists and their own numbers (*II*: 48–9). A further weakening of labor's bargaining power results from destruction of small-scale manufacturing and domestic industry and increased concentration in the sense of "immense industrial establishments, belonging to a very small number of capitalists . . . " (*II*: 136, 165), from the deskilling and displacement of labor in consequence of "machinery" incorporating new technology (*II*: 25, 35, 47, 159–63), and from the use of female and child labor (*I*: 44; *II*: 35–7, 47–8, 149–50). Extreme division of labor generates loss of intelligence, health, and morals thereby destroying labor's ability to make intelligent choices (*II*: 158, 166) – elsewhere, current arrangement is said to "perfect the worker but degrade the man" (*I*: 52–3) – in contrast with the entrepreneur-managers whose intelligence and skill are sharpened by the need to predict the market in uncertain conditions (*II*: 205). And he expresses doubts regarding the validity of the orthodox reemployment argument, citing Sismondi as one of the pessimists to be taken seriously, insisting also that even short-term unemployment is an evil (*II*: 163–4, 167). Much blame is placed on the production of luxuries rather than goods for a mass market – again citing Sismondi – and on production for foreign markets, both characterized by particularly uncertain market conditions and held responsible for the phenomenon of increasingly frequent cyclical fluctuations (*II*: 195–7, 240–1). A broader based system would also reduce the pressure on wage-goods prices generated by competition for scarce supplies on the part of geographically concentrated labor (*II*: 146).

---

[69] Buret (1810?–1842) was a French investigator of pauperism. His initial explorations were recognized by the *Académie des sciences morales et politique*, encouraging him to undertake a first-hand investigation of various French and British cities. He reported on these in the main publication of 1840. For a good account of this work, though limited to its Introduction, see Cottier (1961: 115–38).

Of particular importance is the objection that a falling real wage does not discourage population growth in the orthodox fashion, and this because of a degradation of standards – the case of Ireland, and the impact of Irish emigration to Britain both posited – so that it is unjust to blame laborers for their poverty and to recommend population restraint as the solution (Buret 1840 *I*: 36, 80; *II*: 183). In this context Buret criticizes Malthus, though he himself allows a tendency of population to increase faster than food where faulty institutions discourage moral restraint (*II*: 226–33) – failing (as is so common) to realize that this is precisely Malthus's position.

Striking too are Buret's references to cyclical activity, in fact increasingly frequent trade cycles, as the new norm. Note the first use of the term "crise commerciale" in some contexts not in the narrow sense of upper turning point, but of depression commencing during a particular year, as in a reference to "four great commercial crises over the past 27 years, universal crises affecting the labor market, more or less equally in all major industrial nations. Each lasted several years; that of 1837 is not yet over" (Buret 1840 *II*: 196). In other contexts the term is understood more narrowly, but the sense of the argument is unaffected: "Since the crisis of 1837, the great English manufactures have not attained their earlier levels of activity"(*I*: 71n.). The significant point is that "output no longer expands continuously, but expands and contracts alternately" ("L'augmentation n'est plus constante; elle avance et recule alternativement"). Buret emphasizes that "the so-called commercial crises are so frequently repeated as to become . . . the standard state of industry," entailing "disastrous fluctuations in the demand for labor" (*I*: 29). Indeed, there was evidence of increasingly frequent cycles affecting all industrial countries, as in England where "crises" occur "at increasingly frequent intervals" ("à des intervalles de plus en plus rapprochés"). This pattern constituted an integral part of modern industrial experience (*II*: 196).[70]

Note next an allusion to a reserve army of unemployed: "The industrial war if it is to be successfully waged, requires numerous armies that can be thrown at the same point" (Buret 1840 *I*: 68). These armies "do not even have the security of regular employment; the industry that summons them only providing them with a livelihood when it needs them but then abandons them without scruple" (68–9), implying absorption during prosperity.

Also pertinent from a "Marxian" perspective are several of Buret's methodological principles. First, "no particular class was exclusively responsible for the existence, or worsening, of poverty. . . . Nearly all the causes of poverty were independent of the will of individuals, and no one person could stand accused . . . since they could be traced to institutions, to social custom" ("puisqu'elles tiennent à des institutions, à des habitudes sociales")" (Buret 1840 *I*: 81–2). Second, to fully understand current organization, historical antecedents have to be traced. Thus,

---

[70] It is not clear to me that Buret perceived a degree of frequency approaching a "continuous degenerated state," as proposed in Besomi (2010: 96n.).

"the proletarians, who have no means of existence apart from their wages, are the historical descendents of the feudal serfs, just as the latter descend from the ancient slaves. Their social condition results from a much earlier state of things, from which they have received the wretched legacy of poverty" (*II*: 69). Finally, take note of Buret's objections to the alleged "abstraction" and "scholasticism" attributed to orthodox theory (*I*: 29–30).

Several of the foregoing features are present, and conspicuously so, in the *Outlines*, though Engels makes no mention there of Buret. Interestingly, Marx, in his 1844 manuscripts, expressly cites Buret on the notion of labor as commodity subject to a declining price because of bias in the competition between capitalists and laborers, reflecting the inability of labor to hold back supplies and the replacement of male adults by women and children; on industry as "war," the aim of capitalists being the possession of wealth, not the happiness of men; and on a reserve army (MECW 3: 244–6). Reference is also made to Buret's proposition that "poverty is not so much caused by men as by the power of things" (257).

* * *

Engels acknowledges a wide range of documents consulted to support his personal observations of working-class conditions and related issues in *The Condition of the Working Class*: "I am up to my eyebrows in English newspapers and books upon which I am drawing for my book on the condition of the English proletarians" (to Marx, 19 November 1844; MECW 38: 10). The authors recognized include A. Alison (1840), W. P. Alison (1840, 1844), Bains (1835), Carlyle (1840, 1843), Gaskell (1833), Kay-Shuttleworth (1832), Leach (1844), McCulloch 1844), Owen (1817), Parkinson (1841), Porter (1836, 1838, 1843), Senior (1837), Symons (1839), Ure (1835, 1836), Wade (1833), and Wakefield (1831). Needless to say, references to official reports such as those on sanitary conditions and children's employment abound, as do citations from the bourgeois and radical press.

Noteworthy is the respect shown not only for Leach, "one of the recognised leaders of the Chartists in Manchester," but also for Carlyle (MECW 4: 429),[71] and also the wide range of conservative newspapers and official publications drawn upon in

---

[71] Reviewing Carlyle's *Past and Present* (1843), Engels spells out an objection in terms familiar to us from the *Observations*: "Carlyle recognises the inadequacy of 'competition, demand' and 'supply, Mammonism,' etc., and is far removed from asserting the absolute justification of landownership. So why has he not drawn the straightforward conclusion from all these assumptions and rejected the whole concept of property? ... Why, then, does he not act consistently and decisively, proclaiming the identity of interests the only truly human state of affairs, and thereby putting an end to all difficulties, all imprecision and lack of clarity?" (1844, "The Condition of England . . . "; MECW 3: 466). "In all Carlyle's rhapsodies," he proceeds, "there is not a syllable mentioning the English Socialists."

On the influence of Carlyle, see Marcus (1974: 101–12) and Hunt (2009: 96–8). Hoffman points to a cooling towards Carlyle on Engels's part – and also that of Marx – as early as 1850, and apparent in adjustments made to editions in *The Condition of the Working Class* in the 1880s and 1890s (Carver 1983: 31).

regard to living conditions.[72] In contrast, there is no reference to Watts. Although during his first stay in England (1842–4) Engels had contributed to Owen's *New Moral World*, he provides only a dated reference to Owen: "towards 1817, Robert Owen, then a manufacturer in New Lanark, in Scotland, afterwards founder of English Socialism, began to call the attention of the Government, by memorials and petitions, to the necessity of legislative guarantees for the health of the operatives, and especially of children" (MECW 4: 459). A charge that Owen preceeds with "great consideration for the bourgeoisie . . ." (525), I explore in Chapter Three.

Citations of Adam Smith, particularly on the dynamics of the labor market (above, pp. 47–8), but also on the deadening effect of specialization (MECW 4: 415), point to a first-hand familiarity with the *Wealth of Nations* that is absent in the *Outlines*. The Smithian effect of "competition of capitals" on the profit rate is also conspicuous (see note 33).

We have encountered a sort of multiplier effect in *The Condition of the Working Class* – unattributed by Engels – justifying the generalization of the trade cycle to the economy as a whole (above, p. 52). This feature is less apparent in Wade (1833), to whom Engels acknowledged his indebtedness for the five- to seven-year periodicity.[73]

Stirner (1845) is the sole non-British source specified: "Hence it comes, too, that the social war, the war of each against all, is here openly declared. Just as in Stirners's recent book, people regard each other only as useful objects; each exploits the other, and the end of it all is that the stronger treads the weaker under foot, and that the powerful few, the capitalists, seize everything for themselves, while to the weak many, the poor, scarcely a bare existence remains" (329; see also 564).[74]

Particularly interesting is the possible influence exerted by Eugène Buret's *De La Misère des Classes Laborieuses*. The matter, as I see it, still remains unresolved, as I shall explain.

Andler maintained that *The Condition of the Working Class* "had taken up and recast the investigation that Buret's book had started," and, yet more strongly, that Engels's work "is but a recasting and restatement" ("une refonte et une mise au point") of Buret's two volumes (Andler 1901: 34–5, 79).[75] Dolléans (1953: 217)

---

[72] For a helpful account of Engels's sources from this perspective, see Berg (1980: Chapter 14) and Hunt (2009: 103–4).

[73] The feature is also recognized by Owen, Thompson, and Gray, and by Wade himself in 1826 (Besomi 2008: 625).

[74] For a brief overview of Stirner 1845 (in the English translation *The Ego and Its Own*), see Stedman Jones (2002: 140–4).

[75] Andler, not surprisingly, discerns an unacknowledged influence of Buret on the *Communist Manifesto* (Andler 1901: 99). Laski too notes the *Manifesto*'s silence regarding Buret (1967 [1948]: 46), and further charges Marx and Engels with unfairness toward the English socialists (Hodgskin, Thompson, and Bray), Owen, Saint-Simon, and Fourier (51–4). Ryazanoff's account of these "Great Utopists" plays down the influence of Saint-Simon (1930 [1922]: 231–40).

and Cottier (1961: 115–38) both accepted Andler's position, and Laski asserted, quite generally, that Engels "owed a special debt" to Buret (Laski 1967 [1948]: 46).

Rubel, in discussing *The Condition*, found in Buret an indisputable source for Marx by way of Engels: "There can be no doubt that the insightful evidence provided by Buret influenced Engels, and in consequence Marx" (Rubel 1968: lvii). Rubel appears to ignore the possibility that Marx could have encountered Buret independently. Indeed, apart from the Notebook citations (see above, p. 79), there are several borrowings by Marx from Buret in "Critical marginal notes on the article by a Prussian . . . " completed in Paris, 31 July 1844, and published the following week (MECW 3: 194–6). As for Engels, he is reported to have first encountered Buret's book on his visit to Marx in Paris in August 1844 (Mayer 1934: 195). (His visit to Marx in Brussels in the spring of 1845 when he was correcting proofs of *The Condition* has also been proposed; see on this matter Cottier 1961: 116n.)

Mehring, in contrast, accused Andler of being wildly imaginative (Mehring 1902), and Mayer insisted against Andler that Buret's work had nothing in common with *The Condition*, and that any similarities between the descriptive accounts of British living conditions could be accounted for by use of the same sources such as the Parliamentary reports (Mayer 1934: 195).[76]

I find unconvincing Mayer's thesis that there is no common ground on substance between Engels and Buret. To take his position is to ignore Buret's detailed contributions to technical matters listed above that are so similar to the formulations in the *Outlines* and *The Condition*. Hobsbawm, however, relying on Mayer, insisted that Buret's analysis of poverty differed in a major way from that of Engels, with *The Condition of the Working Class* being "as Engels himself justly claimed, the first book in Britain or any other country which dealt with the working class as a whole and not merely with particular sections and industries. Secondly, and more important, it was not merely a survey of working-class conditions, but a general analysis of the evolution of industrial capitalism, of the social impact of industrialization and its political and social consequences – including the rise of the labour movement" (Hobsbawn 1969: 9).[77] In my judgment, these characteristics describe Buret's study precisely.[78]

---

[76] According to Mayer, Engels later called attention to the features that he shared with Buret: "[Engels] hat spätter selbst hervorgehoben, was daran mit seinem eigenem Eindrucken übereinstimmte" (1934: 195). Regrettably, no supporting reference to the relevant location of the putative remark is provided.

[77] For a similar evaluation of Engels's achievement, see Mehring (1935 [1933]: 132–5).

[78] Hobsbawm's position is particularly difficult to appreciate if we consider the attention he himself calls elsewhere (1968: 48–9) to a broad awareness of contemporary industrialization and some of its consequences, as illustrated by an account of 1844 by Friedrich Harkort, a German liberal businessman, "curiously similar to [that] of other social revolutionaries like Frederick Engels":

As in a sudden flood, medieval constitutions and limitations upon industry disappeared, and statesmen marveled at the grandiose phenomenon which they could neither grasp nor follow.

Hobsbawm further emphasizes the "unassailable" point, also based on Mayer, "that there is no evidence of Engels's acquaintance with Buret's book before his return from England" in late summer 1844 (1969: 9n.). This detail, if substantiated, would certainly clear Engels of any charge that he drew silently from Buret in the *Outlines* (composed from October to November 1843), but it leaves untouched the possibility that he benefited from the book when composing *The Condition of the Working Class* (September 1844 to March 1845).

Mayer is, however, perfectly correct that Engels diverges from Buret in a major way when it comes to the question: "what is to be done?" to avoid an otherwise inevitable revolution (Buret 1840 *I*: 88; also 74). Although Buret refers favorably to Sismondi on the responsibility of the private-property institution for poverty (*I*: 77; also 16–18), and more particularly for the nefarious consequences of the inability of labor to acquire capital (*II*: 224), like Sismondi he does not recommend the wholesale abolition of the institution, calling rather for reform, citing Sismondi himself to the effect that "it is society's obligation to superintend and regulate" ("il appartient à la société de la surveiller et de la régler)." Buret's preference is for steps to encourage the proletariat to acquire capital by way of cooperation, co-partnerships, and other such arrangements – much in the spirit of the later J. S. Mill – and in this manner break the capitalists' class monopoly of property and labor's dependence on capital and thus undermine the "hostility between two hostile interests" (*I*: 83–4, 90–1; *II*: 72–3, 87–91, 126, 136, 340–1, 347, 428). Much is also made of the potential of regulatory Boards of Control at the industry, cantonal, and national levels to prevent unfair business practices, to provide information regarding both domestic and foreign markets designed to reduce instability and speculation resulting from uncertainty, and to encourage good industrial relations (*II*: 355–60, 417–40). Furthermore, we find support of factory legislation (*II*: 358–9), improved property-transfer law (*II*: 364, 366–78), free trade, including abolition of the class-biased Corn Laws (*II*: 91–4), credit control (*II*: 440–5), and national insurance (*II*: 446–7).[79] Engels would have had little patience with most of these reform proposals (see also Churchlich 1990: 82).

The machine obediently served the spirit of man. Yet as machines dwarfed human strength, capital triumphed over labour and created a new form of serfdom.... Mechanization and the incredibly elaborate division of labour diminish the strength and intelligence which is required among the masses, and competition depressed their wages to the minimum of a bare subsistence. In times of those crises of glutted markets, which occur at periods of diminishing length, wages fall below this subsistence minimum. Often work ceases altogether for some time ... and a mass of miserable humanity is exposed to hunger and all the tortures of want. (Harkort 1844: 40–1; English translation in Hobsbawm 1968: 48)

Engels makes no mention of Harkort, though this work was published in Elberfeld, twin town with Barmen, his birthplace and family residence until the 1870s.

[79] A feature of Buret's reformist position is its indifference toward economic growth. Much in the manner of J. S. Mill's formal case for a stationary state, Buret assumes that the nation "possède déjà dans les capitaux accumulés des instruments suffisamment énergique de production" (1840 *II*: 418).

Rodbertus in his *Forderungen,* usually ascribed to 1837, had already called for the replacement of the current system entailing "production for demand" by one of state direction entailing production for "social needs" (Chapter Three, note 64), but this work was only published posthumously (see Rodbertus 1899). However, his *Zur Erkenntniss,* from 1842, where we find in miniature much of the Marxian paradigm (as I shall show in Chapter Two), was available, and it goes unmentioned.

In his editorial notes to *Capital 3,* Engels cites James Gilbart 1834 to the effect that "whatever gives facilities to trade gives facilities to speculation. Trade and speculation are in some cases so nearly allied, that it is impossible to say at what precise point trade ends and speculation begins" (MECW *37:* 404). Engels neglects to mention this work in his 1845 account of the same proposition (above, p. 53).

Finally, Stedman Jones's proposes a specific obligation to Marx that cannot be overlooked: "In *The Condition of the Working Class in England,* written up in the winter of 1844–5, the focus was no longer simply upon private property, individualism and social dissolution. This was now counter-balanced by an emphasis upon the redemptive role of the proletariat, a theme he had probably derived from a reading of Marx's essay in the *Deutsch-Französische Jahrbücher* (German-French Annals),[80] and from his discussions with Marx in Paris in August 1844" (2002: 62).

M. Summary and Conclusion

In the *Outlines of a Critique,* Engels's objections to Ricardo on value bring to mind the objections of those modern readers who mistakenly believe that Ricardo rejected the demand dimension – that his was a "one-legged" theory of value. At least Engels, however, has the high merit of suggesting that a role for demand entered Ricardo's argument almost unwittingly (above, p. 29). Similarly, Engels insisted correctly that Say's approach required allowance for costs, and that Say – despite himself, as it were – was obliged to make that allowance. In fact, any doctrine of value that did not demonstrate how price formation occurred by means of "competition" and the market was a meaningless abstraction. This, however, was to take the orthodox economists on their own (best) terms. For Engels himself, a tendency of market to cost price – an efficient process of allocation – was ruled out in a private-property system by the high instability of both cost and utility elements; only a reformed society could ensure a rational allocation (pp. 31–2). Particularly impressive is the insight that a form of "shadow" pricing of factors would be required in a "rational" system (p. 34), although against this must be set the unhelpful proposition that production decisions would there be based on "the real inherent utility" of goods (above, p. 30).

---

[80] The reference is to Marx's "Contribution to the Critique of Hegel's *Philosophy of Law*" (1844; MECW 3: 185–7).

It also emerges from the *Outlines* that Engels himself appreciated the role allowed to competition for the use of scarce land by the rent doctrine – in itself a commendable insight – though he assumed that the Ricardians thought otherwise, an error committed by Say and repeated to this day (above, p. 32). Most striking is his formulation of the incommensurability of the factor returns in the sense of the absence of an "inherent standard," requiring a solution in terms of "competition" or relative bargaining power (p. 34). Conspicuous in this context is the "centralisation of property" and consequent demise of the middle class and depression of wages to "the very barest necessities" (p. 35). As in the case of allocation so with respect to distribution, only a reformed society entailing abolition of private property would allow a rational solution. Similarly, a perceived bias of "science" toward labor-displacing invention (p. 37) and, more generally, the problem of excessive population growth – recall here the unexpected allowance for a prospective Malthusian problem – could be resolved only in a reformed society (p. 39). The same applies to macroeconomic instability (pp. 40–1).

Claeys proposes that once Engels had begun to champion a revolutionary political path, he himself "had little cause to recall the origins and debts of the *Umrisse*" (1984: 225). However, this neglects to take into account the forecast in this work that the evils attributed to "competition" – particularly cyclical instability – will "finally caus[e] a social revolution such has never been dreamt of in the philosophy of the economists" (above, p. 41); his envisaging, in the context of income bifurcation reflecting business concentration, "a total transformation of social conditions, a fusion of opposed interests, an abolition of private property" (p. 42); and, again, his assertion that population pressure provided "the most powerful economic arguments for a social transformation" (p. 38).

Hutchison surmises that Engels would have regarded certain of his early positions as "dangerous" to fully fledged Marxism, having in mind specifically the emphasis on the role of the scientist that undermines the concept of homogeneous labor power (Hutchison 1981: 5). I reserve judgment, having in mind that the mature Marx himself insisted on the significance of science.

The range of earlier writers who had advanced the subject along lines similar in many respects to those in the *Outlines*, and Engels's indebtedness to them, it has been proposed, explains why Engels "did not make much of his *Outlines*" (Rubel 1968: lvii).[81] This possibility cannot be dismissed. Moreover, this sort of

---

[81] On Engels's later attitude toward the *Outlines*, see his letter to Wilhelm Liebknecht (then editor of *Volkstaat*) dated 13 April 1871: "It is absolutely out of the question for you to reprint my old article.... It is by now quite *obsolete* and full of inaccuracies that could only confuse people. Moreover, it is still written in a Hegelian style which likewise just will not do nowadays. Its sole value is as an historical document" (MECW 44: 136). On the same day, Marx wrote this to Liebknecht: "Engels asks me to tell you that his essay... is now only of historical interest and so no longer has any value as practical propaganda" (135). We shall see in Chapter Seven that Engels's self-deprecation should often be taken with a pinch of salt; that his essay had become wholly "obsolete" is a case in point.

consideration might help explain Marx's hesitancy to acknowledge the *Outlines* on the various details of analysis we have noted. For example, what Engels had to say of volatile market prices in 1844 (above, p. 66) – but also of Ricardo on rent (p. 32) – probably derived from Say; Marx at the time may have found Engels useful, but he did not need him with Say himself at hand. Another possible instance is provided by the Buret case. This hypothesis is supported by the fact that Marx did recognize Engels's contributions of a general methodological order, namely the materialistic conception of historical development in *The Condition of the Working Class* and the advance over Proudhon in the *Outlines* itself, suggesting that some sort of differentiation was made between the subject matter under discussion. Marx silently implied by this contrast that – apart from the broad methodological contribution – the *Outlines* was not to be considered an "original" work. But if his neglect of Engels regarding technical matters was indeed justified along these lines, Marx would be opening himself up to similar criticism considering Buret's temporal priority on so many "Marxian" themes.

Of considerable interest is the importance to be attached in evaluation to analytical "originality." Consider Schumpeter's famous denigration of Adam Smith: "The fact is that the *Wealth of Nations* does not contain a single *analytic* idea, principle, or method that was entirely new in 1776. . . . His mental stature was up to mastering the unwieldy material that flowed from many sources and to subjecting it, with a strong hand, to the rule of a small number of coherent principles" (1954: 184–5). Schumpeter's perspective, in my estimate, unjustifiably minimizes Smith's contribution by focusing unduly on the merit of novelty as such. The same caution applies, though perhaps to a somewhat lesser degree, in the present case. The main consideration here is that the *Outlines* and *The Condition* lay out a great deal of the future Marxian program, a feature of the record justifying our respect for the document whatever the source of some of the elements composing it. At the same time, the document was far from a mere compendium or rearrangement of the observations of others. Engels demonstrated impressive technical insight, particularly in his interpretation of Ricardo and Say on value, in his elaborations of Wade's five- to seven-year endogenous trade cycle in its relation to the secular trend, in the discussion of a reserve army of unemployed, ascribed to technological progress coupled with long-term expansion of employment opportunities and accordingly population, in his insight into shadow pricing, and in his subtle perspective on food shortages. These contributions constitute analytical advance, even if familiarity with Buret's *De la Misère* could be proved. That the *Outlines* was composed when Engels was twenty-three years of age reinforces my admiration for its author.

Marx evidently used the *Principles of Communism* in writing up the *Communist Manifesto*. However, he also had at hand *The Condition*, where the major themes of the *Outlines* appear in more elaborate form, including technical change and its adverse impact on labor, the reserve army, worsening crises, and deteriorating real wages, at least in prospect.[82] The early work of 1844 is of prime importance in the development of Marx's mature position, whether directly or indirectly.

Beyond the detailed features with which we have been concerned here, the Marxian predictions regarding a revolution emerging from the processes of capitalist development – processes generating untenable conditions for labor, including increasing instability and secular depression of living standards – are to be found in Engels's writings during the 1840s, which is before Marx devised his technical notions of "surplus value" and "exploitation." Here is how Hobsbawm expressed the matter: "In Engels [Marx] acquired a partner who [in *The Condition of the Working Class*] brought to the partnership the concept of the 'Industrial Revolution,' an understanding of the dynamics of capitalist economy as it actually existed in Britain, and the rudiments of an economic analysis [in the *Outlines*], all of which led him to predict a future social revolution, to be fomented by an actual working class about which, living and working in Britain in the early 1840s, he knew a great deal" (1998: 24). Engels, one might say, provided the vision and, drawing on a variegated set of sources, went beyond moral indignation into the processes at play.

---

[82] McLellan represents *The Condition of the Working Class* as "the foundation document of what was to become the Marxian socialist tradition," by providing "an empirical basis for several of Marx's later theories" (1993: xix). Certainly Marx made extensive use of the work in *Capital 1* (and earlier in *Theories of Surplus Value*), but this evaluation does not adequately recognize in the *Outlines* the source for the theoretical contribution of the 1845 volume. This is also true of the account by Stedman Jones (1982: 316–17), notwithstanding a good general account of the *Outlines* (304–5).

On Marx's "borrowing" in the *Communist Manifesto* from the *Principles of Communism*, and the dependence of the latter on *The Condition of the Working Class*, see Boyer (1998: 154–5). Boyer does not apparently allow for the high likelihood that Marx had *The Condition* itself at hand. Of the account of cycles, Rubel asserts correctly that Marx was "strongly influenced by these passages [Questions 12 and 13 of the *Principles*], and doubtless also by *The Condition of the Working Class in England*, where Engels described at length the phenomenon of crises" (Rubel 1963: 1578). Henderson recognizes that "virtually everything" in the *Principles of Communism* "had previously appeared in Engels's earlier writings," including the *Outlines* and the *Condition* (1976: 124).

TWO

The Surplus-Value Doctrine, Rodbertus's Charge of Plagiarism, and the Transformation

A. Introduction

This chapter addresses Engels's claim in the Preface to *Capital 2* (1885), in response to the charge of plagiarism by Karl Rodbertus, that the Marxian theory of surplus value based on labor power was already to be found in the *Poverty of Philosophy* (1847) and in "Wage Labour and Capital" (1849; see Prolegomena, p. 13). We encounter the complexity that in his Introduction to the 1891 edition of the latter document and in the correspondence of 1893, Engels seems to dilute this claim and postdate Marx's full comprehension of the surplus-value doctrine to about 1859. However, Engels's case actually turns out to be stronger than he realized: Not only does Marx spell out the essentials in 1849, bar the formal labor-power notion, but the *Grundrisse* (1857–8) – never seen by Engels – contains a most impressive formulation taking full account of labor power.[1] If we then accept further Engels's affirmation that Marx was unfamiliar with Rodbertus until "around 1859," the latter's charge collapses.

Even so, what precisely did Rodbertus have to say regarding the source of surplus value? I shall demonstrate that the formulation in Rodbertus from 1851 is almost identical with that of Marx, as Böhm-Bawerk and others – not only Rodbertus himself – insisted. Engels's approval of its "ironic dismissal" by Marx (MECW 36: 12) is an unjustified reaction. I also take account of Rodbertus's 1842 analysis.

I then review Engels's further efforts to undermine the significance of Rodbertus's contribution by focusing on its unoriginality; and his insistence, by way of contrast, on "labor power" as Marx's main innovation.

---

[1] That Engels should have been unfamiliar with the *Grundrisse* has been ascribed to a breakdown in his health between 1857 and 1860 (Henderson 1976 *1*: 195, 207–8). Also relevant is the fact that Engels still lived in Manchester at this period, whereas Marx was in London. Nonetheless, he was sent materials from the manuscript pertaining to what was published in 1859 (see Marx to Engels, 2 April 1858, MECW *40*: 298–304). Furthermore, Marx intimated to him the significance of some of his researches: "I am, by the way, discovering some nice arguments. E.g. I have completely demolished the theory of profit as hitherto propounded" (Marx to Engels, 16 January; MECW *40*: 249).

Engels's "Prize Essay Competition" (see Prolegomena, p. 14), intended to enhance Marx's reputation against detractors, challenged readers to solve the apparent conflict between uniform profit rates and the "law of value," before publication of a solution in *Capital 3*. I shall evaluate Engels's reception of some of those individuals who took up the challenge and also his response to those who entered the fray after publication of the Transformation solution, which entailed an identity of aggregate surplus value and aggregate price. My final concern is the so-called Historical Transformation problem, which appeared in a "Supplement" to *Capital 3*.

B. Marxian Surplus Value: Engels on Matters of Timing

We first have to evaluate Engels's claim that Marx, in *The Poverty of Philosophy* (1847), had already hit upon the source of surplus value in labor power. To be noted are Marx's extensive citations from John Francis Bray's "remarkable work," *Labour's Wrongs and Labour's Remedy* (1839). Bray starts from the axiom that "[m]en have only two things which they can exchange with each other, namely, labour, and the produce of labour" (1839: 48). From this it followed that profits constituted unpaid labor hours, with the capitalists receiving something for nothing since they themselves provided no services: "the workmen have given the capitalist the labour of a whole year, in exchange for the value of only half a year.... [For] what is it that the capitalist, whether he be manufacturer or landed proprietor, gives in exchange for the labour of the working man? ... The whole transaction ... plainly shews that the capitalists and proprietors do no more than give the working man, for his labour of one week, a part of the wealth which they obtained from him the week before! – which just amounts to giving him *nothing* for *something*" (Bray 1839: 48–9, cited in MECW 6: 138).[2] Now Marx himself says nothing on the technical issue of exploitation,[3] though the citation offers a splendid opportunity to introduce "labor power" into the analysis of surplus conceived as unpaid labor hours. His silence suggests that this technical concept was not yet at hand. There is also a section entitled "Surplus Left by Labour," where Marx cites a statement by Proudhon regarding "[a]n axiom generally admitted by economists ... that all labour must leave a surplus," considered as "universally and absolutely true" – indeed "the corollary of the law of proportion,[4] which may be regarded as the

---

[2] See also Bray (1839: 67, 88, 89, 94, 109–10). Regarding Bray on surplus labor and its sig-
    nificance, see King (1983: 352–3). More generally, King argues the case for perceiving the
    so-called Ricardian socialists as anticipating Marxian doctrine; but for a counterargument,
    see Thompson (1984: 106n.). Whether or not the socialists related the source of surplus value
    to production or to exchange is highly relevant (see Chapter One, p. 76).

[3] "Exploitation" in a general sense is certainly taken for granted by Marx throughout the work.
    In discussing indirect taxation of luxury goods, for example, he remarks in 1847 that industrial
    capital "maintains, reproduces and increases itself by the direct exploitation of labour" (MECW
    6: 196). However, this does not carry us far from a technical point of view.

[4] Proudhon's "law of proportion" refers to the proportionality of prices to labor values.

summary of the whole of economic science" – but "meaningless according to their theory, and . . . not susceptible of any *demonstration*" (1846 *1*: 73, cited in MECW *6*: 152). Unfortunately, Marx proceeds, Proudhon's own proof of the proposition that all labor must generate a surplus – he does not dispute the proposition itself – entailed an illegitimate personification of society (152–3).[5] There follow pages of criticism, but still no substantive statement of Marx's own view of the nature and source of surplus value. Engels's case for 1847 does not seem to be strongly based.[6]

Whereas *Wage Labour and Capital* in the original 1849 version refers throughout to "labour," Engels in his 1891 edition systematically inserts "labour power" in its place. Thus, for example, "wages are the sum of money paid by the bourgeois [the 1891 version uses "capitalist"] for a particular labour time or for a particular output of labour. The bourgeois [1891: "capitalist it seems"], therefore, *buys* their labour with money. They *sell* him their labour for money. [1891: "But this is merely the appearance. In reality what they sell to the capitalist for money is their labour *power*. The capitalist buys this labour power for a day, a week, a month, etc. And after he has bought it, he uses it by having the workers work for the stipulated time."] (MECW *9*: 201). Accordingly, "[w]ages . . . are the *price* of a definite commodity, of labour [1891: "labour power"] . . . [and] determined by the same laws that determine the price of every other commodity" (204).

As in 1847, wages (subject to fluctuations) are determined by subsistence costs: "*Within these fluctuations, however, the price of labour will be determined by the cost of production, by the labour time necessary to produce this commodity – labour* [the 1891 version uses "*labour power*"] (MECW *9*: 209). Here allowance is made for training: "*What, then, is the cost of production of labour* [1891: "*labour power*"]? *It is the cost required for maintaining the worker as a worker and for developing him into a worker.*" Allowance is also made for wear and tear: "in calculating the cost of production of simple labour [1891: "labour power"], there must be included the cost of reproduction, whereby the race of workers is enabled to multiply and to replace worn-out workers by new ones." In sum, "[t]he cost of production of simple labour [1891: "labour power"] . . . amounts to *the cost of existence and reproduction of the worker.*"

The concept of wage advances is conspicuous in the 1849 document, with Engels's editorial adjustments appearing in 1891: "*Wages are, therefore, not the worker's share in the commodity produced by him. Wages are the part of the already*

---

[5] According to Proudhon, "[f]or the true economist, society is a living being, endowed with an intelligence and movement of its own, governed by special laws discovered by observation alone . . ." (1846 *1*: 123; cited in Rubel 1963: 1553).

[6] For this conclusion also see Rubel, who points out that an adjustment at one point of "labour" to read "labour power" in the 1896 re-edition of *Misère de la Philosophie*, "anticipates a later stage of Marx's economic thought" than 1847 (Rubel 1963: 1548). This correction actually appears first in a copy of the work with corrections in Marx's own hand and in a gift copy presented by Marx to N. Utina in 1876 (MECW *6*: 130n.).

existing commodities with which the capitalist buys for himself a definite amount of productive labour [the 1891 version uses "labour power"] (MECW 9: 202). The sale of the commodity "labour" or "the worker's own life-activity . . . in order to secure the necessary *means of subsistence*" is reworded to read as follows: "the exercise of labour power, labour, is the worker's own life-activity . . ." and "the commodity" that is sold to the capitalist is "labour power." In both versions "free labour" is contrasted with the slave and the serf, with the free laborer selling "himself piecemeal" (203), or "sell[ing] at auction eight, ten, twelve, fifteen hours of his life, day after day, to the highest bidder, to the owner of the raw materials, instruments of labour and means of subsistence, that is, to the capitalist. The worker belongs neither to an owner nor to the land, but eight, ten, twelve, fifteen hours of his daily life belong to him who buys them."

Engels added a gloss to Marx's definition of "relative wages," a definition whereby *"[w]ages are . . . not the worker's share in the commodity produced by him [but] . . . the part of already existing commodities with which the capitalist buys for himself a definite amount of productive labour"* (MECW 9: 202). For Engels, "[r]elative wages . . . express the share of direct labour in *the new value* it has created in relation to the share which falls to accumulated labour, to capital" (218n.; emphasis added); only "replacement of the price of the raw materials advanced . . . [and] depreciation of the tools, machinery and other means of labour also advanced" could be said to entail replacement of "*previously existing values*," whereas "both the replacement of the wages and also the surplus profit of the capitalist are, on the whole, taken from the *new value created by the worker's labour* and added to the raw materials. And *in this sense*, in order to compare them with one another, we can regard both wages and profits as shares in the product of the worker." The significance attached to the *advance* of wages is diluted by Engels's addendum; while the broad notion of surplus value that is due to labor is brought into the limelight.

Are Engels's adjustments and glosses to the 1849 document justified? The notion of labor as "the worker's own life-activity," or that of the free laborer's sale "at auction eight, ten, twelve, fifteen hours of his life . . . [which] belongs to him who buys them" – the expressions used by Marx himself in 1849 – are close to the mature concept of "labor power." This impression is reinforced by Marx's discussion of the character of capital: "Capital does not consist in accumulated labour serving living labour as a means for new production" – the traditional view – but "in living labour serving accumulated labour as a means for maintaining and multiplying the exchange value of the latter" (MECW 9: 213). More strikingly, however, the original text refers to the worker's "creative power" in generating surplus value: "The worker receives means of subsistence in exchange for his labour [the 1891 version uses "labour power"], but the capitalist receives in exchange for his means of subsistence labour, the productive activity of the worker, *the creative power whereby the worker not only replaces what he consumes but gives to the accumulated labour a greater value than it previously possessed*" (emphasis added). In elaborating the capital–labor relationship, Marx in fact himself uses the terms "power of the labourer" and "labour power":

Let us take an example: a tenant gives his day labourer five silver groschen a day. For these five silver groschen the labourer works all day on the farmer's field and thus secures him a return of ten silver groschen. . . . [The farmer] has bought with the five silver groschen just that labour and *power of the labourer which produces agricultural products of double value and makes ten silver groschen out of five* [emphasis added]. The day labourer, on the other hand, receives in place of his productive power, the effect of which he has bargained away to the farmer, five silver groschen, which he exchanges for means of subsistence, and these he consumes with greater or less rapidity. The five silver groschen have, therefore, been consumed in a double way, *reproductively* for capital, for they have been exchanged for labour power which produced ten silver groschen, *unproductively* for the worker, for they have been exchanged for means of subsistence which have disappeared forever and the value of which he can only recover by repeating the same exchange with the farmer. (214)

One other passage is similarly suggestive: "Finally, in whatever proportion the capitalist class, the bourgeoisie, whether of one country or of the whole world market, shares the net profit of production within itself, the total amount of this net profit always consists only of the amount by which, on the whole accumulated labour has been increased by living [the 1891 version uses "direct"] labour" (MECW 9: 220). Here we find the proposition that surplus value, pertaining in the first instance to the capitalists, is then redistributed in its various forms – a feature emphasized by Engels – although in 1849 Marx largely identified surplus value with profit (e.g., 218).

It seems fair to conclude with Engels that Marx did maintain in *Wage Labour and Capital* the general principle that "labor power" has a capacity to yield surplus value.[7] Still missing is the notion of surplus expressed formally in terms of the breakdown of the workday between paid and unpaid labor, though Bray to all intents and purposes had already hit upon it. Furthermore, we find little to support Engels's further contention that the "specific forms" of surplus value, in profit, interest and rent, and their explanation, are conspicuous in 1849.

Now Engels in his 1891 Introduction explained that his reissue was "intended practically exclusively for propaganda among workers," for which purpose Marx himself "would certainly have brought the old presentation dating from 1849 into harmony with his new point of view" (MECW 27: 195).[8] The question arises whether by these comments Engels retracted his 1885 attribution to Marx of a full comprehension of the source of surplus value as early as 1849: The expression "new point of view" implies a substantive change by Marx regarding surplus value

---

[7] For a justification of the replacement of "labour" by "labour power" in 1849, also see Rubel (1963: 1548) and Mandel (1967: 53).

[8] For more on this matter, see Chapter Six, p. 292.

sometime after 1849. However, the following formulation in the very same context is ambiguous: "In the forties, Marx had not yet finished his critique of political economy. This took place only towards the end of the fifties. Consequently, his works which appeared before the first part of *A Contribution to the Critique of Political Economy* (1859) differ in some points from those written after 1859, and contain expression and whole sentences which, from the point of view of the later works, appear unfortunate and even incorrect" (194).[9] That Marx's works before and after 1859 "differ in some points" with respect to "certain expressions – "value of labour," "price of labour," "sale of labour" – and "whole sentences" that "appear unfortunate and even incorrect," may suggest a difference in form only, implying comprehension of the substance of surplus value and the need only to correct terminology. In contrast, that more than terminology is intended is implied by the assertion that "[i]n the forties, Marx had not yet finished his critique of political economy. This took place towards the end of the fifties."

At the least, there seems to be some dilution of the claims made on Marx's behalf by Engels's focus on the late 1850s as a key transition date rather than 1849. Furthermore, although Marx's *Critique* of 1859 itself says nothing on labor power as source of surplus value, the dilemma that the labor-power notion was designed to resolve is spelled out: "If the exchange value of a product equals the labour time contained in the product, then the exchange value of a working day is equal to the product it yields, in other words, wages must be equal to the product of labour. But in fact the opposite is true. *Ergo*, this objection amounts to the problem – how does production on the basis of exchange value solely determined by labour time lead to the result that the exchange value of labour is less than the exchange value of the product?" (MECW *29*: 301–2).[10]

---

[9] Engels's pattern of references is confusing. In the 1885 Preface to *Capital 2*, he refers to *Theories of Surplus Value* as *A Contribution to the Critique of Political Economy*. In his 1891 Introduction to *Wage Labour and Capital*, however, he applies the latter title specifically to Marx's 1859 publication. See also the letter of 7 February 1893, cited below.

[10] The labor-power concept itself is mentioned only tangentially in the 1859 publication, in the course of discussing the labor theory of value: "... the labour embodied in exchange values could be called *human* labour *in general*. This abstraction, human labour in general, *exists* in the form of average labour which, in a given society, the average person can perform, productive expenditure of a certain amount of human muscles, nerves, brain, etc. It is *simple* labour which any average individual can be trained to do and which in one way or another he has to perform" (MECW *29*: 272–3); (see also note 31). Conceivably, it is labor power that Marx intended by the following: "Labour itself has exchange value and different types of labour have different exchange values. If one makes exchange value the measure of exchange value, one is caught up in a vicious circle, for the exchange value used as a measure requires in turn a measure. This objection merges into the following problem: given labour time as the intrinsic measure of exchange value, how are wages to be determined on this basis? The theory of wage labour provides the answer to this" (301).

Unpublished preparatory materials do touch on "labour capacity" as the object of exchange in the labor market, with reference to "value-positing use value," but without explicit mention of surplus value (506). Engels, in his newspaper review in 1859 (MECW *16*: 465–77), does not focus on these matters.

A remark of 1893 throws light on Engels's intentions in two respects. It suggests that he indeed intended to postdate Marx's "working out" of the surplus-value doctrine to the late 1850s. He also intended further progress in materials written after the 1859 publication rather than that volume itself, alluding presumably to *Theories of Surplus Value*: "Marx quietly elaborated the theory of surplus value in the fifties, all on his own, and resolutely refused to publish anything on the subject until he was in absolutely no doubt about each of his conclusions. Hence the non-appearance of the second and subsequent installments of *A Contribution to the Critique of Political Economy*" (to V. Y. Shmuilov; 7 February 1893; MECW *50*: 98).

Among modern commentators, Dobb discerns a "shift of emphasis" regarding "alienation,"[11] which is "fully apparent by the time of the *Critique*" and which "follow[s] Marx's more detailed analysis of exploitation and production of surplus value, with its accent on the distinction between labour and labour power and on capitalism as being characteristically a *form* of commodity production in which labour-power itself becomes a commodity'" (1970b: 8–9). Dobb neglects to specify when and where the "more detailed analysis" was accomplished, though evidently he had in mind some time before 1859. He does not, be it noted, specify the 1859 publication itself. One might suppose that he intended the *Grundrisse* of 1857–8, where the surplus-value doctrine based on labor power is expounded in terms of the breakdown of the workday between unpaid and paid hours, a more sophisticated formulation than that of 1849 (see Hollander 2008: 236–7, 240–1, 263). However, Dobb's intentions are unclear, for he writes elsewhere that the *Grundrisse* is "concerned in the main with the sphere of circulation and exchange. Value, for example, is dealt with explicitly only in a fragmentary paragraph which breaks off in the middle of a sentence" (Dobb 1982: 79).

It remains to note that it is not in the documents of the late 1840s but in the *Grundrisse* that Marx first abandons wages-fund reasoning (Hollander 2008: 285–6). If Engels by his adjustments of 1891 to *Wage Labour and Capital* regarding advances (above, p. 90) intended to imply a position adopted by Marx in 1849, he would have been in error.

C. Rodbertus on Surplus Value

Next recall Engels's affirmation that Marx only encountered the *Third Social Letter* (1851) around 1859 when apprized of it by Lassalle, that is to say, after having himself formulated the theory of surplus value based on the labor-power concept. We have confirmed that *Wage Labour and Capital* indeed contains most of the essentials of the mature surplus-value doctrine, and have pointed out that a more

---

[11] And this "whether commodity production per se or appropriation of the product by the capitalist is regarded as the crux of the matter" (Dobb 1970b: 8). The exploitation and surplus-value doctrine, turning on labor power as a commodity, once clarified, shifted the emphasis to the latter.

detailed formulation appears in the *Grundrisse* unknown to Engels. His case is thus stronger than he realized, assuming always that he was justified in affirming that Marx had no earlier inkling of Rodbertus. There remains for us to discern how close Rodbertus's position was in fact to Marx's, and whether what Engels described as Marx's "ironic dismissal" (above, p. 87) was justified.

Rodbertus sets out his own doctrine in 1851 on the basis of a "proposition" represented as "the consistent sequel of the proposition introduced into the science by Smith and placed upon a deeper foundation by the school of Ricardo, the proposition that all commodities economically considered must be regarded solely as the product of labour, as costing nothing but labour" (Rodbertus 1971 [1851]: 70). Similarly, "[l]abour is the original sacrifice, the primary cost, the first and last productive force which is expended upon all products" (112–13). These formulations imply – in Böhm-Bawerk's terms – that "consider[ing] all stages of production as a whole, capital cannot maintain an independent place among the costs of production" (1890: 340). The proposition appears to be in the nature of an axiom – in some contexts applicable when "land and capital belong[s] to society," and distribution is dictated by "a principle of justice according to the work rendered . . . [such] that the value of every product would be determined by the time expended upon its production" (Rodbertus 1971 [1851]: 82–3). Nonetheless, a positive proposition applicable to a competitive-exchange system is also intended, since Rodbertus describes a tendency of prices to labor cost entailing output flows from industries with (initially) low to those with (initially) high returns (117).[12]

Here I must emphasize the striking feature that it is apparently with the rate of return on manufacturing capital that, for Rodbertus, all other returns – including agriculture – must come into line, the manufacturing rate taken as given:

The owners of capital term the last part [the part of revenue going to the manufacture-product] *profit of capital*, and *reckon* it according to the ratio it bears to the amount of capital. . . . This ratio expresses the *rate* of the profit of capital. It sets the standard at the same time for the yield of the revenue of all applications of capital-property. People will not apply capital-property where it does not yield revenue in accordance with this standard; and as capital is required in the creation of raw product also, a part of the profit which falls to the raw product will have to be taken off as revenue or "*ordinary rate of profit,*" *reckoned by this standard,* upon the capital which has been invested. (Rodbertus 1971 [1851]: 98–9)

As for rent: "If there be a portion remaining beyond this, that portion is termed *rent of land,* because it falls to the owner of land purely as such" (99).

Now if the agricultural rate of return is dictated by that emerging in manufacturing with any excess of revenue transferred to the landlord as rent (even on

---

[12] Thus "these shares of the landowners and the capitalists are . . . determined by the relative value of the raw product and the manufacture-product, and this gravitates, as has been shown, towards the cost of the respective products, or according to the law of the productiveness of the respective amounts of labour" (Rodbertus 1971 [1851]: 122).

marginal land), then there must be some constraint at play that prevents capital inflows into agriculture to reduce returns to the average, thereby eliminating rent (at least nondifferential rent). In Böhm-Bawerk's terms, "[w]hat justification has Rodbertus for supposing that the equalization [of profits] will certainly embrace the whole sphere of manufacture, but will come to a halt, as if spellbound, at the boundary of raw production?" (1890: 362). A constraint was to be spelled out formally by Marx in the course of his treatment of Absolute Rent in the early 1860s and thereafter (see Hollander 2008: 29–31, 297–306). Unfortunately, Rodbertus goes on to offer a banal explanation of rent as reflecting faulty reckoning by farmers, who allegedly exclude raw materials when calculating production costs: "while in manufactures the value of the *material*, that is the *whole of the raw product*, is reckoned in with the capital, in raw production it is the land itself which constitutes this material, and land does not come into play as capital" (Rodbertus 1971 [1851]: 101). Marx responded sharply in correspondence: "There's really much in it [Rodbertus 1851] that is good. Except that his attempt to produce a new theory of rent is almost puerile, comical. For he would have us believe that, in agriculture, raw materials are not taken into account because – the German farmer, or so Rodbertus maintains, does not himself regard seed, fodder, etc as expenditure, does not take these production costs into account, i.e., he *reckons wrong*" (Marx to Lassalle, 16 June 1862; MECW *41*: 378).[13] Nevertheless, for all that, Marx did allow that "[p]uerile though Mr. Rodbertus's positive solution may be, it does, nevertheless, tend in the right direction." In *Theories of Surplus Value*, Marx even maintains that his own Absolute Rent solution was arrived at – or, perhaps, could be arrived at – by "stripping away" all of Rodbertus's "nonsense," including the farmer's "wrong calculation," or the "absurd conception that the '*value of the material*' does not form part of the expenditure in (capitalist) agriculture" (MECW *31*: 324–5).[14]

Let us turn next to a further feature of Rodbertus's account, his misreading of Ricardo – the misreading extends back to Smith and forward to "the school of Ricardo" – as considering prices as governed by labor input without even temporary deviation, with Rodbertus himself insisting that such is only an ideal to be achieved in a future state: "That which *Ricardo* assumes to be realized is only what *should* take place, is one of the greatest, and practically also one of the most important of economic *ideas* . . . ; the congruence of the exchange value of products with the quantity of labour which they cost is not a fact, but the grandest economic idea which has ever striven towards realization" (Rodbertus 1971 [1851]: 117–18).

---

[13] See also *Theories of Surplus Value* (MECW *31*: 258–9, 279–80). On the significance of these texts, see Howard and King (1992).

[14] The "real kernel" remaining, then, is this: "When the raw products are sold at their *values*, their value stands above the *average prices* of the other commodities . . . thus leaving an *excess profit* which constitutes *rent*. Furthermore, assuming the same *rate* of surplus value, this means that the ratio of variable capital to constant capital is greater in primary production than it is, on an average, in those spheres of production which belong to industry (which does not prevent it from being higher in some branches of industry than it is in agriculture)" (MECW *31*: 325).

Nonetheless, Rodbertus concludes by reiterating that, in a market system, equilibrium prices will reflect labor inputs, for the *"law of gravitation*... accomplishes even to-day so much as this – that in general the market value of products is in inverse ratio to productiveness; that if with the same expenditure of productive force double the quantity of product is created, the market value of the original quantity of product will at the same time sink to half its former amount" (118). There are, so it seems, no systematic causes generating permanent deviations of normal exchange rates from relative labor inputs. Furthermore, we find that throughout the analysis of the allocation of income between labor and nonlabor recipients and – among the latter – between landowners and capitalists, a strict labor theory of equilibrium values is adopted. It is also to be understood that labor values are expressed in money: "The market value is the exchange value which each product has relative to *all* other products which are exchanged in commerce; and it is controlled by the *general demand and supply of the competitors*. The existence of market value is facilitated by the intervention of a peculiar product, a *product intended for exchange alone, a market commodity* which is preferred to all others, and which, therefore, expresses the market value of all other commodities – the precious metals" (114–15).[15]

Let us take Rodbertus's argument a step further. Labor in the exchange system does not receive the entire value of the national income; rather, "the landowners and the capitalists, or their representatives, the *entrepreneurs*, who engage the workmen in production, under a law which governs wages . . . depresses them far below the value of the product" (Rodbertus 1971 [1851]: 83–4). We have arrived at the matter of surplus value. More specifically, "[r]evenue, according to this theory, includes all income which is derived, without one's own labour, solely from one's possessions" (90).[16] Two conditions must be satisfied for surplus value to exist – a productivity condition and an institutional arrangement ensuring that wage payments fall short of the total available for distribution: "That labour yields such a surplus is due to economic causes, causes that increase the productivity of labour. That this surplus is in whole or in part taken away from the labourers and given to others is due to positive law, which has always allied itself to force, and which now effects this deprivation only by continued coercion" (91). In a situation analogous to slavery, free laborers are obliged to surrender part of their own product in return for the privilege of using the means of production – land and capital (91–2). Briefly stated, "the owners of the production-fund, the landowners and capitalists, share with the real producers, the labourers, in every single product. For positive law declares land and capital to be as peculiarly the property of single individuals as labour-power [*Arbeitskraft*]" – note the expression – "is of the labourer. Consequently the labourers are compelled, in order to be able to produce at all, to enter into

---

[15] See also Rodbertus (1971 [1851]: 81; cited in Chapter Three, pp. 169–70).

[16] "Revenue" is the translator's rendition of Rodbertus's "*Rente*," which includes *all* nonlabor incomes.

a combination with the owners of land and capital, and to share the product of labour with them" (120).

Rodbertus's next represents labor as a commodity under capitalist organization. Not only is the division of the "revenue," or surplus between landowners and capitalists determined by the market, but "the *highest of economic goods*, the essence of all products, *labour*, has also become an object of exchange, the more momentous division between revenue-receivers and labourers is given over to the domination of exchange," with the price of this particular commodity tending to cover the "expenses that are necessary in order to keep up the supply of labour in the market, *i.e.*, in order for the labourer to reproduce his kind" (Rodbertus 1971 [1851]: 123). This notion is restated elsewhere in terms of "necessary wages": "The degrading idea, namely, of 'necessary wages' has been introduced into the science − of wages which comprise only such an amount of commodities as is required by the workman to enable him to continue his work; thus the free labourer has . . . imperceptibly come to be regarded in the light of a slave who costs only as much in the way of sustenance as a machine does in repairs" (93). Rodbertus, however, does not adopt the rigorous Iron Law version of "necessary wages": "This conception of 'necessary wages' does not, however, imply that actual wages cannot fall below that point, nor that it represents a quantity uniform at all times and in all countries" (94).[17] In fact, although "the *measure* of what satisfies [the] most crying wants . . . [is] a *quantity of product* . . . which during a labourer's lifetime in the same country, and taking the average of the seasons, remains a pretty *constant quantity*," over time there typically occurs a degeneration in the minimum itself: "The more populous the country, the more productive its labour, and the greater at the same time the freedom of the individual, the more will the labourer, trade being left to itself, be forced to work 'cheap.' For the more will labour be placed on a level with a commodity subject to the law of competition, and a competition which is harmful; and the more able will the *entrepreneurs* be to 'give out' the work to those who demand the least" (125–6).

Rodbertus, we have seen, described the division between "revenue" − the total of nonwage income or surplus value − and wages as "the more momentous" distributional division. Nonetheless, he also attended to the allocation among the components of surplus value (Rodbertus 1971 [1851]: 96–8, 108–9). According to his "new theory," changes of profit and land rent occur within a total surplus value that is due to labor. This is in contrast to orthodox doctrine, which considered returns to factors as determined by their contributions to output (89). This false view he attributed to a focus on the misleading "surface" manifestations of market relations setting out from the perspective of "*individual* participants" in the market, rather than on "principles which work with silent, unperceived power" based on a

---

[17] But see Falkus: "[Rodbertus's] fundamental proposition taken from Ricardo, was that the working-classes would always receive only a subsistence wage: the 'iron law' of wages. . . . Ferdinand Lassalle took up Rodbertus' 'iron law' of wages" (1987: 218–19).

"social" – we would say "class" – perspective (89–90). The errors of the so-called Say – or the Say–Bastiat – school are rehearsed in a forceful passage that describes the false view of distribution as a "superficial abstraction," and that follows the statement of his own perspective whereby capitalists and landlords obtain parts of surplus value, itself the product of labor:

A false and superficial abstraction has, indeed, in *its* explanation of what landowners and capitalists receive in that compulsory division, pointed back to the special and varied services rendered to production by labour, land, and capital; and, again, has conceived the product created by this combination to be the result of these varied services operating together. But who does not see that this is the grossest *petitio principii* of which any science has ever been guilty, and, it may be added, the most pernicious practical error which still remains for the human understanding to combat! (120–1).

* * *

The high degree of common ground between Rodbertus's and Marx's analyses of surplus value, assuming private-property arrangement, is apparent.[18] To recapitulate: We have pointed to Rodbertus's specification of a labor theory of value involving a tendency based on profit-rate uniformity to proportionality between labor values and prices expressed in money; the depression of the wage rate below the value of the product – itself entirely caused by labor – generating surplus value; wages determined by the cost of producing the "commodity" labor; a falling real-wage trend; an analysis of the elements comprising the surplus; and a concern throughout to understand the processes operating behind the scenes, contrasting with the approach to distribution attributed to Say, which, by focusing on "superficial abstractions," leads to the false view that the incomes of capitalists and landlords reflect the contributions of factors to output rather than deductions from a product that is due to labor. Missing is a formal labor-power concept, though the term is used on occasion and the concept itself is implied by the discussion of the subsistence wage.

The picture drawn by Rodbertus in 1851 is so close to that of Marx that there should be no surprise at Rodbertus's claim to have "shown *virtually in the same way* as Marx, only more briefly and clearly, whence the *surplus-value* of the capitalist *originates*" (Prolegomena, p. 13). Engels, however, reacts begrudgingly. His account of the *Third Social Letter* runs along the following lines: "That 'rent,' his term which lumps together ground rent and profit, does not arise from an 'addition of value' to the value of a commodity, but 'from a deduction of value from wages; in other words, because wages represent only a part of the value of a product,' and if labour is sufficiently productive 'wages need not be equal to the natural exchange value of the product of labour in order to leave enough of this value for the replacing of capital' (!) 'and for rent'" (MECW 36: 12). But he then refers to what he describes as Marx's "ironic dismissal" in *Theories of Surplus Value* (MECW 31: 251) of

---

[18] The same may be said of their visions of communal-property arrangement, as we shall see in Chapter Three.

Rodbertus on surplus value: "Mr. Rodbertus first investigates the situation in a country where there is *no* separation between land ownership and ownership of capital [1971(1851): 79f.] And he here comes to the right conclusion that rent (by which he means the entire *surplus value*) is simply equal to the unpaid labour or the quantity of products which it represents."[19] It is difficult to see how Marx's statement can legitimately be called an "ironic dismissal." (Nonetheless, if we consider that Rodbertus goes out of his way to analyze the elements comprising the surplus, then Marx does mislead by narrowing the scope of his commendation to a "situation . . . where there is *no* separation between land ownership and ownership of capital." This might easily suggest a "dismissal" of the Rodbertus contribution as a whole. Engels perhaps read it in this manner.) He also reports Marx as having responded that "he had no objection" to Rodbertus's claim to having "shown virtually in the same way as Marx, only more briefly and clearly, whence the surplus value of the capitalist originates," and that "he could well afford to let Rodbertus enjoy the pleasure of considering his own presentation the briefer and clearer one" (MECW *36*: 11). This is far from a generous admission that the Marx and Rodbertus positions are substantially the same, and recognized as such by Marx, but admission it is.

Here we must step back. Is there not, after all, a fundamental difference between the schemes? Rodbertus in 1851 adopts the labor theory of equilibrium prices, at least as a tendency (above, p. 96), whereas Marx opposed the notion in the *Grundrisse* (1857–8) – to my knowledge for the first time – insisting on systematic deviations of prices from values, with account taken of differential organic compositions of capital (Hollander 2008: 255–6). Marx himself, in *Theories of Surplus Value* (1861–3), pointed out correctly regarding the 1851 document that "Rodbertus seems to think that competition brings about a normal profit, or average profit or general rate of profit by reducing the commodities to their *real value*; i.e., that it regulates their price relationship in such a manner that the correlative quantities of labour time realised in the various commodities are expressed in money or whatever else happens to be the measure of value" (MECW *31*: 260). Now Marx repeatedly objects to this procedure. His position in this regard, however, did not appear in print until the Transformation materials, designed to justify the surplus value at the *macroeconomic* dimension, were published by Engels after Rodbertus and Marx had both died. *Capital 1* – and it is *Capital 1* that Rodbertus had before him in the 1870s when he charged Marx with plagiarism (Prolegomena, note 8) – proceeds on the assumption that prices *are* proportional to values. I phrase the matter this way because in fact *Capital 1* prices proportionate to values are *disequilibrium* prices with returns on capital unequal (see Hollander 2008: 23–4, 48). However, Rodbertus did not apparently appreciate this feature, presuming – as do so many commentators to this day – that Marx described a system in equilibrium (see his letter to R. Meyer in 1872 cited below).

---

[19] Engels's writes "*important* conclusion" in place of Marx's "right conclusion" (MECW *36*: 13).

Rodbertus's claim to priority over Marx *in print* seems thus far very strong indeed, were it not for two considerations. First, the discussion of the source of surplus value in Marx's publication of 1849 dilutes the claim; second, the price-value deviation, upon which Marx insisted, further weakens any charge that might be directed against him of plagiarism. But we have only taken account of Rodbertus's 1851 contribution. What does the earlier *Zur Erkenntniss* (1842) have to say regarding surplus value?[20]

Here we find the following propositions: "All economic goods cost labor and only labor" ("*Alle wirtschaftlichen Güter kosten Arbeit, und kosten nur Arbeit*"; see Rodbertus 1842: 1); similarly, "[o]nly goods that cost labor are accordingly economic goods" ("*Nur Güter, die Arbeit kosten, sind daher wirthschaftliche Güter*") (6). In a private-property system, however, workers are paid a "subsistence" wage, with the remainder of the product, which is due to labor, enjoyed by landowners and capitalists (72, 127–8). This proposition is also stated in *value* terms (169). Significantly, the same proposition is formulated in terms of the fraction of the workday devoted to produce wage goods, and the remainder, which is *unpaid* labor (133–4). Finally, note the proposition that relative prices necessarily diverge from relative labor inputs considering differential material–labor ratios; what Rodbertus misleadingly refers to as the "Ricardo-McCulloch law" of value must give way to a second "law," that of the tendency to profit-rate uniformity (129–31). Here then we have a formulation of the very problem which Marx's Transformation was designed to solve.[21] Furthermore, in later correspondence, Rodbertus reaffirms the demonstration "that goods do not and cannot exchange merely in proportion to the quantity of labour which has been absorbed by them simply because of the existence of capital," adding "a demonstration that might in case of need be employed against Marx" (to R. Meyer, 7 January 1872, cited in Gide and Rist 1964 [1915]: 425n.).

The fact remains that Rodbertus did not raise the foregoing complexity in the *Third Social Letter* of 1851 (there is an exception to this generalization that I shall consider in Chapter Three). In addition, he does not seem to have realized that the difficulties created for Marx's surplus-value doctrine by price-value deviations apply equally to his own version. Nevertheless, the 1842 document is a remarkable contribution to "Marxian" literature, and it is understandable that Rodbertus believed that Marx had silently used the work. And, it must be said, it is a mystery how Marx could have remained unaware to the end of a work – as Engels maintained was the case – repeatedly referred to in the *Third Social Letter* of 1851, with which he was familiar.[22]

[20] The treatment in 1842 of ideal organization is postponed until Chapter Three.
[21] A deviation of prices from values is also attributed to the circumstance that the relevant costs in price determination pertain to the least-advantageous margin (Rodbertus 1842: 130). The technicalities of this issue are discussed in Hollander (1991).
[22] Rodbertus quotes at length passages from 1842 pointing to the "triviality" of Ricardo's inverse profit–wage relation once rent is set aside by the differential principle; and also to the methodological illegitimacy of proceeding to analyze "the fundamental law which governs the constant fall of profit on capital" by excluding rent when in fact the fall in profits "is due far

D. Engels on Rodbertus's Surplus-Value Doctrine

Engels sought to minimize the significance of Rodbertus on surplus value beyond his citation of Marx's dismissive reaction to the *Third Social Letter* (above, p. 87). He proceeded in the Preface to *Capital 2* by insisting on its unoriginality, Rodbertus having "merely rediscovered a commonplace in his surplus value, or rather his 'rent,'" whereas Marx himself "disdained to claim that he was the first to discover the *fact* of the existence of surplus value" (MECW *36*: 21).[23] Early recognition of that "fact" could be traced back to the Mercantilists, though interpreted by them wrongly, as Adam Smith realized (13). Furthermore, in *Theories of Surplus Value*, Engels cites Marx's estimate of Smith's achievement: "Adam Smith in plain terms describes rent and profit on capital as mere *deductions* from the workman's product or the value of his product, which is equal to the quantity of labour added by him to the material. This deduction however, as Adam Smith has himself previously explained, can only consist of that part of the labour which the workman adds to the materials, over and above the quantity of labour which only pays his wages, or which only provides an equivalent for his wages; that is, the surplus labour, the unpaid part of his labour" (MECW *30*: 391).[24] However, there is this complaint that Marx addresses against Smith, that though he correctly "conceives *surplus value* – that is surplus labour, the excess of labour performed and realized in the commodity *over and above* the paid labour, the labour which has received its equivalent in the wages – as the *general category*, of which profit proper and rent of land are merely branches ... he does not distinguish surplus value as such as a category on its own, distinct from the specific forms it assumes in profit and rent," which was "the source of much error and inadequacy in his inquiry, and of even more in the work of Ricardo" (388–9).

This criticism is mere hair splitting, but Engels found that it "fits Rodbertus to a T. His 'rent' is simply the sum of ground rent and profit. He builds up an entirely erroneous theory of ground rent" – possibly Engels intended here the "almost puerile, comical" explanation mentioned above (p. 95) – "and he accepts

---

more, even according to the Ricardian view of rent and of the increasing unproductiveness of agriculture, to rent than to wages" (1971 [1851]: 20–3; see 1842: 106–8). The recognition of wage differentials in the first paper of *Zur Erkenntniss* is also noted (113n.). Other references to the 1842 document (83n., 115–16) are discussed in Chapter Three.

[23] Hobsbawm comments that "to Foxwell [1887] we ... owe (through the Austrian Menger) the popularization of the German parlour-game of attacking Marx's originality and regarding him as a pillager of Thompson, Hodgskin, Proudhon, Rodbertus, or any other early writers who took the critic's fancy" (1964: 246).

Regarding Rodbertus's own obligations, take note of his identification of the principle of valuation on the basis of labor input with "[t]he constituted value of Proudhon," but his insistence on priority: "I must permit myself the remark that the idea of the constituted value was advanced by me before Proudhon, and that the papers in my work *Zur Erkenntniss . . .* contain nothing but the preliminary investigations necessary for the development of that idea" (1971 [1851]: 83n.).

[24] The attribution to Smith is based on two famous passages relating to the emergence of profit and rent with the transition from early to capitalist society (see Hollander 1992: 74–5).

profit without any examination of it, just as he finds it among his predecessors";
in contrast, "Marx's surplus value, on the contrary, represents the *general form* of
the sum of values appropriated without any equivalent by the owners of the means
of production, and this form splits into the distinct, *converted* forms of profit and
ground rent in accordance with very specific laws, which Marx was the first to
discover" (MECW *36*: 14–15). These laws would only be revealed in *Capital 3*,
where would be seen the "many intermediate links . . . required to arrive from an
understanding of surplus value in general at an understanding of its transformation
into profit and ground rent; in other words at an understanding of the laws of the
distribution of surplus value within the capitalist class" (15).

Engels nonetheless conceded that Rodbertus did carry the matter beyond Smith
by accepting Ricardo's labor theory of value and the inverse wage–profit theorem
deduced therefrom. Rodbertus, however, had gone no further than Ricardo[25] and
was "wholly unaware of the internal contradictions of the Ricardian theory, which
caused the downfall of that school," alluding to neglect of the problem created by
price-value deviations and the failure to distinguish between "labor" and "labor
power" (see below, pp. 105–6). He had also been "misled . . . into raising utopian demands (his *Zur Erkenntniss*) [1842], *etc.*, p. 130), instead of . . . look[ing]
for economic solutions." Rodbertus's "utopian demands" will be taken up in
Chapter Three; here note that the specific reference provided by Engels raises
serious doubts regarding his objectivity. This is precisely where we find Rodbertus's impressive formulation of the discordance between the laws of "value"
and profit-rate uniformity created by unequal labor–capital ratios (above, p. 100)
that should have been warmly applauded as a major advance from a "Marxist"
perspective.

Engels also makes mention of his Preface to the 1885 German edition of *Poverty
of Philosophy* (also published as "Marx and Rodbertus" in *Die Neue Zeit*). There
Engels had allowed that "[t]he simplest socialist appreciation of the Ricardian
theory . . . has led in many cases to insights into the origin and nature of surplus
value which go far beyond Ricardo, as in the case of Rodbertus among others"
(MECW *26*: 281). This is a royal tribute, one might think, and one that scarcely
corresponds with the dismissive remarks in the Preface to *Capital 2*. In fact, though,
he then draws back:

Quite apart from the fact that on this matter he nowhere presents anything which has
not already been said at least as well, before him, his presentation suffers like those
of his predecessors from the fact that he adopts, uncritically and without examining
their content, economic categories – labour, capital, value, etc. – in the crude form,
clinging to their external appearance, in which they were handed down to him by the
economists. He thereby not only cuts himself off from all further development – in
contrast to Marx, who was the first to make something of these propositions so often

---

[25] Here Engels neglects Rodbertus's effort to deal with the problem of *three* variable factors; see
his objections to Ricardo's rent doctrine (1971 [1851]: 69f.).

repeated for the last sixty-four years – but . . . he opens for himself the road leading straight to utopia.[26]

Doubtless the allusion to outdated "economic categories" includes the failure to hit upon "labor power" in place of labor. However, Engels also challenged an alleged failure to consider the value entity properly: "As already noted, Rodbertus adopts the traditional definitions of economic concepts entirely in the form in which they have come down to him from the economists. He does not make the slightest attempt to investigate them. Value is for him 'the valuation of one thing against others according to quantity, this valuation being conceived as measure' (Rodbertus 1842: 61). This, to put it mildly, extremely slovenly definition . . . says absolutely nothing of what [value] is" (MECW 26: 284).[27] All of this presumably justified what Engels understood as Marx's "ironic dismissal" of Rodbertus (above, p. 87).

The Preface to *Capital 2* rehearses a barrage of further complaints regarding Rodbertus's alleged unoriginality. Thus his explanation of commercial crises in terms of the underconsumption of the working class was already to be found in Sismondi's *Nouveaux Principes de l'Économie Politique*, Book IV, Ch. IV (MECW 36: 21–2).[28] Further, "[h]is speculations as to whether wages are derived from capital or income belong to the domain of scholasticism and are definitely settled in Part III of this second book of *Capital*" (22). As for his rent theory, that "remained his

---

[26] The "sixty-four years" comment refers to the anonymous *Source and Remedy of the National Difficulties* (1821), discussed below.

[27] This criticism appears to draw on one of the themes appearing in Marx's marginalia to Adolph Wagner's *Lehrbuch der Politischen Ökonomie* (1879), distinguishing "exchange value" from "value" as such, the latter referring to "the *expenditure of labour power* common to all . . . concrete types of labour," and the former merely its "*form of expression*" (MECW 24: 531, 545; also 551–2).

   Engels points further to Rodbertus's conclusion "that there is no real measure of value and that one has to make do with a substitute measure. Labour could serve as such, but only if products of an equal quantity of labour were always exchanged against products of an equal quantity of labour." (MECW 26: 284, paraphrasing 1842: 61–2). "Consequently," Engels complains, "value and labour remain without any sort of material connection, in spite of the fact that the whole first chapter is taken up to expound to us that commodities 'cost labour' and nothing but labour, and why this is so." This objection is not apparent to the present writer.

[28] Similarly, we see this in *Anti-Dühring*: "The 'under-consumption' explanation of crises originated with Sismondi, and in his exposition it still had a certain meaning. Rodbertus took it from Sismondi, and Herr Dühring has in turn copied it, in his usual vulgarising fashion, from Rodbertus" (MECW 25: 273n.). Engels points in his text to the current (1877) stagnation of the cotton industry as evidence against Rodbertus: " . . . it requires a strong dose of deep-rooted effrontery to explain the present complete stagnation in the yarn and cloth markets by the under-consumption of the English masses and not by the over-production carried on by the English cotton-mill owners." However, for Rodbertus, crises are explained by underconsumption of the masses coupled with increased productivity (see Clark 1971), whereas more seriously, Engels himself, even in *Anti-Dühring* itself, sometimes appealed to underconsumption. (See further on the issue, Chapter Three, note 64.)

exclusive property and may rest in peace until the manuscript of Marx criticizing it is published."

As for socialistic applications of the Ricardian perspective on surplus value, these had been long before "anticipated" in a forty-page pamphlet of 1821 saved from "oblivion" by Marx in *Capital 1*, namely *The Source and Remedy of the National Difficulties*, represented as "the farthest outpost of an entire literature which in the twenties turned the Ricardian theory of value and surplus value against capitalist production in the interest of the proletariat [and] fought the bourgeoisie with its own weapons" (MECW *36*: 15, 17).[29] Rodbertus, for his part, Engels never ceased to insist, had only "utopian" proposals. As for technical matters, Engels cites passages from the pamphlet (1821: 23–6) that point to the concept of interest on capital – intending not only interest proper but also land rent and profits of trade – as " surplus-labour appropriated by the capitalist," increased by efforts to reduce the necessary labor time devoted to labor's maintenance. He notes that the pamphlet-eer's "interest" is precisely the same as Rodbertus's "rent" (MECW *36*: 16). However, if he saw merit in emphasizing the general category of surplus – as, following Marx, he did – then he ought to have commended Rodbertus for that same practice.

Engels also cites Marx's 1861–3 manuscript on the 1821 pamphlet as an advance over Ricardo (MECW *32*: 374, 388–9), and he applies Marx's criticism of the pamphlet to Rodbertus, seeking to demolish the latter's contribution by making a mockery of it:

[Rodbertus], too, remains a captive of the economic categories as he finds them. He, too, applies to surplus value the name of one of its converted sub-forms, rent, and makes it quite indefinite at that. The result of these two mistakes is that he relapsed into economic gibberish, that he does [not] follow up his advance over Ricardo critically, and that instead he is misled into using his unfinished theory, even before it got rid of its egg-shell, as the basis for a utopia with which, as always, he comes too late. The pamphlet appeared in 1821 and anticipated completely Rodbertus' "rent" of 1842. (MECW *36*: 17)

Engels, it will be noted, concedes in this passage some "advance over Ricardo" by Rodbertus, whereas elsewhere in the document he denied any progress whatsoever. Even so, his comments here reflect a word-minded objection to the term "rent" as designation of general surplus value, whereas Rodbertus had in fact carefully distinguished between rent proper and profit and sought to understand these categories.

E. Engels on Marx's Innovation

The efforts made to protect Marx's priority against Rodbertus's allegations of plagiarism created the dilemma that if Rodbertus was unoriginal so too must Marx have been, considering his admitted predecessors: "But what, then, is new in

---

[29] That the British anticapitalist literature, including inter alia Owen, Edmonds, Thompson, Hodgskin, and Ravenstone, was based on Ricardo is questionable (Hollander 1980).

Marx's utterances on surplus value?" Engels asks in the Preface to *Capital* 2. "How is it that Marx's theory of surplus value struck home like a thunderbolt out of a clear sky, and this in all civilised countries, while the theories of all his socialist predecessors, Rodbertus included, vanished without having produced any effect?" (MECW 36: 18). It is again fully allowed that the "*existence* of that part of the value of products which we now call surplus value had been ascertained long before Marx," and that "it had also been stated more or less clearly what it consisted of, namely of the product of the labour for which its appropriator had not given any equivalent" (19–20). However, whereas his predecessors had only "seen a *solution*" – satisfied with the economic fact that surplus value amounted to unpaid labor and focused on the conflict between this fact and "justice" – as in the case of the 1821 pamphleteer and Rodbertus – Marx "saw a *problem*," a need to explain the fact. This required analysis of "labour's value-producing property," particularly the ascertainment of "*what kind* of labour it was that created value, and why and how it did so," necessitating "criticism above all [of] the Ricardian theory of value." Here Engels alludes to labor power – "value was congealed labour of *this* kind," a point Rodbertus "never grasped till his dying day," and the discovery of which solved a problem that had contributed to the collapse of Ricardo's school: "By substituting labour power, the value-producing property, for labour [Marx] solved with one stroke one of the difficulties which brought about the downfall of the Ricardian school, viz., the impossibility of harmonizing the mutual exchange of capital and labour with the Ricardian law that value is determined by labour" (20–1). That labor paid a competitive wage determined by "mutual exchange" nonetheless generated a surplus was one of two "difficulties" relating to surplus value – the second involved the Transformation issue – that had brought about the "shipwreck" of the Ricardian school in 1830 or thereabouts (22).[30] It was Marx's achievement to have reformulated the question "correctly" and thus to have perceived the solution:

First. Labour is the measure of value. However, living labour in its exchange with capital has a lower value than the objectified labour for which it is exchanged. Wages, the value of a definite quantity of living labour, are always less than the value of the product

---

[30] Engels also represents Marx's theory of money as "the first exhaustive one ... [which has been] tacitly accepted everywhere," based on "the property of value imminent in the commodity"; and the transformation of money into capital "based on the purchase and sale of labour power" (MECW 36: 20). He goes on to enumerate Marx's distinction between constant and variable capital, which allowed him to trace "the process of the formation of surplus-value in its minutest details as it really takes place, and thus to explain it – something none of his predecessors had accomplished," for the distinction within capital itself was one "which neither Rodbertus nor the bourgeois economist knew in the least what to do, but which furnishes the key for the solution of the most complicated economic problems, as is strikingly proved again by Book II and will be proved still more by Book III" (21). Beyond this, Marx "analysed surplus-value itself further and found its two forms, absolute and relative surplus-value," showing "that they had played a different, but in either case a decisive role, in the historical development of capitalist production." Moreover, "[o]n the basis of surplus value he developed the first rational theory of wages we have, and for the first time gave an outline of the history of capitalist accumulation and an exposition of its historical tendency."

which this same quantity of living labour produces or in which it is embodied. The question is indeed insoluble, if put in this form. It has been correctly formulated by Marx and thereby answered. It is not labour which has a value. As an activity which creates values it can no more have any special value than gravity can have any special weight, heat any special temperature, electricity any special strength of current. It is not labour which is bought and sold as a commodity but labour *power*. Once labour power becomes a commodity, its value is determined by the labour embodied in it as a social product. This value is equal to the labour socially necessary for its production and reproduction. Hence the purchase and sale of labour power on the basis of its value thus defined does not at all contradict the economic law of value.

Engels's Introduction to the 1891 edition of *Wage Labour and Capital* represents as "totally inadequate" the classical proposition "that the value of a commodity is determined by the labour input contained in it, requisite for its production" (MECW *27*: 196). Marx "was the first thoroughly to investigate the value-creating quality of labour and he discovered in so doing that not all labour apparently, or even really, necessary for the production of a commodity adds to it under all circumstances a magnitude of value which corresponds to the quantity of labour expended." Here Engels presumably intended deviations of prices from values. He continues: "If therefore today we say offhandedly with economists like Ricardo that the value of a commodity is determined by the labour necessary for its production, we always in so doing imply the reservations made by Marx."[31] Beyond this – and more significantly – the source of the "contradiction" allegedly bedeviling classical doctrine is perceived to be (as in 1885) its formulation in terms of "the purchase and sale of labour and of the value of labour"; and the "last offshoot of classical political economy, the Ricardian school, was wrecked mainly by the insolubility of this contradiction. Classical political economy had got into a blind alley. The man who found the way out of this blind alley was Karl Marx" (198). Here Engels is referring to the "buying and selling of labour power" in *Capital*: "What the economists had regarded as the cost of production of 'labour' was the cost of production not of labour but of the living worker himself. And what this worker sold to the capitalist was not his labour. 'As soon as his labour actually begins,' says

---

[31] For further elucidation, Engels refers readers to Marx's *A Contribution to the Critique of Political Economy* (1859) as well as *Capital 1* (Part I, Chapter 1, Sections 1–3). The 1859 reference presumably relates to the affirmation that "[r]egarded as exchange values all commodities are merely definite quantities of *congealed labour time*," specifically of "social labour," with "the different kinds of labour ... reduced to uniform, homogeneous, simple labour" or "*human* labour *in general*.... [I]t is assumed that the labour time contained in a commodity is the labour time *necessary* for its production, namely the labour time required, under the generally prevailing conditions of production, to produce another unit of the same commodity" (MECW *29*: 272–3). But, in fact, Marx specifies elsewhere in his 1859 *Contribution* that prices diverge from values, which he characterizes as a "strange conclusion," which "raises the question how on the basis of exchange value a market price differing from this exchange value comes into being, or rather, how the law of exchange value asserts itself only in its antithesis. This problem is solved in the theory of competition" (302), evidently an allusion to the Transformation.

Marx, 'it has already ceased to belong to him; it can therefore no longer be sold by him' [*Capital* 1, Part VI, Chapter XIX]" (198–9).

The classical economists were totally at sea, so runs the contention, because to talk of the "value" of an hour of labor was tautological (MECW *27*: 196). Nevertheless, Engels goes on to allow that the classics themselves transposed the issue from the "value of labour" to the value of the worker, though "tamper[ing] a little with logic" in doing so. Here he appears to allow to the classics at least an implicit appreciation of labor power, though he still maintained that they were unable to interpret the character of surplus as unpaid labor (197–8). There is a similar allowance when he writes that "labour power is intergrown with [the worker's] person and is inseparable from it. Its cost of production, therefore, coincides with his cost of production; what the economists called the cost of production of labour is really the cost of production of the worker and therewith of his labour power" (199). For all that, he closes by insisting that "[t]he difficulty over which the best economists came to grief, so long as they started out from the value of 'labour,' vanishes as soon as we start out from the value of 'labour *power*' instead" (200). I shall return to Engels's focus on labor power as providing the key to Marxian economics in the concluding section.

F. The Transformation and the "Prize Essay Competition"

Engels in his Preface to *Capital* 2 challenged readers "to demonstrate what Rodbertus's political economy can accomplish," and to "show how an equal average rate of profit can and must come about not only without a violation of the law of value, but rather on the very basis of it" (1885; MECW *36*: 23). The Preface to *Capital* 3 points out that the second challenge alone had been addressed (1894; MECW *37*: 11). However, before we take up some of these offerings and Engels's responses to them in 1894, note his reluctance to reveal the secret before the appearance of *Capital* 3. Thus when responding to one correspondent (N. Danielson) regarding the relation between the rates of surplus value and profit, he focused on a secondary matter entirely, namely Danielson's supposition that "merchant's capital and banker's capital would be impossible, because they would not make any profit" (15 October 1888; MECW *48*: 228). This "formula, that every manufacturer keeps all the surplus value, which he, in the first hand appropriates," he observes, is not how Marx tackled the problem; but he does not reveal the essential point of Marx's solution which is that some manufacturers subsidize others depending on the range of capital compositions. Howard and King regard this response, quite correctly, as "evasive" and even suggest that Engels may have "genuinely forgotten the essentials of Marx's solution" that he had first learned in the correspondence of 1862 (Howard and King 1989: 25). Four years later, though, when it is more likely that the solution was fresh in his mind, Engels also rejected a suggestion to publish it apart: "To print the section [of *Capital* 3] on the rate of profit separately and in advance is quite out of the question, for you should know that in Marx everything is so interrelated that nothing can be torn out of context" (to Conrad Schmidt, 12 September 1892; MECW *49*: 525). Howard and King read this response too as "nothing short of evasive," because on this argument "none of Marx's writings could ever have been published..." (1989: 24–5). There may be something to this, but Engels's refusal can be partly explained by the extreme pressure he was under – almost to the point of panic – finally to bring *Capital 3* to press. Diversions would be intolerable. Furthermore, *Capital 3* was something of a special case, as Engels had earlier intimated to F. A. Sorge: "the third volume will again have the effect of a thunderbolt, since the whole of capitalist production is dealt with in context for the first time and all official bourgeois economics rejected out of hand" (3 June 1885; MECW *47*: 296–7).

Let us turn now to a variety of responses to the challenge, the first by Wilhelm Lexis in *Conrads Jahrbücher* for 1885. Engels allowed that Lexis had, if not solved the problem, at least "correctly *formulated*" it, albeit "somewhat loosely and shallowly" (MECW *37*: 12). This is to be hypercritical, for Lexis actually stated the solution correctly as entailing deviations of prices from values and interindustry transfers of surplus:

"The solution of the contradiction" (between the Ricardo-Marxian law of value and an equal average rate of profit) "is impossible if the various classes of commodities are considered *individually* and if their value is to be equal to their exchange value, and the latter equal or proportional to their price." According to him, the solution is only possible if "we cease measuring the value of individual commodities according to labour, and consider only the production of commodities *as a whole* and their distribution among the aggregate classes of capitalists and workers.... The working class receives but a certain proportion of the total product... the other portion, which falls to the share of the capitalist class, represents the surplus product in Marxian sense, and accordingly... the surplus value. Then the members of the capitalist class divide this total surplus value among themselves not in accordance with the number of workers employed by them, but in proportion to the capital invested by each, the land also being accounted for as capital value."

The Marxian ideal values determined by units of labour incorporated in the commodities do not correspond to prices but may be "regarded as points of departure of a shift which leads to the actual prices. The latter depend on the fact that equal sums of capital demand equal profits." For this reason some capitalists will secure prices higher than the ideal values for their commodities, and others will secure lower prices. "But since the losses and gains of surplus value balance one another within the capitalist class, the total amount of the surplus value is the same as it would be if all prices were proportional to the ideal values." (citations from *Conrads Jahrbücher 11*, 1885)

Engels does, however, refer to Lexis as "a Marxist, disguised as a vulgar economist" (MECW *37*: 14), which can be read as high praise.[32]

---

[32] See also the commendations of Lexis (1885), in Engels to Schmidt, 12 March 1895 (MECW *50*: 463).

A contribution in 1889 by Conrad Schmidt (according to Engels's paraphrase) distinguishes for each product the $(c + v)$ and (s) elements, and maintains that exchange rates relating to the latter category of "surplus" goods are determined by the sums of capital required for their production rather than by *current* labor input ("socially necessary" labor). The average profit rate in the *economy* emerges as the aggregate of all produced surpluses relative to the sum of all capitals, and this is added to the cost prices of the "paid" products, which are determined by current labor input, thus formally satisfying Marx's "law of value" (MECW 37: 14).[33]

Now Schmidt's distinction between paid and surplus product, Engels objected, conflicted with the Marxian view that *both* "must be sold at prices proportionate to the socially necessary labour required and expended in producing them" (MECW 37: 15). Indeed, Schmidt's position implied the orthodox conception of capital – albeit conceived as "accumulated labour of the past" – as an independent factor of production responsible for the creation of surplus on par with current labor. Engels was nonetheless warmly disposed toward Schmidt, for "the rest of his booklet is evidence of the understanding with which he drew further conclusions from the first two volumes of *Capital*," thus neatly turning the achievement to Marx's favor: "His is the honour of independently finding the correct explanation developed by Marx in the third part of the third volume for the hitherto inexplicable sinking tendency of the rate of profit" – an important indication of the significance Engels still attached to Marx's analysis of the falling profit rate – "and, similarly, of explaining the derivation of commercial profit out of industrial surplus value, and of making a great number of observations concerning interest and ground rent, in which he anticipates ideas developed by Marx in the fourth and fifth parts of the third volume."[34]

A third contributor, writing in *Conrads Jahrbücher* in 1892, had "placed his finger on the salient point" (MECW 37: 17). Engels cites the following passage by Peter Fireman, which explains how surplus value, depending on exploitation of labor – unpaid labor – and thus proportional to the labor input, is transferred into a uniform return on capital:

"Simply by selling commodities above their value in all branches of production in which the ratio between . . . constant and variable capital is greatest; but this also implies that commodities are sold below their value in those branches of production in which the ratio between constant and variable capital = c:v is smallest, and that commodities are sold at their true value only in branches in which the ratio of c:v represents a certain mean figure. . . . Is this discrepancy between individual prices and their respective values a refutation of the value principle? By no means. For since the prices of some commodities rise above their value as much as the prices of others fall

[33] On Schmidt, see further Howard and King (1989: 26–8).

[34] Engels also refers to an article of 1892–3 by Schmidt emphasizing "competition" as "produc[ing] the average rate of profit by causing the transfer of capital from branches of production with under-average profit to branches with above-average profit" (MECW 37: 15), which is of course Marx's position. But Engles rejects the attempt to "prove" this result as contrary to Marx's analysis. See also Howard and King (1989: 28).

below it, the total sum of prices remains equal to the total sum of values... in the end this incongruity disappears." This incongruity is a "disturbance"; "however, in the exact sciences it is not customary to regard a predictable disturbance as a refutation of a law."

Despite the accuracy of this formulation in terms of the final Marxian exposition – with Fireman opposing Schmidt's partial application of the law of value – Engels could not bring himself to offer a full commendation, insofar as "the unreservedly cool reception of his able article shows how many interconnecting links would still be needed even after this discovery to enable Fireman to work out a full and comprehensive solution." We are, as always, given to understand that only in *Capital 3* was such a solution to be found.

More broadly, Engels found fault with Fireman's comprehension of Marx's methodology. Fireman based himself, runs the complaint, on "the false assumption" that "one might expect fixed, cut-to-measure, once and for all applicable definitions in Marx's works," whereas "mental images" or "ideas" – *theory* is presumably intended – must be perceived as "subject to change and transformation," being a reflection of *reality* ("things and their interrelations"), which has this character (16). For this reason, the theoretical discourses of *Capital 1* "are not encapsulated in rigid definitions, but are developed in their historical or logical process of formation." Here Engels illustrates in terms of Marx's proceeding from simple (precapitalist) production to capitalist production rather than setting out from the latter. This matter touches implicitly on a *historical* transformation of values into prices; it is elaborated in a "Supplement" by Engels to *Capital 3* (to be discussed presently).[35]

Engels was contemptuous of a charge by Julius Wolf in *Conrads Jahrbücher* for 1891 that the entire "problem" was a spurious one, imagined by Engels and absent from Marx. An industry with a relatively high c/v ratio will in fact experience a relatively high s/v ratio (by way of a productivity effect playing on its v), whereas, precisely because the rate of surplus value in that industry is relatively high, its profit rate may equal that of a second industry having a lower c/v ratio (MECW *37*: 17–18). Engels's reaction was to deny that Wolf had any conception of Marxian economics, though perceiving himself as a follower. He also subverted him in grossly personal terms, referring tangentially to "gossip among professors" suggesting that Schmidt had been unfairly helped by Engels: "Herr Julius Wolf! It may be customary in the world in which you live and strive for the man who publicly poses a problem to others to acquaint his close friends on the sly with its solution. I am quite prepared to believe that you are capable of this sort of thing. But that a man need not stoop to such shabby tricks in my world is proved by the present preface" (18).[36]

---

[35] The text was written during the period from May to June 1895 and appeared in *Die Neue Zeit*, Bd. I, No. 1. 1895–6, after Engels's death.

[36] One other contender is mentioned by Engels, G. C. Stiebeling (1890), but his "solution" has much in common with that of Wolf (MECW *37*: 22–3). That Stiebeling misunderstood Marx,

Even more dismissive was the reaction to Achille Loria. Apart from his claiming in 1886 Marx's conception of history – which dated back to 1845 – "as his own discovery," Loria charged that Marx in fact never had a solution to offer for the apparent contradiction between the law of value and the uniform profit rate in the promised third volume (MECW 37: 19–20). The invective of Engels's reaction is scarcely credible: "What a mountebank one must be to imagine that Marx had need to resort to such miserable tricks," that Marx "was as much a conscious sophist, paralogist, humbug and mountebank as Mr. Loria himself" (21). Engels argues more calmly against Loria's own "solution" of 1890, turning on "the unproductive or commercial capitalist who fulfills the role of profit-rate equalizer" (20).[37]

G. The Historical Transformation: A Theory of Economic History

Let us turn to commentaries made after publication of *Capital 3* to which Engels responded in his Supplement to the volume. Of high interest is Achille Loria's criticism. His main point (1895: 477–9, cited in MECW 37: 876–81) is that Marx abandoned the labor theory while purporting to base himself thereupon: "No economist with any trace of sense has ever concerned himself or will ever want to concern himself with a value which commodities do not sell for *and never can sell for (nè possono vendersi mai)*. . . . In asserting that the value for which commodities *never* sell is proportional to the labour they contain, what does Marx do except repeat in an inverted form the thesis of orthodox economists, that the value for which commodities sell is *not* proportional to the labour expended on them?" (cited in MECW 37: 876). The labor theory is abandoned in *Capital 3*, Loria maintained, notwithstanding the insistence early in *Capital 1* that the exchange rate between two commodities reflects "something common to both" – namely "human labour in the abstract" (see MECW 35: 48). "Was there ever such an utter *reductio ad absurdum*, such complete theoretical bankruptcy? Was ever scientific suicide committed with greater pomp and more solemnity?" (cited in MECW 37: 877).[38] Beyond this, Marx's "solution" in terms of the alleged identity between aggregate value and aggregate price made no sense because value was a *relative* concept: "Matters are not helped by Marx's saying that despite the divergency of individual prices from individual values the total price of all commodities always coincides with their total value, or the amount of labour contained in the totality

---

Engels maintained, was clear from an empirical study of the U.S. profit-rate trend of 1870–80, according to which the profit rate had fallen, whereas Stiebeling "interprets it wrongly and assumes that Marx's theory of a constantly stable rate of profit should be corrected on the basis of experience" – a "stable rate" for Marx being a "figment of Mr. Stiebeling's imagination." For more on Stiebeling, see Howard and King (1989: 28–9).

[37] On Wolf and Loria, see Howard and King (1989: 29–30). Also consult them (34–5) for contestants not mentioned by Engels.

[38] Loria's objection resembles that in our day by Paul Samuelson, to the effect that Marx set out with an erroneous value scheme, erased it, and started anew with a true price scheme (Samuelson 1971: 421).

of the commodities. For inasmuch as value is nothing more than the exchange ratio between one commodity and another, the very concept of a total value is an absurdity, nonsense...a *contradictio in adjecto*..." (cited in MECW 37: 876).[39] Loria found the "solution" so unsatisfactory that he questioned whether it could be the work of Marx at all: "Is it really true that Marx wrote, with the intention of publication, this mixture of disconnected notes that Engels, with pious friendship, has compiled?... [I]t seems to me, that Marx, after publishing his magnificent (*splendido*) book, did not intend to provide it with a successor, or else wanted to leave the completion of the gigantic work to his heirs, outside his own responsibility" (cited in MECW 37: 881n.). Loria's suspicions are certainly unfounded, because Marx's Transformation procedure emerges loud and clear as early as 1857–8 in the *Grundrisse*, and yet louder and clearer in 1861–3 in the *Theories of Surplus Value* (Hollander 2008: 254–6, 293–7).

* * *

Engels scarcely bothers to respond to Loria's representation of a *total* value of commodities as absurd (MECW 37: 878). He does, however, address the initial contention that "commodities do not sell for *and never can sell for*" their labor values, by emphasizing features of a historical Transformation. His statement of position is prefaced by commendation of various writers who had responded positively to the solution spelled out in *Capital 3*, and to this we turn first.

Werner Sombart (1894) is lauded as the first German university professor who "succeeds on the whole in seeing in Marx's writings what Marx really says" (MECW 37: 881). Engels represented the main themes of his achievement this way:

He investigates the importance of value in the Marxian system, and arrives at the following results: Value is not manifest in the exchange relation of capitalistically produced commodities; it does not live in the consciousness of the agents of capitalist production; it is not an empirical, but a mental, a logical fact; the concept of value in its material definiteness in Marx is nothing but the economic expression for the fact of the social productive power of labour as the basis of economic existence; in the final analysis the law of value dominates economic processes in a capitalist economic system, and for this economic system quite generally has the following content: the value of commodities is the specific and historical form in which the productive power of labour, in the last analysis dominating all economic processes, asserts itself as a determining factor.[40]

Nonetheless, there was a deficiency. Sombart's view of "the significance of the law of value for the capitalist form of production," though not wrong, was "too broad and susceptible of a narrower, more precise formulation; in my opinion it by no

---

[39] This objection had been directed long before against Ricardo by Samuel Bailey (1825), and it is even found in our own day (e.g., Itoh 1976).

[40] Weeks contrasts Engels and Marx on "the role of perception and knowledge of labor time" (1981: 55–7). His evidence for Engels's "explain[ing] equivalent exchange on the basis of the knowledge of producers" (55) should be modified by our extract.

means exhausts the entire significance of the law of value for the economic stages of society's development dominated by this law" (881–2). Here Engels was referring to his own perspective on the so-called historical Transformation. The mildness of the reaction is surprising, because in fact Sombart took a firm position in support of the law of value as a "mental" or logical, not "empirical," fact.[41]

In an important letter to Sombart of 11 March 1895, Engels agrees that "[t]he conceptual transitions whereby Marx arrives at the general and equal rate of profit from the various values produced in individual capitalist concerns . . . are wholly foreign to the consciousness of the individual capitalist" (MECW 50: 460). Each individual capitalist merely seeks to maximize his profits, and "[b]ourgeois economics reveals that this pursuit of *bigger* profits on the part of each individual capitalist results in a general and *equal* rate of profit, an approximately *equal* rate of profit for all. But neither capitalists nor bourgeois economists are aware that the real purpose of that pursuit is the equal percentual distribution of the total surplus value over capital as a whole" (461). At this point, however, Engels diverges from this logical dimension to the problem, for he raises this question: "But how did this process of equalization really come about? That is a very interesting point about which Marx himself has little to say." At the same time, Marx did invite further exploration as a matter of principle: "Marx's whole way of thinking is not so much a doctrine as a method. It provides, not so much ready-made dogmas, as aids to further investigation and the method *for* such investigation. Here, then, is a piece of work to be done which Marx himself did not attempt in his first draft." Nonetheless, Marx had made a start (see MECW 37: 175–6), which proved that the concept of value "has, or had, more reality than you ascribe to it. In the early days of exchange when products gradually changed into commodities, exchanges were made *in proportion to value*. For the labour expended on two articles was the sole criterion of quantitative comparison. At that time, then, value *existed in an immediate and real sense*. That this immediate realization of value ceased in exchange, that it now no longer exists, we know" (461–2). He proceeds to conjecture that Sombart would have no "particular difficulty in tracing the intermediate stages, at any rate in broad outline, that led from the above-mentioned real and immediate value to value as represented in the capitalist mode of production, value which is so thoroughly well-concealed that our economists can happily deny its existence. A genuinely historical exposition of this process – which, though admittedly requiring a great deal of research, holds out the prospect of correspondingly rewarding results – would be a most valuable pendant to *Capital*" (462).

A contribution of 1895 by Conrad Schmidt is highly praised in the Supplement for providing a "proof of how the Marxian derivation of average profit from surplus value for the first time gives an answer to the question not even posed by economics up to now: how the magnitude of this average rate of profit is determined, and

---

[41] Cf. Pokorni's notion that Marx's stadial approach in transferring from values to prices is purely "noetical," existing only in the mind or intellect (Pokorni 1985: 113–14).

how it comes about that it is, say 10 or 15% and not 50 or 100%," where surplus value, "first appropriated by the industrial capitalist is the sole and exclusive source from which profit and rent flow" (MECW 37: 882).[42] Nonetheless, as in the case of Sombart, Engels rejected a representation by Conrad Schmidt of Marx's law of value as no more than a "scientific hypothesis":

Schmidt, too, has his formal misgivings regarding the law of value. He calls it a scientific *hypothesis*, set up to explain the actual exchange process, which proves to be the necessary theoretical starting-point, illuminating and indispensable, even in respect of the phenomena of competitive prices which seem in absolute contradiction to it. According to him, without the law of value all theoretical insight into the economic machinery of capitalist reality ceases. And in a private letter that he permits me to quote, Schmidt declares the law of value within the capitalist form of production to be a pure, although theoretically necessary, fiction. (882)[43]

For Engels, "[t]his view . . . is quite incorrect. The law of value has a far greater and more definite significance for capitalist production than of a mere hypothesis, not to mention a fiction, even though a necessary one. . . . Sombart, as well as Schmidt . . . does not make sufficient allowance for the fact that we are dealing here not only with a purely logical process but with a historical process."

In his response to Schmidt dated 12 March 1895 (see note 42), Engels attributes to faulty philosophical training Schmidt's "occasional failure . . . to see the wood for the trees, which is why you reduce the law of values to a fiction, a necessary fiction, in much the same way as Kant reduced the existence of God to a postulate of practical reason" (MECW 50: 463). The main objection turns on the relation perceived by Engels whereby "a concept is by its nature essentially a concept, hence does not ipso facto and *prima facie* correspond to the reality from which it has had first to be abstracted," yet "is always something more than a fiction" (464). In fact, all concepts in economics (and the sciences) are approximations. If, for

---

[42] In correspondence with Schmidt, Engels refers to his article as "first rate," adding that "your demonstration – by quantitative determination – of the specific differences between Marx's theory of profit and that of the earliest political economists, is very well done" (12 March 1895; MECW 50: 466). He had, in fact, also "discovered for himself why it is that the rate of profit tends to fall and how commercial profit is created" (463).

[43] The letter in question, dated 1 March 1895, expresses reservations regarding Marx's argument that establishes the identity aggregate labor values and aggregate prices of production, and concludes that the law of value is a fiction, albeit a necessary fiction in the sense of "a hypothesis which we must necessarily make in order to reach otherwise unattainable results," in the present instance to deduce the law that the general profit rate is determined by the relation between aggregate surplus value and total capital (Howard and King 1989: 47). Necessary fictions were spelled out by Engels himself in *Anti-Dühring* (on which see, e.g., MECW 25: 125, 126–8 on the calculus). There is also an amusing instance in the unpublished *Dialectics of Nature* written between 1873 and 1882 (e.g., MECW 25: 354).

Bernstein had similar misgivings regarding the Transformation solution. If in a capitalist society prices-of-production rule, as Marx insisted, then value "is bereft of all concrete content and becomes a purely abstract concept"; but if "labour value can claim validity only as an intellectual formula or scientific hypothesis, surplus value becomes all the more a mere formula, a formula which rests on a hypothesis" (Bernstein 1993 [1899]: 48).

example, "we were to insist that the rate of profit – say, 14.876934 . . . be exactly the same down to the last decimal point in every business every year, on pain of being reduced to a fiction, we should be grossly mistaking the nature of the rate of profit and of economic laws generally – they none of them have any reality save as an approximation, a tendency, an average, but not an *immediate* reality. This is due partly to the fact that their action is frustrated by the simultaneous action of other laws, but also to some extent by their nature as concepts." In elaborating, Engels illustrates from "the law of value and the distribution of surplus value through the rate of profit," and proceeds: "Both come closest to full realization only in as much as capitalist production has everywhere been fully implemented, i.e. society has been reduced to modern classes of landowners, capitalists (industrialists and traders) and workers, all intermediate stages having been eliminated. This has not yet happened even in England nor will it ever happen – we shouldn't let things get to that pitch" (464–5). England was approaching pure capitalism but would never reach it, Engels alluding, partly in jest, to revolution that would put paid to further capitalist evolution.[44]

But all this is sparring. It is in the Supplement to *Capital 3* where Engels himself offers a provisional historical account of the transition from a system of values to one of prices. He sets out from the Marx reference in the letter to Sombart (above, p. 113) remarking that "[h]ad Marx had an opportunity to go over the third volume once more, he would doubtless have extended this passage considerably. As it stands it gives only a sketchy outline of what is to be said on the point in question" (MECW *37*: 884). The relevant passage reads thus, and it is reproduced by Engels except for the second paragraph:

The exchange of commodities at their values, or approximately at their values, thus requires a much lower stage than their exchange at their prices of production, which requires a definite level of capitalist development.

Whatever the manner in which the prices of various commodities are first mutually fixed or regulated, their movements are always governed by the law of value. If the labour time required for their production happens to shrink, prices fall; if it increases, prices rise, provided other conditions remain the same.

Apart from the domination of prices and price movement by the law of value, it is quite appropriate to regard the values of commodities as not only theoretically but also historically *prius* to the prices of production. This applies to conditions in which the labourer owns his means of production, and this is the condition of the land-owning farmer living off his own labour and the craftsman, in the ancient as well as in the

---

[44] As a further illustration, "total profit and the total surplus value can correspond only approximately," a tendency only, the "unity of concept and phenomenon . . . an essentially endless process" (MECW *50*: 465).

It is doubtful whether Marx perceived his identity of aggregate value and price as an approximation. After all, the logic of his entire case required that such identity be strictly understood. However, it is the basic "law of value" more narrowly perceived as the proportionality of relative prices to labor input that is the main theme of Engels's Supplement to *Capital 3*, specifically the denial that Marx was, in fact, concerned solely with a logical process. The broader issue regarding the identity between aggregate value and price did not arise.

modern world. This agrees also with the view we expressed previously [MECW *29*: 290; *35*: 98] that the evolution of products into commodities arises through exchange between different communities, not between the members of the same community. It holds not only for this primitive condition, but also for subsequent conditions, based on slavery and serfdom, and for the guild organisation of handicrafts, so long as the means of production involved in each branch of production can be transferred from one sphere to another only with difficulty and therefore the various spheres of production are related to one another, within certain limits, as foreign countries or communist communities (MECW *37*: 175–6).[45]

In his own elaboration Engels is rather more precise regarding the sense of the early exchange of commodities at their values. In particular, "the peasant of the Middle Ages knew fairly accurately the labour time required for the manufacture of the articles obtained by him in barter. . . . What had they expended in making these products? Labour and labour alone: to produce the raw material, and to process it they spent nothing but their own labour power; how then could they exchange these products of theirs for those of other labouring producers otherwise than in the ratio of the labour expended on them?" (MECW *37*: 884–5). The same held for exchanges between peasants and urban artisans (885). The estimates of labor inputs entailed by products involving longer processes, regularly interrupted and uncertain, and required of people "who could not calculate," occurred "[o]bviously only by means of a lengthy process of zigzag approximation, often feeling the way here and there in the dark, and, as is usual, learning only through mistakes" (886). Here then is a rather qualified version of the "law of value."

The penetration of money had a twofold effect. On the one hand, "the tendency towards adaptation to the law of value (in the Marxian formulation, *nota bene!*) grows more pronounced on the one hand, while on the other it is already interrupted by the interference of usurers' capital and fleecing by taxation; the periods for which prices, on the average, approach to within a negligible margin of values begin to grow longer" (MECW *37*: 885). The transition to metallic money also rendered "the determination of value by labour time . . . no longer visible upon the surface of commodity exchange" (886). Indeed,

[f]rom the practical point of view, money became the decisive measure of value, all the more as the commodities entering trade became more varied, the more they came from distant countries, and the less, therefore, the labour time necessary for their production could be checked. Money itself usually came first from foreign parts; even when precious metals were obtained within the country, the peasant and artisan were partly unable to estimate approximately the labour employed therein, and partly their own consciousness of the value-measuring property of labour had been fairly well dimmed by the habit of reckoning with money; in the popular mind money began to represent absolute value. (886–7)

[45] Engels comments on Marx's "view" that "the evolution of products into commodities arises through exchange between different commodities": "In 1865, this was merely Marx's 'view.' Today, after the extensive research ranging from Maurer to Morgan into the nature of primitive communities, it is an accepted fact which is hardly anywhere denied" (MECW *37*: 176n.).

Engels thus further undermined his own case for the "law of value" by representing the introduction of money in this fashion. Nonetheless, he asserts with confidence that the law applied for the whole period of "simple commodity production" – preceding the emergence of "the capitalist form of production" – in the sense that "prices gravitate towards the values fixed according to the Marxian law and oscillate around those values, so that the more fully simple commodity production develops, the more the average prices over long periods uninterrupted by external violent disturbances coincide with values within a negligible margin" (887).

We now come to the transition from "simple" to "capitalist" commodity production, with the merchant constituting the "revolutionary element" in the otherwise "stable" environment that comprised the traditional peasant and urban artisanal environments – a stability that Engels himself had earlier brought into question. After a detailed description of the emergence of the merchant, initially "an associate like all his contemporaries" (operating within a merchant, guild, or trading company such as the Genoese, Venetians, or Hanseatics), we have the key proposition that "[h]ere for the first time we meet with a profit and a rate of profit," in fact with an "equal rate of profit" within each trading company and initially for each market area "which in its fully developed form is one of the final results of capitalist production" (MECW 37: 889). A more general equalization later takes place through "competition" and, increasingly, competition between individual merchants (890–1).

Whereas merchant capital made its profit from overseas trade, *production* was undertaken by workers owning their own means of production so that no surplus value to some "capital" entity was yielded – though tribute to feudal lords might be entailed (MECW 37: 891). Subsequently, handicraft producers of export commodities might be compelled to sell to the exporting merchant at prices below values, in which case the law of value ruled "on the average" in the domestic retail trade alone, not in international trade.

The beginnings of the rudiments of capitalist production in shipping, mining, and textiles are then described, and with them "the beginning of the formation of capitalist surplus value" (MECW 37: 892). Special attention is paid to textile contractors "who first brought commodities, directly manufactured for capitalist account, into the market and into competition with the commodities of the same sort made for handicraft account." The merchant might be induced to take on the task of contractor – who supplies the master weaver with yarn to be made into cloth in return for a fixed wage – by the opportunity to make a greater profit at the same selling price as regular merchants: "The merchant capitalist bought the labour power, which still owned its production instruments but no longer the raw material. By thus guaranteeing the weaver regular employment, he could depress the weaver's wage to such a degree that part of the labor time furnished remained unpaid for. The contractor thus became an appropriator of surplus value over and above his commercial profit." He would also tend to undercut his competitors, surrendering a portion of surplus value to the buyer in order to accelerate sales and turnover (893). However, once merchants in general turn to contracting, equality of the profit rate will be reestablished, possibly at a lower level should part of surplus value be transferred to foreign buyers.

The next stage in the "subjugation of industry by capital" entails the transition to manufacturing. Here "the surplus value appropriated by the manufacturing capitalist enables him (or the export merchant who shares with him) to sell cheaper than his competitors" – handicraftsmen – "until the general introduction of the new mode of production, when equalization again takes place. The already existing mercantile rate of profit, even if it is levelled out only locally, remains the Procrustean bed in which the excessive industrial surplus value is lopped off without mercy" (MECW 37: 893). The process is accelerated by the evolution of modern, large-scale industry, which forces production costs even lower, thus eliminating former modes of production:

It is large-scale industry that thus finally conquers the domestic market for capital, puts an end to the small-scale production and natural economy of the self-sufficient peasant family, eliminates direct exchange between small producers, and places the entire nation in the service of capital. Likewise, it equalises the profit rate of the different commercial and industrial branches of business into *one* general rate of profit, and finally ensures industry the position of power due to it in this equalisation by eliminating most of the obstacles formerly hindering the transfer of capital from one branch to another. (894)

The relevant section of the Supplement closes with a statement containing the essential contribution by Engels to the analysis of a historical Transformation from values to prices, for which the account until now amounts to a descriptive introduction:

Thereby the conversion of values into production prices is accomplished for all exchange as a whole. This conversion therefore proceeds according to objective laws, without the consciousness or the intent of the participants. Theoretically there is no difficulty at all in the fact that competition reduces to the general level profits which exceed the general rate, thus again depriving the first industrial appropriator of the surplus value exceeding the average. All the more so in practice, however, for the spheres of production with excessive surplus value, with high variable and low constant capital, i.e., with low capital composition, are by their very nature the ones that are last and least completely subjected to capitalist production, especially agriculture. On the other hand, the rise of production prices above commodity values, which is required to raise the below-average surplus value, contained in the products of the spheres of high capital composition, to the level of the average rate of profit, appears to be extremely difficult theoretically, but is soonest and most easily effected in practice, as we have seen. For when commodities of this class are first produced capitalistically and enter capitalist commerce, they compete with commodities of the same nature produced by precapitalist methods and hence dearer. Thus, even if the capitalist producer renounces a part of the surplus value, he can still obtain the rate of profit prevailing in his locality, which originally had no direct connection with surplus value because it had arisen from merchant capital long before there was any capitalist production at all, and therefore before an industrial rate of profit was possible. (MECW *37*: 894)

The great weight placed on the historical Transformation in one of his last compositions might suggest that Engels intended a displacement of the purely theoretical Transformation. This would certainly not have been acceptable to Marx, who had written that "it is quite appropriate to regard the values of commodities as not only theoretically but also historically *prius* to the prices of production" (above, p. 115).[46] This Engels quoted in introducing his historical disquisition and adopted as his own position. That in defending Marx against his critics Engels should have chosen to elaborate not the theoretical version to which Marx had devoted so much of his attention, but the historical version that, on Engels own account, had been left as a "sketchy outline," is precisely because only the latter stood – as he saw it – in need of elaboration. To be more precise, the closing passage of his historical account takes the theoretical Marxian framework for granted. This applies to surplus envisaged as unpaid labor time, so that in some initial configuration, assuming early capitalist development when labor values rule, the rate of surplus value – and the profit rate – is relatively high in labor-intensive industries; and in the "final" equilibrium, where uniform profit rates pertain, prices fall short of values in labor-intensive sectors and exceed values in those with high organic composition. Unfortunately, having arrived at the key juncture, Engels has very little of substance to say of the actual *historical adjustment* from values to prices of production. What we find is the assertion that capitalist development in the case of the former set of industries (including agriculture) is at a disadvantage relative to the latter. But this, one would think, implies a peculiar constraint on their relative expansion, which should act not to lower returns therein but to maintain them relative to capital-intensive sectors.

Beyond this, note a critical difference between the two versions in the following respect, though it goes unnoticed by Engels. It is that the theoretical version as spelled out in *Capital 3* entails a transition from nonequilibrium values to equilibrium prices (see Hollander 2008: 23–4), whereas the historical version sets out with equilibrium labor ratios.

Particularly striking is the alleged applicability of the "law of value" over an immense period of "from five to seven thousand years," from prehistoric times to the fifteenth century (MECW *37*: 887).[47] This seems to be an unhelpful exaggeration, directed against Loria's position that commodities "do not sell for and

---

[46] We should take this comment into account when evaluating the objection that Engels unjustifiably attributed to Marx his own "logical-historical" method (see Arthur 1996b).

[47] Engels makes the strange assertion, for a Marxist, that it is under *those* conditions that "labour alone is value creating" (MECW *37*: 886). Engels himself, however, restricted this proposition somewhat (see above, pp. 116–7).

never can sell for" their labor values (above, p. 111). Writing to Sombart, Engels is more constrained: "I should delimit [the concept of value] historically by expressly confining [it] to the economic phase in which alone there has and could have been any question of value hitherto – to the social forms in which exchange of *commodities* and production of commodities exist; primitive communism was innocent of value" (11 March 1895; MECW *50*: 460).

Criticisms of Engels's account abound.[48] Take particular note here of several contemporary objections to the historical perspective. First, Bernstein questioned Engels's historical defense of the labor theory as pertaining to a precapitalist era, for Parvus had shown (*Die Neue Zeit*, 1895–6) that "feudal relationships, undifferentiated agriculture, guilds and other monopolies... hindered the formation of a general exchange value based on the labour time of the producers" (Bernstein 1993 [1899]: 49).[49]

Second, recall Sombart's position regarding Marx's law of value having validity only as a "mental" concept, not an "empirical fact" (above, p. 113). This, he believed to be Marx's opinion; but were he mistaken – and we have indeed seen that Marx spoke of the law as a historical reality and not only a theoretical construct – then Marx would have erred, for if in early stages of capitalist development commodities exchanged according to relative labor inputs then the highest rates of exploitation, and therefore of profits, would pertain in labor-intensive industries, whereas the opposite was in fact the case, as in mining. (In modern times too it remains true that the highest returns characterized the capital-intensive industries; see Sombart 1894: 584–6.) This would also be a major objection to Engels's version.

Third, in a review of *Capital 3* by Lexis, of which Engels was unaware, the historical account of the formation of a general rate of profit proposed by Marx is represented as "quite untenable" because there had never been a historical period entailing capitalist organization characterized by differential profit rates:

The equality in the rate of profits (apart from accidental irregularities) is of the essence of capitalistic production. There never has been a social condition in which capitalist methods of production and yet inequality in the rate of profit caused by the different compositions of capital have existed side by side. The equality of profits appears *pari passu* with capitalistic methods of production and in inseparable connection with them; much as, in the embryo, the circulation of the blood develops *pari passu* with the development of shape and form. (Lexis 1895: 10–11)

[48] See the exchange between Morishima and Catephores (1975, 1976) and Meek (1976). Also see Howard and King (1989: 49–50).

[49] See also Howard and King (1989: 74–5) on Bernstein (1901), where he again expressed dissatisfaction with the transformation solution of *Capital 3*, and also with Engels's historical defense of the labor theory, on Conrad Schmidt's grounds that if exchanges according to labor ratios prevailed only in precapitalist societies, then the concept of labor value under capitalism could only be an "abstraction." Also see Angel (1961: 123), on Bernstein's opinion given in 1924 of Marx's solution as "extremely disappointing."

This affirmation would certainly apply to Engels's elaborate account in which coexisting profit-rate differentials apply over centuries.

H. Concluding Remarks

In conclusion let us return to Engels's effort to justify the Marxian enterprise in terms of the centrality accorded by Marx to the labor-power concept (above, pp. 104–6). Marx himself explained in the *Grundrisse* that Ricardo had erred by having the capitalist exchanging not with "labour capacity" – as labor power is called in this context – but with "living labour," thereby unwittingly creating "an insoluble antimony in his system, that a certain amount of living labour is not equal to the commodity which it produces, in which it objectifies itself, even though the value of the commodity equals the amount of labour contained in it" (MECW *28*: 483).[50] Although to my knowledge Engels never read the *Grundrisse* manuscripts, he uses similar language when he asserted in 1891 that classical economics was wrecked mainly by the "insolubility of this contradiction" (above, p. 106).

The weight Engels placed on the labor-power concept as central for comprehension of the surplus-value doctrine should not be understood as downplaying other Marxian contributions. Marx himself considered his analysis of "*the tendency of the profit rate to fall as society progresses*" to be "one of the greatest triumphs over

---

[50] For equivalent statements from a range of Marx's texts before and after the *Grundrisse*, see Hollander (2008: 230, 239–40, 262, 264–5, 287). Of particular interest is a letter to Engels, 24 August 1867, where Marx gives his evaluation of the "best points of my book":

1. (this is fundamental to all understanding of the facts) the *two-fold character of labour* according to whether it is expressed in use-value or exchange-value, which is brought out in the very *First* Chapter; 2. the treatment of *surplus-value regardless of its particular* forms as profit, interest, ground rent, etc. This will be made clear in the second volume especially. The treatment of the particular forms in classical political economy, where they are for ever being jumbled up together with the general form is an *olla potrida* [hodgepodge]. (MECW *42*: 407)

The first point refers to the contrast between labor *power* and labor (see Oakley 1979: 288n.). The second point also appears in a letter of 8 January 1868, as the first of *three* fundamentally new elements of the first volume of *Capital*: "that in contrast to all previous political economy, which from the outset treated the particular fragments of surplus value with their fixed forms of rent, profit and interest as already given, I begin by dealing with the general form of surplus value, in which all these elements are still undifferentiated, in solution as it were" (MECW *42*: 514). The second, as before, relates to labor power: "that the economists, without exception, have missed the simple fact that, if the commodity has the double character of use value and exchange value, then the labour represented in the commodity must also have a double character; thus the bare analysis of labour *sans phrase*, as in Smith, Ricardo, etc., is bound to come up against the inexplicable everywhere. This is, in fact, the whole secret of the critical conception." The third is the assertion, again attending to labor power, "that for the first time wages are shown as the irrational outward form of a hidden relationship, and this is demonstrated exactly in both forms of wages: time wages and piece wages. (It was a help to me that similar formulae are often found in higher mathematics.)" Unfortunately, the extant correspondence contains no reaction by Engels to the latter affirmation.

the *pons asini* of all previous political economy" (to Engels, 30 April 1868; MECW 43: 24). And, of course, Marxian profit-rate theory itself required preliminary comprehension of the surplus-value doctrine. Engels, in fact, insisted to the end on the downward secular trend as an essential feature of Marx's analysis (Preface to *Capital 3* 1894; MECW 37: 23), and in March 1895 he congratulated Schmidt on his keen appreciation of the phenomenon (see note 42), though it is true that the falling profit rate makes no appearance in the account of the close of the cyclical era, which is discussed in Chapters Three and Six.

As for the main issue of this chapter, it must be said that the representation of Ricardo's value theory is a travesty from which Marx manufactured an "insoluble antimony" and that Engels blindly accepted. Ricardo had conspicuously denied the sort of attribution made to him. Thus in elaborating his Labor Theory for the third edition of the *Principles*, he refers to Malthus's criticism that was based on the presumption that he had identified cost and value: "We have the power indeed, arbitrarily, to call the labour which has been employed upon a commodity its real value, but in so doing, we use words in a different sense from that in which they are customarily used; we confound at once the very important distinction between *cost* and *value*; and render it almost impossible to explain with clearness, the main stimulus to the production of wealth, which in fact depends upon this distinction" (Malthus 1820: 61, cited in Ricardo 1951–73 [1821] *1*: 47n.); and he gives his response: "Mr. Malthus appears to think that it is a part of my doctrine, that the cost and value of a thing should be the same; – it is, if he means by cost, 'cost of production' including profits. In the above passage, this is what he does not mean, and therefore he has not clearly understood me." In the text itself, he made protest: "I have not said, because one commodity has cost so much labour bestowed upon it as will cost 1,000 *l.* and another so much as will cost 2,000 *l.* that therefore one would be of the value of 1,000 *l.* and the other of the value of 2,000 *l.* but I have said that their value will be to each other as two to one.... I affirm only, that their relative values will be governed by the relative quantities of labour bestowed on their production" (46–7).[51]

There was, then, no "insoluble antimony" or "contradiction" to be resolved in the first place. Moreover, Ricardo arrived at the general formula that the profit rate is determined by the fraction of the workday devoted to the production of wage goods without formal reference to the cost of "labor power," which in fact is nothing more than the cost of producing the wage basket (see Hollander 1992: 111), as Engels himself occasionally conceded if rather ungraciously (above, p. 107).

Here let us note too that Marx and Engels took for granted that Ricardo's "profit" was indeed a surplus value in the sense that the capitalist recipient undertook no

---

[51] In his *Notes* on Malthus's *Principles*, Ricardo reiterated that "I do not say a portion of [a commodity's] cost measures its exchangeable value – but I say its whole value will be *in proportion* to a portion of its cost" (1951–73 [1820]: 100–1). But Marx and Engels were, of course, unfamiliar with Ricardo's commentary.

effort or task requiring compensation – a surplus that he was unable to explain properly. In fact, Ricardo took no such position. Rather, as he put it in his last (unpublished) paper, one "class gives its labour only to assist towards the production of the commodity and must be paid out of its value the compensation to which it is entitled, the other class makes the advances required in the shape of capital and must receive remuneration from the same source" (1951–73 [1823] 4: 365). There is perhaps a suggestion here of the postponement of present consumption as requiring a return; however, more specifically, the *Principles* itself has it that variation in the profit rate plays on accumulation, that the "motive for accumulation will diminish with every diminution of profit" (1951–73 [1821] 1: 122).[52]

The Marx–Engels account of Ricardo is more justifiable if attached to Rodbertus, who in 1842 did identify cost with labor alone and who envisaged surplus as a simple deduction from value due to labor, the capitalist (and landlord) exerting no effort requiring compensation. However, even Rodbertus did not require the formal notion of labor power to arrive at surplus value. In fact, the labor-power concept was designed only to interpret surplus for those inhabiting the "illusory" world of markets, and had, for Marx himself, no operational significance (Hollander 2008: 58, 76, 265, 287, 288, 290). As for the value of labor power, that is nothing but the labor time required to produce the real wage paid per day. Terms such as the "value-creating" or "wealth-augmenting" potential of labor power are no more than brilliant rhetoric because, when all is said and done, what is entailed is the unexceptionable proposition that in a multifactor system only part of the worker's day is required to reproduce his daily wage goods.

The story recounted here is one of Engels's struggle to defend Marx's reputation as innovator with respect to the essential doctrine of surplus value. It was a difficult task given the numerous predecessors and, particularly, the high degree of common ground between Rodbertus and Marx. Nonetheless, we cannot conclude from this that Marx silently "founded" his doctrine on Rodbertus's work, as Böhm-Bawerk put it and Rodbertus himself believed to be the case, because Marx was already well on his way by the late 1840s. In contrast, a notion of the primacy of the industrial sector in discussing profit-rate uniformity is first formulated by Rodbertus in 1851 (above, p. 94), and by Marx only in the early 1860s (see Hollander 2008: 30). Here the possibility of "debt" becomes particularly interesting – after all, Marx himself allowed that Rodbertus's "positive solution" to rent did "tend in the right direction" (above, p. 95) – but it is not a matter on which Engels focused.

A final word regarding the Transformation. Engels, in his last decade, made much of the phenomenon of "concentration": We shall see in Chapter Five how central it was perceived to be for the granting of welfare reform by the capitalist state. Nevertheless, he did not attempt to incorporate monopoly into the body of

---

[52] Regarding Ricardo's position on capital supply conditions, further see Hollander (1979: 316–26).

Marxian theory (see Baran and Sweezy 1966: 5), the Transformation mechanism turning, of course, in both its theoretical and historical versions, on "competition" and "the elimination of obstacles... hindering the transfer of capital from one branch to another" (above, p. 118). The same, however, might be said of Marx (Hollander 2008: 470–1; see also Howard and King 2008).

THREE

Economic Organization, and the Price Mechanism

A. Introduction

Engels's appreciation of the allocative function of prices in competitive capitalism is demonstrated in the first three substantive sections below. The first establishes the general principles adopted; the second takes account of applications made of the competitive pricing model to housing and credit policy (and also his orthodox approach toward foreign-trade policy); and the third concerns the hostile response made to the "communist" proposals by Karl Rodbertus (1842 and 1851). The documents upon which I draw date to the 1870s, and they reveal a distinct contrast with the position of the early 1840s when Engels emphasized the instability of the market process rather than the equilibrating function of prices (see Chapter One, pp. 30–1).

I turn in Section E to Engels's position on communist organization, drawing on the early writings of 1843–4, including the *Outlines* (reinforcing the claims of priority over Marx made on his behalf in Chapter 1); on *Anti-Dühring* in 1878; and on later formal and informal statements. Here I seek to appreciate Engels's championship of a control system notwithstanding his high respect for the allocative role of markets in a private-property system. Rodbertus's scheme, Engels charged, had improperly neglected to allow for competition notwithstanding its retention of several features of a market system, whereas the reconstructed system he himself had in mind would be one so greatly simplified that a sophisticated allocation mechanism was not required. The discussion of organization is supplemented in Section F by an elaboration of Engels's perspective on Robert Owen. Section G carries the story further with reference to distribution in the communist scheme envisaged by Engels.

Section H focuses on the transition from capitalist organization to the first stage of communism. Entailed is an evolutionary process involving adoption of joint-stock organization on a massive scale, cartelization – and other indexes of what has been called "the decline of the market" – nationalization and direction of production by the capitalist state, and a period under the "dictatorship of the proletariat" characterized by continued, though diminishing, reliance on a capitalist sector.

A misrepresentation of Rodbertus's recommendations of 1842 and 1851 is the concern of Section I. The main outcome is a demonstration of the high degree of common ground between the Rodbertus and the Engels proposals, and also between their visions of prospects for fulfillment, notwithstanding Engels's efforts to differentiate his own contribution. I show, however, that there is merit to Engels's criticisms of certain of Rodbertus's later formulations. Objections to Rodbertus of a historiographical character are briefly reviewed in Section J.

B. The Competitive Price Mechanism I: General Principles

Both static and dynamic features are attached by Engels to the concept of competition. As for the former, he provides an impressive statement of the regulative function of the competitive market. This is in the course of a formal contrast (introduced in the 1885 edition of *Anti-Dühring*) between the "social anarchy of production" in an exchange system and the "social regulation of production under a definite plan" such as he proposed. The mechanism is represented in terms of the operation of "inexorable natural laws" that "work, despite anarchy, in and through anarchy":

Each man produces for himself with such means of production as he may happen to have, and for such exchange as he may require to satisfy his remaining wants. No one knows how much of his particular article is coming on the market, nor how much of it will be wanted. No one knows whether his individual product will meet an actual demand, whether he will be able to make good his costs of production or even to sell his commodity at all. Anarchy reigns in socialised production. But the production of commodities, like every other form of production, has its peculiar, inherent laws inseparable from it; and these laws work, despite anarchy, in and through anarchy. They reveal themselves in the only persistent form of social interrelations, i.e., in exchange, and here they affect the individual producers as compulsory laws of competition. They are, at first, unknown to these producers themselves, and have to be discovered by them gradually and as the result of experience. They work themselves out, therefore, independently of the producers, and in antagonism to them, as inexorable natural laws of their particular form of production (1885, 1894; MECW *25*: 259).[1]

The foregoing entails precapitalist organization, but corresponding "laws" apply to capitalism. However, "with the extension of the production of commodities, and especially with the introduction of the capitalist mode of production, the laws of commodity production, hitherto latent, came into action more openly and

---

[1] For an equivalent statement by Marx – though probably unknown to Engels – see the *Grundrisse* regarding "circulation": "though the individual elements of this movement originate from the conscious will and particular purposes of individuals, nevertheless the totality of the process appears as an objective relationship arising spontaneously; a relationship which results from the interaction of conscious individuals, but which is neither part of their consciousness nor as a whole subsumed under them" (1857–8; MECW *28*: 131–2).

with greater force: "The old bonds were loosened, the old exclusive limits broken through, the producers were more and more turned into independent, isolated producers of commodities. The anarchy of social production became apparent and grew to greater and greater height. But the chief means by aid of which the capitalist mode of production intensified this anarchy of socialised production was the exact opposite of anarchy" (260).

Insistence upon "compulsory laws of competition" governing production decisions, notwithstanding apparent anarchy, suggests the principle of the "invisible hand." Any doubt about Engels's intentions will be removed by a particularly impressive formulation in 1885 of the competitive pricing mechanism as signaling device in the allocative process, with explicit reference to a capitalist environment:

In present-day capitalist society each industrial capitalist produces off his own bat what, how and as much as he likes. The social demand, however, remains an unknown magnitude to him, both in regard to quality, the kind of objects required, and in regard to quantity. That which today cannot be supplied quickly enough, may tomorrow be offered far in excess of the demand. Nevertheless, demand is finally satisfied in one way or another, good or bad, and, taken as a whole production is ultimately geared towards the objects required. How is this evening-out of the contradiction effected? By competition. And how does competition bring about this solution? Simply by depreciating below their labour value those commodities which by their kind or amount are useless for immediately social requirements, and by making the producers feel, through this roundabout means, that they have produced either absolutely useless articles or ostensibly useful articles in unusable, superfluous quantity. Two things follow from this: First, continual deviations of the prices of commodities from their values are the necessary condition in and through which the value of the commodities as such can come into existence. Only though the fluctuations of competition, and consequently of commodity prices, does the law of value of commodity production assert itself and the determination of the value of the commodity by the socially necessary labour time become a reality. . . . Secondly, competition, by bringing into operation the law of value of commodity production in a society of producers who exchange their commodities, precisely thereby brings about the only organization and arrangement of social production which is possible in the circumstances. *Only through the undervaluation or overvaluation of products is it forcibly brought home to the individual commodity producers what society requires or does not require and in what amounts.* ("Marx and Rodbertus," MECW 26: 286–7; emphasis added)

I shall return to this formulation presently (below, p. 136), but at this point let us consider a dynamic feature of competition in *Anti-Dühring* that supplements the allocative function, namely the continuous drive to cut costs, which is familiar to readers of *Capital 1* (e.g., MECW 35: 455, 621) and *Capital 3* (e.g., MECW 37: 638). To note is the emphasis upon the capitalist firm as operative unit: "But the chief means by aid of which the capitalist mode of production intensifies this anarchy of socialized production was the exact opposite of anarchy. It was the increasing organisation of production, upon a social basis, in every individual productive establishment" (MECW 25: 260). Survival is the key function attributed to the capitalist firm:

By this, the old peaceful, stable condition of things was ended. Wherever this organisation of production was introduced into a branch of industry, it brooked no other method of production by its side.... Advantages in natural or artificial conditions of production now decide the existence or non-existence of individual capitalists, as well as of whole industries or countries. He that falls is remorselessly cast aside.... It is the compelling force of anarchy in social production that turns the limitless perfectibility of machinery under modern industry into a compulsory law by which every individual industrial capitalist must perfect his machinery more and more, under penalty of ruin. (260–1)

The drive to cut costs is reflected in an expansion in output in the face of constrained markets: "the ever increasing perfectibility of modern machinery is, by the anarchy of social production, turned into a compulsory law that forces the individual industrial capitalist always to improve his machinery, always to increase its productive force. The bare possibility of extending the field of production is transformed for him into a similar compulsory law.... But the capacity for extension, extensive and intensive, of the markets is primarily governed by quite different laws that work much less energetically. The extension of the markets cannot keep pace with the extension of production" (262–3). (Elsewhere the constraint is related more precisely to limitations on expansion of working-class purchasing power; see, e.g., Chapter Seven, p. 334.) As with Marx (see below, note 63), the inevitable result of the clash is periodic crisis: "The collision becomes inevitable, and as this cannot produce any real solution so long as it does not break in pieces the capitalist mode of production, the collisions become periodic" (263).

A notion of "equilibrium" is clearly implicit in the context of allocation; as we have seen, "taken as a whole production is ultimately geared towards the objects required," and at cost-covering prices. However, equilibrium of a macroeconomic order is also a feature of the cycle. As the matter is expressed in the unpublished *Dialectics of Nature*, "every ten years a crisis restores the equilibrium by destroying not only the means of subsistence, enjoyment and development that have been produced, but also a great part of the productive forces themselves" (1873–82; MECW 25: 584–5, cited Chapter Seven, p. 334). Moreover, even in the dynamic context entailing macroeconomic crises – especially when extended to the international arena – the information-yielding function of prices is accorded a role, for without such data the cyclical problem would be yet more severe:

As soon as the production of commodities has assumed world market dimensions, the evening-out between the individual producers who produce for private account and the market for which they produce, which in respect of quantity and quality of demand is more or less unknown to them, is established by means of a storm on the world market, by a commercial crisis. If now competition is to be forbidden to make the individual producers aware, by a rise or fall in prices, how the world market stands, then they are completely blindfolded.... [T]he producers can no longer learn anything about the state of the market for which they are producing. (1885; "Marx and Rodbertus," MECW 26: 288)

It will be necessary to supplement the foregoing account by an "evolutionary" dimension entailing changes in business organization that results from crisis conditions (see below, p. 162). The main conclusion, though, holds good: Competition generates corrective forces that – "working through anarchy" – nonetheless ensure order, allocative and aggregative, with the latter implying periodic reestablishment of full employment and capacity usage, or (to use a favorite expression of J. S. Mill) periods of "quiescence."[2]

C. The Competitive Price Mechanism II: Applications

Engels's championship of fully fledged communism, to be elaborated presently, in no way implies a failure to appreciate the information-yielding and allocative functions of the competitive price mechanism as it operates, or should be allowed to operate, in a private-property-based system. This emerged in the previous section, but the theme is now pursued further in terms of applications of orthodox price theory to the shortage of working-class housing, to interest-rate control, and to proposals to abolish house rent. Also relevant is the orthodox perspective adopted toward American protectionism.

The Working-Class Housing Shortage

Engels treats working-class housing[3] as a "quite ordinary commodity transaction between two citizens" subject to "the economic laws which govern the sale of commodities in general" (1872, 1887; MECW 23: 320; also 375). The worker thus enters the commodity market as a regular consumer, notwithstanding the formal relation always insisted upon between capital and labor entailing the special category of labor power (318). The analysis is directed against the "bourgeois socialist" Emil Sax, who had no other explanation to offer for the housing shortage than to represent it as "the result of the wickedness of man," as "original sin, so to speak" (341); for "[j]ust as Proudhon takes us from the sphere of economics into the sphere of legal phrases, so our bourgeois socialist takes us . . . from the economic sphere into the moral sphere," whereas moral sermons "immediately evaporate under the influence of private interest and, if necessary, of competition."[4]

---

[2] In principle, this feature can incorporate a "worsening" of cycles, found in some contexts, in the sense of increasing amplitude of cyclical activity.

[3] For a discussion of *The Housing Question* within a broad welfare context, see Chapter Five, Section D. My present concern is with the price-theoretical implications of the study.

[4] Various proposals to abolish rent in the name of the "sense of right" and "justice" are derided as a "rigmarole," meaning no more than that "the practical effects of the economic laws which govern present-day society run contrary to the author's sense of justice and that he cherishes the pious wish that the matter might be so arranged as to remedy this situation" (MECW 23: 322–3). Similarly, "always this justice is but the ideologised, idealised expression of the existing economic relations, now from their conservative, now from the revolutionary angle" (381).

Engels, for his part, insists on an objective microeconomic or price-analytic analysis to explain the housing shortage, in contrast with the vacuity of subjective appeals for increased provision based on "justice" and "right." He sets out from the orthodox demand-based rule that "*[a]ny* investment of capital which satisfies an existing need is profitable if conducted rationally" (MECW 23: 355). What required explanation was "precisely, why the housing question continues to exist *all the same*, why the capitalists . . . do not provide sufficient healthy dwellings for the workers." It was unproductive to blame, as did Sax, "the propertied, higher social classes . . . because they do not make it their business to provide a sufficient supply of good dwellings" (cited, 341). Engels's answer is that it is not in the interests of private providers to solve the problem: "Capital does not *want* to abolish the housing shortage" (355). Such unwillingness reflected the availability of preferable alternatives:

The expansion of the big modern cities gives the land in certain sections of them, particularly in those which are centrally situated, an artificial and often enormously increasing value; the buildings erected in these areas depress this value, instead of increasing it, because they no longer correspond to the changed circumstances; they are pulled down and replaced by others. This takes place above all with centrally located workers' houses, whose rents, even with the greatest overcrowding, can never, or only very slowly, increase above a certain maximum. They are pulled down and in their stead shops, warehouses and public buildings are erected. Through its Haussmann in Paris, Bonapartism exploited this tendency tremendously for swindling and private enrichment. But the spirit of Haussmann has also been abroad in London, Manchester and Liverpool, and seems to feel itself just as much at home in Berlin and Vienna. The result is that the workers are forced out of the centre of the towns towards the outskirts; that workers' dwellings, and small dwellings in general, become rare and expensive and often altogether unobtainable, for under these circumstances the building industry, which is offered a much better field for speculation by more expensive dwelling houses, builds workers' dwellings only by way of exception. (319)

Reacting to Sax's reference to philanthropic and speculative building societies that had yielded net profits of 4 to 6 percent, Engels responded, in this light, that it was unnecessary "to prove . . . that capital invested in workers' houses yields a good profit. The reason why the capitalists do not invest still more than they do in workers' dwellings is that more expensive dwellings bring in still greater profits for their owners. Herr Sax's exhortation to the capitalists, therefore, amounts once again to nothing but a moral sermon" (353).

Marxian features are introduced to preclude the possibility that a capitalist solution might yet be found, given an appropriate change in relative profitability patterns. The problem was inevitable, with its root cause being the capitalist system itself, which undermined any market solution. The housing market was permanently and necessarily turned against labor, the payment of a "subsistence" wage – in the orthodox sense of a "quantity of means of subsistence necessary for their existence and the propagation of their kind" – placing a cap on workers' housing budgets, while the major towns were flooded with "a large reserve army of unemployed," the consequence of labor-displacing machinery and of industrial fluctuations (MECW 23: 340–1). Indeed, considering the more profitable alternative of high-rent accommodation unaffordable by labor, "the house-owner in his capacity as capitalist has not only the right but, by reason of competition, to a certain extent also the duty of ruthlessly making as much out of his property in house rent as he possibly can" (341).

The Abolition of Ground Rent and Interest

The analysis of the housing shortage is supplemented by a more detailed treatment of a proposal by Mülberger (1872) to abolish ground rent – identified with the abolition of private property in land and hence of peculiar significance – and also to reduce the interest rate in the first instance to 1 percent and thereafter to zero by legislation. It may be noted incidentally as an index of Engels's business experience that he focused in this context on the durability feature characterizing a rental contract, namely the sale of the house's "use value" for a certain period, with an eye to time preference: "The piecemeal sale . . . realises the exchange-value only gradually. As a compensation for his renouncing the immediate repayment of the capital advanced and the profit accrued on it, the seller receives an increased price, whose rate is determined by the laws of political economy and not by any means in an arbitrary fashion" (MECW 23: 374).

Engels's primary objection to Mülberger's proposal is that it would be wholly inconsequential from labor's perspective because the creation of surplus value is unaffected; only its distribution between different claimants is at issue. Assuming a constant long-run real wage (at least in the upward direction), Engels concludes that "[t]he mass of unpaid labour taken from the working class" – that is, of surplus value including rent and profit – "would remain exactly the same even if house-owners were to be deprived tomorrow of the possibility of receiving ground rent and interest" (MECW 23: 327). These matters are considered in Chapter Five. Here we consider Mülberger's further proposal to introduce a transitional law reducing the interest rate to 1 percent and subsequently to zero, thereby eliminating "the productivity of capital" and, at the same time, encouraging transfer of housing property to laborers (331).[5] Engels scorned the general idea, appealing again to the theory of surplus value whereby to reduce interest is merely to increase industrial profits, that is to "re-arrange the distribution among the individual capitalists of the unpaid surplus value taken from the working class. It would not give an advantage

---

[5] In an addendum Engels cites Proudhon's *Idée générale de la révolution* (1851: 182–6) as source of the proposal (MECW 23: 387).

Engels also objects to Mülberger's use of the expression "the productivity of capital": "Nothing proves more clearly how completely Proudhon remains enmeshed in bourgeois thinking than the fact that he has taken over this phrase about the productivity of capital. . . . [T]he so-called 'productivity of capital' is nothing but the quality inherent in it (under present-day social relations, without which it would not be capital at all) of being able to appropriate the unpaid labour of wage-workers" (MECW 23: 331). It is quite likely that Mülberger was using the objectionable term ironically.

to the workers against the industrial capitalist, but to the industrial capitalist as against the rentier" (332; also 388). With a zero interest rate, rentiers would simply refuse to lend and invest directly in private or joint-stock companies, leaving the mass of surplus value unchanged (333).[6]

But all this presumed that the interest rate could be effectively regulated by legislation. Engels rejected this presumption on grounds of the operation of competitive market forces that establish the return on loanable funds, with some redirection of investments to minimize the risk of penalty in the event of state intervention in the market:

Proudhon, from his legal standpoint, explains the rate of interest, as he does all economic facts, not by the conditions of social production, but by the state laws in which these conditions receive their general expression. From this point of view, which lacks any inkling of the interconnection between the state laws and the conditions of production in society, these state laws necessarily appear as purely arbitrary orders which at any moment could be replaced just as well by their exact opposites. Nothing is, therefore, easier for Proudhon than to issue a decree – as soon as he has the power to do so – reducing the rate of interest to one per cent. And if all the other social conditions remain as they were, this Proudhonist decree will simply exist on paper only. The rate of interest will continue to be governed by the economic laws to which it is subject today, all decrees notwithstanding. Persons possessing credit will continue to borrow money at two, three, four and more per cent, according to circumstances, just as before, and the only difference will be that rentiers will be very careful to advance money only to persons with whom no litigation is to be expected. (MECW 23: 332)

The project in fact smacked of the usury laws "which have . . . been abolished everywhere because in practice they were continually broken or circumvented, and the state was compelled to admit its impotence against the laws of social production. . . . One sees that the closer Proudhonism is examined the more reactionary it appears" (332–3; see also 388). For the defense of the usury laws we must turn to *The Wealth of Nations*.[7]

Protection versus Free Trade

The foregoing sampling of Engels's applied economics from *The Housing Question* confirms the centrality of the competitive pricing model as a basic tool of analysis. His "Protection and Free Trade" (1888) provides a more general indication of adherence to the tenets of orthodox economics. Here he approaches the question

---

[6] Engels adds the technical point that, on average or in aggregate, even with a positive return on capital, prices reflect labor inputs, implying the Transformation: "In fact, our Proudhonist fails to see that already now, in commodity purchase in bourgeois society, no more is paid on the average than 'the labour necessary to turn over the capital' (it should read, necessary for the production of the commodity in question). Labour is the measure of value of all commodities, and in present-day society – apart from fluctuations of the market – it is absolutely impossible that in the aggregate more should be paid on the average for commodities than the labour necessary for their production" (MECW 23: 333).

[7] Smith's case for a maximum can, however, be shown to take full account of the market process (see Hollander 1999).

from a general developmental perspective, along Infant Industry lines, rather than drawing on features of a characteristically "Marxian" order. He points out that various foreign nations, "subordinating private commercial profit to national exigency... protected their nascent manufactures by high tariffs" (1881, "The French Commercial Treaty," MECW 24: 391). This was not always desirable, but "a short period of Protection is not only justifiable but a matter of absolute necessity" in America, characterized by high inventiveness, an energetic population, and plentiful coal and raw materials (392). "[I]s it to be supposed," he asks rhetorically, "that such a country will expose its young and rising manufactures to a long, protracted, competitive struggle with the old-established industry of England, when, by a short term of some twenty years of protection, she can place them at once on a level with any competitor?" He opines shortly thereafter that such a justification applied no longer; by encouraging the passage from agriculture to manufactures, "protection ought to have done its task for America, and ought to be now becoming a nuisance" (1888, "Protection and Free Trade"; MECW 26: 526).

In other cases no such exceptions are allowed. Thus, for example, he condemned Bismarck's tariff policy introduced in 1879, which applied to a wide range of industrial and agricultural products (1880, "The Socialism of Mr. Bismarck"; MECW 24: 274–5). Of high interest indeed is the general case that "[p]rotection is at best an endless screw, and you never know when you have done with it. By protecting one industry, you directly or indirectly hurt all others, and have therefore to protect them too. By so doing you again damage the industry that you first protected, and have to compensate it; but the compensation reacts, as before, on all other trades, and entitles them to redress, and so on *in infinitum*" (MECW 26: 526–7).[8] This confirms a typically "conservative" orientation in Stigler's sense that it impossible "to impose changes in any one market or industry without causing problems in other markets or industries" (see Chapter Seven, p. 317). In any event, industrial interdependence has major political implications.

Beyond this, technical progress was so rapid and revolutionary "that what may have been yesterday a fairly balanced protective tariff is no longer so to-day," engendering interindustrial and political conflicts to ensure the necessary modifications (MECW 26: 527).[9] However, "the worst of protection" was the fact that

---

[8] Engels continues with an illustration: "America, in this respect, offers us a striking example of the best way to kill an important industry by protection" (MECW 26: 527). Engels draws on data from the Annual Report of the Secretary of the Treasury for 1887, which shows a drastic decline since 1860 in the value of total foreign trade carried by U.S. ships. Engels asserts that the introduction of protection for American shipbuilding in the mid-1860s "has nearly completely driven the American flag from the high seas.... Protection to ship-building has killed both shipping and ship-building." The basis for the assertion is not spelled out.

[9] A fascinating example of the problem is drawn from the Report of the Secretary of the Treasury for 1887. It relates to the inadequacy of the going rates of protective duties against low-cost imports of worsted cloth made possible by new technology (MECW 26: 527–8). The problem, Engels points out, is that "what was protection to home industry yesterday, turns out to-day to be a premium to the foreign importer [of worsted cloth into the United States].... [T]o

"when you once have got it you cannot easily get rid of it. Difficult as is the process of adjustment to an equitable tariff, the return to Free Trade is immensely more difficult," again the consequence of complex industrial interdependencies: "from the conflicting interests of these trades, the most edifying squabbles, lobby intrigues, and parliamentary conspiracies will arise" (528). Again: "you may easily introduce Protection, but you cannot get rid of it again so easily. The legislature, by adopting the protective plan, has created vast interests, for which it is responsible. And not every one of these interests – the various branches of industry – is equally ready, at a given moment, to face open competition. Some will be lagging behind, while others have no longer need of protective nursing. The difference of position will give rise to the usual lobby-plotting, and is in itself a sure guarantee that the protected industries, if Free Trade is resolved upon, will be let down very easy indeed, as was the silk manufacture in England after 1846" (535).

D. The Competitive Price Mechanism III: Objections to Rodbertus

In "Marx and Rodbertus," comprising the Preface to his 1885 edition of the *Poverty of Philosophy*, Engels rejects Karl Rodbertus's version of labor money (as in *Zur Erkenntniss* 1842) precisely because – as he understood the proposal – it neglected the competitive allocation mechanism while retaining central features of the market system. Engels was here, in effect, repeating the sort of complaint that he addressed against Fourier in 1843 (below, p. 141) and against Dühring in 1878 (below, pp. 146–7), which was that they contaminated their schemes with elements of "competition" that they did not allow to function properly.

I can be more specific. Rodbertus – according to Engels's account – retained private property in capital (and land), envisaging state issues of labor certificates advanced to individual capitalists, who would use them to pay their workers. They in turn would use them to purchase goods priced to reflect their labor inputs as required by law: "After the state has thus constituted value – at least for a part of the products, for Rodbertus is also modest – it issues its labour paper money, and gives advances therefrom to the industrial capitalists, with which the latter pay the workers, whereupon the workers buy the products with the labour paper money they have received, and so cause the paper money to flow back to its starting point" (MECW *26*: 285).[10] As for the labor values presumed to rule, Engels wrote this sarcastic comment:

The transition to utopia is now made in the turn of a hand. The "measures," which ensure exchange of commodities according to labour value as the invariable rule, cause

---

amend it, you will have to fight the manufacturers of woollen cloths who profit by this state of things; you will have to open a regular campaign to bring the majority of both Houses of Congress, and eventually the public opinion of the country, round to your views, and the question is, Will that pay?" (528)

[10] That only part of the national income is allocated to private consumption refers to the deductions made by the "public authority" for public goods and the like.

no difficulty. The other utopians of this tendency, from Gray to Proudhon, rack their brains to invent social institutions which would achieve this aim. They attempt at least to solve the economic question in an economic way through the action of the owners themselves who exchange the commodities. For Rodbertus it is much easier. As a good Prussian he appeals to the state: a decree of the state authority orders the reform.[11]

The retention of capitalistic "exploitation" is the essence of Engels's reading of Rodbertus: "Now at last we come to the point where Rodbertus really offers us something new; something which distinguishes him from all his numerous fellow supporters of the labour money exchange economy. They all demand this exchange organisation for the purpose of abolishing the exploitation of wage labour by capital. Every producer is to receive the full labour value of his product. On this they all agree, from Gray to Proudhon. Not at all, says Rodbertus. Wage labour and its exploitation remain" (MECW 26: 288–9). Indeed, "rent and profit are also to continue undiminished. For the landowners and industrial capitalists also exercise certain socially useful or even necessary functions, even if economically unproductive ones, and they receive in the shape of rent and profit a sort of pay on that account – a conception which was ... not new even in 1842" (289).[12] This formulation strikingly expresses the Marx–Engels evaluation of capitalists' activities in general.

A feature of Engels's account relates to deductions from the social product to be undertaken by Rodbertus's bureaucracy. Engels merely points out that "in no conceivable condition of society can the worker receive the full value of his product for consumption.... In a society in which general productive labour is obligatory" – alluding to his own scheme – "the need for a social reserve and accumulation fund would remain and consequently even in that case, the workers, i.e., *all*, would remain in possession and enjoyment of their total product, but each

---

[11] Engels in this context has in mind Gray 1831 (see MECW 26: 283). In point of fact, though, Gray did not rely on the determination of labor values by means of "the action of the owners ... who exchange the commodities," because a conspicuous feature of his scheme is pricing determined by his national Chamber of Commerce (see Thompson 1998: 98–9). More specifically, Gray has his authority taking account not only of labor time but a wide variety of charges including rent and profit: "All goods ... should be transmitted from their respective manufactories to the national warehouses, and here, to the price of material and labour already expended ... should be added the per centage, or profit, fixed by the Chamber of Commerce, to pay the various expenses of rent, interest of capital, management, salaries, depreciation of stock, incidents, and all national charges; and this being done, would form the retail price of goods charges" (Gray 1831: 64). Further, rent and interest are certainly not market-determined prices because Gray's planned constitution entails surrender to the authority of control over private property: "That all the members of this association who shall be possessed of land, or capital, shall have an estimated value put upon the same, and shall consent to receive a fixed annual remuneration for the use thereof, proportionate to its value, in lieu of retaining in their own hands, the chances of gain or loss, by its cultivation or employment" (32).

[12] On the alleged unoriginality of Rodbertus (1842), see also below, Section J. Engels goes further regarding the alleged retention of exploitation: "Rodbertus has need, at least for the next five hundred years, of a privileged class, and so the present rate of surplus value, to express myself correctly, is to remain in existence but is not to be allowed to be increased" (MECW 26: 289).

separate worker would not enjoy the 'full returns of his labour'" (MECW 26: 289).[13] In capitalist society, by contrast, and also in Rodbertus's scheme (which retains exploitation), a "series of economically unproductive but necessary functions have to be met from the fund produced."[14]

In summary, Rodbertus's labor tickets are "advanced" by the state to industrial capitalists, who allocate them to workers employed in privately organized establishments. The recipients spend them on the commodities made available by capitalists at given labor-based prices.[15] Now Rodbertus maintained that all markets would clear, whereas this outcome was, for Engels, rendered inconceivable by its deliberate preclusion of "competition" with its characteristic price signaling to determine the appropriate mix of goods. The passage is already familiar to us as far as concerns the general allocative principle insisted upon (above, p. 127); here I give only what is specifically pertinent to the condemnation of Rodbertus:

To desire, in a society of producers who exchange their commodities, to establish the determination of value by labour time, by forbidding competition to establish this determination of value through pressure on prices in the only way in which it can be established, is therefore merely to prove that, at least in this sphere, one has adopted the usual utopian disdain of economic laws. . . .

But it is precisely this sole regulator that the utopia advocated by Rodbertus among others wishes to abolish. And if we then ask what guarantee we have that [the] necessary quantity and not more of each product will be produced, that we shall not go hungry in regard to corn and meat while we are choked in beet sugar and drowned in potato spirit, that we shall not lack trousers to cover our nakedness while trouser buttons flood by the million – Rodbertus triumphantly shows us his famous calculation, according to which the correct certificate has been handed out for every superfluous pound of sugar, for every unsold barrel of spirit, for every unusable trouser button, a calculation which "works out" exactly, and according to which "all claims will be satisfied and the liquidation correctly brought about" [Rodbertus 1842: 167]. And anyone who does not believe this can apply to the governmental chief revenue office accountant X in Pomerania, who has checked the calculation and found it correct, and who, as one who has never yet been caught lacking with the accounts, is thoroughly trustworthy. (MECW 26: 287–8)

---

[13] Here Engels was, in effect, affirming Marx's representation in 1875 of the Gotha program relating to distribution, based on the "undiminished proceeds of labour" and on "fair distribution," as a crime (1875; MECW 24: 87). As for "an undiminished distribution," labor must be subject to the same "deductions" as under capitalism before distribution for consumption purposes to cover capital maintenance, net investment, insurance, general administration, public-goods provision including education and health services, and welfare relief (84–5).

[14] These deductions from labor's product, Engels adds, had been recognized "by the other labour-money utopians. But they leave the workers to tax themselves for this purpose in the usual democratic way, while Rodbertus, whose whole social reform of 1842 is geared to the Prussian state of that time, refers the whole matter to the decision of the bureaucracy, which determines from above the share of the workers in his own product and graciously permits him to have it" (MECW 26: 289).

[15] The account in Hollander (2008: 398) neglects the role of private capitalists attributed by Engels to Rodbertus.

In a summary dripping with sarcasm, Engels designated the "utopian" plan he attributed to Rodbertus as being "stupid" and "childishly naïve":

If Rodbertus has hitherto always had the misfortune to arrive too late with his new discoveries, this time at least he has the merit of *one* sort of originality: none of his rivals has dared to express the stupidity of the labour money utopia in this childishly naïve transparent, I might say truly Pomeranian, form. Since for every paper certificate a corresponding object of value has been delivered, and no object of value is supplied except in return for a corresponding paper certificate, the sum total of paper certificates must always be covered by the sum total of objects of value. The calculation works out without the smallest remainder, it is correct down to a second of labour time, and no governmental chief revenue office accountant, however many years of faithful service he may have behind him, could prove the slightest error in calculation. What more could one want? (286)[16]

There is much else of high technical interest. Engels pointed to a "contradiction, the antimony of two economic laws," in which "the Ricardian law of value, as Ricardo himself discovered, comes into conflict with the law of the equal rate of profit," alluding to the deviations of equilibrium prices from labor values required to ensure the uniform profit rates that characterize fully fledged competition (MECW *26*: 282).[17] But whereas Ricardo in Chapter 1 of his *Principles* (Sections 4 and 5) – Engels was using the second edition of 1819 – opted for a uniform profit rate, giving up strict labor-determined prices, the "utopians" such as Rodbertus (and also sundry petty-bourgeois reformers) abandoned profit-rate uniformity in favor of labor values. This was in their naïve quest for a just society "in which a single law of commodity production prevails exclusively and in full, but in which the conditions are abolished in which it can prevail at all, viz., the other laws of commodity production and, later, of capitalist production" (283).

Rodbertus's preclusion of a so-called competitive process also undermined his aim of mitigating crises; in fact, it worsened the problem. For however defective the signaling mechanism provided by competitive prices might be considering the "anarchical" character of markets, Rodbertus's alternative was far worse, with his producers then operating "completely blindfolded," particularly in an international environment (cited above, p. 128).

A related objection to Rodbertus's labor certificates helps us better understand Engels's own perspective. I refer to the alleged failure to deal properly with *efficiency* in defining "labor" as well as neglect of the final-demand factor:

Labour, again, is taken uncritically in the form in which it occurs among the economists. And not even that. For, although there is a reference in a couple of words to differences in intensity of labour, labour is still put forward quite generally as something which "costs," hence as something which measures value, quite irrespective of whether it is

---

[16] It would be of interest to learn whether Soviet calculators were at all aware of these passages (see Sowell 2006: 165).

[17] The formulation in terms of two conflicting "laws" might have benefited from Rodbertus (1842: 131).

expended under normal average social conditions or not. Whether the producers take ten days, or only one, to make products which could be made in one day; whether they employ the best or the worst tools; whether they expend their labour time in the production of socially necessary articles and in the socially required quantity, or whether they make quite undesired articles or desired articles in quantities above or below demand – about all this there is not a word: labour is labour, the product of equal labour must be exchanged against the product of equal labour. (MECW 26: 284–5)

Had Rodbertus focused on so-called socially necessary labor and allowed for the demand dimension, then he would have been obliged to confront "the question as to how the adjustment of the production of separate commodity producers to the total social demand takes place, and his whole utopia would thereby have been made impossible" (288).

* * *

In all of this, Engels and Marx were as one. Indeed, the weight placed on the equilibrating function of prices by Engels in the 1870s and 1880s in contrast with the anarchical orientation of 1840s may well reflect the influence of Marx. The technical account of the Transformation – spelled out already in the *Grundrisse* (1857–8), and again in *Theories of Surplus Value* (1861–3), the latter known to Engels – turns strategically on the orthodox pricing mechanism; the analysis is moreover directed against Rodbertus (1851), who "seems to think that competition brings about a normal profit or average profit or general rate of profit by reducing the commodities to their *real value*," that is, relative labor value (*Theories of Surplus Value*; MECW 31: 260). Indeed, much earlier, in *Poverty of Philosophy*, Marx had complained that Proudhon failed to appreciate that "[t]he exchange value of a product depends upon its abundance or its scarcity, but always in relation to demand" (1847; MECW 6: 115). Proudhon "has simply forgotten about *demand*, and that a thing can be scarce and abundant insofar as it is in demand"; his "abundance seems to be something spontaneous. He completely forgets that they are people who produce it, and that it is in their interest never to lose sight of demand" (115–16). As for capital movement between industries, that is dictated by alterations to demand–supply conditions: "it is the *variations in demand and supply* that show the producer what amount of a given commodity he must produce in order to receive at least the cost of production in exchange. And as these variations are continually occurring, there is also a continual movement of withdrawal and application of capital in the different branches of industry" (134). Here Marx appreciatively cited passages from Ricardo on the operation of the allocative mechanism in response to deviations of market from cost price (1951–73 [1821] *1*: 88, 89–90).

Marx then applied what I see as his classical or neoclassical perspective to the labor-based prices proposed by Proudhon for an ideal system: "If . . . he insists on justifying his theory, not as a legislator, but as an economist, he will have to prove that the *time* needed to create a commodity indicates exactly the degree of its *utility* and marks its proportional relation to the demand, and in consequence, to the total amount of wealth" (MECW 6: 132). In brief, Proudhon would have to show that labor values correspond to market-clearing or equilibrium prices, and this he could not do: "since the labour time necessary for the production of an article is not the expression of its degree of utility, the exchange value of this same article, determined beforehand by the labour time embodied in it, can never regulate the correct relation of supply to demand, that is, the proportional relation in the sense M. Proudhon attributes to it at the moment"(134).[18]

E. Communist Organization

There seems at first sight to be some truth to the charge that Engels neglected to specify the character of the future communist society that he envisaged (see Prolegomena, pp. 15–16). For example, he was impatient with Wilhelm Liebknecht, who, as editor of the social-democratic organ *Der Volkstaat*, sought "to make good the shortcomings of our theory, to have an answer to every philistine objection and to have a picture of future society, because that's another thing which your philistine is always pestering them [previous editors] with questions" (Engels to Marx, 28 May 1876; MECW 45: 123). A letter of 21 August 1890 skirts the issue by insisting that "[s]o-called 'socialist society' is not, in my view, to be regarded as something that remains crystallised for all time, but rather as being in process of constant change and transformation like all other social conditions" (MECW 49: 18). Nevertheless, Engels proceeds immediately to insist on the condition of "common ownership . . . of all means of production." At this time he insisted that the key steps would be "socialisation of large-scale industry and large-scale agriculture" (to Bebel, 9–10 November 1891; MECW 49: 294). These specifications do not suggest a disinclination to enter into details regarding the "lower" phase of communism. It is the process of evolution toward the "higher" stage that remains something of a mystery.[19]

There is also insistence that the manner of transition from capitalism to communism in its initial or "lower" phase would depend on circumstances. Thus in 1888 Engels, citing the joint Preface to the *Communist Manifesto*, played down the "practical application" of the Party program: "However much the state of things may have altered during the last 25 years, the general principles laid down in this *Manifesto* are on the whole, as correct to-day as ever. Here and there some detail might be improved. The practical application of the principles

---

[18] Marx's application of standard price-theoretic analysis may be further illustrated by his rejection of the proposals for state confiscation of rent by James Mill and others, a case resembling that of Adam Smith against "a land tax assessed according to a general survey and valuation" (Smith 1976 [1776]: 836), and also by his "Austrian" objections to Napoleon III's plan to regulate French bread prices on grounds, in part, of industry interdependence (Hollander 2008: 204–6, 396–7).

[19] The distributive rule "from each according to his abilities to each according to his needs" would apply in the "higher" phase, the division of labour would be abolished, and in general the scarcity problem would be greatly diminished, though apparently not obliterated ("Critique of the Gotha Programme," 1875; MECW 24: 87). See *Anti-Dühring* (MECW 25: 279–80) for certain features of this phase. Sanderson (1969: 98–109) provides a good coverage.

will depend, as the *Manifesto* itself states, everywhere and at all times on the historical conditions for the time being existing, and, for that reason, no special stress is laid on the revolutionary measures proposed at the end of Section II" (MECW *26*: 517–18). Similarly, in a comment on the evolutionary forces at play within capitalism that ensure a communist outcome – a matter to which I devote Section G – the same message is conveyed: "The more quickly and irrevocably this economic revolution takes place, the more imperative will measures impose themselves which, apparently intended to cure evils that have suddenly assumed vast and intolerable proportions, will eventually result in undermining the foundations of the existing mode of production; and the more rapidly, too, will the working masses obtain a hearing thanks to universal suffrage"; but "*[w]hat* those initial measures will be must depend on local conditions at the time, nor can anything of a general nature be said about them beforehand" (24 March 1891; MECW *49*: 153). Along these lines, Engels rejected a complaint by an Italian critic in 1892 regarding "the error of those socialists who, with Frederick Engels, speak of the imminent coming to power of socialism and do not specify what kind of power" (cited by Engels in his "Reply to the Honourable Giovanni Bovio," MECW *27*: 270). "[Bovio] should be well enough acquainted with German socialism to know that it demands the socialisation of all the means of production" (271), although how this economic revolution "[can] be accomplished . . . will depend on the circumstances in which our party seizes power, on the moment at which and the manner in which that occurs. . . . Meanwhile, if tomorrow, by some accident, our party were called to power, I know perfectly well what I would propose as a programme of action." This is Marx's position precisely, a position eschewing "doctrinaire and of necessity fantastic anticipation of a future revolution's programme" (see Chapter Four, p. 203).

"The Peasant Question in France and Germany" provides examples of the potential complexities that Engels had in mind. With respect to peasant holdings, the ideal course would lie in "the pooling of farms to form co-operative enterprises, in which the exploitation of wage labour will be eliminated more and more, and their gradual transformation into branches of the great national producers' co-operatives with each branch enjoying equal rights and duties" (1894; MECW *27*: 500). However, should the peasant owners prove recalcitrant, "we shall have to . . . address ourselves to their wage workers, among whom we shall not fail to find sympathy. Most likely we shall be able to abstain . . . from resorting to forcible expropriation, and as for the rest to count on future economic developments making even these more stubborn characters amenable to reason." The "big landed estates" entailing "undisguised capitalist production" presented no such complexity, though again the precise course of the transition – including the question of compensation – remained open:

As soon as our Party is in possession of political power, it has simply to expropriate the landed proprietors just like the manufacturers in industry. Whether this expropriation is to be compensated for or not will be to a great extent depend not upon us but the circumstances under which we obtain power, and particularly upon the attitude adopted by these gentry, the big landowners, themselves. We by no means consider compensation as impermissible in any event; Marx told me (and how many times!) that in his opinion we would get off cheapest if we could buy out the whole lot of them.

* * *

It may be said that "socialization of large-scale industry and large-scale agriculture" or, more generally, "of all the means of production" – as in the 1891 correspondence – tell us too little of the future program. However, further details do emerge, preeminently – apart from public ownership – the replacement of the market by central planning. Indications of the position can be found in the early 1840s, placing Engels temporally ahead of Marx in this regard (see Maler 1998: 48).

A prelude is already to be found in a paper of November 1843 on "Progress of Social Reform on the Continent," where Engels asserts that "England, France, and Germany, have all come to the conclusion, that a thorough revolution of social arrangements, based on community of property, has now become an urgent and unavoidable necessity" (MECW 3: 392). Here we encounter a qualification to the praise accorded Fourier (1829) on the "necessity of association," namely that it suffered from a basic "inconsistency" by retaining features of "competition," that is to say of a market mechanism:

In his *Phalanstères* or associated establishments, there are rich and poor, capitalists and working men. The property of all members is placed into a joint stock, the establishment carries on commerce, agricultural and manufacturing industry, and the proceeds are divided among the members; one part as wages of labour, another as reward for skill and talent, and a third as profits of capital. Thus, after all the beautiful theories of association and free labour; after a great deal of indignant declamation against commerce, selfishness, and competition, we have in practice the old competitive system upon an improved plan. (395)

Engels is more enthusiastic toward the "English Socialists" whom he estimated, "in everything bearing on practice, upon the *facts* of the present state of society," as "a long way before us [the Germans].... I may say, besides, that I have met with English socialists with whom I agree upon almost every question" (407).[20]

Unfortunately, Engels did not fulfill a promise "to give an exposition of [the] Communist system" that he himself favored. However, the following year, in *Outlines of a Critique of Political Economy*, he declares for the replacement of "competition" by planning: "In a world worthy of mankind . . . [t]he community will have to calculate what it can produce with the means at its disposal; and in accordance with the relationship of this productive power to the mass of consumers it will determine how far it has to raise or lower production, how far it has to give way to, or curtail, luxury" (1844; MECW 3: 435; see Chapter One, pp. 31–2). At

---

[20] I shall devote the next section to aspects of Engels's perspective on Robert Owens's cooperative proposals as described in various works, including Owen (1821).

this point, and in line with the 1843 publication, readers are invited "to consult the writings of the English Socialists and partly also those of Fourier." As for the former, he probably intended Gray (1831) and Bray (1839).[21]

It is not clear from the foregoing extract, which relates to planning allocations between aggregate investment and consumption, whether Engels intended to allow for a free consumers' market. He in fact appears to rule out consumer sovereignty, because he further maintained that the supersession of private property necessarily implied reliance on communal decision making with regard to production based upon the "inherent utility of the object independent of the parties concerned [in an exchange]," that is, independent of personal judgment and "the freedom of those who exchange" (MECW 3: 426). By way of background, recall the proposition (Chapter One, pp. 29–30) that "value is the relation of production costs to utility. The first application of value is the decision as to whether a thing ought to be produced at all; i.e., as to whether utility counterbalances production costs. Only then can one talk of the application of value to exchange. The production costs of two objects being equal, the deciding factor determining their comparative value will be utility." Engels concludes:

This basis is the only just basis of exchange. But if one proceeds from this basis, who is to decide the utility of the object? The mere opinion of the parties concerned? Then in any event *one* will be cheated. Or are we to assume a determination grounded in the inherent utility of the object independent of the parties concerned, and not apparent to them? If so, the exchange can only be effected by *coercion*, and each party considers itself cheated. The contradiction between the real inherent utility of the thing and the determination of that utility, between the determination of utility and the freedom of those who exchange, cannot be superseded without superseding private property; and once this is superseded, there can no longer be any question of exchange as it exists at present. The practical application of the concept of value will then be increasingly confined to the decision about production, and that is its proper sphere (MECW 3: 426).[22]

There is a further feature of the 1844 account to note. The planning task would include shadow calculations relating to interest and rent based on the productivity contributions of land and capital. Costs are not restricted to direct labor alone:

If . . . we abandon private property, rent is reduced to its truth, to the rational notion which essentially lies at its root. The value of the land divorced from it as rent then reverts to the land itself. This value, to be measured by the productivity of equal areas

---

[21] John Gray (1831) and John Francis Bray (1839) are the two early English writers who contributed most to the analysis of central coordination and control of economic activity in place of a market mechanism, contrasting with reformers championing a high degree of decentralization and the retention of significant features of capitalist arrangement (see Thompson 1998, Chapter 8). Also see note 11 for more information on Gray.

[22] We arrive at the same conclusion when we recall that ignorance of the pattern of consumption was seen as the source of "periodic upheavals" under capitalism, contrasting with the communist solution: "If the producers as such knew how much the consumers required, if they were to organise production, if they were to share it out amongst themselves, then the fluctuations of competition and its tendency to crisis would be impossible" (above, p. 41).

of land subjected to equal applications of labour, is indeed taken into account as part of the production costs when determining the value of products; and like rent, it is the relation of productivity to competition – but to true competition, such as will be developed when its time comes. (MECW 3: 430)

If we abandon private property, then all these unnatural divisions [attributed to capitalism] disappear. The difference between interest and profit disappears; capital is nothing without labour, without movement. The significance of profit is reduced to the weight which capital carries in the determination of the costs of production; and profit thus remains inherent in capital, in the same way as capital itself reverts to its original unity with labour. (431)[23]

On the one hand, these observations raise obvious questions relating to the proposed productivity calculation. On the other hand, the preclusion of demand uncertainties by the control authority would, in principle, greatly simplify the task of calculating productivities.[24]

Let us take leave of the *Outlines*. The replacement of the market mechanism by central planning is already briefly indicated in the joint Marx–Engels production *The German Ideology* (1845–6): "with the abolition of . . . private property, with the communistic regulation of production . . . the power of the relation of supply and demand is dissolved into nothing, and men once more gain control of exchange, production" (MECW 5: 48). It is more fully indicated in Engels's *Principles of Communism* (1847), the forerunner of the *Communist Manifesto*, where the central features of the "new social order" are specified thus: "Above all, it will have to take the running of industry and all branches of production in general out of the hands of separate individuals competing with each other and instead will have to ensure that all these branches of production are run by society as a whole, i.e., for the social good, according to a social plan and with the participation of all members of society. It will therefore do away with competition and replace it by association" (MECW 6: 348). Now "[s]ince the running of industry by individuals had private ownership as its necessary consequence," the transformation implies that "private ownership will also have to be abolished, and in its stead there will be common use of all the instruments of production and the distribution of all products by

---

[23] The second formulation continues by extending the observation to *labor*. Under competition, "the product of labour confronts labour as wages, is separated from it, and is in its turn as usual determined by competition – there being, as we have seen [MECW 3: 431, cited Chapter One, p. 34], no firm standard determining labour's share in production." But under communal arrangement "this unnatural separation also disappears. Labour becomes its own reward, and the true significance of the wages of labour, hitherto alienated comes to light – namely the significance of labour for the determination of the production costs of a thing." The problem I find here is that Engels in some contexts does allude to a firm standard under capitalism, namely subsistence costs.

[24] Costs would also include an allowance for "science," because "in a rational order which has gone beyond the division of interests as it is found with the economist, the mental element certainly belongs among the elements of production[,] and will finds it place, too, in economics among the costs of production" (MECW 3: 428).

common agreement, or the so-called community of property."[25] There is also mention of the abolition of money: "when all capital, all production, and all exchange are concentrated in the hands of the nation, private ownership will have ceased to exist, money will have become superfluous, and production will have so increased and men will have so much changed that the last forms of the old social relations will also be able to fall away" (351).[26]

The Communist Manifesto affirms that the outcome of the transitional program there proposed would be that "all production [is] concentrated in the hands of a vast association of the whole nation" (MECW 6: 505). This is the formulation in the 1888 English edition, namely Samuel Moore's translation edited by Engels. The German editions, however, used the phrase "in the hands of associated individuals," which may conceivably suggest some form of decentralized organization. This is unlikely, however, and central planning seems to be the favored solution, for we also read in the *Manifesto* of the "centralis[ation]" of "all instruments of production in the hands of the State" (504).[27]

---

[25] It is difficult to appreciate the priority accorded industrial organization over property arrangement, for it implies that the former evolves independently of the latter. This implication is spelled out a little earlier: "in the initial stages of its development large-scale industry created free competition, [but] it has now outgrown free competition" (MECW 6: 347).

[26] The allusion to altered character raises the possibility that the entire passage was intended to apply to the "higher" stage of communism. It is also possible, however, that the change in character emerges only after the first steps – communal ownership, central control of activity, and abolition of money – have been taken, with those steps achieved during the "lower" stage. The subsequent texts that I draw upon are less problematic.

   One of the recommended measures formally proposed in the document is "[c]entralisation of the credit and banking systems in the hands of the State by means of a national bank with state capital and the suppression of all private banks and bankers" (MECW 6: 351). If the abolition of money is taken seriously, then the implicit allowance here for a circulating national currency must presumably be a transitional step.

[27] In *Capital 2*, Marx refers to "collective," as distinct from capitalist, production, implying central organization (MECW 36: 450); he also points out that with the elimination of "money capital" – including preeminently credit – "[s]ociety distributes labour power and means of production to the different branches of production" (356). *Capital 3* points to the situation "where production is under the actual, predetermining control of society," with such control "establish[ing] a relation between the volume of social labour time applied in producing definite articles, and the volume of the social want to be satisfied by these articles" (MECW 37: 186). There is also reference to "socialised man, the associated producers, rationally regulating their interchange with Nature, bringing it under their common control" (807). In addition, in his "Inaugural Address to the Working Men's International Association," we have reference to "the great contest between the blind rule of the supply and demand laws which form the political economy of the middle class, and social production controlled by social foresight, which forms the political economy of the working class" (1864; MECW 20: 11), a contrast pointing to a future planning option.

   Brief mention is made of "co-operative societies" in the "Critique of the Gotha Programme" (1875; MECW 24: 93–4), but with no suggestion that they were particularly favored as a feature of communist society. Furthermore, when touching in *The Civil War in France* on "the obtrusive and full-mouthed apostles of co-operative production," alluding to the more intelligent members of the ruling classes seeking to avoid a communist solution to social problems, Marx is careful to specify that it is not competing cooperatives that would be

These features are elaborated by Engels in *Anti-Dühring* 1894 (1878, 1885).[28] The planning notion in general is broached in the course of an overview of trends within late capitalism: "[T]he colossal productive forces created within the capitalist mode of production[,] which the latter can no longer master, are only waiting to be taken possession of by a society organized for co-operative work on a planned basis to ensure to all members of society the means of existence and of the free development of their capacities, and indeed in constantly increasing measure" (MECW *25*: 139). Again, in additions to the text of *Anti-Dühring* made for the pamphlet *Socialism: Utopian and Scientific*, we find the contrast between "the production without any definite plan of capitalist society capitulates to the production upon a definite plan of the invading socialist society" (see below, p. 163). A central plan is explicitly outlined in *Anti-Dühring* in the course of observations regarding industry location: "Only a society which makes it possible for its productive forces to dovetail harmoniously into each other on the basis of one single vast plan can allow industry to be distributed over the whole country in the way best adapted to its own development, and to the maintenance and development of the other elements of production" (282).[29]

It is also clarified that in communist society excluding money and markets, direct procedures suffice to arrive at labor embodiments. The indirect procedures of capitalism involving reference to money prices are avoided by "[d]irect social production and direct distribution [which] preclude all exchange of commodities, therefore also the transformation of the products into commodities (at any rate within the community), and consequently also their transformation into *values*" (MECW *25*: 294).[30] The entire notion of value, in fact, becomes irrelevant.[31]

appropriate but some form of cooperation subject to "a common plan" (1871; MECW *22*: 335). Marx also insisted there, with respect to agriculture, that "the 'social state' will organise production from the onset in such a way that the annual supply of grain is only minimally dependent on changes in the weather. The volume of production – including supply and consumption – will be rationally regulated" (1879, marginal notes to Wagner; MECW *24*: 537).

[28] Marx read and approved of *Anti-Dühring* and in fact collaborated with Engels in various ways (see editorial preface, MECW *25*: xiii; also Stedman Jones 1982: 295). Part II, Chapter X (MECW *6*: 211–43), treating Dühring's "Critical History of Economic Thought," is by Marx.

[29] An embryonic version, combining "urban and rural life," already appears in the *Principles of Communism* (1847; MECW *6*: 351). In *The Housing Question* (1872–3), much is made of the "abolition of the antithesis between town and country," and its replacement by "as uniform a distribution as possible of the population over the whole country," partly with an eye to rescuing the peasantry from "isolation" and "stupor," but more generally to dovetail industrial and agricultural production (MECW *23*: 384).

[30] The qualification "at any rate within the community" should not be lightly passed over. It implies uncertainty regarding the communist scheme with respect to international trading relations. We shall see (below, p. 149) that autarky is envisaged for agriculture; whether this proposal should be generalized is thus open to question.

[31] This is true also of ancient Indian communities and the family communities of the southern Slavs, whose "members are directly associated for production; the work is distributed according to tradition and requirements, and likewise the products to the extent that they are destined for consumption."

All this – fully in line with Marx[32] – is confirmed by further reference to direct calculation by "society" of the labor time required in the production of, say, "a steam-engine . . . or a hundred square yards of cloth of a certain quality" without reference to any "third product" acting as some sort of measure of value:

From the moment when society enters into possession of the means of production and uses them in direct association for production, the labour of each individual, however varied its specifically useful character may be, becomes at the start and directly social labour. The quantity of social labour contained in a product need not then be established in a roundabout way; daily experience shows in a direct way how much of it is required on the average. Society can simply calculate how many hours of labour are contained in a steam-engine, a bushel of wheat of the last harvest, or a hundred square yards of cloth of a certain quality. It could therefore never occur to it still to express the quantities of labour put into the products, quantities which it will then know directly and in their absolute amounts, in a third product, in a measure which, besides, is only relative, fluctuating, inadequate, though formerly unavoidable for lack of a better one, rather than express them in their natural, adequate and absolute measure, *time*. . . . Hence, on the assumption that we made above, society will not assign values to products. It will not express the simple fact that the hundred square yards of cloth have required for their production, say, a thousand hours of labour in the oblique and meaningless way, stating that they have the *value* of a thousand hours of labour.[33]

To fully appreciate the position in *Anti-Dühring*, we must keep in mind a concern that to permit money to circulate would inevitably lead to a reemergence of capitalist organization. For example, unlike Marx's money,[34] Dühring money did not act as a "mere labour certificate" but fulfilled a genuine "monetary" function as far as concerns private saving, with potentially devastating consequences for his

[32] More generally, the absence of markets and exchange in the scheme envisaged, and thus of money and "exchange value" – the indirect measure of labor embodied – in "The Critique of the Gotha Programme" (1875; MECW 24: 85), also figures large much earlier in the *Grundrisse* (1857–8; MECW 28: 92–6), unknown to Engels.

[33] The opening reference to variations in the "specifically useful character" of labor indicates the first, not the mature, stage of communism.

[34] For Marx's adherence to a system involving labor certificates, see, e.g., "The Critique of the Gotha Programme" (1875; MECW 24: 86). Marx's labor certificates would not circulate and so would not constitute *money*, but they would be used solely to redeem consumer goods from the producing authority, a cloakroom function: "The producers may, for all it matters, receive paper vouchers entitling them to withdraw from the social supplies of consumer goods a quantity corresponding to their labour time. These vouchers are not money. They do not circulate" (*Capital 2*; MECW 36: 356). See also note 35 on the position taken in *Capital 1* regarding Owen's "labour money."

A passage in the *Grundrisse* is understood by Foley as expressing the view "that the attempt to reform commodity production by a labor certificate system implies a full socialization of production under central direction," leading him to conclude that, for Marx, "the organization and supervision of work cannot be entrusted to the spontaneous, decentralized, and narrowly self-interested interactions of individuals" (Foley 1986: 165–6). So far, so good. But the passage in question concerns labor certificates that circulate as money (see MECW 28: 92–3). This limitation might be said to imply that labor certificates that do *not* circulate – such as Marx envisaged – would not carry a similar implication, whereas "full socialization of production under central direction" seems to represent Marx's position unconditionally.

communal proposals (MECW 25: 289–90).[35] The retention of money as means of purchase and payment in international trade further encouraged the private motive to accumulate, thereby threatening the entire communal system (290).

A third feature of Engels's proposed communist system as it emerges in *Anti-Dühring* relates to consumer demand. A direct calculation of inputs – involving mainly but not only labor inputs, as we shall see – is fundamental to the central-planning process envisaged, taking for granted "the useful effects of the various articles of consumption":

> It is true that even then it will still be necessary for society to know how much labour each article of consumption requires for its production. It will have to arrange its plan of production in accordance with its means of production, which include, in particular, its labour-powers. The useful effects of the various articles of consumption, compared with one another and with the quantities of labour required for their production, will in the end determine the plan. People will be able to manage everything very simply, without the intervention of much-vaunted "value." (294–5)[36]

But whence the assumed pattern of consumption? Could Engels have intended freedom of consumer choice? Earlier in the text (in passages introduced into the second edition) he had compared the "social anarchy of production" as it existed with the "social regulation of production upon a definite plan, according to the needs of the community and of each individual," referring here to "direct social appropriation, as means to the maintenance and extension of production" and "direct individual appropriation, as means of subsistence and enjoyment" (MECW 25: 267). The reference to "individual" needs or "individual" appropriation, although suggestive, is not definitive; he may merely have intended the contrast between goods satisfying consumption *versus* those satisfying the "needs of the community," or capital goods, with the planners selecting both categories.

---

[35] Engels actually allows that exchanges in Dühring's system between the commune and its members are "effected through the medium of metallic money," but only as a formality because in effect this medium serves "as a mere labour certificate" in the manner of Owen's "labour money" (MECW 25: 288). Engels here cites *Capital 1* on "The Measure of Value" (MECW 35: 104n.) to the effect that Owen's "labour money ... is no more 'money' than a ticket for the theatre.... The certificate of labour is merely evidence of the part taken by the individual in the common labour, and of his right to a certain portion of the common produce destined for consumption." That Dühring's metallic "money" functions only "as a disguised labour certificate" is true to an even greater extent of intercommune exchanges, where "mere book-keeping would suffice" (MECW 25: 288). The problem raised by Engels is that a range of activity nonetheless existed where a true monetary function would be infallibly exercised by Dühring's metallic "tokens." In this respect Owen's scheme had the advantage: "While in Owen's scheme there would have to be a real abuse" – for his tickets to enter into circulation – "in Dühring's scheme the immanent nature of money, which is independent of human volition, would assert itself; the specific, correct use of money would assert itself in spite of the misuse which Herr Dühring tries to impose on it owing to his own ignorance of the nature of money" (291).

[36] The latter refers to external or market-dictated exchange rates, which would have become irrelevant.

Moreover, he had been expatiating on the anarchical character of capitalist production that was due in part to producers' ignorance of markets (259; see above, p. 126), and although we encounter in this context the regulative function attributed to prices, working through "anarchy," there nonetheless remained the enormous waste of resources under capitalism caused by cyclical instability. It is precisely this feature that appears to be the primary consideration in the case for central control of consumption as well as investment; the solution to such wastage resides in implementation of the "social character" of "the products," not only of "the means of production":

This solution can only consist in the practical recognition of the social nature of the modern forces of production, and therefore in the harmonising of the modes of production, appropriation, and exchange with the socialised character of the means of production. And this can only come about by society openly and directly taking possession of the productive forces which have outgrown all control except that of society as a whole. The social character of the means of production *and of the products* today reacts against the producers, periodically disrupts all production and exchange, acts only like a law of nature working blindly forcibly, destructively. But with the taking over by society of the productive forces, the social character of the means of production *and of the products* will be utilised by the producers with a perfect understanding of its nature, and instead of being a source of disturbance and periodical collapse, will become the most powerful lever of production itself. (266; emphasis added)

In my primary passage, the "useful effects of the various articles of consumption, compared with one another" refers on my reading to a ranking by the central controllers of the relative social utilities of various products.[37] This reading is confirmed by Engels's reference in all editions (295n) to his analysis in the *Outlines* (above, pp. 142–3). Nonetheless, how the central authority would assign utility indexes and make the necessary comparisons with costs remains problematic.[38]

In Marx's case, there is a suggestive formulation in *Capital 3* whereby social control "establishes a relation between the volume of social labour time applied in producing definite articles, and the volume of the social want to be satisfied by these

---

[37] However, Lange seems to attribute free consumer choice to the *Anti-Dühring* text in question, and indeed asserts that "[w]ith some benevolent interpretation this statement of Engels may be regarded, indeed, as containing all the essentials of the modern solution," whereby "the production of each commodity has to be carried so far as to make the ratio of the marginal amount of labor used in producing the different commodities equal to the ratio of the marginal utilities (and of the prices) of those commodities" (1938: 133n.).

[38] An addition to the text of *Anti-Dühring*, first printed in the fourth German edition (1891) of the popular *Socialism: Utopian and Scientific*, summarizes under the heading "*Proletarian Revolution*" Engels's position late in the day as championing "[s]ocialised production upon a predetermined plan": "The proletariat seizes the public power, and by means of this transforms the socialised means of production, slipping from the hands of the bourgeoisie, into public property. By this act, the proletariat frees the means of production from the character of capital they have thus far borne, and gives their socialised character complete freedom to work itself out. Socialised production upon a predetermined plan becomes henceforth possible. The development of production makes the existence of different classes of society thenceforth an anachronism" (MECW 25: 642; also MECW 24: 325).

articles" (above, note 27), where the quantity demanded, the "volume of social want," is apparently taken as known. An earlier statement in *Poverty of Philosophy* refering to "social utility" bears a similar reading: "In a future society . . . in which there will no longer be any classes . . . the time of production devoted to an article will be determined by the degree of its social utility" (MECW 6: 134), a known quantity. The remark regarding agriculture in the "Notes on Wagner" (above, note 27) is particularly suggestive.

There is one further feature of the Engels project to note, namely population control from the center. This is expressed in the letter to Kautsky of 1 February 1881 (cited in Chapter One, p. 39). In a typical fashion, Engels adds this: "At all events, it's for those chaps to decide, whether, when and how it's to be done and what means they wish to use. I don't consider myself qualified to supply them with suggestions and advice about this. Indeed, these chaps will, presumably, be every bit as clever as we are" (MECW 46: 57–8).

The character of Engels's control system as it applied to agriculture is indicated in a document entitled "American Food and the Land Question," composed at about the same time as *Anti-Dühring*. Here is described the American "revolution in farming, together with the revolutionised means of transport as invented by the Americans," which exported wheat to Europe "at such low prices that no European farmer can compete with it – at least not while he is expected to pay rent"; and which together with the prospect of similar development in Russia and the Argentine – "all lands equally fit for this modern system of giant farming and cheap production" – could be expected to undermine European agriculture (*The Labour Standard*, 2 July 1881, MECW 24: 398–9). The "upshot of all this," Engels predicts, "will and must be that it will force upon us the nationalisation of the land and its cultivation by co-operative societies under national control. Then, and then alone, it will again pay both the cultivators and the nation to work it, whatever the price of American or any other corn and meat may be" (399). Engels thus envisaged in this context an autarkic regime, with agricultural organized by "co-operatives" controlled from the center apparently precluding intercooperative competition, as we have seen was also Marx's position (above, p. 144). Confirming Engels's stance is a late reference to the establishment in agriculture of "great national producers' co-operatives with each branch enjoying equal rights and duties" (above, p. 140).

It is unlikely that we would be justified to generalize from agriculture to industry as a whole.[39] In a later letter to August Bebel, apparently relating to industry, Engels writes of cooperative organization as only "transitionally" acceptable, and even so subject to national control: "Nor have Marx and I ever doubted that, in the course of transition to a wholly communist economy, widespread use would have to be

---

[39] It is, in fact, far from certain that Engels had thought the matter through, considering his various statements regarding the dovetailing of agricultural and industrial activities (above, p. 145 and note 29).

made of cooperative management as an intermediate stage. Only it will mean so organising things that society, i.e. initially the State, retains ownership of the means of production and thus prevents the particular interests of the cooperatives from taking precedence on those of society as a whole" (20–23 January 1886; MECW *47*: 389; also letter to Bebel, 18–28 March 1875, MECW *45*: 63). Because national control is insisted upon, the question of the role of cooperatives is less significant than in the case of J. S Mill; even cooperatives could be incorporated within Engels's "one single vast plan" (above, p. 145). Note, finally, that in the 1891 Introduction to the third German edition of Marx's *The Civil War in France*, the option of decentralized decision making by "associations" or cooperatives is explicitly excluded:

By 1871, large-scale industry had already so much ceased to be the exceptional case even in Paris, the centre of artistic handicrafts, that by far the most important decree of the Commune instituted an organisation of large-scale industry and even of manufacture which was not only to be based on the association of the workers in each factory, but also to combine all these associations in one great union; in short, an organisation which, as Marx quite rightly says in *The Civil War*, must necessarily have led in the end to communism [MECW *22*: 335], that is to say, the direct opposite of the Proudhon doctrine. And, therefore, the Commune was the grave of the Proudhon school of socialism. (MECW *27*: 188)[40]

Much of the discussion in the later documents repeats and reinforces what had already appeared in the *Outlines* of 1844. The link is remarked upon by Engels himself, who in 1878 refers readers back to the former work. "As long ago as 1844 I stated that the above-mentioned balancing of useful effects and expenditure of labour on making decisions concerning production was all that would be left, in a communist society, of the politico-economic concept of value" (MECW *25*: 295n). Evidently, Engels refers here to MECW *3*: 426 (cited above, p. 142).[41]

$$* * *$$

Hutchison could not appreciate how Engels contrived to condemn Rodbertus on the grounds that he neglected the allocative function of prices, while neglecting to raise the same objection against his own "vacuous" version of communist organization (*Prolegomena*, p. 15). Hutchison was excessively harsh. As we have seen (Section D), Engels's complaint is that Rodbertus rejected the competitive pricing

---

[40] The allusion at the close is to the decentralization that characterizes Proudhon's proposed scheme of equitable exchange between self-governing producers. As for the commune itself, Pokorni emphasizes the limited extent to which the market system was actually superseded even according to Marx's account: "associations of workmen, under reserve of compensation," were allowed to take over only "all [already] closed workshops and factories, whether the respective capitalists had absconded or preferred to strike work" (Pokorni 1993: 30, citing MECW *22*: 339).

[41] Engels asserts, without elaboration, that the "scientific justification for this statement . . . was made possible only by Marx's *Capital*."

mechanism while at the same time he retained significant elements of a market system. This to Engels was an unacceptable halfway house. Like Marx, he perceived of a system excluding money and markets, one involving centralized decisions on investment, output, and pay, and also precluding consumer sovereignty. Production of both capital and consumption goods would be determined by the planners, and the consumption-goods category allocated according to workers' claims based on their labor contributions (possibly rights to a specific bundle of goods were envisaged). This perspective greatly reduces the force of Hutchison's criticisms, because there is no need for an allocative mechanism where both quantities produced and demanded are centrally determined.

The extremely high degree of control envisaged by Engels for his own scheme is also revealed by an objection in all editions of *Anti-Dühring* that Dühring's program of communes countenanced "freedom of movement and obligatory acceptance of new members on the basis of fixed laws and administrative regulations" (Dühring 1876: 322–3, cited in MECW *25*: 275): "There will . . . be rich and poor economic communes, and the levelling out takes place through the population crowding into the rich communes and leaving the poor ones. So that although Herr Dühring wants to eliminate competition in products between the individual communes by means of national organisation of trade, he calmly allows competition among the producers to continue. Things are removed from the sphere of competition, but men remain subject to it."[42] A similar complaint regarding the infiltration of features of "competition" had been addressed much earlier against Fourier (above, p. 141). Furthermore, Engels reacted equally vehemently against a charge by Dühring that Marx "always gives the impression that [collective ownership] means nothing more than corporate ownership by groups of workers," or – more specifically – that by collective ownership Marx means an "ownership which is at once individual and social" (274–5, citing Dühring 1876: 295, 503, 505). These contentions, Engels objects, were an "invention," a "baseless lie."

Now Marx himself assumes labor-based prices in his future communist state (see above, pp. 148–9 and notes 27, 34). We may therefore address the same question to him that Hutchison addressed to Engels: Why not apply to his own scheme the same objection that there is lacking an equilibrating mechanism to ensure market clearing? The answer to such a question would, I propose, reside in the circumstance that his central planning dictates not only production but also consumption patterns. In fact, so insistent is Marx upon the demand dimension as it operates in a capitalist environment and as it ought to be taken into account in various reformist schemes above, (p. 138), that its formal neglect in discussion of his own version of communism can only be accounted for in the manner proposed,

---

[42] It is of high interest that twentieth-century advocates of a socialist planned economy should have recommended a form of market socialism based on self-managed workers' cooperatives, with membership open to all who wish to join. See Breit and Lange (2003 [1934]; I owe this observation to J. E. King.

namely that society assigns consumption rights to specific commodities, leaving nothing to choice – or to chance.[43]

Hutchison's charges against Engels of irresponsibility in opting for communism also neglect the efficiency losses attributed to the market system, particularly those due to cyclical instability, that would be eliminated by "systematic definite organisation" (MECW 25: 270). To this let us add other potential sources of increased efficiency under communism, for one that "it sets free for the community at large a mass of means of production and of products, by doing away with the senseless extravagance of the ruling classes of today and their political representatives" (269). Engels and Marx put more weight on the gains to be expected from the abolition of markets than on the loss of a signaling device that would, they believed, be unnecessary in a system subject to effective central direction of consumption as well as production.[44]

F. The Perspective on Robert Owen

In 1843 Engels had somewhat played down Owen's home-colony or cooperative project as merely an "experiment" ("Progress of Social Reform on the Continent," MECW 3: 398). The following year, he commented on the socialists' lack of "theory," with Owen among those intended: "The English Socialists are purely practical and therefore also propose remedies, home-colonies, etc., rather in the manner of Morison's pills; their philosophy is truly English, sceptical, in other words they despair of theory, and for all practical purposes they cling to the materialism upon which their whole social system is based" (1844, "The Condition of England . . . "; MECW 3: 466–7). Nonetheless, at Elberfeld on 8 February 1845, he represented Owen's cooperative communities as "the most practical and most fully worked out" of proposals designed to ensure "[t]he greatest saving of labour power . . . [by] *fusing of the individual powers* into social collective power, and in

---

[43] See also Pokorni: "[Marx's] certificates do not determine what will be on the shelves; that is the prerogative of planning as an administrative command" (1993: 29).

Maurice Dobb, pointing to Marx's justification of wage differentials in the "lower" stage of communism, has maintained that "as a logical corollary of this there would naturally be a free consumers' market where such money incomes could be spent" (1940: 300). This seems to me unconvincing, because workers might have differential claims to a basket of goods selected by the central planners. Even if free consumer choice is precluded, consumer preferences might, of course, be sought for indirectly in a variety of ways by the planning authority, leading to modifications to the basket if so indicated (Lange 1938: 90–8; Dobb 1970a: 62–3). On this matter, however, Marx was silent.

[44] The avoidance of losses associated with the trade cycle, speculation, and the middle-man, on the one hand, and the role to be allowed science by the planners, on the other, would be the main considerations.

Lichtheim discerns an important contrast between Marx and Engels regarding the impact of communism on productivity, with Engels concentrating to a high degree on the productive potential to be released by abolition of private property in capital (1964: 59). Too little evidence is provided to justify such a sharp contrast.

the kind of organisation which is based on this concentration of powers hitherto opposed to one another" ("Speeches in Elberfeld; MECW 4: 252). Decades later, we find a similarly warm estimate: "in his definite plan for the future, the technical working out of the details is managed with such practical knowledge – ground plan, front and side, and bird's-eye views all included – that the Owen method of social reform once accepted, there is from the practical point of view little to be said against the actual arrangement of details" (1892 [1880]; *Socialism: Utopian and Scientific*'; MECW 24: 296). Furthermore, Owen's "co-operative societies for retail trade and production" proved "that the merchant and the manufacturer are socially quite unnecessary," and his "labor bazaars for the exchange of the products of labour through the medium of labour-notes, whose unit was a single hour of work" anticipated but also superseded Proudhon by not claiming them "to be the panacea for all social ills, but only a first step towards a much more radical revolution of society" (296–7).[45] Owen's labor certificates also met with Engels's approval (see note 35, regarding *Anti-Dühring*; MECW 25: 291).

Maler opines that considering Engels's suspicions regarding specific programs for the future – "utopia begins only when one ventures 'from existing conditions,' to prescribe the *form* in which this or any other antithesis of present-day society is to be resolved" (*The Housing Question*, 1872–3; MECW 23: 384–5) – his enthusiasm for Owen's scheme is difficult to appreciate, other than by perceiving "the founders of socialism" themselves as "remain[ing] locked up in abstract utopia" (1998: 51). There are two considerations to take into account here. First, the "founders" envisaged a centrally planned economy, not a system based on Owen-like communities. Engels's enthusiasm for the latter reflects a wish to controvert charges of impracticability that were commonly directed against plans for communal arrangement in general, coupled with the fundamental qualification that these were "only a first step towards a much more radical revolution in society," such as Engels himself proposed.[46] Second, attention to the context of the citation from *The Housing Question* reduces the anomaly perceived by Maler. There Engels is refuting Proudhon's wish to abolish bourgeois society while the peasantry would remain as currently organized, and he is insisting that the abolition of "the antithesis between town and country" as part of the abolition of capitalism could not be categorized as utopian; rather, utopianism could be charged against reformist schemes, such as Proudhon's, that retained major features of capitalistic arrangement. Recall the same representation of Rodbertus as "utopian" (above, p. 136).

There is, moreover, a further and more critical dimension to Engels's position to take into account. It emerges in *The Condition of the Working Class* at about

---

[45] On a contrast drawn by Engels's between Owen and Saint-Simon, see Chapter Six, p. 293.

[46] Stedman Jones, however, argues for Engels's positive advocacy in his earlier writings of socialist communities *à la* Owen, but he allows that "no hint of this proposal survived into the final version of the Manifesto. . . . How different would 'Communism' have looked, had that proposal remained!" (2002: 67–8).

the same time as the Elberfeld speech. Engels there complains that Owen catered too much to the old system: "English Socialism arose with Owen, a manufacturer, and proceeds therefore with great consideration toward the bourgeoisie and great injustice toward the proletariat in its methods, although it culminates in demanding the abolition of the class antagonism between bourgeoisie and proletariat" (1845; MECW 4: 525). In essence, the English socialists failed to appreciate the process of "historical development" and the essential role of political struggle by the proletariat in the transition to communism. As Ryazanoff put the matter – providing what amounts to a justification of Engels's ambivalence – although Owen "threw himself heart and soul into the proletarian movement... he remained a pacifist utopist, and refused to take part in revolutionary activity.... [This] explains Owen's attitude towards the Chartists, who were struggling for the full political rights of the working class" (1930 [1922]: 240). Here again recall Engels's complaint in 1843 that the English socialists – Owen among them – lacked "theory," and note the objections in the *Communist Manifesto* to Owenites and Fourierists for their opposition to Chartism and their backward looking or "reactionary" orientation (MECW 6: 517).

Finally, Thompson argues that, unlike several other English socialists, Owen "did not develop the idea of exploitation as a systematic process of value abstraction, consciously directed by individual capitalists," or that of "the emiseration of labour [as] the systematic exploitation of one class by another" (Thompson 1984: 77–80; also see 1998: 61). Owen is indeed formally classified in *Socialism: Utopian and Scientific* among the "Utopians," precisely on the grounds that he lacked the "scientific" perspective on socialism (MECW 24: 297).

G. Communist Distribution

The principle of historical materialism is conspicuous in Engels's analysis of distribution. According to this principle, distribution is the dependent variable as he explained in the critique of Dühring: "The materialist conception of history starts from the proposition that the production and, next to production, the exchange of things produced, is the basis of all social structure; that in every society that has appeared in history, the manner in which wealth is distributed and society divided into classes or estates is dependent upon what is produced, how it is produced, and how the products are exchanged" (MECW 25: 254). More specifically – here we encounter the evolutionary dimension – characteristic of each historical stage is growing income inequality, which signals "that the community is already beginning to break up"; this applies quite generally although it is accompanied under capitalism by the emergence of sharp class differences (136–7). The disintegration of the community reflects the circumstance that inequality is inevitable and incorrigible, except by means of a transformation of the mode of production and exchange. As for the capitalist stage, the process had evolved with great rapidity: "modern capitalist production, which is hardly three hundred years old and has become predominant only since the introduction of modern industry, that is, only in the last hundred years, has in this short time brought about antitheses in distribution – concentration of capital in a few hands on the one side and concentration of the propertyless masses in the big towns on the other – which must of necessity bring about its downfall" (137). In this sense, Engels adds, distribution was "not a merely passive result of production and exchange [but] in its turn reacts upon both of these."

From all this there emerges, as with Marx,[47] the irrelevance of any approach to inequality based on appeal to morality and justice; social abuses – "necessary consequences" of the existing mode of production – do not even appear as an injustice to the "exploited masses" until the appropriate historical moment (MECW 25: 137–8). Accordingly, "[t]he task of economic science" – so-called scientific socialism – was "to show that the social abuses which have recently been developing are necessary consequences of the existing mode of production, but at the same time also indications of its approaching dissolution; and to reveal, within the already dissolving economic form of motion, the elements of the future new organisation of production and exchange which will put an end to those abuses" (MECW 25: 138). By contrast, the "new" eighteenth-century science of political economy presented the laws of production and exchange as "eternal laws of nature . . . deduced from the nature of man," not as an expression of the "conditions and requirements of their epoch." Engels had in mind Smith and the Physiocrats (139), but Dühring too was in the same mold, for he "could not offer us anything except a bad translation of Rousseau's theory of equality into the language of socialism, much as one has long been able to hear much more effectively rendered in any workers' tavern in Paris" (141).

Although Engels himself does not hesitate to speak the language of "morality," he insists that all such appeals are useless unless the time is ripe (MECW 25: 145). Thus calls for "the abolition of class antagonisms and class distinctions . . . up to 1830 had left the working and suffering classes cold." This was no longer the case; and Engels's summary explanation contains all the essentials of the Marxian position regarding the "crying contradiction" between the system of distribution based on the advanced capitalist mode of production, and that mode itself – a contradiction ensuring the inevitable "revolution which will put an end to all class distinctions," the account referring to falling real wages and cyclical instability (145–6).

Dühring's failure manifested itself precisely in his use of "force" to understand distributive patterns: "[H]e saves himself the trouble of explaining the various forms of distribution which have hitherto existed, their differences and their causes;

---

[47] We find an early application of the principle stated by Marx in *Poverty of Philosophy* (1847; MECW 6: 159). Proudhon's query why the British laborer had not benefitted from the enormous increase in productivity implied a failure to appreciate that income inequality was a condition for "the development of productive forces." For a discussion of Marx's position, see Hollander 2008: Chapter 13, pp. 387–8).

taken in the lump, they are simply of no account – they rest on oppression, on force" (MECW 25: 144); and also in his appeal to a mutable standard of morality and law: "[H]e thereby transfers the whole theory of distribution from the sphere of economics to that of morality and law, that is, from the sphere of established material facts to that of more or less vacillating opinions and sentiments."[48]

This general orientation is patent also in the 1891 Preface to the first German edition of *Poverty of Philosophy*, which reiterates Marx's position on the matter of "fair" income distribution:

According to the laws of bourgeois economics, the greatest part of the product does *not* belong to the workers who have produced it. If we now say: that is unjust, that ought not to be so, then that has nothing immediately to do with economics. We are merely saying that this economic fact is in contradiction to our sense of morality. Marx, therefore, never based his communist demands upon this, but upon the inevitable collapse of the capitalist mode of production which is daily taking place before our eyes to an ever growing degree; he says only that surplus value consists of unpaid labour, which is a simple fact. ("Marx and Rodbertus"; MECW 26: 281–2)

Indeed, in his contribution "A Fair Day's Wages for a Fair Day's Work" (7 May 1881), Engels defined the very concept of "a fair day's wages" as the subsistence wage, namely "under normal conditions... the sum required to procure to the labourer the means of existence necessary, according to the standard of life of his station and country, to keep himself in working order and to propagate his race" (MECW 24: 376–7).

* * *

Marx rejected "fair" in the sense of "equal" distribution as proposed by the Gotha program, which he assumes applies specifically "to that part of the means of consumption which is divided among the individual producers of the collective" (1875; MECW 24: 85). In the labor-certificate system he himself envisaged, what matters is application of an "equal standard," not the crude equality envisaged by the Party program, and such application implies recognition of the essential inequality of labor:

But one man is superior to another physically or mentally and so supplies more labour in the same time, or can work for a longer time; and labour, to serve as a measure, must be defined by its duration or intensity, otherwise it ceases to be a standard of measurement. This *equal* right is an unequal right for unequal labour. It recognises no class distinctions, because everyone is only a worker like everyone else; but it tacitly

---

[48] Marx estimated that the redistribution envisaged in Proudhon's scheme "would certainly not assure a high degree of comfort for the individual participants" (MECW 6: 159). Engels too implies a similar estimate in *Anti-Dühring* by minimizing both the responsibility of "force" (the term includes state intervention) in aggravating income inequality and its potential to reduce it.

recognises the unequal individual endowment and thus productive capacity of the workers as natural privileges. (86)

Recognition of the natural inequality of labor applied only in the "first phase" of communism, as an inevitable "defect" of a society that has just emerged "after prolonged birth-pangs from capitalist society. Right can never be higher than the economic structure of society and its cultural development which this determines" (87).

The concern here is entirely with natural differences between individuals with regard to physical capacity and mental "talent." Nothing is said either of productivity differentials relating to learned skills or the characteristics attached to various jobs and the attitudes toward them, in the manner of Adam Smith and J. S. Mill in their wage-structure analyses. The contrast is striking. For Smith and Mill the non-pecuniary characteristics explain how, under competitive equilibrium conditions, wage differentials exist despite natural equality. Marx, however, assumes natural inequality and made no appeal to such differentials in the analysis of competitive conditions and a fortiori that of collective organization.[49]

Now Dühring condemned Marx for adopting a typically bourgeois perspective regarding the related matter of "compound labor": "In his lucubrations on value . . . Herr Marx never rids himself of the ghost of a skilled labour-time which lurks in the background. He was unable to effect a thoroughgoing change here because he was hampered by the traditional mode of thought of the educated classes, to whom it necessarily appears monstrous to recognize the labour-time of a porter and that of an architect as of absolutely equal value from the standpoint of economics" (Dühring 1871: 500, cited in *Anti-Dühring*, MECW 25: 183). Engels leaped to Marx's defense, insisting on wage-scale differentials under capitalism – the "higher wages paid for compound labour" – on the grounds that "[i]n a society of private producers, private individuals or their families pay the cost of training the qualified worker" (187). He remarked how fortunate it was for Dühring "that fate did not make him a manufacturer, and thus saved him from fixing the value of his commodities on the basis of this new rule [of treating all labour equally] and thereby running infallibly into the arms of bankruptcy" (185). But the complaint is extended. Dühring applied his rule to his future commune, "entailing the pure, heavenly air of equality and justice." By contrast, under Engels's vision, the planners would ascribe "greater values" to productions of compound labour, though pay differentials would not be recognized: "In a socialistically organised society, these costs [of training] are borne by society, and to it therefore belong the fruits, the greater values produced by compound labour. The worker himself has no claim

[49] Recall here J. S. Mill's distinction between socialism and communism. Under communism, which "forms the extreme limit of Socialism," not only is there an absence of private property, but "the produce is divided and the labour apportioned, as far as possible, equally," i.e., independently of productivity (1965 [1848b] 2: 210). The contrast corresponds to Marx's "higher" and "lower" stages of communism.

to extra pay. And from this, incidentally, follows the moral that at times there is a drawback to the popular demand of the workers for 'the full proceeds of labour'" (187).[50]

Here we have pinned Engels down to a clear-cut statement regarding a central feature of his position on distribution in his communist society. There is no conflict with Marx, who insisted in 1875 on the recognition of "unequal individual endowment and thus productive capacity of the workers as natural privileges," because Engels had in mind not natural endowment but acquired characteristics involving publicly funded training. Furthermore, this solution is the likely one, because a primary purpose of *Anti-Dühring* was to refute the notion ascribed to Dühring of "natural" equality between individuals (MECW *25*: 88–99).[51] Engels did allow that the "idea of equality" still play[ed] an important agitational role in the socialist movement of almost every country" (95), but he insisted that the "real" or scientific content of the proletarian demand was strictly limited to "the abolition of classes" and went no further (99). Claims beyond that were an "absurdity," considering the enormous range of individual character differences. In addition, Engels cites *Capital* to the effect that the idea of equality "already possesses the fixity of a popular prejudice." Needless to say, in the mature phase of communism, workers – that is, all members of society – would be paid not in terms of equal pay per hour whether the work is that of a porter or an architect, as Dühring proposed (nor in terms of Engels's natural differentials), but on a completely different principle, because functional specialization would no longer exist (186).

H. From Capitalism to Communism: An Evolutionary Process

The emergence of communist organization from within capitalism is already expressed by Engels in the *Principles of Communism* (1847). The evolutionist character of development is apparent in what follows: "The abolition of private ownership is indeed the most succinct and characteristic summary of the trans-formation of the entire social system necessarily following from the development of industry, and it is therefore rightly put forward by the Communists as their main demand" (MECW *6*: 348). At this early period he also elaborated a notion of continuum in development that extended from capitalist to postcapitalist organ-ization, justifying proletarian cooperation with the bourgeoisie until the time was ripe for its overthrow:

Through its industry, its commerce and its political institutions, the bourgeoisie is already working everywhere to . . . build up a great nation with common interests, customs and ideas out of the many hitherto mutually independent localities and provinces. The bourgeoisie is already carrying out considerable centralisation. The

---

[50] The term "value" is, of course, inappropriate (see above, p. 145).
[51] Engels maintained that Dühring undermined his own general notion of equality by intro-ducing an entire range of character differences; he also commended Rousseau on inequality (MECW *25*: 90–1).

proletariat, far from suffering any disadvantage from this, will as a result rather be in a position to unite, to feel itself a class, to acquire a proper political point of view within the democracy, and finally to conquer the bourgeoisie. The democratic proletariat not only needs the kind of centralisation begun by the bourgeoisie but will have to extend it very much further. ("The Civil War in Switzerland," November 1847; MECW 6: 372)

The process is subsequently much expanded both by Marx and Engels with respect to the growth of large corporate structures as forerunner of future communist organization.

The general evolutionary theme is nicely stated by Marx in the *Economic Manu- scripts* of 1861–3 with respect to the dissolution of capitalism: "This is an essentially different conception from that of the bourgeois political economists, themselves imprisoned in capitalist preconceptions, who are admittedly able to see how pro- duction is carried on *within* the capital-relation, but not how this *relation* is itself produced, and how at the same time the material conditions for its dissolution are produced within it, thereby removing its *historical justification* as a *necessary form* of economic development, of the production of social wealth" (MECW 34: 466). *The Civil War in France* alludes to an aspect of this evolutionary dimension as defining appropriate action – and the limits to action – on the road to the "new society":

The working class did not expect miracles from the Commune. They have no ready- made utopias to introduce *par décret du peuple*. They know that in order to work out their own emancipation, and along with it that higher form to which present society is irresistibly tending by its own economical agencies, they will have to pass through long struggles, through a series of historic processes, transforming circumstances and men. They have no ideals to realize, but to set free elements of the new society with which old collapsing bourgeois society itself is pregnant." (1871; MECW 22: 335)

Particularly important are observations in *Capital* 3, composed in the 1860s, regarding the joint-stock company as the final stage – "the ultimate development of capitalist production" (MECW 37: 434) – in the transition toward socialism: "The capital, which in itself rests on a social mode of production and presupposes a social concentration of means of production and labour power, is here directly endowed with the form of social capital (capital of directly associated individuals) as distinct from private capital, and its undertakings assume the form of social undertakings as distinct from private undertakings. It is the abolition of capital as private property within the framework of the capitalist mode of production itself." As such, it constitutes "a self-dissolving contradiction, which *prima facie* represents a mere phase of transition to a new form of production. It manifests itself as such a contradiction in its effects. It establishes a monopoly in certain spheres and thereby requires state interference. It reproduces a new financial aristocracy, a new variety of parasites in the shape of promoters, speculators and simply nominal directors; a whole system of swindling and cheating by means of corporation promotion, stock issuance, and stock speculation" (436). "It is," Marx concludes, "private production without the control of private property," implying once again the necessity for state control.

What is said of joint-stock companies as a transitional form "from the capitalist mode of production to the associated one" applied also to the "gradual extension of cooperative enterprises on a more or less national scale" (MECW *37*: 438), with one difference, that "the antagonism is resolved negatively in the one and positively in the other." Treatment of cooperatives as a feature of the final stages of capitalist society on a par with joint-stock organization strengthens my case that it is central control rather than some decentralized decision-making arrangement that Marx had in mind in contemplating communism in its initial stage.

* * *

Engels's version of the disintegration of the capitalist system is found in various articles for *The Labour Standard*. Writing on German, French, and American competition in British textiles and mining and metal works, Engels focuses upon "our present system of using machinery to produce not only manufactured goods, but machines themselves," a process generating "chronic over-production, chronic depression of trade . . . chronic misery and a constant prospect of the workhouse" ("Cotton and Iron," July 1881; MECW *24*: 412). There follows a representation of the essential weakness of the capitalist system – its inability to "direct" an ever-expanding national output in the face of limited markets, creating a situation overwhelmingly detrimental to labor (412–13). As Engels summarized the matter in the next issue, British capitalists had "become unable to manage the immense productive system of this country; . . . they on the one hand expanded production so as to periodically flood all the markets with produce, and on the other became more and more incapable of holding their own against foreign competition" ("Social Classes – Necessary and Superfluous," *The Labour Standard*, December 1881; MECW *24*: 418).

The theme that the capitalist class in Britain had lost its status as progressive vehicle is further elaborated, with particular reference to the displacement of the traditional capitalist-manager within nationalized, joint-stock, and cooperative arrangements:

Now the economical function of the capitalist middle class has been, indeed, to create the modern system of steam manufactures and steam communications, and to crush every economical and political obstacle which delayed or hindered the development of that system. No doubt, as long as the capitalist middle class performed this function it was, under the circumstances, a necessary class. But is it still so? Does it continue to fulfill its essential function as the manager and expander of social production for the benefit of society at large? Let us see.

To begin with the means of communication, we find the telegraphs in the hands of the Government. The railways and a large part of the sea-going steamships are owned, not by individual capitalists who manage their own business, but by joint-stock companies whose business is managed for them by *paid employees*, by servants whose position is to all intents and purposes that of superior better paid workpeople.

As to the directors and shareholders, they both know that the less the former interfere with the management, and the latter with the supervision, the better for the concern. A lax and mostly perfunctory supervision is, indeed, the only function left to the owners of the business. Thus we see that in reality the capitalist owners of these immense establishments have no other action left with regard to them, but to cash the half-yearly dividend warrants. The social function of the capitalist here has been transferred to servants paid by wages; but he continues to pocket, in his dividends, the pay for those functions though he has ceased to perform them. . . .

What is true for railways and steam shipping is becoming more and more true every day for all large manufacturing and trading establishments. "Floating" – transforming large private concerns into limited companies – has been the order of the day for the last ten years and more. From the large Manchester warehouses of the City to the ironworks and coalpits of Wales and the North and the factories of Lancashire, everything has been, or is being, floated. In all Oldham there is scarcely a cotton mill left in private hands; nay, even the retail tradesman is more and more superseded by "co-operative stores," the great majority of which are co-operative in name only – but of that another time. (MECW *24*: 416–17)

The payment of dividends had no further social justification, Engels concluded: "Thus we see that by the very development of the system of capitalists' production the capitalist is superseded quite as much as the handloom-weaver. With this difference, though, that the handloom-weaver is doomed to slow starvation, and the superseded capitalist to slow death from overfeeding." He adds, with his inestimable sense of humor, that "[i]n this they generally are both alike, that neither knows what to do with himself."[52] Indeed, "not only can we manage very well without the interference of the capitalist class in the great industries of the country, but their interference is becoming more and more a nuisance" (418). The perhaps unintended implication of all this is somewhat to undermine the original Marxist perspective on developmental trends – including the underconsumption, cyclical, and downward wage-trend features – that had applied even to a British economy not subject to keen foreign competition in home and foreign markets, for these characteristics appear here as pertaining specifically to an economy so circumstanced.

In *Anti-Dühring*, similarly, the "socialist critique" is said to have demonstrated that the capitalist mode of production "by virtue of its own development, drives towards the point at which it makes itself impossible. This critique proves that the capitalist forms of production and exchange become more and more an intolerable fetter on production itself, that the mode of distribution necessarily determined by those forms has produced a situation among the classes which is daily becoming more intolerable" (MECW *25*: 138–9). The allusion here is to "steadily deteriorating" working-class conditions (see Chapter Five, p. 260), inviting transition to an alternative social system – how the transition would occur is left frustratingly open – to take control of "the colossal productive forces created within the capitalist mode

---

[52] Engels is alluding here to factory organization in general, but subsequently to more elaborate forms, preeminently "the socialisation of great masses of means of production . . . in the different kinds of joint-stock companies" (MECW *25*: 264–5).

of production which the latter can no longer master." Corresponding to the paper on "Social Classes," the text introduces an account of the evolutionary process entailing the increasing importance of joint-stock organization followed by nationalization and "direction of production" by the capitalist state itself. The general context is the compulsion, under competitive pressure, for industrial capitalists to continuously improve machinery in the face of limited markets: "The extension of the markets cannot keep pace with the extension of production," generating periodic crisis (263). Thus, "[t]he fact that the socialised organisation of production within the factory[53] has developed so far that it has become incompatible with the anarchy of production in society, which exists side by side with and dominates it, is brought home to the capitalists themselves by the violent concentration of capital that occurs during crises, through the ruin of many large, and a still greater number of small, capitalists" (264). The consequence is the transformation of business organization:

The period of industrial high pressure, with its unbounded inflation of credit, not less than the crash itself, by the collapse of great capitalist establishments, tends to bring about that form of the socialisation of great masses of means of production which we meet with in the different kinds of joint-stock companies. Many of these means of production and of communication are, from the outset, so colossal that, like the railways, they exclude all other forms of capitalistic exploitation. At a further stage of evolution this form also becomes insufficient: the official representative of capitalist society – the state – will ultimately have to undertake the direction of production. This necessity for conversion into state property is felt first in the great institutions for intercourse and communication – the post office, the telegraphs, the railways. (264–5)[54]

The penultimate sentence is replaced in the pamphlet *Socialism: Utopian and Scientific* by the following elaboration relating to the reorganization of joint-stock companies into "trusts," which, because of their instability, subsequently merge into giant monopolies, as illustrated by British alkali production:

At a further stage of evolution this form also becomes insufficient. The producers on a large scale in a particular branch of industry in a particular country unite in a "Trust," a union for the purpose of regulating production. They determine the total amount to be produced, parcel it out among themselves, and thus enforce the selling price fixed beforehand. But trusts of this kind, as soon as business becomes bad, are generally likely to break up, and, on this very account, compel a yet greater concentration of association. The whole of the particular industry is turned into one giant joint-stock company; internal competition gives place to the internal monopoly of this one company. This has happened in 1890 with the English *alkali* production, which is now, after the fusion of 48 large works, in the hands of one company, conducted upon a single plan, and with a capital of £6,000,000 (MECW *24*: 317; see also MECW *25*: 639).

[53] See also *Socialism, Utopian and Scientific* (1892 [1880]), which contains extracts from *Anti-Dühring* (MECW *24*: 316).

[54] In his very last publication, the Supplement to *Capital 3* written during May and June of 1895, Engels silently carried the theme further by a new centrality accorded the stock exchange (see Chapter Six, p. 284).

But this extreme outcome must prove socially unacceptable – a surprising recognition of the significance of moral suasion: "In the trusts, freedom of competition changes into its very opposite – into monopoly; and the production without any definite plan of capitalist society capitulates to the production upon a definite plan of the invading socialist society. Certainly this is so far still to the benefit and advantage of the capitalists. But in this case the exploitation is so palpable that it must break down. No nation will put up with production conducted by trusts, with so barefaced an exploitation of the community by a small band of dividend-mongers" (MECW *24*: 317–18; see also MECW *25*: 639–40). The solution, once again, is nationalization and direction of production by the state: "In any case, with trusts or without, the official representative of capitalist society – the State – will ultimately have to undertake the direction of production" (318; 640).

The superannuation of the capitalist class as a socially useful agency also appears in the *Anti-Dühring* version of the evolutionary scheme: "If the crises deconstrate the incapacity of the bourgeoisie for managing any longer modern productive forces, the transformation of the great establishmments for production and distribution into joint-stock companies and state property shows how unnecessary the bourgeoisie are for that purpose. All the social functions of the capitalist are now performed by salaried employees" (MECW *25*: 265). The capitalist's sole remaining "social function," Engels wrote sarcastically, was "that of pocketing dividends, tearing off coupons, and gambling on the Stock Exchange, where the different capitalists despoil one another of their capital." He could not resist adding that the process "forces out the capitalists, and reduces them, just as it reduces the workers, to the rank of the surplus population, although not immediately into those of the industrial reserve army."

In an editorial attachment to *Capital 3,* when discussing Marx's observations on the transitional character of joint-stock organization, Engels provided some added details regarding cartelization even on an international scale. As is usual with him, the "overproduction problem" is a central feature of the analysis:

Since Marx wrote the above, new forms of industrial enterprises have developed, as we know, representing the second and third degree of stock companies. The daily growing speed with which production may be enlarged in all fields of large-scale industry today, is offset by the ever-greater slowness with which the market for these increased products expands. . . . Add to this the protective tariff policy, by which every industrial country shuts itself off from all others, particularly from England, and also artificially increases domestic production capacity. The results are a general chronic overproduction, depressed prices, falling and even wholly disappearing profits; in short, the old boasted freedom of competition has reached the end of its tether and must itself announce its obvious, scandalous bankruptcy. (MECW *37*: 435)[55]

---

[55] The details of the new organization are given thus: "The former owners of the more than thirty individual plants have received shares for the appraised value of their entire establishments, totalling about £5 million, which represent the fixed capital of the trust. The technical management remains in the same hands as before, but business control is concentrated in the hands of the general management. The floating capital, totalling about £1 million, was offered to the public for subscription. The total capital is, therefore, £6 million" (MECW *37*: 435–6).

The "new forms" of organization designed to deal with the overproduction phenomenon relate only in the first instance to cartelization: "And in every country this is taking place through the big industrialists of a certain branch joining in a cartel for the regulation of production. A committee fixes the quantity to be produced by each establishment and is the final authority for distributing the incoming orders. Occasionally even international cartels were established, as between the English and German iron industries" (MECW 37: 435). But only in the first instance, because "even this form of association in production did not suffice. The antagonism of interests between the individual firms broke through it only too often, restoring competition. This led in some branches, where the scale of production permitted, to the concentration of the entire production of that branch of industry in *one* big joint-stock company under single management. This has been repeatedly effected in America; in Europe the biggest example so far is the United Alkali Trust, which has brought all British alkali production into the hands of a single business firm." Engels draws the "gratifying" conclusion that "in this branch, which forms the basis of the whole chemical industry, competition has been replaced by monopoly in England, and the road has been paved, most gratifyingly, for future expropriation by the whole of society, the nation" (436).

The "Critique of the Draft Social-Democratic Programme of 1891" – the program intended to replace the Gotha program adopted in 1875 – is particularly instructive. Here Engels recommended removal of the modifier "private" in a reference in the draft to "[t]he planlessness rooted in the nature of capitalist private production": "What is capitalist *private* production? Production by *separate* entrepreneurs, which is increasingly becoming an exception. Capitalist production by *joint-stock companies* is no longer *private* production but production on behalf of many associated people. And when we pass on from joint-stock companies to trusts, which dominate and monopolise whole branches of industry, this puts an end not only to *private production* but also to *planlessness*" (MECW 27: 223–4).

Engels's vision, it may be said, does not necessarily entail central planning because the particular concern appears to be expropriation of individual industries. Nonetheless, it is difficult to conceive of an organization in which all major industries are state owned and individually subject to "planning" without a master plan to coordinate decisions.[56] Furthermore, we have surveyed the considerable evidence throughout Engels's opus pointing to a central-control option.

* * *

Engels regarded the prospective extension of state control as a natural, not a forced, matter arising from the logic of the situation, which explains his representation in *Anti-Dühring* of Bismarckian forms of "state-ownership of industrial establishments" as " a kind of spurious socialism" (MECW 25: 265n.). Furthermore, though even "natural" extensions of state control occurred without disturbing "the

---

[56] Engels's remarks on the integration of cooperatives (above, p. 149) are suggestive.

capitalist relation," because "the workers remain wage-workers," it is part of the process whereby the ultimate "solution" to class conflict would be achieved:

But the transformation, either into joint-stock companies, or into state ownership, does not do away with the capitalistic nature of the productive forces. In the joint-stock companies this is obvious. And the modern state, again, is only the organisation that bourgeois society takes on in order to support the general external conditions of the capitalist mode of production against the encroachments as well of the workers as of individual capitalists. The modern state, no matter what its form, is essentially a capitalist machine, the state of the capitalists, the ideal personification of the total national capital. The more it proceeds to the taking over of productive forces, the more does it actually become the national capitalist, the more citizens does it exploit. The workers remain wage-workers – proletarians. The capitalist relation is not done away with. It is rather brought to a head. But, brought to a head, it topples over. State ownership of the productive forces is not the solution of the conflict, but concealed within it are the technical conditions that form the elements of that solution (265–6).[57]

By "the elements of the solution" provided by nationalization of industry on the part of the capitalist state is intended, partly, that the proletarians – once they seize power – will have already been "shown the way" to proceed with a well-established exemplar at hand: "Whilst the capitalist mode of production more and more completely transforms the great majority of the population into proletarians, it creates the power which, under penalty of its own destruction, is forced to accomplish this revolution. Whilst it forces on more and more the transformation of the vast means of production, already socialised, into state property, it shows itself the way to accomplishing this revolution. *The proletariat seizes political power and turns the means of production in the first instance into state property*. But, in so doing, it abolishes itself as proletariat, abolishes all class distinctions and class antagonisms, abolishes also the state as state" (MECW 25: 267). Here we have a splendid illustration of Engels's position that among the tasks of scientific socialism was its revelation of "the elements [within Capitalism] of the future new organisation of production and exchange which will put an end to ... abuses" (above, p. 155). Engels here has the nationalization program carried

---

[57] See also a letter of 24 March 1891 explaining why state appropriation of land in Germany does not suffice: "[S]o long as the propertied classes remain at the helm, nationalisation never abolishes exploitation but merely changes its form" (MECW 49: 152). Similarly, in "The Socialism of Mr Bismarck," Engels maintains that, notwithstanding nationalization of the railways, "the German Empire is just as completely under the yoke of the Stock Exchange as was the French Empire in its day. It is the stockbrokers who prepare the projects which the Government has to carry out – for the profit of their pockets" (1880: MECW 24: 279). All this apparently assumes that there remains in existence a "bourgeois" class, i.e., that private property in capital is maintained despite nationalization in specific sectors. But the Marx–Engels position on the Paris Commune, and other indications of the importance of democratic control structures, make it virtually certain that Engels would have found equally unacceptable a model entailing wholesale state ownership (leaving at most an insignificant capitalist sector), yet with control in the hands of an elite rather than the proletariat – the Soviet model, for example.

out by the proletariat after achieving power – implying continued reliance, at least temporarily, on a capitalist sector[58] – rather than (as in the accounts of the evolution of late capitalism) as part of a natural process emerging within capitalist arrangement. Presumably both categories of nationalization are intended.

Also relevant to the evolutionary theme are the further developments envisaged once the private-property system had been entirely eliminated. I refer again to Marx's "first phase" and "higher phase" of communism. We have thus seen that in the first phase – as the system has emerged out of capitalism – wage *inequality* is to be recognized; only in the later phase would the egalitarian principle – "From each according to his abilities to each according to his needs" – apply (above, note 19). There is also Engels's express statement that his own and Marx's support for industrial "cooperatives" applied only to a transitional arrangement (above, pp. 149–50).

I. The Rodbertus Proposals Misunderstood

My account in Section D of Rodbertus's labor-money scheme was limited to what was required to appreciate Engels's positive contribution to the functioning of the price mechanism as allocative device. But did Engels represent Rodbertus accurately, when he read him (see above, p. 135) as proposing retention of the exploitative system?

The argument in *Zur Erkenntniss* entails essentially an extended comparison between systems based on private and communal ownership of land and capital, with respect to the working out of "division of labor" – resource allocation we would say – in the broadest sense of the term.[59] As an important instance, Rodbertus has it that the replacement of the private "entrepreneur" by a state official would create no special difficulties; in fact there would be productivity advantages (Rodbertus 1842: 119–20, 124–5, 125–6, 126–7). A primary advantage of public ownership of capital (and land) is perceived to be distributional – the preclusion of "exploitation," whereby the worker is paid less than the value of his product, such as characterizes the capitalist-exchange system (127–8, 169, 171). Goods would be priced by the state authority at labor cost with the sole claim to income based on labor (122–3; cf. 1971 [1851]: 82–3). Productivity improvements in this system would pertain only to labor (72–3, 124–7). The fact of differential labor qualities is noted, but it is not seen as creating an insurmountable problem (5). Furthermore, although the matter is not pursued, it is taken for granted that "utility" is a necessary condition – that the mere exertion of labor is an insufficient condition for valuation. Engels's complaints in these latter respects (see above, pp. 137–8) are exaggerated.

---

[58] On the program of nationalization after a communist takeover, see also the *Communist Manifesto* (Chapter One, p. 63), and a letter of 21 August 1890 (Chapter Four, p. 222).

[59] Rodbertus contrasts this with Smithian of division of labor, which he wrongly identifies with a narrow factory variety (1842: 135).

We must bear these qualifications in mind when we consider the mechanism proposed to achieve the desired outcome, namely the issue by a state authority of "tickets" for labor undertaken, which are to be used to redeem consumer goods from state retail outlets (Rodbertus 1842: 123–4, 164–6, 168).[60] By this device, runs the argument, all claims to income would be "liquidated" or balanced by purchases of final goods:

[T]he necessary measure that the value certified in the note should be actually present in circulation is realised in that only the person who actually delivers a product receives a note, on which is accurately recorded the quantity of labour by which the product was produced. Whoever delivers a product of two days' labour receives a note marked "two days." By the strict observance of this rule in the issue of notes, the [liquidation] condition too would necessarily be fulfilled. For according to our supposition the real value of the goods always coincides with the quantity of labour which their production has cost and this quantity of labour is measured by the usual units of time, and therefore someone who hands in a product on which two days' labour has been expended and receives a certificate for two days, has received, certified or assigned to him neither more nor less value than that which he has in fact supplied. Further, since only the person who has actually put a product into circulation receives such a certificate, it is also certain that the value marked on the note is available for the satisfaction of society. However extensive we imagine the circle of division of labour to be, if this rule is strictly followed, *the sum total of available value* must *be exactly equal to the sum total of certified value*. Since, however, the sum total of certified value is exactly equal to the sum total of value assigned, the latter must *necessarily coincide with the available value, all claims will be satisfied and the liquidation correctly brought about* (1842: 166–7; translation MECW 26: 285–6; Engels's emphasis).

Rodbertus does not go into great detail regarding his control system (1842: 134). However, the authority would be responsible for capital maintenance (124, 169), and problems relating to taxation are touched upon (167). It is not properly clarified whether the tickets would *circulate* as money or be limited to a "cloakroom" function, though the latter seems more likely in the light of the formulation of 1851 (see below, pp. 169–70).

Let us return now to our main concern, namely Engels's assertion that Rodbertus retained the "exploitation" feature by applying his system of labor tickets to a private-property-based system, whereby "the state . . . gives advances [of labor paper money] to the industrial capitalists, with which the latter pay the workers," who in turn "buy the products with the paper money they have received, and so cause the paper money to flow back to its starting point" (MECW 26: 285; above, p. 134). "How very beautifully this is affected," added Engels sarcastically, "one must hear from Rodbertus himself." Now the passage given in evidence – from 1842 (166–7, cited above) – says nothing about this matter. However, there is one passage that does claim that the proposed labor-ticket system might be

---

[60] In an interesting aside, Rodbertus dismisses the potential for forgery of labor tickets (1842: 167).

applied even in a private-property system with the same liquidation results as under communal-property arrangement (169–71).

What are we to make of this? Was Engels correct to charge Rodbertus with recommending from early days the maintenance of exploitation? Rodbertus himself gives the answer in a note attached to the foregoing. He cautions that his case was purely hypothetical, turning on the assumption that goods are priced in a private-property régime according to labor input. In this hypothetical case nothing more is entailed than that capitalists take over claims to income that in a wholly reformed system belong to labor. In actuality, however, the uniform profit-rate principle dictates that prices diverge from values, so that the application of the scheme to a private-property system was irrelevant (171n.).[61] The labor-ticket system proposed in 1842 thus applied solely to a communal-property system, where labor prices are imposed, and Engels's effort to differentiate the Marxian proposals collapses. Above all, his appeal to Ricardo's selection of profit-rate uniformity at the expense of labor values (above p. 137) is otiose, because this represents precisely Rodbertus's position as far as concerns capitalist organization.

* * *

We proceed to the *Social Letters* of 1851 bearing in mind Rodbertus's insistence (encountered below) that this contribution was an elaboration of that of 1842, and also Engels's contention in 1885 that "[f]rom 1842 up to his death, [Rodbertus] went round in circles, always repeating the same ideas which he had already expressed or suggested in his first work, feeling himself unappreciated, finding himself plundered, where there was nothing to plunder, and finally refusing, not without intention, to recognise that in essence he had only rediscovered what had already been discovered long before" ("Marx and Rodbertus"; MECW 26: 290).[62] It is particularly important that we consider the two documents together because Rodbertus's charge of plagiarism against Marx (see Prolegomena, pp. 12–13) refers to both. That the main themes of the 1851 document are already to be found in 1842 will be apparent from the account that follows, though in some cases – particularly with respect to the question of the monetary function of labor tickets – the 1851 version is rather clearer.

The purpose of the proposed socialization of private property of land and capital was primarily to ensure that "the result of increased productiveness would accrue solely to the benefit of the labourers, so that their income would increase

---

[61] Nevertheless, Rodbertus contends elsewhere that prices would be unaffected by the abolition of profit and rent (1842: 132–3), which is scarcely consistent with the present text.

[62] Engels's love–hate sentiment toward Rodbertus emerges in a letter to Kautsky, dated 17 October 1884: "I am . . . ploughing through the whole of *Zur Erkenntniss* again. It will repay the trouble; only by a really close investigation does one properly appreciate the stupendousness of the nonsense preached here, nonsense that literally overwhelms the few flashes of insight which, though admittedly not new, are nevertheless accurate and, for Germany, commendable. *Capital*, Book II, will be very illuminating on this point" (MECW 47: 206).

in direct proportion to the increase of productiveness"; by contrast, the private-property institution, "with its law governing wages, has the effect of throwing all the benefits arising from increased productiveness exclusively into the hands of the landowners and capitalists" (Rodbertus 1971 [1851]: 86–7). Communal ownership was also seen as the primary solution to the problem of pauperism that was due to underconsumption and cycles.[63]

First, in the system envisaged – and as with the Marx–Engels version – the individual's claim to income would uniquely reflect his labor contribution, with allowance made for differential strength and skill (Rodbertus 1971 [1851]: 79–80). Second, and more specifically, the wage payment would be made by means of labor certificates "attesting to the time expended," which would be used to redeem consumer goods – priced according to labor input – "from the storehouses of the State" (83). Here Rodbertus attaches a note identifying the principle according to which, assuming communal ownership of capital and land, "the value of every product would be determined by the time expended on its production" with "the constituted value of Proudhon." However, he is careful to add this: "I must permit myself to remark that the idea of the constituted value was advanced by me before Proudhon, and that the papers in my work *Zur Erkenntniss*... contain nothing but the preliminary investigations necessary for the development of that idea" (83n.).

Third, responsibility for the direction of production would fall to a "public authority"(Rodbertus 1971 [1851]: 80).[64] This is contrasted with the capitalist-exchange system wherein the "sale or exchange of products" – and the production process in general – is "effected through the medium of money":

[U]nder present conditions where the national property is, by the institution of land and capital ownership, divided up among private owners, *the interest of these owners* takes the place of such an authority; these owners likewise applying those parts of the national property which now belong to them, to the production of things intended to meet the needs of society.... [Under these conditions] in place of such an order [of the public authority] there necessarily intervene, besides the like economic work of transportation, also the *legal business of the sale or exchange of products*, trade and with it money; so that to-day the movement of national production, from beginning to end,

---

[63] Eduard Bernstein correctly perceived that Marx's statement in *Capital* 3 (composed 1864–5) regarding "[t]he ultimate reason for all real crises" – that it "always remains the poverty and restricted consumption of the masses as opposed to the drive of capitalist production to develop the productive forces as though only the absolute consuming power of society constituted their limit" (MECW 37: 483) – had in common with Rodbertus's approach that crises are "caused not simply by underconsumption by the masses but by this in conjunction with the rising productivity of labour" (Bernstein 1993 [1899]: 81). How far Marx actually stood by this formulation is discussed in Hollander (2008: 145–50).

[64] There is also the authority's responsibility for public goods – "to satisfy the needs arising through the existence of society as such" (1971 [1851]: 87). Finally, the authority would be responsible for capital maintenance, taking care "that one part of the national production should always be devoted to replacing the capital which has been consumed or impaired in the process of production, and only the remaining portion be used for producing the national income, *i.e.*, the products required to satisfy social needs" (82).

i.e., from the first stroke of work applied to the raw material up to the completion of the product, is carried on by a series of property transfers effected through the medium of money. (80–1)

The implication of this last passage is that a fully functioning *money* such as circulates in the capitalist-exchange system is irrelevant for the control system envisaged by Rodbertus. The labor certificates would not circulate but only fulfill a cloakroom function. It is also certainly Rodbertus's position that the public authority selects the bill of goods to be produced – that it "direct[s] the national production in accordance with national needs, or . . . regulate[s] the application of the national property in the most advantageous manner" (80) – at the labor prices imposed, which implies that little, if anything, is left to the (direct) revelation of consumer preferences; similarly, and with the same implication, retail outlets are operated by the authority.[65] To that extent, there is little that distinguishes the Rodbertus scheme from the Marx–Engels version.

There remains one further matter. Rodbertus refers in 1851 to the last paper in *Zur Erkenntniss* with respect to the details of the device of labor certificates constituting "receipts" for labor supplied and at the same time "drafts" entitling a claim for an equivalent amount of product (116n.). This note is attached to a passage concerning the hypothetical introduction into a capitalist-exchange system of labor certificates – "*[w]ere it possible . . . to determine the market value according to the quantity of labour which the products have cost*":

[G]old and silver perform the *office of money*, the conception of which is by no means that of a market commodity. The essence of money consists solely in its being a *certificate* of the market value which anyone has given away in his exchange-product, and which, in turn, he can realize as a *draft upon just the same amount of market value*. *Were it possible, therefore, to determine the market value according to the quantity of labour which the products have cost*, a money could be introduced which would answer perfectly to its conception. It would consist of strips of paper, which would constitute accurate *receipts* for the quantity of labour which each one had in trade delivered in his products, and therefore also *drafts* entitling him to obtain in trade the same quantity in return. (115–16)

But the 1842 analysis explicitly excludes the possibility that prices correspond to values in a capitalist-exchange system (above, p. 168).[66] The labor-certificate system applies, therefore, solely to a fully reconstituted system, and the irrelevance

---

[65] See on this matter Gide and Rist: "[A]fter 1837 [*Forderungen*] we find Rodbertus proposing the substitution of a system of State direction for the system of natural liberty, and his whole work is an attempt to justify the introduction of such a system," including the proposal "to set up production for social need as a substitute for production for demand" (1964 [1915]: 421).

[66] We have seen in Chapter Two, p. 98, that Rodbertus assumed a tendency to profit-rate uniformity characterized by an equality of prices and values, thereby implying identical capital–labor ratios throughout. The passage now under discussion in effect relaxes this latter implication.

of Engels's charge that Rodbertus countenanced "exploitation" in his contributions of 1842 and 1851 is confirmed.

* * *

At this point we may refer to an editorial note attached to the third (1883) German edition of *Capital,* where Engels complains that Rodbertus had reverted to "ideological commonplaces" when he opined in a late letter (published posthumously in 1881) that because "we still know no other social organization," he proposed treatment of "the acts of the industrial capitalist as economic and political functions, that have been delegated to him with his capital," and profits as "a form of salary" subject to *regulation,* and specifically as returns that "may be reduced if they take too much from wages" (MECW 35: 532n.). It does indeed appear that Rodbertus turned away from the earlier case for the abolition of private property in capital and land: "[R]ecoil[ing] from his own solution...the ardent socialist becomes a simple State Socialist," is how Gide and Rist expressed the matter (1964 [1915]: 429). We thus encounter in *Der Normal-Arbeitstag* (1871) the proposal for the state issue of labor tickets to private entrepreneurs to be distributed appropriately (430), which Rodbertus had mentioned earlier but only as an unacceptable hypothesis.[67] It is this later perspective that Engels imposes on the early Rodbertus.[68]

---

[67] Citations by Böhm-Bawerk from *Zur Erklärung* (Rodbertus 1868–9) also indicate that "notwithstanding the very severe theoretical judgment that he pronounces on profit in describing it as plunder, Rodbertus will not hear of abolishing either private property in capital or profit on capital" (Böhm-Bawerk 1890: 336). However, some of the evidence for Rodbertus's "later" position is already found in *Das Kapital* in 1852, published posthumously (1884 [1852]: 176, 187, cited in Gide and Rist 1964 [1915]: 429).

[68] *Der Normal-Arbeitstag* (1871) is described by Engels as Rodbertus's "social testament" ("Marx and Rodbertus," MECW 26: 283). Gonner made the point that Rodbertus sought in 1871 "the practical means whereby he hoped society might be secured and labour safeguarded in the enjoyment of its due without any radical subversion of the present system" (1899: 202).

Rodbertus had apparently abandoned (or forgotten) his earlier objection that deviations of prices from values in an enterprise system rendered irrelevant the ticket scheme based on values proposed for such a system. Nonetheless, he may not have turned his back entirely on the original radical proposal for the abolition of private ownership, but merely sought a provisional "compromise." This is indicated in the posthumously published *Das Kapital* (1852): "And so I believe that just as history is nothing but a series of compromises, the first problem that awaits economic science at the present moment is that of effecting some kind of a working compromise between labour, capital and property" (cited in Gide and Rist 1964 [1915]: 430n.). Similarly, in correspondence with R. Meyer of 18 September 1873, he wrote that the great problem "is to help us to pass by a peaceful evolution from our present system, which is based upon private property in land and capital, to that superior social order which must succeed it in the natural course of history, which will be based upon desert and the mere ownership of income, and which is already showing itself in various aspects of social life, as if it were already on the point of coming into operation" (430n.).

On the provisional character of Rodbertus's "compromise," see Menger (1962 [1899]: 89–90). Menger points out that "[e]ventually...[Rodbertus] believed that private ownership of land and capital would die out [citing *Das Kapital* 1884 (1852): 219, 221], and he himself gave in his posthumous work on capital a sketch of his proposals in the event of a communistic establishment [136–60]."

J. Historiographical Objections to Rodbertus's "Utopia"

We encounter in the context of socialist application the same insistence by Engels on Rodbertus's unoriginality, coupled with a rejection of the charge of plagiarism against Marx, encountered in Chapter Two with respect to the technicalities of surplus value. The Preface to the 1885 edition of *Poverty of Philosophy* provides a convenient entry into the topic.

Engels points to a note by Marx in *A Contribution to the Critique of Political Economy* attached to a statement of the problem that if goods exchange according to labor input, then wages should absorb the entire product rather than fall short: "This objection, which was advanced against Ricardo by economists, was later taken up by socialists. Assuming that the formula was theoretically sound, they alleged that practice stood in conflict with the theory and demanded that bourgeois society should draw the practical conclusions supposedly arising from its theoretical principles. In this way at least English socialists [since 1821] turned Ricardo's formula of exchange value against political economy" (1859; MECW *29*: 301n., cited in Engels MECW *26*: 280–1). *Zur Erkenntniss* was at most a novelty in Germany but nowhere else: "If, therefore, in 1842, Rodbertus for his part drew socialist conclusions from the above propositions, that was certainly a very considerable step forward for a German at that time, but it could rank as a new discovery only for Germany at best" (279–80).

The allusion to 1821 (Engels, 279) is to the anonymous "Letter to Lord John Russell," so much admired by Marx. And "[t]hat such an application of the Ricardian theory was far from new," Engels continued, was further proved by Marx in 1847 against Proudhon, "who suffered from a similar conceit" (280), considering socialist applications of Ricardian theory by, inter alia, Hodgskin (1827), Thompson (1824), and Edmonds (1828); and by Bray (1839).[69] Engels also refers readers to Marx's treatment in 1859 (MECW *29*: 320–3) of "the *first* labour money exchange utopia" devised by John Gray in 1831 (291). Only someone infected by "Prussian local bigotry" could have been unaware of this socialist literature (280). Furthermore, Marx's *Zur Kritik* of 1859 had been published in Berlin, so Rodbertus had even less excuse when he made a claim to originality and charged Marx with plagiarism: "Rodbertus, therefore, had sufficient opportunity of convincing himself whether his discoveries of 1842 were really new. Instead, he proclaims them again and again and regards them as so incomparable that it never occurs to him that Marx might have drawn his conclusions from Ricardo independently, just as well as Rodbertus himself. Absolutely impossible! Marx had 'plundered' him" (281).[70] Furthermore, earlier "utopian" schemes had not only been "theoretically propagated" but actually "tried in practice" in England in the thirties – presumably an allusion to Owen; and yet Rodbertus in 1842 and again in 1871 – as well as Proudhon in 1846 – and the "horde of careerists who in the name of Rodbertus set

---

[69] See also Chapter One, p. 76 and above p. 142 on the English Socialists.
[70] For Rodbertus's charge of plagiarism, see Prolegomena, note 8.

out to exploit Prussian state socialism" – all claimed his work "as the latest truth" (283).[71]

Engels tries to be fair. He reiterates that Rodbertus's work of 1842 was an achievement, if limited to Germany: "For the time when Rodbertus' *Zur Erkenntniss*, etc., appeared, it was certainly an important book. His development of Ricardo's theory of value in that one direction was a very promising beginning. Even if it was new only for him and for Germany, still as a whole, it stands on a par with the achievements of the better ones among his English predecessors (290).[72] Rodbertus, however, had made no technical breakthrough in the manner of Marx – turning rather to "utopia-building," a matter addressed in Chapter Two (p. 102) – Engels alluding in particular to an alleged failure to appreciate the nature of surplus value: "Rodbertus, who is otherwise always ready, whether rightly or not, to adopt the national standpoint and to survey the relations of individual producers from the high watchtower of general social considerations, is anxious to avoid doing so here," with respect to the question of the character of "labor," and this, Engels opines, "because any investigation of labour seen from its property of creating value would be bound to put insuperable obstacles in his way" (285).

K. Concluding Remarks

Engels's exposition of the allocative role of the competitive price mechanism is impressive (above, pp. 126–7, 136–7). We have suggested that his complaint regarding Rodbertus's neglect of the operation of that mechanism in his ideal labor-ticket system would apply to a lesser extent to his own control system, which precluded free consumer choice (p. 151). Nonetheless, there remains the naïve belief that the planners are capable of making accurate estimates of labor inputs required, the distribution of labor tickets according to pay differentials, and the corresponding consumption quotas – that all this could be achieved, as Engels thought, "very simply" (above, p. 147). But in point of fact, the planning task he himself envisaged is rather more complex, for planners would have to make allowance in their cost calculations, as shadow or accounting returns, for interest and rent based on the estimated productivity contribution of land and capital and not only for labor (above, pp. 142–3).[73] Engels, it emerges, may have had a deeper appreciation of the planning problem than Marx in this respect.

[71] The latter reference is to those responsible for the posthumous publication of Rodbertus's *Das Kapital* 1884, composed in 1852, preeminently Adolph Wagner. (See editorial note 146, MECW *26*: 648.)

[72] See also the letter to Kautsky of 17 October 1884 (cited above, note 62).

[73] Whether Marx stood by his early statement, in *Poverty of Philosophy*, that in communist society "use will no longer be determined by the *minimum* time of production" (see Chapter One, p. 70) is by no means certain; after all, his letter to Kugelmann, dated 11 July 1868, talks of a universal problem of achieving efficiency (see Chapter Seven, p. 319). In any event, though, Engels did not apparently accept the point in question (see Chapter One, pp. 31–2 and note 3, and above pp. 141–2 on his *Outlines*); and *Anti-Dühring* expresses continued concern with efficient allocation: "It will still be necessary for society to know how much labour each article of consumption requires for its production" (above, p. 147).

We have been unable to attribute to Engels a clear-cut position on international trading relations (above, p. 145 and note 30). Autarky is envisaged for agriculture, but its extension to industry as a whole may not have been countenanced. How the control system could be protected assuming an open economy remains an open question, but recall that Engels himself had raised an aspect of the issue when criticizing Dühring. The details of the proposed linkages between town and country, which go back to the 1840s and are restated in *The Housing Question* (above, note 29), are never properly clarified.

There remains a further consideration. Some explanation is called for to account for the failure on the part of both Engels and Marx to provide a concerted exposition of their vision of communist organization so that one is obliged to draw for information from a wide variety of statements, many of which criticize the schemes of others. Now we do find convincing rationalizations of the refusal to spell out formally the character of the final stage of communist society, rationalizations turning on the ever-unfolding historical process that could never be known in any detail (see, e.g., Foley 1986: 158–60; Sweezy 1987: 444–5; Maler 1998: 51). However, our concern throughout has been with the "first" stage of communism as it emerges out of capitalism. There is no doubt of their reticence in advertising their intentions, though both Marx and Engels provide considerably more detail of the scheme they envisaged for that stage than many critics suppose. For this reticence I am able to offer only tentative suggestions.

The sophistication of the evolutionary dimension describing, and to some extent accounting for, the transition from competitive to monopoly capitalism (see above, pp. 161–3) sits uncomfortably beside the simplicity of the plan for the first stage of communism, although the latter is supposed to emerge from the final stages of the former system. Indeed, its very simplicity renders it patently inappropriate for major economies such as England, France, Germany, and the United States, especially if international trading relations are taken into account. In brief, there is something of the "utopian" to their plan. Much the same point has been made by Rigby when he concludes that "Marx and Engels' communism came to suffer from the same weaknesses as the utopian socialism against which they had originally defined their own outlook" (1992: 207). Awareness of this deficiency may have encouraged the strategy of reticence, our heroes not totally convinced by their own scheme.[74]

See Pokorni (1993: 30–1), for an excellent account of some of the vageries of Marx's position, particularly with regard to the relevant time horizon to be adopted by the planning authority in arriving at investment versus consumption decisions, and to the determination of what constitues "social needs" or legitimate consumption. Bober denies that Marx perceived labor value as a guide to communist organization (1965: 285–8), but his case turns on the sense accorded the notion that "value" is no longer a relevant category (see above, p. 145).

[74] "Scientific" socialism – as Engels has it in *Socialism: Utopian and Scientific* – entails the interpretation of nonwage incomes under capitalism in terms of surplus value envisaged as unpaid labor and the perspective provided by the principles of historical materialism, but has little to do with the character of future communist arrangement.

There are doubtless other considerations. Note the expressions of concern in a circular letter written by Engels, and signed also by Marx, that concentration on the character of "the future social order" detracted from what is required for proper analysis of topical issues (17–18 September 1879; MECW 45: 400); this is reminiscent of Bernstein's concern (see Epilogue, pp. 346, 348). Furthermore, at the end of his life, Engels cautioned the French socialist party to avoid premature commitments, doubting in the case at hand whether it was "wise to promise 40 million annually to the peasants in a form and for a purpose so clearly defined. The peasants could one day present us with this promissory note, and at a time when we might have better uses for such a sum" (3 March 1895; MECW 50: 454; also see Chapter Four, p. 218).

In closing, let us return to the accuracy of Engels's account of Rodbertus. It has emerged that his criticisms turn out to have been inapplicable to Rodbertus's scheme, in its early formulations of 1842 and 1851 and for precisely the same reason that it is inapplicable to his own. The two control systems are very similar, and Engels's efforts to distinguish them are unconvincing. By the same token, regarding deductions from national product before consumption allowances can be considered, it is difficult to appreciate his objection that Rodbertus in 1842 "refers the whole matter to the decision of the bureaucracy" (above, p. 136 and note 14), as if this were not true of his own scheme. Also irrelevant is the charge against Rodbertus that, in his 1842 and 1851 contributions, he countenanced retention of an "exploitative" system by recommending the distribution of tickets by the central authority to "industrial capitalists with which the latter pay the workers" (p. 134). The ticket system in Rodbertus's earlier writings was inapplicable in a capitalist-exchange environment.

Beyond this, although Engels's representation of Rodbertus as reverting late in the day to "ideological commonplaces" (above, p. 171) may be valid, the charge can be returned to the sender. After all, Engels (like Marx) himself took a cautious, evolutionary, stance toward the demise of capitalism, countenancing the toleration of a capitalist sector even after a political take-over by the proletariat, and this for an undefined intermediate period (pp. 165–6). This takes us directly to Engels's "revisionism," to be explored in the two chapters that follow.

FOUR

"Revisionism" I. Constitutional Reform
versus Revolution

A. Introduction

The general context for this chapter was set out in the Prolegomena, and I can proceed to substance. I focus in Section B on *The Condition of the Working Class in England* (1845), where Engels expresses the likelihood of violent revolution at the next cyclical crisis – notwithstanding an expectation that the Chartists' demands for an extended franchise would be met – with some hope that the communists might restrain the violence. Other statements are ambiguous regarding the manner of achievement of proletarian rule, but by 1847–8 the prospect of a successful constitutional outcome is viewed seriously, while the important *Principles of Communism* (1847) advises the prospective proletarian majority to undertake the dismantling of the private-property system. The realization of "democracy" by constitutional means had already occurred in the eastern states of the United States, whereas government intransigence rendered the prospect less promising in France.

Much the same picture emerges from Marx's *Poverty of Philosophy* of 1847, where union activity combined with Chartist political activity is championed; and a Marx paper of October 1847 elaborates the achievement by constitutional means of "political equality" in the eastern United States. The joint *Communist Manifesto* itself justifies communist support for constitutional reform measures and calls for cooperation between the bourgeoisie and the proletariat.

Section C principally concerns Marx's *The Class Struggles in France 1848–1850*, which expresses disappointment at the failure of the June 1848 uprising. Though Marx continued to countenance cooperation with a variety of reformers, he rejected their claims that a "revolutionary collision" could be avoided in France, pointing to the intransigence of the ruling classes as evidenced by their withdrawal of the universal-suffrage provisions instituted earlier. By contrast, papers by both Marx and Engels in 1850 and 1852 reveal their continued confidence in meaningful progress toward universal suffrage in Britain as a result of Chartist agitation.

Materials dating to the 1860s and an anti-Proudhon paper of 1873, considered in Section D, remove any remaining doubt regarding Marx's appreciation of major progress on the constitutional front in Britain – "Insurrection would be madness when peaceful agitation would more swiftly and surely do the work" – Germany, and the United States. Surprisingly, considering the events of 1870 and their aftermath, Marx even envisaged the possibility that British experience would be repeated in France. All this comes to a head in May 1880 in a striking endorsement of the potential for effective constitutional reform extending to the achievement by means of universal suffrage of collective ownership of the means of production.

As I show in Section E, Engels followed the same line to some extent in *The Housing Question* of 1872 and in a marked manner in articles of 1874 and thereafter. Section F places his 1895 Introduction to *The Class Struggles in France* in perspective. It must be seen as part of a continuum, wholly in line with Marx, extending back to the 1840s. This takes us to qualifications to Engels's revisionism in Sections G and H.

B. Evidence from the 1840s: Chartism and Constitutional Reform

In a newspaper article of November 1842, Engels opined that "the middle class will never renounce its occupation of the House of Commons by agreeing to universal suffrage" – a main plank of the Chartist program[1] "since it would immediately be outvoted by the huge number of unpropertied ... " ("The English View of the Internal Crisis"; MECW 2: 368). There was a possibility that, with time, Chartism might gain some hold "among educated people," but this prospect could not be taken seriously because the middle class was devoted to "the preservation of the *status quo*; in England's present condition, 'legal progress' and universal suffrage would inevitably result in a revolution" (369). Within very few years the prospect came to be viewed differently.

The Holy Family – formally a joint production but largely by Marx – represents the Chartist movement as "the political expression of public opinion among the workers" (1844–5; MECW 4: 15). We must keep in mind this supportive position when we approach *The Condition of the Working Class*, where Engels makes it very clear that the achievement of the Six Points of the Charter would ensure a democratic political structure and "proletarian law," thereby at least implying a first step in the transformation of society:

Since the working-men do not respect the law, but simply submit to its power when they cannot change it, it is most natural that they should at least propose alterations in it, that they should wish to put a proletarian law in the place of the legal fabric of the

---

[1] The *People's Charter*, published on 8 May 1838, consisted of six clauses: universal suffrage for men at twenty-one years of age, annual elections to Parliament, secret ballot, equal constituencies, abolition of property qualifications for candidates, and salaries for members. Petitions for the Charter were rejected by Parliament in 1839 and 1842, and in 1847–8 the Chartists renewed a mass campaign, on which see Saville (1987, 1994: Chapter 6).

bourgeoisie. This proposed law is the People's Charter, which in form is purely political, and demands a democratic basis for the House of Commons. Chartism is the compact form of their opposition to the bourgeoisie. In the Unions and turnouts opposition always remained isolated: it was single working-men or sections who fought a single bourgeois. . . . But in Chartism it is the whole working-class which arises against the bourgeoisie, and attacks, first of all, the political power, the legislative rampart with which the bourgeoisie has surrounded itself. . . . These six points, which are all limited to the reconstitution of the House of Commons, are sufficient to overthrow the whole English Constitution, Queen and Lords included. (1845; MECW 4: 517–18)[2]

Furthermore, following Engels's exposition of a worsening of the cyclical pattern and increasing bifurcation of income distribution between an expanding proletariat and "a few millionaires" (see Chapter 1, p. 57), we find a prediction of the adoption of the Chartists' demands and a proletarian majority in Parliament by constitutional means with an uncertain "revolutionary" sequel: "The commercial crises, the mightiest levers for all independent development of the proletariat, will probably shorten the process [of social transformation], acting in concert with foreign competition and the deepening ruin of the lower middle-class. I think the people will not endure more than one more crisis. The next one, in 1846 or 1847, will probably bring with it the repeal of the Corn Laws [1887: and it did] and the enactment of the Charter. What revolutionary movements the Charter may give rise to remains to be seen" (580–1).

Engels proceeds immediately to speculate that the crisis expected in 1852–3, assuming the standard pattern, would signal "revolution" and this apparently of a violent nature:

But, by the time of the next following crisis, which, according to the analogy of its predecessors, must break out in 1852 or 1853, unless delayed perhaps by the repeal of the Corn Laws or hastened by other influences, such as foreign competition – by the time this crisis arrives, the English people will have had enough of being plundered by the capitalists and left to starve when the capitalists no longer require their services. If, up to that time, the English bourgeoisie does not pause to reflect – and to all appearance it certainly will not do so – a revolution will follow with which none hitherto known can be compared (MECW 4: 581).[3]

---

[2] Drawing on this passage, Saville rightly observes that although "[t]he acceptance of parliamentarianism was unquestioned" even by radical representatives of the Chartists, nevertheless the movement "took it for granted, without being at all precise in elaboration, that the achievement of the six points – the democratization of the political structure – would be the first major step towards a new kind of political structure" (1987: 213–14). On the political organization of the working class from the perspective of Chartism in various Engels and Marx texts, see Ryazanoff (1930 [1922]: 116–18).

[3] Elsewhere in the same document Engels opines that Corn Law repeal, by extending the rule of "free competition," would necessitate (rather than delay) a "radical transformation of the social order": "Like the operatives, the agricultural labourers are thoroughly indifferent to the repeal or non-repeal of the Corn Laws. Yet the question is an important one for both. That is to say – by the repeal of the Corn Laws, free competition, the present social economy is carried to its extreme point; all further development within the present order comes to an end, and the only possible step farther is a radical transformation of the social order" (MECW 4: 555). In the 1887 edition, he adds a note: "This has been literally fulfilled. After a period

Although the concessions by the bourgeoisie intended by the foregoing warning are not spelled out, presumably they extend beyond mere enactment of the Charter, which was envisaged as occurring in 1846–7. In any event, Engels adds that "[e]ven the union of a part of the bourgeoisie with the proletariat, even a general reform of the bourgeoisie, would not help matters," because any such reform could at best only be "lukewarm." "The prejudices of a whole class cannot be laid aside like an old coat: least of all, those of the stable, narrow, selfish English bourgeoisie. These are all inferences which may be drawn with the greatest certainty: conclusions, the premises for which are undeniable facts, partly of historical development, partly facts inherent in human nature. Prophecy is nowhere so easy as in England, where all the component elements of society are clearly defined and sharply separated."[4] Apparently, even proletarian control of Parliament would not suffice to prevent a "war of the poor against the rich" which, "now carried on in detail and indirectly, will become direct and universal. It is too late for a peaceful solution. The classes are divided more and more sharply, the spirit of resistance penetrates the workers, the bitterness intensifies, the guerilla skirmishes become concentrated in more important battles, and soon a slight impulse will suffice to set the avalanche in motion. Then, indeed, will the war-cry resound through the land: 'War to the mansion, peace to the cottage!'– but then it will be too late for the rich to beware" (582–3).

For all that, Engels expressed himself strongly against gratuitous violence: "The revolution must come; it is already too late to bring about a peaceful solution; but it can be made more gently than that prophesied in the foregoing pages. This depends, however, more upon the development of the proletariat than upon that of the bourgeoisie. In proportion, as the proletariat absorbs socialistic and communistic elements, will the revolution diminish in bloodshed, revenge and savagery" (MECW 4: 581). He envisaged the communists exerting a moderating influence:

Communism is a question of humanity and not of the workers alone. Besides, it does not occur to any Communist to wish to revenge himself upon individuals, or to believe that, in general, the single bourgeois can act otherwise, under existing circumstances, than he does act. English Socialism, i.e., Communism, rests directly upon the irresponsibility of the individual. Thus the more the English workers absorb communistic ideas, the more superfluous becomes their present bitterness, which, should it continue so violent as at present, could accomplish nothing; and the more their action against the bourgeoisie

of unexampled extension of trade, Free Trade has landed England in a crisis, which began in 1878, and is still increasing in energy in 1886."

   Whereas Engels refers in 1845 to the "indifference" of labor (both agricultural and industrial) to Corn Law repeal, in *The Holy Family*, it is a matter of labor's positive hostility toward the Anti-Corn-Law League (1844–5; MECW 4: 15).

4   Engels had similarly accounted in 1843 for differences between French and English communism or socialism, the terms are used interchangeably, by reference to "the difference of the French and English national character and government" ("Progress of Social Reform on the Continent"; MECW 3: 398). The character difference favored a moderate outcome in the English case (397).

will lose its savage cruelty.... And as Communism stands above the strife between bourgeoisie and proletariat, it will be easier for the better elements of the bourgeoisie (which are, however, deplorably few, and can look for recruits only among the rising generation) to unite with it than with purely proletarian Chartism. (582)[5]

Thompson has written that "1848 was to see the third and final abortive effort to effect a substantial measure of political reform by way of petitioning Parliament and, in the aftermath of that failure, a number of Chartists" – preeminently J. B. O'Brien, Ernest Jones, and G. J. Harney – "came to believe that if Chartism was to be made a potent political force once again, it would be necessary to fuse Chartist demands with an economic programme clearly indicative of the kind of social transformation that might be effected once political power has been won" (Thompson 1998: 111). This program Thompson designates as "Chartist Socialism." However, he allows that an integration of Chartist political objectives with an anticapitalist political economy was, in some measure, already available prior to 1848 in the writing of O'Brien (112). Now *The Condition of the Working Class* of 1845 in fact itself perceives that the Chartist movement, following the repression of an "unintentional revolt" in 1842, was beginning to take on elements of a "Socialist" orientation: "The 'Six Points' which for the Radical bourgeois are the beginning and end of the matter, which are meant, at the utmost, to call forth certain further reforms of the Constitution, are for the proletarian a mere means to further ends.... There is no longer a mere politician among the Chartists, even though their Socialism is very little developed" (MECW 4: 522, 524). The document represents most of the leadership as "already Communist" (582).[6]

Mention should be made next of a marginal note by Engels to the joint *The German Ideology* (1845–6) alluding to the proletarian acquisition of "political power" as a first step toward total social transformation: "every class which is aiming at domination, even when its domination, as is the case with the proletariat, leads to the abolition of the old form of society in its entirety and of domination in general, must first conquer political power in order to represent its interest in turn as the general interest, which in the first moment it is forced to do" (MECW 5: 47).[7] There is no explicit commitment here to the particular means

---

[5] Engels's formulations also play down deliberate violence on the part of the Chartists during the "uprising" of 1842 (MECW 4: 522).

[6] The Chartist case for universal suffrage is said by Thompson to be "the wish to secure the means of affecting a fundamental shift in the balance of economic power in favour of labour" (Thompson 1998: 130). This formulation implies retention of the class system and its reform in favor of labor. Immediately thereafter, though, Thompson cites the aim as that of effecting "'THE ABOLITION OF CLASSES AND THE SOVEREIGNTY OF LABOUR.' This was what set it apart from almost all of what had gone before and that is what was truly significant in its legacy for the future." The contrast is essential in approaching the possible influence of Marx–Engels on Chartist policy prescription. (See note 21 for further information.)

[7] Rubel reports that Marx claimed fathering recognition of a stage between capitalism and socialism characterized by the "dictatorship of the proletariat" (Rubel 1968: cxxviii). Here, however, we have Engels responsible for such a period.

whereby political domination by the proletariat is to be initially achieved, though the constitutional option is not excluded. This issue is not Engels's main concern, which is rather to convey the message that the acquisition of power, however achieved, is but the means toward a higher end. Again, in late 1845, Engels made this declaration: "*Democracy nowadays is communism.* . . . Democracy has become the proletarian principle, the principle of the masses" (1846, "The Festival of Nations in London," MECW 6: 5). This declaration has been interpreted as indicating support for universal suffrage as a step toward the dictatorship of the proletariat and thence communism, with Engels expressing the position of the Communist Correspondence Committee that he had founded with Marx in Brussels (Hunt 2009: 134–5). This might well be the case, though the central message is rather that democracy "should not be understood simply in a political sense," for "social equality of rights is implicit in democracy" (MECW 6: 4–5), a principle holding good independent of the manner by which "democracy" is achieved.

In his "Draft of a Communist Confession of Faith" – the draft program discussed at the First Congress of the Communist League in London in June 1847 – Engels objected to "conspiracies" and to "deliberate and arbitrary" action based merely on "will" and "leadership," alluding to Blanqui's position; at the same time, he again opined that the intransigence of the propertied classes "in almost all countries" would probably force "the oppressed proletariat" to revolution:

Question 6: *How do you wish to prepare the way for your community of property?*
    Answer: By enlightening and uniting the proletariat.

Question 14: *Let us go back to the sixth question. As you wish to prepare for community of property by the enlightening and uniting of the proletariat, then you reject revolution?*
    Answer: We are convinced not only of the uselessness but even of the harmfulness of all conspiracies. We are also aware that revolutions are not made deliberately and arbitrarily but that everywhere and at all times they are the necessary consequences of circumstances which are not in any way whatever dependent either on the will or on the leadership of individual parties or of whole classes. But we also see that the development of the proletariat in almost all countries of the world is forcibly repressed by the possessing classes and thus a revolution is being forcibly worked for by the opponents of communism. If, in the end, the oppressed proletariat is thus driven into a revolution, then we will defend the cause of the proletariat just as well by our deeds as now by our words. (MECW 6: 96, 101–2)

This is not a statement of the *inevitability* of revolution in the literal sense even in the case of "almost all countries" and a fortiori in that of the unspecified exceptions, where a reform-minded bourgeoisie might conceivably render revolution unnecessary. It merely states a matter of likelihood.

Engels's answer to Question 16, "*How do you think the transition from the present situation to community of property is to be effected?*," is vague enough to cover all options: "The first, fundamental condition for the introduction of community of property is the political liberation of the proletariat through a democratic constitution" (MECW 6: 102). If this response assumes that the proletariat has taken at least provisional control by way of literal revolution, then the framing of a "democratic constitution" relates to the postrevolutionary period with the nature of the constitution left an open question, whether for example there would be allowed some representation by the bourgeoisie. But the inclusive response to Question 14 and the position adopted in 1845 suggest that by "political liberation" Engels may have intended the granting of a "democratic constitution," that is, of universal suffrage, by a reform-minded or fearful bourgeoisie, the granting of the Charter in effect.

Engels drew on his "confession" when composing the *Principles of Communism* in October 1847 – the basis for the *Communist Manifesto*. In answer to the question *"Will it be possible to bring about the abolition of private property by peaceful methods?"* (MECW 6: 349), he goes so far as to assert that "[i]t is to be desired that this could happen, and Communists certainly would be the last to resist it"; in contrast, "they also see that the development of the proletariat is in nearly every civilised country forcibly suppressed, and that thus the opponents of the Communists are working with all their might towards a revolution." A reform-minded bourgeoisie thus might make revolution in the literal sense unnecessary. It is true that Engels had just rehearsed the theme that the industrialization process generates the numbers, the concentration, and thus the power of the proletariat, along with growing discontent in consequence of labor-displacing machinery and the "depress[ion] of wages to their minimum," to "prepar[e] a social revolution by the proletariat" (346), but this does not necessarily preclude the achievement of political control by constitutional means. Similarly, the negative answer given to Question 17, *"Will it be possible to abolish private property at one stroke?,"* does not rule out that the "impending revolution," to which Engels also refers, relates to establishment of proletarian control by way of the ballot box, the new authority then setting in motion the gradual dismantling of the private-property system: "No, such a thing would be just as impossible as at *one* stroke to increase the existing productive forces to the degree necessary for instituting community of property. Hence, the proletarian revolution, which in all probability is impending, will transform existing society only gradually, and be able to abolish private property only when the necessary quantity of the means of production has been created" (350).[8]

The prospect of violence expressed in *The Condition of the Working Class* – and this notwithstanding the granting of the Charter – seems now to be moderated. Engels's response to Question 18, *"What will be the course of this revolution?"* (it provides the October counterpart to Question 16 in June), similarly suggests acquisition of proletarian power by way of universal suffrage (as in 1845), at least

---

[8]   The *Communist Manifesto* and the *Principles of Communism* upon which it is based both assume *proletarian control* or "democracy" and outline the measures to be undertaken, including reduction of the private sector; i.e., it is relevant to a stage preceding fully fledged public ownership and central control.

in the British case. Once again, though, it cannot be positively precluded that "the political rule of the proletariat" is perceived as resulting from literal revolution:

Answer: In the first place it will inaugurate a *democratic constitution* and thereby, directly or indirectly, the political rule of the proletariat. Directly in England, where the proletariat already constitutes the majority of the people. Indirectly in France and in Germany, where the majority of the people consists not only of proletarians but also of small peasants and urban petty bourgeois, who are only now being proletarianised and in all their political interests are becoming more and more dependent on the proletariat and therefore soon will have to conform to the demands of the proletariat (MECW 6: 350).

What follows in the *Principles of Communism* clarifies Engels's position on the manner of transition to proletarian control. In answer to Question 24, "*In what way do Communists differ from socialists?*," Engels expressed the willingness of "genuine" communists to cooperate with "democratic socialists" who "in the same way as the Communists desire part of the measures listed in Question [18],"[9] albeit not "as a means of transition to communism but as measures sufficient to abolish the misery of present society and to cause its evils to disappear. These *democratic socialists* are either proletarians who are not yet sufficiently enlightened regarding the conditions of the emancipation of their class, or they are members of the petty bourgeoisie, a class which, until the winning of democracy and the realisation of the socialist measures following upon it, has in many respects the same interest as the proletariat" (MECW 6: 355–6). Consistently with the view taken in *The Condition of the Working Class* of the Chartist masses as believing in some form of embryonic socialism (above, p. 180), the Chartists – categorized as "democratic socialists" – "who are all workers," are said to be "incalculably nearer to the Communists than are the democratic petty bourgeois or so-called radicals" (356). There no hint in all this of the prospect, or desirability, of violent revolution in the achievement of proletarian control.

Engels's positive response to the election to Parliament of Feargus O'Connor (though himself no socialist) further confirms that his support for cooperation with the Chartists in the light of their commendable orientation toward "political economy" in no way detracted from his support of their political program as encapsulated in the Six Points: "You will judge for yourselves to whom French democracy ought to give its sympathy; to the Chartists, sincere democrats without ulterior motives, or to the radical bourgeois who so carefully avoid using the

---

[9] The "measures" referred to in the response to Question 18 (MECW 6: 350–1) are almost identical to the *Communist Manifesto* proposals. In his earlier draft of the *Principles*, Engels specifies as the "first measure" after "democracy" had been established, the "[g]uaranteeing [of] the subsistence of the proletariat," which would be achieved "I. By limiting private property in such a way that it gradually prepares the way for its transformation into social property, e.g., by progressive taxation, limitation of the right of inheritance in favour of the state, etc., etc. II. By employing workers in national workshops and factories and on national estates. III. By educating all children at the expense of the state" (MECW 6: 102).

words *people's charter, universal suffrage*, and limit themselves to proclaiming that they are partisans of *complete suffrage!*" – a meaningless generalisation designed to detract workers from the specific demands of the Charter ("The Chartist Banquet," November 1847; MECW 6: 361).[10] Again: "The opening of the recently elected Parliament that counts among its members distinguished representatives of the People's Party could not but produce extraordinary excitement in the ranks of democracy" ("The Chartist Movement," November 1847; 383). Furthermore, Engels reports favorably a resolution of The Society of Fraternal Democrats to support the Chartist agitation: "the English people will be unable effectively to support democracy's struggle in other countries until it has won democratic government for itself" so that "our society, established to succour the militant democracy of every country, is duty-bound to come to the aid of the English democrats in their effort to obtain an electoral reform on the basis of the Charter" (384).

The ambiguity of several earlier texts has now dissipated with the prospect of proletarian control achieved constitutionally enhanced by the course of events. But a word of caution is advised. Although the main object of the Chartist movement was Parliamentary reform, "agitation" toward that end was not always peaceful or legal, as a convenient chronological table of events prepared in 1886 spells out (MECW 26: 566–77).[11] Engels's sympathies are clear, but whether the Charter "be carried by physical or moral force," as he expressed it retrospectively in 1885 – doubtless having in mind here the Chartist slogan "peaceably if we may, forcibly if we must" – is not the major issue, which is rather the principle of constitutional change to enlarge the electorate: "The working masses of the towns demanded their share of political power – the People's Charter; they were supported by the majority of the small trading class, and the only difference between the two was whether the Charter should be carried by physical or by moral force" ("England in 1845 and in 1885," *The Commonweal*, March 1885; MECW 26: 295).

The Parliamentary route again emerges in the support for Harney's position favoring universal suffrage brought about largely by proletarian effort, for Engels mistrusted bourgeois reformers whose proposals were designed to detract the working class from its primary objective – majority rule – and the subsequent reforms that would inevitably follow: "Were they desirous, as they profess to be, of promoting your welfare, they would aid you to obtain sovereign power" by supporting the People's Charter. "They well know that if you controlled the

---

[10] For a vignette of O'Connor as Chartist leader, see Saville (1987: 212–13, 215).

[11] Engels, soon after arriving in England in 1842, became friendly with George Julian Harney, described as being at that time "a Jacobin in an English setting" (Saville 1987: 56). Harney is also cited as calling in 1848 on Englishmen to "at once set about the work – peacefully and legally – of struggling for their Charter" (79). Be that as it may, in *The Condition of the Working Class* Engels had referred to the disturbances of August 1842 as an "unintentional revolt" (MECW 4: 522). Further, his "Chartist Agitation," written at the time of the 1847 disturbances, refers to wholly legal protest meetings and petitions, one of which extended to moderate land reform (MECW 6: 412–14). J. S. Mill too played down the violent element in the Chartist demonstrations of April 1848 ("England and Ireland," Mill 1963–91 [1848b] 25: 1099).

legislature, all the reforms they seek – and reforms of much greater importance – would be forthwith effected. How then can they call themselves your friends, while refusing you the suffrage?" ("The Chartist Movement," January 1848; MECW 6: 466). Universal suffrage attained constitutionally within capitalist arrangement would, as is by now a standard theme, be an insufficient achievement, the first step only on the road to "very definite" social reform.[12]

Engels reiterated at this time (in a joint paper with Marx) that "[o]f all countries, England is the one where the contradiction between the proletariat and the bourgeoisie is most highly developed" ("On Poland," December 1847; MECW 6: 389). Further, "the first decisive blow which will lead to the victory of democracy, to the liberation of all European nations, will be struck by the English Chartists," precisely because it is in England that the class struggle is the most intense – a standard application of the principle of historical materialism whereby modern industry and use of machinery creates "a single great class with common interests, the class of the proletariat" and sets it face to face against "a single class, the bourgeoisie"; for the aristocracy having lost power in England the "struggle" was "simplified" to the extent that "it will be possible to decide it by one single heavy blow."[13] Now by

[12] See also a comment of November 1847 touching on the French press: "Of all Parisian daily papers, there is . . . but one which will not be satisfied with anything less than Universal Suffrage, and which, by the term 'Republic,' understands not merely 'Political Reforms,' which will, after all, leave the working classes as miserable as before – but Social Reforms, and very definite ones too. This paper is the *Réforme*" ("The Reform Movement in France," MECW 6: 380). Similarly, "the enemy once beaten, they must establish measures that will guarantee the stability of their conquest; that will destroy not only the political, but the social power of capital, that will guarantee their social welfare, along with their political strength" (381). On Engels's contributions at this time to the socialist press, see Saville (1987: 57).

[13] This formulation may perhaps be understood as recognition of the possibility of arriving at socialism in one country. This is unlikely, though, for Engels adds that "not only in England; in all other countries [machinery] has had the same effect on the workers. In Belgium, in America, in France, in Germany, it has evened out the position of all workers and daily continues to do so more and more; in all these countries the workers now have the same interest, which is the overthrow of the class that oppresses them – the bourgeoisie. . . . Because the condition of the workers of all countries is the same, because their interests are the same, their enemies the same, they must also fight together, they must oppose the brotherhood of the bourgeoisie of all nations with a brotherhood of the workers of all nations" (MECW 6: 390). A little earlier Engels had expressed a similar view of proletarian internationalism, arguing that although "[t]he fantasies about a European Republic, perpetual peace under political organisation, have become just as ridiculous as the phrases about uniting the nations under the aegis of universal free trade . . . the proletarians of all nations, without too much ceremony, are already *really* beginning *to fraternise* under the banner of communist democracy," and this because in contrast with the bourgeoisie "the proletarians in all countries have one and the same interest, one and the same enemy, and one and the same struggle. The great mass of the proletarians are, by their very nature, free from national prejudices and their whole disposition and movement is essentially humanitarian, anti-nationalist. Only the proletarians can destroy nationality, only the awakening proletariat can bring about fraternisation between the different nations" (1846, "The Festival of Nations in London"; MECW 6: 6). See also the joint "Address of the Central Authority to the League of Communists," March 1850, MECW *10*: 281 (cited below, p. 221).

this – or by the "first decisive blow which will lead to the victory of democracy" – is intended nothing more than the achievement of a majority in Parliament by way of the franchise. That the "struggle" would be decided by "one single heavy blow" refers to the circumstance that the proletariat faces the bourgeoisie with no third party – the aristocracy – to complicate matters. It is not a reference to revolution in the literal sense.

America had advanced yet further than England in one respect, for there "a democratic constitution has been introduced" (*Principles of Communism*; MECW 6: 356). The Communists were advised to cooperate "with the party that will turn this constitution against the bourgeoisie and use it in the interest of the proletariat, that is, with the national agrarian reformers." As for Germany, where "the decisive struggle between the bourgeoisie and the absolute monarchy is still to come," and "Communists cannot count on the decisive struggle between themselves and the bourgeoisie until the bourgeoisie rules," a strategy of temporary accommodation with the industrial or liberal bourgeoisie is recommended, though "they must ever be on their guard" not to lose sight of the ultimate goal. An article of September 1847 accords the democratic press in Germany the task of showing "the inadequacy of the constitutional system that brings the bourgeoisie to the helm" since "the conquest of political power by the proletarians, small peasants and urban petty bourgeoisie is the first condition for the application of [the] means" whereby "social oppression . . . can be eliminated" ("The Communists and Karl Heinzen"; MECW 6: 294). It also recommends that the democratic press examine "the extent to which a rapid realisation of democracy may be expected, what resources the [Communist] party can command and what other parties it must ally itself with as long as it is too weak to act alone."

All this points to conquest of political power by the proletariat by means of the ballot box; only the rapidity of its achievement was in question in the German case. That "democracy" would be achieved by constitutional means – in "all civilised countries," be it noted – after which the communist program could be put into practice, is unambiguously confirmed thus:

Far from starting futile quarrels with the democrats, in the present circumstances, the Communists for the time being rather take the field as democrats themselves in all practical party matters. In all civilised countries, democracy has as its necessary consequence the political rule of the proletariat, and the political rule of the proletariat is the first condition for all communist measures. . . . Indeed, understandings will be possible concerning many measures which are to be carried out in the interests of the previously oppressed classes immediately after democracy has been achieved, e.g., the running of large-scale industry and the railways by the state, the education of all children at state expense, etc. (MECW 6: 299)

In the French case, Engels refers to the great promise of the democratic reform movement that had the British model at hand: "May democrats of all lands follow the same example! Everywhere democracy marches forward. In France, banquet follows banquet in favour of electoral reform; and the movement is developing on such a scale that it must lead to a happy result" ("The Chartist Banquet," November 1847; MECW 6: 363). However, while reiterating his support for French parliamentary reform, Engels distinguished – as always – between genuine democrats (even if not proletarian), who championed fully fledged universal suffrage, and "treacherous" middle-class reformers, who paid lip service only to parliamentary reform ("Split in the Camp," November 1847; 385–7). These bourgeois radicals "would under certain circumstances, and with certain restrictions, perhaps, consent to give the people the suffrage; but let them never think of profiting by the gift by passing measures which would essentially alter the actual mode of production and distribution of wealth – which would, in course of time, give to the entire people the command of the productive powers of the country, and do away with all individual 'employers'!" ("The 'Satisfied' Majority," January 1848; 440–1). Here Engels insists once again that universal suffrage, achieved constitutionally, would still be a first step only in a process toward the ultimate transition from the private-property system.

To Engels's delight and surprise, the workers participated in the street fighting that broke out in February 1848 directed by the bourgeoisie against the Guizot government and in favor of "reform" ("Revolution in Paris," February 1848; MECW 6: 558). Engels in fact attributed to proletarian action the collapse of the monarchy that followed, which opened the road to "the age of democracy." France, however, was rather a special case, for there "the situation is more sharply defined, more revolutionary than elsewhere" ("The Movements of 1847," January 1848; 527). In any event, even in France the February violence was not directed at the overthrow of the bourgeoisie. The declaration that follows regarding the British and American working classes as in "open revolution rebellion against the ruling bourgeoisie" is mere rhetoric:

[The bourgeois] really believe that they are working on their own behalf! They are so short-sighted as to fancy that through their triumph the world will assume its final configuration. Yet nothing is more clear, than that they are everywhere preparing the way for *us*, for the democrats and the Communists; than that they will at most win a few years of troubled enjoyment, only to be then immediately overthrown. Behind them stands everywhere the proletariat, sometimes participating in their endeavours and partly in their illusions, as in Italy and Switzerland, sometimes silent and reserved, but secretly preparing the overthrow of the bourgeoisie, as in France and Germany; finally, in Britain and America, in open rebellion against the ruling bourgeoisie. (MECW 6: 528)[14]

"Open rebellion" cannot be read literally. After all, the Chartists – though sometimes engaged in violence – were demanding constitutional reform, and the *Principles of Communism* had commended the fact that in the United States "a

---

[14] The predominance of the English bourgeoisie over the aristocracy, despite appearance, is insisted upon: "The present bourgeois or manufacturers' parliament . . . will change the old feudal-looking England into a more or less modern country of bourgeois organisation. . . . It will complete the victory of the English industrial bourgeoisie" (MECW 6: 526).

democratic constitution has been introduced" (above, p. 186). For all that, the purely tactical objective of cooperation on the constitutional front is apparent.

* * *

The language of Marx's *The Poverty of Philosophy* (1847) sometimes evokes violent revolution: "is it at all surprising that a society founded on the *opposition* of classes should culminate in brutal *contradiction*, the shock of body against body, as its final dénouement?. . . . [O]n the eve of every general reshuffling of society, the last word of social science will always be: 'le combat ou la mort; la lutte sanguinaire ou le néant' (George Sand)" (MECW 6: 212). Yet Marx looked positively on unionism combined with political activity, according the legalist Chartists pride of place: "The organisation of . . . strikes, combinations, and *trades unions* went on simultaneously with the political struggles of the workers, who now constitute a large political party, under the name of *Chartists*" (210). But conceivably by the clash of classes in "its final dénouement" was intended the period after the proletariat comes to power, with such power achieved in the first instance by constitutional means.

Marx had no illusions. The principle of historical materialism taught that the mere achievement by the proletariat of "political rule" would be of no lasting significance unless the "material conditions" are ripe for the "definitive overthrow" of the bourgeoisie ("Moralising Criticism and Critical Morality," October 1847; MECW 6: 319). Furthermore, he implies that only in the United States – where political equality had been achieved – were material conditions ripe for a "definitive overthrow," for "[n]owhere . . . does *social* inequality obtrude itself more harshly than in the eastern states of North America, because nowhere is it less disguised by political inequality" (323). Unfortunately, he leaves open the character of the final dénouement itself, committing himself only to a (hopeful) prediction regarding falling standards: "If pauperism has not yet developed there as much as in England, this is explained by economic circumstances which it is not our task to elucidate further here. Meanwhile, pauperism is making the most gratifying progress."

In further commentary early in 1848, Marx warned that the "political consti-tution of North America" – such as the Chartists were seeking by their quest for universal suffrage – could not be attained prematurely in Belgium or other con-tinental countries where a "great national" workers' party did not yet exist ("The *Débat Social* on the Democratic Association," February 1848; MECW 6: 539). The Chartist campaign, by contrast, "presupposed a long and arduous unification of the English workers into a class." These remarks suggest the prospect of success-ful constitutional reform enhancing proletarian political power, which would be subject, of course, to attainment of the appropriate stage in capitalist development.

* * *

Let us turn to the *Communist Manifesto* itself. Here, as in Engels's *Principles of Communism*, we have an account of the impact of modern industrial development on the proletariat – improved communication, "concentration," deskilling, and the downward trend and increasing instability of the real wage – whose quantitative expansion and coherence are reflected in unionization that extends increasingly to the national level and that promises the establishment of a workers' political party; and though "[t]his organisation of the proletarians into a class, and consequently into a political party, is constantly being upset again by the competition between the workers themselves . . . it ever rises up again, stronger, firmer, mightier" (MECW 6: 493). Moreover, intrabourgeois domestic rivalry – for there were sections "antagonistic to the progress of industry" – and international rivalry obliged "appeal to the proletariat . . . for its help," thereby drag[ging] it into the political arena." Finally, "near the decisive hour" the "dissolution" of the ruling class is such that "a portion of the bourgeois ideologists" – those "who have raised themselves to the level of comprehending theoretically the historical movement as a whole" – "joins the revolutionary class" (494). To be noted more specifically are the *Manifesto's* hostility, on the one hand, toward a variety of "critical-utopian" socialists of the day, for "violently oppos[ing] all political action on the part of the working class" (517), and its support, on the other hand, for the constitutional reform measures proposed by the Chartists in England, the Agrarian Reformers in America, and the Social Democrats in France (518).

We have here clear intimation of a stage entailing cooperation between bourgeoisie and proletariat, the former obliged by force of circumstance to contribute to the political advancement of the latter. In a comment on Germany, the authors again emphasize that the bourgeoisie in its struggle "against the absolute monarchy, the feudal squirearchy, and the petty bourgeoisie" was obliged to contribute to proletarian political progress, whereas the Communists "never cease, for a single instant, to instil into the working class the clearest possible recognition of the hostile antagonism between bourgeoisie and proletariat, in order that the German workers may straightway use, as so many weapons against the bourgeoisie, the social and political conditions that the bourgeoisie must necessarily introduce along with its supremacy, and in order that, after the fall of the reactionary classes in Germany, the fight against the bourgeoisie itself may immediately begin" (MECW 6: 519).

What, though, of the character of the "fight against the bourgeoisie"? The account refers more specifically to "open revolution . . . where the violent overthrow of the bourgeoisie lays the foundation for the sway of the proletariat" (495). Similarly, the expected "bourgeois revolution in Germany will be but the prelude to an immediately following proletarian revolution," the Communists "openly declar[ing] that their ends can be attained only by the forcible overthrow of all existing social conditions" (519). This is followed by the most famous of Marxian declarations: "Let the ruling classes tremble at a Communistic revolution. The proletarians have nothing to lose but their chains. They have a world to win."[15]

---

[15] Let us not enter into the complex issue of the relation of the communists to the proletarian class except to note the declaration that "[t]he Communists . . . are on the one hand, practically, the most advanced and resolute section of the working-class parties of every country, that section which pushes forward all others; on the other hand, theoretically, they have over the great mass

However, the "violent" overthrow of the bourgeoisie might occur after the proletariat has achieved political power constitutionally. Such a reading is suggested by the declaration that "the first step in the revolution of the working class is to raise the proletariat to the position of the ruling class, to win the battle of democracy" (504). Furthermore, similar expressions encountered in the independent formulations by Engels and Marx lend themselves readily to such an interpretation. In sum, already in the late 1840s both countenanced the achievement of proletarian political control by constitutional means, as a first step to "the final dénouement."

C. Evidence from the 1850s: Universal Suffrage in France versus England

Marx's *The Class Struggles in France, 1848–1850*[16] of 1850 constitutes a sort of coroner's post mortem regarding the failure of the June 1848 insurrection. It contains a number of important generalizations regarding political matters.

In the first place, the appropriate combination of circumstances required for a successful uprising had been absent so that the French workers had acted prematurely on June 23 (MECW *10*: 56).[17] The key to any future success would be the achievement by the proletariat of "that extensive national existence which can raise its revolution to a national one," and this in turn depended on the primacy of the industrial bourgeoisie over both the "finance aristocracy" and agriculture; in fact, what industrial advance had been already achieved in France was artificial, "its command even of the national market [maintained] only through a more or less modified system of prohibitive tariffs." By contrast, "[i]n England – and the largest French manufacturers are petty bourgeois compared with their English rivals – we really find the manufacturers, a Cobden, a Bright, at the head of the crusade against the bank and the stock-exchange aristocracy" (116). Nothing could be expected from the French proletariat without prior domination of world markets by the industrialists in what promised to be a long drawn-out process (117).

Despite the obstacles in the way of early success, "the *proletariat* increasingly organises itself around *revolutionary Socialism*, around *Communism*, for which the

---

of the proletariat the advantage of clearly understanding the line of march, the conditions, and the ultimate general results of the proletarian movement" (MECW *6*: 497). And yet the communists are also said "not [to] set up any sectarian [German editions have "separate"] principles of their own, by which to shape and mould the proletarian movement." The same pragmatic approach is apparent years later in a retrospective comment: "Had we from 1864–73 insisted on working together only with those who openly adopted our platform – Where should we be to-day? I think all our practice has shown that it is possible to work along with the general movement of the working class at every one of its stages without giving up or hiding our own distinct position and even organization" (27 January 1887, MECW *48*: 9; similarly, 28 December 1886, MECW *47*: 541).

[16] This title is Engels's choice; the material first appeared in Marx's short-lived journal *Neue Rheinische Zeitung. Politisch-ökonomische Revue.*

[17] June 1848 is represented as a failed *proletarian* revolution against "the self-constituted bourgeois republic," and June 1849 as a failure of the petty bourgeoisie against the "party of Order" (MECW *10*: 99–100).

bourgeoisie itself has invented the name of *Blanqui*" – referring to misapplication of Blanqui's name by the conservatives – having as its objective "common, social production," and declaring "*the permanence of the revolution, the class dictatorship of the proletariat as the necessary transit point to the abolition of class distinctions generally,* to the abolition of all the relations of production on which they rest, to the abolition of all the social relations that correspond to these relations of production, to the revolutionising of all the ideas that result from these social relations" (MECW *10*: 126–7).[18]

Now the analysis of the failures of June 1848 examines obstacles impeding a "class dictatorship" initially achieved by violent revolutionary activity.[19] However, "the permanence of the revolution" is also consistent with a warning that any attempt to undermine the "class dictatorship" (and along with it a fully fledged communist program) would never be countenanced by the communists, even should the "class

---

[18] This is apparently the first use by Marx of the term "dictatorship of the proletariat." Although he might perhaps be read as attributing the expression to Blanqui, this is unlikely because Blanqui himself never used it (see Johnstone 1983: 49–50; Draper 1986: 35). Draper appreciates that for Marx and Engels, "*from beginning to end of their careers and without any exception, 'dictatorship of the proletariat' meant nothing more and nothing less than 'rule of the proletariat,' the 'conquest of political power' by the working class, the establishment of a workers' state in the first post revolutionary period*" (Draper 1986: 213).

Our primary concern is with "dictatorship" as an expression of proletarian political control of the state apparatus, in precisely this sense – whether achieved initially in a peaceful manner, by means of the electoral process, or by revolution – rather than with the precise system of government then to be put into place. But see below, pp. 199–200 and note 32.

On the "permanence of the revolution," see also the Marx–Engels Address of the Central Authority to the League of Communists in March 1850 with respect to the utter insufficiency of the limited demands of the German petty-bourgeois reformists (MECW *10*: 281; below, p. 221).

[19] The March 1850 address to the League of Communists (see previous note) is explicit regarding the need for "arming the proletariat" in Germany, and this in part to ensure ultimate hegemony over the bourgeois democrats with whom an alliance was necessitated by temporary weakness.

In *The Class Struggles in France* and in a joint review, "May to October [1850]," the matter of right timing of revolutionary activity in relation to the trade cycle is raised. Renewed prosperity during the course of 1848 and 1849 promised failure should any new attempt be made: "With this general prosperity . . . there can be no talk of a real revolution. Such a revolution is only possible in the periods when *both . . . factors,* the *modern* productive *forces* and the *bourgeois forms of production,* come *in collision* with each other. . . . *A new revolution is possible only in consequence of a new crisis. It is, however, just as certain as this crisis*" (MECW *10*: 135; 510). This argument is introduced by a passage relating to the dependence of Continental on British industrial activity, and greater sensitivity to revolutionary outbreak in crisis periods at the Continental periphery than the British centre: "[W]hile . . . the crises first produce revolutions on the Continent, the foundation for these is, nevertheless, always laid in England. Violent outbreaks must naturally occur rather in the extremities of the bourgeois body than in its heart, since the possibility of adjustment is greater here than there" (134; 509). Here the authors add a comment in the reverse direction: "On the other hand, the degree to which Continental revolutions react on England is at the same time the barometer which indicates how far these revolutions really call in question the bourgeois conditions of life, or how far they only hit their political formations" (134–5; 509–10). See also Marx–Engels, "January to February [1850]" (MECW *10*: 257–70) for the political significance of cycles.

dictatorship" entail a working-class parliamentary majority ensured by universal suffrage. We must then return to the central issue for us – the potential for constitutional reform within capitalist society.

Consider as background Marx's approach toward the formation of the Social Democratic or "red" party early in 1849, a coalition comprising the revolutionary proletariat in conjunction with petty bourgeois and peasant groupings (MECW 10: 96–7). Although it was, in part, the weakness of the proletariat that obliged it to enter into coalitions with the "socialist sects" and "doctrinaires of its emancipation" (98), it was also true that "the friends of reform of all shades... were compelled to group themselves round the banner of the most extreme party of revolution, round the *red flag*," deceiving themselves with the belief that "revolutionary collisions" could be avoided (126). But "revolutionary collisions" could not be avoided because the "big bourgeoisie" would never tolerate constraints on untrammelled capitalist development. This was apparent in the fact that it reversed itself on the matter of universal suffrage, instituted prior to the 1848–9 uprising, once it came to realize what was truly involved: "[D]oes not universal suffrage put an end to all stability, does it not every moment question all the powers that be, does it not annihilate authority, does it not threaten to elevate anarchy itself to the position of authority?" (131). Lukes (1983: 114) draws attention to an important passage where Marx points to a "fundamental contradiction" in the draft constitution proposed just before the June outbreak:

The classes whose social slavery the constitution is to perpetuate, proletariat, peasantry, petty bourgeoisie, it puts in possession of political power through universal suffrage. And from the class whose old social power it sanctions, the bourgeoisie, it withdraws the political guarantees of this power. It forces the political rule of the bourgeoisie into democratic conditions, which at every moment help the hostile classes to victory and jeopardize the very foundations of bourgeois society. (MECW 10: 79)

But the French bourgeois state now appeared in its true light, as unable to tolerate genuine legislative reform. The anomalous situation, Marx explains elsewhere at this time, was corrected by the new electoral law of 31 May 1850, which outlawed universal suffrage and thereby removed more than three million voters from the rolls (*The Eighteenth Brumaire of Louis Bonaparte*, 1852; MECW 11: 146).[20] Further, a series of articles in 1850 by Engels for *The Democratic Review* spells out month

[20] Some of Marx's most remarkable prose describes the manner in which the repressive measures taken by the bourgeoisie – apart from the new suffrage law he considers restrictions on the "revolutionary press," control of popular meetings, and military interference in the judiciary – were turned against the proletariat after the December takeover: "It repressed every stirring in society by means of the state power, every stirring in its society is suppressed by the state power" (MECW 11: 182). That the proletariat did not then rise up is explained by various maneuvers on the part of Louis Bonaparte; nonetheless, Marx declared (without elaboration) that his "overthrow of the parliamentary republic contains within itself the germ of the triumph of the proletarian revolution" (184).

The importance of this document for appreciating "the *particular* role played by political struggles and events – needless to say within the framework of their *general* dependence on economic conditions," is later emphasized by Engels in an attempt to get the doctrine of

by month the process by which "the conspiracy" of universal suffrage, as it was now viewed by the authorities, was withdrawn (MECW 10: 26, 32, 33, 34).

All this must be placed in proper context. The perceived infeasibility of constitutional reform – necessitating the violent overthrow of the bourgeoisie at the appropriate time – specifically reflects an evaluation of the events in France during 1848–9. In Britain, by contrast, meaningful constitutional progress was still countenanced, and indeed represented as an essential preliminary for a successful "revolutionary" outcome. To this we turn next.

* * *

In joint overview of the political turmoil of the period from May to October 1850, Marx and Engels point to signs of a split in the Chartist movement between "a purely democratic faction" led by Feargus O'Connor, including "the labour aristocracy" and some members of the petty bourgeoisie, "whose programme is limited to the People's Charter and a number of petty bourgeois reforms," and the "revolutionary" faction – which included "[t]he mass of workers who live in truly proletarian conditions" – under the leadership of Harney and Ernest Jones (MECW 10: 514).[21] (The second grouping entails Thompson's "Chartist

historical materialism straight (27 October 1890; MECW 49: 63), as is clarified in Chapter Seven, note 15.

[21] The term "aristocracy of trades" or "of industry" has been traced to William Thompson (1827). See Lapides (1987: 197). The central issue between the factions mentioned in my text turned on land redistribution versus nationalization: "O'Connor and his party want to use the Charter to accommodate some of the workers on small plots of land and eventually to parcel out all the land in Great Britain.... The revolutionary faction... insists that it should not be distributed but remain national property" (MECW 10: 515).

Saville has commented that "during the last years of the forties... the developing ideas of 'The Charter and Something More' can be discerned in the speeches and writings of the left-wing of the Chartist leadership" (1987: 215). Cole's position that "the Socialism of Ernest Jones as it developed after 1848, was in its essentials that of Marx" (Cole 1962: 151) is disputed by Thompson (1998: 154); and Saville maintains that "[w]hile Marx and Engels can be credited with some influence upon the ideas of Ernest Jones, who drafted the 1851 [Chartist] programme, its intellectual lineage can be clearly traced in the speeches and writings of the earlier years" (1987: 215–16). In support of Cole, however, we may refer to Jones's position on trade unionism, which corresponds closely with that of Marx and Engels during the 1840s (see Chapter One, p. 62). Thus trades unions for Jones at their best were a means of developing working-class consciousness (Jones 1851: 326–7), but they were ineffectual in maintaining wages considering ongoing mechanization, the elimination of small concerns, the inflow of women and children into the work force, the intensification of labor, and natural population growth (422). Indeed, the typical union was at fault in teaching members "to believe that their wages could be kept up without a political change" (342). Similarly, for Harney, whose *The Red Republican* published the first English-language edition of the *Communist Manifesto*, the "reforms" proposed by the Charter "are utterly valueless, unless associated with such social changes as will enable the great body of the community to command the actual sovereignty of society" (Harney 1966 [1850]: 1). The end sought after was abolition of the class-based system, "not the mere improvement of the social life of our class" (131). For Harney's position in historical context, see Finn (1993).

Saville attributes the breakdown of the Chartist movement after mid-century partly to the absence of a "coherent political strategy" or a "tradition of insurrection," and partly

Socialists"; above, p. 180). The point to note is that the authors appreciated the necessity for cooperation with the mere reformists on the specific grounds that "[t]he revolutionary movement proper cannot begin in Britain until the Charter has been carried through" (515–16). Further, though they write somewhat disparagingly of the Charter, it is only in the sense that proletarian demands must go much further. In fact, a joint review of Carlyle's *Latter-Day Pamphlets* at this period rejects his hostile allusions to (in their paraphrase) a "superstitious English belief in the infallibility of parliamentary government" (MECW *10*: 305).

An Engels paper of 1850 on the 1847 Factory Act is relevant for us at this juncture. Here he refers favorably to the workers' transfer of support from "reactionary" landowning forces to the industrial capitalists with regard inter alia to extension of the suffrage, a transition based on an "instinctive" perception that they were thereby hastening the development, and thus the ultimate collapse, of the industrial system:

They have learnt that the bourgeois industrialists are still in the first instance the class which alone is capable of marching at the head of the movement at the present moment, and that it would be a vain task to work against them in this progressive mission. For this reason . . . the workers are now much more inclined to support them in their agitation for the complete implementation of Free Trade, financial reform and extension of the franchise, than to allow themselves to be decoyed once again by philanthropic allurements to the banner of the united reactionaries. They feel that their day can only come when the industrialists have worn themselves out, and hence their instinct is correct in hastening the process of development which will give the industrialists power and thus prepare their fall. ("The English Ten Hours' Bill"; MECW *10*: 298)[22]

Moreover, "restoration" of the 1847 Factory Act following its de facto "annulment" – a matter I shall elaborate in Chapter Five – was desirable, provided it was enacted under the "exclusive political rule of the working class," and this presupposed a universal franchise:

But because of this they [the working class] do not forget that in the industrialists they are bringing to power their own direct enemies, and that they can achieve their own liberation only through toppling the industrialists and conquering political power for themselves. The annulment of the Ten Hours' Bill has once more proved this to them in the most striking fashion. The restoration of this Bill can only have any significance now under the rule of universal franchise, and universal franchise in an England

to repressive measures by the state (1987: 220–2). For Engels, the breakdown reflected "the fact that the English proletariat is actually becoming more and more bourgeois" (see below, p. 205). Of particular concern to Engels at this time was Jones's attempt to reinvigorate the Chartist movement on the basis of cooperation with the bourgeois radicals.

22 The industrialists' willingness to allow the franchise, at least to a reliable section of the working class, is represented as part of a strategy to gain control over the "English state machine" at the expense of the traditional property owners, "the aristocracy, the Church, the sinecures and the semi-feudal system of jurisprudence" (MECW *10*: 296).

two-thirds of whose inhabitants are industrial proletarians means the exclusive political rule of the working class with all the revolutionary changes in social conditions which are inseparable from it.[23]

In a second paper of 1850 on the Factory Acts, Engels opined that "[t]he working classes, the very first day they get political power, will have to pass far more stringent measures against over-working women and children than a Ten Hours', or even an Eight Hours' Bill"; for they had been taught by the de facto abrogation of the 1847 bill that "*no lasting benefit whatever can be obtained for them by others, but that they must obtain it themselves by conquering, first of all, political power . . .* [and] that *under no circumstances have they any guarantee for bettering their social position unless by Universal Suffrage,* which would enable them to seat a *Majority of Working Men* in the House of Commons" ("The Ten Hours' Question"; MECW *10*: 274–5). There is a strong suggestion in all this that Engels had in mind the stage to which the *Communist Manifesto* itself applied (see note 8) when the proletariat would be firmly in control and in a position to dictate a series of "revolutionary changes in social conditions."

Articles written in 1850 for *The Democratic Review* regarding France are further indicative. In April the prognosis for a proletarian revolutionary victory in France was still good: "[T]he government, forced to attack universal suffrage will thereby give the people an occasion for a combat, in which there is for the proletarians the certainty of victory" ("Letters from France"; MECW *10*: 32). By June, the failure of the proletariat to react to the retraction of universal suffrage had become apparent, its passivity reflecting a dependency on reformist-minded Socialists – "the old socialist tradition," though this dependency was in the process of dissolution and violent revolution was inevitable in the face of capitalist intransigence (35). In sharp contrast, universal suffrage once granted in Britain could not conceivably be retracted – and this because of national character:

It really is a curious fact, that Universal Suffrage in France, won easily in 1848, has been annihilated far more easily in 1850. Such ups and downs, however, correspond much with the French character, and occur very often in French history. In England such a thing would be impossible. Universal Suffrage, once established there, would be won for ever. No government would dare to touch it. Only think of the minister who should be foolish enough to consider seriously re-establishing the Corn Laws. The immense laughter of the whole nation would hurl him down. (34)

---

[23] Engels's paper closes with a declaration that the ruling proletariat would approach the question of hours as part and parcel of a total transformation:

The first consequence of the proletarian revolution in England will be the centralisation of large-scale industry in the hands of the state, that is, the ruling proletariat, and with the centralisation of industry all the conditions of competition, which nowadays bring the regulation of labour time into conflict with the progress of industry, fall away. And thus the only solution to the Ten Hours question, as to every question depending on the antagonism between capital and wage labour, lies in the *proletarian revolution.* (MECW *10*: 300)

Achievement of universal (male) suffrage in Britain, and this by constitutional means, was thus treated as tantamount to permanent proletarian control, a proletarian "dictatorship"no less.

A proposed electoral reform bill is described by Engels shortly thereafter as "the most important" of issues before Parliament, albeit of no *direct* consequence for the proletariat, affecting "solely how much of their political power will be retained by the reactionary or conservative classes, i.e. the landed aristocracy, the rentiers, the stock-exchange speculators, the colonial landowners, the shipping magnates and a section of the merchants and bankers, and how much they will surrender to the industrial bourgeoisie, which heads all the progressive and revolutionary classes" ("England," January 1852; MECW *11*: 206).[24] Nonetheless, "[t]he proletariat, whose independent struggle for its own interests against the industrial bourgeoisie will not begin until such time as the political supremacy of that class is established, the proletariat will in any circumstances also derive some advantage from this electoral reform" (208).[25]

* * *

A word next on Marx's version of the theme. He explains in August 1852 to an American audience that "the complete annihilation of Old England as an aristocratic country is the end which [the industrial bourgeoisie] follows up with more or less consciousness. Its nearest object, however, is the attainment of a Parliamentary reform which should transfer to its hands the legislative power necessary for such a revolution" ("The Chartists," *New York Daily Tribune*; MECW *11*: 334).[26] When the industrialists "will have conquered exclusive political dominion, when political dominion and economical supremacy will be united in the same hands, when therefore, the struggle against capital [by the proletariat] will no longer be distinct from the struggle against the existing Government – from that very moment will date the *social revolution of England*" (335). Now because Marx proceeds immediately to the Chartists with particular reference to universal suffrage as synonymous with proletarian political power, it is evidently a constitutional "revolution" that is envisaged:

We now come to the *Chartists*, the politically active portion of the British *working class*. The six points of the Charter which they contend for contain nothing but the demand

---

[24] Russell's 1852 bill was in fact aborted, and shortly afterward a second reform bill was also withdrawn.

[25] "How great this advantage will be," Engels adds, "depends simply on whether the debate and eventual establishment of electoral reform occurs *before* the trade crisis breaks or rather coincides with it; for the proletariat, for the time being, only plays an active part, at the front of the stage, at great moments of decision, like Fate in classical tragedy" (MECW *11*: 208–9).

[26] In this process the industrial bourgeoisie – unlike "excitable Frenchmen" – prefer to "compromise with the vanishing opponent" (the aristocracy) "rather than to strengthen the arising enemy" (the working class), "to whom the future belongs, by concessions of a more than apparent importance," but "historical necessity" pushed them onward in their "mission" to destroy Old England (MECW *11*: 334–5).

of *Universal Suffrage*, and of the conditions without which Universal Suffrage would be illusory for the working class; such as the ballot, payment of members, annual general elections. But Universal Suffrage is the equivalent for political power for the working class of England, where the proletariat forms the large majority of the population, where, in a long, though underground civil war, it has gained a clear consciousness of its position as a class, and where even the rural districts know no longer any peasants, but only landlords, industrial capitalists (farmers) and hired laborers. The carrying of Universal Suffrage in England would, therefore, be a far more socialistic measure than anything which has been honored with that name on the Continent. (335–6)[27]

Marx closes regarding England: "Its inevitable result, here, is *the political supremacy of the working class*," further confirming our reading of this and equivalent forms of expression encountered throughout our texts.

In June 1855 Marx wrote to the same effect, and with equal assurance, of a change in attitude in Britain toward universal suffrage since the early 1840s when support for it had reflected in part a deceptive strategy of the radical bourgeoisie: "Since that day there has no longer been any doubt about the meaning of universal suffrage.... It is the *Charter* of the people and implies the assumption of political power as a means of satisfying their social needs. Universal suffrage, which was regarded as the motto of universal brotherhood in the France of 1848, has become a battle cry in England. There universal suffrage was the direct content of the revolution; here, revolution is the direct content of the universal suffrage" (1855, "The Association for Administrative Reform," MECW *14*: 243). Marx in fact concludes that this trend reflected the outcome of British industrial development: "An examination of the history of universal suffrage in England will show that it casts off its idealistic features at the same rate as modern society with its immense contradictions develops in the country, contradictions that are produced by industrial progress."

Brophy records that the editors of MEGA[2] (see Bibliography, p. 377) "call attention to Marx's meditations on the differing roles of universal suffrage for French and Chartist politics in an article from June 1855, which reveals a wavering consideration that British workers might achieve power through peaceful parliamentary means" (2007: 532). "Wavering consideration" is the last term to use to describe Marx's position.

D. Marx's Revisionism in the 1860s and Thereafter

Brief allusions to constitutional reform will be found in Marx's "Inaugural Address to the Working Men's International Association" – the First International – in September 1864. Mention is there made of the impact on British opinion exerted by the post-1848 events on the continent, including a weakening of working-class morale such that "[a]ll the efforts made at keeping up, or remodelling the Chartist

---

[27] The particular complexity of French politics is described by Marx in *The Eighteenth Brumaire* (1852; MECW *11*: 181–97).

Movement, failed signally.... [N]ever before seemed the English working class so thoroughly reconciled to a state of political nullity" (MECW *20*: 10). This state of affairs had by 1864 been transformed: "To conquer political power" – one notes the terminology of the *Communist Manifesto* (above, pp. 189–90) – "has become the great duty of the working classes. They seem to have comprehended this, for in England, Germany, Italy, and France there have taken place simultaneous revivals, and simultaneous efforts are being made at the political reorganisation of the working men's party" (12).[28] All this is consistent with approval of renewed participation in legal constitutional processes. Such participation is strongly confirmed by the Third Annual Report (1867) of the Association, signed by Marx for Germany and in which parliamentary reform is represented as "an indispensable stepping stone to that complete emancipation of the working classes from the domination of capital which is the aim of the International Working Men's Association. One step has undoubtedly been gained by the Act of 1867" (MECW *20*: 432).[29] This act – albeit only a step toward fully fledged universal (male) suffrage ensuring a proletarian majority – was "sufficiently comprehensive to enable the

[28] Marx here makes much of the absolute numbers of the proletariat, not only their "combination," "knowledge," and international cooperation between national parties. We may appreciate in this light his citing the massive emigration from Britain as a factor *weakening* rather than strengthening labor (MECW *20*: 10). By the same token, in his Amsterdam speech of September 1872 on the Hague Congress, Marx commends the transfer of the seat of the General Council of the International to New York – as he had proposed – on the grounds that "America is becoming the world of workers *par excellence*; that every year half a million men, workers, emigrate to that other continent, and that the International must vigorously take root in that soil where the worker predominates" (MECW *23*: 255).

Much more was in fact involved by the transfer. It went hand in hand with the expulsion of Bakunin on grounds, Marx wrote from The Hague, of his "creation within our Association of a secret society, the *Alliance of Socialist Democracy*, which claimed to direct the International to aims contrary to its principles" (12 September 1872, to the Editor of *Le Corsaire*; MECW *23*: 257). See also Marx to Friedrich Bolte, 23 November 1871 (MECW *44*: 255). An account by Engels appears in his "Karl Marx" (1877; MECW *24*: 190–1). Also relevant are his "The Bakunists at Work" (1873; MECW *23*: 581–98), and a letter to Sorge regarding "the Bakunist adventurers" (12–17 September 1874; MECW *45*: 41–2). On Bakunin, see Ryazanoff (1930 [1922]: 196–7), King (2002: 217, 220–1), and Hunt (2009: 256–60).

An excellent modern account of Marx's "strange decision" to transfer the General Council to New York is provided by Collins, who stresses – apart from the concern with the Bakunist "contagion" – Marx's wish to retire temporarily from politics and his unwillingness to leave the General Council in London under the influence of leaders who flirted with the idea of collaboration with the liberal bourgeoisie and who favored a labor party with trade-union affiliations (1967: 257–75). Engels was represented at this time by some opponents as Marx's "evil genius," the accusations including his alleged "packing" of The Hague delegates to ensure a pro-Marx outcome (269).

[29] Gladstone's Reform legislation of 1866 was designed to enfranchise the "respectable" urban working class. It was defeated. However, Disraeli's 1867 Reform Act went much further, enfranchising nearly 60 percent of adult males in the boroughs, thereby adding 1.12 million to the existing U.K. electorate of 1.4 million (see Matthew 1985: 256; also MECW *20*: 513 n. 337. The first election under the new provisions took place in 1868 and the second in 1874 (see note 38, for later suffrage data). For the broader picture surrounding Disraeli's Act, see Cowling (1967) and Briggs (1990: 272–303).

working classes to politically combine for class purposes within the precincts of the Constitution, and exercise a direct influence upon the Legislature in matters of social and economical reform, in as far as they affect the labour question."

This remarkably moderate formulation focuses quite deliberately on constitutionality and, to that extent and by extension, might be thought to imply that the loss of a working-class majority at the polls would be acceptable as a matter of democratic principle. This, however, is uncertain. Universal suffrage of an order ensuring a proletarian majority might have been identified by Marx with *permanent* proletarian control, as it was by Engels (above, p. 196).

An interview accorded *The World* newspaper on 3 July 1871 raises the same question. Marx there declares the general objective of the International to be "[t]he economical emancipation of the working class by the conquest of political power," and its use in "the attainment of social ends" (MECW 22: 601). Such "conquest" in England was to be achieved by peaceful means, for there "the way to show political power lies open to the working class" and "[i]nsurrection would be madness where peaceful agitation would more swiftly and surely do the work," whereas in France "a hundred laws of repression and a mortal antagonism between classes seem to necessitate the violent solution of social war" (602).[30] But again, it not properly clarified whether the *maintenance* of proletarian political power in Britain, as distinct from its initial *achievement*, would be subject to constitutional principles. The same may be said of a speech on the Seventh Anniversary of the International, as reported in *The World* of 15 October, which spells out the contrast between the two nations. In France "[t]he working classes would have to conquer the right to emancipate themselves on the battlefield" (634); but England – where the Chartist movement "had been started with the consent and assistance of middle-class radicals" – is represented as "the only country where the working class was sufficiently developed and organized to turn universal suffrage to its own proper account."[31] (The representation of Britain as a unique case proves, we shall see, to be an exaggeration.)

By Spring 1871, France had yielded one instance of proletarian control achieved by violent means – the Paris Commune. In *The Civil War in France* (written in April and May) the "Dictatorship of the Proletariat" is understood (MECW 22: 331–6) – in Miliband's terms – "not only as a form of *régime*, in which the proletariat would exercise the sort of hegemony hitherto exercised by the bourgeoisie, with

---

[30] *The Civil War in France* (1871) brilliantly describes the devastating overthrow of the Paris Commune by the new French Republic in cooperation with German occupation forces. The French proletariat would learn from experience that "there can be neither peace nor truce possible between the working men of France and the appropriators of their produce" (MECW 22: 354).

[31] This formulation perhaps supports the notion of revolution in one country (see above, notes 13 and 19). Even so, at this time Marx also recommended that the International concern itself with the Irish question, because the best way to weaken the English ruling class was to undermine their Irish properties (letter dated 9 April 1870; MECW 43: 473–5).

the actual task of government left to others, but also as a form of *government*, with the working class actually governing, and fulfilling many of the tasks hitherto performed by the state" (Miliband 1983: 130; see also Ryazanoff 1930 [1922]: 179; Draper 1986: 269–74; Tabak 2000).[32] For all that, Marx conceded that "the working class cannot simply lay hold of the ready-made State machinery and wield it for its own purposes" (MECW 22: 328).[33] And he was most cautious: "The working class did not expect miracles from the Commune. They have no ready-made utopias to introduce *par décret du people*" (335), as we have seen in Chapter Three (p. 159).[34]

[32] A possible allusion to this sort of perspective may be the reference to rendering "the revolution permanent" by the proletariat "conquer[ing] state power," in the Marx–Engels Address of the Central Authority to the League of Communists in 1850 (see below, p. 221, and note 18).

   Marx might have had second thoughts regarding the significance of the commune as proof of the effectiveness of proletarian control *as a form of government*, for he wrote in correspondence of 1882 of the commune as "merely an uprising of one city in exceptional circumstances, the majority ... [being] in no sense socialist, nor could it have been" (22 February; MECW 46: 66).

   It is unclear to which version of the "dictatorship" Engels adhered when he closed his 1891 Introduction to the German edition of *The Civil War in France*: "Of late, the German [Social Democratic] philistine has once more been filled with wholesome terror at the words: Dictatorship of the proletariat. Well and good, gentlemen, do you want to know what this dictatorship looks like. Look at the Paris Commune. That was the Dictatorship of the Proletariat" (MECW 27: 191).

[33] This is cited passage in the jointly written Preface to the 1872 German edition of the *Manifesto* (MECW 23:175). The Preface is, however, somewhat ambiguous regarding the implications of the Commune experience and might be read as illustrating the promise, at least in France, of the efficacy of literal revolution, though on balance this seems unlikely (MECW 23: 174–5).

[34] Rather surprisingly at first sight, considering his case for central planning discussed in Chapter Three, is Marx's commendation of the decentralization feature of the Commune constitution: "The Paris Commune was, of course, to serve as a model to all the great industrial centres of France. The communal *régime* once established in Paris and the secondary centres, the old centralized Government would in the provinces, too, have to give way to the self-government of the producers" (MECW 22: 332). In contrast, Marx does add a significant qualification:

   The few but important functions which still would remain for a central government were not to be suppressed, as has been intentionally mis-stated, but were to be discharged by Communal, and therefore strictly responsible agents. The unity of the nation was not to be broken, but, on the contrary, to be organized by the Communal constitution.... While the merely repressive organs of the old governmental [State] power were to be amputated, its legitimate functions were to be wrested from an authority usurping pre-eminence over society itself, and restored to the responsible agents of society. (332–3)

   Ryazanoff expresses the matter well: "The Commune should not merely have assumed parliamentary functions, but should have become a working corporation combining both the executive and legislative powers. The old centralized organization should have yielded place to self-governing bodies in the provincial districts likewise. The unity of the nation, far from being in any way tampered with by such institutions, would have been strengthened by communal organization of this type; unity would, indeed, have become a tangible fact, thanks to the abolition of the bourgeois State power which only masquerades as the fulfillment of that unity" (1930 [1922]: 194–5).

As for Britain, Marx was aware of obstacles impeding workers' entry into Parliament: "The Members receiving no subsidy, and the worker having nothing but the proceeds of his labour to live on, Parliament is closed to him, and the Bourgeoisie, stubbornly refusing to pay an allowance to Members, knows full well that this is the way to prevent the working class from being represented" (Speech at the London Conference of the International, 20 September 1871; MECW *22*: 617). Nevertheless, he insisted on the importance of working-class membership: "If their voices are stifled . . . the effect of this severity and intolerance on the people is profound." An example is given from Germany (where universal suffrage was introduced by Bismarck in 1866): "[I]f, like Bebel and Liebknecht, they are able to speak from this platform, the entire world can hear them – in one way or the other it means considerable publicity for our principles. . . . The governments are hostile to us. We must answer them by using every possible means at our disposal, getting workers into parliament is so much gaining over them." Marx's support for the constitutional achievement of proletarian "power" in Germany seems apparent from this account – and this notwithstanding the debacle of 1848 – belying his representation elsewhere at the same time of England as a unique case.

Similarly indicative are Marx's remarks of September 1872 commending a resolution based on proposals by himself and Engels regarding "the necessity for the working classes to fight the old disintegrating society on the political as well as the social field" ("On the Hague Congress," MECW *23*: 254). The resolution in question was adopted as one of the articles of the Association: "This constitution of the working class into a political party is indispensable in order to insure the triumph of the social revolution, and of its ultimate end, the abolition of classes. . . . The lords of land and the lords of capital will always use their political privileges for the defence and perpetuation of their economical monopolies, and for the enslavement of labour. The conquest of political power has therefore become the great duty of the working class" (cited in Marx and Engels, "Resolutions of the General Congress held at The Hague," MECW *23*: 243). Such "conquest" might be attained, Marx opined, by "peaceful means," at least in America, England, and (perhaps) Holland: "We know that the institutions, customs and traditions in the different countries must be taken into account; and we do not deny the existence of countries like America, England, and if I knew your institutions better I might add Holland, where the workers may achieve their aims by peaceful means" ("On the Hague Congress," MECW *23*: 255). The conspicuous omission of Germany conceivably implies an element of uncertainty, which indeed seems to be reinforced in a later unpublished comment induced by Bismarck's Anti-Socialist Laws (considered below). (Engels, we shall find, is also hesitant regarding German prospects but in the end adopts a rather positive view of the constitutional option, taking account of the abandonment of the anti-Socialist Law.)

Relevant for our theme is a letter from Marx at this time that is addressed to Friedrich Bolte. It elaborates the interdependency between the political and social objectives of the proletariat.[35] The political dimension to worker agitation for reforms relating to factory hours provides a case in point:

The political movement of the working class naturally has as its final object the conquest of political power for this class, and this requires, of course, a previous organisation of the working class developed up to a certain point, which arises from the economic struggles themselves.... The movement to force through an eight-hour *law*, etc.... is a *political* movement. And in this way, out of the separate economic movements of the workers there grows up everywhere a *political movement*, that is to say a movement of the *class*, with the object of achieving its interests in a general form, in a form possessing general, socially binding force. (23 November 1871; MECW 44: 258)

Whether the "conquest of political power," the achievement by the proletariat of its own class interests "in a form possessing general socially binding force," was envisaged as occurring by constitutional means is not explicitly indicated, but it seems to be implied by the formulation.

We return to the Hague Congress speech, which Marx concluded by declaring "that in most countries on the Continent it is force which must be the lever of our revolution; it is force which will have to be resorted to for a time in order to establish the rule of the workers" (MECW 23: 255). France, one might suppose, would fall into this category. In fact, though, an essay on "Political Indifferentism" in 1873 against the Proudhonists seems to envisage a reclassification of the French case. Here Marx reverts to his refutation in *Poverty of Philosophy* of Proudhon's "sophisms against the working-class movement" (see Chapter Five for his position regarding unions), but he adds a new condemnation in the light of Proudhon's anarchical *De la capacité politique des classes ouvrières* (1868a), a work opposed to all forms of compromise with the state, including political organization within the law, because (in Marx's paraphrase) "[a]ll peaceful movements, such as those in which English and American workers have the bad habit of engaging, are ... to be despised" (MECW 23: 392).[36] Further, such a reclassification is confirmed in his "Preamble to the Programme of the French Workers' Party" of May 1880 on universal suffrage as "instrument of emancipation" toward the "collective appropriation" of the means of production (MECW 24: 340). This outcome "can only spring from the revolutionary action of the producing class – or proletariat – organised into an independent political party," which organization "must be striven for, using all the

[35] Marx focuses at times on the contrast between objectives, rather than the linkage between them, as for example in *Capital* itself: "The factory hands, especially since 1838, had made the Ten-Hours' Bill their economic, as they had made the Charter their political, election-cry" (MECW 35: 286).

[36] Even should the proletariat turn to violence in their political struggle, "replac[ing] the dictatorship of the bourgeois class with their own revolutionary dictatorship," they would, according to the Proudhonists, Marx writes sarcastically, be "guilty of the terrible crime of *lèse-principe*," for "instead of laying down their arms and abolishing the State, [they] give to the State a revolutionary and transitory form" (MECW 23: 393).

means at the disposal of the proletariat, including above all universal suffrage, thus transformed from the instrument of deception which it has been hitherto into an instrument of emancipation."

Here we must refer to an important clarification of 1878 appearing in a draft commentary on Bismarck's Anti-Socialist Law, unpublished at the time, to the effect that the "peaceful" achievement of proletarian control via the suffrage may not be possible, considering the likely reaction to any imminent social transformation:

If in England, for instance, or the United States, the working class were to gain a majority in Parliament or Congress, they could, by lawful means, rid themselves of such laws and institutions as impeded their development, though they could only do insofar as society had reached a sufficiently mature development. However, the "peaceful" movement might be transformed into a "forcible" one by resistance on the part of those interested in restoring the former state of affairs; if (as in the American Civil War and French Revolution) they are put down by *force*, it is as rebels against "lawful" force. ("Parliamentary Debate on the Anti-Socialist Law," MECW *24*: 248)

As we shall see, this justification of defensive violence was to become an important consideration for Engels.

Beyond this allowance for defensive violence, Marx did not eschew the language of violent revolution at this late stage, as in a letter dated early 1881 referring to the "fury" of the masses (22 February 1881; MECW *46*: 67). The context is a refusal to be specific about the precise course of future revolutionary developments, warning against any "doctrinaire and of necessity fantastic anticipation of a future revolution's programme [which] only serves to distract from the present struggle." The future would look after itself:

Scientific insight into the inevitable disintegration, now steadily taking place before our eyes, of the prevailing social order; the masses themselves, their fury mounting under the lash of the old governmental bogies; the gigantic and positive advances simultaneously taking place in the development of the means of production – all this is sufficient guarantee that the moment a truly proletarian revolution breaks out, the conditions for its immediate initial (if certainly not idyllic) *modus operandi* will also be there.

Accordingly, "the critical conjuncture for a new international working men's association has not yet arrived; hence I consider all labour congresses and/or socialist congresses, in so far as they do not relate to the immediate, actual conditions obtaining in this or that specific nation, to be not only useless but harmful." Marx's practical, cautious, and nondoctrinaire approach – his Bernsteinian approach, in fact – is apparent. He also, unfortunately, leaves open here not only the course the "revolution" would or should take, but the question that has largely exercised us – whether it would initially be achieved by constitutional or other means.

E. Engels's Revisionism, 1865–1894

Engels's contribution to revisionist options over the three decades from 1865 to 1894 commences with observations regarding universal suffrage made when approaching the Prussian "military question," preeminently conscription. Engels seems very clear at first glance: "The more workers who are trained in the use of weapons the better. Universal conscription is the necessary and natural corollary of universal suffrage; it puts the voters in a position of being able to enforce their decisions gun in hand against any attempt at a coup d'état" ("The Prussian Military Question and the German Workers' Party," 1865; MECW *20*: 67). But this justifies defensive violence, not violence in the achievement of political power. As for the support of universal suffrage, the matter is complex; Engels proceeds to insist that all "will depend on what kind of aims the workers' party, i.e., that part of the working class which has become aware of its common class interests, is striving for in the interests of that class" (69). Support for universal suffrage was thus conditional on the requirement that those aims be acceptable, as they happened to be in the Prussian case: "It seems that the most advanced workers in Germany are demanding the emancipation of the workers from the capitalists by the transfer of state capital to associations of workers, so that production can be organised, without capitalists, for general account; and as a means to the achievement of this end: the conquest of political power by universal direct suffrage." This formulation in fact reflects advice offered by Marx, who had objected to an earlier draft that laid out more specific worker demands in France and England, as well as Germany, on the grounds that Engels might be misunderstood as recommending a Lassallian reform program (letter to Engels dated 11 February 1865; MECW *42*: 86–7). Marx's proposed reformulation, as adopted by Engels, "doesn't commit you at all, which is all to the good, as later on you yourself criticise universal suffrage if not accompanied by the requisite conditions."

Also significant are the tactical gains to be made by playing off the "reactionary" party of hereditary nobles against the bourgeoisie. In one passage of high relevance to us, the workers' party is advised to take full advantage of the bourgeoisie's support (albeit for its own ends) not only of universal suffrage but of freedom of the press and of assembly: "The bourgeoisie cannot win political power for itself nor give this political power constitutional and legal forms without putting weapons into the hands of the proletariat.... [T]he proletariat will thereby also acquire all the weapons it needs for its ultimate victory. With freedom of the press and the right of assembly and association it will win universal suffrage, and with universal, direct suffrage, in conjunction with the above tools of agitation, it will win everything else" (1865, "The Prussian Military Question"; MECW *20*: 77). Again the key qualification emerges. Engels's enthusiasm for universal suffrage supposed a politically reliable workers' party: "It is . . . in the interests of the workers to support the bourgeoisie in its struggle against all reactionary elements, *as long as it remains true to itself.* Every gain which the bourgeoisie extracts from reaction, eventually benefits the working class, if that condition is fulfilled." The condition was evidently considered as satisfied in Prussia, because Bismarck's 1867 Constitution, which introduced universal suffrage for adult males, is received enthusiastically as in a review of *Capital 1*: "Universal suffrage has added to our present parliamentary parties a new one, the *Social-Democratic Party.* ... It would be foolish to continue to treat the existence, activity and doctrines of such a party with genteel silence in a country where universal suffrage has placed the final decision into the hands of the most numerous and poorest classes" (1867; MECW *20*: 210). Significantly, it is taken for granted in a second review "that none of the deputies that have been elected by German workers will proceed to discuss this bill" – a bill relating to factory hours – "without previously making themselves thoroughly conversant with *Marx's* book. ... Marx's book gives them all the material in ready form" (236). There was no better token of working-class reliability!

Relevant to the foregoing themes is *The Housing Question* (1872). Here Engels attended to efforts by English industrialists to bypass social legislation – such as the 1858 Local Government Act – represented as "of importance only because in the hands of a government dominated by or under the pressure of the workers, a government which would at last really administer it, it will be a powerful weapon for making a breach in the existing social state of things" (MECW *23*: 361). Presumably a proletarian majority in Parliament would ensure the requisite "pressure," and certainly Engels did not preclude at this time a constitutional path to proletarian "domination." For when discussing "the spirit of German scientific socialism," or Marxian political economy, he insisted on "the necessity of political action by the proletariat and of its dictatorship as the transition to the abolition of classes and, with them of the state – views such as had already been expressed in the *Communist Manifesto* and since then on innumerable occasions" (370); and we have shown that in the *Manifesto* and elsewhere the constitutional option to arrive at the so-called "dictatorship" has been fully allowed for. That "spirit of German scientific socialism" was the driving force behind the German Social Democratic Party a genuine proletarian party pursuing "class policy," one "necessarily striving to establish *its* rule, the rule of the working class, hence 'class domination'" – "necessarily" in the sense that "each political party sets out to establish its rule in the state" (372). Here the formation of a proletarian party is envisaged as "the primary condition of its struggle, and the dictatorship of the proletariat as the immediate aim of the struggle," all reminiscent of the documents of 1847 and 1848 with their allowances for a constitutional path to working-class control. Particularly revealing is the representation in this context of the *Chartists* as the first "real proletarian party."

Note here dispirited remarks to Marx from 7 October 1858 "that the English proletariat is actually becoming more and more bourgeois" (MECW *40*: 344), and from 8 April 1863 "that the English proletariat's revolutionary energy has all but completely evaporated and the English proletarian has declared himself in full agreement with the dominancy of the bourgeoisie" (MECW *41*: 465).[37] This perspective seems to be subsequently modified. At least an article of February 1874 ("The English Elections") takes the constitutional option a step forward, reflecting allowance for the recent British national elections, the new Parliament being the first elected by secret ballot – a major Chartist demand – and the second elected under the provisions of the 1867 Reform Act (see note 29). Engels here set out to explain why it was "particularly the big industrial cities and factory districts, where the workers are now absolutely in the majority, that send Conservatives to Parliament" (MECW *23*: 611). One answer is that, despite all appearance, the outcome in fact constituted a protest vote against capitalist employers: "the secret ballot has enabled a large number of workers who usually were politically passive to vote with impunity against their exploiters and against the party in which they rightly see that of the big barons of industry, namely, the Liberal Party," that Party "represent[ing] large-scale industry as opposed to big landed property and high finance" (612). This is far from the full picture, though. That only two working-class MPs were elected reflected the absence of a working-class political party, and this Engels accounted for in an extraordinary manner:

[T]hat no separate political working-class party has existed in England since the down-fall of the Chartist Party in the fifties . . . is understandable in a country in which the working class has shared more than anywhere else in the advantages of the immense expansion of its large-scale industry. Nor could it have been otherwise in an England that ruled the world market; and certainly not in a country where the ruling classes have set themselves the task of carrying out, parallel with other concessions, one point of the Chartists' programme, the People's Charter, after another. (613)

For two points of the Charter had already been adopted: the secret ballot and the abolition of property qualifications for the candidates, while the third, universal suffrage, had been approximated. Only annual elections, payment of members of Parliament, and equal electoral areas remained to be fulfilled.

Despite the major political (and material) advance within capitalism achieved even without direct proletarian representation, Engels still believed that the election of working-class members organized as a party was inevitable. By accepting the blandishments of the bourgeoisie to acquire a parliamentary seat for themselves, the "labour leaders" (chairmen and secretaries of trades unions and working men's political societies) had prevented the election of as many as sixty working-class members (MECW *23*: 614). Nevertheless, the 1874 elections – returning two working-class members and also Irish Home Rule members – had "indisputably ushered in a new phase in English political development" (616). The labor leaders

---

[37] I surmise that Engels's pessimism reflected the effective collapse of the Chartist movement with economic prosperity in the 1850s and also the moderation shown by ex-Chartists and radicals who looked to the Liberal party to support their aims now limited to household suffrage (see Matthew 1985: 256). On this matter, see Nimtz (1999: 214–15).

could only delay, not prevent, the formation of an active proletarian party and its participation in parliamentary affairs.

It is also helpful to have in mind here, once more, Engels's emphasis on the friction between aristocracy and bourgeoisie of which labor was taking advantage, but which delayed the onset of "real revolutionary" activity: "Britain will certainly not experience violent socialist agitations such as occur in other countries, where the ruling classes simply constitute, in relation to the workers, a great, reactionary, compact and inexorable mass. But once the working classes are no longer able to draw any profit from the rival competition between the interests of the landed aristocracy and the interests of the industrial bourgeoisie, because the competition will no longer exist, then we shall have in Britain too the start of the real revolutionary period" ("British Agricultural Labourers," June 1877; MECW 24: 180). "The social movement in Britain," Engels concluded, "is slow, it is evolutionist, not revolutionary, but is nevertheless a movement forward," confirming one of the major themes developed in Chapter Three. However, a letter to Bernstein shortly thereafter suggests that even the muted optimism expressed in 1874 and 1877 was premature; nothing could "conceal the fact that at this moment a genuine workers' movement in the continental sense is non-existent here" (17 June 1879; MECW 45: 361).

The willingness of the bourgeoisie to make meaningful concessions to labor emerges again in a newspaper article of 1881 and is accounted for by the fear generated by the Chartist experiment: "Thus the working class of Great Britain for years fought ardently and even violently for the People's Charter, which was to give it . . . political power; it was defeated, but the struggle had made such an impression upon the victorious middle class that this class, since then, was only too glad to buy a prolonged armistice at the price of ever-repeated concessions to the working people" ("Trades Unions," The Labour Standard, May 1881; MECW 24: 386). Yet once more Engels did not disguise his continued disappointment at labor's failure to take advantage of the opportunities offered by the enfranchisement of "the greater portion of the organised working class" (386–7). The British unions continued as always to concern themselves exclusively with the achievement of higher wages and shorter hours for their members, whereas "it is not the lowness of wages which forms the fundamental evil, but the wages system itself" (387). The "struggle for high wages and short hours" was only a means to the higher end, albeit – Engels probably intended the political experience gained – "a very necessary and effective means." He nonetheless predicted, hopefully, that if the trades unions did not come to this awareness there would inevitably arise "a general Union, a political organisation of the working class as a whole" to claim "its full share of representation in Parliament," once again confirming support for the constitutional route to proletarian power.

The creation of a "working man's party" in England would merely introduce there what already existed in Belgium, Holland, Italy, France, and also Germany, where recent repressive measures by Bismarck had been to no avail ("A Working

Men's Party," *The Labour Standard,* July 1881; MECW *24*: 405). Even in America, where upward mobility out of the working class was comparatively easy, such a party existed. The lack of a British equivalent was a mystery because the potential for major reforms that would be released thereby was so patently evident, the working class having already achieved most of the Chartist demands and that for equal electoral districts was "distinctly in sight, a promised reform of the present Government" (406). "And if," Engels proceeds, "the mere recollection of a past political organisation of the working class could effect these political reforms, and a series of social reforms besides, what will the actual presence of a working men's political party do, backed by forty or fifty representatives in Parliament?.... The workpeople of England have but to will, and they are the masters to carry every reform, social and political, which their situation requires." It was "purely the fault of the workers themselves," he lamented, "that they have not had 40 or 50 representatives of their own in Parliament since 1868" ("The Abdication of the Bourgeoisie," October 1889; MECW *26*: 546).

Engels had no explanation for the absence at this time of a working man's party – the Independent Labour Party was created only in 1893 – especially because (as he puts it in another article) "the working class has a majority in all large towns and manufacturing districts" ("Two Model Town Councils," *The Labour Standard,* June 1881: MECW *24*: 396). "And if," he proceeds, "you once have working men in Parliament, in the Town Councils and Local Boards of Guardians, etc., how long will it be ere you will have also working men magistrates?" Even so, the capitalist class had been prepared to surrender much of their legislative power. This fact is, as in "A Working Men's Party," explained by fear:

In every struggle of class against class, the next end fought for is political power; the ruling class defends its political supremacy, that is to say its safe majority in the Legislature; the inferior class fights for, first a share, then the whole of that power, in order to become enabled to change existing laws in conformity with their own interests and requirements. Thus the working class of Great Britain for years fought ardently and even violently for the People's Charter, which was to give it that political power; it was defeated, but the struggle had made such an impression upon the victorious middle class that this class, since then, was only too glad to buy a prolonged armistice at the price of ever-repeated concessions to the working people. ("Trades Unions"; MECW *24*: 386)

An appreciation of the major advances that had been achieved by labor with the direct support of the industrial bourgeoisie – which had learned "that the middle class can never obtain full social and political power over the nation except by the help of the working class" – will be found in the important comparative study of 1885, "England in 1845 and in 1885" (MECW *26*: 297). Indeed, "a gradual change came over the relations between both classes," with Engels's illustrations including progressive constitutional legislation: "The 'Abolition of the Property Qualification' and 'Vote by Ballot' are now the law of the land. The Reform Acts of 1867 and 1884 make a near approach to 'universal suffrage,' at least such as it now exists in Germany." Taking account of prospective legislation, the entire Chartist program would be satisfied: "the Redistribution Bill now before Parliament[38] creates 'equal electoral districts' – on the whole not more unequal than those of France or Germany; 'payment of members' and shorter, if not actually 'annual parliaments,' are visibly looming in the distance – and yet there are people who say that Chartism is dead." All this is confirmed in the 1892 Introduction to the English edition of *Socialism: Utopian and Scientific* (1892):

[Working-class] claims to the franchise . . . gradually became irresistible; while the Whig leaders of the Liberals "funked," Disraeli showed his superiority by making the Tories seize the favorable moment and introduce household suffrage in the boroughs, along with a redistribution of seats. Then followed the ballot; then in 1884 the extension of household suffrage to the counties and a fresh redistribution of seats, by which electoral districts were to some extent equalised. All these measures considerably increased the electoral power of the working class, so much so that in at least 150 to 200 constituencies that class now furnishes the majority of voters. (MECW *27*: 299)

A striking observation in the correspondence of 1890 relates to the significance of the political dimension in answer to those who, misunderstanding the principle of historical materialism, believed "that we deny that the political, etc., reflections of the economic trends have any effect whatsoever on that trend itself" (27 October 1890; MECW *49*: 63). One had only to look at the section in *Capital* on the working day "where legislation, which is, after all, a political act, appears in such an uncompromising light. Or at the section on the history of the bourgeoisie (Chapter 24). Otherwise why should we be fighting for the political dictatorship of the proletariat if political power is economically powerless? Might (i.e. state power) is also an economic force!" Again, the following year: "steps of a truly liberating nature will not be possible until the economic revolution has made the great majority of the workers alive to their situation and thus paved the way for their political rule. The other classes can only patch up or palliate. And this process of clarifying the workers' minds is daily gaining momentum and in 5 or 10 years' time the various parliaments will look very different from what they do today" (24 March 1891; MECW *49*: 153).

Engels's "revisionist" comments of June 1891 on a draft of the German Social Democratic Party program – the Erfurt program (Prolegomena, p. 18) – are very outspoken regarding the constitutional option, though with exception apparently made for Germany:

One can conceive that the old society may develop peacefully into the new one in countries where the representatives of the people concentrate all power in their hands, where, if one has the support of the majority of the people, one can do as one sees fit in a constitutional way: in democratic republics such as France and the U.S.A., in

---

[38] Engels was referring to the Third Reform Act of 1884, which extended the householder and lodger franchise from the boroughs to the countryside, enfranchising nearly 70 percent of males in the counties and nearly doubling the voting population of the United Kingdom and Ireland from just over 3 million men in 1883 to almost 6 million in 1885. The radical implications of the 1884 legislation, supplemented by the Redistribution of Seats Act of 1885, are summarized by Cannadine (1992: 40; also Matthew 1985: 258–9).

monarchies such as Britain, where the imminent abdication of the dynasty in return for financial compensation is discussed in the press daily and where this dynasty is powerless against the people. But in Germany where the government is almost omnipotent and the Reichstag and all other representative bodies have no real power, to advocate such a thing in Germany, when, moreover, there is no need to do so, means removing the fig-leaf from absolutism and becoming oneself a screen for its nakedness. (MECW 27: 226)

Engels concluded that "[i]f one thing is certain, it is that our party and the working class can only come to power under the form of a democratic republic.... But the fact that in Germany it is not permitted to advance even a republican party programme openly, proves how totally mistaken is the belief that a republic, and not only a republic, but also communist society, can be established in a cosy, peaceful way" (227).

Notwithstanding this formulation, Engels was not dogmatic about a German exception to a constitutional option. After all, he had just warned against premature armed action following the excellent results obtained by the Social Democratic party at the polls early in 1890, which made it the second strongest in the German Empire: "At the moment when...the whole social and political situation, when even all their enemies have to work for the Social Democrats, as though they were paid by them – at this moment should discipline and self-control fail, and should we throw ourselves upon the outstretched sword? Never!" ("What Now?" February–March 1890; MECW 27: 10). Again, late in 1891 he expresses his hope that "there will be strife between the landed mobility and the bourgeoisie, and between the protectionist bourgeoisie...and the bourgeoisie favouring free trade...; the stability of the ministries and of the country's domestic policy will be shattered, in other words there will be movement, struggle, vitality, and it is our party that will reap the whole benefit. If things take this turn, our party will be able to come to power round about 1898" (letter to Paul Lafargue, 2 September 1891; MECW 49: 235–6).[39] All this without revolutionary action. Similarly: "Represented by two deputies and one hundred thousand votes from 1866, when universal suffrage opened up to it the doors of the Reichstag, today it has 35 deputies and a million-and-a-half voters, a figure which none of the other parties reached in the elections of 1890.... [T]his party today has reached the point where it is possible to determine the date when it will come to power almost by mathematical calculation" ("Socialism in Germany," 1892; MECW 27: 239–40). Once more Engels appealed for restraint, provided that the authorities did not resort to violent repression:

How many times have the bourgeois called on us to renounce the use of revolutionary means for ever, to remain within the law, now that the exceptional [Anti-Socialist] law has been dropped and one law has been re-established for all, including the socialists?

---

[39] Elsewhere Engels asserted that "[w]e German socialists...would come to power in 10 years' time provided peace is preserved..." (to Bebel, 24, 26 October 1891; MECW 49: 270).

Unfortunately we are not in a position to oblige *messieurs les bourgeois*. Be that as it may, for the time being it is not we who are being destroyed by legality. It is working so well for us that we would be mad to spurn it as long as the situation lasts. It remains to be seen whether it will be the bourgeois and their government who will be the first to turn their back on the law in order to crush us by violence. That is what we shall be waiting for. You shoot first, *messieurs les bourgeois*. (240–1)[40]

This same message with respect to Germany is repeated in 1895, as we shall see.

A comment on developments in France further confirms Engels's commitment to the constitutional path: "As you will have seen from the municipal elections in May and the departmental elections in July, the French are increasingly following in the footsteps of the Germans and learning to make use of universal suffrage instead of inveighing against it" (to Sorge, 23 August 1892; MECW *49*: 508). By late 1893 he felt able to assert that the trend to universal suffrage throughout Western and Central Europe was unstoppable: "there can be no question of a settlement being reached [in Austria] on the basis of some sort of half-baked electoral reform. Once the ball is rolling, the impulsion will communicate itself to all around it, and thus one country will immediately affect its neighbour" (11 October 1893; MECW *50*: 202; cf. 206, 212). More specifically with respect to Austria, Engels stated that what "matters most in Austria is the campaign for universal suffrage, that weapon which, in the hands of class-conscious workers, has a longer range and a surer aim than a small-calibre magazine rifle in the hands of a trained soldier.... [I]f the workers show the political judgment, the patience and perseverance, the unanimity and discipline with which they have already won so many fine victories, then the ultimate victory will surely be theirs. The whole of historical necessity, both economic and political, is on their side" ("To the Fourth Austrian Party Congress," March 1894; MECW *27*: 442).

As for Britain, by the early 1890s Engels's enthusiasm for the progress of parliamentary reform knew no bounds: Gladstone "must... introduce one man one vote by drawing up a sensible electoral register which will ensure the workers do in fact get what was promised them on paper in general terms in 1867 and 1884 but was subsequently retracted in matters of detail, i.e. a $1–1\frac{1}{2}$ million increase in the Labour electorate" (to Regina Bernstein, 25 July 1892; MECW *49*: 482). Again, the next year: "Up till now progress has been splendid and Gladstone will have to capitulate to the workers. Most important of all are the political measures, namely the extension of the franchise for working men by implementing what is presently on paper and which would increase the Labour vote by 50 per cent, the curtailment of the duration of Parliament (now seven years!) and the payment of electoral

---

[40] Regarding Belgium, Engels warned that "the danger with countries possessing a revolutionary past, inasmuch as any new region invaded by socialism is tempted to have its revolution within 24 hours.... All that the Walloons, in particular, comprehend is rioting and in this they are nearly always the losers. Consider the struggles of the Belgian miners; organisation nil or virtually nil, irrepressibly impatient, hence doomed to defeat" (to Lafargue, 19 May 1891; MECW *49*: 191).

expenses and M.P.'s salaries out of public funds" (to Bebel, 9 February 1893; MECW *50*: 104). The Liberals, he concluded – alluding not only to the franchise but to "a whole number of juridical and economic measures for the benefit of workers" – "recognise that, to make sure of governing at the present time, they can do nothing but increase the political power of the working class who will naturally kick them out afterwards" (to Paul Lafargue, 25 February 1893; MECW *50*: 114).[41] In fact, the same held true of the Conservatives who would have to "win the working-class vote by political or economic concessions"; both parties "cannot help extending the power of the working class, and hastening the time which will eliminate both the one and the other" (115). Engels's support for the constitutional path, as always (see above, pp. 204–5), was strictly bounded by the presumption that achievement of proletarian power would guarantee the elimination of the class system.

At this point we anticipate the conclusion to Chapter Five regarding Engels's judgment in the 1885 document "England in 1845 and in 1885" that future prospects for labor's *welfare* were dim, if we consider emerging features of what some later economic historians labeled the "Great Depression," leading him to predict that "there will be Socialism again in England" not seen since the "dying-out of Owenism" (MECW *26*: 301). The Preface to the first English edition of *Capital* (1886) similarly points to the replacement of the cyclical pattern recurrent from 1825 to 1867 by a state of "permanent and chronic depression," with the same implication: "we can almost calculate the moment when the unemployed losing patience will take their own fate into their own hands" (MECW *35*: 36). (In correspondence, too, he declared that "the more quickly [England's] domination of the world market is utterly destroyed, the sooner will the workers over here come to power"; 30 August 1892, MECW *49*: 513.) Might Engels then after all have envisaged violent revolution in Britain? I think not. He proceeds in his 1886 Preface to commend Marx's early prescience in finding England to be the only European country "where the inevitable social revolution might be effected entirely by peaceful and legal means," albeit that the English ruling classes could hardly be expected "to submit, without a 'pro-slavery rebellion,' to this peaceful and legal revolution." Later editions of *The Condition of the Working Class* attribute to "youthful ardor" the original opinion of 1845 (above, p. 179) that a "peaceful solution" was "too late" (Appendix to the 1887 American edition, MECW *26*: 404; Preface to the 1892 English edition, MECW *27*: 262).[42]

---

[41] Engels's enthusiasm was somewhat premature, because the relevant draft legislation was rejected subsequently by the House of Lords (editorial note MECW *50*: 564 n. 162).
  An extra-Parliamentary dimension should also be taken into account: "it's a blessing that Paris and London . . . have municipal councils that are *all too aware* of their dependence on the Labour vote" (to Bebel, 8 March 1892; MECW *49*: 374).

[42] In the American Appendix Engels also admits that, from the perspective of mature scientific communism, the original version of 1845 took a naïve position regarding the prospect of "emancipation" undertaken jointly by the wealthy and working classes (MECW *26*: 404). However, Engels reacted sharply to an earlier rumor that he had actually "disowned" the book (to Marx, 8 April 1863; MECW *41*: 465).

F. The 1895 Introduction to *The Class Struggles in France*

There only remains to consider the 1895 Introduction to *The Class Struggles in France, 1848–1850* so often represented as marking a major "revisionist" break-away from Marx. Any such reading collapses in the face of the facts that have emerged above. In the first place, both Marx and Engels recognized early on the potentiality for achieving proletarian political supremacy by constitutional means, subject always to circumstances propitious for the granting of universal suffrage. The Introduction itself recalls that "*The Communist Manifesto* had already pro-claimed the winning of universal suffrage, of democracy, as one of the first and most important tasks of the militant proletariat" (MECW *27*: 515).[43] Second, the promise of constitutional progress toward the "dictatorship of the proletariat" is reiterated in the early 1890s with respect to an ever-widening range of West European countries and the United States in the light of extensions of the fran-chise. The 1895 document, we conclude, must be read as part of a continuum as far as concerns the case for constitutionality.

We turn now to the Introduction in its own right. There Engels expressed his admiration for Marx's "first attempt" – in *The Class Struggles* published in the *Neue Rheinische Zeitung* (MECW *10*: 45–145; discussed above, pp. 190–2) – to apply his materialist conception of history by "trac[ing] political events back to effects of what were, in the final analysis, economic causes" (MECW *27*: 506). There is a problem with this retroactive view, which ascribes confidence to Marx early in 1850 in the prospect of an imminent and successful proletarian revolution, whereas in fact Marx had then attributed the collapse of the Paris uprising of June 1848 to the fact that industry – and with it a self-conscious proletariat force – had not yet achieved an appropriate level of development (MECW *10*: 116–17; above p. 190). Engels did, however, allow a change in outlook emerging shortly thereafter in the joint article "May to October [1850]": "Whereas in the first three articles... there was still the expectation of an early new upsurge of revolutionary vigour, the historical review written by Marx and myself [numbers 5–6 of the *Neue Rhein-ische Zeitung*, Autumn 1850; MECW *10*: 490–532]... breaks with these illusions once and for all" (MECW *27*: 507–8). Specifically, the joint contribution expressed the realization that "at least the *first* chapter of the revolutionary period was closed and that nothing was to be expected until the outbreak of a new world economic crisis."[44] For this reason, "we were excommunicated, as traitors to the revolution" (510). Yet experience since 1850 had proven even this modified position to have been faulty in that "the state of economic development on the Continent at that time was not, by a long way, ripe for the elimination of capitalist production" (512). With the exception of England and select continental centers, the general establishment of "big industry," and with it an organized proletariat, was only

---

[43] For similar use of the term "militant" in November 1847, see above (p. 184).
[44] See above note 19 on this position.

achieved subsequently: "[History] has proved this by the economic revolution which, since 1848, has seized the whole of the Continent, and has caused big industry to take real root in France, Austria, Hungary, Poland and, recently, in Russia, while it has made Germany positively an industrial country of the first rank – all on a capitalist basis, which in the year 1848, therefore, still had great capacity for expansion." It is, he goes on, "precisely this industrial revolution which... has created a genuine bourgeois and a genuine large-scale industrial proletariat and has pushed them into the foreground of social development."

Now Engels rejected violent revolution in the transformed environment, for experience "has not merely dispelled the erroneous notions we then held; it has also completely transformed the conditions under which the proletariat has to fight. The mode of struggle of 1848 is today obsolete in every respect" (MECW 27: 510). In effect declaring war on the Blanquists,[45] Engels emphasized opportunities for working within the system to achieve proletarian gains. In elaborating this theme, special attention is given to the impact of universal suffrage, especially in the case of Germany since its introduction in 1866 when "Bismarck found himself compelled to introduce this franchise as the only means of interesting the mass of the people in his plans" (515). Indeed, "[w]ith this successful utilisation of universal suffrage... an entirely new method of proletarian struggle came into operation, and this method quickly took on a more tangible form.... [T]he bourgeoisie and the government came to be much more afraid of the legal than of the illegal action of the workers' party, of the results of elections than of those of rebellion" (516).[46]

Engels does not actually specify which social gains had been or might be obtained by labor by means of the franchise. He focuses rather on the "astonishing growth

---

[45] Blanqui denounced legalist or constitutional procedures of arriving at a "dictatorship," and his vision of the latter differed entirely from that of our author. Here are Engels's words:

Blanqui is essentially a political revolutionary, a socialist only in sentiment, because of his sympathy for the sufferings of the people, but he has neither socialist theory nor definite practical proposals for social reforms. In his political activities he was essentially a "man of action," believing that, if a small well-organised minority should attempt to affect a revolutionary uprising at the right moment, it might, after scoring a few initial successes, carry the mass of the people and thus accomplish a victorious revolution.... Since Blanqui regards every revolution as a coup de main by a small revolutionary minority, it automatically follows that its victory must inevitably be succeeded by the establishment of a dictatorship – not, it should be well noted, of the entire revolutionary class, the proletariat, but of the small number of those who accomplished the coup and who themselves are, at first, organised under the dictatorship of one or several individuals. ("Refugee Literature" 1874; MECW 24: 13)

For a modern account, see Cole (1962: 158–67).

[46] The effect extended far and wide: "It was found that the state institutions, in which the rule of the bourgeoisie is organised, offer the working class still further levers to fight these very state institutions. The workers took part in elections to particular diets, to municipal councils and to trades courts; they contested with the bourgeoisie every post in the occupation of which a sufficient part of the proletariat had a say" (MECW 27: 516).

of the [Social Democratic] party," reflecting "the intelligent use which the German workers made of the universal suffrage introduced in 1866" and illustrated by their compelling the abrogation of Bismarck's "Anti-Socialist Law" of 1878 (MECW 27: 514–15).[47] He does, however, cite Marx's "Preamble to the Programme of the French Workers' Party" of May 1880 on universal suffrage as "instrument of emancipation" (516); and the full passage, it will be recalled, makes clear the ultimate object of the exercise, namely the "collective appropriation" of the means of production, which "can only spring from the revolutionary action of the producing class – or proletariat – organised into an independent political party." This organization "must be striven for, using all the means at the disposal of the proletariat, including above all universal suffrage, thus transformed from the instrument of deception which it has been hitherto into an instrument of emancipation" (above, p. 202).

Engels, it may be added, points out that in France universal suffrage had long existed but "had fallen into disrepute through the way it had been abused by the Bonapartist government. After the Commune [1870–71] there was no workers' party to make use of it" (MECW 27: 515). Nonetheless, there had been progress along the legislative route; for even in France, with an insurrectionary tradition dating back a century, "the Socialists are realising more and more that no lasting victory is possible for them unless they first win over the great mass of the people, i.e. the peasants in this instance. Slow propaganda work and parliamentary activity are recognised here, too, as the immediate tasks of the party" (520–1). In Germany, the prospects were much brighter and the proletariat might achieve entirely by legal means, and as early as 1900, a parliamentary majority "beyond the control of the prevailing governmental system" and "before which all other powers will have to bow, whether they like it or not" – here we have, be it noted, one application of the celebrated "dictatorship of the proletariat" – cautioning only that no excuse should be given to the capitalist state to take repressive action and hold up the process (521–2). Once again Engels concludes: "The irony of world history turns everything upside down. We, the 'revolutionaries,' the 'overthrowers' – we are thriving far better on legal methods than on illegal methods and overthrow. The parties of order, as they call themselves, are perishing under the legal conditions created by themselves" (522).[48]

---

[47] See Engels on this repressive measure, in "Bismarck and the German Working Men's Party," *The Labour Standard,* July 1881 (MECW 24: 407–9). The law was passed in October 1878, periodically renewed, and then repealed in October 1890.

[48] It remains to note that this same appeal for restraint appears in a letter to Lafargue at this very time regarding Germany: "In any case, we are striding towards a crisis. . . . As for us, our policy should be not to let ourselves be provoked at this point. . . . Today our Party would be fighting alone against all the others, rallied around the government under the banner of social order; in two or three years we will have on our side the peasants and the petty-bourgeois crushed by taxation. The battle corps does not engage in frontline battles but reserves itself for the critical moment" (to Lafargue 26 February 1895; MECW 50: 447).

G. Limits to Constitutional Revisionism

Why the bourgeoisie would agree to universal suffrage is a question not properly addressed in the Marx–Engels papers of the early 1850s regarding the British case. Such generosity is problematic considering the fact (emerging in Chapter Five) that at this very period Engels and Marx had small hopes for meaningful *social* reform under contemporary capitalist arrangement. All we have to go on is Engels's rationalization that allowing the franchise hastened victory over the aristocracy (above, p. 187), and his recourse to national character to explain that universal suffrage in Britain once granted could not conceivably be withdrawn (above, p. 195).[49] We must remember, however, that the prospect at that time for major constitutional progress was poor, as Engels as well as Marx emphasized; in his retrospective of 1885 Engels points out that the French Revolution of 1848 "saved the English middle class" by putting paid to immediate Chartist victory: "At the very moment Chartism was bound to assert itself in its full strength, it collapsed internally.... The action [the German edition used "political action"] of the working class was thrust into the background" ("England in 1845 and in 1885," *The Commonweal*, March 1885; MECW *26*: 295–6). But this is no longer the case in the documents dating to the early 1880s, where fear – with only the memory of the Chartists at play – is said to have motivated major constitutional concessions (above, p. 207).[50]

The constitutional option thus emerges unmistakably long before 1895. How are we to account for the neglect or minimization of this fact in so many of the commentaries that insist on 1895 as an essential transition date? The rhetoric of

[49] Differences in national character are a pervasive theme, as they had been in the early 1840s (see above, p. 179). For example, Engels represents the German bourgeoisie as "stupid and cowardly," the French as "the most mercenary and pleasure-seeking of all," and the English as having the "keenest sense of class, i.e., sense of politics," ready to make concessions to the workers by extending the suffrage ("The Abdication of the Bourgeoisie," 1889; MECW *26*: 546). The situation, however, was not static. With the passivity of the English bourgeoisie during the London dock strike of 1889 in mind (on which see Chapter Five, p. 265), Engels observed that "the English bourgeoisie (into which the so-called aristocracy has been absorbed and assimilated) exhibited until recently a certain talent for doing justice to its position as leading class at least to some degree. This now seems to be changing more and more" (547). As Henderson phrased the matter, this episode showed for Engels "that the middle classes in England were declining and were no longer able to fulfill the function assigned to them by Karl Marx in his theory of the class struggle," which included the task of abolishing feudal institutions (Henderson 1976: 695).

[50] Engels also touches on the matter when discussing Bismarck's introduction of universal suffrage in 1866. It was partly a matter of creating a counterweight against the powerful remnants of "decaying feudalism," while "fear of the dangerously growing working-class movement did the rest" ("The Role of Force in History" 1887–8; MECW *26*: 502). In some contexts relating to Britain, however, the "old parties" – the Conservatives and Liberals – are represented as ready to make concessions to the new Labour party simply as an accidental matter relating to the mechanics of the political process (to Laura Lafargue, 7 July 1892; MECW *49*: 468).

"revolution" and "dictatorship" has done much to disguise the revisionism apparent throughout the range of Marx–Engels documents extending over nearly half a century. In particular, whereas the ubiquitous term "revolution" seems to suggest *violent* transition, it is frequently intended to convey "social revolution" achieved by constitutional means. The rhetoric of the *Communist Manifesto* – "Let the ruling classes tremble at a Communistic revolution" – is misleading, bearing in mind that this same document expressed strong support for the constitutional movements in Britain and America (and at this time in France) whereby "the conquest of political power by the proletariat" – or "win[ning] the battle of democracy" – would be achieved (above, p. 190). As Marx himself put the matter in 1852, "[u]niversal suffrage is the equivalent for political power for the working class in England.... Its inevitable result, here, is *the political supremacy of the working class*" (p. 197). In 1871, he says: "Insurrection would be madness where peaceful agitation would more swiftly and surely do the work" (p. 199), and in 1872 that the "conquest" of political power might be achieved by "peaceful means" (p. 201); or yet again in 1880 that proletarian political activity even in France must include all means, "including above all universal suffrage" (p. 203).[51]

That there is nothing particularly novel in Engels's 1895 Introduction to *The Class Struggles in France* in this respect is not to say that Marx or Engels positively excluded violent revolution in the achievement of proletarian control – only that very much depended on ruling circumstances, including the stage in national development achieved, the cyclical phases, and even national character and custom (see also below, p. 224). The contrast between Britain and France after the failures of June 1848 is sharply drawn, for in the one case the constitutional option is promising and in the other "force" alone would sooner or later have to be resorted to achieve proletarian control (pp. 191–3). Certainly some expressions used at this period – especially regarding the worsening of cyclical instability in consequence of capitalist development – suggest violent revolution (a matter addressed in Chapter Five). *Capital 1* itself yields several striking instances: "Force is the midwife of every old society pregnant with a new one" (MECW 35: 739); and the "knell of capitalist private property sounds" (750). The same holds true at a much later date, as is clear from the letter of early 1881 where Marx writes of a certain prospect of mounting proletarian "fury" (above, p. 203). All the more important, then, is it to be fully alert to the allowances that proletarian power might be, and was likely to be, achieved by constitutional means, and that universal suffrage might be, and was likely to be, the "instrument of emancipation" toward the "collective appropriation" of the means of production (p. 202).

Note next that Engels's flexibility regarding practical policy reflects tactics in a general sense of the term: "[T]he first objective of the labour movement," he

---

[51] Engels condemned terrorist "acts of folly" by "fanatics," such as a Fenian bomb placed in Clerkenwell Prison that caused civilian casualties (letter to Marx, 19 December 1867; MECW 42: 505–6).

wrote in correspondence of 1893, "is the conquest of political power for and by the working class. Once we are agreed on that, differences of opinion between upright men, in full command of their wits, as to the ways and means of struggle are unlikely to give rise to a dispute over principles. In my view the best tactics in any given country are those which lead most quickly and surely to the goal" (14 March 1893; MECW *50*: 119).[52] Indeed, when evaluating reformist proposals relating to hours and minimum wages, Engels was concerned not to commit the party – referring here to the French Socialist party – in any definitive way, thereby indicating tactical concerns with a vengeance:

I see these proposals simply as a means of propaganda, since with the present house there is no chance of seeing them accepted. From this point of view, we would first have to assure ourselves of their efficacy, and then determine whether or not they might be of interest for future action by the party when we are in a position to proceed to positive legislative activity. It is from this angle that I have formulated my criticism, and here I find just one point that seems to me to be dubious; whether it is wise to promise 40 million annually to the peasants in a form and for a purpose so clearly defined. The peasants could one day present us with this promissory note, and at a time when we might have better uses for such a sum. (3 March 1895; MECW *50*: 454)[53]

Beyond this, though, the insistence in the 1895 Introduction on legality as the route to proletarian power was a tactical matter in the literal sense, reflecting allowance for recent advances in military technology that gave the advantage in any violent encounter to the armed forces of the state: "[T]he conditions of the struggle had changed fundamentally. Rebellion in the old style, street fighting with barricades, which decided the issue everywhere up to 1848, had become largely outdated" (MECW *27*: 517).[54] But here he steps back somewhat from

---

[52] For an emphasis on this dimension, see Steger (1999) and Wilde (1999).

[53] On Engels's evaluation of the alternatives appropriate for adoption by various national working-class parties, see Concheiro (1998: 171–2).

 An earlier letter on advisable Social Democratic voting patterns raises several difficulties. Engels had there recommended support for "questions that immediately involve the relation of workers to capitalists," including factory legislation and hours, and "[p]]erhaps also improvements in the purely bourgeois sense such as constitute a positive step forward," including "standardisation of coins, and weights, freedom of movement, extension of personal freedom, etc." (to Bebel, 24 November 1879; MECW *45*: 423). These illustrations reveal Engels's priorities. There are his doubts regarding advisable voting in the case of "bourgeois" concerns relating to personal freedom; but his primary concern, he goes on to specify, was with "all other economic questions, such as protective tariffs, nationalisation of railways, assurance companies, etc. Social Demoratic deputies must always uphold the vital principle of consenting to nothing that increases the power of the government vis-à-vis the people . . . and hence abstention . . . is automatically called for" (423–4). The problem we face is that elsewhere Engels represents nationalization as an integral element in the natural course of evolution of capitalism to be supported for that reason (see Chapter Three, Section H). Similarly, protection by Continental states was supported in other contexts as providing a stimulus to capitalist development and thus hastening its ultimate collapse (see Appendix to Chapter Five, pp. 359–60).

[54] The theme appears three years earlier in correspondence with Paul Lafargue: The new weaponry was ideal "for curbing the so-called revolutionary inclinations, on whose outbursts our governments count. The era of barricades and street fighting has gone for good; *if*

his moderate position by going on to ask this question: "Does that mean that in the future street fighting will not longer play any role? Certainly not. It only means that the conditions since 1848 have become far more unfavourable for civilian fighters and far more favourable for the military" (519). He points out that throughout Continental Europe, including Russia, and in Latin countries, "the German example of utilising the suffrage, of winning all posts accessible to us, has been imitated," but he adds that "[o]f course, our foreign comrades do not in the least renounce their right to revolution" (520–1). He also adds a veiled warning that the government might, even without the excuse provided by illegal action, take repressive action: "Breach of the constitution, dictatorship, return to absolutism" (523); but he leaves the matter open: "If, therefore, you break the constitution of the Reich, Social-Democracy is free, and can do as it pleases with regard to you." "You shoot first, *messieurs les bourgeois*" is how he expressed the warning in 1892 (above, p. 211).

To Engels's distress, his qualifications were omitted from the excerpts published by *Vorwärts*, the organ of the SPD, whose Central Committee headed by Wilhelm Liebknecht wished to avoid problems in the light of pending anti-agitational legislation.[55] Engels explained his position to Kautsky: "I was amazed to see today in the *Vorwärts* an excerpt from my 'Introduction' that had been *printed without my prior knowledge* and tricked out in such a way as to present me as a peace-loving proponent of legality *quand même*. Which is all the more reason why I should like it to appear in its entirety in the *Neue Zeit* in order that this disgraceful impression may be erased" (1 April 1895; MECW 50: 486). He made further explanation to Paul Lafargue: "I preach those tactics only for the *Germany of today* and even then with many *reservations*. For France, Belgium, Italy, Austria, such tactics could not be followed as a whole and, for Germany, they could become inapplicable tomorrow" (3 April 1895; 490).

Engels evidently found himself in a severe quandary,[56] but it is not one that emerged for the first time in 1895. For example, so conciliatory is Engels's position in *The Labour Standard* for 1881 in terms of what had been achieved by way of the parliamentary process, and what might be achieved if only the working class

---

the military fight, resistance becomes madness. Hence the necessity to find new revolutionary tactics. I have pondered over this for some time and am not yet settled in my mind" (3 November 1892; MECW 50: 21–2). A year later, he writes this to Kautsky in Vienna: "You say yourself that barricades are out of date, though" – Engels adds – "they might come in handy again as soon as a third or two-fifths of the army had turned socialist and it was imperative that they be given an opportunity of changing sides" (3 November 1893; 225).

[55] See Collier (1996: 37). The complaints refer to unauthorized omissions from the 1895 Introduction in the version published by *Vorwärts*.

Other modifications had been conceded by Engels with regret. Writing to Kautsky, he allowed that "[m]y text has suffered to some extent from the apprehensive objections, inspired by the Subversion Bill, of our friends in Berlin – objections of which, in the circumstances, I could not but take into account" (25 March 1895; MECW 50: 480).

[56] The "chronic dilemma" facing Marxists in general is splendidly described in Tuchman (1967: 478–80).

was willing to become more active on the political front, that one is left wondering whether anything at all is left of the ultimate communist objective. There is, after all, nothing very radical in his appeal "to give the working classes a turn for the next twenty-five years" – in place of the "absolute reign" of Manchester School Free Trade doctrines – since "they could not manage worse" ("Cotton and Iron," July 1881; MECW *24*: 414).[57] In fact, one might be led to suppose so total a commitment to parliamentary principles that even a reversal of a working-class majority at the polls would be tolerated: "give the working classes a turn" is all that is demanded. Similarly, in 1891 Engels proposed to Kautsky a modification to a draft program to the effect that "what [the proletarians] need for their economic struggles and their organisation as a militant class is a measure of political freedom and equal rights that will grow with their successes" (28 September 1891; MECW *49*: 240), which is scarcely very radical. (We recall the same tone in several of Marx's formulations in the late 1860s and early 1870s; above, pp. 198–9).

If these observations reflect Engels's considered position rather than temporary dejection in the light of immediate prospects, his concern at being misrepresented by *Vorwärts* would be inexplicable. But two considerations require attention. First, Engels never deviated from the conditional character of his support for universal suffrage, first expressed in 1865, conditional, that is, on a proletarian majority toeing the party line (above, pp. 204–5, 212).[58] This qualification is reflected in the circular letter dated 17–18 September 1879, signed by Marx and Engels but written by Engels, addressed to several leaders of the German Social Democratic Party, protesting at the voting behavior of a Reichstag party member, Max Kayser (MECW *45*: 397–401). Kayser's offense was to have voted for indirect taxes (in support of protective tariffs), against the party program, and also for granting Bismarck funds, against party tactics (399). Engels's position is enunciated in the course of his rejection of criticisms by Eduard Bernstein and others of Carl Hirsch, who, in his short-lived newspaper *Die Laterne*, had condemned Kayser along these lines. Hirsch had every right to condemn Kayser, Engels insisted, "[o]r has German Social-Democracy indeed been infected with the parliamentary disease, believing that, with the popular vote, the Holy Ghost is poured upon those elected,

---

[57] Rather unexpected is a remark at this time regarding the responsibility for the British Empire that would fall to a constitutionally elected proletariat: "in England, where the industrial and agricultural working class forms the immense majority of the people, democracy means the dominion of the working class, neither more nor less. Let, then, that working class prepare itself for the task in store for it, – the ruling of this great empire; let them understand the responsibilities which inevitably will fall to their share" ("A Working Men's Party," 1881; MECW *24*: 405).

[58] Laski maintained that Marx and Engels "could not . . . have envisaged the Communist Party acting as a dictatorship over the working class and excluding all other parties from the right to share in, and influence over, the exercise of power" (1967 [1948]: 66). This is a difficult issue. Other parties might be tolerated, but not to the point of constituting a genuine alternative; after all, even the "proletarian majority" had to toe the line. It is true, however, that Engels must not be identified with Blanqui with regard to the character of the "dictatorship of the proletariat" (see note 45).

that meetings of the faction are transformed into infallible councils and factional resolutions into sacrosanct dogma?" (400). Pace Nimtz (2000: 255–9), this episode is not evidence of Engels's hostility toward universal suffrage and parliamentary activity as a means to achieve proletarian control, but rather points to insistence on "party discipline" by the proletarian party.[59]

Second, Engels's concern that he had been misrepresented can be appreciated by focusing on his unshaken commitment to the ultimate objective of a proletarian "dictatorship" – however achieved – namely a control economy in a classless society. All this goes back to the 1840s, when a "democratic constitution" is favored as the best means, in some circumstances, to that specific end (above, pp. 181, 184–5).[60] The joint "Address of the Central Authority to the League of Communists" in March 1850 with respect to the insufficiency of petty-bourgeois reformist demands is particularly instructive:

[I]t is our interest and our task to make the revolution permanent, until all more or less possessing classes have been forced out of their position of dominance, the proletariat has conquered state power, and the association of proletarians, not only in one country but in all the dominant countries of the world, has advanced so far that competition among the proletarians in these countries has ceased and that at least the decisive productive forces are concentrated in the hands of the proletarians. For us the issue cannot be the alteration of private property but only its annihilation, not the smoothing over of class antagonisms but the abolition of classes, not the improvement of the existing society but the foundation of a new one. (MECW *10*: 281)

In 1881 we find repeated in "Trades Unions" the quite standard proposition that "it is not the lowness of wages which forms the fundamental evil, but the wages system itself" (above, p. 207).[61] Here, too, the parliamentary route toward the establishment of the so-called dictatorship of the proletariat and the eradication of the "fundamental evil" is spelled out with admirable clarity: "In every struggle of class against class, the next end fought for is political power; the ruling class defends its political supremacy, that is to say its safe majority in the Legislature; the inferior class fights for, first a share, then the whole of that power, in order to become enabled to change existing laws in conformity with their own interests

---

[59] Marx's account of the episode similarly refers to the parliamentary faction that reportedly authorized Kayser to speak as "already so far infected with parliamentary cretinism as to believe themselves above criticism and to denounce criticism as a *crime de lèse majesté!*" (to Sorge, 19 September 1879; MECW *45*: 414).

For all that, Engels showed some flexibility with respect to party discipline in general. In a comment to Plekhanov, he advised "let us not require too much orthodoxy! The party is too large, and the theory of Marx has become too widespread for relatively isolated muddle headed persons to do too much harm in the West. In your part of the world it is different, as it was with us in 1845–59" (26 February 1895; MECW *50*: 451).

On the Marx–Engels notion of "party," see Hobsbawm (1982b: 237–8).

[60] See also Engels's remark of 1850 that, once the 1847 Factory Act had passed, "the labour movement concentrate[d] wholly on achieving the political rule of the proletariat as the prime means of transforming the whole of existing society" (MECW *10*: 293).

[61] For an elaboration of this theme, see Chapter Five, Section F.

and requirements" (above, p. 208). By contrast, Marx seems to have been less san-
guine about the untrammeled ability of the proletariat to introduce a communist
legislative program even when it possessed a firm majority. Discussing the English
and American cases, he enters a qualification: "They could, by lawful means, rid
themselves of such laws and institutions as impeded their development, though
they could only do so insofar as society had reached a sufficiently mature development" (1878; "Parliamentary Debate on the Anti-Socialist Law"; MECW *24*: 248).
Could he have intended that public opinion had to be taken into consideration?

The case for "common ownership" as final objective, with emphasis on the
"gradual" implementation of the program once the proletariat had "gained "political supremacy," will be found reiterated in Engels's correspondence of the 1890s:

> The crucial difference between [socialist] society and conditions today consists, of
> course, in the organisation of production on the basis of common ownership, initially
> by the nation, of all means of production. I see absolutely no difficulty in carrying out
> this revolution over a period, i.e. gradually.... Assuming... that we have an adequate
> number of supporters among the masses, the socialisation of large-scale industry and
> of the farms on the big estates can be carried out very quickly, once we have gained
> political supremacy. The rest will soon follow at a faster or slower pace. And when the
> large sources of production are ours, we shall be masters of the situation. (21 August
> 1890; MECW *49*: 18–19)

To another German correspondent, Engels opined that bourgeois reformist measures in response to requirements generated by capitalist economic development –
he intended technical change and labor displacement in particular – must undermine capitalist organization at the very time when proletarian parliamentary power
would have been achieved (this also apparently a consequence of capitalist economic development), paving the way for a radical transformation:

> The more quickly and irrevocably this economic revolution takes place, the more
> imperative will measures impose themselves which, apparently intended to cure evils
> that have suddenly assumed vast and intolerable proportions, will eventually result in
> undermining the foundations of the existing mode of production; and the more rapidly,
> too, will the working masses obtain a hearing thanks to universal suffrage.... [A]s I see
> it, steps of a truly liberating nature will not be possible until the economic revolution
> has made the great majority of the workers alive to their situation and thus paved the
> way for their political rule. The other classes can only patch up or palliate. (24 March
> 1891; 153)[62]

Accordingly, current proposals relating to expropriation of land in Germany would
not suffice. Engels complained to Paul Lafargue in France of the "nominally 'socialist' radicals in the Chamber... the detritus of Proudhonism and, as such, the

---

[62] Engels goes on to assert that "this process of clarifying the workers' minds is daily gaining
momentum and in 5 or 10 years' time the various parliaments will look very different from
what they do today" (MECW *49*: 153).

avowed opponents of the socialisation of the means of production" (31 October 1891; 281).

At the same time, it is true, Engels objected that Kautsky's proposed designation for the forthcoming Erfurt Congress of bourgeois opponents as "one reactionary mass" – a Lassallian phrase – neglected the major reformist measures, as illustrated by the extended franchise in Britain: "Take the Englishmen of the two official parties who have vastly extended the suffrage and brought about a fivefold increase in the number of voters, who have evened out the size of constituencies and introduced compulsory and improved schooling, who at every session still vote not only for bourgeois reforms but also for one concession after another in favour of the working man – their progress may be slow and sluggish but nobody can condemn them out of hand as '*one* reactionary mass'" (14 October 1891; MECW *49*: 262).[63] But these reforms – and others that the bourgeoisie might propose even after the "revolution" (implying proletarian political control) – have to be understood as taking place within "a system that was [my emphasis] in *the process of being overthrown*," though with a hint of doubt with respect to the final outcome in England: "[W]e have no right to present a tendency in gradual process of realisation as an already accomplished fact, the less so in that in England, for example, such a tendency will *never* quite get to the point of becoming a fact. Come the revolution over here, the bourgeoisie would still be prepared to introduce all sorts of minor reforms, though by then it would be quite pointless to insist on minor reforms in a system that was in the process of being overthrown" (262).[64] To Engels's delight, Kautsky obliged and removed the offending phrase (letter to Kautsky, 25 October 1891; 273).

The correspondence of the 1890s does express disappointment with the slow awakening of a proletarian "consciousness," particularly in Britain, where the course of events raised new doubts regarding the rapidity of achievement of a proletarian majority committed to a communist program, reminiscent of Engels's

---

[63] On objections to Lassalle on these grounds, see Engels to Bebel, 18–28 March 1875 (MECW *45*: 61, 73). The draft legislation was in fact rejected by the Reichstag in May 1895 (for details see the editorial note in MECW *50*: 593 n. 428).

[64] In a revealing remark to Kautsky on the Erfurt Congress, Engels insisted that support for various reform measures in the Party program must be understood as applying to a *future* socialist régime, though it was strategic to demand them immediately:

The practical demands contain all kinds of snags; many of them seem philistine – if applied to conditions today – but now that we occupy a position of power we can reply quite rightly that they will certainly not be implemented until we come to the helm and that they will then assume quite a different character. As for instance, free legal advice. A six hours' working day up till the age of 18 obviously ought to have gone in – as also the banning of night work for women and of any sort of work at the very least one month before and 6 weeks after a confinement. (3 December 1891; MECW *49*: 315)

Discussing the expropriation of big landed proprietors once "our Party is in possession of political power," Engels recalled that "[w]e by no means consider compensation as impermissible in any event; Marx told me (and how many times!) that in his opinion we would get off cheapest if we could buy out the whole lot of them" (1894, "The Peasant Question in France and Germany"; MECW *27*: 500).

dispirited remark to Marx in 1863 (above, pp. 205–6).[65] Thus he made complaint to Sorge: "What is most repellent here is the workers' deeply ingrained sense of middle-class *'respectability.'* The division of society into innumerable, incontestably recognised grades, each having its own pride but also an innate respect for its *'betters'* and *'superiors,'* is so old and so firmly established that it's still pretty easy for the middle classes to practice their allurements" (7 December 1889; MECW *48*: 418). In 1892, immediately after outlining the success of the working class at the polls following the 1884 extensions to the suffrage, he commented that "parliamentary government is a capital school for teaching respect for tradition," and that the middle class, who "had been compelled to incorporate the better part of the People's Charter in the Statutes of the United Kingdom," were engaged in efforts to keep the masses in order "by moral means" (Introduction to *Socialism: Utopian and Scientific*, April 1892; MECW *27*: 299–300). Nonetheless, tradition, though "a great retarding force . . . [was] sure to be broken down; and thus religion will be no lasting safeguard to capitalist society" (300).

* * *

That Engels's revisionism never diluted the final objective of the "dictatorship of the proletariat," namely to set in motion a program designed to ensure a total social transformation, is also evident from his evaluation in the 1895 Introduction of the joint contribution of 1850 to the *Neue Rheinische Zeitung* (above, p. 213):

What gives our work quite special significance is the fact that it was the first to express the formula in which, by common agreement, the workers' parties of all countries in the world briefly summarise their demand for economic transformation: the appropriation of the means of production by society. In the second chapter, in connection with the "right to work" . . . it is said [MECW *10*: 78]: "but behind the right to work stands the power over capital; behind the power over capital, the *appropriation of the means of production*, their subjection to the associated working class and, therefore, the abolition of wage labour, of capital and of their mutual relations." (MECW *27*: 508)

Account must also be taken when we are evaluating the extent of Engels's revisionism of the fact that he addressed as an immediate problem the provision of skilled personnel to operate the new system to be set in place once proletarian power had been achieved. One indication will be found in the letter of 21 August 1890:

The fact that our working men are up to it is borne out by their many productive and distributive associations which . . . are managed no worse and far more honestly

---

[65] Engels's concerns were well founded. For example, in the 1874 elections, "striking Conservative gains were recorded in great manufacturing towns, such as Manchester, Leeds, Bradford, Oldham, Newcastle-upon-Tyne, Nottingham, Stoke-on-Trent, Wakefield, Wigan, Warrington, Stalybridge, and Northampton, as well as in the large populous London districts such as Chelsea, Greenwich, Marylebone, Southwark, and, most important of all, the vast constituency of Tower Hamlets" (Briggs 1990: 298).

than the joint-stock companies of the middle classes. I fail to see how you can talk of inadequate education among the masses in Germany, now that our workers have given such striking proof of political maturity in their victorious struggle against the Anti-Socialist Law.... Admittedly we are still short of technicians, agronomists, engineers, chemists, architects, etc., but if the worst comes to the worst we can buy them, just as the capitalists do, and if a stern example is made of a traitor or two – of whom there will assuredly be some in such company – they will find it in their interest to cease robbing us. (MECW 49: 18–19)

We find an optimistic tone regarding the supply of managerial skills available for the planned economy in a letter of 26 October 1891 to Bebel:

If we are to take over and operate the means of production, we need people who are technically trained and plenty of them. These we have not got, and have even been pretty glad hitherto to have been largely spared the company of the "educated." Now things have changed. Now we are strong enough to absorb and digest any quantity of educated riff-raff and I would predict that in the next 8 or 10 years we shall recruit enough young technicians, doctors, jurists and schoolmasters for the factories and large estates to be managed for the nation by party members. In which case our accession to power will take place quite naturally and will run a – relatively – smooth course. (272)[66]

Anticipating the Soviet preoccupation with "wrecking" is the mention above of the "stern example" that might have to be made "of a traitor or two" among the specialist personnel required by socialist industry. This raises once again the question of legitimate violence. In the event of a so-called premature acquisition of proletarian power, a "reign of terror" would have to be unleashed to deal with sabotage by the professional elite: "If... we come to the helm prematurely and as a result of war, the technicians will be our principal opponents and will deceive and betray us at every turn; we should have to inaugurate a reign of terror against them and would lose out all the same. This is what *always* happened to the French revolutionaries, if on a smaller scale; even in everyday administration they had to leave the subordinate, really operative, posts to their former reactionary incumbents – men who hampered and paralysed everything" (MECW 49: 272).[67] This may be something of a special case, limited specifically to a premature takeover. However,

---

[66] See also a letter of 19 July 1893 regarding practical industrial and agricultural issues, including hours and training of labor for agricultural tasks (MECW 50: 168–71).

[67] Responding to Bebel's more optimistic view of the prospective loyalty to the socialist cause of German scientists, teachers, officials, and technicians (see MECW 49: 612 n. 353), Engels made this objection: "I am glad to hear that so much sympathy is already felt for us in technologically educated circles. But from what I experienced in 1848 and 1870/71 of the French Republicans, who were after all themselves bourgeois, I know only too well just how far one gets with such silent hangers-on and sympathisers – in time of danger" (9–10 November 1891; 294). The danger was particularly acute "in relation to so important a business as the socialisation of large-scale industry and large-scale agriculture".

there are more general allowances for violent means to protect a proletarian "dictatorship" – whether achieved via the ballot box or revolution – against reactionary
counter-revolution, which suggests a further qualification to Engels's revisionism.
For example, there is his early warning – based on the French experience of 1830 –
that "the enemy once beaten" still remains a danger ("The Reform Movement in
France," November 1847; MECW 6: 381). A reference in "The Communists and
Karl Heinzen" (September to October 1847; MECW 6: 295) to the maintenance of
proletarian achievements "by force of arms" makes the point explicitly.[68] Similarly,
"if the victorious party does not want to have fought in vain, it must maintain
this rule by means of the terror which its arms inspire in the reactionaries"
("On Authority," 1873; MECW 23: 425). Further, Engels justifies the state – pace
objections to this institution by the anarchists – as the (transitional) instrument "to
keep down one's enemies by force" (to Bebel, 18–28 March 1875; MECW 45: 64), a
theme elaborated in *Anti-Dühring* (MECW 25: 267–8). Precisely the same attitude
is expressed in a letter of 1892 to Paul Lafargue – recently elected to the French
Chamber of Deputies – alluding to "armed revolution" in the event that the bourgeoisie reverts to force against a constitutionally elected working-class majority;
in fact, the passage confirms in a striking manner Engels's support for the "slower
and more boring" path to proletarian power rather than literal "revolution," but
it also points out that such an achievement would probably encourage "the rulers
to overthrow legality," signaling the opportune moment for "armed [counter]
revolution":

Do you realise now what a splendid weapon you in France have had in your hands for
forty years in universal suffrage; if only people had known how to use it! It's slower
and more boring than the call to revolution, but it's ten times more sure, and what is
even better, it indicates with the most perfect accuracy the day when a call to armed
revolution has to be made; it's even ten to one that universal suffrage, intelligently used
by the workers, will drive the rulers to overthrow legality, that is, to put us in the most
favourable position to make the revolution. (12 November 1892; MECW 50: 29)

This text is taken by Nimtz as evidence against "all of the social democratic efforts to
make [Engels] a reformist" (2000: 261). However, Nimtz's interpretation implies
that Engels was wholly unconcerned with achieving a proletarian majority in
Parliament (Prolegomena, p. 19), whereas the passage points to universal suffrage
as the means of achieving proletarian control or "dictatorship" rather than by way
of violent overthrow of the legal authority. Indeed, it is to counter reactionary

---

[68] See also the reference to "the forcible overthrow of all existing social conditions" (above, p. 189).
For all that, Engels expressed his concern in 1870 with the prospect of useless cruelty in Paris, as
is clear from a letter to Marx in which he condemns the Reign of Terror of 1793 and attributes
it to "the bourgeois frightened out of their wits and setting out to comport themselves like
patriots," and to "the mob of the underworld" (4 September 1870; MECW 44: 63).
    On the role allowed coercion during the transition period to full communism, see Popper
(1983 [1945]: 328 n. 6) and Duncan (1973: 180–1).

efforts to overthrow the legal authority that violence is justified, wholly consistent with the position established in the mid-1840s.[69]

H. Concluding Remarks

In taking the foregoing line, Engels was following a precedent set by Marx, who in a first draft of "The Civil War in France" (1871) represents the Commune in Paris and other great towns as having achieved provisional proletarian power (in this case, of course, by non-Parliamentary means) subject to the prospect of reaction and consequentially of defensive counterattack (MECW *22*: 491). Marx there opines that reactionary outbreaks would be only sporadic once communist organization had achieved national status and, he hints, not even unwelcome: "The communal organization once firmly established on a national scale, the catastrophes it might still have to undergo, would be sporadic slaveholders' insurrections, which, while for a moment interrupting the work of peaceful progress, would only accelerate the movement, by putting the sword into the hand of the Social Revolution." There is also Marx's draft on the Reichstag debate on Bismarck's Anti-Socialist Law in 1878 (above, p. 203). Violent means of maintaining power once achieved are certainly not ruled out.

Some of Engels's pronouncements appear to justify "preventive" revolutionary activity against efforts to abolish universal suffrage by reactionaries fearful of the mere prospect of a proletarian majority. For example, a "new Anti-Socialist Law" as envisaged by Bismarck's replacement as Chancellor "can only strengthen the party in proportion to the individual existences it destroys. Anyone who has got the better of Bismarck need have no fear of his successor. . . . If Caprivi does away with universal suffrage he will destroy a great empire, namely that of the Hohenzollerns" (19 July 1893; MECW *50*: 168).[70] Such an eventuality, however, does not efface a

---

[69] The democratic component in Nimtz's title actually refers to internal Party matters (2000: 258, 266–7, 275, 298), notwithstanding that his Preface itself defines democracy in standard liberal terms as the "institution of 'universal suffrage,' the 'responsibility of the state apparatus to the elected parliament,' and the acquisition of civil liberties" (vii). Indeed, were Engels disinterested in the achievement by the proletariat of a parliamentary majority, as Nimtz maintains, it is difficult to see how he (and Marx) can be represented as contributing to the "democratic breakthrough" in the *liberal* sense of the expression. King, who reads Nimtz as making out a case for Engels and Marx as "consistent and thoroughgoing democrats," not surprisingly finds that Nimtz undermines any such position as he proceeds (King 2002: 220).

[70] See also "Socialism in Germany" (1892): "One fine day the German bourgeois and their government . . . witnessing the ever increasing advances of socialism, will resort to illegality and violence. To what avail? [T]here is no force in the world which can wipe out a party of two million men spread out over the entire surface-area of a large empire. Counter-revolutionary violence will be able to slow down the victory of socialism by a few years; but only in order to make it all the more complete when it comes" (MECW *27*: 241). There are allusions in 1895 to attempts by the German landowning class to instigate illegal responses by Socialist members of the Reichstag as an excuse to undertake a coup d' état (MECW *50*: 419, 423, 426).

preference under increasingly appropriate conditions for arriving at a proletarian "dictatorship" by way of appeal to the electorate.[71]

There is a further qualification to Engels's revisionism. Although he seems to have countenanced in his final years a constitutional transformation of society in Germany, "like all Marxists at all times, he considered the peaceful, or even gradual perspectives in some countries in the general context of a world situation in which the 'old-fashioned' revolutionary developments of some regions – Engels thought of Russia – would react back upon the non-revolutionary ones" (Hobsbawm 1964: 341n.). We encounter an instance of this perspective in Engels's criticism of Bernstein and his colleagues in 1879 (above, p. 220): "If, therefore, the 5–600,000 Social-Democratic voters, 1/10 to 1/8 of the total electorate . . . have sense enough not to beat their heads against a wall and attempt a 'bloody revolution' with odds at one to ten, this is supposed to prove that they will, for all time, continue to *deny* themselves all chance of exploiting some violent upheaval abroad, a sudden wave of revolutionary fervour engendered thereby, or even a people's *victory* arising therefrom!" (MECW *45*: 404). The jointly written Preface to the 1882 Russian edition of the *Communist Manifesto* makes the point in question (see Appendix to Chapter Seven, p. 370).

I close with a final qualification of no small importance, for it suggests Engels's order of priorities. Thus in his objections to the draft Gotha program he played down "legislation by the people" relative to "administration by the people": "That a host of somewhat muddled and *purely democratic demands* should figure in the programme, some of them being of a purely fashionable nature – for instance 'legislation by the people' such as exists in Switzerland and does more harm than good, if it can be said to do anything at all. *Administration* by the people – that would at least be something. Similarly omitted is the first prerequisite of all liberty – that all officials be responsible for all their official actions to every citizen before the ordinary courts and in accordance with common laws" (to Bebel, 18–28 March 1875; MECW *45*: 63). Marx's appreciation of the Paris Commune had in fact turned to some degree on this dimension (1871; MECW *22*: 331–6; see above pp. 199–200).

---

[71] Even the passage in *The Origin of the Family* upon which Nimtz bases much of his case for Parliamentarian activity as mere "gauge" (2000: 260, see Prolegomena, p. 19) can be read as referring to the achievement of a Parliamentary majority by an independent proletarian party, and a warning to the opposition that such a majority presaged the end of capitalist arrangement:

[T]he possessing class rules directly through the medium of universal suffrage. As long as the oppressed class, in our case, therefore, the proletariat, is not yet ripe to emancipate itself, it will in its majority regard the existing order of society as the only one possible and, politically, will form the tail of the capitalist, class, its extreme Left wing. To the extent, however, that this class matures for its self-emancipation, it constitutes itself as a party of its own and elects its own representatives, not those of the capitalists. Thus, universal suffrage is the gauge of the maturity of the working class. It cannot and never will be anything more in the present-day state; but that is sufficient. On the day the thermometer of universal suffrage registers boiling point among the workers, both they and the capitalists will know where they stand. (MECW *26*: 272)

FIVE

"Revisionism" II. Social Reform

A. Introduction

This chapter extends the discussion of "revisionism" from the constitutional to the welfare front. What concessions, if any, could be expected from the bourgeoisie in terms of its willingness and ability to improve working-class well-being?

Section B specifies the principles of social reform emerging in the late 1840s and early 1850s. Measures championed in Engels's *Principles of Communism* and then in the *Communist Manifesto* as part of a program to be introduced once the proletariat had acquired political control of the state apparatus – the Factory Acts in particular – were unacceptable if adopted by the bourgeois régime itself, for such measures restrained capitalist development. Those measures that, to the contrary, gave capitalist development free rein – free trade is a prime instance – were acceptable though their perceived consequence might be to worsen working-class living conditions, precisely because by encouraging capitalist development they thereby also hastened its demise. As for unions, they were countenanced by Engels in *The Condition of the Working Class* (1845) and by Marx in the *Poverty of Philosophy* (1847), not as a counteracting or modifying force capable of reversing the downward wage trend but as an inevitable consequence of capitalist industrialization providing political training to a united, nationally organized, work force.

Marx's *The Class Struggles in France* of 1850 again opposes the range of reforms proposed in the *Communist Manifesto* as obstructing capitalist development. However, now the focus of attention is on the refusal of the bourgeois state to tolerate reform as proven by British as well as French experience. (That effective constitutional reform was recognized by Marx at this time, at least in Britain, reinforces the desirability of treating welfare apart from constitutional considerations.) The same picture emerges in two contributions of 1850 by Engels relating to the recently enacted Ten Hours' Bill. This he opposed on the standard grounds that it would restrain capitalist development. As with Marx, though, this undesirable effect did not come into play because the restrictions on hours imposed by the 1847 act were sidestepped in practice. Engels in fact applauded efforts to thwart the legislation.

Section C brings evidence from the 1860s and 1870s – an important address of 1864, *Capital* itself, and "Political Indifferentism" (1873) – revealing Marx's recognition of major welfare advances in the British case. The contrast with 1850 is remarkable, as Marx now emphasizes the real gains to adult male labor from factory legislation that he applauded, setting aside his own and Engels's earlier belief that such measures would never be tolerated in practice. That the factory magnates had now become reconciled to the inevitable indeed reflected the impact of ever-increasing proletarian power. Marx in fact treats social welfare legislation as one of his "tendencies working with iron necessity towards inevitable results" (below, p. 243), putting a completely different gloss on the canvas than that normally encountered.

This new stance is not yet reflected in Engels's *The Housing Question* (1872–3), discussed in Section D. Indeed, his main concern was to deny the potential of various projects to improve the real wage, wholly in line with Marx in this regard. Nevertheless, he does touch on the broader aspects of social reform with particular reference to housing. Much as in the 1850s, this is envisaged as reactionary by restraining capitalist development. The capitalist state in any event was both unable and unwilling to remedy "the housing calamity."

Section E documents the emergence of a clear "revisionist" stance by Engels in 1874 and in various papers of the 1880s. Here significant social reforms are recognized, notwithstanding in Britain the absence of a formal working-class political party equivalent to the Continental Social Democrats. Like Marx, Engels stressed the necessitarian character of these welfare trends. His positive estimate at this period of the potential to ensure that workers would receive improved real wages by unionization goes beyond Marx's allowances for welfare improvement, which relate solely to labor's "physical and moral regeneration." So too does his recognition, documented in Section F, of the unionization of unskilled London dock and gas workers and the consequential modest improvement in their earnings as well as work conditions. Deterioration in the case of the mass of unskilled labor remains a feature of the account.

As I argued in Chapter Four, at no time did Engels abandon the ultimate Marxian objective – the complete dismantling of capitalist institutions. Nonetheless, secularly rising real wages and improving conditions, even if limited to unionized industrial workers, compromised this outcome, especially considering the promise of unionization more broadly. This dilemma is described in Section G; as I show in Section H, it is resolved by Engels in terms of the perceived setting in of secular decline with the end of Britain's industrial monopoly, coupled with a threat to living standards that emanated from imminent Chinese immigration on a massive scale. Welfare gains were unsustainable.

B. Principles of Reform: Early Statements

Engels's *Principles of Communism* (October 1847) formulates a fundamental principle of social reform: The very same measures appearing as part of a program to dismantle the private-property system were otherwise unacceptable. "Democracy would be quite useless to the proletariat if it were not immediately used as a means of carrying through further measures directly attacking private ownership and securing the means of subsistence of the proletariat" (MECW 6: 350). The "democratic socialists" supported part of the program to appear shortly in the *Communist Manifesto* – which assumes proletarian control of the state apparatus (see Chapter Four, note 8) – not "as a means of transition to communism but as measures sufficient to abolish the misery of present society and to cause its evils to disappear" (355).

What is said of the "democratic socialists" held true a fortiori of the "bourgeois" or "reactionary" socialists who sought to "preserve present society." The objection here is not merely that their proposals cannot succeed in improving living conditions within capitalist society, "the evils" being "inseparable from it" and "bound up with it" – for this incapacity was equally the case with free trade and unionization, which were nonetheless favored, as we shall see – but that they "would retain the foundations of present society" (MECW 6: 355). The *Communist Manifesto* itself reacts in just this way to a variety of so-called reactionary, conservative, democratic, or bourgeois socialists – Proudhon falls into the latter category – and "hole-and-corner reformers of every imaginable kind" (513).

Engels's "The Communists and Karl Heinzen" (1847) reinforces the hostility toward reform measures introduced by the capitalist state, even if they are identical to those proposed in the communist program as measures designed to liquidate private property: "All measures to restrict competition and the accumulation of capital in the hands of individuals, all restriction or suppression of the law of inheritance, all organisation of labour by the state, etc., all these measures are not only possible as revolutionary measures, but actually necessary.... They are possible as preparatory steps, temporary transitional stages towards the abolition of private property, but not in any other way" (MECW 6: 295). Reform measures designed to ensure "a peaceful bourgeois condition" were "reactionary" by seeking to restrain or even reverse *capitalist* development, though such attempts would inevitably fail in the long run: "All measures... which start from the basis of private property and which are nevertheless directed against free competition" – described at this time as "the ultimate, highest and most developed form of existence of private property"[1] – "are reactionary and tend to restore more primitive stages in the development of property, and for that reason they must finally be defeated once more by competition and result in the restoration of the present situation" (295–6). That such so-called arbitrary reform measures must ultimately fail turns on the principle of historical materialism: "Herr Heinzen of course imagines that property relations, the law of inheritance, etc., can at will be altered and trimmed to shape.

---

[1] Even in 1847 Engels recognized the trend to "centralisation," and in the 1860s, joint-stock organization was said by Marx to constitute "the ultimate development of capitalist production" (see Chapter Three, Section H).

Herr Heinzen ... may, of course, not know that the property relations of any given era are the necessary result of the mode of production and exchange of that era" (296).

* * *

The approach toward free trade illustrates a further aspect of the Marx–Engels perspective on social policy. As reported by Engels, Marx (in a speech prepared for delivery in September 1847) maintained that the "laws" of "classical" political economy are increasingly approximated as a free-trade regime is adopted: "If you wish to read in the book of the future, open Smith, Say, Ricardo. There you will find described, as clearly as possible, the condition which awaits the working man under the reign of perfect Free Trade" ("Speech of Dr. Marx on Protection, Free Trade and the Working Classes," in Engels, "The Free Trade Congress at Brussels"; MECW 6: 289).[2] Despite the range of attributions, Marx had Ricardo especially in mind when he elaborated the minimum wage principle as the rule in a fully operative free-trade regime: "This law, that the lowest level of wages is the natural price of the commodity of labour, will realise itself in the same measure with Ricardo's supposition that Free Trade will become a reality" (290). There is also reference to Malthus in the further proposition that with free trade his "law of population" will, along with the other laws of economics, come into its own. Marx arrives at this conclusion: "Either you must disavow the whole of political economy as it exists at present, or you must allow that under the freedom of trade the whole severity of the laws of political economy will be applied to the working classes." But precisely because the capitalist system would be given free reign to expand – and on a worldwide scale – with this very consequence, Marx favored free trade: "by Free Trade all economical laws, with their most astounding contradictions, will act upon a larger scale, upon a greater extent of territory, upon the territory of the whole earth; and because from the uniting of all these contradictions into a single group, where they stand face to face, will result the struggle which will itself eventuate in the emancipation of the proletarians."

Marx's "Speech on the Question of Free Trade," delivered in Brussels on 9 January 1848, takes for granted that the growth of capital in consequence of free trade implies increased "concentration" or "centralization," and, correspondingly, adoption of machine processes, greater division of labor, and loss of skills, all working to depress the real wage (MECW 6: 459). This process was reinforced by inflows into the work force from the lower middle classes with the declining interest rate, one of the further consequences attributed to increased accumulation. Furthermore, with the "progress of industry" the subsistence basket itself deteriorates, for "as means are constantly found for the maintenance of labour on cheaper and more wretched food, the minimum of wages is constantly

---

[2] The speech, prepared for the International Congress of Economists in Brussels, was not delivered, but extracts were published by Engels in *The Northern Star* in October.

sinking" (463). Once again Marx concludes that by allowing free reign to capital, the "laws" relating to subsistence wages come fully into their own, "the whole severity of the economic laws . . . fall[ing] upon the workers." The efficiency advantages obtained were irrelevant to the principal issue: "It is really difficult to understand the presumption of the Free Traders who imagine that the more advantageous application of capital will abolish the antagonism between industrial capitalists and wage-workers. On the contrary. The only result will be that the antagonism of these two classes will stand out more clearly." Brief reference is also made to overproduction: "[T]he more productive capital grows, the more it is compelled to produce for a market whose requirements it does not know, – the more production outstrips consumption, the more supply tries to force demand" (459–60). This generates crisis, which in turn "hastens the concentration of capital," thereby adding to the proletariat (460).

Marx strongly supported free trade from a "revolutionary standpoint," although in consequence the exploitative system operates on terms increasingly unfavorable to labor. "[G]enerally speaking, the Protective system in these days is conservative, while the Free Trade system works destructively. It breaks up old nationalities and carries antagonism of proletariat and bourgeoisie to the uttermost point. In a word, the Free Trade system hastens the Social Revolution. In this revolutionary sense alone, gentlemen, I am in favour of Free Trade" (465).[3]

Engels rehearsed the theme in 1850. He identified the "free trade" movement itself with the Manchester School, and he attributed to it the view that low earnings were essential for successful exportation and growth – essentially, one might say, a mercantilist position ("The Ten Hours' Question," MECW *10*: 271–3; "The English Ten Hours' Bill," MECW *10*: 295–6).[4] He favored free trade on Marx's ground that it allowed industrial capitalism the unhindered scope to destroy itself by overproducing in the face of limited markets, with the inevitable outcome – that is, increasingly severe cycles and ultimate collapse (299).

---

[3] An identical analysis of the negative effects of free trade on labor's welfare is given by Georg Weerth in a speech at the Congress of Economists held in Brussels, 18 September 1847. (See the paraphrase provided by Engels in his paper "The Free Trade Congress at Brussels" mentioned above; MECW *6*: 284–5.) Coincidences are not unknown, and this might be one. However, there is reason to believe that the common analysis was no coincidence. Marx (as well as Engels) attended the congress and doubtless heard Weerth's presentation, which in any event was published in full on 29 September 1847 in *Atelier Démocratique* (see letter of Engels to Marx informing him of the publication, 28–30 September, MECW *38*: 125; also editorial note 162, p. 589). It is important, therefore, to stress that the conclusions drawn from the analysis are not identical, with Weerth warning the bourgeoisie that other steps must be taken to improve labor's welfare because free trade would not help, without which revolution would result (cited by Engels, MECW *6*: 285).

[4] See also much later: "There was no secret made, in those times, of what was aimed at by the repeal of the Corn Laws. To reduce the price of bread, and thereby the money rate of wages, would enable British manufacturers to defy all and every competition with which wicked or ignorant foreigners threatened them" ("The French Commercial Treaty," 1881; MECW *24*: 391).

Related considerations emerge from the treatment of trade unions. Here Engels takes temporal precedence over Marx: "Engels was the first who endeavoured to give a theoretical exposition of the course of trade union development among the workers. Differing from the economists and socialists of his day, he showed as early as 1845 that trade unions are the inevitable result of the struggle between workers and industrialists, and that trade unions must form the basis of all working-class organisation" (Ryazanoff 1930 [1922]: 113; see also Henderson 1989: 62–3). This evaluation is based upon the discussion in *The Condition of the Working Class* of efforts "to deal, *en masse*, as a power, with the employers" designed to maintain the rate of wages "uniform in each trade throughout the country," restrict labor supply by limiting the number of apprentices, and "counteract, as far as possible, the indirect wages reductions which the manufacturers brought about by means of new tools and machinery" (1845; MECW 4: 504). But though a form of working-class organization arising from capitalist development itself, unions "naturally cannot alter the economic law according to which wages are determined by the relation between supply and demand in the labour market" (505). Unions sought to reduce labor supply and also competition between workers by the enforcement of uniform wages, but in fact "remain powerless against all *great* forces" that influence the supply–demand relation. This weakness is manifest in periods of crisis when competition between manufacturers to cut costs is at a pitch; only "*under average conditions*" are efforts to cut wages "somewhat restricted by the opposition of the working-men," whereas "in a time of considerable increase in the demand for labour, [a union] cannot fix the rate of wages higher than would be reached spontaneously by the competion of the capitalists among themselves."

Although Engels saw a modest potential for unions as far as concerns wages, his support was unstinted from the educational perspective. The true significance of unions was their role as training ground; strikes were "the strongest proof that the decisive battle between bourgeoisie and proletariat is approaching. They are the military school of the working-men in which they prepare themselves for the great struggle which cannot be avoided; they are the pronunciamentos of single branches of industry that these too have joined the labour movement" (MECW 4: 512).

Like Engels, Marx in *Poverty of Philosophy* (1847) represented combination in terms effectively of historical materialism, as a natural consequence of a developing competitive capitalist system rather than as a constraint on capitalist development. He went further by positing that the legalization of combination is forced upon the legislature: "[I]t is the economic system which has forced Parliament to grant this legal authorisation. . . . The more modern industry and competition develop, the more elements there are which call forth and strengthen combination, and as soon as combination becomes an economic fact, daily gaining in solidity, it is bound before long to become a legal fact" (MECW 6: 209). Marx points to the success of British unionization extending far beyond the "passing strike" by "partial combinations," to *trades unions* and beyond that even toward a national organization along with the Chartists' formation of a working-class political party (210; see Chapter Four, p. 188).

What, though, of the effectiveness of unions with respect to real *wages*? There is mention of the encouragement of labor-saving technology, but unfortunately Marx does not say whether it is in response to actual wage increases or to avoid pressure to raise wages; nevertheless, although counterproductive to that extent, "[i]f combinations and strikes had no other effect than that of making the efforts of mechanical genius react against them, they would still exercise an immense influence on the development of industry" (MECW 6: 207).[5] The advantage presumably entails precipitating the final demise of capitalism. However, as with Engels, it is the political rather than the wage effects of unions that are accorded precedence (210–11).

The representation of unionization as a necessary feature of capitalist development, reflecting the increasingly bitter class struggle, is elaborated in the *Communist Manifesto*. Here is spelled out the process of increasing "concentration" of labor in masses receiving, because of the obliteration of skills, a uniform rate of pay that tends downward "to the same low level" in consequence of improved machinery while also increasingly subject to cyclical instability (MECW 6: 492). Under these conditions – all part and parcel of the industrialization process – "the collisions between individual workmen and individual bourgeois take more and more the character of collisions between two classes" (492–3). Even a successful effort to maintain the wage rate could be "only for a time" (493); for "[t]he modern labourer" – unlike the serf or the petty bourgeois of earlier times – "instead of rising with the progress of industry, sinks deeper and deeper below the conditions of existence of his own class. He becomes a pauper, and pauperism develops more rapidly than population and wealth" (495).

Factory legislation presents us with a problem. As mentioned in Chapter Four (p. 189), the authors of the *Communist Manifesto* represent the "organisation of the proletarians into a class, and consequently into a political party," as a natural outcome of capitalist development, which "compels legislative recognition of particular interests of the workers," who profit from the "divisions among the bourgeoisie itself" (MECW 6: 493). "Thus the Ten Hours' Bill in England was carried." From this perspective the legislation should have been championed on the same grounds as unionization. This was later to be the case, by Marx in the 1860s and Engels shortly thereafter. However, I shall show presently that in two

---

[5] Labor-displacing technology is ascribed to the economists as an argument to dissuade workers from forming unions: "The economists say to the workers: Do not combine. By combination you hinder the regular progress of industry, you prevent manufacturers from carrying out their orders, you disturb trade and you precipitate the invasion of machines which, by rendering your labour in part useless, force you to accept a still lower wage" (MECW 6: 209).

papers of 1850 on recent factory legislation, Engels did not yet take this line but condemned the regulations as "reactionary."

* * *

In his *The Class Struggles in France* (1850), Marx represents reformist measures proposed by those he classified as "bourgeois socialists" – credit institutions, progressive taxation, limitation of inheritance, nationalization of industry, state support of "association" – as a program to ensure "the peaceful achievement" of their objective to *"forcibly stem the growth of capital"* (MECW *10*: 126).[6] These "reactionary" steps must fail "just as certainly as all moral indignation and all enthusiastic proclamations of the democrats" (135). The inevitable failure reflects in some formulations the uncontrollable force of ongoing capitalist development (see above p. 231 regarding Engels's reaction to Heinzen), but in the present context Marx intended rather a refusal of the capitalist state to tolerate them.[7] Thus several reformist enactments introduced by the French National Assembly before the outbreaks of 1848–9 were withdrawn or reversed immediately thereafter. Such was true of the so-called "right to work" – an "absurdity" from the bourgeois viewpoint originally enacted out of fear of the working class – which was then whittled down to a mere "right to public relief" (77–8). Progressive taxation Marx represented as a purely intrabourgeois matter of little consequence to labor (78). Even this was reversed by the "big-bourgeoisie."

As for Britain, we find in the joint "May to October" of 1850 a similar if less dramatic picture of reform measures proposed but not instituted: "[E]ach spell of prosperity is a time when Whiggery comes into its own.... The ministry brings before Parliament little hole-and-corner reform bills which it knows will be rejected by the Upper House or which it withdraws itself at the end of the session on the pretext of insufficient time" (MECW *10*: 510). Measures enacted by Sir Robert Peel during the 1840s were designed to strengthen the industrial bourgeoisie at the expense of the financial and landed aristocracy: "Thus it was with the Catholic emancipation and the police reform, by which he increased the political power of the bourgeoisie; with the bank laws of 1818 and 1844, which strengthened the finance aristocracy; with the tariff reform of 1842 and the free-trade laws of 1846, by which the landed aristocracy was positively sacrificed to the industrial bourgeoisie" (512). These enactments, it is implied, were of little interest to labor.

Of the highest interest to labor was factory legislation, particularly the Ten Hours' Bill of 1847, which applied to the workday of female workers and juveniles

---

[6] Similarly, a joint "Address of the Central Authority to the League of Communists" (March 1850), condemns the reform program of the "democratic petty bourgeoisie" for striving "for a change of social conditions by means of which the existing society will be made as tolerable and comfortable as possible for them – the "revolutionary proletarians" (MECW *10*: 280). On this document, see below, p. 240.

[7] This is in line with an earlier formulation of 1844 regarding prospects for social reform ("Critical Marginal Notes on the Article by a Prussian"; MECW *3*: 189–206).

younger than eighteen. Noteworthy here is a joint paper pertaining to "January to February" of 1850, which remarks that with the business upturn commencing in Spring 1849 when "factories are overloaded with orders and are working at an accelerated rate . . . every means is being sought to dodge the Ten Hours' Bill and gain new hours of labour" (264). This demonstrated the impossibility of achieving in practice any effective progress under capitalist organization that is beneficial to labor. This is the theme of two papers by Engels in 1850 – "The Ten Hours' Question" and "The English Ten Hours' Bill."

Engels points in the first of these papers to "the cool, heartless, political economist, the paid servant of those who fattened upon this system, and [who] proved by a series of conclusions, as undeniable and as stringent as the rule of three, that, under penalty of 'ruining the country,' there was no means of interfering in any way in the system" (MECW *10*: 272). Yet this is Engels's position too, for he insists that "under the present social system" England depended upon manufacturing prosperity and therefore "upon the most unlimited freedom of buying and selling, and of turning to the greatest possible profit all the resources of the country" (272–3). This in turn required "reducing the cost of the working man, in reducing the cost of his sustenance (free trade in corn, etc.), or in merely reducing his wages to the lowest possible level. Thus, in all cases, the working man is the loser – thus, England can only be saved by the ruin of her working people!" (273). The Ten Hours' Bill from this point of view was "a false step, an impolitic, and even reactionary measure." However, it "bore within itself the germ of its own destruction," as evidenced by the manner in which the manufacturers – who had "virtually secured their ascendency, by forcing free trade in corn, and in navigation, through parliament" (274) – were able to negate the intention of the legislation, by re-introducing the relay system and forcing the Home Secretary to order the factory inspectors to turn a blind eye to infractions of the law; and when "the growing demand for their produce made the remonstrances of some troublesome inspectors insupportable, they brought the question before the Court of Exchequer, which, by one single judgment, destroyed, to the last vestige, the Ten Hours' Bill," proving that the judges were "the paid servants of the ruling class" (274; also 288).

The increased strength of the industrial interests since 1847 when the bill was enacted is one consideration accounting for its "defeat" in 1850. The bill had been initially "carried by the *reactionary* opponents of free trade, by the allied landed, funded, colonial and shipping interest; by the combined aristocracy and those portions of the bourgeoisie who themselves dreaded the ascendency of the free-trading manufacturers" (MECW *10*: 273). What support the working class gave the short-time movement reflected not efforts by the genuine industrial proletarians, but those of "moderate, respectable, church-and-king men . . . inclined mostly towards some sort of sentimental Toryism." The 1847 legislation proved not that the working classes were strong but "that the manufacturers were not strong enough to do as they liked" (274).

As Engels put the matter in his second paper, the bill was initially passed "as a piece of chicanery that the aristocrats and a faction of the Peelites and the Whigs put over on the manufacturers to avenge themselves for the great victory which these had wrested from them in the repeal of the Corn Laws" (MECW *10*: 293). This was despite the growing strength of the industrial bourgeoisie, as evidenced by the 1832 Reform Act, which admitted middle-class urban voters to the Lower House (294). However, more than "vengeance" on the part of the landed aristocracy was at play. Engels represents earlier factory legislation as required of the state "to curb the manufacturers' utterly ruthless frenzy for exploitation, which was trampling all the requirements of civilised society underfoot" (291). These initial restrictions were inadequate and easily circumvented, so that "[o]nly half a century after the introduction of large-scale industry, when the stream of industrial development had found a regular course for itself, only in 1833 was it possible to bring in an effective law that to some extent curbed at least the most blatant excesses." Nonetheless, if one asks *why* a bourgeois state should be at all concerned, the answer once again is that the manufacturers were not yet strong enough to oppose the pressures exerted by "sentimental Tories" and "softhearted ideologues" (Sadler in the 1820s and Lord Ashley and Oastler in the 1830s), "joined by all sections of society whose interests were suffering and whose existence was being threatened by the industrial upheaval. The bankers, stockjobbers, shipowners and merchants, the landed aristocracy, the big West Indian landowners and the petty bourgeoisie . . . ," and also by working-class Tories, "respectable folk who felt a pious abhorrence towards Chartism and socialism" (291–2). The working class as a whole thus suffered a serious "adulteration," though "[i]t was quite natural, especially at the start of the industrial upheaval, that the workers, who were in direct conflict only with the industrial bourgeoisie" – handweaving is cited – "should ally themselves with the aristocracy and the other factions of the bourgeoisie by whom they were not directly exploited and who were also struggling against the industrial bourgeoisie" (293).[8]

The legislation, which "significantly restrict[ed] the rapid development of the wealth, the influence, and the social and political power of the manufacturers," nonetheless "gave the workers . . . exclusively physical advantages. It protected their health from being too rapidly ruined. But it gave them nothing which could make them dangerous to their reactionary allies; it neither gave them political power nor altered their social position as wage-labourers" (MECW *10*: 292). Be that as

---

[8] This position of 1850 differs from that in the *Communist Manifesto*, which represents the factory legislation as the outcome of the "organisation of the proletarians into a class . . . compel[ling] legislative recognition of particular interests of the workers" (cited above, p. 235) – apparently those in the advanced industrial sector – a perspective implying proletarian force, which was itself the outcome of capitalist development. One also discerns a contrast with a comment of 1847 by Engels on massive Irish immigration: "This means that the competition between the workers will become stronger, and it would not be at all surprising if the present crisis caused such an uproar that it compelled the government to grant reforms of a most important nature" ("The Commercial Crisis in England," *La Réforme*, November 1847; MECW *6*: 309).

it may, the Ten Hours' Bill was "indispensable for the workers" without which "a whole generation ... will be physically ruined" (298). Now this poses a problem because Engels also represented the 1847 legislation as inoperative in practice. One explanation may be that under the "relay" or "shift" system designed to bypass the legal restriction – a system whereby women and juveniles remained in the factory for the length of the adult male's day, but worked only at intervals – no "single individual covered by the Ten Hours' Bill work[ed] more than ten hours daily" (297), and this would be to their physical benefit, though irrelevant for the current generation of adult males.[9]

More is involved in the initial passage of the 1847 act than the weakness of the industrialists relative to the "reactionaries." There is the specifically economic feature that it coincided with a *quiescent* phase of the trade cycle – I use J. S. Mill's phrase – "in which industry is still labouring sufficiently under the consequences of over-production to be able to set only a part of its resources in motion, in which the manufacturers themselves therefore do not allow full-time working" (MECW *10*: 296). It was with the upswing that industry insisted on the "unrestricted disposal for all its resources," for "[w]hat would become of the industrialists during the next crisis if they were not permitted to exploit the brief period of prosperity with all their might? The Ten Hours' Bill had to succumb." Here we are brought back to the theme encountered in the discussion of free trade (above, p. 233) – that unfettered activity hastens the collapse of the capitalist system, with emphasis now placed on the free reign to overproduce in the face of limited markets, thereby generating worsening cycles and "inevitable" revolution (299).

The denial by Engels, in common with Marx, of any scope for effective social reform under capitalism contrasts with the positive view taken at the same time of prospects for legislative reform in Britain, if not in France. In any event, the de facto undermining of the factory legislation revealed to the workers the bank-ruptcy of their long-standing alliance with various old-time "reactionaries"; and – "instinctively" realizing that by allowing their employers scope for overproduction they would be hastening the collapse of the capitalist system – it convinced them of the need to cooperate with the industrialists: "They have learnt that the bour-geois industrialists are still in the first instance the class which alone is capable of marching at the head of the movement at the present moment, and that it would be a vain task to work against them in this progressive mission.... They feel that their day can only come when the industrialists have worn themselves out, and hence their instinct is correct in hastening the process of development which will give the industrialists power and thus prepare their fall" (MECW *10*: 298). Accordingly, they "are now much more inclined to support them in their agitation

---

[9] The factory legislation dealt solely with the employment of women and children (and the law was not extended beyond the textile trades until 1867). See, however, the later remark by Jevons that though the Factory and Workshop Act of 1878 still covered only children, young persons, and women, "[i]ndirectly ... a large number of workmen fell practically under restriction" (Jevons 1910 [1882]: 66).

for the complete implementation of Free Trade, financial reform and extension of the franchise, than to allow themselves to be decoyed once again by philanthropic allurements to the banner of the united reactionaries."

Engels even appears to suggest that working-class support of the industrialists extended to their undermining of the 1847 factory legislation. He maintains that the factory issue is transformed assuming universal suffrage and a guarantee of "the exclusive political rule of the working class with all the revolutionary changes in social conditions which are inseparable from it" (MECW *10*: 298; see Chapter Four, p. 195). Then the legislation would be part and parcel of the dismantling of the capitalist system: "The Ten Hours' Bill demanded by the workers today is thus quite different from the one which has just been overruled by the Court of Exchequer. It is no longer an isolated attempt to cripple industrial development, it is a link in a long chain of measures which will revolutionise the whole of the present form of society and gradually destroy the class antagonisms which have hitherto existed; it is not a reactionary measure, but a revolutionary one" (298–9). All in all, it is remarkable to find Engels condemning the 1847 bill as a measure "attempt[ing] to cripple industrial development" and applauding – and attributing the same sentiment to the proletariat – industrialists' schemes to thwart the legislation in practice.

* * *

The joint "Address of the Central Authority to the League of Communists" in March 1850 raises a problem. Here we find the complaint that "[f]ar from desiring to transform the whole of society for the revolutionary proletarians, the democratic petty bourgeois strive for a change in social conditions by means of which the existing society will be made as tolerable and comfortable as possible for them" (MECW *10*: 280). The reformists' program focused "on a diminution of state expenditure by curtailing the bureaucracy and shifting the bulk of the taxes on to the big landowners and bourgeois." Beyond this, "they demand the abolition of the pressure of big capital on small, through public credit institutions and laws against usury... [in order] to obtain advances on favourable conditions from the state instead of from the capitalists.... The domination and speedy increase of capital is further to be counteracted partly by restricting the right of inheritance and partly by transferring as many jobs of work as possible to the state." The strategy toward labor was simply one of *bribery*: "[T]he democratic petty bourgeois only desire better wages and a more secure existence for the workers and hope to achieve this through partial employment by the state and through charity measures." Nonetheless, the workers, who were in no position to "propose any directly communist measures," are advised by Engels to cooperate with the "democrats," though in the sense of taking their program further (286). They were to "[c]ompel the democrats to interfere in as many spheres as possible of the hitherto existing social order, to disturb its regular course and to ... concentrate the utmost possible productive forces, means of transport, factories, railways, etc., in the hands of the state"; and to "carry to the extreme the proposals of the democrats, who in any case will not act in a revolutionary but in a merely reformist manner, and transform them into direct attacks upon private property." For example, there would be state confiscation rather than purchase of railways and factories; steeply progressive rather than proportional taxation, in order to ruin "big capital"; and measures to ensure state bankruptcy, rather than mere regulation of state debt. Now these recommendations pose a problem for which I have no explanation. They propose all manner of policy measures that presumably would constrain capitalistic growth, on which grounds such interventions are condemned as a matter of high principle in other documents of the same period, as we have seen.

C. On Marx's Revisionism: The 1860s and 1870s

I have spelled out elsewhere in some detail Marx's "revisionism" with respect to welfare, as it emerged during the 1860s and 1870s (Hollander 2008: 449–61). A briefer formulation will suffice for our present purposes, commencing with Marx's assertion in September 1864 regarding Britain "that the misery of the working masses has not diminished" since 1848, despite "unrivalled" development of industry and commerce ("Inaugural Address of the Working Men's International Association"; MECW *20*: 5). So too in the "industrious and progressive countries of the Continent, only "a minority of the working classes got their real wages somewhat advanced . . . [while] everywhere the great mass of the working classes were sinking down to a lower depth, at the same rate, at least, that those above them were rising in the social scale" (9). This is the forecast: "[E]very fresh development of the productive powers of labour must tend to deepen social contrasts and point [sic] social antagonisms." This evaluation is reinforced the following year by the declaration that "the very development of modern industry must progressively turn the scale in favour of the capitalist against the working man, and . . . sink the average standard of wages . . . more or less to its *minimum limit*," a trend that union activity could not prevent; "they are retarding the downward movement, but not changing its direction" (*Value, Price and Profit*, 1865; MECW *20*: 148).[10]

In striking contrast, Marx recognized the "immense . . . benefits" to labor of factory legislation: "After a thirty years' struggle, fought with most admirable perseverance, the English working classes, improving a momentaneous split between the landlords and money-lords, succeeded in carrying the Ten Hours' Bill. The immense physical, moral, and intellectual benefits hence accruing to the factory operatives, half-yearly chronicled in the reports of the inspectors of factories, are

---

[10] To the pressures depressing real wages Irish immigration must be added: "Ireland is steadily supplying its surplus [population] for the English labour market, and thus forcing down the wages and material and moral position of the English working class" (9 April 1870; MECW *43*: 474). This is represented not as a disturbing cause but as reflecting English bourgeois "concentration of leaseholding" in Ireland.

now acknowledged on all sides" (1864; "Inaugural Address of the Working Men's International Association," MECW *20*: 10). Taking a broader view, "the marvelous success of this working men's measure" refuted middle-class predictions made "[t]hrough their most notorious organs of science, such as Dr. Ure, Professor Senior . . . that any legal restriction of the hours of labour must sound the death knell of British industry . . . " (10–11).[11] Yet more significant were the profound implications of the legislation for "the great contest between the blind rule of the supply and demand laws which form the political economy of the middle class, and social production controlled by social foresight, which forms the political economy of the working class" (11). It was in fact "the first time that in broad daylight the political economy of the middle class succumbed to the political economy of the working class."

We are here witness to a sea change in the evaluation of the effectiveness of social-reform measures within capitalist organization, because in 1850 Marx and Engels had denied that industrialists would tolerate factory legislation in practice and emphasized the devices designed to bypass the 1847 regulations.[12] Moreover, whereas in his two papers of 1850 on the issue Engels had opined that the effective application of the Ten Hours' Act would hold back industrial growth (above, pp. 237, 239–40), Marx's remark in 1864 on Ure and Senior asserts explicitly that British industry had not been restrained. Striking too is the representation of the 1847 legislation as a proletarian victory – again in contrast to Engels's earlier interpretation – and a step from market toward "social" organization. Finally, the "immense physical and moral benefits," which in 1850 had been recognized even by Engels in the case of juveniles and female factory workers, are now extended it seems quite generally.[13]

There were limits, though, to what could be achieved. For example, Marx's inaugural address of September 1864 is only a little more positive than in 1852 (see *The Eighteenth Brumaire*, MECW *11*: 110–11) regarding cooperatives. Although Marx recognized the expansion of the British cooperative movement of 1848–64 and thought it "excellent in principle, and . . . useful in practice," he reiterates an earlier theme that because "kept within the narrow circle of the casual efforts of

---

[11] Neither Marx nor Engels identified a fall in hours with a rise in the wage rate, as did Senior, at least implicitly (see Hollander 2008: 450n.). They were right to take this position, because the legislation made no provision for rates of pay; conceivably take-home earnings per day or week might fall, to correspond with the shorter workday, thereby precluding a real-wage increase.

[12] In a letter of early 1860 to Engels, Marx had qualified the "benefits": "The state of health of the workers (adults) has improved since your *Condition of the Working Class* . . . whereas that of children (mortality) has deteriorated" (MECW *41*: 5).

[13] A letter to Engels in August 1863 warns of the need for "control" to ensure the gains made: "Since you wrote your book about England, a second *Children's Employment Commission Report* [1863] has at long last appeared. It shows that all those horrors that were banished from certain spheres of industry by the Factory Acts, have proliferated with redoubled vigour wherever there is no control!" (MECW *41*: 490).

private workmen," it was unable "to arrest the growth in geometrical progression of monopoly, to free the masses, [or] even to perceptibly lighten the burden of their miseries" (MECW *20*: 11–12). To have effects of this order, "co-operative labour ought to be developed to national dimensions, and consequently, to be fostered by national means"; and this would never be countenanced by "the lords of land and the lords of capital [who] will always use their political privileges for the defence and perpetuation of their economical monopolies" (12). That we should end up with a denial of prospects for truly radical reform extending to communal ownership is scarcely surprising.

Marx in *Capital* questioned Gladstone's position in his budget speech of 16 April 1863 that real wages had risen since 1843 (see the Appendix), basing his objection on evidence of a rise in prices in the period 1860–2 of some 20 percent compared with the period 1851–3 and a further "progressive rise" in wage-goods prices over the following three years, 1863–5 (MECW *35*: 646). He also cited Gladstone's less optimistic budget speech of 7 April 1864, and Fawcett's view that "the rich grow rapidly richer, whilst there is no perceptible advance in the comfort enjoyed by the industrial classes," money-wage increases being largely balanced by rising wage-goods prices (Fawcett 1865: 67–82). By contrast, and in line with the 1864 address, the British Factory Acts are represented in the Preface to the first German edition of *Capital* as having ensured a meaningful improvement in labor's welfare; thus in Germany "the condition of things is much worse than in England, because the counterpoise of the Factory Acts is wanting" (MECW *35*: 9). Here too we find a paean of praise for the quest to "get at the truth" regarding social conditions, specifically in the British case a quest involving government, parliament, and inspectorate. Underlying the national contrast were the "natural laws of capitalist production" entailing "tendencies working with iron necessity towards inevitable results," the more advanced industrially showing the less advanced "the image of its own future." The social legislation was imposed upon the ruling classes by the ever-growing power of organized labor: "In England the progress of social disintegration is palpable.... Apart from higher motives" – for these are not denied – "their own most important interests dictate to the classes that are for the nonce the ruling ones, the removal of all legally removable hindrances to the free development of the working class" (9–10). The same course "must re-act on the Continent [where] it will take a form more brutal or more humane, according to the degree of development of the working class itself."

All this is much reinforced in the discussion of "The Struggle for the Normal Working Day" in the body of *Capital*. First to be noted is a formal rationalization of intervention by the state – albeit a creature of the capitalist class – entailing the public-goods property, for under competitive conditions each individual employer tends to force the limits of his workers and has to be restrained for the good of the whole: "Capital is reckless of the health or length of life of the labourer, unless under compulsion from society.... Free competition brings out the inherent laws of capitalist production, in the shape of external coercive laws having power over every individual capitalist" (MECW 35: 275–6).[14] This rationalization, however, scarcely accounts for the timing of the interventions.

"Pressures from without" are said to have compelled the legislature to take effective action. This may allude to some extent to the broad moral considerations that Leonard Horner insisted on (in Reports of Insp. of Factories, for 31 December 1841; MECW 35: 283n.). But taking center stage is the necessitarian character attributed to the factory interventions, which "developed gradually out of circumstances as natural laws of the modern mode of production. Their formulation, official recognition, and proclamation by the State, were the result of a long struggle of classes" (287–8). We are apparently now to attribute the reforms largely to the growth of proletarian power, itself a necessary consequence of modern industrial development. The same story underlies the Ten Hours' Bill of 1847 itself – though it still did not formally cover adult males (288).

The theme of legislative intervention to regulate and make uniform the workday as necessitated by the very nature of industrial development is elaborated in an overview of British experience, emphasizing the efforts of a class of proletarians, rather than isolated workers, engaged in a successful protracted "civil war" against capital; again the public-goods character is apparent, this time from labor's perspective:

The history of the regulation of the working day in certain branches of production, and the struggle still going on in others in regard to this regulation, prove conclusively that the isolated labourer, the labourer as "free" vendor of his labour power, when capitalist production has once attained a certain stage, succumbs without any power of resistance. The creation of a normal working day is, therefore, the product of a protracted civil war, more or less dissembled, between the capitalist class and the working class. As the contest takes place in the arena of modern industry, it first breaks out in the home of that industry – England. (MECW 35: 303)

Also implicit is the standard "classical" position whereby the legislation actually reinforced the competitive character of the labor contract, because in the absence of social control the individual laborer is far from a "free" agent on a par with his employer (306).[15] In defense, "the labourers must put their heads together, and, as a class, compel the passing of a law, an all-powerful social barrier that shall prevent the very workers from selling, by voluntary contract with capital, themselves and their families into slavery and death."

We recall, by way of contrast, that in the joint Marx–Engels contribution of early 1850 and in the two papers by Engels of that year, the efforts "to dodge" the regulations of 1847 were seen as a successful reaction by employers, especially upon the upturn of activity beginning in 1849 (above, p. 237). What we have in *Capital* is insistence upon the failure of that reaction, a failure that is due to working-class

---

[14] Furthermore, "however much the individual manufacturer might give the reign to the old lust for gain, the spokesmen and the political leaders of the manufacturing class ordered a change of front and of speech towards the workpeople" (MECW 35: 286). For more on the public-goods property, see Hollander (2008: 452–3) and Howard and King (2008: 227).

[15] Here Marx cites Engels, "The English Ten Hours' Bill" (MECW 10: 288).

counterthreats (MECW 35: 296). There had been employer resistance – Marx cites Engels's account of the episode – whereby "the Ten Hours' Act was effectively abolished." But this reaction, he goes on to explain, was short lived: "[T]he gradually surging revolt of the working class compelled Parliament to shorten compulsorily the hours of labour, and to begin by imposing a normal working day on factories proper" (412).

Conspicuous in all this is the success of working-class pressure, and this despite the absence of representation in Parliament. That Marx intended success in the very real sense of improvement to working-class welfare is clear from the following striking passage relating to the effect of the Act of 1850 as modified by that of 1853, reiterating what was already insisted upon in the Inaugural Address of 1864: "[T]he principle had triumphed with its victory in those great branches of industry which form the most characteristic creation of the modern mode of production. Their wonderful development from 1853 to 1860, hand in hand with *the physical and moral regeneration of the factory workers,* struck the most purblind" (MECW 35: 300; emphasis added). Again one notes that the most impressive advances achieved by labor in terms of its "physical and moral regeneration" occurred in the most advanced industries. Marx goes on to allude to further progress since 1860: "It will be easily understood that after the factory magnates had resigned themselves and become reconciled to the inevitable, the power of resistance of capital gradually weakened, whilst at the same time the power of attack of the working class grew with the number of its allies in the classes of society not immediately interested in the question. Hence the comparatively rapid advance since 1860." Extensions of the act in 1863 and further proposals to cover all the important branches of industry – except for agriculture, mining, and transportation – illustrate that advance (302).[16]

That the "factory magnates" should have become thus "reconciled to the inevitable" is thus explained in terms of fear of an increasingly class-conscious proletariat. Perhaps Marx was concerned that he had written prematurely, though, because he adds a note to the second edition (1873): "Since 1866, when I wrote the above passages, a reaction has set in" (MECW 35: 302n.). Yet it is difficult to imagine that by this he came to withdraw the proposition that effective welfare legislation accompanied the development of modern industry, and indeed was its necessary consequence. Interesting indeed is Marx's recognition that several Owenite proposals once widely disparaged as "utopian" – limited workday, children's education combined with work, and cooperation – had become normal features of the capitalist system (304n.).

* * *

"Instructions" drawn up by Marx in August 1866 for the delegates of the Provisional General Council of the International in preparation for the Geneva meetings in September suggest a more positive, if still cautious, evaluation of the merits of

---

[16] In a retrospect of 1890–1 regarding the extensions of the Factory Acts in 1863, Engels was rather more qualified. See below, note 50.

cooperatives, compared with earlier expressions of skepticism (above, pp. 242–3). Two specific recommendations are made. First, that workers should "embark in *co-operative production* rather than in *co-operative stores*. The latter touch but the surface of the present economical system, the former attacks its groundwork" (MECW *20*: 190). Second, that "to prevent co-operative societies from degenerating into ordinary middle-class joint stock companies (*sociétés par actions*), all workmen employed, whether shareholders or not, ought to share alike. As a mere temporary expedient, we are willing to allow shareholders a low rate of interest." That cooperative associations were indeed significant as a transitional form to socialist production is expressed in *Capital 3* itself: "The capitalist stock companies, as much as the cooperative factories, should be considered as transitional forms from the capitalist mode of production to the associated one, with the only distinction that the antagonism is resolved negatively in the one and positively in the other" (MECW *37*: 438).

The "Instructions" of August 1866 also throws light on Marx's position regarding unions, and it reiterates his own and Engels's position adopted in the 1840s. The emphasis is partly on their role in countering capitalists' bargaining advantage by restricting competition between individual laborers: "This activity of the Trades' Unions is not only legitimate, it is necessary. It cannot be dispensed with so long as the present system of production lasts" (MECW *20*: 191). More important is their role as a political training ground: "If the Trades' Unions are required for the guerilla fights between capital and labour, they are still more important as *organised agencies for superseding the very system of wages labour and capital rule.*" Eduard Bernstein, who emphasized Marx's caution regarding cooperatives, found his general practice to be "predominantly political, and . . . directed at the seizure of political power" (Bernstein 1993 [1899]: 110). Moreover, "as a matter of principle, almost the only significance it attaches to the trade-union movement is as a direct form of the class struggle of the workers."[17]

There is, however, evidence from the early 1870s that Marx was losing confidence in the British unions and was looking rather to the International.[18] An interview accorded *The World* on 3 July 1871 downplays "every known workmen's organization": "The working classes remain poor amid the increase of wealth, wretched amid the increase of luxury. Their material privation dwarfs their moral as well as their physical stature. They cannot rely on others for a remedy.... They must revise the relations between themselves and the capitalists and landlords, and that means they must transform society.... To establish a perfect solidarity between these organizations" – Marx includes in addition to workmen's organizations, "land and labor leagues, trade and friendly societies, co-operative stores

---

[17] The significance of the latter is incidentally confirmed in the apparent approval of the evaluation by the Factory Inspectorate that by making the workers "masters of their own time" the Factory Acts "have given them a moral energy which is directing them to the eventual possession of political power" (Reports for 31 October 1859, in cited MECW *35*: 307n.).

[18] Marx and Engels joined the General Council of the International in 1870.

and co-operative production" – "is the business of the International Association" (MECW 22: 602–3). In addition, at the session of the London conference of the International in September, Marx represented trades unions as "an aristocratic minority" (MECW 22: 614).[19]

Clearly, then, there were limits to what could be achieved by union activity within capitalist arrangement by way of material and even political benefit. Transformation of society was still the order of day – as I concluded in Chapter Four – and cooperation between national proletariats would be an essential feature in its achievement. Nevertheless, this qualification does not efface what is described in *Capital* as "the physical and moral regeneration of the factory workers" in consequence of social legislation by the bourgeois state (above, p. 245), a "revisionist" perspective contrasting sharply with the pessimism of 1850 and conveying the new message that reaction had failed. Marx certainly does not suddenly revert in the early 1870s to Proudhonist nihilism regarding working-class activity within the bourgeois state, as is apparent from his "Political Indifference" of 1873 (Hollander 2008: 459–60). It is noteworthy, for example, that he finds even *local* strike activity to be rendered more effective by international cooperation: "Formerly, when a strike took place in one country, it was defeated by the importation of workmen from another. The International has nearly stopped all that" (*The World*, 18 July 1871; MECW 22: 602).

A letter addressed to Friedrich Bolte confirms the political dimension to worker agitation for reforms relating to factory conditions (see Chapter Four, p. 202). Some read the letter as expressing opposition to reformist measures within capitalist arrangement (see Prolegomena, p. 21), but the only indication of such opposition appears in remarks addressed specifically against Bakunin's program (MECW 44: 255) and cannot be generalized.

Finally, note an indication of prospects for welfare reform in Marx's "Preamble to the Programme of the French Workers' Party" of May 1880. This late document champions "the revolutionary action of the producing class – or proletariat – organized into an independent political party" and "using all the means at the disposal of the proletariat including above all universal suffrage" to achieve the ultimate proletarian objective, namely "collective appropriation" of the means of production (see Chapter Four, pp. 202–3). Nevertheless, Marx introduced as a "*minimum* programme" for the party a series of reform demands within going capitalist arrangement potentially achievable by means of the ballot box: factory regulations including Monday holidays, restrictions of hours for adults and juveniles, abolition of child labor, minimum wages, nondiscriminatory pay between the sexes, state finance of scientific and technological education, exclusive worker control of their mutual societies, and employer contributions to insurance (MECW 24:

---

[19] On Marx's failure to convert the trade unionists on the General Council to his economic doctrines, see Henderson (1989: 69). The attitude of Marx and Engels toward the Paris Commune antagonized several trade union leaders, most of whom represented societies of skilled craftsmen.

340–1). The original concern not to constrain capitalist development by reformist legislation has faded away, presumably because of a sense that the entire system was under threat of imminent collapse.

D. *The Housing Question*: 1872–1873

I have demonstrated Marx's tendency toward "revisionism," dating back to the 1860s and apparent in *Capital* itself, regarding social progress but not extending to recognition of improved real wages. Engels's *The Housing Question* (1872–3),[20] to which I turn next, is uncompromising with regard to the ineffectiveness of social reform measures in a capitalist régime, at least from the wages perspective. Beyond this, moreover, he continues to represent reformist measures as "reactionary."

The document rejects a proposal by a "Proudhonist" (Arthur Mülberger) to transform rental into installment payments to the end finally of eliminating rent from the working-class budget. Mülberger had taken "an enormous step backward in comparison with the whole course of development of German socialism, which delivered a decisive blow precisely to the Proudhonist ideas as far back as twenty-five years ago" (alluding to *Poverty of Philosophy*; MECW *23*: 317). From the Marxian perspective the housing issue was secondary: "The housing shortage from which the workers and part of the petty bourgeoisie suffer in our modern big cities is one of the innumerable *smaller*, secondary evils which result from the present-day capitalist mode of production" (318). The problem was not "a direct result of the exploitation of the worker *as* worker by the capitalist," the "cornerstone" of which entailed the purchase of "labour power . . . at its value" and extraction of "much more than its value by making the worker work longer than is necessary to reproduce the price paid for the labour power"; on this view, how that surplus value was parceled out amongst "those who do not work" was irrelevant to the worker.[21] Again:

The Proudhonist finds it a crime against eternal justice that the house-owner can without working obtain ground rent and interest out of the capital he has invested in the house. He decrees that this must cease, that capital invested in houses shall no longer yield interest; nor ground rent either, so far as it represents landed property. Now . . . the capitalist mode of production, the basis of present-day society, is in no way affected thereby. The pivot on which the exploitation of the worker turns is the sale of his labour power to the capitalist and the use which the capitalist makes of this transaction, the fact that he compels the worker to produce far more than the paid value of his labour power amounts to. It is this transaction between capitalist and worker which produces all the surplus value afterwards divided in the form of ground rent, commercial profit, [the 1887 version adds "interest on capital,"] taxes, etc., among the diverse varieties of capitalists and their servitors. (327)

---

[20] The study, written from May 1872 to January 1873, appeared first as a series of articles in *Der Volkstaat* and in reprints 1872–3. It was reissued in 1887 with modifications.

[21] For the latter point Engels refers readers to Marx's *Capital* "where this was propounded for the first time" (MECW *23*: 318). As for the surplus-value doctrine itself, Proudhon had shown "absolutely no clearness" (336; see below, p. 251).

In brief, any proposal that left untouched the capitalist institution itself, and accordingly still tolerated "exploitation," was unworthy of consideration. It is a matter of all or nothing.

A more specific objection turns on the constant-wage principle. To begin with, note a downplaying by Engels of the problem of high rents as a working-class problem, insofar as any upward pressure on a wage-goods price will ultimately be compensated by a money-wage increase: "[A]s soon as a certain average measure of cheating" – this alludes to price or quality of merchandise – "has become the social rule in any place, it must in the long run be adjusted by a corresponding increase in wages" (MECW 23: 318).[22] This formulation actually allows for some fall in the real wage even over the long run, because the "evil" must reach a "certain level" before activating a wage correction. That this downward flexibility of the real wage has no counterpart in the reverse direction becomes clear from Engels's insistence that the proposed solution to the "housing question" provided by worker ownership could, at best, only be temporary because the benefit to labor will ultimately be lost to capitalist-employers: "Every reduction in the cost of production of labour power, that is to say, every permanent price reduction in the worker's necessities of life is equivalent 'on the basis of the iron laws of the doctrine of national economy' to a depression of the value of labour power and will therefore finally result in a corresponding drop in wages" (345). In brief, "the worker would pay for his own house, but not, as formerly, in money to the house-owner, but in unpaid labour to the factory owner for whom he works."[23]

The expression "iron laws of the doctrine of national economy" is taken from a formulation by Emil Sax (1869): "By social economy we mean the doctrine of national economy in its application to social questions; or . . . the totality of the ways and means which this science offers us for *raising the so-called (!) propertyless classes to the level of the propertied classes, on the basis of its 'iron' laws within the*

---

[22] To describe the pricing process in terms of "cheating" is not representative of the Marx–Engels position, but the argument regarding wage adjustment is unaffected.

[23] See also Engels's addendum to his paper referring to Mülberger's debt to Proudhon in proposing "that the solution of the housing problem consists in everyone becoming the owner instead of the tenant of his dwelling [and] that this solution shall be put into effect by passing a law turning rent payments into installment payments on the purchase price of the dwelling" (MECW 23: 387). Both points were "borrowed from Proudhon, as anyone can see in the *Idée générale de la révolution* [1868b] p. 199 et. seq., where on p. 203 a project of the law in question is to be found already drafted." (At Marx's request, Engels in 1851 had made a study of the first edition of Proudhon's work on its appearance, including the proposal to turn tenant into owner; see MECW 11: 560–1.)

Engels cites an 1872 Spanish account of various European installment plans actually in operation, which emphasizes their profitability to speculators: "Proudhon proposed that tenants should be converted into buyers on the installment plan, that the rent paid annually be booked as an installment on the redemption payment of the value of the particular dwelling, so that after a certain time the tenant would become its owner. This method, which Proudhon considered very revolutionary, is being put into operation in all countries by companies of speculators who thus secure double and treble the value of the houses by raising the rents" (MECW 23: 329).

framework of the order of society at present prevailing" (cited in MECW 23: 339; Engels's exclamation). However, it is Engels who specifically posited the constant real wage as an "iron law" of capitalism, directing it against Sax and Mülberger as axiomatic: "[I]f the cost of production of labour power were reduced, would not the price of labour power be bound to fall?" (336).

Engels generalized broadly from the case of housing: "[W]hat has been said above applies to all so-called social reforms which can be reduced to savings schemes or to cheapening the means of subsistence of the worker. Either they become general and then they are followed by a corresponding reduction of wages or they remain quite isolated experiments," proving "that their realisation on an extensive scale is incompatible with the existing capitalist mode of production" (MECW 23: 345). Thus there is a reduction in the costs of wage goods in consequence of consumers' cooperatives: "in the long run wages would fall in that area . . . in the same proportion as the means of subsistence in question enter into the budget of the workers" (345–6). Here is a further instance: "Give *every* worker an independent income . . . achieved by saving, and his weekly wage must finally fall. . . . Therefore, the more he saves the less he will receive in wages. He saves, therefore, not in his own interest but in the interest of the capitalist" (346).

Engels provides us also with a glimpse into his position on a wide variety of issues in commenting on Mülberger's generalization from housing: "Such and similar questions, it would seem to us, are well worth the attention of the Social-Democracy. . . . Let us seek to clarify its mind, as here on the housing question, so also on other and equally important questions, such as *credit, state debts, private debts, taxes*" (cited MECW 23: 335). By way of "anticipation," Engels suggests how Mülberger would approach these matters: "[I]t all amounts to what has already been said: interest on capital is to be abolished and with that the interest on public and private debt disappears, credit will be gratis, etc." (335–6). These were exactly Proudhon's recommendations,[24] which Engels held to be "just as absurd economically and just as essentially bourgeois as his solution to the housing problem" (388). This evaluation entailed a coupling of the view that the working class was unaffected by credit at reduced or even zero interest, considering the quantitative insignificance of credit for that class, with the constant real-wage doctrine: "And if he did . . . obtain some advantage from it, that is to say, if the cost of production of labour power were reduced, would not the price of labour power be bound to fall?" (336). Similarly, taxation "interests the bourgeoisie very much but the worker only very little. What the worker pays in taxes goes in the long run into the cost of production of labour power and must therefore be compensated for by the capitalist." Engels closes by striking at the true target – Proudhon himself: "Our Proudhonist [Mülberger] has not a word to say about the great question

[24] As they appeared in Proudhon's *Idée générale*, Engels citing "credit, page 182; state debts, page 186; private debts, p. 196 – just as much as his [Mülberger's] articles on the housing question coincided with the passages I quoted from the same book" (MECW 23: 388).

which really concerns the workers, that of the relation between capitalist and wage-worker, the question of how it comes about that the capitalist can enrich himself by the labour of his workers. True enough, his lord and master did occupy himself with it, but introduced absolutely no clearness into the matter. Even in his latest writings he has got essentially no farther than he was in his *Philosophie de la Misère*, which Marx so strikingly reduced to nothingness in 1847."

* * *

The outcome thus far is that the housing scheme in question, and similar reform measures, cannot raise the long-run real wage. There is, though, the further proposition that, when viewed in terms of scientific socialism and the historical development of capitalism, the proposal emerged in its true light as positively reactionary. It would have the effect of turning the clock back in favor of pre-capitalist domestic industry, whereas "[i]t is precisely modern large-scale industry which has turned the worker ... into a completely propertyless proletarian, liberated from all traditional fetters, *a free outlaw*; it is precisely this economic revolution which has created the sole conditions under which the exploitation of the working class in its final form, in capitalist production, can be overthrown" (MECW 23: 323; also 382). Mülberger – the "tearful Proudhonist" – "bewails the driving of the workers from hearth and home as though it were a great retrogression instead of being the very first condition of their intellectual emancipation." However, the "intellectual emancipation" of the proletarian of 1872 – that he was indeed "on an infinitely higher level than the rural domestic weaver of 1772" – positively does not relate to material benefit, for "the situation of the workers has on the whole become materially worse since the introduction of capitalist production on a large scale ..." (324), an evaluation retained in the 1887 edition.

Further objections are directed against worker-ownership proposals advanced by Emil Sax, with Engels referring back to the charge in the *Communist Manifesto* that "the bourgeois socialists are desirous of 'redressing social grievances, in order to secure the continued existence of bourgeois society'; they want '*a bourgeoisie without a proletariat*' [MECW 6: 513].... Herr Sax formulates the problem in exactly the same fashion ... " (MECW 23: 340). The case is made out specifically against Sax as representative of the "bourgeois socialists": "In such a society the housing shortage is no accident; it is a necessary institution and can be abolished together with all its effects on health, etc., only if the whole social order from which it springs is fundamentally refashioned. That, however, bourgeois socialism dare not know. It *dare* not explain the housing shortage as arising from the existing conditions" (341). Worse, his proposals threatened to undermine workers' bargaining power by acting as a fetter on their mobility, thereby reinforcing capitalist institutions: "Herr Sax ... falsely impute[s] to the workers of our big cities a longing to own land.... For our workers in the big cities freedom of movement is the prime condition of existence, and land ownership can only be a fetter to them. Give them their own houses ... and you break their power of resistance to the wage cutting of the factory owners" (344). Even should an individual worker "be able to sell his house on occasion... during a big strike [the 1887 version uses "or general industrial crisis"] all the houses belonging to the workers affected would have to be put up for sale and would therefore find no purchasers or be sold off below their cost price."

But all this poses a difficulty. Although *The Housing Question* shows the same general "pessimism" regarding prospects for reform as do Engels's early papers on factory regulation, there is a difference. Engels had then opposed the Factory Acts as a constraint on capitalist growth, while supporting reforms – preeminently free trade – that allowed capitalism its head (above, pp. 232–3, 240). On these grounds he ought to have relished Sax's proposal to the extent that (as Engels charged) it would undermine labor's "power of resistance to the wage cutting of the factory owners." I have no explanation.

It was Sax's hope, as reported by Engels, that the home-ownership plan would help dissipate "the proletarian bitterness, the hatred... the dangerous confusion of ideas" relating to capitalism, thus engendering on labor's part an interest in retaining the system (cited in MECW *23*: 346). Engels for his part denied that the proposal enhanced labor's positive stake in capitalism, Sax "*falsely* imput[ing] to the workers of our big cities a longing to own land." Workers themselves were alert to the damaging implications of home ownership for their bargaining power, and any initial illusions would be destroyed by experience. Thus in response to a contention that workers qua property owners could more easily acquire credit, Engels referred to the contrary experience of small peasants (344). He also cites the Spanish authority (see above, note 23) to the effect that the installment-plan proposal "which Proudhon considered very revolutionary, is being put into operation in all countries by companies of speculators who then secure double and treble the value of the houses by raising the rents.... Thus the Proudhon plan, far from bringing the working class any relief, even turned directly against it" (cited in MECW *23*: 329–30). Of all this the workers were aware.

We must, however, also note that the same authority is cited by Engels regarding the political objective behind a range of ownership schemes to strengthen classes other than, and potentially hostile to, the urban proletariat: "The cleverest leaders of the ruling class have always directed their efforts towards increasing the number of small owners in order to build an army for themselves against the proletariat" (cited in MECW *23*: 329). Engels might conceivably be expressing here some latent concern with a prospect of increased outward movement from the urban proletariat in consequence of the measures in question, though against this we must note a downplaying of such mobility apart from exceptional cases, as we shall see.

A further consideration ensured against working-class enthusiasm for reformist measures, namely the downward real-wage trend. German scientific socialism described "the development on the one hand, of a class whose conditions of life necessarily drive it to social revolution, the proletariat, and, on the other hand, of productive forces which, having grown beyond the framework of capitalist society, must necessarily burst that framework" (MECW *23*: 377). Now "the conditions of life" presumably include the real wage; further, we have encountered the contention that "the situation of the worker has on the whole become materially worse since the introduction of capitalist production on a large scale" (above, p. 251). There was nothing that could be done to alter the outcome, as the proletariat (so it is implied) appreciated.

The falling real-wage trend is similarly drawn on to deny the efficacy of cooperative "self-help" measures by labor – preeminently building societies that act as a sort of savings bank. Building cooperatives were not essentially workers' societies; their chief aim was to provide "a more profitable mortgage investment for the savings of the *petty bourgeoisie*, at a good rate of interest," with a "prospect of dividends from speculation in real estate" (MECW *23*: 357). A degree of upward mobility is allowed, but only exceptionally in the case of select categories such as clerks. Taking account of family size, one finds that the general wage trend is downward (and uncertain), precluding the requisite accumulation of funds out of income (358).

E. Engels's Revisionism: 1872–1895

Engels maintained in *The Housing Question* much the same skepticism regarding reform potential as he did in 1850. Indeed, reinforcing that position is a charge that Emil Sax naively believed that "an Act of Parliament only requires to become legally effective in order to be carried immediately into practice" (MECW *23*: 360). He allowed that in England "the state officials entrusted with the preparation and execution of social legislation are usually distinguished by a strict sense of duty" (albeit "in a lesser degree today than twenty or thirty years ago"), but even so the administration of the Local Government Act of 1858 fell to the notoriously corrupt and nepotistic urban authorities that had thwarted its application as far as possible, while it was "the principle of every *Liberal* government in England to propose social reform laws only when compelled to do so and, if at all possible, to avoid carrying into effect those already existing" (361). In fact, "the state as it exists today is neither able nor willing to do anything to remedy the housing calamity," for "[t]he state is nothing but the organised collective power of the possessing classes, the landowners and the capitalist, as against the exploited classes, the peasants and the workers" (362). (The "collective capitalist" would at best "see to it that the measure of superficial palliation which has become customary is carried into execution everywhere uniformly.") A little later Engels again reverts in effect to the uncompromising position of 1850 when he comments on the clearing of the worst of the Manchester areas – those described in *The Condition of the Working Class* – that no social benefits could possibly emanate from the capitalist state: "The same economic necessity which produced them [poor housing conditions] in the first place produces them in the next place also. As long as the capitalist mode of production continues to exist it is folly to hope for an isolated settlement of the housing question or of any of the social questions affecting the lot of the workers" (368).

In all this, Engels lagged behind Marx, who in *Capital* itself had abandoned the notion that industrialists would inevitably undermine reformist legislation. Yet strange to relate in *The Housing Question* itself, Engels rationalized the advanced state of British social legislation (as did Marx) as a normal feature of capitalist development: "England is the motherland of modern large-scale industry; the capitalist mode of production has developed there most freely and extensively of all, its consequences show themselves there most glaringly of all and therefore it is likewise there that they first produced a reaction in the sphere of legislation. The best proof of this is factory legislation" (MECW *23*: 360). Apparently, it is the effectiveness of legal enactments that remained in question.

A surprisingly positive view of what labor might expect, on the wages front, in England at least, is apparent in a newspaper interview in April in which Engels describes the widespread implications for the general wage of the recent formation of an English agricultural union: "The union of agricultural labourers was for the frightened landlords and farmers what the *International* is for the reactionary governments of Europe.... And they mounted an opposition, but in vain; the union, helped by the counsel and by the experience of the resistance societies of the industrial workers, grew and became more solid every day" ("Letters from London," MECW *23*: 149). The bourgeoisie supported the effort, considering the "state of great industrial prosperity in which it needs many workers. [Consequently], nearly all the agricultural labourers on strike found themselves transported to the towns, where they were employed and paid much better than they could have been on the land." Engels waxed lyrical regarding the outcome: "Hence the strike was completely successful, with the landlords and farmers of all England spontaneously raising labourers' wages by 25 and 30 per cent." Further, although the successful strike is partly explained here by "great industrial prosperity," which might be temporary, it is the permanent outcome that is emphasized: "From this first great victory will date a new era in the intellectual and social life of the rural proletariat, which has entered as a mass into the movement of the urban proletarians against the tyranny of capital." We have then in 1872 evidence of uncertainty, which may well reflect opinion in a state of flux.[25]

An unambiguous "revisionist" stance is also apparent in "The English Elections" of February 1874, where Engels explains the fact that "no separate political working-class party had existed in England since the downfall of the Chartist Party in the fifties," by the circumstance that "the working class has shared more than anywhere else in the advantages of the immense expansion of its large-scale industry" in an "England that ruled the world market" (MECW *23*: 613; see Chapter Four, p. 206).

---

[25] See Sanderson (1969: 59–60) for comments to similar effect. Sanderson refers to Engels's – and Marx's – "theory of political institutions as instruments of class oppression," but he also cites evidence of uncertainty regarding the intended applicability of this "theory" to particular cases.

This certainly implies real-wage improvements.[26] The same lament and the same rationale are expressed to Kautsky eight years later: "You ask me what the English workers think of colonial policy. Well, exactly what they think of any policy – the same as what the middle classes think. There is, after all, no labour party here, only conservatives and liberal radicals, and the workers cheerfully go snacks in England's monopoly of the world market and colonies" (12 September 1882; MECW 46: 322).[27]

A letter to Bebel dated March 1875, conflicting sharply with the "iron law" passages of *The Housing Question* (above, p. 250), takes us a step further:

[O]ur people have allowed themselves to be saddled with the Lassallean "iron law of wages" which is based on a completely outmoded economic view, namely that on average the worker receives only the *minimum* wage because, according to the Malthusian theory of population, there are always too many workers (such was Lassalle's reasoning). Now in *Capital* Marx has amply demonstrated that the laws governing wages are very complex, that, according to circumstances, now this law, now that, holds sway, that they are therefore by no means iron but are, on the contrary, exceedingly elastic, and that the subject really cannot be dismissed in a few words, as Lassalle imagined. Malthus' argument, upon which the law Lassalle derived from him and Ricardo (whom he misinterpreted) is based . . . is exhaustively refuted by Marx in the section on "Accumulation of Capital" (MECW 45: 62).[28]

---

[26] Unfortunately, Engels provided no data on real wages per capita or employment. (Whether he intended in the present context the elite of the workers or the "labor aristocracy" is discussed below.)

Wood's near-contemporary estimate of 1909 indicates a significant real-wage increase 1850–1902, with allowance made for variation in (cyclical) unemployment and for the significant reduction in hours in 1875 and 1902. That the working-class "standard of comfort" rose considerably is supported by evidence of increase in consumption per head, 1860–1902 (1962 [1909]: 141). Similarly, Saul's index of British real wages shows an increase from c. 135 in 1875 to c. 180 in 1900 (1850 = 100; Saul 1985: 31). This trend makes no allowance for unemployment, but also recorded is an increase in the wage share in the sum of wages and profits from 52.3 percent in 1870–4 to 62.2 percent in 1890–4 (Saul 1985: 33). Saul records, by contrast, a slight fall on balance in the real wage, comparing 1914 with 1896. For a comprehensive review of real-wage trends and the difficulties and ambiguities of measurement, taking particular account of the celebrated indexes devised by Bowley and Weinstein as well as Wood, see Boyer (2004).

Whether, and to what degree, British wage earners benefited from foreign investment (1870–1914) is a matter of debate (see Strachey 1959: 120–1). On the difficulties of arriving at estimates of the net gains from Empire to Britain as a whole, 1870–1914, see Edelstein (2004).

[27] In 1879 Engels told Bernstein that no "genuine labour movement in the continental sense" exists in England, and he lamented the ban on participation in politics by union regulations that ruled out activities "on the part of the working class as a class. Politically the workers are divided into Conservatives and Liberal-Radicals, into supporters of a Disraeli (Beaconsfield) administration and supporters of a Gladstone administration" (17 June 1879; MECW 45: 360–1).

[28] See also a later formulation of 1891 against Brentano: "Mr. Brentano must know that in the first volume of *Capital* Marx specifically denied all and every responsibility for any conclusions drawn by Lassalle, and that in the same book Marx describes the law of wages as a function

Several publications of 1881 in *The Labour Standard* elaborate the potential of labor unions to ensure real-wage gains for their members.[29]

The discussion represents orthodoxy as defining a "fair day's wages, under normal conditions" as "the sum required to procure to the labourer the means of existence necessary, according to the standard of life of his station and country, to keep himself in working order and to propagate his race. The actual rate of wages, with the fluctuations of trade, may be sometimes above, sometimes below this rate; but under fair conditions, that rate ought to be the average of all oscillations" ("A Fair Day's Wages for a Fair Day's Work," *The Labour Standard*, May 1881; MECW *24*: 376–7).[30] Engels protests that there is no "fairness" here because the competition presumed to be at play is biased against labor in two respects; first, the capitalist "can afford to wait, and live upon his capital" in the course of bargaining, and second because of the pressure exerted by the reserve army: "[u]ntil the very last man, woman, or child of this army of reserve shall have found work – which happens in times of frantic over-production alone – until then will its competition keep down wages, and by its existence alone strengthen the power of Capital in its struggle with Labour" (377).[31]

This, however, is in the absence of trades unions. In a second paper Engels explains that because the "standard of life" itself is not rigidly fixed but tends to fall – in part because of the advantages enjoyed by employers – the organization into unions of otherwise disorganized groups of workers permits the maintenance, even increase, of the standard; in fact, "[T]rades Unions in England, as well as in every other manufacturing country, are a necessity for the working classes in their struggle against capital" ("The Wages System," *The Labour Standard*, May 1881, MECW *24*: 380). The full statement is extraordinarily positive, if we consider the earlier statement on the depressing effects on earnings of the industrial reserve:

The average rate of wages is equal to the sum of necessaries sufficient to keep up the race of workmen in a certain country according to the standard of life habitual in that country. That standard of life may be very different for different classes of workmen.

of different variables and very elastic, and thus anything but iron" ("In the Case of Brentano versus Marx," MECW *27*: 117).

To cite *Capital* on the "elasticity" of the wage is misleading because Marx, in rejecting the so-called "iron" law of wages, was concerned to counter the alleged universality of the Malthusian position: "[E]very special historic mode of production has its own special laws of population, historically valid within its limits alone. An abstract law of population exists for plants and animals only, and only in so far as man has not interfered with them" (MECW *35*: 626). The issue of wage "elasticity" that preoccupied Engels relates, by contrast, to an assumed capitalist reality.

[29] On Engels's *Labour Standard* contributions, see Henderson (1989: 72). Engels was in the end disappointed by the journal's failure to follow his recommendation to urge trade unionists to establish a parliamentary party.

[30] Similarly, "a fair day's work" is the number of hours and degree of intensity "which expends one day's full working power of the workman without encroaching upon his capacity for the same amount of work for the next and following days" (MECW *24*: 377).

[31] See also below, p. 296.

The great merit of Trades Unions, in their struggle to keep up the rate of wages and to reduce working hours, is that they tend to keep up and to raise the standard of life. There are many trades in the East-end of London whose labour is not more [sic] skilled and quite as hard as that of bricklayers and bricklayers' labourers, yet they hardly earn half the wages of these. Why? Simply because a powerful organisation enables the one set to maintain a comparatively high standard of life as the rule by which their wages are measured; while the other set, disorganised and powerless, have to submit not only to unavoidable but also to arbitrary encroachments of their employers: their standard of life is gradually reduced, they learn how to live on less and less wages, and their wages naturally fall to that level which they themselves have learnt to accept as sufficient (380).[32]

This paper goes on to elaborate the exertion by unions of countervailing power in the bargaining process, neutralizing the advantages enjoyed by the capitalist against individual employees; for "[t]he law of wages . . . is not inexorable with certain limits. There is at every time (great depression excepted) for every trade a certain latitude within which the rate of wages may be modified by the results of the struggle between the two contending parties." Here Engels expounds what is, in effect, the orthodox view.

Let us return to "the great merit of Trades Unions," that of "tend[ing] to keep up and to raise the standard of life." What are we to make of it, when we recall the downward pressures exerted by ongoing secular development? Now in his third paper ("Trades Unions"), Engels reverts to the "law" of secularly declining real wages in consequence of increasing organic composition of capital, but he clarifies that this process of secular decline toward some kind of "absolute minimum" applied specifically to unorganized labor:

[I]n trades without organisation of the workpeople, wages tend constantly to fall and the working hours tend constantly to increase. Slowly, but surely, this process goes on. Times of prosperity may now and then interrupt it, but times of bad trade hasten it

---

[32] In a further article, Engels elaborates that though the "rate of wages is governed by a distinct and well-defined law of social economy" – he refers indeed to an "irrefutable" law of wages – it is "elastic" with the emphasis placed, however, on the standard of life as subject to downward pressure: "The rate of wages can be lowered, in a particular trade, either directly, by gradually accustoming the workpeople of that trade to a lower standard of life, or, indirectly, by increasing the number of working hours per day (or the intensity of work during the same working hours) without increasing the pay" ("Trades Unions," *The Labour Standard*, May 1881; MECW 24: 382–3).

Engels prefaces the observation by reference to Ricardo's profit–wage relation: "The produce of labour, after deducting all expenses, is divided, as David Ricardo has irrefutably proved, into two shares: the one forms the labourer's wages, the other the capitalist's profits. . . . To deny that it is the interest of the capitalist to reduce wages, would be tantamount to say that it is not his interest to increase his profits" (382). Downward pressure on the wage "receives a fresh stimulus from the competition of capitalists of the same trade amongst each other. Each one of them tries to undersell his competitors, and unless he is to sacrifice his profits he must try and reduce wages. Thus, the pressure upon the rate of wages brought about by the interest of every individual capitalist is increased tenfold by the competition amongst them. What was before a matter of more or less profit, now becomes a matter of necessity" (383).

on all the more afterwards. The workpeople gradually get accustomed to a lower and lower standard of life. While the length of working day more and more approaches the possible maximum, the wages come nearer and nearer to their absolute minimum – the sum below which it becomes absolutely impossible for the workman to live and to reproduce his race ("Trades Unions," *The Labour Standard*, May 1881, MECW *24*: 383; emphasis added).[33]

Engels closes a historical overview by affirming that, dating from the legalization of unions in 1824, "[l]abour became a power in England. The formerly helpless mass, divided against itself, was no longer so. To the strength given by union and common action soon was added the force of a well-filled exchequer – 'resistance money,' as our French brethren expressively call it. The entire position of things now changed. For the capitalist it became a risky thing to indulge in a reduction of wages or an increase of working hours" (384).[34] The allowance for accumulated reserves of union funds implies a potential to save out of wages, labor apparently sharing in the surplus.

In a Note to the German edition of *The Poverty of Philosophy* of 1885, Engels explains that when Marx wrote in 1847 that "[e]conomists and socialists are in agreement on one point: the condemnation of *combinations*," albeit for different reasons, he intended "the socialists of that time: the Fourierists in France, the Owenites in England" (MECW *6*: 209n.). Here Engels is not being entirely candid, for the ineffectualness of unions had been his own and Marx's position not only in the 1840s but long thereafter. Indeed, in taking the new line, Engels diverges not only from Marx in *Value, Price and Profit* (1865) that unions could not reverse but at best could only slow down the rate of decline in the real wage, but from his own *The Housing Question*. How far then did Engels go? One passage in "Trades Unions" suggests that he stepped back somewhat by asserting that any gains obtained by means of unions – supplemented by factory legislation – will be periodically reversed, in consequence of disparate bargaining power:

Thus it is through the action of Trades Unions that the law of wages is enforced as against the employers, and that the workpeople of any well-organised trade are enabled to obtain, at least approximately, the full value of the working power which

---

[33] Engels allows "a temporary exception" to falling real wages at the beginning of the century; but after 1815 – here he identifies the onset of the sequences of industrial cycles – the downward wage trend set in: "When the general peace, in 1815, re-established regularity of trade, the decennial fluctuations between prosperity, over-production and commercial panic began. Whatever advantages the workpeople had preserved from old prosperous times, and perhaps even increased during the period of frantic over-production, were now taken from them during the period of bad trade and panic; and soon the manufacturing population of England submitted to *the general law that the wages of unorganised labour constantly tend towards the absolute minimum*" (MECW *24*: 383–4; emphasis added).

[34] Engels also accepted the standard orthodox case that whereas "[c]apitalists are always organised [and] need in most cases no formal union, no rules, officers, etc.... the workpeople from the very beginning cannot do without a strong organisation, well-defined by rules and delegating its authority to officers and committees. The Act of 1824 rendered these organisations legal" (MECW *24*: 384).

they hire to their employer; and that, with the help of State laws, the hours of labour are made at least not to exceed too much that maximum length beyond which the working power is prematurely exhausted. This, however, is the utmost Trades Unions, as at present organised, can hope to obtain, and that by constant struggle only, by an immense waste of strength and money; and then the fluctuations of trade, once every ten years at least, break down for the moment what has been conquered, and the fight has to be fought over again. It is a vicious circle from which there is no issue. (MECW 24: 385)

Again, in an article "Cotton and Iron," Engels allows some real-wage increase in those unionized trades – "here, as in other trades, if the condition of the workpeople has not become worse, and in some instances even better, it is due exclusively to their own efforts – to strong organisation and hard-fought strikes"; but what follows implies that any improvements are effaced during the cyclical downturn: "We know that after a few short years of prosperity about and after 1874 there was a complete collapse of the cotton and iron trades; factories were closed, furnaces blown out, and where production was continued short time was the rule. Such periods of collapse had been known before; they recur, on an average, once in every ten years; they last their time, to be relieved by a new period of prosperity, and so on" (*The Labour Standard*, July 1881; MECW 24: 411). A letter to Bernstein expresses similar doubts: "For a number of years the English workers' movement has been going round and round bootlessly in a confined circle of strikes for wages and the reduction of working hours – not, mark you, as an expedient and a means of propaganda and organisation, but as the ultimate aim" (17 June 1879; MECW 45: 360). Indeed, these strikes "were, as often as not, deliberately engineered by the capitalists in the late years of depression so as to have an excuse for closing down their factories, strikes in which the working class makes no progress whatsoever" (361).

Yet Engels by no means retracted his allowance for permanent real-wage improvement. To the American translator of *The Condition of the Working Class* he refers, early in 1885 with respect to Britain, to "the improved position [since 1845] of a more or less privileged minority, to the certainly not alleviated misery of the great body" (10 February 1885; MECW 47: 259). The important retrospect "England in 1845 and in 1885" adds to this clarification. The generalization that no "permanent improvement" in real wages had occurred over the years 1845–85 did not apply either to "the factory hands" who had benefited permanently from factory legislation in particular, or to workers organized in the "great Trades' Unions" – an "aristocracy" composed largely of adult males – who had also achieved permanent gains:

And the conditions of the working class during this period? There was temporary improvement even for the great mass. But this improvement always was reduced to the old level by the influx of the great body of the unemployed reserve, by the constant superseding of hands by new machinery, by the immigration of the agricultural population, now, too, more and more superseded by machines.

A permanent improvement can be recognised for two "protected" sections only of the working class. Firstly, the factory hands. The fixing by Act of Parliament of their working day within relatively rational limits [German translation: normal working day in their favour], has restored [German translation: has restored to a certain extent] their physical constitution and endowed them with a moral superiority, enhanced by their local concentration. They are undoubtedly better off than before 1848....

Secondly, the great Trades' Unions. They are the organisations of those trades in which the labour of *grown-up men* predominates, or is alone applicable. Here the competition neither of women and children nor of machinery has so far weakened their organised strength. The engineers, the carpenters and joiners, the bricklayers, are each of them a power, to that extent that, as in the case of the bricklayers and bricklayers' labourers, they can even successfully resist the introduction of machinery. That their condition has remarkably improved since 1848 there can be no doubt.... They form an aristocracy among the working class; they have succeeded in enforcing for themselves a relatively comfortable position, and they accept it as final. (*The Commonweal*, March 1885; MECW *26*: 298–9)

But as to the "great mass" of workers in the East end, other major towns, smaller towns, and agriculture, "[t]he law which reduces the *value* of labor-power to the value of the necessary means of subsistence, and the other law which reduces its *average price* as a rule to the minimum of those means of subsistence: these laws act upon them with the irresistible force of an automatic engine, which crushes them between its wheels" (299). All this is cited verbatim in the Prefaces to the 1892 editions of *The Condition of the Working Class in England* (MECW *27*: 265–6; 317–18). An unqualified statement in *Anti-Dühring*, in 1894 as in earlier editions, regarding "propertyless wage-workers, whose number is constantly increasing and whose conditions, taken as a whole, are steadily deteriorating" (MECW *25*: 139), presumably refers to unorganized labor.

An objection made in the 1891 "Critique of the German Social Democratic (Erfurt) Programme" to a general proposition that "[t]he number and the *misery* of the proletariat increase continuously" is suggestive but ambiguous: "This is incorrect when put in such a categorical way. The organisation of the workers and their constantly growing resistance" – presumably referring to unionization[35] – will possibly check the *increase of misery* to a certain extent. However, what *certainly* does increase is the *insecurity of existence*" (MECW *27*: 223).[36] To "check the increase of misery" conceivably implies a rise in the real wage, though read literally it suggests no more than a decelerated decline.

Engels surely misleads when he dismisses as exceptions industrial workers with regard to labor conditions and the "labor aristocracy" of unionized workers with regard to earnings, for these categories encompass the strategically important

---

[35] In his letter to Bebel of 18–28 March 1875, Engels uses the expression "organisation of the working class as a class through the medium of trade unions" (MECW *45*: 63).
[36] For common ground with Bernstein, see the Epilogue, note 7.

advanced sectors of the economy acquiring a significance out of proportion to their quantitative dimensions.[37] An important point for us is that the progress enjoyed by these categories had been achieved, according to the 1885 overview, with the support of the industrial bourgeoisie that had learned "that the middle class can never obtain full social and political power over the nation except by the help of the working class. Thus a gradual change came over the relations between both classes" (MECW *26*: 297). The 1892 Prefaces to *The Condition* go considerably further by attributing the progress of reform to support from large companies as part of the "concentration" process with the object of creating barriers to entry by raising labor costs. This elaboration emerges in the course of a historical overview of British economic development since "the dawn of a new industrial epoch," which set in after the crisis of 1847 and entailed a truly world market focused initially "around one manufacturing centre – England.... No wonder England's industrial progress was colossal and unparalleled, and such that the status of 1844 now appears to us as comparatively primitive and insignificant" (MECW *27*: 258). There were profound consequences for reform:

And in proportion as this increase took place, in the same proportion did manufacturing industry become apparently moralised. The competition of manufacturer against manufacturer by means of petty thefts upon the workpeople did no longer pay. Trade had outgrown such low means of making money; they were not worth while practising for the manufacturing millionaire, and served merely to keep alive the competition of smaller traders, thankful to pick up a penny wherever they could. Thus the truck system was suppressed, the Ten Hours' Bill was enacted, and a number of other secondary reforms introduced – much against the spirit of Free Trade and unbridled competition, but quite as much in favour of the giant-capitalist in his competition with his less favoured brother. Moreover, the larger the concern, and with it the number of hands, the greater the loss and inconvenience caused by every conflict between master and men; and thus a new spirit came over the masters, especially the large ones, which taught them to avoid unnecessary squabbles, to acquiesce in the existence and power of Trades Unions, and finally even to discover in strikes – at opportune times – a powerful means to serve their own ends. The largest manufacturers, formerly the leaders of the war against the working-class, were now the foremost to preach peace and harmony. And for a very good reason. The fact is that all these concessions to justice and philanthropy were nothing else but means to accelerate the concentration of capital in the hands of the few, for whom the niggardly extra extortions of former years had lost all importance and had become actual nuisances; and to crush all the quicker and all

---

[37] See further on the "labor aristocracy," below, pp. 270–2.

A significant datum from the Factory Inspector's Report for 1886, referred by Bernstein (1993 [1899]: 66), entails 4.4 million persons in factories and workshops subject to the Factory Acts out of 9 million actively engaged in industry, omitting transport, or some 48 percent. Those covered by the legislation were employed in approximately 161,000 factories and workshops, an average of some twenty-seven or twenty-eight workers per establishment, which scarcely supports Engels's hypothesis relating progress on the regulation of hours to "concentration."

the safer their smaller competitors who could not make both ends meet without such perquisites. (258–9; see also 311)[38]

Accordingly, "the development of production on the basis of the capitalistic system has of itself sufficed – at least in the leading industries, for in the more unimportant branches this is far from being the case – to do away with all those minor grievances which aggravated the workman's fate during its earlier stages" (259; also 311).[39]

Engels's illustrations of this social transformation, albeit that the "great mass" had not benefited other than occasionally, cover most of the episodes that have concerned us:

The Factory Acts, once the bugbear of all manufacturers, were not only willingly submitted to, but their expansion into acts regulating almost all trades, was tolerated. Trades' Unions, lately considered inventions of the devil himself, were now petted and patronised as perfectly legitimate institutions and as useful means of spreading sound economical doctrines amongst the workers. Even strikes, than which nothing had been more nefarious up to 1848, were now gradually found out to be occasionally very useful, especially when provoked by the masters themselves, at their own time. Of the legal enactments, placing the workman at a lower level or at a disadvantage with regard to the master, at least the most revolting were repealed. (1885; MECW 26: 297)

Let us turn to Engels's support for the Eight-Hour campaign of the early 1890s. The matter is complex. To be noted is the observation that not all factory workers favored reduced hours, though their concerns were diminishing: "So proud were the factory workers of the North of their old Ten Hours' Bill that it was largely they who opposed the eight hour day. . . . This is now changing; the masses are gradually being converted to 8 hours while the leaders with their 10 hours are beginning to

---

[38] Engels's interpretation is also found in his editorial notes to *Capital 3*. A modern case entails a charge against the United Mine Workers of America of conspiring with corporations to raise wages as a means of limiting entry; see Williamson (1968). Rogerson (1984) considers the incentives for a monopolist to increased fixed costs to the same end.

   In an earlier evaluation, Engels attributes effective Prussian reform measures to efforts by the "reactionary" party to "provoke" the bourgeoisie ("The Prussian Military Question and the German Workers' Party," 1865; MECW 20: 76). Specifically: "Concerning the *social* concessions that reaction could offer to the workers – reduction of working hours in the factories, improved operation of the factory acts, the right of association, etc. – experience in every country has shown that reaction makes such propositions without the workers having to offer the slightest thing in return."

[39] Engels concludes – rather curiously, because by so doing he plays down the welfare achievements he had just allowed and neglects the implications of the expansion of the advanced industrial (and unionized) sectors – that this development "renders more and more evident the great central fact that the cause of the miserable condition of the working-class is to be sought, not in these minor grievances, but *in the capitalistic system itself*" (MECW 27: 259; 311).

find themselves out on a limb" (to Kautsky, 12 August 1892; MECW *49*: 494–5).[40] Nevertheless, Engels considered this "conversion" a mixed blessing, based on the state of trade rather than ideology: "[A] period of slack trade and the manufacturers' threat to knock 10 per cent off wages has suddenly cured the Lancashire cotton operatives of their enthusiasm for 10 hours and opened their eyes to the advantages of the 8 hour day. Even the leaders are already said to have switched horses. Thus the 8 hour day has triumphed in England. The resistance of those factory hands who enjoyed the protection of the 10 hour day was the principal weapon in the bourgeois arsenal" (to Bebel, 14 August 1892; 497).[41]

In late 1889 Engels lamented that "[w]hat is most repellent here is the workers' deeply ingrained sense of middle-class "*respectability*" (to Sorge, 7 December 1889; MECW *48*: 418). Little had changed since he had complained to Marx some thirty years earlier "that the English proletariat is actually becoming more and more bourgeois" (Chapter Four, p. 205). Now, with reference to the textile workers, he lamented further that they are "deeply infected with the Parliamentary spirit of compromise.... Thus the sudden awakening of the Eight Hours' enthusiasm (3 years ago considered an impossibility, you know, by the very people who now clamour loudest after it) has almost succeeded in giving a reactionary character to that cry. It is to be the universal panacea" (to Laura Lafargue, 11 September 1892; MECW *49*: 520). The reference to Parliament is no mere flourish, when we recall from Chapter Four (see pp. 204, 212) the faith placed in universal suffrage, for a proletarian majority had to be reliable and sure to vote appropriately for a communist program.[42]

---

[40] See also letters dated 14 and 30 September 1891 to Sorge:

> The Trades Union Congress in Newcastle has also been a great victory [September 1891]. The old Unions with the textile workers at their head, together with the entire reactionary party that exists among the workers, had mustered all their forces in order to overturn the eight hours resolution of 1890. They failed, having secured no more than one insignificant, fleeting concession. That is crucial. There is still much confusion, but there's no stopping things now and the bourgeois papers fully recognise the defeat of the bourgeois labour party, recognise it with dismay and a wailing and gnashing of teeth. (MECW *49*: 238)

> The Trades Union Congress was also a success. The "old" unions did everything in their power to get the Liverpudlian eight hours resolution overturned and their failure to do more than whittle away a small fragment of it is of itself a defeat for them and their middle-class allies. You ought to have seen the liberal papers, in particular the Scottish ones, and the way they wrung their hands over the aberrations of the English working man and his lapse into socialism. (250)

> The references here to the "1890" or "Liverpudlian" resolution are to the eight-hours resolution at the Congress of the British Trade Unions meeting, held in Liverpool, in September 1890.

[41] The "advantages" of the eight-hour day are not spelled out. The slack cotton trade is attributed to American competition ("The American Presidential Election," November 1892; MECW *27*: 330) and to continental and Indian competition (letter dated 30 August 1892; MECW *49*: 513).

[42] The subsequent history of the "New Union" leadership would have confirmed Engels's worst fears, as "the revolutionary Marxists who led the Dockers and Gas-Workers ... were increasingly replaced by much milder socialists ... " (Hobsbawm 1964: 191; also 327–8).

F. Further Extensions: Unskilled Labor and the "New Unionism"

Thus far we have encountered recognition of welfare and real-wage advance solely in the advanced industrial sectors. Now let us consider evidence indicating that, by the early 1890s, Engels had begun to allow for some welfare progress even with respect to unskilled labor. Here I introduce the matter of "New Unionism," which broadened the base of the trade union movement by organizing semi-skilled and unskilled workers in the public utilities. Engels wrote lyrically of these developments in the 1892 Prefaces to *The Condition of the Working Class in England* regarding "the revival of the East End of London":

That immense haunt of misery is no longer the stagnant pool it was six years ago. It has shaken off its torpid despair, has returned to life, and has become the home of what is called the "New Unionism," that is to say, of the organisation of the great mass of "unskilled" workers.... The old Unions preserve the traditions of the time when they were founded, and look upon the wages system as a once-for-all established, final fact, which they at best can modify in the interest of their members. The new Unions were founded at a time when the faith in the eternity of the wages system was severely shaken; their founders and promoters were Socialists either consciously or by feeling; the masses, whose adhesion gave them strength, were rough, neglected, looked down upon by the working-class aristocracy; but they had this immense advantage, that *their minds were virgin soil*, entirely free from the inherited "respectable" bourgeois prejudices which hampered the brains of the better situated "old" Unionists. And thus we see now these new Unions taking the lead of the working-class movement generally, and more and more taking in tow the rich and proud "old" Unions.... [F]or all the faults committed in past, present and future, the revival of the East End of London remains one of the greatest and most fruitful facts of this *fin de siècle*, and glad and proud I am to have lived to see it. (MECW *27*: 268–9; 321)

Engels's enthusiasm clearly reflects the prospect, as he interpreted the evidence, of a growing proletarian force prepared to entertain the demise of the "wages system."[43] This also emerges from a further comparison of the "new" and the "old" unions: "The latter, encompassing 'skilled' workers, are exclusive; they bar all workers who have not received a guild training, and thereby themselves give rise to competition from those not in the guild; they are rich, but the richer they become, the more they degenerate into mere health-insurance and death benefit funds; they are conservative and they steer clear above all of... socialism, as far and as long as they can" ("May 4 [1890] in London"; MECW *27*: 62). By contrast, "[t]he new

---

[43] For the "revolutionary" dimension to "New Unionism," see also the correspondence of 1889 and 1890 (e.g., MECW *48*: 422, 436–7, 494, 496). Eleanor (Tussy) Marx-Aveling, Marx's youngest daughter, appears as a leading character (see Hobsbawm 1964: 327, Kapp 1976: 318–35, 735–6; Lapides 1987: xvii). It is worth mentioning that favorable trade conditions in the late 1880s, with unemployment down to 2 percent, contributed to the phenomenon of new unionism (Matthew 1985: 260). The depression of the early 1890s had correspondingly adverse effects (Hobsbawm 1964: 181). On the new phenomenon more generally, see Hunt (2009: 332–4).

'unskilled' unions ... admit *every* worker in the given trade; they are essentially, and the gas workers even exclusively, unions geared to organising and funding strikes. And while they are not socialist to a man, they nevertheless absolutely insist on being led by socialists and no others."

Nevertheless, the prospect of reform of the capitalist system is by no means dismissed as irrelevant in the new circumstances. Ongoing reformist modifications to the capitalist system evidently played their part for Engels, who described the successful London dock strike of August to September 1889 for higher wages and improved conditions as "the greatest event to have taken place in England since the last Reform Bills," namely since the electoral reforms of 1867 and 1884 (letter to Kautsky, 15 September 1889; MECW *48*: 377).[44] He ascribed "the universal sympathy shown by the press, and even by the philistines" to "[h]atred of the monopolistic Dock Companies," and also to "[t]he knowledge *that the Dockers are voters* and need to be cajoled if the 16 to 18 East End M.P.s of Liberal and Conservative complexion wish to be re-elected (which they won't be; this time there'll be Labour M.P.s)." For all that, the gas workers' strike of the same year for an eight-hour day Engels found to be only partially successful and under threat.[45]

In further correspondence, Engels represents the welfare demands of the "new" unionists, including an eight-hour day, as merely "provisional, considering the prospective transition to socialism"; and although the rank-and-file "don't yet

---

[44] On the dockers, see Hobsbawm (1964: 204–30). Bertrand Russell, in his *Autobiography*, recalls an account he heard in summer 1889 of "the latest news of a great dock strike that was then in progress. This dock strike was of considerable interest and importance because it marked the penetration of Trade Unionism to a lower level than that previous reached" (Russell 1968: 93).

Engels argues in "The Abdication of the Bourgeoisie" (5 October 1889) that the bourgeoisie had failed in its task to counter residuals of "feudalism" wherever they exist, as in the case of "the dock monopoly and the feudal port constitution," and left the task to the dock workers (MECW *26*: 548–9).

[45] On the gas workers, see Hobsbawm (1964: 158–78).

Engels goes on to explain that in 1889 "the gas workers won an eight-hour working day here in London, but in an unsuccessful strike lost it again in the southern part of the city, acquiring sufficient proof that this gain is by no means safe for all times in the northern part either" ("May 4 [1890] in London"; MECW *27*: 62).

The attitudes toward the eight-hour day on the part of the "new" and "old" unions are distinguished in an account of the May Day celebrations in 1890, with the former calling for a statutory reduction in hours at the *standard* daily wage, i.e., with no pay cut, the latter prepared to accept a pro-rata reduction in the daily wage to be compensated by overtime rates beyond eight hours (63). The distinction is explained in correspondence some two years later: "Now the eight-hour day advocated by the majority on the Trades Council merely implies payment of the ordinary [hourly] wage for 8 hours, any work over and above this being payable as overtime at one and a half times or twice the ordinary rate; thus the eight hour day advocated by these people is quite different from our own ... " (to Kautsky, 20 April 1892; MECW *49*: 403). Eleanor Marx-Aveling made the same point to Paul Lafargue: "do not forget the very important fact that the Legal Eight Hours Day demanded by Shipton and Co. [London Trades Council] is not *our* Legal Eight Hours Day. They only want the 8 hours day legalised in order that over-time may be more highly paid" (15 April 1892: 560).

know what their ultimate goal will be.... this obscure presentiment is deep-seated enough for them to choose *only* avowed socialists for their leaders.... [U]nlike the old Trades Unions, they greet with derision any reference to an identity of interests between capital and labour" (to Sorge, 7 December 1889; MECW *48*: 417).[46] A letter to Kautsky of 18 September 1890 carries the same message (MECW *49*: 26). Nonetheless, although the reforms may have been "provisional," one notes the significance Engels placed on legal confirmation of the gains within the going system: "The gas workers – the best of the new Unions – were greatly in favour of the 8 hours demonstration for, besides having fought for and secured an 8 hour day for themselves, they have also learnt how insecure in practice is such an achievement, liable as it is to being revised by the capitalists at the first opportunity; for the gas workers as for the Miners, the main thing is that it should be *legally* established" (to Sorge, 30 April 1890; *48*: 488–9). The prospect of reform within capitalism is still taken very seriously indeed.[47]

Recognition of welfare progress, at least in Britain, can already be found to some degree in the 1887 edition of *The Housing Question*. The passage in question is quite general and may be relevant to the unskilled, not only the élite: "In recent English Acts of Parliament giving the London building authorities the right of expropriation for the purpose of new street construction, a certain amount of consideration is given to the workers thus turned out of their homes. A provision has been inserted that the new buildings to be erected must be suitable for housing those classes of the population previously living there. Big five or six storey tenement houses are therefore erected for the workers on the least valuable sites and in this way the letter of the law is complied with" (MECW *23*: 362). Engels reserved judgment regarding the future effectiveness of the legislation in question, but he does not dismiss it out of hand as necessarily ineffectual: "It remains to be seen how this arrangement will work, for the workers are quite unaccustomed to it and in the midst of the old conditions in London these buildings represent a completely foreign development. At best, however, they will provide new dwellings for hardly a quarter of the workers actually evicted by the building operations."[48] Five years

---

[46] Engels adds this: "I hope there won't be any general elections for the next three years . . . so that the labour movement can develop still further and, perhaps, mature more quickly as a result of the bad trading conditions that will surely come as a backlash of the present boom. Then the next parliament might boast between 20 and 40 labour M.P.s" (MECW *48*: 417–18). How this fits in with the end of cycles there is unclear (see note 59).

[47] As for the Eight-Hour campaign with regard to the *factory sector*, to be noted is the observation that not all factory workers favored reduced hours, though their concerns were diminishing (see letter to Kautsky, 12 August 1892; cited above, pp. 262–3). However, this "conversion," important though it was, was based less on ideology than on the state of trade (see letter to Bebel, 14 August 1892; cited above, p. 263).

[48] Engels did not, however, take the opportunity to revise, in the light of the somewhat more optimistic British outlook, his pessimistic projections regarding Germany as German capitalist development progressed. On the contrary, he reinforced them in a note to the new edition regarding home-ownership projects, drawing on a letter dated 28 November 1886 from Eleanor Marx-Aveling in Indianapolis, describing the heavy mortgage debts there entailed, such that

later, in the Preface to the 1892 English edition of *The Condition of the Working Class*, he allowed that "the most crying abuses" described in the 1845 original – the chronic epidemics due to foul or nonexistent sanitation – had "either disappeared or [had] been made less conspicuous" by drainage schemes, slum clearance, and wide roads, although the improvements are attributed to concern of the bourgeois "to save himself and family" from disease (MECW *27*: 260). As for housing, Engels refers back to the 1885 Report of the Royal Commission on the Housing of the Poor as evidence that "no substantial improvement has taken place."

Finally, a remark in correspondence regarding the London dock workers' strike of 1889 possibly suggests a small upward secular movement in the real wage: "It's the old story – when business is good, demand compels the masters to be accommodating, when it is bad, they exploit the excessive supply of labour to contest all these concessions again. On the whole, however, the resistance of the workers increases as they become better organised, – so much so, in fact, that the general situation – on average – improves slightly and no crisis can lastingly drag the workers down to or below zero, the nadir of the previous crisis" (24 March 1891; MECW *49*: 152). Nonetheless, even this modest allowance is subject to the qualification that "it would be difficult to say what would happen if at any time we were to experience a prolonged, chronic, general industrial crisis of 5 or 6 years' duration."[49]

G. A Grand Dilemma

I have established that Marx and Engels, writing in the late 1840s and early 1850s, recognized the progressive factory legislation enacted by the British Parliament but emphasised the practical impediments imposed by the industrialists rendering such measures a dead letter. We encountered a major change of viewpoint in the 1860s on Marx's part – apparent in *Capital* itself – who, despite continued pessimism regarding the course of real wages, outlined the positive consequences for labor emanating from the effective operation of the Factory Acts. Moreover, he now welcomed such legislation envisaged as forced on Parliament by working-class pressure contrasting with his hostility in 1850 based on the grounds that capitalist development would be thereby restrained.

Engels's adoption of this "revisionist" position regarding effective and desirable reform is somewhat delayed, with *The Housing Question* of 1872 still taking for granted the ineffectiveness of social reform measures. A more positive perspective is apparent in 1874 and again in papers of 1881–5, where Engels acknowledges

---

workers "become the slaves of their employers. They are tied to their houses, they cannot go away, and must put up with whatever working conditions are offered them" (MECW *23*: 330n.).

[49] The specific issue related to the liberty of unions to "negotiate wage settlements with the entrepreneurs direct and on everyone's behalf" – an aim achieved in the 1889 dock strike (MECW *49*: 151–2).

progress with respect to improved working conditions; whereas the 1887 edition of *The Housing Question* is rather noncommittal regarding the new housing estates for London workers, the 1892 edition of *The Condition of the Working Class* describes enthusiastically the success of urban renewal schemes, rendering outdated the original account of Manchester in 1845. Some allowance is also made in the 1881–5 papers for real-wage increase in the factories and unionized trades. Subsequently improvement is noted even in the unskilled sector under pressure of the "New Union" movement with respect to hours and possibly, though to a limited degree, pay. (As early as 1872 Engels described the success of an agricultural union in raising wages.) It is surprising that Engels did not recognize the "revisionism" apparent in *Capital* immediately upon its appearance, but that he did ultimately come to do so amply confirms that his 1895 Introduction to Marx's *The Class Struggles in France* constitutes no radical change of position late in the day, and certainly no "deception" of Marx such as has been attributed to him (Prolegomena, p. 17).

With respect to the ability of unions to ensure improved real wages for their members, including specific categories of unskilled workers, we find Engels taking a somewhat more positive view than had Marx – at least Marx in the mid-1860s. References as late as 1894 to "steadily deteriorating" conditions refer to the "great mass" of unprotected workers (above, pp. 260, 262).

I have tried to appreciate the reasons offered why the capitalists, and their organ the State, ultimately complied in granting reform measures. What stands out is the representation of social reform as a necessary feature of advanced capitalism: "all these concessions to justice and philanthropy," Engels wrote in the 1892 Prefaces to *The Condition of the Working Class* of the Factory Acts and acceptance of unions, were "but means to accelerate the concentration of capital in the hands of the few" (above, p. 261). Now both Marx and Engels had already intimated in the 1840s that formal legalization of unions and factory legislation were necessary features of capitalist development, although practical implementation of the latter was quite another matter (above, pp. 234–5). In *Capital 1*, however, Marx represents the effective Ten Hours' legislation of 1863 as a necessary consequence of the development of modern industry and corresponding "struggle of classes" (p. 244).[50] Engels carries the argument a step further.

---

[50] Nonetheless, Engels wrote in 1891 in rather qualified fashion regarding the 1863 legislation:

The factory legislation of the forties had decisively improved the lot of those workers subject to it. But in 1863 this benefitted only the workers employed in wool, linen and silk, altogether about 270,000, while the cotton operatives were starving.... Further: in branches of work in which full male strength and sometimes dexterity are indispensable, the resistance of the workers, organised in trade associations, had forced through for themselves a share of the proceeds of the favourable business period, and it may be said that on the average for *these* branches or work, involving heavy male labour, the living standard of the workers had risen decisively, though it is still ridiculous to describe this improvement as "unexampled" ("In the Case of Brentano versus Marx"; MECW 27: 130).

I might add a further rationale offered in 1892, namely that important local government reforms had been introduced as assurance against "genuine" socialism: "[I]t's a blessing that Paris and London, at any rate, have municipal councils that are all too aware of their dependence on the Labour vote, and are the less inclined to put up any serious resistance to demands, realisable even today, such as employment on public works, shorter working hours, wages in accordance with trades union demands, etc., etc., in that these represent the best means of safeguarding the masses against worse socialist – genuinely socialist – heresies" (to Bebel, 8 March 1892; MECW 49: 374).[51] This cynical comment does not negate the assurance of welfare advance within capitalism.

* * *

The evidence presented above points directly away from von Mises's view that "Marx and the school of orthodox Marxism" grew increasingly opposed to social-reform measures within capitalist organization in later years (Prolegomena, p. 21). Unfortunately, the proletariat's growing dissatisfaction with capitalism also plays a necessary role in the Marxist vision, entailing in Engels's terms "the development of a class whose conditions of life necessarily drive it to social revolution" (above, p. 252). An important application of the theme emerges in late correspondence from London with Sorge:

The movement over there [America], just like the one in this country and now, too, in the mining districts of Germany, cannot be produced by exhortation alone. It's the facts themselves that will have to bring all this home to the chaps, after which, however, things will move fast – fastest, of course, where an organised and theoretically educated section of the proletariat already exists, as in Germany. Today the coal miners belong to us, potentially and of necessity; in the Ruhr, the process is well under way, the Aachen and Saar Basins will follow, then Saxony, then Lower Silesia and, finally, the Wasserpolaken of Upper Silesia. Considering our party's position in Germany, all that was needed to call forth an irresistible movement was the impulse arising out of the miners' own living conditions. (8 February 1890; MECW 48: 447)

We should certainly not forget the standard position encountered in *The Housing Question* (above, pp. 248–9) that any improvement in labor's condition is a secondary matter so long as the exploitative wages system itself remained untouched. The "Wages System" of 1881 again spells out the issue:

[T]he Trades Unions do not attack the wages system. But it is not the highness or lowness of wages which constitutes the economical degradation of the working class: this degradation is comprised in the fact that, instead of receiving for its labour the full

---

[51] A later comment regarding draft proposals placed by Socialist deputies before the French National Assembly affirms the desirable propaganda effect of reformist legislation: "[A]n eight-hour working day and a minimum wage for workers, etc., employed by the state, corresponds more or less to what has been instituted here by the County Council, and in part also by the ministries of war and the navy. A measure very useful both as an example for the capitalists, and as a means of propaganda" (5 March 1895; MECW 50: 453).

produce of this labour, the working class has to be satisfied with a portion of its own produce called wages. The capitalist pockets the whole produce (paying the labourer out of it) because he is the owner of the means of labour. And, therefore, there is no real redemption for the working class until it becomes owner of all the means of work – land, raw material, machinery, etc. – and thereby also the owner of THE WHOLE OF THE PRODUCE OF ITS OWN LABOUR. (MECW 24: 381; also 379–80)

There is a corresponding emphasis on the "exploitative" feature of the "capitalist system itself" in the Appendix to the 1887 American and the 1892 British editions of *The Condition of the Working Class* focusing on profit as unpaid labor hours or "surplus value which costs the capitalist nothing" (MECW 26: 401; 27: 259). Although in these contexts there is some intimation also of workers' "miserable" condition, the refrain turning on the technical sense of "exploitation" in no way negates the perceived fact of welfare progress or resolves the dilemma that progress under capitalism with respect to working conditions and real wages compromises the transition to communism by generating what has been called "class collaboration."

Let us first step back for perspective. As early as 1850, Marx and Engels had expressed their concern that a wing of the Chartist movement comprising the "labour aristocracy," and in collaboration with the petty bourgeoisie, merely sought passage of the Charter and minor reforms. This was in opposition to the "revolutionary" faction of the movement that consisted of "the mass of the workers who live in truly proletarian conditions" (Chapter Four, p. 193). Engels in fact attributed the collapse of the movement to this clash of perspective. The problem is elaborated in 1858, but with respect to the *embourgeoisement* of the British working class as a whole: "the English proletariat is actually becoming more and more bourgeois" (Chapter Four, p. 205). This phenomenon is explained in 1874 and 1882 in terms of Britain's "monopoly of the world market and colonies" (above, p. 255), implying a broadly based improvement in living standards. The matter is complex, and how seriously to take the implication of general real-wage advance is open to question if we consider Engels's insistence throughout the 1880s until his death upon secular deterioration in the well-being of the unorganized masses (above, p. 268). Some allowance must be made for an admission in 1885 that "even the great mass had at least a temporary share now and then" in the benefits of the monopoly (below p. 274). Nonetheless on balance the trend towards "*embourgeoisement*" and the rationale offered appear to relate to the upper echelons of the working class – factory and unionized workers.[52]

---

[52] The empirical investigation by Hobsbawm suggests the difficulty at arriving at reliable orders of magnitude. By "labour aristocracy" Hobsbawm understood "certain distinctive upper strata of the working class, better paid, better treated and generally regarded as more 'respectable' and politically moderate than the mass of the proletariat" (1964: 272), though the main criteria are the level and regularity of earnings because of the difficulties in quantifying more subjective criteria (273). He adds, however, that "it is probably unsafe to conclude anything

Thus Engels had confidence that the dock and gas workers could not be so easily bribed (above, p. 264).

An account of the development of class collaboration by Lenin in 1915 allows us to perceive Engels's position more clearly, by way of contrast:

The collapse of the Second International [1914] is the collapse of socialist opportunism. The latter has grown as a product of the preceding "peaceful" period in the development of the labour movement. That period taught the working class to utilize such important means of struggle as parliamentarianism and all legal opportunities, create mass economic and political organizations, a widespread labour press, etc.; on the other hand, the period engendered a tendency to repudiate the class struggle and to preach a class truce, repudiate the socialist revolution, repudiate the very principle of illegal organizations, recognize bourgeois patriotism, etc. Certain strata of the working class (the bureaucracy of the labour movement and the labour aristocracy, who get a fraction of the profits from the exploitation of the colonies and from the privileged position of their "fatherlands" in the world market) . . . have proved the social mainstay of these tendencies and channels of bourgeois influence over the proletariat. (Lenin 1964 [1915]: 161)

The phraseology suggests an Engels influence, but even so there would be this difference, that Lenin describes class collaboration dating from late in the century, whereas Engels's account reflects a perceived reality setting in decades earlier, at least as early as 1858 where the charge of embourgeoisement is first encountered. Furthermore, as Hobsbawm notes, Lenin neglected to explain why the masses should have followed a minority "upper stratum"; he suggests that this can be accounted for by the beginnings of a dissolution of the differential as all workers began to enjoy the revenue generated by imperialism (Hobsbawm 1970: 209–10).[53] Now we have seen that Engels tended to limit the charge of class collaboration reflecting improved conditions to the working-class aristocracy. To explain why the masses would follow the upper strata in their attitude toward capitalism in

from our survey except that the labour aristocracy averaged between, say, 10 and 20 percent of the total size of the working class, though in individual regions or industries it might be larger or smaller" (290).

Moorhouse objects that Hobsbawm "draws far too neat an equation between high wages and a quiescent labour force" (1978: 72), for there are "much more fundamental forces that maintained (and maintain) class subordination in British society" than the "economistic" criteria Hobsbawm employed (82). He does not, however, offer a detailed alternative. For a summary and evaluation of the literature on these and related issues, see Perkin (1978).

The correspondence discerned by Engels between the labor aristocracy and unionization seems to be justified, at least before the rise of the New Unions in 1889. Hobsbawm relies in part on what data there are on unionization to obtain his estimate of the magnitude of the aristocracy (Hobsbawm 1964: 275, 279–80, 287–9).

[53] See also Hobsbawm on the dissolution of the traditional "labour aristocracy" accompanied by a general "class collaboration" with the extension of privileges to the entire working class that occurred after 1914 (1964: 300–3).

the 1850s, one would have to rely on behavioral attitudes of a sociological order unrelated to the level (or stability) of real wages.[54]

H. The Resolution: Economic Stagnation and Immigration

I turn now to Engels's solution to the dilemma, namely that progressive reforms and rising living standards in the case of factory and unionized workers undermined prospects in Britain of proletarian hostility toward capitalist organization.[55] It lies in a perception that British industrial primacy was now under threat, so that what advantages had admittedly been enjoyed by labor were unsustainable.[56]

We recall from Section B that the case for free trade in the late 1840s had turned on its liberation of the forces ensuring rapid capitalist development. To be added now is Engels's view, first expressed in the early 1880s, that free trade was no longer a valid option for Britain, considering imminent, if not actual, competition from foreign sources ("The French Commercial Treaty," June 1881; MECW *24*: 389–93). In "England in 1845 and in 1885," Engels describes the early years of what economic historians once labeled "The Great Depression," which set in after the mid-1870s following several decades of successful free-trade policy and "rule of the manufacturing capitalists":

But then a change came. The crash of 1866 was, indeed, followed by a slight and short revival about 1873; but that did not last. We did not, indeed, pass through the full crisis at the time it was due, in 1877 or 1878; but we have had, ever since 1876, a chronic state of stagnation in all dominant branches of industry. Neither will the full crash come; nor will the period of longed-for prosperity to which we used to be entitled before and after it. A dull depression, a chronic glut of all markets for all trades, that is what we have been living in for nearly ten years (1885, MECW *26*: 299).

The "manufacturing monopoly enjoyed by England for nearly a century" was "irretrievably broken up," the future promising nothing but aggravated overproduction (300).[57]

---

[54] Engels denied upward mobility out of the working class (see above, p. 252), focusing rather, as he often did, on downward mobility into the working class; and he doubtless would have subscribed to J. S. Mill's notion of "non-competing groups" (see Chapter Four, p. 224).

[55] The possibility must be entertained that the increase in "insecurity of existence," alluded to in 1891, could be relied upon to undermine class collaboration, even should the "increase of misery" be somewhat mitigated by unionization (above p. 260). However, Engels's response to the dilemma, now to be spelled out – that any progress enjoyed by labor was temporary only – implies that he himself did not rely to any great degree on this line.

[56] The dilemma was also faced by Marx, who realized that the working class would not turn to socialism under conditions of capitalist prosperity; he, too, did not expect prosperity to last (Rigby 1987: 136). The dilemma sharpened with the passage of time, though, and Engels provided specific rationalizations drawn from contemporary events to justify the evaluation of prospects for labor.

[57] Engels cites Palgrave: "I am not the first to point this out. Already in 1883, at the Southport meeting of the British Association, Mr. Inglis Palgrave, the President of the Economical section, stated plainly that 'the days of the great trade profits in England were over, and there was a

Much the same depressing forecast applied to agriculture; Engels elaborated in another paper of 1881 a parallel threat to British corn and cattle from American imports: "The price of corn is now determined by the cost of production in America, plus the cost of transport... [and] American meat and American cattle are sent over in ever-increasing quantities," while "[w]ith the present state of science and the rapid progress made in its application, we may be sure that in a very few years – at the very latest – Australian and South American beef and mutton will be brought over in a perfect state of preservation and in enormous quantities" ("American Food and the Land Question," June 1881; MECW *24*: 398).[58] It is allowed that the "system of land exhaustion" practiced in the Far West could not continue forever; any limitations, however, would not be felt for a century, while there were lands aplenty in South Russia and the Argentine all "fit for this modern system of giant farming and cheap production" (398–9).

The primary outcome for us of the challenge to British competitiveness is the dire consequence for employment, for "what is to become of the 'hands' when England's immense export trade begins to shrink down every year instead of expanding?" ("The French Commercial Treaty," 1881; MECW *24*: 392). The revolution would now follow, the supersession of British industrial power "break[ing] the last link which still binds the English working class to the English middle class. This link was

pause in the progress of several great branches of industrial labour. *The country might almost be said to be entering the non-progressive state* '" (MECW *26*: 300).

For the perceived end of the cyclical era, see also "Marx and Rodbertus": "Since England's monopoly of the world market is being increasingly shattered by the participation of France, Germany and, above all, of America in world trade, a new form of evening-out appears to come into operation. The period of general prosperity preceding the crisis still fails to appear. If it should remain absent altogether, then chronic stagnation must necessarily become the normal condition of modern industry, with only insignificant fluctuations" (1885; MECW *26*: 288n.).

See Appendix B: III for some later evaluations of British experience in the last quarter of the nineteenth century.

[58] Engels emphasized the threat to continental as well as British farming, though it was subject to different landed arrangement; 1879 is mentioned as the first year when the effect of major corn imports from America was experienced, in that "for the first time the British farmer had a bad crop and low prices of wheat at the same time" (MECW *24*: 398). The article commences with an important overview regarding cycles: "Since autumn 1837 we have been quite accustomed to see money panics and commercial crises imported from New York into England. At least one out of every two of the decennial revulsions of industry broke out in America. But that America should also upset the time-honoured relations of British agriculture, revolutionise the immemorial feudal relations between landlord and tenant at will, smash up English rents, and lay waste English farms, was a sight reserved for the last quarter of the nineteenth century" (397).

For data on the remarkable increase in wheat and meat imports, beginning, however, in the 1860s, see Turner (2004: 134–8). Turner observes that a slump in domestic wheat yields in the 1880s, "the darkest decade of the agricultural depression," did not lead to price increase because "British prices were determined now more by external considerations" (141). For the decline in rents per acre, commencing in the early 1880s, see Turner (2004: 141). For a nuanced account of the impact on meat prices exerted by imports, distinguishing between different categories, see Saul (1985).

their common working of a national monopoly. That monopoly once destroyed, the British working class will be compelled to take in hand its own interests, its own salvation, and to make an end of the wages system. Let us hope it will not wait until then" (393). The same vision of secular decline in consequence of foreign competition bringing to an end that "cooperation" between labor and capital that had brought about real-wage gains, at least for a "privileged minority" of the working class, is touched upon in the letter of 10 February 1885 (cited above p. 259), for there Engels also insists on "the impending change for the worse which must necessarily follow from the break-down of the industrial monopoly of England in consequence of the increasing competition in the markets of the world, of Continental Europe and especially of America" (MECW 47: 259).

With the inevitable loss of what advantages they had (very partially) shared with the capitalists, labor would at last turn to socialism, a matter I anticipated at the close of Chapter Four, as is explained in "England in 1845 and in 1885":

The truth is this: during the period of England's industrial monopoly the English working class have to a certain extent shared in the benefits of the monopoly. These benefits were very unequally parcelled out amongst them; the privileged minority pocketed most, but even the great mass had at least a temporary share now and then. And that is the reason why since the dying-out of Owenism there has been no Socialism in England. With the breakdown of that monopoly the English working class will lose that privileged position; it will find itself generally – the privileged and leading minority not excepted – on a level with its fellow-workers abroad. And that is the reason why there will be Socialism again in England. (1885; MECW 26: 301)

Similarly, Engels's Preface of 1886 to the first English edition of *Capital 1* elaborates the replacement of the cyclical pattern recurrent from 1825 to 1867 by "a permanent and chronic depression," with dire consequences for labor: "The decennial cycle of stagnation, prosperity, over-production and crisis, ever recurrent from 1825 to 1867, seems indeed to have run its course; but only to land us in the slough of despond of a permanent and chronic depression. . . . [W]e can almost calculate the moment when the unemployed losing patience will take their own fate into their own hands" (MECW 35: 35).

This, then, is the primary qualification to Engels's "revisionism" dating from at least 1874 that recognized welfare progress, including real-wage improvement, under capitalist organization at least for English factory and unionized labor.[59]

---

[59] The prognosis is considerably qualified in other contexts. Thus in a letter to Bebel in Germany, dated 18 January 1884, we find reference to secular stagnation in England but also intimations of an imminent crisis: "In this country, too, industry has taken a different character. The ten-year cycle would seem to have been disrupted since 1870, when American and German competition began to destroy England's monopoly in the world market. Since 1868 business has been slack in the main branches, while production has been gradually increasing; and now, here and in America, we appear to be on the eve of another crisis which has not, in England, been preceded by a period of prosperity" (MECW 47: 82). (This pattern is said to provide "the secret behind the sudden emergence of the socialist movement over here – sudden, although it has been slowly maturing for the past 3 years.") In his letter to Bebel of 8 March 1892 (above,

In taking this line Engels was actually unearthing a forty-year-old theme. *The Holy Family* contains brief remarks on the undermining of Britain's international competitiveness and on centralization with their dire consequences for labor (1845; MECW 4: 14). Further, *The Condition of the Working Class* elaborates the worsening outlook for labor given the prospect of American industrial preeminence (rejecting McCulloch's position in this respect).[60] In the event of an undermining of British competitiveness – and provided "the present conditions remain unchanged" (an important proviso indeed) – the "proletariat must become forever superfluous and has no other choice than to starve or to rebel" (MECW 4: 580). Late in the day, Engels took pride in this early prescience: "The wonder is, not that a good many of [the 'prophesies'] proved wrong, but that so many of them proved right, and that the critical state of English trade, to be brought on by Continental and especially American competition, which I then foresaw – though in too short a period – has now actually come to pass" (Preface to 1892 English edition, MECW 27: 262; see also the Appendix to the 1887 American edition, MECW 26: 402).

In a newspaper contribution at this time, Engels further opined that should "the centre of gravity" in textiles and iron pass to America, as it would with the introduction there of free trade, then "England will become either a second Holland, whose bourgeoisie live on their former greatness, and whose proletariat shrivels, or – it will reorganise itself along socialist lines. The first is not possible, the English proletariat will not put up with it, it is far too numerous and developed for this. Only the second remains. *The fall of protective tariffs in America means the ultimate victory of socialism in England*" (1892; "The American Presidential Election," MECW 27: 330). As he wrote to an Austrian correspondent, "[b]y promoting your industry . . . you will be doing England a service; the more quickly her domination of the world market is utterly destroyed, the sooner will the workers over here come to power. Continental and American competition (and likewise Indian) has finally precipitated a crisis in Lancashire, the first of its consequences being the prompt conversion of the workers to the eight-hour day" (to Victor Adler, 30 August 1892; MECW 49: 513).

Let us return to the resolution of Engels's dilemma, and specifically to a further perceived threat pertaining to Europe as a whole and also to America, namely the

---

p. 269), Engels points out that "unemployment might well get worse next year. For protection has had exactly the same effect as free trade – the flooding of individual national markets and this almost everywhere, though it's not so bad over here as where you are" (MECW 49: 373). But in England, too, "where we have come through two or three insidious little crises since 1867, we would at last seem to be heading for another acute one." These remarks are nonetheless compatible with the demise of the regular cyclical pattern, whereas other letters still seem to take such a pattern for granted (e.g., 7 December 1889, above note 46; 24 March 1891, above p. 267; 14 August 1892, above p. 263).

For important qualifications in notes to *Capital 3* to the prospect of permanent stagnation, see Chapter Six, p. 282.

[60] McCulloch (1837b: 221–38).

threat of massive immigration from China with the destruction there of small agri-culture and domestic industry: "The consequence will be a wholesale emigration such as the world has not yet seen, a flooding of America, Asia and Europe by the hated Chinaman, a competition for work with the American, Australian and European workman on the basis of the Chinese standard of life, the lowest of all" (22 September 1892; MECW 49: 538). Once again, the resolution of all these dark prospects was found to be in the adoption of socialism: "and if," Engels goes on to warn, "the system of production has not been changed in Europe before that time, it will have to be changed then."

The Japan–China war, two years later, generated a yet more specific prediction. China's modernization – enforced by European and Japanese intervention[61] – would displace millions, "[a]nd then the Chinese Coolies will be everywhere, in Europe as well as America and Australia, and will try to reduce wages and the standard of living of our working men to the Chinese level. And then the time will come for our European workmen. And the English will be the first to suffer from this invasion and *to fight*. I fully expect that this Japan–Chinese War will hasten our victory in Europe by five years at least" (to Laura Lafargue, September 1894; MECW 50: 347–8). As Engels wrote to Sorge in the United States, "in your country as in ours, Chinese competition will, as soon as it reaches massive proportions, quickly bring things to a head and thus the conquest of China by capitalism will at the same time provide the impulse for the overthrow of capitalism in Europe and America" (10 November 1894; 359). The Chinese were playing the role accorded the Irish in 1845: "the Irish have . . . discovered the minimum of the necessities of life, and are now making the English workers acquainted with it" (MECW 4: 390–1, cited in Chapter One, p. 55).

I. Concluding Remarks

The "revisionist" papers dating from the early 1870s and recognizing some welfare progress under capitalist organization, at least for British factory and unionized workers and a little later even for some unskilled and agricultural labor, must be read in the light of the qualification that the system held no future promise for labor. There is no reasonable sense in which the 1895 Introduction to the reissue of *The Class Struggles in France* can be considered as a "tragic deception" of Marx. It is also important to recall Engels's perception in the early 1880s that the cap-italist class in Britain no longer constituted a progressive vehicle, considering the displacement over recent years of the traditional individual capitalist-manager

---

[61] More than foreign intervention would have been entailed, considering Marx's declaration in the Preface to *Capital 1*: "Intrinsically, it is not a question of the higher or lower degree of development of the social antagonisms that result from the natural laws of capitalist production. It is a question of these laws themselves, of these tendencies working with iron necessity towards inevitable results. The country that is more developed industrially only shows, to the less developed, the image of its own future" (MECW 35: 9).

by nationalized, or joint-stock, or cooperative ventures (see Chapter Three, pp. 160–4). Capitalist organization itself was becoming an irrelevance.

There is a further dimension to Engels's perspective regarding prospects for the achievement of communism. It is the remarkable forecast in 1887 of a worldwide conflagration in consequence of the arms race – "the systematic development of mutual one-upmanship in armaments" – that would guarantee Europe-wide proletarian victory, despite inevitable but temporary setbacks.

Engels sets out with a focus on Prussia: "the only war left for Prussia–Germany to wage will be a world war, a world war, moreover, of an extent and violence hitherto unimagined. Eight to ten million soldiers will be at each other's throats and in the process they will strip Europe barer than a swarm of locusts" ("Introduction to Sigismund Borkheim," 1887; MECW *26*: 451). The war would end, he closes,

in universal bankruptcy; collapse of the old states and their conventional political wisdom to the point where crowns will roll into the gutters by the dozen, and no one will be around to pick them up; the absolute impossibility of foreseeing how it will all end and who will emerge as victor from the battle. Only one consequence is absolutely certain; universal exhaustion and the creation of the conditions for the ultimate victory of the working class.

That is the prospect for the moment when the systematic development of mutual one-upmanship in armaments reaches its climax and finally brings forth its inevitable fruits. This is the pass, my worthy princes and statesmen, to which you in your wisdom have brought our ancient Europe. And when no alternative is left to you but to strike up the last dance of war – that will be no skin off your noses. The war may push us [the communists] into the background for a while, it may wrest many a conquered base from our hands. But once you have unleashed the forces you will be unable to restrain, things can take their course: by the end of the tragedy you will be ruined and the victory of the proletariat will either have already been achieved or else inevitable.[62]

Such an outcome would doubtless put to rest Engels's disappointment with the British working class, and it would settle the uncertainties regarding the transition to communism spelled out in my text. Unfortunately, in the end Engels abandoned the prediction: "The Franco-Russian alliance is becoming more and more lenitive. . . . At the same time the Triple Alliance [Germany, Austria–Hungary, Italy]

---

[62] On this Lenin wrote the following in *Pravda*: "Nobody, thank God, believes in miracles nowadays. Miraculous prophecy is a fairy-tale. But scientific prophecy is a fact. And in these days, when we so very often encounter shameful despondency and even despair around us, it is useful to recall one scientific prophecy which has come true" (1965b [1918] *27*: 494). Lenin was particularly impressed by Engels's allusions to the likelihood of temporary setbacks to the movement, expressed in my passage. This is also the theme with which Mayer closes his biography (1969 [1936]: 332).

In his brilliantly original *Lenin. The Novel*, Alan Brien has his protagonist describing in 1922 Marx's explanation of "the workings of a new machine," alluding to the methodology of historical materialism, as "clairvoyance on an heroic scale, comparable only to Copernicus or Darwin," but adding that "without disrespect" to Marx, "as an exact chronicler of the epoch yet to appear, no one can equal Engels, the Nostradamus of Socialism" (Brien 1988: 664). "Lenin" cites a version of the passages from *The Peasant War in Germany* given in my text.

has ceased to exist except on paper.... So that, with the complete revolution in weapons since 1870 and, in consequence, of tactics, there is a total uncertainty about the outcome of a war where so many imponderables are involved and regarding which all the calculations made in advance are based on fictitious quantities. In these circumstances we seem to be assured of peace" (to Paul Lafargue, 22 January 1895; MECW 50: 428).

We are left then with reliance, in the British case, on secular depression and mass immigration as the proposed solutions to the dilemma of working-class *embour-geoisement*. Engels, unfortunately, is not out of the woods. Secular depression would not ensure a transition to communism either in America or the European nations responsible for the undermining of British competiveness. As for the prospect of massive Chinese immigration, that turns on the displacement of labor "with the conquest of China by capitalism," as Engels himself pointed out.

SIX

The Engels–Marx Relation

A. Introduction

This chapter on aspects of the Marx–Engels relationship sets out in Section B by questioning the merits of a commonly encountered representation of Engels as little more than Marx's mouthpiece. Nonetheless, his role in the production of *Capital* itself is shown in Section C to parallel that of James Mill with regard to Ricardo's *Principles*. More generally, we find in Section D that as propagandist he frequently appears to be "more royalist than the king," particularly with respect to the surplus-value doctrine. His own evaluation of his contribution to the Marxist enterprise, including the doctrine of historical materialism, is the subject matter of Section E. Finally, I examine his performance as editor, taking under consideration, but dismissing, doubts regarding the reliability of his edition of *Capital 3* in the light of the original Marx manuscripts of 1864–5 now published in the MEGA^2 edition.

B. His Master's Voice?

Let us turn first to a commonly encountered underestimation, even dismissal, of Engels's contribution to the Marxian enterprise (see the Prolegomena, pp. 2, 22). Regarding matters of technical detail, I would suggest that there is nothing "pedestrian" about the recognition in the *Outlines* of the "Marshallian" notion of long-run price entailing both blades of the scissors, and the contention that Ricardo and Say, implicitly or unwittingly, were obliged to make allowance for the omitted blade to make any sense of their own respective doctrines (Chapter One, pp. 29, 65, 83). By the same token, there is his analysis of rent in terms of productivity and "competition" and, more specifically, his appreciation that differential rent turns on land scarcity (pp. 32–3). His early perception of scientific progress as the source of a problem of excess population relative to means of employment, in place of the "Malthusian" problem (pp. 37, 39–40, 84), cannot be dismissed. It was not dismissed by Marx. Similarly, *The Condition of the Working Class* provides important critical observations on the proper direction of causality in Malthusian doctrine (p. 48). Recall, too, the evidence provided in Chapter Three of Engels's profound understanding of the information-yielding and allocative role of prices in a capitalist-exchange system equal to anything found in Marx.

But much broader claims can be made on Engels's behalf. As I argued in the first essay, the Marxian predictions regarding the evolution of capitalism are spelled out in the early 1840s, with Engels not only providing the overall "vision" but also elaborating some of the main processes at play. *The Outlines*, for example, elaborates the subsistence-wage concept in terms of labor's bargaining disadvantage, the process of centralization exacerbated by ever-worsening crises, bifurcation of income entailing the demise of the middle class, and inflows into the working class exerting additional downward pressure on the wage, all leading to "a total transformation of social conditions" – in other words, "a social revolution such as has never been dreamt of in the philosophy of the economists" (Chapter One, p. 41). The relation of cycle to trend (in the context of overproduction) is also explored (p. 41). Of particular significance is the recognition in *The Condition of the Working Class* of a positive effect on aggregate demand for industrial labor exerted by mechanization, such that any displacement is more than compensated for, with rapid population growth a consequence (pp. 49, 56). A downward real-wage trend under these conditions can only result from forces at play degrading minimum standards such as Irish immigration (p. 55), in addition to the increasing inflows from the middle classes already found in the *Outlines*. Completing the picture of industrial development are the superposition of cycles on an upward trend of capital, employment, and population, and the reserve army of unemployed, which is perceived as a force available to service capitalists' exceptional requirements at peak levels of cyclical activity (54). The requisite labor supply to meet long-term industrial growth derives on this view from population growth rather than the pool of unemployed (pp. 54, 70). All of this reemerges in the later Marx, who based his falling real-wage forecast on rapid growth in population, considering the net expansion of demand accompanying accumulation subject to mechanization (Hollander 2008: 94–102).

Although *The Communist Manifesto* of 1848 was formulated by Marx, much of its technical substance derives from Engels's *Principles of Communism* of 1847 (see Chapter One, pp. 58–64). The main themes of the *Manifesto* already found in the *Principles* or *The Condition of the Working Class* include the matter of regularly repeated crises that threaten the existence of bourgeois society; the treatment of the "commodity" labor, including its pricing in terms of its production costs, namely subsistence; the destruction of the lower middle classes; the "concentration of labor" with a consequential growth of its political and social power; the deterioration of living standards – more specifically "pauperism" – and prospective revolution. There is too a discussion of deskilling in consequence of mechanization, allowing increasing entry of women and children into the work force and thereby exacerbating the adult male immizeration trend. In addition, the analysis in the *Communist Manifesto* of the nature and effects of globalization was originally conceived by Engels in the *Principles* (Chapter One, pp. 60–1).

Taking a yet broader perspective, we see that further qualification of the standard position is in order. Although the predictive potential of the engine of analysis incorporating the methodology of historical materialism may certainly be called into question, Engels deserves credit for admitting that several of his forecasts regarding a violent revolutionary outcome were ill timed (Chapter Four, p. 212). The same applies to some of his other predictions. There is too his discernment of conspicuous structural changes in the capitalist economy since Marx composed *Capital* in the 1860s. A number of instances from the editorial notes to *Capital 3* will be recorded here.

When discussing the actualization on a worldwide scale of the "general principle of competition to 'buy in the cheapest market,'" Marx had been skeptical regarding "a common, all-embracing and far-sighted control of the production of raw materials," and treated attempts to form cartels or "associations to regulate production" as, in practice, "a pious wish . . . or limited to exceptional co-operation in times of great stress and confusion" (1894; MECW 37: 121). Although he closes with a concession to the older view, Engels enters a major modification and also exploits the opportunity to champion "regulation" of production, although not of course by the capitalist class:

Since the above was written (1865), competition on the world market has been considerably intensified by the rapid development of industry in all civilised countries, especially in America and Germany. The fact that the rapidly and enormously expanding productive forces today outgrow the control of the laws of the capitalist mode of commodity exchange, within which they are supposed to operate, impresses itself more and more even on the minds of the capitalists. This is disclosed especially by two symptoms. First, by the new and general mania for a protective tariff, which differs from the old protectionism in that now articles fit for export are those best protected. And secondly, by the trusts of manufacturers of whole spheres of production which regulate production, and thus prices and profits. It goes without saying that these experiments are practicable only so long as the economic climate is relatively favourable. The first storm must upset them and prove that, although production assuredly needs regulation, it is certainly not the capitalist class which is fitted for that task. Meanwhile, the trusts have no other mission but to see to it that the little fish are swallowed by the big fish still more rapidly than before. (121–2n.)

We should recall here his observations, also made in notes to *Capital 3*, regarding the "trust" movement as entailing a transition from joint-stock organization envisaged as an aspect of the evolutionary process carried beyond the stage where Marx had taken it (see Chapter Three, pp. 162–4).

Recall, too, that Engels perceived not merely a change in the periodicity of cycles but, more significantly, the close of the cyclical era (Chapter Five, p. 274). The importance of this perception cannot be exaggerated because in 1873 Marx made very much indeed of the standard cyclical pattern.[1] Note, however, that Engels appears to qualify his position regarding permanent stagnation. Thus in a lengthy note to *Capital 3* he describes the replacement of the regular ten-year cycle by "a more chronic, long drawn out, alternation between a relatively short and slight business improvement and a relatively long, indecisive depression – taking place in the various industrial countries at different times" (1894; MECW 37: 488n.). Even this reading of events is not firmly offered, if we consider his introduction of the prospect of an "unparalleled" world crash: "But perhaps it is only a matter of a prolongation of the duration of the cycle.[2] In the early years of world commerce, 1815–47, it can be shown that these cycles lasted about five years; from 1847–67 the cycle is clearly ten years; is it possible that we are now in the preparatory stage of a new world crash of unparalleled vehemence?" This prospect is linked to the evolution of a "real world market." Globalization – as we now call it – reduces, on the one hand, the problem of "local overspeculation" and *local* crises:

Many things seem to point in this direction. Since the last general crisis of 1867 profound changes have taken place. The colossal expansion of the means of transportation and communication – ocean liners, railways, electrical telegraphs, the Suez Canal – has made a real world market a fact. The former monopoly of England in industry has been challenged by a number of competing industrial countries; infinitely greater and varied fields have been opened in all parts of the world for the investment of surplus

---

[1] See Marx's Afterword to the second German (1873) edition of *Capital 1*: "The contradictions inherent in the movement of capitalist society impress themselves upon the practical bourgeois most strikingly in the changes of the periodic cycle, through which modern industry runs, and whose crowning point is the universal crisis. That crisis is once again approaching, although as yet but in its preliminary stage; and by the universality of its theatre and the intensity of its action it will drum dialectics even into the heads of the mushroom-upstarts of the new, holy Prusso-German empire" (1873, MECW 35: 20).

A note to this paragraph appearing in the French edition (tr. Joseph Roy) of 1872–5, *Le Capital*, justifies the prediction made therein: "The Postface to the second German edition is dated 24 January 1873, and it was only some time after publication that the crisis there predicted broke out in Austria, the United States and Germany. Many people believe wrongly that the general crisis has been forestalled, so to speak, by partial albeit violent explosions. On the contrary, the phenomenon of general crisis is reaching its apogee. England will be the locus of the central explosion, whose effect will be felt universally" (Rubel 1963: 559n.). A letter to N. Danielson, dated 15 November 1878, reinforces the justification:

The English crisis which I predicted on p. 351 of the French edition, note – has at last come to a head during the past few weeks. Some of my friends – theoreticians and businessmen – had asked me to omit that note because they thought it unfounded. So convinced were they that the crises in the north and south of America and those in Germany and Austria were bound, as it were, to "cancel out" the English crisis. . . . The most interesting field for the economist is now certainly to be found in the United States, and, above all, during the period of 1873 (since the crash in September) until 1878 – the period of chronic crisis. (MECW 45: 344)

There is, however, an implicit suggestion in *Capital 3* that the regular cyclical pattern would be mitigated by the trend toward monopoly (see Hollander 2008: 471).

[2] Schumpeter perhaps had this in mind when he suggested that "some anticipation of Kondratieff's work on Long Cycles" might be discerned in Engels's writings (Schumpeter 1950: 41n.).

European capital, so that it is far more widely distributed and local overspeculation may be more easily overcome. By means of all this, most of the old breeding grounds of crises and opportunities for their development have been eliminated or strongly reduced. (1894; MECW *37*: 488n.)

But, so runs the contention – for Engels provides no proper justification – the prospect of "the ultimate general industrial war" was enhanced: "At the same time, competition in the domestic market recedes before the cartels and trusts, while in the foreign market it is restricted by protective tariffs, with which all major industrial countries, England excepted, surround themselves. But these protective tariffs are nothing but preparations for the ultimate general industrial war, which shall decide who has supremacy on the world market." Thus, Engels concludes, "every factor which works against a repetition of the old crisis, carries within itself the germ of a far more powerful future crisis," apparently on a world scale.[3] At the end of the day Engels had, in one sense, managed to strengthen rather than undermine the Marxian vision.

Also reflecting new globalization trends is a modification Engels made to Marx's discussion of fraudulent commercial practices involving the purchase of commodities in order to generate discountable drafts convertible into money (1894; MECW *37*: 407). Marx had relied on evidence dating to 1847 relating to the East Indian trade, and this was no longer valid: "This fraudulent procedure remained in vogue so long as goods to and from India had to round the Cape in sailing vessels. But ever since they are being shipped in steamboats via the Suez Canal this method of fabricating fictitious capital has been deprived of its basis – the long freight voyage. And ever since the telegraph informs the English businessman about the Indian market and the Indian merchant about the English market, on the same day this method has become totally impracticable."[4] Because Engels related aggregative instability to information deficiencies, especially with regard to foreign markets (see Chapter One, pp. 41, 52; Chapter Three, p. 128), these improvements take on particular significance as potentially mitigating cycles.

---

[3] Howard and King cite an early draft of Engels's 1892 edition of *The Condition of the Working Class* that similarly indicated his expectation of a "gigantic crisis": "The absence of crisis since 1868 [is] also attributable to the expansion of the world market, which distributed the excess English and European capital *over the entire world* in transport equipment and the like. Thus a crisis due to overspecialization in railways, banks, etc., or in special American equipment or in the Indian trade became impossible, though small crises, like the Argentinean one, [have been] possible for the last three years. But all this goes to show that a gigantic crisis is preparing itself" (1989: 11). In contrast, the notion of permanent depression, peculiar to Britain rather than of global dimension, and due to foreign competition, appears in the 1887 and 1892 editions of *The Condition of the Working Class*, which reproduce the text of "England in 1845 and in 1885" of 1885 (see MECW *26*: 648n. 153).

[4] Stock-company fraud, however, remained very much alive. In an editorial note to *Capital 3*, Engels remarks on Marx's text (composed in the late 1860s) regarding this issue; "the entire Panama swindle [1888] is here correctly anticipated, fully twenty years before it occurred" (MECW *37*: 437).

There were, additionally, major changes to industrial organization since the composition of *Capital*, and many of them were fraught with implications for the stock market. This matter Engels elaborates in his Supplement:

The position of the stock exchange in capitalist production in general is clear from Volume III, Part 5, especially Chapter 27 [MECW 37: 432–9]. But since 1865, when the book was written, a change has taken place which today assigns a considerably increased and constantly growing role to the stock exchange, and which, as it develops, tends to concentrate all production, industrial as well as agricultural, and all commerce, the means of communication as well as the functions of exchange, in the hands of stock exchange operators, so that the stock exchange becomes the most prominent representative of capitalist production itself. (1894; MECW 37: 894–5)

The impact extended far and wide: "Now all foreign investments in the form of shares. To mention England alone: American railways, North and South (consult the stocklist). . . . Then colonisation. Today this is purely a subsidiary of the stock exchange, in whose interests the European powers divided Africa a few years ago" (896–7).

Perelman criticizes Engels's dismissal of stock exchanges as an institution entailing a zero-sum game (1987: 204–5). In fact, though, Engels himself makes the point that such a criticism was no longer relevant: "At that time [1865], the stock exchange was still a place where the capitalists took away each other's accumulated capital" 1894; MECW 37: 895). "Now it is otherwise," by virtue of its new role of encouraging "expansion of production."[5]

Finally, although Engels may have lagged somewhat behind Marx in recognizing welfare progress as a feature inherent in capitalist development – Marx, as I proposed in Chapters Four and Five, was the *first* "revisionist" – he did come to recognize real-wage increase in the factories and unionized trades, whereas Marx hesitated; he also noted significant advances in the unskilled sectors, reflecting the New Union movement (Chapter Five, pp. 264–7).

As for future prospects, and in the light of the evolving evidence, Engels carried further Marx's late questioning of the progressive function assigned to the bourgeoisie (Chapter Three, pp. 160–2). In addition, we have encountered his impressive insights into problems likely to beset any communist régime taking power prematurely, including bottlenecks in the supply of skilled technicians and the opportunities for "wrecking" that arise therefrom on the part of opponents of the communist state (Chapter Four, p. 225). This warning appeared in 1891, but forty years earlier Engels had made out the same sort of case in more general but equally impressive terms:

---

[5] See also a note regarding the apparent "doubling and trebling of capital," already discerned by Marx, but that had "developed considerably further in recent years, for instance, through financial trusts, which already occupy a heading of their own in the report of the London Stock exchange" (1894; MECW 37: 470–1n.).

The worst thing that can befall the leader of an extreme party is to be compelled to assume power at a time when the movement is not yet ripe for the domination of the class he represents and for the measures this domination implies.... [H]e necessarily finds himself in an unsolvable dilemma. What he *can* do contradicts all his previous actions and principles and the immediate interests of his party, and what he *ought* to do cannot be done. In a word, he is compelled to represent not his party or his class, but the class for whose domination the movement is then ripe. (*The Peasant War in Germany*, 1850; MECW *10*: 469–70)

C. Engels's Contribution to *Capital*: Form or Substance?

Engels, we have seen, had much to offer in his early days, even on a theoretical plane. From this point of view, the following advice offered to Marx at an early stage in the composition of *Capital* comes as something of a surprise: "Do try for once to be a little less conscientious with regard to your own stuff; it is, in any case, far too good for the wretched public. The *main* thing is that it should be written and published; the shortcomings that catch your eye certainly won't be apparent to the jackasses" (31 January 1860; MECW *41*:14). At the same time, we must not forget that Marx allowed himself too readily to be diverted from the main task at hand, and that Engels knew his man.

Engels himself made only a few contributions to Marxian theory while Marx was engaged with *Capital*.[6] Sometimes, for example, he requests clarification of theoretical concepts as when he was "by no means clear about the existence of 'absolute' rent" – and promised to write further on the matter (8 August 1862; MECW *41*: 402). This led Marx to make a provisional elaboration (9 August; 403–4; see Hollander 2008: 299–300) while awaiting comments promised by Engels. However, the extant correspondence contains nothing further from Engels on the matter, which may partly be accounted for by business difficulties during the cotton famine: "What with the cotton pother, the theory of rent has really proved too abstract for me. I shall have to consider the thing when I eventually get a little more peace and quiet" (9 September; MECW *41*: 414). Marx's request for "objections" to his version of the *Tableau Economique* (6 July 1863; MECW *41*: 485) also apparently went unanswered.

There is, however, an exchange regarding the life cycle of fixed capital (and its relevance to cyclical fluctuations) in which Engels, drawing on his businessman's perspective, was in his element. The story commences with a request in 1858 from Marx: "Can you tell me how often machinery has to be replaced in, say, your factory? Babbage maintains [in 1835, *On the Economy of Machinery and Manufactures*, p. 285] that in Manchester the bulk of machinery is renovated on average every 5 years. This seems to me somewhat startling and not quite trustworthy. The average

---

[6] In fact, in 1858 Engels commended the "arrangement" of *A Contribution* (in manuscript), but he admitted that "all abstract reasoning is now completely foreign to me" (9 April 1858; MECW *40*: 304).

period for the replacement of machinery is *one* important factor in explaining the multi-year cycle which has been a feature of industrial development ever since the consolidation of big industry" (2 March 1858; MECW *40*: 278). Engels's well-reasoned reply confirms Marx's skepticism: "Babbage's assertion is so absurd that were it true, England's industrial capital must continually diminish," considering that a five-year replacement period "would, of course, vastly increase the cost price of all articles – more, almost, than it would be increased by wages – in which case where is the advantage of machinery?" (4 March; 281). As for his own estimate, the "most reliable criterion is the percentage by which a manufacturer writes down his machinery each year for wear and tear and repairs, thus recovering the entire cost of his machines within a given period. This percentage is normally 7 $\frac{1}{2}$, in which case the machinery will be paid for over 13 $\frac{1}{3}$ years by an annual deduction from profits, i.e. will be replaceable without loss" (279–80). But, in an impressive passage that draws directly upon his own expertise in cotton manufacturing, Engels spells out the difficulties in fixing upon a precise estimate and rejects the identification of the rate of economic depreciation with the rate at which machinery in the physical sense disappears from use:

Now, 13 $\frac{1}{3}$ years is admittedly a long time in the course of which numerous bankruptcies and changes occur; you may enter other branches, sell your old machinery, introduce new improvements, but if this calculation wasn't more or less right, practice would have changed it long ago. Nor does the old machinery that has been sold promptly become old iron; it finds takers among the small spinners, etc., etc., who continue to use it. We ourselves have machines in operation that are certainly 20 years old and, when one occasionally takes a glance inside some of the more ancient and ramshackle concerns up here, one can see antiquated stuff that must be 30 years old at least. Moreover, in the case of most machines, only a few of the components wear out to the extent that they have to be replaced after 5 or 6 years. And even after 15 years, provided the basic principle of a machine has not been superseded by new inventions, there is relatively little difficulty in replacing worn out parts (I refer here to spinning and flyer frames), so that it is hard to set a definite term on the effective life of such machinery. Again, over the last 20 years improvements in spinning machinery have not been such as to preclude the incorporation of almost all of them in the existing *structure* of the machines, since nearly all are minor innovations. (Admittedly, in the case of carding, the enlargement of the carding cylinder was a major improvement which supplanted the old machines where *good* qualities were concerned, but for ordinary qualities the old machinery will be perfectly adequate for a long time yet). (280–1)[7]

Marx, in his response, ignored the sophistication of Engels's qualifications, taking instead the thirteen-year figure relating to full depreciation of equipment in the accounting sense as constituting at least one circumstance governing cyclical periodicity: "My best thanks for your *éclaircissements* about machinery. The figure of 13 years corresponds closely enough to the theory, since it establishes a *unit* for one epoch of industrial reproduction which *plus ou moins* coincides with the

---

[7]   I wish this fine passage had been on hand when I investigated DuPont rayon manufacture (Hollander 1965).

period in which major crises recur; needless to say their course is also determined by factors of a quite different kind, depending on their period of reproduction" (5 March 1858; MECW 40: 282).

Some four years later Marx again requested help. Taking the average life of machinery as twelve years, he raises a question to which Engels "as a practical man, must have the answer" (20 August 1862; MECW 41: 411), albeit that the question is in fact rather of a theoretical nature: "[I]n the course of those 12 years does not $^1/_{12}$ of the machinery have to be replaced *in natura* each year? Now, what becomes of this fund, which yearly replaces $^1/_{12}$ of the machinery? Is it not, in fact, an accumulation fund to extend reproduction aside from any conversion of revenue into capital? Does not the existence of this fund *partly* account for the *very different* rate at which capital accumulates in nations with advanced capitalist production and hence a great deal of *capital fixe*, and those where this is not the case?" (411–12). In response Engels wrote perfunctorily that "I rather suspect you have gone off the rails. Depreciation time is not, of course, the same for all machines" (9 September; MECW 41: 414). A promised elaboration is not forthcoming, but his general objection confirms the qualifications of 1858, which had cast doubt on the proposed basis for cyclical movements in capital replacement.[8]

Such objections are not typical. On the whole, Engels praised Marx's manuscript of *Capital 1* to high heaven but was critical of the book's "structure":

I have now worked through as far as sheet 36 approx., and I congratulate you on the comprehensive way in which the most complex economic problems are elucidated simply and almost sensuously merely by arranging them suitably and by placing them in the right context. Likewise, in respect of subject-matter, on the quite splendid exposition of the relationship between labour and capital – for the first time here in its full context and complete. I was also greatly diverted to see how you have worked your way into the language of technology, which must surely have given you much trouble and on which account I had various misgivings. I have corrected several slips of the pen in pencil in the margin, and also ventured to make a few conjectures. But how could you leave the *outward* structure of the book in its present form! (23 August 1867; MECW 42: 405–6)

Regarding the so-called form of value, at the outset of *Capital*, Engels's sense of humor is revealed when he remarks that "Sheet 2 [of the proofs] in particular has the marks of your carbuncles rather firmly stamped upon it, but there is not much that can be done about it now and I think you should not deal with it any further in the supplement, as your philistine really is not accustomed to this kind of abstract thinking and will certainly not torment himself for the sake of the form of value"

---

[8] As Perelman has pointed out, "Marx never absorbed Engels' lessons on the turnover of plant and equipment... [but] frequently referred to the decennial cycles brought on by the pattern of renewing fixed capital" (Perelman 1987: 127).

   An important editorial clarification by Engels in *Capital 3* relates to the implicit assumption in the discussion of the falling profit rate, namely that "capital is turned over exactly in one year" (MECW 37: 225; also 54).

(16 June 1867; MECW *42*: 381).[9] Without doubt, this has proven a valid evaluation of likely "philistine" reaction. Marx went only part way toward accommodating Engels with respect to the organization of the material (22 June 1867; MECW *42*: 384–5; see Carver 1989: 248).

Engels found the analyses of "The Transformation of Money into Capital" and "Production of Surplus-Value" to be "the best, as far as presentation and content are concerned" (24 June 1867; MECW *42*: 386). Nonetheless, we should take note of his serious misgivings regarding the exposition of the origin of surplus in unpaid labor power, which comes as a surprise because precisely this matter, we have seen in Chapter Two, was regarded as the essential Marxian contribution:

With regard to the production of surplus-value, another point: the manufacturer, and with him the vulgar economist, will immediately interject: if the capitalist only pays the worker the price of 6 hours for his 12 hours' labour, no surplus-value can be produced, since in that case each hour of the factory worker's labour counts only $= \frac{1}{2}$ an hour's labour, $=$ the amount which has been paid for, and only that value can be embodied in the value of the labour product. Whereupon there will follow the usual formula by way of example: so much for raw materials, so much for wear and tear, so much for wages (wages *actually paid* per hour's actual product), etc. Atrociously superficial though this argument may be, however much it may equate exchange-value with price, and value of labour with labour-wage, and absurd though its premise may be that if for one hour's labour only half an hour is paid, then only $\frac{1}{2}$ hour's worth goes into the value, I do, nevertheless, find it surprising that you have not already taken it into account, for you will *most certainly* be immediately confronted with this objection, and it is better to anticipate it. Perhaps you return to it in the following sheets. (26 June 1867; MECW *42*: 388–9)[10]

These evaluations of Marx's proofs of *Capital 1* are of the same order as those made by James Mill when he was reviewing the manuscript of Ricardo's *Principles* (Hollander 1979: 189–90).[11] Similar too was Mill's readiness to adopt extreme or unqualified versions of Ricardian doctrine (Hollander 1992: 180, 333–4), and this to ensure effective use of economic theory for propaganda purposes, as we shall presently see.

* * *

[9] For more on the "form of value," see Engels's letter of 9 September 1867 (MECW *42*: 423).
[10] The following remark by Marx himself, however, expresses precisely the same concern:

Proudhon has sown total confusion in people's minds on that subject [the theory of value]. They believe that a commodity is sold for its value if it is sold for its *prix de revient* [prime cost] $=$ price of the means of production which have been consumed in it, $+$ wages (or price of the labour added to the means of production). They do not see that the unpaid labour which is contained in the commodity constitutes just as fundamental an element of value as the labour which has been paid for, and that this element of value now takes the form of profit, etc. They have no idea what wages are. Without an understanding of the nature of value, arguments about the working day, etc., in short, the factory laws, have no basis. (to V. Schily, 30 November 1867; MECW *42*: 488)

[11] Also relevant are later concerns with style pertaining to the French version of *Capital,* on which matter see Rubel (1963: 538–9).

Let us turn now to the two volumes published by Engels in 1885 and 1894. Strange as it may appear, it was only after Marx's death in 1883 that Engels became aware of the materials on which he was to base his edition (see Engels to Lavrov, 2 April 1883; MECW 47: 3). Indeed, he had little idea of what progress Marx had been making over the entire period from 1867 to 1883. "You ask," he wrote to Bebel, "why I of all people should not have been told how far the thing had got. It is quite simple: had I known, I should have pestered him night and day until it was all finished and printed. And Marx knew that better than anyone else. He knew besides that, if the worst came to the worst, as has now happened, the ms. could be edited by me in the spirit in which he would have done it himself, indeed he told Tussy [Eleanor Marx] as much" (30 August; MECW 47: 53). Again, regarding what was to become *Capital 3*: "It is almost inconceivable how a man who had such tremendous discoveries, such an entire and complete scientific revolution in his head, could keep it there for 20 years. For the ms. I am working at, has been written either before, or at the same time, as the *first volume*; and the essential part of it is already in the old manuscript of 1860–1862" (to Laura Lafargue, 8 March 1885; MECW 47: 264). The latter allusion is to the *Economic Manuscripts* of 1861–3, the central part of which consists of what later was to be called *Theories of Surplus Value.* That Engels was aware of the contents of this document is of particular significance, because he was right to say that much of *Capital 3* is already to be found therein (Hollander 2008: Part Four).

Only at the outset of the period from 1867 to 1883 do we find some relevant correspondence with Marx, and it deals entirely with "practical" business matters. This suggests the degree to which Marx himself evaluated Engels's usefulness to him at this time. Thus he said with regard to an accumulation or sinking fund: "Now, as a manufacturer, you must know what you do with the returns on *capital fixe before* the time it has to be replaced *in natura.* And you must answer this point for me without theorising, *in purely practical terms*" (Marx to Engels, 24 August 1867; MECW 42: 408).[12] Again, "[s]ince practice is better than all theory,

---

[12] Marx had reminded Engels of his inadequate response in 1862 (see above, p. 287) regarding treatment of the replacement fund, and he pushed for a fuller explanation: "Many years ago I wrote to you that it seemed to me that in this manner an accumulation fund was being built up, since in the intervening period the capitalist was of course using the returned money, before replacing the *capital fixe* with it. You disagreed with this somewhat superficially in a letter" (24 August 1867; MECW 42: 408). A provisional response, focusing on business practice regarding the writing off of machinery, was forthcoming from Engels (26 August; 409). Significantly, Engels admits that "regarding the economic significance of the matter, I am none too clear about it, I do not see how the manufacturer is supposed to be able to cheat the other partners in the surplus-value, that is, the ultimate consumers, by thus falsely representing the position – in the long run. *Nota bene*, as a rule, machinery is depreciated at $7\frac{1}{2}$%, which assumes a useful life of approximately 13 years." Two full sets of schedules for machinery depreciation are sent the following day (410–13).

Immediately after publication of *Capital 1*, Marx raised a related question: "How do you calculate the turnover of the circulating part of capital (i.e. raw material, auxiliary materials, wages)? How great then is the circulating capital advanced? I would like to receive this

I would ask you to describe to me very precisely (with examples) how you run your business quant à banquier, etc.," with reference to "the method in purchasing (cotton, etc.) . . . sales. . . . Settlements . . . " (14 November 1868; MECW *43*: 160).

The picture alters only a little when we take into account Engels's allowances (discussed in Chapter Three) for a new empirical reality with respect to secular stagnation, international trade, and industrial organization, for they are essentially of a descriptive order. Some of Engels's elaborations in these respects do, however, unwittingly tend to undermine the Marxian doctrine he did so much to propagate. Thus, for example, the processes of monopolization (trusts and cartels) and protectionism do not sit well with the essential competitive assumption of the basic theory. We have also noted (Chapter Two, p. 122) the absence of any reference to Marx's falling profit-rate trend in the discussion of the transition from cycles to secular stagnation, which concerns rather the changes in industrial organization under way.

Allowance, though, should certainly be made for Engels's own discussion in *Capital 3* (Part I, Chapter IV) of "the effect of [capital] turnover on the rate of profit" (MECW *37*: 73–80), which carries forward Marx's own discussion in Part II of *Capital 2*. Of particular interest are recognition of the positive effects on the profit rate of reductions in the turnover rate (see below, p. 309) and observations regarding the need for statistical confirmations of orders of magnitude, containing reference to Manchester practice drawn from a review of *Capital 2* by Lexis (see editorial note MECW *37*: 904 n. 16) – we have seen that Marx had pressed Engels for information on business practice relevant to turnover – and to American practice:

Since very few capitalists ever think of making calculations of this sort with reference to their own business, statistics is almost completely silent about the relation of the constant portion of the total social capital to its variable portion. Only the American census gives what is possible under modern conditions, namely the sum of wages paid in each line of business and the profits realised. Questionable as they may be, being based on the industrialist's own uncontrolled statements, they are nevertheless very valuable and the only records available to us on this subject. In Europe we are far too delicate to expect such revelations from our major industrialists. (MECW *37*: 80)

Engels also contributed arithmetical examples of both intensive and extensive differential rent to supplement Marx's analysis (Chapter 43); his treatment closed with observations regarding current agricultural trends, particularly increasing foreign competition (713–14). These explorations indicate an awareness of the

---

answered in detail, even illustrated, particularly the turnover calculation of the circulating capital advanced" (7 May 1868; MECW *43*: 31). Here – as with the average life of machinery – Engels responds in a rather noncommittal fashion: "I do not really know what you mean by this," but presuming the question relates to "how much circulating capital is in business," he replies that this "differs in almost all cases," depending on such issues as the prosperity of the firm that permits it to make use of spare funds in, say, the purchase of cotton if an opportunity arises, and on the availability of credit (10 May; MECW *43*: 32). However, he does suggest a rough average – for an investment in machines, a mill owner "can get along with one–fifth to one–quarter of the fixed capital."

limitations of arithmetical examples and hint at the promise of a more generalized, mathematical, procedure (e.g., 704).[13] Nonetheless, this chapter as well as the treatment of Marx's own texts in *Capital 3* – considered below in my discussion of Engels as editor – confirm a disinclination to push the matter any further.[14]

Account must now be taken of the "Supplement" to *Capital 3*, which outlines the elements of a historical Transformation elaborated in my Chapter Two. Following Marx's suggestion, it amounts to an attempt to bring real time into the picture by envisaging a genuine analysis of economic history – something more than a descriptive account – somewhat in the same spirit as the undertaking by John Hicks in *A Theory of Economic History* (1969). Unlike Marx himself, though, who at least recognized the major problem that *inputs* are not transformed (Hollander 2008: 22), Engels nowhere addresses the defects of the "theoretical" Transformation that he spent decades defending and propagandizing; it must also not be forgotten that it is precisely this theoretical structure that governed the historical Transformation (see Chapter Two, p. 119).

Engels's particular concern with applications contributes substantially toward a balanced overview. Here note Mayer's general point:

[Engels] saw in himself a certain indolence "*en fait de théorie*," which proved to him that he was not qualified to work out an economic or philosophical system and to grapple it together with hooks of steel. It is true that he had a natural talent for observing theoretical connexions, but he was content to grasp them by intuition, to understand the direction in which they pointed, and especially to draw inferences from them to action – for action was for him the crown of life. . . . He could give himself up with passionate interest to scientific study. But the faculties of research and of logical analysis were less developed in him than the talent for stimulating, disseminating, and popularizing, in the noblest sense of the word." (1969 [1934]: 329–30)[15]

---

[13] Vollgraf and Jungnickel refer to Engels's skepticism regarding formulae (2002 [1994]: 63). The present context suggests otherwise, and so too do the comments in Chapter Three.

[14] Indicative of Engels's small interest in purely theoretical matters in later years is his rather casual perspective on cycles. Schumpeter in his harsh evaluation (Prolegomena, pp. 22–3) cites as evidence for the prosecution Engels's uncritical adoption in *Anti-Dühring* of the underconsumption approach (Schumpeter 1950: 39n.). He had in mind the naïve approval of Fourier's "self-explanatory phrase *crises pléthoriques*," which follows upon an assertion that "[t]he extension of the markets cannot keep pace with the extension of production" (MECW *25*: 263). However, Engels objected to this approach elsewhere in *Anti-Dühring* itself, at least the version propounded by Rodbertus (see Chapter Two, note 28), his objections following Marx's lines (see Hollander 2008: 149–50). His position on underconsumption is thus unclear.

In *Capital 2* Engels attached a note to Marx's conclusion that "capitalist production comprises conditions independent of good or bad will, conditions which permit the working class to enjoy that relative prosperity only momentarily, and at that always only as the harbinger of a coming crisis" (MECW *36*: 410), reading simply "*Ad notam* for possible followers of the Rodbertian theory of crises."

[15] Commenting on the composition of *Anti-Dühring*, Engels pointed out that "the tenth chapter of the part on economics ("From *Kritische Geschichte*") was written by Marx. . . . As a matter of fact, we had always been accustomed to help each other out in special subjects" (Preface to second edition 1885; MECW 25: 9). By implication, Engels had a lesser competence and

Carver has observed yet more specifically that "in presenting Marx to the public Engels generally concentrated on delineating Marx's method and setting an intellectual context for his work... and its consequences for political action" (1989: 232). This seems a fair evaluation subject only to the important rider that some of Engels's most impressive applications entailed the functioning of the competitive price system in general and the housing and credit markets in particular, and the issue of free trade versus protection, in terms that would be at home in any "orthodox" text, be it classical or neoclassical (See Chapter Three). In some respects, the applications have very much in common with the "Austrian" outlook on interventionism whether by domestic price control or protection. However, in all this Engels was traveling along a road already laid out by Marx himself.

D. "More Royalist than the King"

I return to my comparison of the Engels–Marx relationship with that between James Mill and Ricardo (above, p. 288). The point I wish to make now relates to Engels's treatment of Marx's surplus-value doctrine with its focus on labor power, and his insistence on a solution to the price-value dilemma to be forthcoming in *Capital 3*. As for the first issue, Marx was aware of the weak points in the surplus-value doctrine and valiantly sought to protect it (see Hollander 2008: 465–9); Engels, by contrast, proceeded in an uncritical fashion in most of his expositions of the doctrine.[16] The impression he conveys is of someone engaged in propaganda rather than science. Engels himself said so quite candidly when describing his editorial replacement of "labour" by "labour power" in some contexts (see below, p. 303).

Engels was more royalist than the king in a further respect. Marx was prepared to allow some credit to Rodbertus for appreciation of the source of surplus value. The recognition in 1861–3 that the latter had reached the "right conclusion" is perhaps sufficiently limited in its application to the case in which land and capital ownership are not yet separated to justify the description "ironic dismissal," as Engels put it (Chapter Two, p. 99). But in contrast with Engels, who was determined to grant as little as possible to Rodbertus – a concern extending to matters of ideology far beyond the purely technical problem of surplus value – Marx allowed in 1862 that there was "really much in [the *Third Social Letter*] that is good.... Puerile though Mr. Rodbertus's positive solution [to rent] may be, it does, nevertheless, tend in the right direction" (p. 95). What is more important, he publicly conceded in *Capital 1* that "in spite of its erroneous theory of rent," Rodbertus's book "sees through the nature of capitalist production" (MECW *35*: 532n.), leading Engels in

---

interest in the history of doctrine. See also the elaboration in the Preface to the third edition regarding "Marx's own revelations from the history of economics" (15).

[16] O'Neill provides an amusing description of the view sometimes taken of the Marx–Engels relationship: He contrasts "the stiff and ponderous Engels" and "his intellectually more supple partner" (1996: 47).

an editorial note attached to the third German edition of 1883 to enter the following caution:

It may be seen from this how favourably Marx judged his predecessors, whenever he found in them real progress, or new and sound ideas. The subsequent publication of Rodbertus' letters to Rud. Meyer has shown that *the above acknowledgement by Marx wants restricting to some extent.* In those letters this passage occurs: "Capital must be rescued not only from labour, but from itself, and that will be best effected, by treating the acts of the industrial capitalist, as economic and political functions, that have been delegated to him with his capital, and by treating his profit as a form of salary, because we still know no other social organisation. But salaries may be regulated and may also be reduced if they take too much from wages. The irruption of Marx into Society, as I may call his book, must be warded off.... Altogether, Marx's book is not so much an investigation into capital, as a polemic against the present form of capital, a form which he confounds with the concept itself of capital" (*Briefe, &c., von Dr. Rodbertus-Jagetzow, herrausgg. Von Dr. Rud. Meyer*, Berlin, 1881, I. Bd. pp. 111, 48. Brief von Rodbertus). *To such ideological commonplaces did the bold attack by Rodbertus in his "social letters" finally dwindle down.* (emphasis added)[17]

A telling instance of Engels's concern with proper classification is provided by his defense of Saint-Simon against Marx's comparison in *Capital 3* of the latter, to his disadvantage, with Owen, all Saint-Simon's works (except the very last of 1825, the year of his death) described as "mere encomiums of modern bourgeois society.... What a difference compared with the contemporaneous writings of Owen" (MECW 37: 600).[18] "Marx would surely have modified this passage considerably, had he reworked his manuscript," Engels maintained, for "[l]ater Marx spoke only with admiration of the genius and encyclopaedic mind of Saint-Simon"; he also provided an environmental rationale both for Saint-Simon and Owen: "When in his earlier works the latter ignores the antithesis between the bourgeoisie and the proletariat, which was just then coming into existence in France, when he includes among the *travailleurs* that part of the bourgeoisie which was active in production, this corresponds to Fourier's conception of attempting to reconcile capital and labour and is explained by the economic and political situation of France in those days. The fact that Owen was more far-sighted in this respect is due to his different environment, for he lived in a period of industrial revolution and of acutely sharpening class antagonisms." A paean of praise for Saint-Simon, of

---

[17] The ideological dimension is found also in Engels's frequent allusions to Rodbertus as Pomeranian landowner, which is quite in line with Marx's remarks in *Theories of Surplus Value* (e.g., MECW 31: 382–6). In pointing to Sismondi's priority regarding the underconsumption problem (see Chapter Two, p. 103), Engels makes this addition: "However, Sismondi always had the world market in mind, while Rodbertus's horizon does not extend beyond the Prussian border" (MECW 36: 22).

[18] See also Marx on Owen in 1867: "[Owen] not only practically made the factory system the sole foundation of his experiments, but also declared that system to be theoretically the starting-point of the social revolution" (MECW 35: 505n.).

which incidentally Marx was aware, will also be found in *Socialism: Utopian and Scientific* (1880; MECW *24*: 290–3).

The "Prize Essay Competition" and its sequence, discussed in Chapter Two, provides an instance of Engels's assumption of the role of official censor. Nothing would do except the solution to the perceived conflict between the laws of value and profit-rate uniformity precisely as given in *Capital 3*. The achievements of those who had arrived more or less at the "correct" solution were measured in terms of proximity to the master's formulation: "The outcome of the entire investigation shows . . . that it is the Marxian school alone which has accomplished something. If Fireman and Conrad Schmidt read this third book, each one, for his part, may well be satisfied with his own work" (MECW *37*: 23).[19] As Howard and King put it, "[t]he theory of ideology, initially developed by [Engels] and Marx in the 1840s, allowed no role for 'vulgar economists' to contribute to the development of political economy as a science" (1989: 37).[20] And none it seems, to one such as Lexis, who was "disguised as a vulgar economist" (Chapter Two, p. 108). It must, unfortunately, be said that this contradicts the fine-sounding principle that "Marx's whole way of thinking is not so much a doctrine as a method. It provides not so much ready-made dogmas, as aids to further investigation and the method *for* such investigation" (p. 113). In any event, though, all this was for public consumption; Engels knew better, because his formal declarations were belied by the centrality he himself accorded the orthodox pricing mechanism in so many contexts.

E. Engels's Self-Evaluation

There remains for us to consider Berlin's notion of Engels's "total uncompetitiveness in relation to [Marx]" and "absence of all desire to resist the impact of that powerful personality," or Schumpeter's notion of Engels's "self-effacing loyalty" (Prolegomena, p. 22). Does this not ring true? After all, he himself described the *Communist Manifesto* as "essentially" the work of Marx ("Karl Marx," 1869; MECW *21*: 61). Further consider the self-evaluation written to a correspondent soon after Marx's death:

[M]y misfortune is that since we lost Marx I have been supposed to represent him. I have spent a lifetime doing what I was fitted for, namely playing second fiddle, and indeed I believe I acquitted myself reasonably well. And I was happy to have so splendid a first fiddle as Marx. But now that I am suddenly expected to take Marx's place in matters of theory and play first fiddle, there will inevitably be blunders and no one is more aware of that than I. And not until the times get somewhat more turbulent shall we really be aware of what we have lost in Marx. Not one of us possesses the breadth of vision that enabled him, at the very moment when rapid action was called for, invariably to hit upon the right solution at once to get to the heart of the matter.

---

[19] On Fireman and Schmidt, see Chapter Two, Section F.
[20] Howard and King go further, charging Engels with "freezing" the development of Marxian political economy for a decade by his procrastination in bringing out *Capital 3* (1989: 16).

In more peaceful times it could happen that events proved me right and him wrong, but at a revolutionary juncture his judgment was virtually infallible. (15 October 1884; MECW 47: 202)[21]

Again, alluding to "the mode of outlook expounded" in *Anti-Dühring*, namely scientific socialism, Engels wrote this in the Preface of 1885: "I must note in passing that inasmuch as in this book was founded and developed in far greater measure by Marx, and only in an insignificant degree by myself, it was self-understood between us that this exposition of mine should not be issued without his knowledge. I read the whole manuscript to him before it was printed" MECW 25: 9).[22] A similar tone is struck in a letter expressing a preference not to have a book dedicated to him; "at present I happen to be in a frame of mind which makes me think my merits grossly overrated in some quarters. If one is so fortunate as to collaborate for forty years with a greater man and measure oneself against him day by day, one is given the chance of evaluating one's own achievements in accordance with a true standard. And I feel instinctively that to place any undue emphasis on my own activities is unwittingly to detract from what we all of us owe to Marx" (29 August 1887; MECW 48: 97). Writing to Sorge regarding the forthcoming seventieth-birthday celebrations, he protested against "all the unnecessary fuss which I cannot abide even at the best of times. And after all, I am, to a large extent, simply the chap who is reaping what Marx has sown in the way of fame" (26 November 1890; MECW 49: 73).[23]

If the Berlin–Schumpeter perspective is valid, then Engels's self-assessments fall into place – he merely recognized his own "pedestrianism." Nonetheless, once the significance of his early contribution and other instances of independent thought are taken into account, the matter becomes more complex. In fact, there were limits even to his modesty.[24] As I shall now show, positive claims were made by Engels for various contributions.

---

[21] The reference to "theory" in this passage should be understood to include "scientific socialism" as a whole, rather than economic theory narrowly conceived. The original is translated thus by Henderson: "No one realizes better than I do that I am likely to make some mistakes now that I must suddenly step into Marx's shoes as an interpreter of his theories and as leader of the orchestra" (Henderson 1976: 657).

[22] Marx had expressed his approval. See, for example, his letter to a correspondent referring to *Anti-Dühring* as "very important for a true appreciation of German Socialism" (3 October 1878; MECW 45: 334). Regarding an earlier serialization of the work, he stated that "[t]here's much to be learnt from Engels' positive exposés, not only by ordinary workers . . . but even by scientifically educated people" (11 April 1877; 218). See Nimtz (2000: 255) on Marx's commendation.

[23] On learning from Kautsky that Rudolf Meyer proposed to describe him in an article as the "oldest and greatest of the living political economists," Engels protested: "To apply that epithet to me is really very silly. You would be doing a kindness to me and certainly to others as well, if you pointed out to him, at any rate for future guidance, that he must accustom himself to our less grandiose terminology" (17 May 1892; MECW 49: 416).

[24] Ryazanoff describes a dimension to Engels's character in an account of his relations with largely working-class members of the General Council of the International meeting in London in the early 1870s – "his haughty air of intellectual superiority" – that, if accurate, would support this conclusion (Riazanov 1973 [1927]: 202–3; also Collins 1967: 268–9).

In correspondence of 1851, for example, Engels commended Marx's explorations into rent as "absolutely right," while adding "[y]ou will remember that, in the *Deutsch-Französische Jahrbücher*, I already invoked the progress made by scientific agriculture as against the theory of increasing infertility – of course very crude and not at all closely argued" (29 January 1851; MECW *38*: 271). More formally, Engels alludes in *Anti-Dühring* to his early appreciation of aspects of communal arrangement with regard to "value": "As long ago as 1844 I stated that the above-mentioned balancing of useful effects and expenditure of labour on making decisions concerning production was all that would be left, in a communist society, of the politico-economic concept of value" (see Chapter Three, p. 150). There is, though, a bow in Marx's direction: "The scientific justification for this statement, however, as can be seen, was made possible only by Marx's *Capital*" (Chapter Three, note 41).[25] We also find in *Anti-Dühring* some claim to the reserve army concept as it appeared in *The Condition of the Working Class*, in the reference to "the displacement of millions of manual by a few machine-workers... [and] more and more of the machine-workers themselves," resulting in "the production of a number of available wage-workers in excess of the average needs of capital, the formation of a complete industrial reserve army, as I called it in 1845, available at the times when industry is working at high pressure, to be cast out upon the street when the inevitable crash comes, a constant dead weight upon the limbs of the working class in its struggle for existence with capital, a regulator for the keeping of wages down to the low level that suits the interests of capital" (MECW *25*: 261).

A self-congratulatory reference will be found in one of the 1892 Prefaces to *The Condition of the Working Class*: "The wonder is, not that a good many of [the 'prophesies'] proved wrong, but that so many of them proved right, and that the critical state of English trade, to be brought on by Continental and especially American competition, which I then foresaw – though in too short a period – has now actually come to pass" (Chapter Five, p. 275). Furthermore, Engels maintained in 1887 that the original 1845 version "was justified precisely by the fact that industrial conditions in present-day America coincide almost entirely with those in the England of the forties, that is those described by myself" ("The Labor Movement in America"; MECW *26*: 434n.). And in 1888, he wrote with some pride of his having rightly envisaged several years earlier that Infant Industry protection in the United States could be justified for a quarter of a century and no more (MECW *26*: 526). Also recall his positive reference in correspondence of 1881 to his attitude in 1844 toward population control under communism (Chapter One, pp. 38–9).

The tension between Engels's natural modesty and his claim to recognition is already apparent. It emerges in a variety of other contexts as well. Thus he chided a correspondent for dubbing the author of *The Condition of the Working Class* as "the father of descriptive economics": "You will find descriptive economics in Petty, Boisguillebert, Vauban, and Adam Smith, to name only a few. Such accounts,

---

[25] Engels had actually gone further, recommending allowance also for rent and interest in the communist calculation (see Chapter One, p. 34).

notably of proletarian conditions, were written by Frenchmen and Englishmen before I did mine. It was just that I was lucky enough to be precipitated into the heart of modern large-scale industry and to be the first whose eyes were opened to its implications – at any rate the most immediate ones" (29 August 1887; MECW 48: 97). This surely is a major claim.

Another major claim appears in an editorial adjustment to *Poverty of Philosophy* in the German edition of 1885.[26] To Marx's proposition that "the natural price of labour is no other than the minimum wage" (MECW 6: 125; see Hollander 2008: 206), Engels attached a note taking for granted that Marx intended "labour power" but claiming for himself priority for the major proposition, namely the subsistence wage: "The thesis that the 'natural,' i.e., normal, price of labour power coincides with the minimum wage, i.e., with the equivalent in value of the means of subsistence absolutely indispensable for the life and procreation of the worker, was first put forward by me in *Outlines of a Critique of Political Economy (Deutsche-Französische Jahrbücher*, Paris, 1844) and in *The Condition of the Working Class in England* [MECW 3: 420–31, 440–3; 4: 375–88]. As seen here, Marx at that time accepted the thesis. Lassalle took it over from both of us" (MECW 6: 125n.).[27] This claim is, however, in one respect problematic. The closest Engels comes in his *Outlines* is the proposition that "only the very barest necessities, the mere means of subsistence, fall to the lot of the labourer" (Chapter One, p. 35), with no mention of the *value* of subsistence. The discussion in *The Condition of the Working Class* is more extensive, but again there is no emphasis on the *value* of the wage and a fortiori none on the value of *labor power* (pp. 45–7). Thus, although at least one clear claim for priority must be somewhat discounted,[28] that Engels made the claim at all is the salient point.

[26] For further details see MECW 6: xviii, 672–4 and Rubel (1963: 3–5, 1546). Engels called the reply to Proudhon "our programme" (letter to Marx, 25–26 October, 1847; MECW 38: 134). Marx attempted to republish the entire work in 1880, thus indicating that he stood by it. The first German translation appeared in 1885, edited and prefaced by Engels, who took account of corrections in Marx's hand made sometime before 1876 in a copy of the 1847 edition.

[27] Rubel observes of Engels's reference to Lassalle, "Lassalle's 'borrowing,' of which Engels was speaking, is none other than the 'iron law of wages,' formulated in 1863, which passed into the program of the German Workers' party, adopted at the Gotha unification Congress (1875)" (Rubel 1963: 1547).

[28] Engels himself already used the term "labour power" in the *Outlines* (e.g., Chapter One, pp. 35, 37), but without any implication regarding the source of surplus value.

Engels proceeds to a correction by Marx in *Capital* relating to the depression of the price of labor power "below its value": "Although, however, in reality wages have a constant tendency to approach the minimum, the above thesis is nevertheless incorrect. The fact that labour power is regularly and on the average paid below its value cannot alter its value. In *Capital*, Marx has put the above thesis right (Section on the Buying and Selling of Labour Power) and also (Chapter 25: *The General Law of Capitalist Accumulation*) analysed the circumstances which permit capitalist production to depress the price of labour power more and more below its value" (MECW 6: 125n.). As for the "correction" attributed to Marx, the problem is that Marx there allowed explicitly for the possible degradation of standards, that is, reduction in the value of labor (labor power) itself, in the event that the market wage fell below the original value of labor for a considerable time (see Hollander 2008: 94). Strangely, Engels himself in *The Condition of the Working Class* refers to degradation of standards (Chapter One, pp. 45–6).

Similarly, after taking the initiative in the publication in *Die Neue Zeit* of Marx's "Critique of the Gotha Programme" – on which see my discussion in Chapter Three – Engels wrote to Sorge, with evident satisfaction, that "[t]he Berlin correspondent of the Vienna *Arbeiter-Zeitung*... actually thanks me for the service I have rendered the party" (11 February 1891; MECW *49*: 126), and to Kautsky, editor of *Die Neue Zeit*: "don't forget that it was I, after all, who first instigated the thing" (23 February 1891; MECW *49*: 133). On learning of a party plan to publish a volume of Marx's "minor works," he protested that "I cannot allow them to steal a march on me by bringing out in this piecemeal fashion the complete edition to whose ultimate publication *I* am committed" (to Kautsky, 29 June 1891; MECW *49*: 210). Furthermore, he vehemently objected when apprized by a third party of the project by Bernstein, Kautsky, and others to publish a *History of Socialism* – the first volume of which appeared in 1895 – without seeking his collaboration: "Of all the people then living there was only one, I think I may say, whose collaboration was absolutely necessary, and that person was myself. I might even say that, without my help, a work of this nature cannot today be anything but incomplete and inadequate. And this you knew as well as I did. But of all those who might have been of use to you, I and I alone was the only one *not* invited to collaborate" (to Kautsky, 21 May 1895; MECW *50*: 511).[29]

Particularly significant is Engels's pride in his *Socialism: Utopian and Scientific*, first published in French in 1880: "A German edition... is something I have long had in mind, particularly now that I have seen what a regular revolution the thing has wrought in the minds of many of the better people in France" (to Bernstein, 9 August 1882; MECW 46: 300). The work, he repeated to Sorge, had "made a tremendous impression in France" (9 November; 369).

Finally, I turn to the "materialist conception of history," so designated by Engels in his review of Marx's *A Contribution to the Critique of Political Economy* on its appearance (*Das Volk*, 1859; MECW *16*: 469). Although Marx there recognized Engels's contribution to the doctrine in *The Condition of the Working Class*, he insisted on his own independent achievement (in the *Deutsch-Französiche Jahrbücher*) in 1844: "My inquiry led me to the conclusion that neither legal relations nor political forms could be comprehended whether by themselves or on

---

[29] Engels refused a request by Kautsky to contribute an article on the First International: "had the roles been reversed, I should have reflected for a very, very long time before coming to you with a request such as this one. Is it really so terribly difficult to see that everyone must bear the consequences of his own actions?... If there is no room for me here, it is only because you wanted it so" (MECW *50*: 511). His generous character is revealed by the fact that he did not permit this episode to sour his relationship with Kautsky or Bernstein regarding other matters, as the remainder of the letter indicates. Kautsky explained in reply that the original decision not to ask Engels for a contribution reflected a wish not to disturb his preparation of *Capital* 3 for the press (see MECW *50*: 610n. 601). Kapp attributes the decision to knowledge of his terminal illness and a wish not to intrude at such a time (1976: 594). The dramatic Mary Burns episode, which nearly led to a Marx–Engels rupture, certainly shows that there were limits to Engels's amenability, even regarding Marx. For Marx's letter of 8 January 1863 that caused the furor, see MECW (*41*: 442–3).

the basis of a so-called general development of the human mind, but that on the contrary they originate in the material conditions of life" (MECW *29*: 262). The joint *German Ideology* conveniently summarizes the doctrine (1845–6; MECW *5*: 53–4).[30]

In his 1859 review, Engels refers to Marx's position as a "revolutionary discovery," and he cites (or paraphrases) the text of *A Contribution*, including the prognosti-cation – as a component of the full doctrine – of "the prospect of a gigantic revolution." I spell out the Marxian doctrine as understood by Engels, because "historical materialism" means different things to different people:

The proposition that "the process of social, political and intellectual life in general is determined by the mode of production of material life" [MECW *29*: 263]; that all social and political relations, all religious and legal systems, all theoretical conceptions which arise in the course of history can only be understood if the material conditions of life obtaining during the relevant epoch have been understood and the former are traced back to these material conditions – this proposition was a revolutionary discovery not only for economics but also for all historical sciences. . . . "It is not the consciousness of men that determines their being, but their social being that determines their con-sciousness" [263]. This proposition . . . leads to highly revolutionary consequences not only in the sphere of theory but also in that of practice. "At a certain stage in their development, the material productive forces of society come into conflict with the existing relations of production or – which merely expresses the same thing in legal terms – with the property relations within the framework of which they have operated hitherto. From forms of development of the productive forces these relations turn into their fetters. Then begins an epoch of *social revolutions*. The change in the economic foundation leads sooner or later to the transformation of the whole immense super-structure. . . . The bourgeois relations of production are the last antagonistic form of the social process of production . . . but the productive forces developing within bourgeois society create also the material conditions for a solution of this antagonism" [263]. The prospect of a gigantic revolution, the most gigantic revolution that has ever taken place, therefore presents itself to us as soon as we pursue our materialist thesis further and apply it to the present time. (MECW *16*: 469–70)

His introduction to the 1888 edition of the *Communist Manifesto* attributes to Marx "the fundamental proposition which forms its nucleus," actually a tripartite proposition, elaborating the role of class struggle:

[1] That in every historical epoch, the prevailing mode of economic production and exchange, and the social organisation necessarily following from it, form the basis upon which is built up, and from which alone can be explained, the political and intellectual history of that epoch; [2] that consequently the whole history of mankind (since the dissolution of primitive tribal society, holding land in common ownership) has been a history of class struggles, contests between exploiting and exploited, ruling and oppressed classes; [3] that the history of these class struggles forms a series of evolution in which, nowadays, a stage has been reached where the exploited and oppressed class – the proletariat – cannot attain its emancipation from the sway of the exploiting and

---

[30] For a helpful account of the development of the doctrine, see Oakley (1984, Chapter 3.)

ruling class – the bourgeoisie – without, at the same time, and once and for all, emancipating society at large from all exploitation, oppression, class-distinctions and class struggles (MECW 26: 517).[31]

For all that, Engels does proceed to reclaim some of the glory for himself, though leaving it to the reader to substantiate the claim: "This proposition which, in my opinion, is destined to do for history what Darwin's has done for biology, we, both of us, had been gradually approaching for some years before 1845. How far I had independently progressed towards it, is best shown by my 'Condition of the Working Class in England.' But when I again met Marx at Brussels in spring, 1845, he had it already worked out, and put it before me, in terms almost as clear as those in which I have stated it here" (517). Engels, it seems, was putting himself into the shade, yet allowing readers a glimpse of the actual sequence of events. Also indicating a certain pride in his own contribution is the insistence in late correspondence that the account of the doctrine in *Anti-Dühring* and *Ludwig Feuerbach* was "so far as I know, the most exhaustive in existence" (to Joseph Bloch, 21 September 1890; MECW 49: 36). As we shall see in Chapter Seven, he was confident enough to represent himself in this context as senior living authority, willing to accept responsibility for having in the past – along with Marx – misled readers, and to carry further than Marx had done the qualifications to be admitted (below, p. 330).

How much of the materialist doctrine is actually to be found in *The Condition of the Working Class*? Certainly the second and third elements of the tripartite version are clear enough, though the second largely in relation to the specific "contest" between exploiting and exploited as it manifested itself in contemporary society. (On prospective revolution, see Chapter One, pp. 57–8) But the first and crucial element – in Marx's terms, the subjection of the "forms of social consciousness" to the "mode of production" – is also apparent, as Hobsbawm has well explained (1969: 9–10, 12–13), though again in terms of local circumstances, temporal and geographical. This limitation is spelled out by Engels himself in 1885. Marx was the first to perceive the general significance of the materialistic perspective, whereas Engels's contribution recognized a more limited range of application based on his Manchester experience: "Marx had not only arrived at the same view, but had already, in the *Deutsch-Französische Jahrbücher* (1844), generalised it to the effect that it is not the state which conditions and regulates civil society, but civil society which conditions and regulates the state, and, consequently, that policy and its history are to be explained from the economic relations and their development, and not the other way round" ("On the History of the Communist League," 1885;

---

[31] Possony (1954: xiv–xvii) refers to Engels's statement of the "fundamental proposition" as entailing three separate ideas, each of which was not in fact original with Marx. Bonar goes back to the seventeenth century, citing James Harrington as a pioneer (1922: 350). For a minimization – in my view unjustified – of Marx's contribution to the doctrine, see, e.g., Avineri (1968: 65f) and Carver (1981: 62f.). Avineri takes too seriously the fact that Marx did not coin or use the precise term "historical materialism."

MECW *26*: 317–18). Engels goes on to explain that "[w]hen, in the spring of 1845, we met again in Brussels, Marx had already fully developed his materialist theory of history in its main features from the above-mentioned foundations, and we now applied ourselves to the detailed elaboration of the newly won outlook in the most varied directions. This discovery, which revolutionised the science of history and, as we have seen, is essentially the work of Marx – a discovery in which I can claim for myself only a very small share – was, however, of immediate importance for the contemporary workers' movement of the time". (318).

Ludwig Feuerbach contains a revealing so-called "personal explanation," attached to a text regarding the materialistic doctrine as "essentially connected with the name of Marx," which comments on a "[l]ately repeated reference... made to my share in this theory" (1888 [1886]; MECW *26*: 382):

I cannot deny that both before and during my forty years' collaboration with Marx I had a certain independent share in laying the foundations of the theory, and more particularly in its elaboration. But the greater part of its leading basic principles, especially in the realm of economics and history, and, above all, their final trenchant formulation, belongs to Marx. What I contributed – at any rate with the exception of my work in a few special fields – Marx could very well have done without me. What Marx accomplished I would not have achieved. Marx stood higher, saw further, and took a wider and quicker view than all the rest of us. Marx was a genius; we others were at best talented. Without him the theory would not be by far what it is today. It therefore rightly bears his name. (382n.)

The declaration "Marx was a genius; we others were at best talented" did not appear in the original version appearing in *Die Neue Zeit* in 1886; it was especially added in the book version of 1888. Even so, one cannot simply ignore the claim "that both before and during my forty years' collaboration with Marx I had a certain independent share in laying the foundations of the theory, and more particularly in its elaboration."[32] Stedman Jones has well argued that "without Engels' work on England, the formulation of a Marxist theory would at the least, have been much slower than it actually was," because Engels provided "the raw components which dramatised the inadequacies of the previous theory and formed a large part of the nucleus of the propositions to which the new theory was addressed" (1982: 316–17; see also 296–7).

I shall have more to say in Chapter Seven on Engels's perspective after Marx's death regarding the doctrine of historical materialism. For now, two late letters are particularly pertinent to our general concern with Engels's self-evaluation. First,

---

[32] In a letter dated 7 February 1893, Engels advises V. Shmuilov that "[a]s to the *genesis* of historical materialism, you will, in my opinion, find everything you want in my *Feuerbach*... – the appendix by Marx *is*, of course, itself the genesis!" (MECW *50*: 98). The Appendix reprints Marx's "Theses on Feuerbach" – Engels's title – written in Brussels in April 1845 and found in Marx's notebooks of 1844–7 (MECW *5*: 3–8; and editorial comment, 585 n. 1). These brief notes include the criticism – it illustrates the general principle involved – that Feuerbach "does not see that the 'religious sentiment' is itself a social product, and that the abstract individual which he analyses belongs to a particular form of society" (5).

writing on 14 July 1893 to congratulate Mehring on his comprehension of the doctrine, Engels adds this:

If I have any criticism to make, it is that you accord me more merit than I deserve, even if one takes account of what I may, perhaps, have found out for myself – in course of time – but which Marx, with his swifter _coup d'oeil_ and greater discernment, discovered much more quickly. If one has been fortunate enough to spend forty years collaborating with a man like Marx, one tends, during one's lifetime to receive less recognition than one feels is due to one; when the greater man dies, however, the lesser may easily come to be overrated – and that is exactly what seems to have happened in my case; all this will eventually be put right by history, and by then one will be safely out of the way and know nothing at all about it. (MECW 50: 163)

Notwithstanding his designation of Marx as the "greater man," Engels expressly admits to a sense that he had been _inadequately_ recognized during Marx's lifetime.

The second letter I have in mind, to W. Borgius dated 25 January 1894, goes a step further, as it alludes to the restricted role allowed "great men" in history: "The fact that such and such a man, and he alone, should arise at a particular time in any given country, is, of course, purely fortuitous. But if we eliminate him, a replacement will be called for and such a replacement will be found.... That Napoleon, this particular Corsican, was the military dictator rendered necessary by a French Republic bled white by her own wars, was fortuitous; but that, in the absence of a Napoleon, someone else would have taken his place is proved by the fact that the moment someone becomes necessary – Caesar, Augustus, Cromwell, etc. – he invariably turns up" (MECW 50: 266). Indeed, the proposition that no particular individual is indispensable in the historical process is actually spelled out with respect to Marx himself as "discoverer" of the doctrine of historical materialism: "If it was Marx who discovered the materialist view of history, the work of Thierry, Mignet, Guizot and every English historiographer prior to 1850 goes to show that efforts were being made in that direction, while the discovery of the same view by Morgan shows that the time was ripe for it and that it was _bound_ to be discovered."[33] We thus find Engels, at the end, seriously diluting the status accorded the master. Even so, Engels still insisted that the _Origin of the Family_ – though based on Morgan – made use of Marx's notes following his design (1884; MECW 26: 131), leading Bonar to remark perceptively that Engels "is never beyond suspicion of allowing his modesty to wrong him, a generous fault which might be counted a virtue if it did not hinder his critics from being sure whom they are criticizing" (1922: 349).

The propensity to emphasize his secondary status via-à-vis Marx was, however, at least to some degree, simply a matter of strategy rather than a sense of inadequacy. As I show in Chapter Five and further elaborate in the Epilogue when

---

[33] The last reference is to Lewis H. Morgan (1877), on which see a brief remark by Engels in the 1885 Preface to _Anti-Dühring_ (MECW 25: 10). Engels relied on Morgan in his _Origin of the Family, Private Property and the State_ (1884; MECW 26: 129–276).

contrasting Engels with Bernstein, we find Engels fighting valiantly in the last decade of his life to close the breach created in the standard revolutionary account by the "revisionist" orientation. The point to note now is that Engels's unflinching commitment to a final overthrow of the capitalist-exchange system justified his "self-effacing loyalty" – Schumpeter's term – to one who had proven himself a brilliant strategist in dangerous times: "In more peaceful times," Engels explained, "it could happen that events proved me right and [Marx] wrong, but at a revolutionary juncture his judgment was virtually infallible" (above, p. 295). Engels was acutely aware that of the two of them, it was Marx who had proven himself to be indispensable at critical junctures.

F. Engels as Editor

I shall now sum up several of my main conclusions in terms of a particularly sensitive theme, namely the character of Engels's editorship of Marx's work. Did Engels's practice in some of his own work of presenting strong or unqualified versions of Marxian doctrine in order to score points in contemporary debate manifest itself in his editing of Marx's manuscripts? Can it fairly be concluded, as some do conclude, that by straight-jacketing Marx, and narrowing the open-endedness of Marxian theory, Engels positively distorted Marx's position? Much of the secondary literature regarding this issue turns on his treatment of *Capital 3*, but first let us briefly consider a broader range of texts.

Wage Labour and Capital, in the original 1849 version, refers throughout to "labor," but there are systematic, and silent, editorial insertions of "labour power" in its place in the 1891 edition (see Chapter Two, p. 89). There I concluded that in his original formulation Marx did maintain the general principle that labor power has a capacity to yield surplus value, justifying Engels's interpretation. However, in view of a remarkably frank statement by Engels in his 1891 Introduction of the principle of textual amendment he had adopted, we cannot leave the matter here. Had he intended in reissuing the materials to address a "general public" concerned with Marx's "intellectual development," he would "not have dreamed of altering a word of them"; but their publication was "intended practically exclusively for propaganda among workers," for which purpose Marx himself "would certainly have brought the old presentation from 1849 into harmony with his new point of view... undertaking *for this edition* the few alterations and additions which are required in order to obtain this object in all essential points" (MECW 27: 194–5).[34] This was not then "the pamphlet as Marx wrote it in 1849 but approximately as he would have written it in 1891." His alterations, Engels explained, turned "on one point," that "[a]ccording to the original, the worker sells his *labour* to the capitalist

---

[34] See also Engels to Kautsky, 17 March 1891: "*Wage Labour and Capital* was written in pre-surplus value terminology which cannot possibly be allowed to stand today in a propaganda piece running to 10,000 copies" (MECW 49: 145).

for wages; according to the present text he sells his labour *power*."[35] It was "not a case here of mere juggling with words, but rather one of the most important points in the whole of political economy." In the light of this candid admission we can forgive Engels much, especially because his adjustments to *Wage Labour and Capital* appear to be broadly justified.

Let us now turn to the *Communist Manifesto*. The *Collected Works* edition of the document that I used in Chapter One prints the first English edition of 1888, translated from the first (1848) German edition by Samuel Moore, and edited and supplied with notes by Engels. Carver provides an alternative translation (1998: 14–40), basing it on early pamphlet editions to avoid Engels's "framing of the text with introductions and . . . doctrinal 'corrections' in footnotes," such "corrections" and "additions" constituting deliberate "updating and aligning [of] the work according to [Engels's] view of what current doctrine was supposed to be" (Carver 1998: 55, 61). Splendid though the new translation is in its own right, it does not seem that Engels's modifications were of a major order distorting the 1848 version on the issues that concern us (see Chapter One, p. 61), whereas Carver himself properly recognizes the reliance of the *Manifesto* on Engels's own *Principles of Communism* (Carver 1998: 57), a dependency I have demonstrated at some length (pp. 61–4).

Engels's Prefaces to the 1888 English and the 1890 German editions of the *Communist Manifesto* (MECW *26*: 512–18; *27*: 53–60) emphasize the contemporary relevance of the document; this sharply contrasts with the position adopted by himself and Marx in the Preface to the 1872 American version (MECW *23*: 174–5), which had perceived the political situation as entirely altered since 1848. (On this issue, see Carver 1998: 60; Thatcher 1998: 64.) This change is indicative of a degree of independence on Engels's part and should not be viewed as a distortion.

* * *

My principal task remains to address the charge that "in the editorial work Engels did on Marx's *Capital*, he abused (consciously or unconsciously) the trust Marx placed in him as the literary executor of the Marxian legacy," to cite Arthur's formulation of the issue (Arthur 1996a: 173). It will help materially to bear in mind here the status of the later volumes.

Engels had proposed in 1866 that the material that now appears in *Capital 1* be published apart from the rest to avoid delay (see Engels to Marx, 10 February; MECW *42*: 226). Marx explained in reply that "[a]lthough finished, the manuscript" – presumably referring to the *entire* extant documentation – "gigantic in its present form, could not be made ready for publication by anybody but me, not

---

[35] Similarly, Engels closes his Preface to the 1885 edition of Marx's *Poverty of Philosophy* with the observation that "[i]t is hardly necessary to point out that the terminology used in this work does not entirely coincide with that in *Capital*. Thus this work still speaks of *labour* as a commodity, of the purchase and sale of labour, instead of labour *power*" (MECW *26*: 291).

even by you" (13 February; Padover 1979: 205).[36] He nonetheless accepted Engels's advice: "I agree with you and shall get the first volume to Meissner as soon as possible" (MECW *42*: 228). However, he gave this explanation to a correspondent: "In fact, *privatim*, I began by writing *Capital* in a sequence (starting with the 3rd, historical section)" – this latter is a reference to the *Theories of Surplus Value* (also known as the *Economic Manuscripts*) – "quite the reverse of that in which it was presented to the public, saving only that the first [published] volume – the last I tackled – was got ready for the press straight away, whereas the two others remained in the very rough form which all research originally assumes" (3 November 1877; MECW *45*: 287).[37]

The salient point is that the theoretical materials appearing in the last two volumes were under preparation even before *Capital 1* was published. In Engels's terms, "[b]etween 1863 and 1867, Marx . . . completed the first draft of the two last volumes of *Capital* and prepared the first volume for the printer" (MECW *37*: 7); as for the documentation comprising *Capital 3*, Engels explains in the Preface to *Capital 2* that "[i]t was written, at least the greater part of it, in 1864 and 1865. Only after this manuscript had been completed in its essential parts did Marx undertake the elaboration of Book I, the first volume published in 1867" (1885; MECW *36*: 7). Now to say the manuscript was "completed in its essential parts" does not necessarily imply a polished state; in fact, in the Preface to *Capital 3* Engels makes it clear that the texts from which he worked amounted to a "first extremely incomplete draft" (1894; MECW *37*: 6). Similarly, he refers in the supplement to the third volume to the materials in question as "a hastily sketched and partly incomplete first draft" (1895; MECW *37*: 876). These remarks belie a charge by Rubel that Engels conveyed a misleading impression by implying that the last two volumes constituted a pretty complete coverage of what Marx left to posterity, when Marx himself considered his task to be "inachevé" (incomplete) not only in form but in substance (Rubel 1968: 502; also cxxi–cxxvi, 868).[38]

---

[36] This appears in a similar fashion in the Rubel translation (Rubel 1968: cxiv; also Heinrich 1996: 465–6). The MECW translation, however, reads less sensibly: "Although ready, the manuscript which in its present form is gigantic, is not fit for publishing for anyone but myself, not even for you" (13 February 1866; MECW *42*: 227).

[37] Marx here intimates that his plan, at the time *Capital 1* appeared in 1867, was to publish the remaining theoretical materials in a single volume; this was to be followed by a third volume containing history of thought. This is confirmed in the Preface to the first German edition of 1867: "The second volume of this work will treat of the process of the circulation of capital (Book II), and of the varied forms assumed by capital in the course of its development (Book III), the third and last volume (Book IV), the history of the theory" (MECW *35*: 11). In fact, until the very end, Marx presumed that the materials edited by Engels, and ultimately published as *Capital 2* and *Capital 3*, would appear as a single volume (Rubel 1968: cxvii).

[38] Notwithstanding, Rubel and Manale opine that Volume 3 is "the smoothest and best written" of the three volumes (1973: 212). The negative evaluation of *Capital 3* goes back a long way. Thus Bernstein maintained that Volume 3 in its entirety was a "rough skeleton of what Marx intended . . . to produce" (1894–5: 334, cited in Vollgraf and Jungnickel 2002 [1994]: 35).

Rubel's criticisms go further. On the one hand, he emphasizes that "Engels wrote much that Marx no doubt was unable to accept uncritically" (Rubel 1981: 23), and on the other that he neglected a very large body of Marx's work including the Paris and Brussels manuscripts of 1844 and the *Grundrisse* of 1857–8 (24).[39] He further objects that Engels failed to incorporate into the 1890 German edition of *Capital 1* all the modifications proposed by Marx for the French edition 1872–5. Above all, he questions whether Engels's edition of the last two volumes of *Capital* accurately reflects Marx's intentions, and basing his view on the original Marx manuscripts dating to 1864–5 offers alternative readings in the Bibliothèque de la Pléiade series (Rubel 1968: cxxvi, 502, 868). The implication is that Engels, one way or another, distorted Marx's message by his editorial interventions. Let us consider these charges.

As for *Capital 1*, Arthur has pointed to Engels's efforts to take account of the 1872–5 French edition in preparing the English version of 1887 in order to fulfill Marx's preferences (Arthur 1996b: 176–8).[40] Although Arthur questions some of Engels's editorial decisions, he points out that "the anti-Engels faction . . . trip up" in many of their objections, and he concludes that "much of the work [Engels] did on Volume I cannot be faulted" (199). Anderson objects that Arthur neglected to mention Engels's failure to incorporate fully a specific "List of Changes" Marx himself prepared for the French edition, changes that corrected errors marring that edition and to be avoided in later versions (Anderson 1999: 249; see also 1983). This deficiency, however, should not be exaggerated. As Marx himself pointed out, the proposed corrections "ne concerne, sauf quelques exceptions, que la première section du livre" (cited in Rubel 1963: 539–40).[41]

Arthur does, however, protest strongly against the practice of perceiving Marx and Engels "as one person" (Arthur 1996b: 174; also 188–90). He illustrates by what he sees as Engels's illegitimate ascription to Marx of the "logical-historical method" in his 1859 review of *A Contribution to the Critique of Political Economy* (see MECW *16*: 465–71).[42] He similarly takes issue with a related ascription to

---

[39] For the complaint that Engels should have taken the *Grundrisse* into account, see also Rubel (1968: cxxv.) Marx had in fact briefly informed Engels that he was engaged in "collating my economic studies so that I at least get the outlines [*Grundrisse*] clear before the *déluge*" (8 December 1857; MECW *40*: 217), and again "I am engaged in . . . [e]laborating the outlines of political economy" (18 December; MECW *40*: 224).

[40] Engels himself acknowledged Marx's preference for the French edition (see his Preface to the 1887 English edition, MECW *35*: 33). His efforts to take account of both that version and the 1887 English version in preparing the fourth 1890 German edition are briefly indicated in the Preface to the latter (37).

[41] Rubel published the French edition as translated by Joseph Roy in the Bibliothèque de la Pléiade series, but he incorporated Marx's list of errata. See Rolf Hecker et al. in MEGA² II/8 (1989) for a detailed account of the precise extent to which Engels incorporated Marx's desired changes.

[42] Arthur refers to an unpublished *Introduction to the Critique of Political Economy* composed by Marx in 1857, and apparently unknown to Engels, which appears to deny the so-called "logical-historical method"; "it would be . . . wrong to let economic categories succeed each

Marx by Meek of a "*logical* transition in *Capital* (from the commodity relation as such to the 'capitalistically modified' form of this relation) . . . presented by him as the 'mirror-image' of a *historical* transition (from 'simple' to 'capitalist' commodity production)" (citing Meek 1975: xv). Both the "logical-historical method" and "simple commodity production" are, maintains Arthur, Engels's inventions, referring here to the Preface to *Capital 3*, where Engels invented "simple commodity production" to describe Marx's discussion at the outset of *Capital 1* (MECW *37*: 16). Heinrich similarly takes issue both with Engels's notion of exchanges occurring according to labor ratios over several millennia of precapitalist organization and with his attribution of this idea to an "incidental" statement in *Capital 1* (at MECW *37*: 176, cited Chapter Two, pp. 115–16), whereby "it is quite appropriate to regard the values of commodities as not only theoretically but also historically *prius* to the prices of production" (Heinrich 1996: 896).[43]

We have considered aspects of this issue in Chapter Two in the context of the historical Transformation (above, pp. 115–19). In my view, Arthur fails to make a convincing case; he also goes too far when he concludes that "from the very first line Marx is presupposing that his object is capitalist production and that the commodity is its basic unit of output whose conditions of existence he traces" (1996b: 193). There are enough indications in the early chapters of *Capital 1* to justify Engels's interpretation in terms of "simple commodity production," if not this precise expression (see, e.g., MECW *35*: 70, 72, 84, 87, 93). Arthur is certainly right to raise the question whether the so-called law of value could possibly apply under precapitalist conditions lacking mobility (1996b: 186, 191–3), but such a problem concerns Marx no less than Engels.[44] Furthermore, we cannot simply dismiss Marx's assertion in this same context (MECW *37*: 175) that "[t]he exchange of commodities at their values, or approximately at their values . . . requires a much lower stage than their exchange at their prices of production." Nor can we neglect Engels's own restriction of the scope of the value concept when writing to Sombart on 11 March 1895: "I should delimit [it] historically by expressly confining [it] to the economic phase in which alone there has and could have been any question of value hitherto – to the social forms in which exchange of *commodities* and

---

other in the order in which they were historically decisive"(cited in Arthur 1996: 180). That Marx approved the 1859 review with its message to the contrary, Arthur suggests, reflects his uncertainty regarding the issue (185–6).

[43] Weeks had similarly argued for a divergence of Engels from Marx regarding the applicability of the "law of value" for millennia before the emergence of capitalist society (Weeks 1981: 50–5). Weeks's sharp contrast between Marx and Engels on the "role of perception and knowledge of labor time" requires modification (see Chapter Two, note 40).

[44] There is, in fact, a qualification by Engels himself that is pertinent in principle, though not formally concerned with value. In one of his reviews of *Capital I*, he asserted that "[a]fter this work it will no longer be possible . . . to apply laws which are valid for modern large-scale industry, conditioned by free competition, without further ado to the conditions of antiquity, or the guilds of the Middle Ages" (MECW *20*: 217).

production of commodities exist; primitive communism was innocent of value" (cited Chapter Two, p. 120).

With respect to *Capital 3* in particular, objections to the Engels edition have been renewed with a vengeance since the publication in 1992 in the *Marx–Engels Gesamtausgabe* edition (MEGA², volume II/4.2) of Marx's 1864–5 manuscript (upon which Engels had relied). Thus Heinrich calls for a return to the original material and the decanonization of the Engels version: "Engels's edition can no longer be considered to be volume III of Marx's *Capital;* it is not Marx's text 'in the full genuineness of his own presentation,' as Engels claimed in the supplement [MECW 37: 875], but a strong editing of this presentation, a pre-interpreted textbook edition of Marx's manuscript.... [T]he text he presented is by no means the third volume of *Capital.* Every future discussion of Marx's economic theory will have to refer back to Marx's original manuscript" (Heinrich 1996: 464–5).

Heinrich also expresses a degree of nihilism with respect to Marx himself in opining that he left few settled positions – as we have seen, this had earlier been suggested by Rubel – any impression to the contrary being due to Engels's misuse of the original source material: "But even this manuscript [of 1864–5] also cannot simply be considered to be the third volume of *Capital.* ... Marx was nowhere near solving all the *conceptual* problems" (1996: 465). Roth takes a similar position: "One of the conclusions that these papers[45] justify is that none of these Marx texts gives a systematic and concise presentation of his thought. He did not decide which of his various ways of treating the issues was the 'right' one; therefore, an 'authorized version,' in terms of an editor, does not really exist. There are merely fragments available.... Thus ... none of them can offer us a systematic presentation of what he thought" (2002: 65).[46] Similarly, Vollgraf and Jungnickel, following an account of Engels's interventions, refer to "the old dogma of the unity of Marx–Engels thought" (2002 [1994]: 68), concluding that "it is clear that Marx was in the midst of an open-ended process of research fermenting over many pages. It is also evident that his original text is at variance with various chords first struck by Engels's edition of 1894 which then continued to resonate down through the history of its influence" (2002: 37; also 67).[47] Finally, most recently, Musto has written of "[t]he intense editing activity on which Engels focused his efforts in the period between 1885–1914 [which] resulted in a transition from a very rough text, mainly comprising 'thoughts recorded *in statu nascendi*' and preliminary notes, to an organic text of systematic theory," and which "[n]ot surprisingly ... resulted in many errors of interpretation" (2009: 265–6).

---

[45] In addition to the 1864–5 material, Roth intends here Marx's document "The Rate of Surplus Value and the Rate of Profit Rendered Mathematically" and related manuscripts published in MEGA² II/14 (see below, note 49).

[46] See also Herres and Roth on Marx's "failed life" (2005: 64).

[47] For a critique of Vollgraff and Jungnickel, see Vygodskii (2002). A helpful summary of literature relating to "Engels as Editor" is provided in Roth and Mosely (2002).

I can be more specific regarding the main objections to Engels's edition. The complaint that Engels distorted Marx's position by extending the applicability of the "law of value" to precapitalistic commodity production has already been addressed and found wanting. A second major complaint relates to Engels's representation in Part III of *Capital 3* of "The Law of the Tendency of the Rate of Profit to Fall" (comprising Chapters XIII, XIV, and XV), with Engels allegedly presenting a more definite construct than had Marx in the original version of 1864–5 (Heinrich 1996: 459–60; Roth 2002: 67; Vollgraf and Jungnickel 2002 [1994]: 37). However, Roth allows that "Engels adopted Marx's method of discussing the various influences on the rate of profit" (2002: 68). Further, while maintaining that Engels "upgraded" the material regarding the falling rate of profit, Heinrich nonetheless concedes that the basic argument of the first two chapters of Part III – "The Law as Such" and "Counteracting Tendencies" – do "follow Marx's argumentation," thereby limiting the complaint to the link between the decline in the profit rate and crisis in the third chapter, the Engels version allegedly according it a systematic relevance absent in the original.

Now no reader of the chapters concerned with the logic of the falling profit rate could possibly come away with the notion that Marx's case is clear cut; Engels's version properly leaves the open-ended character of the argument intact (see Hollander 2008, Chapter 4). Indeed, Seigel has suggested that Engels weakened rather than strengthened the case for a falling profit rate by various rearrangements of the original materials. By transferring pages that reaffirm the validity of the law from their original order after the discussion of "Counteracting Influences" to Chapter XIII, he gave "the factors working against the law a more independent place in the argument than Marx had" (Seigel 1978: 339; see also Perelman 1985: 484–5, 1987: 53). Seigel also points out (1978: 343–4) that the chapter written by Engels on "The Effect of Turnover on the Rate of Profit" (Part I, Chapter IV), to fill a gap left by Marx, makes the case that the shortening of turnover periods of capital investment by a variety of improvements militates against a downward profit-rate trend. At the same time, Seigel is careful to add that Engels was not necessarily distorting Marx's intentions because there is evidence in the original texts of Marx's own doubts; "his editing of Marx's manuscripts may have expressed more than just his own doubts" (1978: 344–5).

As for Chapter XV of *Capital 3*, that too retains the complexities regarding the linkage between the falling profit rate and breakdown (Hollander 2008: 132–3, 471), namely a weakening of the motive to capital accumulation with the fall in the rate of return – "its fall checks the formation of new independent capitals" – creating a "threat" to the capitalist system, and also a "breed[ing] of overproduction, speculation, crises, and surplus capital" (MECW 37: 240), the first relating to reduced net investment and the second to cyclical fluctuations in capacity usage. Engels certainly allows Marx's voice to be heard, although the falling profit rate due to the distinctly Marxian logic entailing rising organic composition is absent from his own accounts of the close of the cyclical era and the prospective demise of capitalism (see Chapter Five, pp. 272–4).

That the harsh objections to Engels's edition of *Capital 3* are overdone is confirmed by the early version found in the *Grundrisse* (1857–8). This document provides independent evidence of the major progress already made by Marx in the late 1850s and supports the veracity of the Engels version, including his representation of the very high significance for Marx of the profit-rate trend – considered by Marx in 1857–8 as "one of the most striking phenomena of modern production" (MECW *28*: 479) – and its theoretical substantiation along the lines provided in 1894 (see Hollander 2008: 110, 252–4). In short, Engels's neglect of the *Grundrisse*, which Rubel believed detracted from his reconstruction of Marx's intellectual evolution (above, p. 306), suggests a different conclusion: Had this work been taken into account it would have strengthened, not undermined, the defense of Marx against charges that he had no solution to the "antinomy" between the law of value and profit-rate uniformity. There is certainly no "distortion" here, merely a failure to make the case as strong as it actually was. Similarly increasing our confidence in the Engel's edition is the fact that the document comprising twenty-three notebooks written between August 1861 and June 1863, which Engels always hoped to edit (10 April 1895; MECW *50*: 493), contains a substantial body of positive economics fully consonant with the main themes of *Capital 3* (Hollander 2008: 306–11). These literary origins lend support to Sowell's protest that "it is completely misleading to depict *Capital* as an analytically unfinished work, even though it was, in a literary sense, far from a finished piece of writing when Marx died in 1883" (Sowell 2006: 172).

The "mathematical" chapter in *Capital 3*, "The Relation of the Rate of Profit to the Rate of Surplus Value" (MECW *37*: 52–73), calls for comment at this point. Engels's Preface to the volume explains the provenance of the chapter, making mention of a Marx manuscript:

There was a series of uncompleted mathematical calculations for Chapter III, as well as a whole, almost complete, notebook dating from the seventies, which presents the relation of the rate of surplus value to the rate of profit in the form of equations. My friend Samuel Moore... undertook to edit this notebook for me, a work for which he was far better equipped, being an old Cambridge mathematician. It was from his summary, with occasional use of the main manuscript, that I then compiled Chapter III. (MECW *37*: 8)

This explanation is further elaborated in an important footnote at the close of the chapter itself, describing a specific omission from the notebook:

The manuscript contains also very detailed calculations of the difference between the rate of surplus value and the rate of profit ($s'-p'$), which has very interesting peculiarities, and whose movement indicates where the two rates draw apart or approach one another. These movements may also be represented by curves. I am not reproducing this material because it is of less importance to the immediate purposes of this work, and because it is enough here to call attention to this fact for readers who wish to pursue this point further. (MECW *37*: 73n.)

Although he certainly does not dismiss such investigations as unimportant, rather the contrary,[48] Engels is perfectly candid here about his editorial decision to exclude the detailed mathematical elaborations. One may regret the decision, but there is no gainsaying an eminently fair representation of the facts of the matter; Engels, had he wished, might have remained silent about the existence of Marx's explorations.

The 1885 Preface to *Anti-Dühring* notes once again that "Marx was well versed in mathematics" (MECW *25*: 11). Despite efforts to correct the deficiency, Engels admitted his own limitations. Having in mind the need for a sound theoretical exposition of the development of the natural sciences, he expressed the hope "to find some later opportunity to put together and publish the results which I have arrived at, perhaps in conjunction with the extremely important mathematical manuscripts left by Marx" (13). Conceivably he would have included in the tentatively projected collection the notebook on the relation of the rates of profit and surplus value "in the form of equations."[49]

* * *

Writing to Sombart in March 1895, Engels insisted that *Capital 3* presented the work of Marx faithfully: "I must . . . thank you for the high esteem in which you must hold me if you take the view that I could have turned Volume III into something better than it is. But I am unable to share that opinion and believe I have done my duty by presenting Marx in Marx's own words, even at the risk of expecting the reader to do rather more thinking for himself" (MECW *50*: 462). In his Supplement, written from May to June 1895, Engels explains that in editing Volume 3 he had sought "to produce as authentic a text as possible, to demonstrate the new results obtained by Marx in Marx's own words as far as possible, to intervene myself only where absolutely unavoidable, and even then to leave the reader in no doubt as to who was talking to him" (MECW *37*: 875). The scope of his "intervention" was limited "to eliminate difficulties in understanding, to bring more to the fore important aspects whose significance is not strikingly enough evident in the text, and to make some important additions to the text written in 1865 to fit the state of affairs in 1895" (876). For the reasons given above, I find that Engels's work on Volume 3 is fully consonant with his intentions.

While some 6 to 8 percent of Marx's text of *Capital 3* is actually by Engels, 90 percent of the interpolations – "from the tiniest scrap of a sentence to entire

---

[48] See also Engel's grave-side speech: "in every single field which Marx investigated – and he investigated very many fields, none of them superficially – in every field, even in that of mathematics, he made independent discoveries" (1883; MECW *24*: 468).

[49] That document is now published in MEGA² II/14 (2003: 19–150). See Roth (2002: 67–8) for an account of the third chapter in *Capital 3* in the light of this document and various others dealing with the same topic. She reports that the conclusions in the Engels version are stated somewhat more strongly than they are in the original.

chapters" – are "marked" as such, according to Vollgraf and Jungnickel (2002 [1994]: 52–3). This datum suggests that Engels was certainly not engaged in a deliberate campaign to mislead readers as to authorship. Even Vollgraf and Jungnickel themselves, critical though they are, allow that "Engel's editing work did not conceal the fact that the third volume had remained a torso and the manuscript remained a draft, even in its published version" (62). Indeed, Roth and Mosely read the Vollgraf–Jungnickel critique as taking a rather moderate position: "They come to the conclusion that Engels in fact preserved the characteristics of the draft by and large, but that he did, however, make a number of changes which conceal the complete extent of the questions left unanswered and studies left unfinished [by Marx]" (2002: 6). This fair assessment scarcely justifies a superannuation of the MECW version.[50]

* * *

I close with two qualifications. The dating of *Capital 2* source materials, particularly the "departmental" analysis (see Hollander 2008: 68–84), is rather more complex than that for those of *Capital 3*. Engels referred to a "first draft" prepared between 1863 and 1867, but he also allowed that Marx worked on relevant materials (if rather desultorily) in 1870 and thereafter, in fact as late as 1877–8 (MECW 36: 7–9). Eduard Bernstein made much of the later dating of *Capital 2* (1993 [1899]: 81). Rubel, who concedes that *Capital 3* largely predates 1868, insists of *Capital 2* that "tout reste pratiquement à faire" after the appearance of *Capital 1* in 1867 (Rubel 1968: 501; also cxvii–cxviii), most of the *Capital 2* materials dating to 1875–8 (cxiii). Similarly, Rubel and Manale designate *Capital 2* as "rudimentary" (1973: 212).

There is, then, general agreement that the middle volume is the latest of the three, standing somewhat apart from the rest as a set of exploratory exercises and very much open ended. If the claim that Engels accorded the original text of *Capital* more of a structure than it merited can be justified at all, it would be more valid with respect to *Capital 2* than the main themes of *Capital 3*, though there do remain sufficient loose ends in the departmental analysis to somewhat dilute any such evaluation (see Hollander 2008: 68–83).

Second, although it is safe for most of the central Marxian themes to consider *Capital 1* and *Capital 3* as, so the speak, a single unit that relies heavily on the early documents of 1857–8 and 1861–3, it is also the case that Marx worked much

---

[50] Howard and King question whether Rubel's edition – recall that this edition, like the MEGA edition, is based on the original *Capital 3* document of 1864–5 – necessitates "any fundamental reassessment" of the standard view of Marx's political economy based on the Engels version (1989: 16). Oakley is more reserved, and although he refuses to commit himself regarding "the relative merits of the Engels and Rubel editions of *Capital*, Books II and III," he does maintain that Rubel's endeavors "do serve to re-emphasise the very important point that *Capital* must be read as an incomplete work of uncertain bibliographical and substantive status" (1983: 126).

later on materials published by Engels toward the end of *Capital 3*. Like much of *Capital 2*, they remain in a very unfinished state. This applies, for example, to Chapter 49, "Concerning the Analysis of the Process of Production" (MECW 37: 818–38), which touches on the question whether (as Adam Smith believed) the entire national income can be resolved into wages, profit, and rent. This chapter, which draws heavily on the "simple reproduction" notions of *Capital 2,* proved a veritable nightmare to Engels, as is well explained by Rubel (1968: 1844). The analysis of credit in Part V of *Capital 3* has also been the subject of considerable stricture, some of which is doubtless justified (Rubel 1968: cxxiv; Heinrich 1996: 460–3).[51] Nevertheless, these two allowances scarcely justify an indictment of Engels's editorial work as a whole.

---

[51] On the especially patchy sections in *Capital 3*, Bernstein commented that the "more Engels attempted to put things here in order, the more these sections threatened to lose the character he so carefully sought to preserve for the book, namely, that it remain Marx's product in all essential points" (cited in Vollgraf and Jungnickel 2002 [1994]: 67).

SEVEN

A Methodological Overview

A. Introduction

My first five chapters demonstrated Engels's impressive contributions in the 1840s to Marxian economic analysis appearing in the *Outlines of Political Economy, The Condition of the Working Class*, and the *Principles of Communism*; justified his defense of Marx against charges of plagiarism regarding surplus-value doctrine, perceived (along with the doctrine of historical materialism) as the essence of scientific socialism; rationalized his objections to the "utopian" socialists for proposing organizational arrangements that lack a price mechanism, notwithstanding his own case for a central-control system; and analyzed his so-called revisionism, attending to the scope for (and desirability of) constitutional and welfare reform within capitalism, and to the serious implications of such progress for a communist outcome. (Precisely how my positions on these matters relate to other treatments of Engels's political economy is conveniently summarized in the Prolegomena.) Chapter Six pulled some of the threads of my account together by focusing on facets of Engels's relationship with Marx, including his work as Marx's editor. (Again, my contribution in relation to the secondary literature is clarified in the Prolegomena.) I shall complete the synthesis in this concluding chapter by surveying the methodological implications of Engels's contribution to Marxian political economy.

In Section B, considerable common ground is shown to exist between Engels's view of the character of "political economy" – much of what we say applies equally to Marx – and that of the tradition represented by Lionel Robbins, namely the contrast between value-free economic analysis and value-laden prescription. This parallel has not, to my knowledge, been addressed in the literature. Also conspicuous, I shall argue, is the "conservative" nature of several of Engels's applications of price theory – again, the same is true of Marx – using the term in the sense spelled out by George Stigler.

The Marxian theoretical corpus obviously extends beyond the pricing and allocation mechanism upon which Robbins focused. What I refer to as Engels's conservative application of distinctive Marxian theoretical features relating to the labor market is illustrated in Section C. Here I confirm that Engels did not always live up to the principle of value-free analysis, frequently adopting extreme or unqualified versions of particular Marxian structures for "propaganda" purposes.

Peculiar to Marxian political economy is its perception of the theoretical organon as predictive device – generating, in the growth context, forecasts of falling real-wage and profit rates – contrasting with the classical or neoclassical variety, which makes no pretension to historical prediction. Prediction regarding welfare prospects under capitalism is a further major theme, though conspicuous here (as shown in Chapter Five) is the dramatic reversal in later years of the early presumption, then accorded the status almost of doctrinal principle, that social reform under capitalism was inconceivable. More generally, the evolutionary dimension describing and accounting for the transition from competitive to monopoly capitalism (the so-called decline of the market), and ultimately to communism, entails prediction with a vengeance. These matters are reviewed in Section D. Here I also recall the Marx–Engels perspective regarding possibilities of arriving at communism by way of the constitutional option (discussed in Chapter Four), considering the political concessions by the British ruling classes forced on them by the growing proletarian power that was generated by the transformation of industry structure. At the same time, of increasing concern to Engels was the *embourgeoisement* of the British proletariat, reflected in conservative voting habits, encouraged by a degree of wage improvement in addition to ongoing welfare legislation (discussed in Chapter Five). These trends undermined the concept of economic "determinism," understood as the inevitability that a communist order would emerge from mature capitalism according to the principles of historical materialism entailing the contrast between economic "base" and political "superstructure." In effect, the political superstructure seemed to be taking on a life of its own, thus thwarting the "inevitable" outcome.

As I show in Section E, Engels's late restatements of historical materialism in correspondence claim that he and Marx had always intended the interdependence between base and superstructure. I show this claim to be open to question. In any event, Engels seems insufficiently aware of the extent to which such a reading threatens the doctrine. Compounding the problem is his frequent appeal, not limited to writings after 1883, to behavioral patterns at play in the evolution of capitalism divorced from the economic base. I deal with this characteristic in Section F. An Appendix is devoted to the prospect of an alternative, Russian, route to communism to that perceived as relevant in Britain and Western Europe. Any such projection, which would in the event further muddy the methodological waters, is, however, shown not to have been given much credence by either Marx or Engels.

B. The Unduly Neglected Price-Theoretical Component

Lionel Robbins famously insisted on a sharp distinction between value-free economic analysis and description, and necessarily value-laden prescription, ascribing this perspective to a tradition represented in particular by von Mises and Wicksteed (Robbins 1935, 1976). He pointed out that the two were treated by Adam Smith and the nineteenth-century Classics as falling within a single designation, "political economy," to describe not only "how the economic system actually worked, or could work, but also how, according to the assumptions of the author, it ought to be made, or allowed, to work." Modern practice, by contrast, designates the analysis and description of economic phenomena as "economics," reserving the term "political economy" for "the discussion of what is desirable in the way of policy as a distinct, though related, speculative area" (Robbins 1976: 1–2). In either case, the link turns on the fact that "to prescribe what is desirable" requires "knowledge of what is possible – of what effects are likely to follow from what specific types of individual or political action," so that "discussion of the problems of what is practically desirable . . . should be conducted against a background of relevant scientific knowledge," in the sense of "a collection of value-free generalizations about the way in which the economic system works" (2–3).

Several texts encountered in the present work justify the contention that Engels (like Marx) subscribed to the foregoing perspective regarding value-free analysis, and the necessity for prescription to take it into account. Recall first from Chapter Three the objection on price-theoretical grounds to Rodbertus's reform proposals entailing the imposition by the state of labor values, despite his retention of elements of capitalist organization in a halfway house arrangement. (This parallels Marx's criticisms of Proudhon's reform proposals.) Rodbertus is charged with "utopianism" precisely because, by proposing a market system subject to controlled prices, he "adopted the usual utopian disdain of economic laws" (Chapter Three, p. 136). His preclusion of a market mechanism, above all of a signaling device to equilibrate quantities supplied and demanded, undermined his plan to impose labor-based prices by authority. This objection reflects not only the requirement to base policy prescription upon analysis taking account of the "laws" of political economy, but also the objective character attributed to the laws of competitive pricing. After all, the value judgments regarding ends acceptable to Engels and Marx differed entirely from those of orthodox economists applying the identical pricing model; their opposition to state intervention was differently motivated.[1]

---

[1] There are other indications of the "neutrality" of analysis as such. We have, for example, Engels's representation of the Fabians as "a well-meaning gang of eddicated [sic] middle-class folk who have refuted Marx with Jevons' worthless vulgar economics – so vulgar that you can make anything of it, including socialism" (to Sorge, 8 February 1890; MECW 48: 449). Similarly, "the Fabian Society positively pullulates with Jevons-Mengerians who look down with infinite contempt on a Marx they have long since outdistanced" (to C. Schmidt, 12 September 1892; MECW 49: 526). Engels commended Schmidt for his critique (in Schmidt 1891–2) of the Jevons–Menger psychological orientation (to Kautsky, 29 September 1892; 553). Also in the Preface to *Capital 3* Engels refers to the "plausible vulgar socialism . . . built in England on the foundation of Jevons's and Menger's theory of use value and marginal utility" (1894; MECW 37: 13).

Also recall the strong opposition on the part of both Engels and Marx to approaching income distribution in terms of morality and justice. They insisted – with respect to communist no less than capitalist organization – both on the essential deductions from national product before recognition of consumption allowances could be contemplated and on the economic necessity for "inequality" with respect to wage differentials (Chapter Three, pp. 156–8, 166). All of this indicates a value-free orientation with regard to analysis, and the requirement to take account of such analysis when one is evaluating economic organization.[2] Similarly indicative is the "Austrian" quality of their analyses emerging in objections to interventionist proposals on the grounds that they neglected interdependencies between industries that necessitate further, unimagined, interventions to support the initial step (Chapter Three, pp. 133–4).

* * *

I may elaborate the position thus far by reference to George Stigler's familiar quest for the "cause of professional conservatism." This he isolated in the economist's scientific training, for "the professional study of economics makes one politically conservative, in the sense of one who wishes most economic activity to be conducted by private enterprise, and who believes that abuses of private power will usually be checked, and incitements to efficiency and progress usually provided, by the forces of competition" (1965 [1959]: 52–3). Alternatively expressed, the economist's conservatism is traced to "the effect of a sort of "natural selectivity" engendered by the study of economics (59). Specifically,

[h]e is drilled in the problems of *all* economic systems and in the methods by which a price system solves these problems. It becomes impossible for the trained economist to believe that a small group of selfish capitalists dictates the main outlines of the allocation of resources and the determination of outputs. It becomes impossible for him to believe that men of good will can by their individual actions stem inflation, or that it is possible to impose changes in any one market or industry without causing problems in other markets or industries. He cannot unblushingly repeat slogans such as "production for use rather than for profit." He cannot believe that a change in the *form* of social organization will eliminate basic economic problems" (1965 [1959]: 59–60).

This sort of training was absorbed by Marx and Engels, directly or indirectly, through study of the classical literature, and it was applied in a "conservative" manner in campaigning against naïve reformist proposals. In Engels's case, this is apparent from his criticisms of Rodbertus's labor-ticket scheme, and equally from his

---

2 Similarly, with respect to descriptive economics, there is Engels's insistence in 1891 that Marx "never based his communist demands" on a charge of "unfair" income distribution under going conditions, "but upon the inevitable collapse of the capitalist mode of production which is daily taking place before our eyes to an ever growing degree," referring to evidence of the decline of the market; "he says only that surplus value consists of unpaid labour, which is a simple fact" (cited in Chapter Three, p. 156).

objections to protectionism and to rent and interest-rate control (Chapter Three, pp. 129–34, 134–8), on the objective grounds that price-control measures could not succeed in their objective and that market interdependence was highly pertinent to policy evaluation. From this point of view Engels (like Marx) emerges as defender of the status quo, rejecting anything short of full-fledged communism. As for the mixed systems proposed by various socialist reformers, they feared their degeneration into fully fledged capitalism.[3]

Needless to say, there are sharp differences between this and, say, Adam Smith's stance. Smith justified government intervention in the price system as a means to ensure a framework within which the private-property and free-market arrangement might operate to the social good. The position of Engels and Marx is far more complex. They had no desire to see corrected the defects of the private-property system to better allow its functioning from a welfare point of view. Indeed, we have found in Chapter Five that major policy measures – such as factory legislation and free trade – were evaluated in terms of the likelihood that their effect would be to encourage or impede the development of capitalism and thus expedite or delay its collapse. In these terms a measure might be supported even if its consequence might be detrimental to working-class welfare.

It may be objected that, because at no time was Engels swayed from his absolute commitment to central control in place of the market system – in Mayer's terms, from his "unshakable faith in the final victory of communism" (1969 [1936]: 328; also 331–2) – he can scarcely be classified, as I propose, as a conservative in Stigler's sense. The objection is invalid, though these contrasting ends must never be lost from sight. As pointed out, Engels's "conservatism" is manifested in his rejection of compromise arrangements entailing what we call today a "mixed economy." Beyond this, though, it is precisely the appreciation of the significance of the pricing mechanism that lies behind the radical simplifications he proposed for future economic arrangement, including the preclusion of free consumer choice; and his concern (as with Marx) was to devise a system that would provide an alternative to market-price signaling to ensure balance between demands and supplies by central control of both.

I have adopted this perspective in response to Hutchison's complaint that Engels failed to direct the same objection against his own scheme that he directed against Rodbertus's, namely its lack of a pricing mechanism yielding market-clearing equilibrium (Chapter Three, pp. 150–1). In any event, Engels made some allowance for "shadow prices" in his early perception of communist arrangement, indicating an awareness of a crucial aspect of a universal economic problem (pp. 142–3, 173).

---

[3] Two qualifications are in order. First, the course of events forced upon Marx and Engels a recognition of the effectiveness of capitalistic welfare reform (with particular reference to monopoly capitalism); second, even a "dictatorship of the proletariat" might tolerate – at least temporarily – a capitalist sector and introduce tax reform and the like, namely the measures recommended in the *Communist Manifesto*. Such reforms could be tolerated because communist political control would be ensured.

Similarly, his notion of autarky, formally expressed in discussing agriculture but in principle applicable more widely (pp. 145n30, 149, 174), does not reflect neglect or ignorance of the pricing mechanism. To the contrary, it indicates a quest for a system avoiding that mechanism. In addition, at the broadest level, the exclusion of a circulating medium from the communist scheme is based precisely on a concern that its allowance must lead to the ultimate demise of the scheme because of the uncontrollable pressures released thereby (pp. 146–7).[4]

The point at hand may be rephrased in terms of a comment by Marx to Kugelmann regarding the universal problem of resource (labor) scarcity – even designated as a "natural law" – the consequent allocative problem, and the specificity of the solution under capitalism:

[E]very child knows . . . that the amounts of products corresponding to the differing amounts of needs demand differing and quantitatively determined amounts of society's aggregate labour. It is self-evident that this necessity of the distribution of social labour in specific proportions is certainly not abolished by the specific form of social production; it can only change its form of manifestation. Natural laws cannot be abolished at all. The only thing that can change, under historically differing conditions, is the form in which those laws assert themselves. And the form in which this proportional distribution of labour asserts itself in a state of society in which the interconnection of social labour expresses itself as the private exchange of the individual products of labour, is precisely the exchange value of these products. (11 July 1868; MECW 43: 68)

The universality of the problem of resource allocation and also the solution in a private-enterprise economy are here made strikingly clear. My point has been that in a central-control system (so Engels and Marx maintained) the problem would ideally be resolved by alternative means, avoiding any need for an allocative price mechanism.

It is instructive, from the foregoing perspective, to perceive the Marx–Engels communist scheme as one entailing several features of a "war economy," in the sense of the term adopted by Robbins, as an alternative to the price mechanism:

There can be no question that, in a situation such as a major war, a centrally planned economy whose output has some rational significance is both conceivable and practically possible. The aim is simple: to win the war. The essential problem is therefore to produce for domestic consumption in terms of food, clothing and so on the minimum means necessary to sustain morale and health for the non-military population – quantities which to some extent can be *technically* estimated – leaving all the rest of the productive potential for the war effort. Doubtless there are profound problems arising from scarcities of materials and services even here; and the use of markets and prices in special sectors may be desirable. But the nature of the aims and the urgencies of the situation make the very idea of running a major war by the price mechanism alone a little ridiculous. (Robbins 1976: 144)

---

[4] This is not to suggest, of course, that Marx and Engels wholly got to grips with prospective planning problems (see, e.g., Chapter Three, p. 148).

Although the parallel does not hold good in all respects – what, for example, corresponds to the ultimate objective of "winning the war"? – it does apply to the positing by the Marx–Engels conception of a highly simplified régime that avoids a pricing mechanism to ensure market clearing, to the allocation of rights to a specific basket of goods decided upon centrally rather than by free consumer choice, and to the treatment of final consumption as a residual after social ends have been met. The essential difference is that Marx and Engels were, in effect, proposing a war economy not for an emergency situation but permanently, or at least into the foreseeable future once their scheme had been put in place.

Lord Robbins refers broadly to "relevant scientific knowledge" in regard to value-free economics, analytical and descriptive (above, p. 316). My account of the centrality for Engels of the competitive pricing mechanism in evaluating Rodbertus's scheme for social reorganization may leave an impression that the "relevant" body of theory he applied – the same observation holds good of Marx with regard to his critique of Proudhon – amounts specifically to classical price theory, or the so-called neoclassical variety, for that matter.[5] But the account is certainly not intended to represent the alpha and omega of Marxian political economy, but rather to take under consideration a price-theoretical component that is lacking in the secondary expositions of Marx and Engels of which I am aware. Let us take the story a step further in the next section.

C. Engels's Applied Economics: The "Marxian Component"

We must now determine how far my conclusions hold good, once we allow for the more familiar "Marxian" doctrine. Here I have in mind Engels's own complaint, expressed in a letter to Marx, that Liebknecht intended to be "as independent of us theoretically as possible," in which regard "considering his complete ignorance of theory, he has always been far more successful than he himself is aware" (28 May 1876; MECW 45: 123). Again, the joint circular letter of September 1879 insists that sound policy deliberation required preliminary "study of the new science" (MECW 45: 407).[6] Also relevant is an objection in the same letter that the Party leadership had no idea how to deal with practical issues such as protection, the analysis of which required precise "knowledge of conditions in German industry and the latter's position in the world market" (400); this objection suggested an appeal for "objectivity" in approaching application.

My discussion relates to the sampling in Chapter Three of applications of so-called relevant theory to trade policy and to reform proposals regarding the housing and credit markets. The use made of distinctively "Marxian" theory varies from case to case. Thus it plays no part in "Protection and Free Trade" (1888), which precedes

---

[5] To the extent that my case is well made out, the celebrated Marxian designation of 1830 as marking a transition from "scientific" to "apologetic" economics must be understood as referring to the use made of analysis, rather than the analysis as such.

[6] For a discussion of this letter, see Chapter Four, p. 220, and Epilogue pp. 345–6.

in terms of standard or orthodox development economics (Chapter Three, pp. 132–3). Further, in *The Housing Question* (1872–3; 1887), proposals to regulate the interest rate by legislation are rejected on grounds of the operation of competitive market forces that establish the return on loanable funds: "The rate of interest will continue to be governed by the economic laws to which it is subject today, all decrees notwithstanding" (p. 132). In fact, the "great plan to deprive capital of its 'productivity' is as old as the... *usury laws* which aim at nothing else but limiting the rate of interest, and which have since been abolished everywhere because in practice they were continually broken or circumvented, and the state was compelled to admit its impotence against the laws of social production."

Nonetheless, Marxian components are certainly called upon in *The Housing Question*. The competitive pricing model as basic tool of analysis is coupled with appeal to a particularly strong version of Marxian wage theory, to ongoing labor-displacing "machinery," and to regular trade cycles, in accounting for laborers' depressed purchasing power and consequently the low profitability of investment in working-class housing relative to higher-class categories, rendering the housing shortage intractable in a market system (Chapter Three, pp. 130–1). More generally, measures that merely affect the distribution of "surplus value" (such as proposals to abolish house rent and interest) were judged irrelevant from labor's perspective, considering the assumed constancy of the long-run real wage. Beyond this, even increased housing provision reflected in reduced living costs, should it occur, would be of little avail to labor in the long run, the wage doctrine proving the impossibility of a permanently raise in living standards.

* * *

The condemnation of Rodbertus as "utopian" for his alleged "disdain of economic laws" should not be identified with a criticism of various reformist schemes to improve real wages on grounds of neglect of the economic "law" of wage determination. The objection to Rodbertus concerns the theory of allocation, and it makes no pretense at forecasts regarding the position of demand or supply schedules in commodity markets. The criticism regarding wages concerns such forecasts, with the 1872 Engels imposing something akin to subsistence reasoning – very much reminiscent of pseudo- or textbook Malthusianism.

One would be excused for concluding that Engels's position was engraved in stone, because the perspective of *The Housing Question* in 1872 merely rehearses the position maintained in *The Condition of the Working Class* that union activity "cannot alter the economic law according to which wages are determined by the relation between supply and demand in the labour market" (Chapter Five, p. 234). Nonetheless, there are signs of movement. In his interview in April 1872, Engels spoke enthusiastically of wage increases granted to organized agricultural workers (p. 254). Later, in the letter to Bebel of 1875 he opposed the "iron law of wages," appealing to the notion of "elastic" laws appearing in *Capital 1* (p. 255 and note 28). This qualification is further elaborated in 1881; "the law of wages... is not inexorable with certain limits," but there exists a "latitude within which the rate of wages may be modified by the results of the struggle between the two contending parties" (p. 257). It is true that as late as 1885, and even 1892, Engels still refers to laws that "act upon [workers] with the irresistible force of an automatic engine, which crushes them between its wheels" (260). However, this applied to the unskilled rather than to industrial and unionized workers, and in the end even unskilled labor was beginning to enjoy improved real wages under New Union pressure (p. 264).

By allowing for "elasticity" regarding earnings prospects, Engels weakened treatment of the Marxian model as predictive device; this allowance, if taken seriously, implies a conception of the model as engine of analysis that indicates what may occur under alternative assumptions. (I shall return to this matter in discussing the forecast of capitalism's demise; below, pp. 326–8.) But also undermined is the notion, conspicuous in *The Housing Question*, of "economic law" as justifying a case against the potential of reformist measures and institutions.[7] Now because in 1872, the very year that document was first published, Engels made allowance elsewhere for real-wage increases, it is difficult to say whether he took his own case seriously. However, as there are no substantive changes admitted in the version of 1887, I am obliged to question Engels's motives in denying the feasibility of reform measures to improve working-class housing by appeal to a "law" of the labor market that he himself had come to reject. Compounding the charge is the fact that all editions of *Anti-Dühring* (1878, 1885, 1894) reproduce the empirically superannuated version of "steadily deteriorating" conditions, which – together with the increasing inability of the capitalist class to fulfill their organizational function – supposedly ensured a transition to communism (Chapter Five, p. 260).

If charged with lack of candor for continuing to posit the infeasibility of real-wage improvement though aware of evidence to the contrary, Engels might well have pointed to his further forecast that all improvement could at best be temporary, considering the onset of secular depression and prospective mass immigration from China (pp. 272–6). However, this is to give him the full benefit of the doubt, whereas we cannot preclude a propensity to draw on strong versions of Marxian theory, especially with regard to wages, as it suited his immediate purpose, which was to educate the working classes in appropriate attitudes. Needless to say, to this extent the value-free character of analysis was severely compromised.

Although Marx, too, continued to insist in *Capital 1* on falling real wages (Chapter Five, p. 243), my criticism applies to a lesser extent because the time span remaining for him to modify the evaluation was more limited than it was in Engels's case. This excuse is not, however, available when it comes to factory legislation. It is true that these reforms were represented by Marx as the outcome of increasing proletarian power, allowing a formal reconciliation with continued insistence

---

[7]   I have documented Marx's dramatic abandonment of the inconceivability of effective welfare progress within capitalism in discussing factory legislation: For the "first time . . . in broad daylight the political economy of the middle class succumbed to the political economy of the working class," in the "great contest between the blind rule of the laws of supply and demand which form the political economy of the middle class, and social production, controlled by foresight, which forms the political economy of the working class" (Chapter Five, p. 242).

upon "tendencies working with iron necessity towards inevitable results" and the "natural laws of the modern mode of production" (pp. 243–4) and protecting the principle of historical materialism, which insists on the predominance of the economic "base." Nonetheless, this perspective implies a volte-face relative to the 1840s regarding the character of economic "laws," which at that time were said to preclude such reformist possibilities. As Marx himself put it (see note 7), the "political economy of the middle class" entailing the laws of the market was in the process of surrendering to the "political economy of the working class" entailing the laws of a planned economy.

Apart from his frequent use of strong versions of Marxian wages theory, Engels also applies typically Marxian conceptions to the interpretation of the labor–capital nexus, conspicuously the notion of surplus value as unpaid labor, when discussing abolition of house rent and interest. Recall here from the Prolegomena and from Chapter Two that "scientific" as distinct from "utopian" socialism is defined precisely in terms of a proper appreciation of surplus value. Recall, too, the well-known position that no reform is meaningful that leaves unaltered the capitalistic wage contract, however favorable real wages may be (Chapter Five, pp. 269–70). Nevertheless, these features do not directly touch upon the positive economic analysis and the applications based upon it that have preoccupied us thus far in this chapter.

D. Political Economy in the Historical Context

The political economy found appropriate in the historical context has a "conservative" character reflecting the evolutionary processes at play. It corresponds to the conservatism encountered in applications of theory to the commodity and labor markets, assuming a given capitalist organization. This characteristic is spelled out by Engels himself in his account of dialectical philosophy in *Ludwig Feuerbach*: "It has, however, also a conservative side: it recognises that definite stages of cognition and society are justified for their time and circumstances" (MECW *26*: 360).[8] The conservative principle is thus conceded, notwithstanding a qualification that Engels hastened to add: "but only so far. The conservatism of this outlook is relative; its revolutionary character is absolute – the only absolute dialectical philosophy admits."

A criticism of the English socialists in *The Condition of the Working Class* is indicative of the point at hand: "They acknowledge no historical development, and wish to place the nation in a state of Communism at once, overnight, not by the unavoidable march of its political development up to the point at which this transition becomes both possible and necessary" (MECW *4*: 525; see also

---

[8] A striking illustration is provided by the perspective on colonialism, for Marx and Engels were far more restrained in their support for national liberation movements – in the modern terminology – than might have been expected. As Hunt summarizes the matter, "neither Marx nor Engels felt able to support fully the struggle for independence since the demands of economic progress and imperial modernity superseded any narrow Indian rights to self-governance" (2009: 226).

Chapter Three, p. 154). In *Anti-Dühring* Engels insisted that "the appropriation by society of all the means of production . . . could become possible, could become a historical necessity, only when the actual conditions for its realisation were there. Like every other social advance, it becomes practicable, not by men understanding that the existence of classes is in contradiction to justice, equality, etc., not by the mere willingness to abolish these classes, but by virtue of certain new economic conditions" (MECW 25: 268). The general principle is also applied to the period after the communists had achieved power and the state had taken possession of the means of production; the state would then "die out" naturally, pace the "agitators," including the anarchists who sought "the abolition of the state out of hand." Further, although it is true that the *Principles of Communism* (1847) implies that the foundations for a social transformation, manifested in enormous productive capacity, were actually in place, allowing communist society "to increase these productive forces in a short time to an infinite extent" (Chapter One, p. 63), Engels nevertheless answers the question whether it "[i]t will . . . be possible to abolish private property at one stroke," firmly in the negative (Chapter Four, p. 182). It is a striking concession to insist on the retention of private-property institutions after the achievement of proletarian political rule, in order to ensure that degree of expansion of productive capacity required for the successful implementation of communist arrangement. This position is confirmed by insistence in the *Principles* on the "gradual expropriation of landed proprietors, factory owners, railway and shipping magnates," with the further remarkable qualification that it be done "partly through competition on the part of state industry and partly through compensation in assignations" (MECW 6: 350; see also Chapter One, p. 64). The "first radical onslaught upon private ownership," as Engels put it (351), is much less radical than one might be led to believe. In the *Communist Manifesto* too, "the proletariat will use its political supremacy to wrest, by degrees, all capital from the bourgeoisie" (MECW 6: 504).

Let us return to the matter of historical prediction, having in mind a declaration in *Anti-Dühring* that "[p]olitical economy is . . . essentially a *historical* science. It deals with material which is historical, that is, constantly changing," which prefaces a concern to establish that "[t]he mode of production and exchange in a definite historical society, and the historical conditions that have given birth to this society, determine the mode of distribution of its products," while distribution "is not a merely passive result of production and exchange; it in its turn reacts upon both of these" (MECW 25: 135–7). This latter relation is illustrated by the phenomenon of "modern capitalist production," which has "brought about antitheses in distribution – concentration of capital in a few hands on the one side and concentration of the propertyless masses in the big towns on the other – which must of necessity bring about its downfall" (137).[9] Although we have here a "deterministic"

---

[9] Recall here the difference perceived by Claeys between Engels and Watts on the character of the tendency toward concentration (Chapter One, note 61).

prediction of the inevitable collapse of capitalism, it soon becomes apparent that Engels himself had little confidence in the posited playback of distribution upon organization. In any event, the character of the so-called downfall of capitalism – whether by constitutional or violent means – is left an open question.

We observed in the analysis of constitutional reform (Chapter Four), how conspicuous was the interplay of the continuously evolving political and economic factors with considerable weight placed on the functioning of the political "super-structure." Thus Engels had by 1895 reached the conclusion that "[t]he mode of struggle of 1848" was "obsolete in every respect," considering the open route to communist power via the polls coupled with the tactical advantages increasingly enjoyed by the modern state against uprisings, with both trends attributed to capitalist development (MECW *27*: 510; see Chapter Four, p. 214). However, the interplay of the political and economic dimensions enters by a second route. Engels could not take a transition to communism for granted, considering his ever-growing concern with the reliability of the British working class attracted by improving wages (reflecting the success of unions) and working conditions (reflecting bourgeois welfare reforms). It is true that these trends were related to the transition from competitive to monopoly capitalism (Chapter Five, pp. 261–2), and to this extent the predominance of the economic "base" was protected. But a communist finale was nonetheless now in doubt. This threat was met by appeal to an imminent end to British industrial progress coupled with the prospect of massive Chinese immigration and – at least temporarily – that of world war, bringing to an end working-class progress within capitalism (pp. 277–8).[10] (One may suppose that under sufficiently dire circumstances the constitutional option would become wholly irrelevant, leaving violent revolution as the only alternative.)

Despite his formal resolution of the dilemma, Engels's uncertainty regarding the future is apparent. He recalls in 1895 that when, in 1850, he and Marx had declared – against the "illusions" of the "vulgar democrats" – that "at least the *first* chapter of the revolutionary period was closed and that nothing was to be expected until the outbreak of a new world economic crisis," they had been "excommunicated, as traitors to the revolution" (Chapter Four, p. 213). He candidly admits that even their evaluation had been refuted by events: "history has proved us wrong. . . . It has made it clear that the state of economic development on the Continent at that time was not, by a long way, ripe for the elimination of capitalist production" (MECW *27*: 512). The growth of the proletariat and its organs – a feature of capitalist development, for "the grave-diggers of the Revolution of 1848 had become the

---

[10] Although such appeal might suggest a grasping at straws, a more sympathetic interpretation would interpret the proffered solution to the dilemma presented by real-wage and welfare progress under capitalism in terms of globalization trends – British industrial superiority undermined by American and European technological development, and Chinese workers displaced by the adoption in China of capitalistic arrangement. For Marx, similarly, Irish immigration to England resulted from the imposition in Ireland of large-scale capitalist farming.

executors of its will" (513) – would finally provide the key to success; but the experience of the Paris Commune, when "power fell, quite of itself and quite undisputed, into the hands of the working class... proved how impossible even then, twenty years after the time described in our work, this rule of the working class still was" (514). And although, with the impact of foreign competition on British industry in mind, Engels remarked that "[t]he wonder is, not that a good many of [his prophesies] proved wrong, but that so many of them proved right" (Chapter Five, p. 275.) – for this particular "prophesy" goes back to the 1840s – what stands out in all this is the high degree of uncertainty regarding the future. True enough, in 1892 he asserted that the German Social Democratic Party "has reached the point where it is possible to determine the date when it will come to power almost by mathematical calculation," suggesting near certainty (Chapter Four, p. 210). This, however, was for public consumption, as is apparent from the explanation to Bebel at this time regarding reports that he had positively predicted the collapse of bourgeois society by 1898: "There must have been a little mistake somewhere. All I said was that by '98 we might possibly have come to the helm. Should this *not* happen, bourgeois society might continue to potter along as it is for a bit, until such time as an impulse from without causes the whole rotten structure to come crashing down. In still air a dilapidated old wreck of that sort can survive for a couple of decades even when it is to all intents and purposes defunct" (26 October 1891; MECW *49*: 271). Nonetheless, "I should have been exceedingly careful about making predictions of this nature. . . . [T]he possibility of our coming to power is merely a calculation of probability in accordance with mathematical laws."[11]

Yet for all the doubts and qualifications regarding the specific timing of events, prediction was in the blood, which is scarcely surprising in that the Marxian theoretical apparatus was purported to constitute, in principle, a forecasting, not merely an analytical engine (see further, Blaug 1982, Chapter 2). Thus in the Preface to *Capital 1* Marx refers to the "natural laws of capitalist production" entailing "tendencies working with iron necessity towards inevitable results," such that "[t]he country that is more developed industrially only shows, to the less developed, the image

---

[11] What precisely was intended by this reference to "mathematical probability" is open to conjecture, but conceivably Engels had in mind Quételet's predictions based on statistical probabilities (Quételet 1842 [1835]). Marx refers to Quételet regarding the prediction of different sorts of crime based on statistical probabilities in "Capital Punishment" (1853; MECW *11*: 497), and regarding urban health (correspondence, 11 March 1858; MECW *40*: 286). In a letter to Kugelmann, he opined that Quételet had "rendered great services in the past by demonstrating that even the apparently casual incidents of social life possess an inner necessity through their periodic recurrence and their periodic average incidence. But he was never successful in interpreting this necessity" (3 March 1869; MECW *43*: 232). His familiarity with Quételet's statistical regularities is clear in *Capital* itself (MECW *35*: 328n.; MECW *37*: 847), and it would certainly have been known to Engels because Marx mentions "Quételet's average man" in correspondence with Engels (21 August 1875; MECW *45*: 82). There is also an implicit reference to the concept in the joint *The German Ideology* (1845–6; MECW *5*: 80).

of its own future" (MECW 35: 9).[12] He also makes this statement: "One nation can and should learn from others. And even when a society has got upon the right track for the discovery of the natural laws of its movement – and it is the ultimate aim of this work, to lay bare the economic law of motion of modern society – it can neither clear by bold leaps, nor remove by legal enactments, the obstacles offered by the successive phases of its normal development" (10).[13] A striking instance of the principle is the forecast of a similar pattern in the United States to what he then believed to be under way in Britain, including a prospective real-wage decline: "Capitalistic production advances there with giant strides, even though the lowering of wages and the dependence of the wage worker are yet far from being brought down to the normal European level" (MECW 35: 760).

Engels adopted this prognosis. In his Appendix to the 1887 American edition of *The Condition of the Working Class*, he identified features of the contemporary American economy in 1887 with that of Britain in 1844, pointing to "two circumstances which for a long time prevented the *unavoidable consequences* of the Capitalist system from showing themselves in the full glare of day in America," namely "easy access to the ownership of cheap land and the influx of immigration," the latter serving as wage labor (MECW 26: 402; emphasis added). But, as for the first, "[t]he great safety-valve against the formation of a permanent proletarian class has practically ceased to act" (402–3), and all the characteristic features of capitalist development were apparent (403). Less than a year later in his Preface to the American edition, Engels confirmed his prognosis: "that I anticipated a working class movement on a national scale, my 'Appendix' shows; but no one could then foresee that in such a short time the [labor] movement would burst out with such irresistible force, would spread with the rapidity of a prairie-fire, would shake American society to its very foundations" ("The Labor Movement in America," 1887; MECW 26: 435). We recall that he found the original *The Condition of the Working Class* to be "justified precisely by the fact that industrial conditions in present-day America coincide almost entirely with those in the England of the forties, that is those described by myself" (see Chapter Six, p. 296).

Now Shaw takes the position that *Capital* "underwrites the claim that socialism is 'inevitable,' but by the same token it does not empower one to predict the arrival of socialism at any particular time or place – only to affirm that the tendency of

---

[12] Marx's strong statements regarding "iron necessity" – and Engels's adherence to them – must be taken seriously, but Hacking is perhaps going too far when he attributes to Marx actual use of Quételet in the derivation of necessitarian laws: "Marx fabricat[ed] an iron necessity out of the very same numerals, the identical official statistics, that I have incorporated into an account of the taming of chance"; or again, that he "read the statistics of Engel or Quételet or Farr with indifference, divining with their aid the underlying laws of society that bind it in a totally nonstatistical necessity" (Hacking 1990: 8, 132). Marx, I would say, did not allow the statistical work of Quételet to damage the notion of necessitarian laws at which he had arrived independently.

[13] Marx immediately adds this elusive consolation: "But it can shorten and lessen the birth-pangs," thereby opening up a range of potentialities for intervention.

capitalist development is such as to bring it about" (1983: 209–10). We have indeed found that both Engels and Marx frequently admit their inability to arrive at a *specific* prediction in any particular case with respect to the collapse of capitalism, a concession that ought to be a matter for congratulation. In approaching predictions with regard to the course of real wages under capitalism, Engels himself came to allow a degree of "elasticity," thereby weakening the original insistence on a downward trend (above, p. 322). More significantly, he himself in notes to the manuscript *Dialectics of Nature* represented the testing of hypotheses against the evidence as the essence of "scientific" procedure: "The form of development of natural science . . . is the *hypothesis*. A new fact is observed which makes impossible the previous method of explaining the facts belonging to the same group. From this moment onwards new methods of explanation are required – at first based on only a limited number of facts and observations. Further observational material weeds out these hypotheses, doing away with some, and correcting others, until finally the law is established in a pure form" (1873–82; MECW 25: 520). The case for the testing of hypotheses is argued more generally, "since all human knowledge develops in a much twisted curve; and in the historical sciences also . . . theories displace one another."[14] Nonetheless, when Hunt, with this "proto-Popperian" stance in minds, defends Engels against the charge that he was "that narrow-minded, mechanistic architect of dialect materialism which twentieth-century Soviet ideology so exalted" (Hunt 2009: 365–6), he perhaps overlooked that this admirable open-mindedness in principle renders meaningless the "inevitability" of a final communist outcome upon which Engels also firmly insisted, even if he was unable to fix the date. Engels, it seems, wanted to have it both ways.

E. On the Late Formulation of Historical Materialism

Our studies of constitutional and welfare reform in Chapters Four and Five have brought to light the heavy weight that was placed on the political dimension, the so-called superstructure, in the representation of the evolution of capitalist development. This orientation clashes with any strong statement of the doctrine of historical materialism, and in fact in late correspondence Engels insisted that the materialist view had always been the qualified proposition that the "determining factor in history, is, in the final analysis, the production and reproduction of actual

---

[14] In *Anti-Dühring*, we find an equally impressive insistence on the relativity of knowledge and a rejection of any finality of outcome: "Mankind . . . finds itself faced with a contradiction: on the one hand, it has to gain an exhaustive knowledge of the world system in all its interrelations; and on the other hand, because of the nature both of men and of the world system, this task can never be completely fulfilled. But this contradiction . . . is also the main lever of all intellectual advance, and finds its solution continuously, day by day, in the endless progressive development of humanity" (MECW 25: 35–6). Again, "the knowledge which has an unconditional claim to truth is realised in a series of relative errors; neither the one nor the other can be fully realised except through an unending duration of human existence" (80). All this is in accordance with the principle of scientific progress; also see O'Neill (1996) and Hunt (2009: 366).

life. More than that was never maintained either by Marx or myself. Now if someone distorts this by declaring the economic moment to be the only determining factor, he changes that proposition into a meaningless, abstract, ridiculous piece of jargon" (to Joseph Bloch, 21–2 September 1890; MECW 49: 34). He refers in justification to some of Marx's original statements in *The Eighteenth Brumaire*, and in *Capital*,[15] and to the "most exhaustive" treatment of which he was aware, namely that provided in his own *Anti-Dühring* and his *Ludwig Feuerbach* (MECW 49: 36; see Chapter Six, p. 300).[16] While condemning "some younger writers" – including some "more recent 'Marxists'" – who "attribute more importance to the economic aspect than is its due," he accepted the blame (along with Marx) for having encouraged their faulty position: "We had to stress this leading principle in the face of opponents who denied it, and we did not always have the time, space or opportunity to do justice to the other factors that interacted upon each other."[17]

Now *Anti-Dühring*, already in the first edition of 1878, indeed formulates the materialist conception of history in the qualified manner Engels describes. Thus the playing out of events since the 1830s had led to a realization that

all past history was the history of class struggle; that these warring classes of society are always the products of the modes of production and of exchange – in a word, of the *economic* conditions of their time; that the economic structure of society always furnishes the real basis, starting from which we can alone work out the *ultimate* (emphasis added) explanation of the whole superstructure of juridical and political institutions as well as of the religious, philosophical, and other ideas of a given historical period. (MECW 25: 26)

Furthermore,

The materialist conception of history starts from the proposition that the production and, next to production, the exchange of things produced, is the basis of all social structure; that in every society that has appeared in history, the manner in which wealth is distributed and society divided into classes or estates is dependent upon what is produced, how it is produced, and how the products are exchanged. From this point of view the *final causes* (emphasis added) of all social changes and political revolutions are to be sought, not in men's brains, not in men's better insight into eternal truth and justice, but in changes in the modes of production and exchange. They are to be sought, not in the *philosophy*, but in the *economics* of each particular epoch. (254)

---

[15] These references are further expanded in a letter to Conrad Schmidt, in the light of criticism of the doctrine by Paul Barth (1890). *The Eighteenth Brumaire*, Engels there pointed out, "is devoted almost exclusively to the particular role played by political struggles and events – needless to say within the framework of their *general* dependence on economic conditions" (27 October 1890; MECW 49: 63). As for *Capital 1*, examples are drawn from the discussion there of factory legislation, "a political act," and of the history of the bourgeoisie, which Engels designates as "Chapter 24"; he probably intended Part VIII as a whole (see editorial suggestion 578 n. 78). (On this letter, see further Chapter Four, p. 209.) Bernstein expressed a high opinion of this letter (1993 [1899]: 16).

[16] See also the references to his own formulations in a letter to W. Borgius, 25 January 1894 (MECW 50: 267).

[17] Engels added the assurance that when one was dealing with applications to specific historical episodes, "there was no possibility of error" (MECW 49: 36).

There is, then, nothing newly added, only an insistence on getting the record straight, when Engels insisted in 1890 upon economic causes as "leading" or "determining," reflecting what in 1878 had been designated the "ultimate" or "final" explanation, with no intention of excluding – in Bernstein's convincing terms – other "attendant causes, of another kind, causes of the second and third degree [such that] the longer the series of such causes the more limited, both qualitatively and quantitatively, is the determining force of the ultimate causes" (1993 [1899]: 14–15). Rather, the true significance of Engels's late representation of the doctrine extends beyond allowance for political and other influences while insisting on the economic influence as "determining" factor, and even beyond allowance for "other factors that interacted upon each other." The novelty lies in an insistence upon mutual interaction between political and economic factors, in effect between superstructure and base. This position is to be found in his letter to Schmidt of 27 October 1890:

What all these gentlemen lack is dialectics. All they ever see is cause on the one hand and effect on the other. But what they fail to see is that this is an empty abstraction, that in the real world such metaphysically polar opposites exist only in a crisis, that instead the whole great process takes place solely and entirely in the form of interplay – if of very unequal forces of which the economic trend is by far the strongest, the oldest and the most vital – and that here nothing is absolute and everything relative. So far as they are concerned, Hegel might never have existed. (MECW 49: 63)

In fact, in Socialism: Utopian and Scientific, Engels had already expressed the general methodological principle that "cause and effect are conceptions which only hold good in their application to individual cases; but as soon as we consider the individual cases in their general connection with the universe as a whole, they run into each other, and they become confounded when we contemplate that universal action and reaction in which causes and effects are eternally changing places, so that what is effect here and now will be cause there and then, and vice versa" (1892 [1880]; MECW 24: 301). In a late letter to Franz Mehring regarding historical materialism, he congratulated Mehring for having himself provided an excellent formulation of the doctrine in his Die Lessing-Legende (1919 [1893]), complaining of the "undialectical conception of cause and effect as rigidly opposite poles, quite regardless of any interaction. The ['ideologists'] forget, often almost deliberately, that an historical element, once it is ushered into the world by other, ultimately economic, causes, will react in its turn, and may exert a reciprocal influence on its environment and even upon its own causes. Cf. Barth, for example, on the priestly caste and religion" (14 July 1893; MECW 50: 165).

Engels in this letter accepts the blame as "senior culprit" – doubtless intending senior living culprit – for not making the case for the economic influence as strong as it might have been. The case would have been strengthened had the expositors emphasized the psychological fact that thought processes tended to remain in the realm of the mind and so were inherently biased against tracing "political, legal, and other ideological conceptions" to their true source in economic reality

(MECW 50: 164–5). More important is an attempt the following year, in his letter to Borgius, to reduce the nihilistic effect of the allowances regarding mutual causality. Here Engels elaborates the nature of causal interdependence he intended by the proposition that although "[p]olitical, juridical, philosophical, religious, literary, artistic, etc., development is based on economic development . . . each of these also reacts upon the others and upon the economic basis," which "is not to say that the economic situation is the *cause* and that it *alone* is *active* while everything else is mere passive effect, but rather that there is reciprocal action based, *in the final analysis*, on economic necessity which invariably prevails. The state, for instance, exerts its influence through protective tariffs, free trade, good or bad fiscal systems" (25 January 1894; 265). In brief, "the effect of the economic situation is not, as is sometimes conveniently supposed, automatic; rather, men make their own history, but in a given environment by which they are conditioned, and on the basis of extant and actual relations of which economic relations, no matter how much they may be influenced by others of a political and ideological nature, are ultimately the determining factor and represent the unbroken clue which alone can lead to comprehension" (266). Here the allowance for a degree of interplay between base and superstructure is combined with reiterated insistence on the base as the "ultimate" causal force at play "in the final analysis."

Rigby has observed that "Engels was . . . obliged to deny, at the end of his life, a reductionist version of historical materialism and to establish what he and Marx has 'intended' to say," adding that "[w]hether this was Marx's 'intent' is largely irrelevant. The point is that Engels offered a legitimate reading of Marx as a proponent of 'dialectical interaction'" (1987:185). But, in fact, one is hard pressed to cite formulations by Marx of the interdependence between base and superstructure that Engels intended.[18] An important methodological overview of *Capital* adopts rather a strong version of the undiluted doctrine. I have in mind Marx's approving citation of a Russian reviewer of *Capital 1* (I. I. Kaufmann), given in the Afterword to the Second German edition (1873).

To be noted first is the representation of historical development by Kaufmann as "a process of natural history," envisaged in strictly necessitarian terms:

Marx only troubles himself about one thing: to show, by rigid scientific investigation, the necessity of successive determinate orders of social conditions, and to establish, as impartially as possible, the facts that serve him for fundamental starting-points. For

---

[18] A passage in *Capital 3* qualifying the concept of economic base deserves mention. After formulating the standard materialist conception whereby "[t]he specific economic form, in which unpaid surplus labour is pumped out of direct producers, determines the relationship of rulers and ruled," Marx adds this statement: "This does not prevent the same economic basis – the same from the standpoint of its main conditions – due to innumerable different empirical circumstances, natural environment, racial relations, external historical influences, etc., from showing infinite variations and gradations in appearance, which can be ascertained only by analysis of the empirically given circumstances" (MECW 37: 777–8). However, this qualification does not assert a relationship of interdependence between political superstructure and economic base. In any event, Marx retained a strong version of economic base *in principle*, relegating the qualification to a secondary, descriptive, sphere.

this it is quite enough, if he proves, at the same time, both the necessity of the present order of things, and the necessity of another order into which the first must inevitably pass over; and this all the same, whether men believe or do not believe it, whether they are conscious or unconscious of it. Marx treats the social movement as a process of natural history, governed by laws not only independent of human will, consciousness and intelligence, but rather, on the contrary, determining that will, consciousness and intelligence.... [M]ost important of all is the rigid analysis of the series of successions, of the sequences and concatenations in which the different stages of such an evolution present themselves. (MECW 35: 18)[19]

Here the reviewer confirms Marx's rejection of economics as a science analogous to physics and chemistry – the concern is entirely with economic development rather than allocation – in favor of a biological analogy:

But it will be said...the general laws of economic life are one and the same, no matter whether they are applied to the present or the past. This Marx directly denies. According to him, such abstract laws do not exist.... On the contrary, in his opinion every historical period has laws of its own.... As soon as society has outlived a given period of development, and is passing over from one given stage to another, it begins to be subject to other laws. In a word, economic life offers us a phenomenon analogous to the history of evolution in other branches of biology.... The old economists misunderstood the nature of economic laws when they likened them to the laws of physics and chemistry.... A more thorough analysis of phenomena shows that social organisms differ among themselves as fundamentally as plants or animals.... [As a specific instance, Marx] denies that the law of population is the same at all times and places. He asserts, on the contrary, that every stage of development has its own law of population. (MECW 35: 18–19).

The citation then focuses, more generally, on Marx's concentration in *Capital* on capitalist development, the laws relevant to it, and its transformation, providing thereby an archetype for other possible investigations:

With the varying degree of development of productive power, social conditions and the laws governing them vary too. Whilst Marx set himself the task of following and explaining from this point of view the economic system established by the sway of capital, he is only formulating, in a strictly scientific manner, the aim that every accurate investigation into economic life must have.... The scientific value of such an inquiry lies in the disclosing of the special laws that regulate the origin, existence, development, death of a given social organism and its replacement by another and higher one. And it is this value that, in point of fact, Marx's book has. (MECW 35: 19)

In none of this is there even a hint of mutual interdependence between non-economic and economic factors. "Social conditions and the laws governing them" are determined by the "degree of development of productive power" in a one-way street.

---

[19] Marx points out that the reviewer's account appears after citation from his work of 1859. Nonetheless, he clearly accepted the account as valid for *Capital*, the main subject of the review.

The qualified view of the doctrine taking account of what Rigby terms "dialectical interaction" is Engels's late contribution. The problem created is that once mutual causality is allowed, even if the "ultimate" supremacy in some sense of "economic relations" is insisted upon, it becomes far from clear what precisely the doctrine amounts to. Carver has well expressed the problem: "Engels's defence of his 'materialistic interpretation of history' was analytically indeterminate and ultimately dogmatic, because interaction between base and superstructure was never distinguished from ultimate causation of the base" (1981: 67; see also Kolakowski 2005: 298–300 and Hunt 2009: 217).[20]

It deserves emphasis that in none of his late formal presentations, as distinct from his letters, does Engels spell out the new complexity. Even though he cites *Anti-Dühring* and *Ludwig Feuerbach* as providing the "most exhaustive treatment" of the doctrine known to him (above, p. 329), the statements of economic determinism in the second and third editions of *Anti-Dühring* do not differ from those of 1878, which omit mention of dialectic interdependence between base and superstructure.

Before turning to *Ludwig Feuerbach*, let us take note of the Notes and Fragments relating to Engels's incomplete manuscript *Dialectics of Nature* composed between 1873 and 1882).[21] As with Marx, we find rejected the notion of "eternal natural laws of society"; the Malthusian theory of population again provides the prime instance (MECW 25: 584).[22] Engels does not object to the biological analogy – a reference to the "complexity" of social development implies it; it is the unqualified transference from biology to society that he rejects, particularly the social relevance

---

[20] For an alternative view, which plays down the qualifications to the doctrine, see Bober (1965: 306–7).

[21] For insights into Engels's perspective on the natural sciences, see Lukács (1971 [1921]: 128–32), McLellan (1977: 69; 2007: 10–12), Stedman Jones (1982: 294–5), Carver (1983: 126, 151; 1989: 249; 1999: 17–36), Rabinbach (1992: 81–2), Benton (1996), Sayers (1996), Manicas (1999), O'Neill (1996), and Kolakowski (2005: 308–26, 328–30, 536–7). Hunley (1991: 47–64) offers a useful evaluation of an extensive secondary literature.

[22] A representative statement by Engels to the same effect is given in *Anti-Dühring*: Political economy "must first investigate the special laws of each individual stage in the evolution of production and exchange, and only when it has completed this investigation will it be able to establish the few quite general laws which hold good for production and exchange in general" (1875; MECW 25: 135–6). He illustrates "general laws" by reference to the general theory of money, but he neglects to mention Marx's designation of the problem of resource scarcity as a universal "natural law" (above, p. 319).

Engels, most interestingly, finds the origin of the allegedly fallacious idea of eternal social laws as originating in questionable ideas relating to society, first transferred to nature, and then transferred back to society:

The whole Darwinian theory of the struggle for existence is simply the transference from society to organic nature of Hobbes' theory of *bellum omnium contra omnes* and of the economic theory of competition, as well as the Malthusian theory of population. When once this feat has been accomplished (the unconditional justification for which, especially as regards the Malthusian theory, is still very questionable), it is very easy to transfer these theories back again from natural history to the history of society, and altogether too naïve to maintain that thereby these assertions have been proved as eternal natural laws of society. (MECW 25: 584)

of a Darwinian "struggle for existence": "it is absolutely childish to desire to sum up the whole manifold wealth of historical development and complexity in the meager and one-sided phrase 'struggle for existence.' That says less than nothing."[23]

Engels closes with an eminently clear summary of the standard Marxian perspective on the evolution of capitalism, with special reference to secular underconsumption (reflecting the restricted expansion of labor's income), and the consequential trade cycle characterized by recurring crises every ten years and entailing a destructive process that "restores the equilibrium" and this dispite mention elsewhere of the obsolescence of the cycle:

Finally, under the capitalist mode of production, production reaches such a high level that society can no longer consume the means of subsistence, enjoyment and development that have been produced, because for the great mass of producers access to these means is artificially and forcibly barred; and therefore every ten years a crisis restores the equilibrium by destroying not only the means of subsistence, enjoyment and development that have been produced, but also a great part of the productive forces themselves. (MECW 25: 584–5)

What can only very loosely be designated "the struggle for existence," in this reading, amounts to the protection of productive capacity by the abolition of capitalist organization: "Hence the so-called struggle for existence assumes *the* form: to *protect* the products and productive forces produced by bourgeois capitalist society against the destructive, ravaging effect of this capitalist social order, by taking control of social production and distribution out of the hands of the ruling capitalist class, which has become incapable of this function, and transferring it to the producing masses – and that is the socialist revolution" (585).[24]

Engels concludes more generally that "[t]he conception of history as a series of class struggles is already much richer in content and deeper than merely reducing it to weakly distinguished phases of the struggle for existence." The class-struggle conception itself, however, remains on the books. So too does the "necessary" outcome of the class struggle in the replacement of capitalism by communism. *Economic determinism is alive and well in the late public statements.*

[23] This position is rationalized in terms of man's distinctive activity as producer:

Let us accept for a moment the phrase "struggle for existence," for argument's sake. The most that the animal can achieve is to *collect*; man *produces*, he prepares the means of subsistence, in the widest sense of the words, which without him nature would not have produced. This makes impossible any unqualified transference of the laws of life in animal societies to human society. Production soon brings it about that the so-called struggle for existence no longer turns on pure means of existence, but on means of enjoyment and development. Here – where the means of development are socially produced – the categories taken from the animal kingdom are already totally inapplicable. (MECW 25: 584)

[24] On more specific matters we find that Engels does apply the struggle-for-existence principle, conspicuously regarding competition as manifested in competitive cost cutting: "He that falls is remorselessly cast aside. It is the Darwinian struggle of the individual for existence transferred from nature to society with intensified violence. The conditions of existence natural to the animal appear as the final term of human development" (*Anti-Dühring*; MECW 25: 260). For the general context of this affirmation, see Chapter Three (p. 162).

Another feature of Engels's perspective on Darwin's "epoch-making book" entails the undermining of the established notion of immutable species, "the previous basis for all regularity in biology," by setting out "from the widest existing basis of chance," namely "the infinite, accidental differences between individuals within a single species, differences which become accentuated until they break through the character of the species, and whose immediate causes even can be demonstrated only in extremely few cases (the material on chance occurrences accumulated in the meantime has suppressed and shattered the old idea of necessity)" (MECW 25: 501). Thus "[c]hance overthrows necessity, as conceived hitherto. The previous idea of necessity breaks down. To retain it means dictatorially to impose on nature as a law a human arbitrary determination that is in contradiction to itself and to reality." Now, this latter proposition, if extended to social development, might have put in question the necessitarian character of social process. But we must be cautious. In the first place, Engels was not rejecting out of hand the notion of necessitarian law in science, but rather "the previous idea of necessity," insisting on according some role to chance; and second, law is said to rule supreme in human affairs, although here too a role for chance is allowed.[25]

This is confirmed in *Ludwig Feuerbach*. The contrast between nature, governed by "blind, unconscious agencies acting upon one another, out of whose interplay the general law comes into operation" and human history, wherein "the actors are all endowed with consciousness," is here said to be of small consequence, because consciousness is more apparent than real in its effects; and although "accident" or "chance" reflecting the clash of wills appears to be decisive, in fact historical events are subject to "innate general laws" or "inner, hidden laws [which] only have to be discovered":

[T]his distinction, important as it is for historical investigation, particularly of individual epochs and events, cannot alter the fact that the course of history is governed by innate general laws. For here, too, on the whole, in spite of the consciously desired aims of all individuals, accident apparently reigns on the surface. What is desired happens but rarely; in the majority of instances the numerous desired ends cross and conflict with one another, or these ends themselves are from the outset impracticable or the means of attaining them are insufficient. Thus the conflicts of innumerable individual wills and individual actions in the domain of history lead to a state of affairs quite similar to that prevailing in the realm of unconscious nature. The ends of the actions are desired, but the results which actually follow from these actions are not desired; or when they do seem to correspond to the desired end, they ultimately have consequences quite other than those desired. Historical events thus appear on the whole to be likewise governed by chance. But wherever on the surface chance holds sway, it is always governed by inner, hidden laws and these laws only have to be discovered. (1888; MECW 26: 387)[26]

---

[25] See above notes 11 and 12.

[26] A formulation of the same general theme by Marx appears in the *Grundrisse* – unknown, of course, to Engels (MECW 28: 131–2).

Kolakowski allows that although Engels's theme "is in harmony with many of Marx's statements," nonetheless "the philosophical bases of Marx's Marxism" are incompatible "with

Engels is in essence formulating a version of the so-called invisible hand when he concludes that "the many individual wills active in history for the most part produce results quite other than those desired – often quite the opposite; . . . their motives, therefore, in relation to the total result are likewise of only secondary importance" (388).[27] All in all, the insistence upon necessitarian "laws" of development remains intact.

We do encounter an acknowledgment that "even in our modern era, with its gigantic means of production and communication, the state is not an independent domain with independent development, but one whose existence as well as development is to be explained *in the last resort* by the economic conditions of life of society" (MECW 26: 391; emphasis added). However, Engels goes no further by way of qualification in his important summary of the doctrine (388–97). The acknowledgment is far from a recognition of "dialectical interaction" between base and superstructure upon which he himself insisted in late correspondence.

F. On the Behavioral Assumptions

The qualifications to the doctrine of historical determinism emerging in correspondence of the 1890s did not, I have concluded, leave a mark on Engels's formal texts. The doctrine was, however, already under threat much earlier from another direction, for we have encountered numerous instances of Engels's own presumption that when it comes to behavior an economic determinant is frequently entirely inoperative. Appeal to ethnicity provides a key instance. Thus, for example, France and England differ in that in England alone universal suffrage once granted could not possibly be retracted: "No government would dare to touch it," anymore than it would dare to reintroduce agricultural protection: "The immense laughter of the whole nation would hurl [the minister] down" (Chapter Four, p. 195). There is also Marx's amusing allusion to "excitable Frenchmen" as a determining factor in

---

belief in general laws of nature having, as particular applications, the history of mankind and also the rules of thought, identified with psychological or physiological regularities of the brains. Whereas Engels, broadly speaking, believed that man could be explained in terms of natural history and the laws of evolution to which he was subject, and which he was capable of knowing in themselves, Marx's view was that nature as we know it is an extension of man, an organ of practical activity," meaning that "[w]e cannot contemplate the subject in itself, free from historical involvement; the *cogito* is an impossibility" (2005: 328–9). None of this, in my view, diminishes the significance of Marx's approval of Kaufmann's representation of his position as one perceiving historical development as a process of natural history. It is, however, unclear whether Kolakowski himself goes so far as to maintain that "the development of society and above all its revolutionary transformation would be the effect of 'natural laws,' which is the opposite of Marx's view," or whether he is ascribing this view to certain "Marxist critics" (334).

27 An interesting application of the general principle is given in *Dialectics of Nature*: "Let us not . . . flatter ourselves overmuch on account of our human victories over nature," having in mind "unforeseen effects" of productive activities, deforestation being a prime instance of neglect of the laws of nature (MECW 25: 460).

French industrial relations (note 26). A striking illustration involves the insistence on a wage scale – whether under capitalism or communism – to reflect "natural" differentials, again a position shared with Marx (Chapter Three, p. 158). At no time does Engels attempt to avoid the conclusion that character is to this extent *not* reducible to economic pressures. By way of contrast, recall that Adam Smith had sought to account for apparent character differences in terms of occupational loci (see Hollander 1977), very much in the spirit of "historical materialism" in its unqualified version.[28]

A further illustration of my theme is provided by the immensely impressive prediction of world war mentioned at the close of Chapter Five. Unfortunately, no proper attempt is made to dovetail it with the trends that relate to evolving capitalism. We have to this extent the introduction of a *deus ex machina* or appeal to a massive "disturbing cause." This is not to say that no attempt was made to appreciate antecedent circumstances. After all, at about this time, though in a different context, Engels insisted that "[t]here is no point in complaining about historical events. On the contrary, the problem is to comprehend their causes and hence also their effects" (1885; Preface to "Karl Marx before the Cologne Jury," MECW *26*: 307). In the case at hand, however, considerable weight is placed on the attitudes of the aristocratic Prussian officer class (1887; "Introduction to Borkheim," MECW *26*: 450). In a companion piece this weighting is confirmed, though extended to France: "We find ourselves face to face with a terrible danger. We are threatened by a war in which those who loathe it and have only common interests – the French proletariat and the German proletariat – will be forced to butcher each other. What is the real cause of this state of things? It is militarism, it is the introduction of the Prussian military system in all the major countries of the Continent" (1887; Letter to the Organising Committee of the International Festival in Paris, MECW *26*: 443). "Patriotic frenzy," as exploited by Bismarck, plays a part in "The Role of Force in History" (written 1887–8; MECW *26*: 503–4). None of this addresses the features of an evolving capitalism in a global context responsible for the danger, which is the least that one expects from a sophisticated expositor of historical materialism. Most surprising is the absence of concerted attention to empire building as a feature, notwithstanding reference elsewhere to the seventeenth-century and eighteenth-century experience of commercial wars originating in colonial expansion (*Anti-Dühring*; MECW *25*: 260), and keen awareness of contemporary colonial activity.[29]

Engels's position on science is tangentially relevant. Thus he wrote famously that "from the very beginning the origin and development of the sciences has been

---

[28] In the spirit of Adam Smith, Bernstein ascribed the perceived intellectual contrast between German and English workers not to temperament, but to "a difference in conditions of life" (1921 [1918]: 276).

[29] See, for example, the letter to Kautsky, 12 September 1882 (cited Chapter Five, p. 255). I owe to J. E. King the observation that Kautsky "offered probably the first clear economic interpretation of imperialism by any Marxist" in his article "Tongking" (1884), on which see Howard and King (1989: 92, 104).

determined by production" (*Dialectics of Nature*; MECW 25: 465). However, this is to exaggerate the demand-induced incentives, because in the *Dialectics* itself, and also in *Anti-Dühring*, the detailed account of the progress of the sciences turns rather on "supply-side" considerations internal to the scientific venture and unrelated to the demands of production (Rosenberg 1974: 726–7).[30]

But we must be cautious. The full story is not as one sided as the foregoing instances suggest. Thus we note Engels's references to "tradition" when evaluating prospects for the transition to communism in the British case, and the element of wishful thinking in the assertion that tradition, though "a great retarding force," was "sure to be broken down; and thus religion will be no lasting safeguard to capitalist society" (Chapter Four, p. 224).[31] "Tradition" is here treated as a dependent variable. Indeed, even the characteristics of the "Anglo-Saxon race" are at one point said to be subject to evolutionary pressures (to Sorge, 16 January 1895; MECW 50: 422).

What, though, of the British proletariat's bourgeois outlook as expressed, for example, in the letter to Marx of 8 March 1858? (Cited in Chapter Four, p. 205.) Here we do encounter explicit appeal to economic forces to explain behavior, the lament closing with the aside that "[f]or a nation which exploits the entire world this is, of course, justified to some extent." This suggests that, with the breakdown of British world domination, bourgeois behavior would be corrected. The later article "The English Elections" of 1874 makes a similar projection (Chapter Four, p. 206; Chapter Five, p. 254). Similarly, the reliance placed on the prospect of secular depression, imminent massive immigration, and even world war to solve the dilemma presented by improving working-class conditions under capitalism and corresponding *embourgeoisement* silently takes for granted an economic base to behavior patterns. It is difficult to discern a consistent perspective.

G. A Final Summation

Schumpeter unfairly represented Engels, solely on the basis of brief grave-side remarks (MECW 24: 467–8), as giving either an erroneous or a "piteously trivial" account of Marx's intentions regarding the doctrine of historical materialism (1950: 11).[32] Engels showed himself to be far more sophisticated in his interpretation of

---

[30] Even where Engels insists on an economic base, as in the case of applied military research, he does not necessarily get the relevant prediction right. Thus in *Anti-Dühring* he spells out the economic forces that dictated the development of the great battleship, but then he proceeds – on the basis of so-called inherent dialectical laws of motion – to predict its imminent demise in consequence of the newly developed torpedo (MECW 25: 159–61).

[31] On Engels's strong tendency to wishful thinking, including his perspective on working-class attitudes, see Wilde (1999: 203, 209).

[32] Schumpeter's reading of Engels's eulogy is wholly misleading. Schumpeter rightly denied that Marx ever maintained the view that "men are, consciously or unconsciously, wholly or primarily, actuated by economic motives," but he proceeds to assert that "[e]ven his friends Engels, at the open grave of Marx, defined the theory in question as meaning precisely that

Marx, and a fortiori in formulating his own reading of the doctrine. Nonetheless, we have also seen that his late recognition of a mutual dependence between base and superstructure did not leave a mark on his formal writings; thus although he opened the door for a serious undermining of the materialist doctrine, he himself failed to carry the argument through effectively. We have also noticed a challenge to the doctrine of long standing – inadequately recognized in the literature – namely that posed by Engels's frequent appeals to national and natural character differentials in accounting for the course of events.[33] How far he himself was aware of the extensiveness of such allowances is an open question.[34] In any event, the commonly encountered opinion that Engels was more of an "economic determinist" than Marx is hardly convincing, as also proves to be the case with regard to their respective positions on Russia (see Appendix C).

Even where differences can be shown to exist between Marx and Engels, there is no reason to credit the charge of deliberate or even unintentional distortion of Marxian doctrine. In any specific instance Engels may have been elaborating his own position with no intention of ascribing it to Marx.[35] This is true, in particular, of the descriptive accounts of a new empirical reality given in Engels's editorial notes to *Capital 3*, as well as in the Supplement to that volume, particularly a perceived superannuation of the cyclical pattern (see Chapter Five, p. 274). It is also true of topics left in abeyance by Marx, which Engels analyzed in some detail; the chapter on the effects on the profit rate of capital turnover provides a conspicuous example (MECW *37*: 73–80). Each instance should be considered in its own right, with credit accorded Engels for adopting an original position whenever this can be shown, and certainly without treachery entering the picture.

The case that Engels deserves to be taken seriously in his own right is greatly reinforced by his exceptional contribution in the 1840s to the foundations of the entire Marxian enterprise, entailing not only the "vision" but also the provision of some of the building blocks, as I have demonstrated in the first chapter. Thereafter,

individuals and groups are swayed primarily by economic motives" (1950: 11). In fact, Engels said nothing of motivation in his brief account of Marx's "discovery," to the effect that "the degree of economic development attained by a given people or during a given epoch form the foundation upon which the state institutions, the legal conceptions, art, and even the ideas on religion, of the people concerned have been evolved, and in the light of which they must, therefore, be explained, instead of *vice versa*, as had hitherto been the case" (17 March 1883; MECW *24*: 467–8).

[33] We have seen that the challenge emerges also in the Marx texts (above, pp. 336–7). In addition to his appeal to natural differences with respect to labor note his treating "racial relations" on a par with the "natural environment" (above, note 18).

[34] Adam Smith provides an earlier example of an author who does not gather together the qualifications made piecemeal, and trace out explicitly the implications flowing from the accumulated effect of those qualifications. Thus Viner wrote of "the extent to which Smith acknowledged exceptions to the doctrine of a natural harmony in the economic order even when left to its natural course. Smith, himself, never brought these together; but if this is done, they make a surprisingly comprehensive list" (1958 [1927]): 228).

[35] For a perspective similar to my own, see Vygodskii (2002: 81–2).

his positive contribution to theoretical economics is less impressive; it may be regretted that he should have devoted his huge energies to a defense of the doctrine of surplus value often in its least defensible form, with the propagandist objective of affording the working class a simplified and easily understood creed, an objective he himself was the first to admit (Chapter Six, pp. 303–4). It is indeed an exquisite irony that his most impressive applications of theory relate not to strictly Marxian analysis but to the failure of socialist "utopians" to appreciate the economics of resource allocation.

EPILOGUE

The Immediate Legacy

Engels at one time thought of both Eduard Bernstein and Karl Kautsky as promising heirs, the former having served the cause well as editor of *Der Sozialdemokrat* from 1881 to 1890, the latter as editor of *Die Neue Zeit* from 1883 and in the forefront in the bitter dispute with those prepared to compromise with Bismarckian state socialism. Engels advised and contributed to both journals and considered their editors suitable for the task of preparing a fair copy of the "fourth volume" of *Capital*, later known as *Theories of Surplus Value*.[1] He was also happy to rely on Bernstein to provide a full response to Paul Barth's criticisms in 1890 of historical materialism (see MECW *49*: 63). A brief comparison between the positions of Engels and those of his younger colleagues will serve to sharpen our comprehension of Engels.

A. Engels and Bernstein

In his Preface to the first English translation of *The Preconditions of Socialism*,[2] Bernstein advised that his book "can, all in all, be regarded as an exposition of the theoretical and political tendencies of the German social democratic revisionists" (1961 [1909]: viii).[3] As for doctrinal matters, he feared from the outset that he

---

[1] Engels to Kautsky, 28 January 1889 (MECW *48*: 257–9). Because Bernstein was overworked and unwell, the task would have to fall to Kautsky. This plan did not materialize, and if Engels did not appoint Kautsky one of his literary executors (along with Bernstein and Bebel) as once planned, it was because of Kautsky's failure to produce a "fair copy" in the stipulated time (see Engels to Laura Lafargue, 17 December 1894; MECW *50*: 387). The work was published by Kautsky over the period 1905–10.

[2] Two English translations are available: One is by E. C. Harvey in 1909, republished in 1961, under the title *Evolutionary Socialism*; the other is by H. Tudor in 1993. I cite from the latter.

[3] Much of the material relates to British and European conditions generally. Its substance appeared in a series of articles in 1896 in *Die Neue Zeit*, where Bernstein argued for a revision in the program of the German Social Democratic Party. Henderson (1976 *2*: 731–2) observes that Bernstein's arguments resembles those of Karl Höchberg, who Engels condemned

might be misunderstood; he explained that "the *further development and elaboration of Marxist doctrine must begin with criticism of it*"; for "[t]he duty of the disciples" consisted in isolating and removing defects in the theory, not "perpetually repeating the words of the masters" (1993 [1899]: 28).[4] At the same time, he insisted that recognition of the defects "does not necessarily mean the destruction of the doctrine." The key point is the proposal to recognize the phenomenon of surplus but without recourse to the strict labor theory – very much in the spirit, in our day, of Lange or Robinson or Sraffa or Morishima (see Hollander 2008: 486–7). In this way nothing is lost, whereas key features of economic reality – considered in the aggregate – might be captured: "*Whether or not Marx's theory of value is correct has no bearing whatsoever on the demonstration of surplus labour. It is in this respect not a demonstrative argument but merely a means of analysis and illustration*" (1993 [1899]: 52).[5]

Now Bernstein asserted, though without supporting evidence, that "[t]he surplus product is increasing everywhere; but the ratio of its increase to the increase of wages-capital is, at present, declining in the most advanced countries" (Bernstein 1993 [1899]: 53). He represents as excessively "narrow" Marx's perception of the industrial and mercantile functions to be recognized as responsible for the creation of social surplus, by his exclusion of several that are "by their nature indispensable to the social life of modern times" (54). He also firmly rejected the Marxian identification of the rates of surplus value and of exploitation: "The labour theory of value is misleading above all in that it appears again and again as a yardstick for the exploitation of the worker by the capitalist, an error furthered by amongst other things, the characterisation of the rate of surplus value as the rate of exploitation" (55). To the contrary, "[n]owadays . . . we find the best-placed workers, members of the 'labour aristocracy,' precisely in those trades with a very high rate of surplus value, and the most infamously exploited workers in those with a very low rate" (55–6).

Several other original Marxian empirical evaluations were challenged. Thus Bernstein refuted the notion that the average size of industrial establishments had increased:

If the relentless advance of technology and the centralisation of businesses in an increasing number of branches of industry is a fact the significance of which even obdurate reactionaries can hardly ignore nowadays, it is a no-less-well-established fact that in a whole range of branches of industry small and medium-sized businesses prove to be quite capable of surviving alongside large companies. Also, there is in industry

---

as peddling "petty-bourgeois socialism" (Engels to Bebel, 16 December 1879; MECW 45: 431).

    For Bernstein's overall position, see also Schumpeter (1950: 346–7), Gay (1952: 160–5), Cole (1956: 276–96), Angel (1961: 177–262), Tudor (1988, 1993), Howard and King (1989: 71–7), Steger (1997), Kolakowski (2005: 433–46), and McLellan (2007: 23–6).

[4] See Chapter Two, p. 120 and note 49 for certain of his theoretical objections.

[5] See also Bernstein (1901: 372–4), cited in Howard and King (1989: 75).

no pattern of development that holds equally for all branches. Companies which are completely mechanised remain as small and medium-sized businesses, while branches of the arts and crafts, which were thought to be safe for small businesses, are all of a sudden, irretrievably lost to big business. (1993 [1899]: 69)[6]

More generally, it was "quite wrong to suppose that the present development shows a relative or indeed absolute decrease in the number of property-owners" (61; also 200). Logic supported the facts of the case, for otherwise it would be difficult to account for the absorption of the increasing flow of goods due to technical progress (61–2). He also rejected the related theme of labor impoverishment, the "completely out-dated idea that the realisation of socialism depends on an increasingly rapid reduction in the number of the very rich and on the growing impoverishment of the masses" (168). He refers to "[t]he struggle of trade unionists for an improvement in their living standard," and he observes that "[a]lthough the shorter working day does not directly cause a reduction in the work done for the current wage – it is well known that in many cases the opposite happens – it does indirectly lead to an increase in demands for a better standard of living for the workers, and so makes a rise in wages necessary" (136–7). Bernstein was scarcely diverging from Engels in his later writings on real-wage trends, as we have seen in Chapter Five.[7]

Specifically addressing some of Engels's late formulations in the editorial notes to *Capital 3* (on which matter see Chapter Six, pp. 281–3), Bernstein insisted that "[n]o signs of a worldwide economic crash of unprecedented violence have been detected, nor can the improvement of trade between crises be character-ized as particularly short-lived" (1993 [1899]: 83–4). Indeed, the joint question arose, "(1) whether the enormous geographical expansion of the world market in conjunction with the extraordinary reduction in the time required for transport and the transmission of news have not so increased the possibilities of *level-ling out* disturbances, and (2) whether the enormously increased wealth of the European industrial states in conjunction with the elasticity of the modern credit system and the rise of industrial cartels have not so limited the *reactive force* of local or individual disturbances on the general state of business that, at least for some time, general trade crises similar to the earlier ones are to be regarded as unlikely" (84). On the whole, it was "impossible to decide a priori the ultimate relation of these forces to one another, or their development" (96); but "[u]nless

---

[6] It has recently been asserted that the prediction according to which "[t]he market was in irreversible long-run decline . . . lay at the heart of Eduard Bernstein's revisionist challenge to the official position of the Second International" (Howard and King 2008: 217). My passage suggests a far more complex position.

[7] There is a further point of contact. Bernstein had maintained in an earlier publication that while real wages were improving absolutely, if not relatively, labor was subject to increasing insecurity (1893 [1890]: 134–5). Engels had similarly objected to the 1891 draft of the German Social Democratic Programme that the trade union movement "will possibly check the *increase of misery* to a certain extent. However, what *certainly* does increase is the *insecurity of existence*" (Chapter Five, p. 260).

unforeseen *external* events bring about a general crisis . . . there is no compelling reason to conclude, on purely economic grounds, that such a crisis is imminent. Local and partial recessions are unavoidable. Thanks to the present organisation and expansion of the world market, and thanks particularly to the great *expansion in food production*, a general stagnation is not unavoidable. . . . Perhaps nothing has contributed so much to the mitigation of business crises, or to the prevention of their increase, as the fall in rents and food prices" (96–7).[8] Nonetheless, Bernstein was fully aware of Engels's own uncertainties regarding the future cyclical pattern (spelled out in Chapter Seven, p. 334), insisting only that the question still remained unanswered (83).

As for the question of welfare improvement, Bernstein drew heavily on Marx himself, referring to the recognition in *Capital* of the "physical and moral regeneration" of the Lancashire textile workers as a result of the Factory Act of 1847, which "suggests not hopelessness but capability for improvement in the condition of the worker" (1993 [1899]: 196). Indeed, "the legislation described has been not weakened but improved and made more general since 1866 when this was written, and has further been supplemented by laws and institutions working in the same direction." Take note of Bernstein's citation of a passage by Marx in *The Civil War in France* (1871), where he maintained (as Bernstein accurately interpreted it) that "the movement, the series of processes, is everything, while in comparison any goal fixed in detail before the event is immaterial" (192).[9]

Bernstein also reminded his critics how far Engels and Marx had moved from the early radicalism Bernstein found in the *Communist Manifesto* based on the prospect "of an immanent collapse of bourgeois society" (1993 [1899]: 1).[10] An illegitimate short-circuiting of the time required by the evolution of modern society had been "recognised without reservation by Friedrich Engels, the co-author of the *Manifesto*, in his preface to *The Class War in France*" (2; on this matter, see Chapter Four, pp. 213–14). Again, "[i]n 1872 Marx and Engels stated in their preface to the new edition of *The Communist Manifesto* that the Paris Commune in particular had proved that 'the working class cannot simply lay hold of the ready-made state machinery and wield it for their own purposes.' And in 1895, Friedrich Engels

---

[8] Gneuss emphasizes that, in all this, it is not merely a questioning of *facts* that is at issue, but a questioning of the "laws" of historical development, that is, the doctrine of historical materialism itself (1962: 35–8). Engels's letters to Bloch, Schmidt, and Borgius qualifying the doctrine (see Chapter Seven, pp. 328–31) were published in 1903 in *Dokumente des Sozialismus*, which was edited by Bernstein.

[9] For the passage in question (MECW 22: 335), see Chapter Three (p. 159); also Chapter Four (p. 200).

Bernstein also remarks on the "greatest similarity to the federalism of Proudhon" exhibited by Marx's decentralist remarks on the communal constitution (see Chapter Four, note 34). Perhaps so, but not to be neglected is the presumption of central control.

[10] "Nevertheless, Bernstein does recognize Engels's reference in 1895 (see Chapter Four, p. 213) "to the fact that the *Communist Manifesto* has 'proclaimed the winning of universal suffrage, of democracy, as one of the first and most important tasks of the militant proletariat" (1993 [1899]: 4).

explained in detail, in his preface to *The Class Struggles*, that the time for surprise political attacks, or 'revolutions carried through by small conscious minorities at the head of unconscious masses' had now passed" (1993 [1899]: 3, also 152). Indeed, "so thoroughly convinced" was Engels "that tactics geared to a catastrophe have had its day that he considers *a revision* to *abandon them* to be due even in the Latin countries where tradition is much more favourable to them than in Germany" (4). The conditions of class war had been transformed in Engels's own judgment.[11]

It has been said that the circular letter of September 1879 (Chapter Four, p. 220), sent by Engels to leaders of the Social Democratic Party, constituted a "major programmatic statement against opportunism or what would later be called reformism or revisionism," and this with Bernstein in mind (Nimtz 2000: 258). Certainly the letter lambasts Bernstein – one of a trio of Zürich journalists proposing a new Party newspaper that would be opposed to "political radicalism" and "adopt a line that is socialist on principle" (Bernstein, cited in MECW 45: 398) – as "too moderate" (401). By calling for "an influx of supporters from the ranks of the educated and propertied classes" especially as Reichstag members (cited on p. 403), the Zürich trio also apparently denied the merits of "a workers' party." This policy Engels rejected, referring to the *Communist Manifesto* where entry of people from the ruling class was to be tolerated subject to their commitment to the "militant proletariat" (407). Furthermore,"[a]t the founding of the International we expressly formulated the battle cry: The emancipation of the working class must be achieved by the working class itself" (408, citing Marx, "Provisional Rules," October 1864; MECW 20: 14). Engels accordingly called for the resignation or dismissal from office of Bernstein and other Party leaders if it was indeed their position "to combat the party's proletarian character" (403). He closed in like terms: "If the new party organ is to adopt a policy that corresponds to the opinions of these gentlemen, if it is bourgeois and not proletarian, then all we could do – much though we might regret it – would be publicly to declare ourselves opposed to it and abandon the solidarity with which we have hitherto represented the German party abroad. But we hope it won't come to *that*" (408).

Now Engels was not engaged here in a call to arms and revolution, as a casual reading might suggest. He does cite the Zürich trio as applauding the Party for "showing that it does not wish to pursue the path of forcible, bloody revolution, but rather . . . to tread the path of legality, i.e., of reform" (MECW 45: 404). But he himself admitted (above, p. 228) that Social Democratic voters "have sense enough not to break their heads against a wall and attempt a 'bloody revolution' with the odds of one to ten"; he insisted only that that all options should be left open, and that Social Democrats not "*deny* themselves all chance of exploiting some violent upheaval abroad, a sudden wave of revolutionary fervour engendered thereby."

---

[11] Gneuss observes that "in his address to the Stuttgart congress of the SPD [1898], Bernstein referred explicitly to Engels's Preface to clear himself from the charge of heresy" (1962: 35). The Foreword to *The Preconditions* comprises this address.

A mild alternative is also proposed when responding to the Zürich trio's declaration that although they had no wish "to relinquish our party and our programme . . . we shall have enough to do for years to come if we concentrate our whole strength, our entire energies, on the attainment of certain immediate objectives which must in any case be won before there can be any thought of realising more ambitious aspirations" (cited on p. 405), which is Bernstein's trademark philosophy. Engels merely proposed participation in polemic, that is, in "resolute political opposition . . . laying stress on ambitious goals which are calculated to frighten off the bourgeoisie," rather than have the party "devote all its strength and energies to those petty-bourgeois stop-gap reforms which provide new props for the old social order and which might, perhaps, transform the ultimate catastrophe into a gradual, piecemeal and, as far as possible, peaceable process of dissolution" (406). Considering the conspicuous omission of a call to actual revolutionary activity, we see that "ultimate catastrophe" has the flavor of wishful thinking.

Given the extensive common ground, with respect to welfare improvement in particular, it is all the more important to reiterate that Engels sought to provide assurances that what progress had been achieved could not be maintained in the future, considering the prospect of increasing foreign industrial competition and massive immigration that I spelled out in Chapter Five. In addition, though, his ideal for the future differed wholly from Bernstein's, a matter properly emphasized by Tudor (1993: xxvi–xxviii). This latter contrast requires particular attention, for Lichtheim maintains that Engels by 1895 "had fully accepted the democratic viewpoint," and Sowell and Carver ascribe to Marx and Engels a fully fledged democratic perspective of the nineteenth-century liberal variety (see Prolegomena, p. 18). Now for this to be the case, we would have to believe that Engels had abandoned the entire concept of a proletarian "dictatorship," accepting the possibility that a majority of working-class voters might refuse to support a communist program designed to dismantle – not merely reform or modify – the private-property system or, more generally, might vote a proletarian government out of office. However, we have seen that Engels's support for universal suffrage was conditional upon the existence of a "reliable" workers' party (Chapter Four, p. 204). He was certainly troubled by continued manifestations in the early 1890s of labor's unreliability (Chapter Four, pp. 223–4), yet he took it on faith that sooner or later "revolutionary"-minded parliamentary proletarian majorities prepared to implement a communist program would emerge in Britain and on the Continent. Sympathetic though he was toward Engels, even Hobsbawm nonetheless represented his position as "tragic":

Engels clearly saw himself not as abandoning revolution but simply as adapting the revolutionary strategy and tactics to a changed situation, as he and Marx had done all their lives. It was the discovery that the growth of mass social-democratic parties did not lead to some form of confrontation but to some form of integration of the movement into the existing system, which threw doubt on his analysis. If he is to be criticized, it is for underestimating this possibility. . . . It was the tragedy of Engels' last years, as we can now see, that his lucid, realistic and often immensely perspicacious comments on the concrete situation of the movement served not to influence its practice, but to reinforce a general doctrine increasingly separate from it (1982b: 244).

Bernstein's position, by contrast, resembles in major respects J. S. Mill's "liberalism."[12] Thus he placed great weight on individual freedom and responsibility, education, social experimentation, local-government initiative ("municipal socialism"), and cooperation: "[W]ith respect to liberalism as a historical movement, socialism is its legitimate heir, not only chronologically, but also intellectually," as revealed "in every question of principle on which Social Democracy has had to take a stand" (Bernstein 1993 [1899]: 147). A Millian dimension also emerges in the insistence that the fact that the number of wealthy people increases – pace the standard Marxian contention – was irrelevant for labor: "it is only speculative theory that is affected by this question. It has no bearing whatsoever on the actual aspirations of the workers. It affects neither their struggle for political democracy, nor their struggle for democracy in industry" (200–1). These practical considerations did "not depend on concentration of capital in the hands of a diminishing number of magnates, nor on the whole dialectical scaffolding of which this is a plank. Rather it depends on the growth of social wealth and of the social productive forces, in conjunction with general social progress, and in particular the intellectual and moral advance of the working class itself" (201).

The "right of revolution" is taken for granted by Bernstein, but as "a purely speculative right"; and "a democratic socialistic party of reform" is advised to "emancipate itself from phraseology that is, in fact, obsolete" (1993 [1899]: 186). "We look in vain," he complained of the Marxist literature, "for any investigation into the question as to what can, in principle, be expected from legal and what from revolutionary action" (204), and he himself opined that "[a]s soon as a

---

[12] For an extensive literature on Bernstein and the liberal connection, see Steger (1997: 7). Whereas for Engels and Marx universal suffrage was to be the means of achieving a "proletarian dictatorship," J. S. Mill supported the general principle of universal suffrage with safeguards including an educational qualification requirement and some means of protecting minority groups. Thus, for example, a letter to William Lovett (a Chartist leader), 27 July 1842, expresses concern with "class legislation," engendered by "a legislature absolutely controlled by one class, even when that class numerically exceeds all others taken together" (Mill 1963–91 *13*: 533). Also see *Thoughts on Parliamentary Reform* (1963–91 [1859a] *19*: 330), "Recent Writers on Reform" (1859b: 363–4), and *Considerations on Representative Government* (1861: 477). A letter dated 17 April 1865 summarizes Mill's position: "I would open the suffrage to all grown persons, both men & women, who can read, write, & perform a sum in the rule of three, & who have not, within some small number of years, received parish relief. At the same time, utterly abominating all class ascendancy, I would not vote for giving the suffrage in such a manner that any class, even though it be the most numerous, could swamp all other classes taken together" (1963–91 *16*: 1032). Until the details of a system "practically the best adapted to secure to every portion of the community its just share of influence, while preventing any class from acquiring an unjust degree of preponderance either by means of property of or numbers," Mill was "prepared to support a measure which would give to the labouring classes a clear half of the national representation."

nation has reached a political state of affairs where the rights of the propertied minority have ceased to be a serious impediment to social progress, where the negative tasks of political action take second place to the positive, the appeal to violent revolution becomes pointless" (205). He denied in his 1909 Foreword that his work implied "that we abandon the taking of political power by the politically and economically organised proletariat" (1). "Nobody," he protested, "ever questioned the necessity for the working class to fight for democracy" (4). But, he asked, "must the proletariat take power only by means of a political catastrophe? And does this mean the appropriation and use of state power exclusively by the proletariat against the whole non-proletarian world?" (3). Further, in his original text, he represented the franchise for the Reichstag as "Social Democracy's most effective means of asserting its demands, apart from propaganda by voice and pen" (184).

Extension of expropriation rights at the local level, provided the franchise becomes democratic, was necessary "if a socialist municipal policy is to be possible" (Bernstein 1993 [1899]: 182). As far as concerns the national level, though, there is a strong warning against extensive nationalization of industry at least without serious preparation of the preliminary groundwork: "If democracy is not to outdo centralised absolutism in fostering bureaucracy, it must be based on a highly differentiated system of self-government with the relevant economic responsibilities devolved to all units of government as well as to all adult citizens. Nothing is more harmful to the healthy development of democracy than enforced uniformity and excessive protectionism" (151–2). In the absence of such arrangement, "the so-called social appropriation of the means of production would result in nothing but a massive devastation of productive forces, senseless experimentation, and pointless violence. The political rule of the working class could, in fact, be implemented only in the form of a dictatorial, revolutionary central power supported by the terrorist dictatorship of revolutionary clubs" (152). Elsewhere, Bernstein questions the ability of the state to take over even the larger undertakings: "Imagine the huge resources of judgment, expertise, and managerial talent which a government or national assembly must have at its command to be equal to even just the direction or economic control of such a gigantic organism!" (102). In fact, the whole matter is relegated to the sidelines: "nationalisation of all means of production" might be the ultimate aim of "revolutionary socialism... but not for practical political socialism which gives goals which are nearer at hand priority over distant ones" (191). All this is scarcely surprising considering the masthead principle: "that which is usually termed the final goal of socialism is nothing to me, the movement is everything" (190).[13]

---

[13] In the 1909 Preface to the English edition, Bernstein expressed this view very strongly indeed when summarizing the intention of the work:

It is the strong accentuation of what in Germany is called the GEGENWARTARBEIT – the every-day work of the socialist party – that work in the furrows of the field which by many

Two complexities regarding Bernstein's position may be raised here. First, he is none too clear regarding the "ends" of Social Democracy. Thus elaborating in the Foreword the foregoing dictum, he insisted that he did not intend to "express indifference towards the ultimate implementation of socialist principles, but only indifference – or, more correctly, lack of anxiety – to 'how' things would ultimately take shape" (Bernstein 1993 [1899]: 5). But what are the "socialist principles" in question? What follows includes "expropriation of the capitalists" but only as means to an uncertain end; certainly there is little positive enthusiasm for the Social Democratic program:

At no time has my interest in the future gone beyond general principles, and detailed depictions of the future were never something I could read through to the end. It is present tasks and those of the immediate future which occupy my thoughts and energies; perspectives beyond that concern me only insofar as they suggest guidelines for the most effective action in this regard.

The seizure of political power by the working classes and the expropriation of the capitalists are not in themselves final goals but merely the means to achieve certain goals and fulfil certain aspirations. As such, they are demands in the programme of Social Democracy, and nobody questions them. The circumstances in which they will be fulfilled cannot be predicted. We can only fight for their realisation. But the taking of political power cannot be achieved without political *rights*, and the most important tactical problem which German Social Democracy has to solve at the present is, it seems to me, *the best way to extend the political and industrial rights* of the German working man. (Bernstein 1993 [1899]: 5)

The problem was immediately noted in a review by Bonar: "The principles of Mr. Bernstein, in fact, seem to give us not Social Democracy, but Democracy without Socialism, without what has hitherto passed for Socialism in Germany or even (Protean as it has been) in our own country. 'We are all Socialists,' Mr. Bernstein not less than the most of us, and not much more" (Bonar 1899: 553).[14]

My second point relates to Bernstein's apparent neglect of the possibility that a working-class electoral majority, once achieved, might turn out a socialist party at the polls. (His immediate concern was rather the danger that the authorities would curtail the franchise for the Reichstag; 1993 [1899]: 184.) However, although he

is regarded as mere stop-gap work compared with the great coming upheaval, and of which much as been done consequently in a half-hearted way only. Unable to believe in finalities at all, I cannot believe in a final aim of socialism. But I strongly believe in the socialist movement, in the march forward of the working classes, who step by step must work our their emancipation by changing society from the domain of a commercial landholding oligarchy to a real democracy which in all its departments is guided by the interests of those who work and create. (1961 [1909]: viii–ix)

[14] See also the summary by Angel: "Bernstein retained of Marxism in the end only that which might appear acceptable to the bourgeois left" (1961: 431). "Nothing could be found therein"– referring to his revised and reformed Marxism – "that prevented bourgeois liberals from joining." But see Przeworski: "Bernstein's famous renunciation of ultimate goals did not imply that they would remain unfulfilled, but only that the way to realize them was to concentrate on proximate aims" (1985: 30).

did not formally address the issue, the entire spirit of his work points toward the acceptance of such an eventuality: "Is there any sense, for example, in maintaining the phrase 'dictatorship of the proletariat' at a time when representatives of Social Democracy have in practice placed themselves wherever possible in the arena of parliamentary work, in the struggle for a representation of the people which adequately reflects their numbers, and in the struggle for popular participation in legislation – all of which is inconsistent with dictatorship" (145).[15] Here the contrast with Engels, whose support for universal suffrage was conditional on the proletariat faithfully following the party line, is most apparent. In any event, for Bernstein "Social Democracy does not depend exclusively on the franchise and parliamentary activity. It also has a large and fertile field of activity outside parliament" (185).

It is not surprising that Bernstein, a close friend of Engels[16] and aware of the limits to the latter's revisionism and the elasticity of his own, should have delayed such a full spelling out of his views – they first appear in articles of 1896 – until after Engels's death (Gay 1952: 55; Howard and King 1989: 73). The essential difference between his own stance and that of Marx and Engels, despite the various modifications they had come to accept regarding "practical questions" as distinct – so it is implied – from matters of principle, is well expressed by Bernstein himself:

I am well aware that it deviates in several important particulars from the views to be found in the theory of Karl Marx and Friedrich Engels – whose writings have exercised the greatest influence on my views as a socialist, and one of whom – Friedrich Engels – not only honoured me with his personal friendship until his death but also showed beyond the grave, in his testamentary arrangements, a proof of his confidence in me. This difference in our ways of seeing things is not of recent date; it is the product of an inner struggle which lasted for years, and I have in my hand the proof that this was no secret from Friedrich Engels. Moreover, although I must protect Engels from the imputation that he had become so narrow-minded as to exact from his friends an unconditional adherence to his views, it will be understood from the foregoing why I have, until now, done everything possible to avoid expressing my disagreement as a critique of the doctrine propounded by Marx and Engels. Until now, this was all the easier, because, as regards the practical questions at issue here, Marx and Engels themselves considerably modified their views in the course of time. (1993 [1899]: 7)

As Bernstein here intimates, Engels was long aware of Bernstein's transition[17] – as he saw it – from a reliable comrade-in-arms to one who had come to have a "comical respect for the Fabians," represented as "self-styled" labor candidates "dab[ling] in Possibilist programmes of municipal reform" (12, 14 August 1892;

---

[15] The dilemma faced by Bernstein, and Social Democrats generally, is well expressed in Gneuss (1962) and in Przeworski (1985: 16).

[16] See the extract below regarding Engels's "testamentary arrangements." For Engels's appointment of Bernstein as executor, see MECW (*50*: 537).

[17] Gay points to an index of the transition provided by Bernstein's remark that "my own theoretical development has led me spiritually closer to Lassalle" (Preface to *Ferdinand Lassalle* 1904, cited in Gay 1952: 55n.).

MECW *49*: 494, 497).[18] Recall Engels's own (Bernsteinian) disclaimer regarding an immediate preoccupation with matters of principle when only "the ways and means of struggle" were under consideration (14 March 1893, cited in Chapter Four, p. 218), but note also his concern that Bernstein "from his writing desk, discourses in doctrinaire fashion on questions of immediate practical moment" (to Kautsky, 3 November 1893; MECW *50*: 224–5). Support for reform, in brief, had been turned by Bernstein from legitimate *means* to illegitimate *end*.

This sort of reaction only masked the severe dilemma created by the evolutionary perspective insisted on by Marx and Engels themselves, for any practical differences with Bernstein had been greatly diluted thereby.[19] The revolution must come, they insisted, but when was another matter. Thus, for example, we find Engels objecting to the French Socialists Millerand and Jaurès, who, while paying lip service to communism, offered "a highly platonic socialist programme," wherein "the *socialisation des moyens de production* still remained an innocent chimera which might perhaps acquire practical significance three or four generations hence,

[18] Bernstein himself denied a Fabian influence (McLellan 2007: 24; but see Angel 1961: 106–9). On Fabian Socialism, see the classic account in Cole (1956: 104–78). Hobsbawm maintains that Bernstein, who "derived his 'revisionism' from English experience and Fabian contacts," saw them – mistakenly – "as merely a particularly empirical, hard-headed and anti-romantic group within the British socialist movement, and for this reason the pioneers of the rejection or revision of doctrinaire Marxism" (Hobsbawm 1964: 264–5).

Engels's remark to Sorge (8 February 1890) regarding the Fabian refutation of Marx in favor of a "socialism" based on Jevonian logic (see Chapter Seven, note 1) continues thus: "As in America, its chief object is to convert your *bourgeois* to socialism, and to introduce the thing *peacefully* and *constitutionally*" (MECW *48*: 449). In the light of the ample evidence to the contrary that we have considered, it is improbable that this formulation was intended as a general case against peaceful and constitutional progress; it insists rather that the Fabian and Engels ideals of socialism have little in common. And beyond this, "[t]he means employed by the Fabian Society," Engels wrote at this time, "are indistinguishable from those employed in corrupt parliamentary politics: money, intrigue, careerism, i.e., after the English fashion. . . . There is nothing one can tell the workers to beware that these chaps are not already practising" (to Kautsky, 4 September 1892; MECW *49*: 516).

Engels tried to explain away Bernstein's position by reference to his nervous indisposition: "I also suspect that his unduly high opinion of the Fabians is partly attributable to his illness and that this will subside" (to Bebel, 20 August 1892; MECW *49*: 502–3). Engels was genuinely concerned not to cause Bernstein distress, and he had some hope of his return to full reliability. He asked Bebel "to observe caution *vis-à-vis* K. Kautsky in regard to Ede," who was showing signs of recovery: "should [Kautsky's] letters suggest to Ede that we were secretly conspiring to counteract his enthusiasm for Fabianism, it might bring about a serious relapse" (502). Also, "I believe that what he now needs most of all is something to liven and cheer him up in order that his soundness of judgement may once more gain complete control over his still somewhat excessive aspirations after justice" (to Kautsky, 26 January 1893; MECW *50*: 92). Engels would have been thoroughly disappointed had he lived to read *The Preconditions of Socialism*.

Engels certainly did not despise municipal reform, provided it was part of a broader and genuine Socialist campaign (to Laura Lafargue, 28 March 1895; MECW *50*: 484).

[19] Bonar actually cites Engels as maintaining that "Communism is not a doctrine, but a movement" (1922: 334n.). Bernstein, as we know, interpreted Marx in this fashion. But the fact remains, of course, that Marx and Engels were to the end very much committed to communism as doctrine, and in that commitment lay the difference with Bernstein.

but certainly not any sooner" (17 July 1894; MECW *50*: 324–5).[20] Engels may have expected the transformation sooner rather than later, but he was quite unable to say how much sooner, and – as Bernstein pointed out – had admitted having in the past illegitimately short-circuited the time required by evolutionary processes. There were also the obvious problems whether, to what extent, and by what means the evolutionary process might legitimately be accelerated. That Engels so much missed the leadership of the master tactician (see Chapter Six, p. 303) is easy to appreciate, though the dilemma was raised and left unanswered in *Capital*, where Marx had asserted that although it was possible neither "to clear by bold leaps nor remove by legal enactments, the obstacles offered by the successive phases of its normal development, it was possible to "shorten and lessen the birth-pangs" (cited Chapter Seven, note 13).

B. Engels and Kautsky

Engels ranked Karl Kautsky as "theorist" above Bernstein for "far too much of [Bernstein's] time is taken up by practical activities for him to be able to participate in, and further his knowledge of the theoretical side as much as he would no doubt like and be capable of doing. And there is, after all, so much still to be done here in the way of theory, especially in the field of economic history and its links with political history, as with the history of law, religion, literature and civilisation generally when the only sure guide through the labyrinth of facts is a clear theoretical insight" (Engels to Conrad Schmidt, 17 October 1889; MECW *48*: 391–2).

Like Engels, Kautsky insisted on the ultimate communist objective, at least during Engels's lifetime and for several years thereafter. Bernstein in his 1909 Preface to the English edition of *The Preconditions of Socialism* refers to Kautsky's reaction on the appearance of the German edition in 1899: "Karl Kautsky denounced it as an abandonment of the fundamental principles and conception of scientific socialism" (1961 [1909]: vii). The fact remains, however, that Kautsky also subscribed to Engels's evolutionism, which entailed a presumption – wishful thinking is perhaps a more accurate term – that communism would come within a "reasonably" short time or a "comparatively few years," without forcing the pace. These two strands are so well expressed in an appreciation of Engels in 1887 that I give it in its entirety:

Engels has always succeeded in keeping himself free from illusions. This he can do because behind him lies the experience of half a hundred years, in which the world has changed more than in any previous hundred years. These experiences have made him a cool, quiet observer. The whole development during his later years has made him certain that the proletariat will become the determining force in the life of the state within a comparatively few years in the lands of capitalistic civilization. To be

---

[20] Within a few months, Engels's view of Jaurès altered: "Jaurès is on the right road. He is *learning* Marxism, and he should not be hurried too much. However, he has already made good progress, much more than I had dared hope" (to Plekhanov, 26 February 1895; MECW *50*: 451).

sure, there are many and great obstacles yet to be overcome, but the dynamic forces of present historic development in the economic and political spheres are such that these obstacles will not prove insurmountable. We cannot wish anything better, said Engels, than that existing relations will be allowed to develop further in their present direction. Then our victory is certain within a reasonable time. The worst to happen would be a leap into uncertainty, which, while having the appearance of an advance, would in reality set us still further back; or that some event should put the Social Democracy to an extreme test before its strength were sufficiently developed; or that the thoughts of the people should be given a new direction. Such an event would mean war, which would arouse race hate and destroy the international solidarity.

Such elementary events naturally cannot be advanced or hindered according to our desire. When they do occur we must seek as far as possible to exploit them in our interest. What we must seek to avoid at such times is an "adventurous policy" on the part of our own party. We must not attempt to forcibly surprise natural development or to diplomatically outwit it. "We have learned to wait," said Engels to me, "and you in turn must learn to wait your time." But by such waiting he did not mean waiting with folded arms and open mouth until one of the roasted doves of spontaneous development should fly down the throat, but a waiting in tireless labor – labor of organization and propaganda. Quietly and decisively, with faith in our own good cause, without either prophecy or hesitancy, we must toil on, without rest, to weld the mass of the proletariat more firmly and clearly together and to fill them with a more clear self-consciousness. We have not only to teach, but also learn much – very much to learn. (Kautsky 1899 [1887]: 26–7)

It is significant as a confirmation of Engels's own revisionism that he approved this formulation (letter to Kautsky, 17 August 1887; MECW *48*: 96; see 546 n. 155) and took the trouble of mailing a copy to Sorge in America (109).[21]

This moderate statement contrasts with Schumpeter's representation of Kautsky as holding "a position that can be described only in ecclesiastical terms, upholding the 'revolutionary' doctrine against revisionism as he was later to uphold orthodoxy against the Bolshevik heretics" (Schumpeter 1950: 347n.).[22] A possible reconciliation between these perspectives is suggested by a contrast drawn by Kautsky in his 1899 review of Bernstein's revisionism – as already formulated in

---

[21] Engels also thanked Kautsky for a seventieth birthday appreciation in *Die Neue Zeit*, albeit "all too flattering" (13 December 1890; MECW *49*: 90).

[22] See also Joll: "Bernstein's criticisms of Marx were answered by Karl Kautsky in a doctrinal duel worthy of the early Church" (1974: 93). Patrick Goode similarly represents Kautsky's *The Road to Power* (1909) as "restat[ing] the need for the working class to undertake direct revolutionary action against the state power" (1983: 249). Further, McLellan writes of Kautsky's "insistence on the reality of class conflict and the consequent impossibility of forging links with the bourgeoisie.... Reforms could not deal with the fundamental reality of class conflict and the granting of democratic rights could never provide a substitute for revolution" (2007: 32). But Cole's position is very close to my own:

Kautsky ... appeared, in the 1890s, to be the defender of revolutionary Marxism against every sort of compromise. But, though he insisted on the proletarian basis of the party, and often used phrases which seemed to rank him with the advocates of proletarian dictatorship, he in fact envisaged the overthrow of the existing state and the proletarian conquest of political power mainly in terms of a peaceful advance by propagandist and parliamentary action, and

articles published between 1896 and 1898 – between Germany, where he found Bernstein's position regarding gradual progress toward "socialism" inappropriate, and France and Britain, where there existed a tradition of "democracy" (see Henderson 1976 2: 732; also Howard and King 1989: 84–5). Further, in *The Dictatorship of the Proletariat* (1919 [1918]), he denied that Marx necessarily intended "dictatorship" in a literal sense, allowing once more for a peaceable transition, at least in Britain and America (Service 2000: 376, 387). It is also pertinent that Engels persuaded Kautsky to remove his proposed designation for the Erfurt Congress of bourgeois opponents as "one reactionary mass" as inaccurate and impolitic (Chapter Four, p. 223).[23] Considering his earlier faith in Kautsky, it is small wonder that Lenin, responding to *The Dictatorship of the Proletariat*, should place him ahead of Bernstein in his gallery of rogues: "The renegade Bernstein has proved to be a mere puppy compared with the renegade Kautsky" (Lenin 1965a [1918]: 242).[24] The wonder is that it took him so long to reach this conclusion, considering Kautsky's early appreciation of Engels as a moderate, and his own concessions to Bernstein regarding Britain and France.

One particular difference between Engels and Kautsky requires comment. Kolakowski refers, though without citation, to Kautsky's denial that the intensity of the class struggle is a function of absolute poverty, so that "[t]he theory of absolute pauperization of the working class was . . . not an essential part of Marxist doctrine, such that the latter would have to be abandoned if the theory proved to be untrue" (2005: 389). As for Engels, although he recognized increasing insecurity of existence (Chapter Five, p. 260), he took the threat posed by rising wages

agreed with Liebknecht in regarding the essence of the revolution as consisting rather in the end accomplished than in the means. (1956: 268)

Kolakowski similarly refers to Kautsky's "centrist position, based on his scientific attitude and reluctance to take decisions without rational foundation, amount[ing] in practice to acceptance of the reformist standpoint" (2005: 391). He also represents Kautsky as "profoundly attached to democratic values; he hated violence and war, and, while recognizing that future forms of the class struggle could not be foreseen, he hoped that mankind would advance into the realm of socialist freedom as a result of peaceful pressure, without violence or bloodshed" (397–8).

[23] Howard and King appear to neglect this episode when they write, *tout court*, that "Kautsky was right to argue that the various non-proletarian classes and groups constituted – potentially if not yet actually – a single reactionary mass in opposition to the working class, and that socialism could be won only through the independent action of the proletariat, fighting alone against all other classes" (1989: 85).

[24] Lenin read Bernstein's *Preconditions of Socialism* and Kautsky's reaction on their appearance, and he had then referred to Bernstein's position as "heresy" (Clark 1989: 54–5). At that stage Kautsky was evidently not yet perceived as a traitor – to the contrary (Service 2000: 123–4). The reversal of attitude first emerges when Kautsky refused to break with the German Social Democratic Party over the vote on war credits in August 1914 (226, 248), and when he remained unconvinced by Lenin's position that the working classes could be easily induced to revolutionary activity (238). For his bitter attack on Kautsky's "Social-Democracy in Wartime" (*Die Neue Zeit*, 2 October 1914), see Lenin 1964 [1914].

seriously and sought to meet it by the argument that such improvement could not be sustained.

So much for the manner of transition to communism, in which regard Lenin might have accorded Engels and Marx themselves high ranking as "renegades," considering their "revisionism" that I have recorded in this book. As for the future communist state, it should be noted that, in later years, Kautsky became far more catholic in his perceptions (see Kowalik 1987), moving away from Engels's strict central control and absence of a circulating medium and closer to Bernstein's open-ended perspective, thereby further fueling Lenin's disgust.

Appendix A: Prolegomena: A Brief Chronology

28 November 1820: FE born at Barmen-Elberfeld, Prussian province of the Rhineland.

August 1838–March 1841: Business training in Bremen.

September 1841–October 1842: Voluntary military service in Berlin; joins group of Young Hegelians ("The Free").

November 1842: Meets with KM in Cologne office of the *Rheinische Zeitung*.

December 1842–August 1844: Commercial training at "Ermen & Engels" in Manchester; meets Mary Burns – his companion from Summer 1845.

October–November 1843: Composes the *Outlines of a Critique of Political Economy*.

November 1843: First mentions KM in print, in the *New Moral World* newspaper.

February 1844: His *Outlines* published by KM in *Deutsch-Französische Jahrbücher* (first and only number of the journal).

Late August–early September 1844: Second meeting with KM, in Paris; beginning of Marx–Engels collaboration.

September 1844: Returns to Barmen.

September 1844–March 1845: Composes *The Condition of the Working Class in England*.

April 1845: Joins KM in Brussels (until 1848).

July–August 1845: Visits Manchester with KM.

January 1846: FE and KM found the Communist Correspondence Committee (Brussels).

January 1847: FE and KM invited to join the "League of the Just" (a communist group organized in 1836–8) in Paris.

June 1847: The League reorganized as the League of Communists; London Congress adopts FE's "Draft of a Communist Confession of Faith" as provisional basis of its new program.

December 1847: FE's *Principles of Communism* accepted as basis of final version of the program; KM asked by Communist League to prepare document for publication.

February 1848: FE and KM return to Cologne; FE works on the editorial staff of the *Neue Rheinische Zeitung* founded by KM and becomes an editor later in the year.

[1849: KM deported from Prussia. Leaves for Paris, and then London.]

May 1849: Participates in Elberfeld uprising against Prussians; indicted.

June 1849: Participates against Prussians in Baden and Palatinate campaigns.

November 1849: Emigrates to London to join KM.

November 1850: Returns to Manchester as employee of "Ermen & Engels," representing the Engels family.

6–7 January 1863: Death of Mary Burns; thereafter FE lived with Lizzie Burns, Mary's sister.

[28 September 1864: KM participates in founding of International Working Men's Association, the First International.]

September 1864–June 1869: Partner in "Ermen & Engels."

September 1870: Settles in London. Elected to the General Council of the IWMA.

12 September 1878. Death of Lizzie Burns (FE married LB on 11 September).

[14 March 1883: Death of KM.]

1883: Publication of *Capital 2*.

1889: Participates in founding of the Second International.

1894: Publication of *Capital 3*.

5 August 1895: Death of FE.

Appendix B: Chapter 5

I. Engels and International Trade Policy

I devote this appendix to Engels's position on international trade, extending the discussion in Chapter Five, pp. 232–3 regarding principles of reform. I take note first of his review in 1888 of Marx's position of the 1840s: "[B]ecause Free Trade is the natural, the normal atmosphere for this historical evolution" – the process described by Marx – "the economic medium in which the conditions for the inevitable social revolution will be the soonest created, – for this reason, and for this alone, did Marx declare in favor of Free Trade" ("Protection and Free Trade" (1888; MECW 26: 524; see editorial note MECW 6: 696 n. 246). By insisting on this feature, Engels implies that at other periods or places the same objective might not justify free trade.

Consider a letter to Bebel in Berlin of 8 March 1892. Here Engels remarks that "unemployment [in Germany] might well get worse next year. For protectionism has had exactly the same effect as free trade – the flooding of individual national markets and this almost everywhere, although it's not so bad over here as where you are" (MECW 49: 373). Later, on 30 August he writes in response to a remark by Victor Adler regarding the rapid industrial progress of Austria and Hungary behind a tariff: "What you say . . . has pleased me immensely. That is the only solid basis for the advancement of our movement. And it is also the only good aspect of protectionism – at any rate in the case of most of the continental countries and of America. Large-scale industry, big capitalists and large masses of proletarians are being artificially nurtured, the centralisation of capital is being speeded up and the middle classes destroyed" (MECW 49: 513).[1] These remarks point directly away

---

[1] However, this had not been the case in Germany, where "protective tariffs were . . . unnecessary, having been introduced at the precise moment when Germany was establishing herself in the world market and it is *that* process which they have disrupted" (MECW 49: 513). Yet this clear-cut statement is then qualified, for tariffs are said to have "filled a number of gaps in German industry which otherwise would have remained unfilled." Were they to be now abandoned, Germany "would be far better able to compete [in the world market] than hitherto." Also note that Engels no longer justified protection in the American case: "Both in Germany and

from the free trade régime proposed in the 1840s for Britain, but with precisely the same intent – the speeding up of capitalist evolution toward its extinction. In the lengthy note introduced into *Capital 3* (MECW *37*: 435, discussed in Chapter Three, p. 163), Engels regards protection as the policy of "every industrial country," apart from England, with the disastrous – though desirable – results indicative of the collapse of capitalism, namely "general chronic overproduction, depressed prices, falling and even wholly disappearing profits."

Howard and King discern a conflict between the 1888 endorsement of free trade along the standard Marxian lines and the passage in *Capital 3* whereby the collapse of capitalism arrives by way of monopolies protected behind tariffs (1989: 15). However, the perceived conflict disappears if, as I propose, the 1888 argument is not read as a clear-cut endorsement of Marx's free trade position of the 1840s, but one conditional upon the circumstances of that period. This interpretation is amply confirmed at the close of "Protection and Free Trade," where Engels explicitly raises the question of the correct "socialist" position on the issue. The choice interested socialists only indirectly "inasmuch as we must desire the present system of production to develop and expand as freely and as quickly as possible; because along with it will develop also those economic phenomena which are its necessary consequences, and which must destroy the whole system" (MECW *26*: 535). Those consequences are conveniently spelled out, with the supercession of trade cycles recognized only as one possibility, as

misery of the great mass of the people, in consequence of overproduction; this over-production engendering either periodical gluts and revulsions, accompanied by panic, or else a chronic stagnation of trade; division of society into a small class of large cap-italists, and a large one of practically hereditary wage-slaves, proletarians, who while their numbers increase constantly, are at the same time constantly being superseded by new labor-saving machinery; in short, society brought to a deadlock, out of which there is no escaping but by a complete remodelling of the economic structure which forms its basis. (MECW *26*: 535)

Marx had some forty years earlier "pronounced, in principle, in favor of Free Trade as the more progressive plan," or the plan which "would soonest bring capitalist society to that deadlock." But protection would not, at least in current circumstances, hinder this outcome, or "hurt the prospects of Socialism in the least.... Whether you try the Protectionist or the Free Trade plan will make no difference in the end, and hardly any in the length of respite left to you until the day when the end will come" (536). In other words, "[p]rotection is a plan for artificially manufacturing manufacturers, and therefore also a plan for artificially manufacturing wage-laborers... the class which is fated one day to destroy the system itself."

in America protective tariffs are now simply a hindrance because they hinder those countries from taking their proper place in the world market. In America, therefore, they are bound to be abandoned before long and Germany is bound to follow suit."

II. Two Contemporary Estimates of the Real-Wage Trend

1. William Gladstone (1863–4)

In his Inaugural Address to the International Working Men's Association, 28 September 1864 (MECW *20*: 7), and in *Capital* itself (MECW *35*: 645–6), Marx objected to Gladstone's budget speech of 16 April 1863 regarding a rising real-wage trend, 1843–63 (Chapter Five, p. 243). The original *Morning Star* report runs as follows:

In ten years, from 1842 to 1852 inclusive, the taxable income of the country increased by 6 per cent., as nearly as I can make out – a very considerable increase in ten years. But in eight years from 1853 to 1861 the income of the country again increased from the basis taken in 1853 by 20 per cent. The fact is so astonishing as to be almost incredible.... I must say, for one, I should look with apprehension and with pain upon this intoxicating augmentation of wealth and power, if it were my belief that it was confined to the classes who are in easy circumstances. This great increase of wealth takes no cognizance at all of the condition of the labouring population. The augmentation is an augmentation entirely confined to classes of property. But that augmentation must be of indirect benefit to the labouring population, because it cheapens the commodities which go to the general consumption. So that we have this profound, and I almost say, inestimable consolation – while the rich have been growing richer, the poor have been growing less poor. At any rate, whether the extremes are less extreme than they were I do not presume to say, but the average condition of the British labourer, we have the happiness to know, has improved during the last twenty years in a degree that we know to be extraordinary, and that we may almost pronounce to be unexampled in the history of any country or any age. (17 April 1863, p. 6)

Now Marx was right to complain that the ambiguities in Gladstone's next budget speech – that of 7 April 1864 as reported in *The Times* – cast doubt on the reliability of his first confident evaluation of improvement. On the one hand, Gladstone applauds a perceived reduction in pauperism as an index of recent growth of "national wealth": "The pauperism of the country, excluding that in Lancashire, has not only not been stationary, but has decreased since the year 1848–49" (*The Times*, 8 April 1864, p. 6). In making a case for "our duty to practice public economy," however, he introduces qualifications: "Just now I read amid the cheers of the House the statement that our paupers are reduced in number to somewhat about 840,000 [sic]. That amount, however, does not include persons relieved by private charity, but only comprises those who are driven to the last necessity of resorting to the poor-house. That then is a great number; but, besides there are many of the labouring classes who struggle manfully but with difficulty to maintain themselves in a position above paupers.... In many cases wages have much increased, though in many other places they have not." A further note of doubt is introduced when Gladstone insists on the obligation to reduce the burden of the national debt: "The debt appears to me to be a very inflexible and formidable burden, grave and serious even in the midst of our wealth and prosperity, and likely to become still more grave and serious in its pressures if our prosperity

Table 1. *Comparison of wages fifty years ago and at present time [c. 1835–c. 1880]*

Occupation	Place	Wages per week		Increase or decrease		
		Fifty years ago	Present times	Amount		Percent
Carpenters	Manchester	24/-	34/-	10/-	(+)	42
Carpenters	Glasgow	14/-	26/-	12/-	(+)	85
Bricklayers	Manchester	24/-	36/-	12/-	(+)	50
Bricklayers	Glasgow	15/-	27/-	12/-	(+)	80
Masons	Manchester	24/-	29/10	5/10	(+)	24
Masons	Glasgow	14/-	23/8	9/8	(+)	69
Miners	Staffordshire	2/8	4/-	1/4	(+)	50
Pattern weavers	Huddersfield	16/-	25/-	9/-	(+)	55
Wool scourers	Huddersfield	17/-	22/-	5/-	(+)	30
Mule spinners	Huddersfield	25/6	30/-	4/6	(+)	20
Weavers	Huddersfield	12/-	26/-	14/-	(+)	115
Warpers and beamers	Huddersfield	17/-	27/-	10/-	(+)	58
Winders and reelers	Huddersfield	6/-	11/-	5/-	(+)	83
Weavers (men)	Bradford	8/3	20/6	12/3	(+)	150
Reeling and warping	Bradford	7/9	15/6	7/9	(+)	100
Spinning (children)	Bradford	4/5	11/6	7/1	(+)	160

Note: The comparison is from "Miscellaneous Statistics of the United Kingdom" and Porter's "Progress of the Nation."
Source: Giffen 1904 (1883): 388.

turned out be less permanent and less stable than most of us are disposed to believe" (p. 5).[2]

2. Robert Giffen (1883)

A more serious estimate of wage trends, extending over nearly half a century, is by Robert Giffen in "The Progress of the Working Classes."[3] His data (see Table 1) showed that in most cases per capita money wages – "the individual income of the working classes" – had risen by 50 percent to at least 100 percent, with a mean percentage increase of over 70 percent (Giffen 1904 [1883]: 388, 412). Appreciation

---

[2] Because the essential point emerges in both versions that Gladstone insisted on *rising* real wages, it is difficult to see any basis for Lujo Brentano's charge that Marx, in the Inaugural Address and in *Capital*, deliberately falsified Gladstone's speech. See Engels's defense "In the Case of Brentano versus Marx" (1890–1; MECW *27*: 95–176, esp. 126).

[3] Engels was aware of Giffen (see, e.g., his letter dated 11 April 1883, MECW *47*: 5), but I can find no evidence that he was familiar with the study of wage trends.

of Table 1 requires attention to the following: Money wages per week had increased over a period when (1) hours worked per week had fallen by nearly 20 percent in textiles, engineering and house building (388, 391); (2) the price of wheat had declined and was subject to less instability, with periodic famine prices becoming irrelevant (392–6); (3) the prices of other wage goods including clothing had declined (396), while the upward trend in meat prices and house rent did not neutralize the gains, especially when allowance is made for the increase in quality of housing (396–9); and (4) when expenditures for miscellaneous civil purposes by the state (including education, the post office, and factory inspection) and by local government (sanitation and education, including libraries, in addition to poor relief) had risen (399–400).

Evidence of improvement in the general "condition of the people," corroborating the increase in "the means of improvement," includes a falling death rate with an impact on the mean duration of life over the period 1838–80 (Giffen 1904 [1883]: 400–2). Further corroborative data are provided relating to education, pauperism, crime and savings banks (404–7), as well as industrial and provident cooperative societies (407). Special attention is accorded wealth diffusion, particularly the contention "that the capitalist classes... secure for themselves all the benefits of the modern advance in wealth; the rich, it is said, are becoming richer, and the poor are becoming poorer" (408). This contention is rejected as reflecting a false supposition that the capitalist class remained unchanged in number, whereas in fact "they receive recruits from period to period" as evidenced by the number of probates granted in 1881 compared with corresponding data for 1838 (409). The comparison revealed a more than doubling in the number of estates (broadly, an index of the numbers comprising the capitalist classes), that is, faster than that of the population, though with the increase of capital per head of the capitalist class in the United Kingdom rising by only 15 percent and in England by 19 percent, contrasting with "the individual income of the working classes" that had increased from 50 to 100 percent (411–12).

Table 2 concerns income-tax assessments under Schedule D, Part I: Trades and Professions (excluding public companies), namely earnings of individuals "having wealth of some kind" (Giffen 1904 [1883]: 413). These data indicate greater diffusion of wealth – comparing 1879–80 and 1843 – with the "increase in all classes, from the lowest to the highest... between two and three times, or rather more than three times, with the exception of the highest class of all, where the numbers, however, are quite inconsiderable" (413). Giffen perceives evidence here of a growing *middle class*: "while the increase of personal property per head of the capitalist class, according to the probate returns, is comparatively small, being only about 15 per cent., yet there is an increase of the number of people receiving good incomes from trades and professions out of all proportion to the increase of population. We cannot but infer from this that the number of the moderately rich is increasing, and that there is little foundation for the assertion that the rich are becoming richer" (414). He adds that a case might be made to consider the

Table 2. *Number of persons at different amounts of*
income charged under Schedule D in 1843 and 1879–80
[in England]

Income (£)	1843	1879–80
150–200	39,366	130,101
200–300	28,370	88,445
300–400	13,429	39,896
400–500	6,781	16,501
500–600	4,780	11,317
600–700	2,672	6,894
700–800	1,874	4,054
800–900	1,442	3,595
900–1,000	894	1,396
1,000–2,000	4,228	10,352
2,000–3,000	1,235	3,131
3,000–4,000	526	1,430
4,000–5,000	339	758
5,000–10,000	493	1,439
10,000–50,000	200	785
50,000+	8	68
TOTAL	106,637	320,162

Note: Incomes under £150 are omitted for want of satisfactory data
relating to incomes not subject to assessment.
Source: Giffen 1904 (1883): 413.

lower-income earners, say from £150 to £1,000 per annum, as falling within the
working classes, indicating an increase "out of all proportion to the increase of
population." In any event "[t]he working classes have had large additions to their
means; capital has increased in about equal ratio; but the increase of capital per
head of the capitalist classes is by no means so great as the increase of working-class
incomes" (414).

Using income-tax data Giffen proceeds to provide a rough estimate of the trend
in income 1843–81 from "idle capital" and "income which is derived not so much
from the capital itself as from the labour bestowed in using the capital," referring
largely to "wages of superintendence and salaries" (Giffen 1904 [1883]: (415–16).
His data, laid out in Table 3, implied that "a very large part of the increase of the
income-tax income in the last forty years is not an increase of the income from capital at all in any proper sense of the word"; rather, "the increase in the income from
capital is only about two-thirds of the total increase" (417). And since such increase
was "at a less rate than the increase of the capital itself," Giffen concluded that:

the working classes have not been losing in the last fifty years through the fruits of
their labour being increasingly appropriated to capital. On the contrary, the income
from capital has at least no more than kept pace with the increase of capital itself,

Table 3. *Analysis of the income tax returns for the undermentioned years*

	1881		1862		1843	
Schedule	From capital	From salaries, etc.	From capital	From salaries, etc.	From capital	From salaries, etc.
A						
Land, tithes, etc., exclusive of houses	70	nil	60	nil	57	nil
Messuages, etc.	117	nil	62	nil	41	nil
B						
Occupation of land	25	44	22½	38½	20	36
C	40	nil	29	nil	29	nil
D (Part I)	64	100	32	49	29½	46½
D (Part II)	91	nil	47	nil	12	nil
E	nil	33	nil	20	nil	11
TOTAL	407	177	252½	107½	188½	93½

Note: Analysis shows the estimated income from capital on the one side, and the estimated income from wages of superintendence and salaries on the other side; it is given in millions of pounds. A Messuage is a dwelling house with outbuildings and adjacent land.
Source: Giffen 1904 (1883): 416.

while the increase of capital per head, as we have seen, is very little; so that it may be doubted whether the income of the individual capitalist from capital has on the average increased at all.... [I]t would not be far short of the mark to say that almost the whole of the great material improvement of the last fifty years has gone to the masses. The share of capital is a very small one. And what has not gone to the workmen, so called, has gone to remunerate people who are really workmen also, the persons whose incomes are returned under Schedule D as from "Trades and Professions." (417)

III. Further Opinion Regarding the Late-Nineteenth-Century British Economy

Later research has brought into question the meaningfulness of the term "Great Depression" to describe the period 1873 through 1896. Beales made the important observation – gainsaying Engels's perception of the close of the cyclical era – that "the period embraces three slumps and two intervening recoveries. The peak of the good years was reached in 1872, and the succeeding slump lasted till 1879. Three years of improvement then followed. The second spasm of depression lasted from 1882 to 1886. It was succeeded by four years of recovery, after which the third phase of depression pursued its course, lasting from 1890 till 1896." (Beales 1954 [1934]: 411). As for the shorter term, an upturn in activity is apparent from late 1879 with major orders from the United States for iron (Rostow 1948: 201, 210). More recent investigation of the unemployment rate suggests similarly that "before

1914 there was a fairly regular cycle consistent with other cyclical indicators, with unemployment rates reaching 6 to 8 per cent in depressions and falling to 3 or 4 per cent in booms" (Hatton 2004: 348). However, Saul notes that, extracting from cyclical variation, "[u]nemployment during 1874–95 was clearly higher than during 1851–73 and 1896–1914, the figures being 7.2 per cent compared with 5 per cent and 5.4 percent respectively" (1985: 30), although he sees nothing significant about the 1873 and 1896 brackets (see below).

Giffen at the time took a more optimistic view than Engels of the likely effects of increasing American competition (Giffen 1904 [1877] *1*: 116–17), and he traces out the implications of the (doubtful) contention that English manufacturing was in decline. Other contemporaries, including Marshall and also the *Economist* and two Royal Commissions, were equally skeptical (Rostow 1948: 58). Beales observes that although "[t]here may have been, as Giffen suggested, a slight falling off of the real rate of material progress in this country . . . the outstanding fact, or group of facts, in the quarter-century was the rapid industrialization of other countries and the further industrialization of this" (1954 [1934]: 413). "The period of the so-called 'great depression,'" he concludes, "was a period of progress in circumstances of great difficulty" that "might be dubbed a period of 'lean years' in contrast with the preceding good years, if profit were the main criterion of progress. In no final sense, however, was that period one of retrogression" (415).

Saul's representation of the Great Depression as a "myth" runs along different lines. His main contentions are that the movements of pertinent indexes do not always coincide with each other or relate necessarily to the starting and closing dates in question, and more particularly that although "the last quarter or so of the nineteenth century was a watershed for Britain as competition developed overseas and the rate of growth markedly slackened . . . the process was probably under way before 1870 and most certainly continued unabated – at least in statistical terms – after 1900" (1985: 54). Unfortunately, Saul is difficult to pin down because he also notes that "growth for the years from 1873 to 1899 was only fractionally below that for the previous seventeen years," strengthening "the argument that the concept of a 'Great Depression' in real terms is a myth. . . . [I]t is after 1899 that the long-run decline in the rate of growth manifests itself. . . . At the international level, too, the statistics show Britain lagging only slightly at the end of the century but much more seriously thereafter" (57). Crafts, however, questions the notion of a sharp reduction in trend growth 1899–1913 (2004: 13–14).

On the quality and character of British entrepreneurship in the late nineteenth and early twentieth centuries, especially its alleged "failure' in the face of foreign competition, see Nicholas (2004). His conclusion supports Engels's position on this matter: "In Britain there was too much inheritance as social structure and family capitalism preserved the *status quo*, insufficient luck in terms of resource endowments and market size, and too little effort on the part of entrepreneurs to break out of existing paths of development" (252). A rather different view is taken by Magee: "Failure, in the sense of a rapid loss of markets, was an issue in only those industries for which upon reflection it can be see that the nation was not well suited. Elsewhere British manufacturers appear to have held their own" (2004: 98).[4] Regarding the initial years 1873–9, account should be taken of major technical progress in the British coal, iron, and ship-building industries (Rostow 1948: 212).

[4] Saul too takes a similar position, referring to "the undoubted fact that in important sectors of industry [Britain] was fast making good her technological deficiencies in the decade before 1914.... [T]he industrial structure and its skills were in process of far-reaching readjustment by 1914" (1985: 51–2). Subsequently, Saul appears to take a more qualified position (71–2).

Appendix C: Chapter 7

Marx and Engels on an Alternative Russian Option

Of high interest in the light of Engels's "unavoidable developmental path" or Marx's "tendencies working with iron necessity towards inevitable results" are prospects for a transition to communism in Russia based upon the peasant commune (the *obshchina*), rather than upon capitalist development. The possibility that Russia might achieve communism without passing through a capitalist stage has been attributed to Marx (see, e.g., Howard and King 1989: 138; also 1985: 233). This attribution is based in part on a letter of 1877 (responding to a critical review of *Capital*) opining that "if Russia continues along the path it has followed since 1861" – an allusion to incipient capitalistic progress – "it will miss the finest chance that history has offered to a nation, only to undergo all the fatal vicissitude of a capitalist system" ("Letter to *Otechestvenniye Zapiski*"; MECW 24: 199). By implication, the "finest chance" relates to the commune option, and this is how it has often been understood in the literature. This remark is actually crossed out in Marx's manuscript (199n.), and it is not clear why or by whom; however, what follows immediately makes much the same point. Thus Marx points out that his Chapter 26 ("The Secret of Primitive Accumulation") concerned specifically Western European experience, and it had concluded in the following terms:

> In the history of primitive accumulation, all revolutions are epoch-making that act as levers for the capitalist class in course of formation; but, above all, those moments when great masses of men are suddenly and forcibly torn from their means of subsistence, and hurled as free and "unattached" proletarians on the labour market. The expropriation of the agricultural producer, of the peasant, from the soil, is the basis of the whole process. The history of this expropriation, in different countries, assumes different aspects, and runs through its various phases in different orders of succession, and at different periods. In England alone, which we take as our example, has it the classic form. (MECW 35: 707)

Likewise, he explains that his Chapter 32 ("Historical Tendency of Capitalist Accumulation"), which provided a "historical sketch of the genesis of capitalism in

Western Europe," was never intended as "a historico-philosophical theory of general development, imposed by fate on all peoples, whatever the historical circumstances in which they are placed, in order to eventually attain this economic formation which, with a tremendous leap of the productive forces of social labour, assures the most integral development of every individual producer" (MECW *24*: 200). Apparently he alludes to a communist outcome based on a noncapitalist foundation.

When evaluating these texts, we should insist upon two qualifications. First, the foregoing possibility is scarcely allowed with conviction, for the sole reference Marx gives in his letter of an allegedly flexible position is to the discussion in *Capital* of the "destiny of the plebeians of Ancient Rome . . . originally free peasants cultivating their own plots of land on their own account," who "became not wage labourers but an idle '*mob*' . . . and alongside them there developed a mode of production that was not capitalist but based on slavery. Thus events strikingly analogous, but occurring in different historical milieux, led to quite disparate results" (MECW *24*: 200–1). None of this allows for an alternative path to communism other than the European one, and we are inclined to conclude that Marx's musings regarding such a possibility should not be taken too seriously.[1]

Second, the degree of freedom allowed in the letter is not extended generally, for it remains a fundamental principle that should capitalist development take firm hold in Russia – whether or not it will do so remains an open question – its evolution into communism would inevitably follow: "If Russia is tending to become a capitalist nation . . . – and in recent years it has gone to great pains to move in this direction – it will not succeed without having first transformed a large portion of its peasants into proletarians; and after that, once it has been placed in the bosom of the capitalist system, it will be subjected to its pitiless laws, like other profane peoples" (MECW *24*: 200). Accordingly, Marx stood by his summary of position in the chapter on "the historical tendency of capitalist accumulation," that capitalism "'itself begets its own negation with the inexorability which governs the metamorphoses of nature' [MECW *35*: 751]; that it has itself created the elements of a new economic order, by giving the greatest impulse at once to the productive forces of social labour and to the integral development of every individual producer; that capitalist property, which actually rests already on a collective mode of production, can only be transformed into social property."

We should bear these two limitations in mind when considering Marx's approval of the reading of his methodology by I. I. Kaufmann (MECW *35*: 18; above, pp. 331–2). Whereas the first qualification plays down the necessitarian character of the establishment of the "present order of things," namely capitalist organization,

---

[1] See also Avineri regarding Asian development: "Though it is theoretically obvious that once capitalism is introduced from the outside into non-European society, the next step should be a development toward socialism, Marx nowhere makes an explicit suggestion to that effect" (Avineri 1969: 22). For an alternative evaluation, see Stedman Jones (2002: 184n.) and Aarons (2009: 165–6).

the second in effect represents *Capital* as an exposition of the necessary "laws" that become pertinent once capitalist organization is taken for granted as the starting point. This same perspective is also apparent in a celebrated letter to Vera Zasulich of 8 March 1881.[2] Here Marx cites the French edition of *Capital* (1872–5) to the effect that, in addition to England, "all the other countries of Western Europe are undergoing the same process" of capitalist expropriation of the independent agricultural producer – alluding to expropriation of peasant-owned land – and insists on a different situation in Russia (MECW 46: 71). In Western Europe the initial transition was from "[p]rivate property, based on personal labour" to "capitalist private property"– as explained in *Capital* – whereas "[i]n the case of the Russian peasants, their communal property would... have to be transformed into private property." It is thus not the case that Marx took no final position on the matter, as Stedman Jones maintained (1982: 292). For Marx, there could be no transition to communist organization based directly on the rural commune; the end point would have to be reached by an intermediate stage entailing capitalistic ownership.

Let us turn to Engels. Howard and King maintain that "Engels's writings... stress to a far greater degree than those of Marx himself the indispensability of Western political leadership for the realization of populist ideas. There is also evidence to suggest that Engels never took the [populist] prospect very seriously, even before Marx's death. After 1883 his position hardened even further" regarding the potential of a "populist path" to communism avoiding the capitalist stage (1989: 139–40). This interpretation is based partly on the Preface to the 1882 (Russian) edition of the *Communist Manifesto*, which, though under the names of Marx and Engels, is said to have been "drafted" by Engels. Here a successful *obshchina* route to communism, taking account of its actual weak state in consequence of Russian capitalist developments, is said to presuppose a "complement" in Western revolution, which itself required an initial stimulus from Russia:

Now the question is: can the Russian *obshchina*, a form of primeval common ownership of land, even if greatly undermined [by capitalist developments], pass directly to the higher form of communist common ownership? Or must it, conversely, first pass through the same process of dissolution as constitutes the historical development of the West?

The only possible answer today is this: If the Russian Revolution [overthrow of the Czar] becomes the signal for a proletarian revolution in the West, so that the two complement each other, the present Russian common ownership of land may serve as the starting point for communist development. (MECW 24: 426; also reproduced 1890, MECW 27: 54)

For my part, I see no reason to believe that Engels was the sole responsible author of the Preface, Marx merely lending his name. That it was "drafted" by Engels proves

---

[2] Zasulich's initial request that Marx comment on the possible fate of the rural commune (16 February 1881) and several drafts of his reply are printed and discussed in Shanin (1983, Part II). See also for these drafts MECW 24 (346–69).

nothing.[3] Indeed, in the Preface to the Fourth German edition (1890), Engels expressly specifies that the Preface "was written by Marx and myself" (MECW *27*: 53). Certainly, there is no evidence of a "hardening" of position regarding the *obshchina* route to communism relative to Marx, who, we have seen, denied in 1867 and again in 1877 the prospect of a transition to communism avoiding the stage of capitalism.

An Engels letter of 1893 refers both to Marx's letter in 1877 and to the 1882 Preface and actually cites Marx as sole author, though evidently this is not to be taken seriously. However, Engels now maintains that any such possibility was no longer relevant, for the disappointing progress made by the Western proletarian movement was allowing time for the progress of Russian capitalism, thus rendering the *obshchina* option increasingly irrelevant:

No doubt the commune and to a certain extent the artel, contained germs which under certain conditions might have developed and saved Russia the necessity of passing through the torments of the capitalistic *régime*. . . . I fully subscribe to our author's letter [Marx, 1877]. . . . But in his, as well as in my opinion, the first condition required to bring this about was the impulse from without, the change of economic system in the Occident of Europe, the destruction of the capitalist system in the countries where it had originated. Our author [sic] said in a certain preface to a certain old manifesto, in January 1882, replying to the question whether the Russian commune might not be the starting-point of a higher social development: if the change of economic system in Russia coincides with a change of economic system in the West – so that the two complement each other, the present Russian common ownership of land may serve as the starting-point for communist development.

If we in the West had been quicker in our own economic development, if we had been able to upset the capitalistic regime some ten or twenty years ago, there might have been time yet for Russia to cut short the tendency of her own evolution towards capitalism. Unfortunately we are too slow, and those economic consequences of the capitalistic system which must bring it up to the critical point, are only just now developing in the various countries about us: while England is fast losing her industrial monopoly, France and Germany are approaching the industrial level of England, and America bids fair to drive them all out of the world's market both for industrial and agricultural produce. (to Nikolai Danielson, 24 February 1893; MECW *50*: 110–11)

The rapid progress of Russian capitalism and the likelihood that this, and not the *obshchina* option, was the prelude to communism following the irrevocable laws of capitalist development might be said to amount to a "hardening" of position; however, here there is no change regarding matters of principle, merely an evaluation of empirical reality regarding the poor fortunes of the *obshchina* under the pressure of rapid capitalist advance.[4]

---

[3] The facsimile of the original document – lost soon after submission – appears in the Russian edition of the *Communist Manifesto* 1948 (see MECW *24*: 649 n. 480).

[4] Even so, be it noted, Engels still makes allowance for a possible, if very partial or localized, role for the *obshchina*; "with you, the commune fades away, and we can only hope that the change to a better system, with us, may come soon enough to save, at least in some of the remoter portions of your country, institutions which may, under these circumstances, be called upon

Engels's 1894 Afterward to his "On Social Relations in Russia [1875]" reserves judgment regarding the resilience of the commune system; nonetheless, even assuming the best case possible, a successful transition to communism in Russia based on the commune would still require a "sudden change of direction in Western Europe," confirming the position of 1882 (MECW *27*: 433). Further, the interdependence of the Western and Russian patterns of development there emphasized is again apparent, insofar as the overthrow of the Czarist régime – a requirement for progress by the peasantry – would encourage proletarian revolution in the West, which in turn is represented as a necessary condition for a "socialist transformation" in Russia.

Now at this point we encounter a feature not apparent in the earlier formulations of 1882 and 1893. The aforementioned condition is said to apply whether such transformation "proceed[ed] from the commune *or from capitalism*" (emphasis added). Engels had little confidence in a communist outcome in Russia, even one based on capitalist development, without a Western complement:

Whether enough of this commune has been saved so that, if the occasion arises, as Marx and I still hoped in 1882, it could become the point of departure for communist development, in harmony with a sudden change of direction in Western Europe, I do not presume to say. But this much is certain: if a remnant of this commune is to be preserved, the first condition is the fall of tsarist despotism – revolution in Russia. This will not only tear the great mass of the nation, the peasants, away from the isolation of their villages . . . ; it will also give the labour movement of the West fresh impetus and create new, better conditions in which to carry on the struggle, thus hastening the victory of the modern industrial proletariat, without which present-day Russia can never achieve a socialist transformation, whether proceeding from the commune or from capitalism. (MECW *27*: 433)[5]

Here Engels, in effect, is illustrating an evaluation made in the late 1840s of a small likelihood of achieving socialism in one country (Chapter Four, note 13). To this extent he emerges, in this context at least, as somewhat less "deterministic" than Marx, who took for granted a communist outcome in Russia, provided capitalist development there had taken hold, and this independently of external events.[6]

---

to fulfill a great future. But facts are facts, and we must not forget that these chances are getting less and less every year" (MECW *50*: 111).

[5] Whether Engels intended violent or constitutional change by "a proletarian revolution in the West" in 1882, the "destruction of the capitalist system" in the West in 1893, a "sudden change of direction in Western Europe" and the "victory of the modern industrial proletariat" in 1894 is not relevant here. The issue was treated in Chapter Four.

[6] For an instance of the view of Engels as *more* "deterministic" than Marx, see Lichtheim (1964: 59–60); for a counterview, see Hobsbawm (1998: 27–8).

Bibliography of Works Cited

MECW refers to the English-language *Marx–Engels Collected Works*, published jointly in fifty volumes (1975–2004) by Lawrence and Wishart, London; International Publishers, New York; and Progress Publishers and the Institute of Marxism-Leninism (subsequently the Russian Independent Institute of Social and National Problems), Moscow.

* * *

A. Works by Engels

"Schelling and Revelation: Critique of the Latest Attempt of Reaction Against the Free Philosophy." 1842. MECW 2: 189–240.

"The English View of the Internal Crisis." 1842. MECW 2: 368–9.

"Letters from London." 1843. MECW 3: 379–91.

"Progress of Social Reform on the Continent." 1843. MECW 3: 392–408.

Outlines of a Critique of Political Economy. 1844. MECW 3: 418–43.

"The Condition of England. *Past and Present* by Thomas Carlyle (1843)." 1844. MECW 3: 445–68.

"The Condition of England. The Eighteenth Century." 1844. MECW 3: 469–513.

"Speeches in Elberfeld." 1845. MECW 4: 244–64.

The Condition of the Working Class in England. 1845. MECW 4: 295–583.

Correspondence. 1847–95. MECW 38–50.

"The Festival of Nations in London." 1846. MECW 6: 3–14.

Draft of a "Communist Confession of Faith." 1847. MECW 6: 96–103.

"The Free Trade Congress at Brussels." 1847. MECW 6: 282–90.

"The Communists and Karl Heinzen." 1847. MECW 6: 291–306.

"The Commercial Crisis in England." 1847. MECW 6: 307–9.

Principles of Communism. 1847. MECW 6: 341–57.

"The Chartist Banquet." 1847. MECW 6: 361–3.

"The Civil War in Switzerland." 1847. MECW 6: 367–74.

"The Reform Movement in France." 1847. MECW 6: 375–82.

"The Chartist Movement." 1847. MECW 6: 383–4.

"Split in the Camp." 1847. MECW 6: 385–7.

"Chartist Agitation." 1847. MECW 6: 412–14.

"The 'Satisfied' Majority." 1848. MECW 6: 438–44.

"The Chartist Movement." 1848. MECW 6: 466–7.

373

"The Movements of 1847." 1848. MECW *6*: 520–9.

"Revolution in Paris." 1848. MECW *6*: 556–8.

"Letters from France." 1850. MECW *10*: 17–40.

"The Ten Hours' Question." 1850. MECW *10*: 271–6.

"The English Ten Hours' Bill." 1850. MECW *10*: 288–300.

The Peasant War in Germany. 1850. MECW *10*: 397–482.

Critical Review (ms) of Proudhon's *Idée générale de la revolution au XIX e siècle.* 1851. MECW *11*: 545–70.

"England." 1852. MECW *11*: 198–209.

Review of Marx's *A Contribution to the Critique of Political Economy.* 1859. MECW *16*: 465–77.

"The Prussian Military Question and the German Workers' Party." 1865. MECW *20*: 37–79.

Review of *Capital 1.* 1867. MECW *20*: 210–13.

Review of *Capital 1.* 1868. MECW *20*: 231–7.

"Karl Marx." 1869. MECW *21*: 59–64.

"Letters from London." 1872. MECW *23*: 148–50.

The Housing Question. 1872–3. (Revised 1887.) MECW *23*: 315–91.

Dialectics of Nature (ms). 1873–82. MECW *25*: 311–588.

"On Authority." 1873. MECW *23*: 422–5.

"The Bakunists at Work: An Account of the Spanish Revolt in the Summer of 1873." 1873. MECW *23*: 581–98.

"The English Elections." 1874. MECW *23*: 611–16.

"Refugee Literature." 1874. MECW *24*: 3–50.

"British Agricultural Labourers." 1877. MECW *24*: 179–80.

"Karl Marx." 1877. MECW *24*: 183–95.

Anti-Dühring. 1878. See entry under 1894 (1878, 1885).

"The Socialism of Mr. Bismarck." 1880. MECW *24*: 272–80.

Socialism: Utopian and Scientific. 1880. See entry for 1892 (1880).

"A Fair Day's Wages for a Fair Day's Work." 1881. MECW *24*: 376–8.

"The Wages System." 1881. MECW *24*: 379–81.

"Trades Unions." 1881. MECW *24*: 382–8.

"The French Commercial Treaty." 1881. MECW *24*: 389–93.

"Two Model Town Councils." 1881. MECW *24*: 394–6.

"American Food and the Land Question." 1881. MECW *24*: 397–9.

"A Working Men's Party." 1881. MECW *24*: 404–6.

"Bismarck and the German Working Men's Party." 1881. MECW *24*: 407–9.

"Cotton and Iron." 1881. MECW *24*: 411–14.

"Social Classes – Necessary and Superfluous." 1881. MECW *24*: 415–18.

Eulogy at Karl Marx's Funeral. 1883. MECW *24*: 467–71.

The Origin of the Family, Private Property and the State, in the Light of the Researches of Lewis H. Morgan. 1884. MECW *26*: 129–276.

"England in 1845 and in 1885." 1885. MECW *26*: 295–301.

"On the History of the Communist League." 1885. MECW *26*: 312–30.

Chronological Table of Chartist Agitation. 1886. MECW *26*: 566–77.

"Marx and Rodbertus." Preface to first German Edition of Marx's *The Poverty of Philosophy.* 1885. MECW *26*: 278–91.

Preface to "Karl Marx before the Cologne Jury [1849]." 1885. MECW *26*: 304–10.

Preface to *Capital 2.* 1885. MECW *36*: 5–23.

Preface to first English edition of *Capital 1.* 1886. MECW *35*: 30–6.

Appendix to American edition of *The Condition of the Working Class in England*. 1887. MECW *26*: 399–405.

"The Labor Movement in America." Preface to American edition of *The Condition of the Working Class in England*. 1887. MECW *26*: 434–42.

Letter to the Organising Committee of the International Festival in Paris. MECW *26*: 443–4.

Introduction to Sigismund Borkheim.... 1887. MECW *26*: 446–51.

Ludwig Feuerbach and the End of Classical German Philosophy. 1888 (1886). MECW *26*: 353–98.

"The Role of Force in History." 1887–8. MECW *26*: 453–510.

Introduction to English edition of the *Manifesto of the Communist Party*. 1888. MECW *26*: 512–18.

"Protection and Free Trade" (Preface to Marx's Speech on the Question of Free Trade 1848). 1888. MECW *26*: 521–36.

Interview to *New Yorker Volkzeitung*. 1888. MECW *26*: 626–7.

"The Abdication of the Bourgeoisie." 1889. MECW *26*: 546–50.

"What Now?" 1890. MECW *27*: 7–10.

Preface to the Fourth German edition of the *Communist Manifesto*. 1890. MECW *27*: 53–60.

"May 4 in London." 1890. MECW *27*: 61–6.

"In the Case of Brentano versus Marx." 1891. MECW *27*: 95–131.

Introduction to German edition of Marx's *The Civil War in France*. 1891. MECW *27*: 179–91.

Introduction to "Wage Labour and Capital." 1891. MECW *27*: 194–201.

"A Critique of the Draft Social-Democratic Programme (Erfurt)." 1891. MECW *27*: 217–32.

"Socialism in Germany." 1892. MECW *27*: 235–50.

Preface to English edition of *The Condition of the Working Class in England in 1844*. 1892. MECW *27*: 257–69.

"Reply to the Honourable Giovanni Bovio." 1892. MECW *27*: 270–2.

Socialism: Utopian and Scientific. 1892 (1880). MECW *24*: 281–325.

Introduction to *Socialism: Utopian and Scientific*.1892. MECW *27*: 278–302.

Preface to Second German edition of *The Condition of the Working Class in England*. 1892. MECW *27*: 307–23.

"The American Presidential Election." 1892. MECW *27*: 329–31.

Message to the German Workers on May Day. 1893. MECW *27*: 394–5.

Preface to *Capital 3*. 1894. MECW *37*: 5–23.

Anti-Dühring. Herr Eugen Dühring's "Revolution in Science." 1894 (1878, 1885). 3rd ed. MECW *25*: 1–309. (Part II, Chapter X: 211–43 is by Marx.)

Afterword to "On Social Relations in Russia" (1875). 1894. MECW *27*: 421–33.

The Third Volume of Karl Marx's *Capital*. 1894. MECW *27*: 434.

On the Contents of the Third Volume of *Capital*. 1894. MECW *27*: 435–6.

To the Fourth Austrian Party Congress. 1894. MECW *27*: 442.

"The Peasant Question in France and Germany." 1894. MECW *27*: 481–502.

"Law of Value and Rate of Profit." Supplement to *Capital 3*. 1895. MECW *37*: 873–97.

Introduction to Marx's *The Class Struggles in France 1848–1850*. 1895. MECW *27*: 506–24.

B. Works by Engels and Marx

The Holy Family or Critique of Critical Criticism against Bruno Bauer and Company. 1845. MECW *4*: 4–211.

The Germany Ideology. 1845–6. MECW *5*: 19–539.

"On Poland." 1847. MECW *6*: 388–90.

Manifesto of the Communist Party. 1848. MECW *6*: 477–519.
"January to February." 1850. MECW *10*: 257–70.
Address of the Central Authority to the League of Communists. 1850. MECW *10*: 277–87.
Review of *Latter-Day Pamphlets*, ed. Thomas Carlyle. 1850. MECW *10*: 301–10.
"May to October." 1850. MECW *10*: 490–532.
Preface to German edition of the *Manifesto of the Communist Party.* 1872. MECW *23*: 174–5.
"Resolutions of the General Congress held at The Hague" (September). 1872. MECW *23*: 243–53.
Preface to Second Russian edition of the *Communist Manifesto.* 1882. MECW *24*: 425–6.

C. Works by Marx

"Contribution to the Critique of Hegel's *Philosophy of Law.*" 1844. MECW *3*: 175–87.
Critical marginal notes on the article "The King of Prussia and Social Reform by a Prussian [1844]." 1844. MECW *3*: 189–206.
Comments on James Mill. 1844. MECW *3*: 211–28.
Economic and Philosophic Manuscripts. 1844. MECW *3*: 229–346.
Summary of Frederick Engels' Article, "Outlines of a Critique of Political Economy." 1844. MECW *3*: 375–6.
"Theses on Feuerbach." 1845. MECW *5*: 3–8.
The Poverty of Philosophy. An Answer to the "Philosophy of Poverty" by M. Proudhon. 1847. MECW *6*: 105–212.
Speech (undelivered) on Protection, Free Trade and the Working Classes. 1847. In Engels, "The Free Trade Congress at Brussels." MECW *6*: 287–90.
"Moralising Criticism and Critical Morality." 1847. MECW *6*: 312–40.
"Wages." 1847. MECW *6*: 415–37.
"Speech on the Question of Free Trade." 1848. MECW *6*: 450–65.
"The *Débat Social* on the Democratic Association." 1848. MECW *6*: 537–9.
"Wage Labour and Capital." 1849. MECW *9*: 197–228.
The Class Struggles in France, 1848–1850. 1850. MECW *10*: 45–145.
The Eighteenth Brumaire of Louis Bonaparte. 1852. MECW *11*: 99–197.
"The Chartists." 1852. MECW *11*: 333–41.
"Capital Punishment – Mr. Cobden's pamphlet – Regulations of the Bank of England." 1853. MECW *11*: 495–501.
"The Association for Administrative Reform." 1855. MECW *14*: 240–4.
Outlines of the Critique of Political Economy. (Grundrisse der Kritik der Politischen Ökonomie.) 1857–8. MECW *28*; *29*: 5–251.
"Project for the Regulation of the Price of Bread in France." 1858. MECW *16*: 110–14.
A Contribution to the Critique of Political Economy. 1859. MECW *29*: 257–417.
Economic Manuscripts. 1861–63. *MECW 30–34.* Includes *Theories of Surplus Value, 30*: 348–451; *31*; *32*; *33*: 7–371.
Correspondence. 1862–82. MECW *41–46.*
Inaugural Address of the Working Men's International Association. 1864. MECW *20*: 3–13.
Provisional Rules of the Working Men's International Association. 1864. MECW *20*: 14–16.
Value, Price and Profit. 1865. MECW *20*: 101–49.
Instructions for the Delegates of the Provisional General Council of the International. 1867. MECW *20*: 185–94.
Capital: A Critique of Political Economy 1. 1867. MECW *35*.
The Civil War in France. 1871. 3rd ed. MECW *22*: 307–59.
First Drafts of *The Civil War in France.* 1871. MECW *22*: 437–514.

Interview with *The World* Correspondent. 1871. MECW *22*: 600–6.

Speech at the London Conference of the International. 1871. MECW *22*: 614–17.

Speech on the Seventh Anniversary of the International. 1871. MECW *22*: 633–4.

"On the Hague Congress." 1872. MECW *23*: 254–6.

Le Capital. Traduction de M. J. Roy. 1872–5. Paris: Maurice Lachâtre et Cie.

To the editor of *Le Corsair.* 1872. MECW *23*: 257–8.

"Political Indifferentism." 1873. MECW *23*: 392–7.

Afterword to second German edition of *Capital 1.* 1873. MECW *35*: 12–20.

"Critique of the Gotha Programme. Marginal Notes on the Unity Program of the German Workers' Party." 1875. MECW *24*: 81–99.

Letter to *Otechestvenniye Zapiski.* 1877. MECW *24*: 196–201.

"The Parliamentary Debate on the Anti-Socialist Law" (Outline of an article). 1878. MECW *24*: 240–50.

"Preamble to the Programme of the French Workers' Party." 1880. MECW *24*: 340–1.

Introduction to Engels, *Socialism, Utopian and Scientific.* 1880. MECW *24*: 335–9.

Marginal notes to Adolphe Wagner. 1879. (Completed after January 1881.) MECW *24*: 531–59.

Capital: A Critique of Political Economy 2. 1885. MECW *36*.

Capital: A Critique of Political Economy 3. 1894. MECW *37*.

* * *

Karl Marx. Oeuvres. M. Rubel, ed. Paris: Gallimard. Édition de la Pléiade:

Économie I. 1963 (cited as Marx 1963).
Économie II. 1968 (cited as Marx 1968).
Économie III. 1982 (cited as Marx 1982).

Notes de lecture. 1844. *Marx 1968*: 7–43.

* * *

Karl Marx/ Friedrich Engels Gesamtausgabe. The Internationalen Marx–Engels Stiftung:

MEGA² II/8. 1989. *Das Kapital: Kritik der politischen Ökonomie.* Erste Band. Berlin: Dietz Verlag.

MEGA² II/4.2. 1992. *Ökonomische Manuskripte 1863–1867.* Berlin: Dietz Verlag.

MEGA² II/14. 2003. *Manuskripte und redaktionelle Texte zum dritten Buch des "Kapitals," 1871 bis 1895.* Berlin: Akademie Verlag.

D. Works Cited by Engels

Anon. 1821. *The Source and Remedy of the National Difficulties: A Letter to Lord John Russell.* London: Rodwell and Martin.

Alison, A. 1840. *The Principles of Population and Their Connection with Human Happiness.* Edinburgh: W. Blackwood.

Alison, W. P. 1840. *Observations on the Management of the Poor in Scotland, and Its Effects on the Health of the Great Towns.* Edinburgh: W. Blackwood.

Alison, W. P. 1844. "Notes on the Report of the Royal Commissioners on the Operation of the Poor Laws in Scotland, 1844." *Journal of the Statistical Society of London 7*: 316–18.

Annual Report of the Secretary of the Treasury. 1887. Washington, pp. xxviii–xxix.

Baines, E. 1835. *History of Cotton Manufacture in Great Britain.* London: Fisher, Fisher and Jackson.

Barth, P. 1890. *Die Geschichtsphilosophie Hegels und der Hegelianer bis auf Marx und Hartmann.* Leipzig: R. Reisland.

Bray, J. F. 1839. *Labour's Wrongs and Labour's Remedy.* Leeds: David Green, Briggate.

Carlyle, T. 1840. *Chartism.* London: J. Fraser.

Carlyle, T. 1843. *Past and Present.* London: Chapman and Hall.

Dühring, E. 1871. *Kritische Geschichte der Nationalökonomie und des Sozialismus.* Berlin: Grieben.

Dühring, E. 1876. *Cursus der National- und Sozialökonomie.* Leipzig: T. Grieben.

Edmonds, T. R. 1828. *Practical, Moral and Political Economy.* London: E. Wilson.

Feuerbach, L. 1841. *Das Wesen des Christenthums.* Leipzig: Otto Wigand.

Fireman, P. 1892. "Kritik der Marx'schen Werttheorie." *Jahrbücher für Nationalökonomie und Statistik 58*: 793–808.

Fourier, F. M. C. 1829. *Le Nouveau Monde industriel et sociétaire.* Paris: Bossange.

Gaskell, P. 1833. *The Manufacturing Population of England.* London: Baldwin and Cradock.

Gilbart, J. W. 1834. *The History and Principles of Banking.* London: Longman, Rees, Orme, Brown, Green and Longmans.

Gray, J. 1831. *The Social System: A Treatise on the Principle of Exchange.* Edinburgh: W. Tate.

Hansard Parliamentary Debates. 1844. Third Series. Vol. LXXIII. Sir James Graham and Lord Ashley on the Ten Hours' Bill, 15 March.

Hess, M. 1842. "Über eine in England bevorstehende Katastrophe." *Rheinische Zeitung 177.* 26 June.

Hodgskin, T. 1827. *Popular Political Economy.* London: C. and W. Tait.

Kay-Shuttleworth, J. P. 1832. *The Moral and Physical Condition of the Working Classes Employed in the Cotton Manufacture in Manchester.* 2nd ed. London: Ridgway.

Leach, J. 1844. *Stubborn Facts from the Factories by a Manchester Operative.* London: John Ollivier.

Lexis, W. 1885. "Die Marx'sche Kapitaltheorie." *Conrads Jahrbücher (Jahrbücher für Nationalökonomie und Statistik) 11*: 452–65.

Loria, A. 1886. *La teoria economica della costituzione politica.* Turin: Bocca.

Loria, A. 1890. "Review of Schmidt 1889." *Jahrbücher für Nationalökonomie und Statistik 20*: 272f.

Loria, A. 1895. "L'opera postuma di Carlo Marx." *Nuova Antologia 1*: 460–96.

McCulloch, J. R. 1837a. *A Statistical Account of the British Empire.* London: Charles Knight.

McCulloch, J. R. 1844. *A Dictionary Practical, Theoretical and Historical of Commerce and Commercial Navigation.* New ed. London: Longman, Brown, Green and Longmans.

Mehring, F. 1919 (1893). *Die Lessing-Legende.* Stuttgart: Dietz.

Morgan, L. H. 1877. *Ancient Society, or Researches in the Lines of Human Progress from Savagery, through Barbarism to Civilisation.* London: MacMillan.

Mülberger, A. 1872. *Die Wohnungsfrage. Eine sociale Skizze.* Leipzig: Separat-Abdruck aus dem Volksstaat.

Owen, R. 1817. *Observations on the Effect of the Manufacturing System.* 2nd ed. London: Longman, Hurst, Reese, Orme and Brown.

Parkinson, R. 1841. *On the Present Condition of the Labouring Poor in Manchester.* 3rd ed. London and Manchester: Simpkin, Marshall & Company.

Porter, G. R. 1836, 1838, 1843. *The Progress of the Nation.* 3 Volumes. London: Charles Knight.

Proudhon, P.-J. 1840. *Qu'est la proprieté? Ou Recherches sur le principe du droit et du gouvernement.* Paris: Garnier.

Proudhon, P.-J. 1851. *Idée générale de la révolution au XIX e siècle.* Paris: Garnier.

Proudhon, P.-J. 1846. *Système des contradictions économiques, ou Philosophie de la misère.* Paris: Guillaumin.

Proudhon, P.-J. 1868a. *De la capacité politique des classes ouvrières.* Nouvelle édition. Paris: Lacroix.

Proudhon, P.-J. 1868b. *Idée générale de la revolution au XIX e siècle.* Nouvelle édition. Paris: Librairie Internationale.

Ricardo, D. 1819. *Principles of Political Economy.* 2nd ed. London: J. Murray.

Rodbertus-Jagetzow, J. K. 1842. *Zur Erkenntniss unsrer staatswirthschaftlichen Zustände. I.* Neubrandenberg und Friedland: G. Barnewitz.

Rodbertus-Jagetzow, J. K. 1971 (1851). *Soziale Briefe an von Kirchmann. Dritte Brief.* Berlin: F. Gerhard. English trans. Julia Franklin 1898 as *Overproduction and Crises.* New York: Swan Sonnenschein.

Rodbertus-Jagetzow, J. K. 1871. *Der Normal-Arbeitstag.* Berlin: G. Hickethier.

Rodbertus-Jagetzow, J. K. 1881. *Briefe und sozialpolitsche Aufsaetze.* Berlin: Rudolf Meyer.

Rousseau, J.-J. 1755. *Discours sur l'origine et les fondemens de l'inégalite parmi les hommes.* Amsterdam: Marc Michel Rey.

Sax, E. 1869. *Die Wohnungszustände der arbeiten Klassen und ihre Reform.* Vienna: Pichler's Witwe & Sohn.

Schmidt, C. 1889. *Die Durchschnittsprofitrate auf Grundlage des Marx'schen Werthgesetzes.* Stuttgart: Dietz.

Schmidt, C. 1891–2. "Die psychologische Richtung in der neueren National-Ökonomie." *Die Neue Zeit 10.* 2 Band. Nr. 40, 41.

Schmidt, C. 1892–3. "Die Durchschnittsprofitrate und das Marx'sche Werthgesetz." *Die Neue Zeit 11.* Nr. 3, 4.

Schmidt, C. 1895. "Der dritte Band des 'Kapital.'" In *Sozialpolitsches Centralblatt* No. 22. 25 February.

Senior, N. W. 1837. *Letters on the Factory Acts.* London: B. Fellowes.

Sismondi, J. C. L. Simonde de. 1827. *Nouveaux Principes de l'Économie Politique.* 2nd ed. Paris: Delaunay.

Smith, A. 1976 (1776). *An Inquiry into the Nature and Causes of the Wealth of Nations.* Oxford: Oxford University Press.

Sombart, W. 1894. "Zur Kritik des Ökonomischen System von Karl Marx." *Archiv für soziale Gesetzgebung und Statistik 7:* 584–6.

Stiebeling, G. C. 1890. *Das Werthgesetz und die Profitrate.* New York: Heinrichs.

Stirner, M. 1845. *Der Einzige und sein Eigenthum.* Leipzig: Otto Wigand.

Thompson, T. P. 1826. *The True Theory of Rent in Opposition to Mr. Ricardo and Others.* London: R. Heward.

Thompson, W. 1824. *An Inquiry into the Principles of the Distribution of Wealth.* London: Longman, Hurst, Rees, Orme, Brown and Green.

Ure, A. 1835. *The Philosophy of Manufactures or, an Exposition of the Scientific, Moral, and Commercial Economy of the Factory System of Great Britain.* London: Charles Knight.

Ure, A. 1836. *The Cotton Manufacture of Great Britain Systematically Investigated.* London: Charles Knight.

Wade, J. 1833. *History of the Middle and Working Classes.* London: Effingham Wilson.

Wakefield, E. G. 1831. *Swing Unmasked; or, the Causes of Rural Incendiarism.* London: E. Wilson.

Watts, J. 1842. *The Facts and Fictions of Political Economists*. Manchester: A. Heywood.

Wolf, J. 1891. "Das Rätsel der Durchschnittsprofitrate bei Marx." *Jahrbücher für Nationalökonomie und Statistik 57*: 352–67.

E. Other References

Aarons, E. 2009. *Hayek versus Marx and Today's Challenges*. London & New York: Routledge.

Anderson, K. 1983. "The 'Unknown' Marx's *Capital*, Volume I: The French Edition of 1872–75, 100 Years Later." *Review of Radical Political Economics 15*: 71–80.

Anderson, K. 1999. Review of Arthur, ed. *Engels Today. Science and Society 63*: 247–50.

Andler, C. 1901 (nd). *Le Manifeste Communiste de Karl Marx et Friedrich Engels. Introduction historique et commentaire*. Paris: Les éditions Rieder.

Andréas, B. 1963. *Le Manifeste Communiste de Marx et Engels: Histoire et Bibliographie 1848–1918*. Milano: Feltrinelli Editore.

Angel, P. 1961. *Eduard Bernstein et l'évolution du socialisme allemande*. Paris: Marcel Didier.

Arthur, C. J., ed. 1996a. *Engels Today: A Centenary Appreciation*. Basingstoke: Macmillan.

Arthur, C. J. 1996b. "Engels as Interpreter of Marx's Economics." In C. J. Arthur, ed. *Engels Today*, 173–210.

Avineri, S. 1968. *The Social and Political Thought of Karl Marx*. Cambridge: Cambridge University Press.

Avineri, S. 1969. *Introduction to Karl Marx on Colonialism and Modernization*, 1–31. New York: Anchor Books.

Babbage, C. 1835. *On the Economy of Machinery and Manufactures*. London: Charles Knight.

Bakunin, M. 1973 (1872). "The International and Karl Marx." In S. Dolgoff, ed. *Bakunin on Anarchy: Selected Works of the Founder of World Anarchism*, 286–320. London: Allen & Unwin.

Baran, P. A. and P. M. Sweezy. 1996. *Monopoly Capitalism: An Essay on the American Economic and Social Order*. New York & London: Monthly Review Press.

Beales, H. L. 1954 (1934). "The 'Great Depression' in Industry and Trade." In E. M. Carus-Wilson, ed. *Essays in Economic History 1*: 406–15. London: Edward Arnold.

Beamish, R. 1998. "The making of the *Manifesto*." *The Socialist Register 34*: 218–39.

Benton, T. 1996. "Engels and the Politics of Nature." In C. J. Arthur, ed. *Engels Today*, 67–93.

Berg, M. 1980. *The Machinery Question and the Making of Political Economy*. Cambridge: Cambridge University Press.

Berlin, I. 1963. *Karl Marx. His Life and Environment*. 3rd ed. Oxford: Oxford University Press.

Bernstein, E. 1893 (1890). *Ferdinand Lassalle as a Social Reformer*. Trans. E. Marx-Aveling. London: Swan Sonnenschein.

Bernstein, E. 1894–5. "Der dritte Band des 'Kapital'." *Die Neue Zeit 13 (1)*: 33–8.

Bernstein, E. 1899. "Arbeitswert oder Nutzwert." *Die Neue Zeit 17*: 548–54.

Bernstein, E. 1901. *Zur Geschichte und Theorie des Sozialismus*. Gesammelte Abhandlungen. Berlin: Edelheim.

Bernstein, E., ed. 1903. *Dokumente des Sozialismus 3*. Stuttgart: Dietz.

Bernstein, E. 1904. *Ferdinand Lassalle und seine Beteutung für die Arbeiterklasse*. Berlin: Buchhandlung Vorwärts.

Bernstein, E. 1921 (1918). *My Years in Exile: Reminiscences of a Socialist*. Trans. B. Miall. New York: Harcourt, Brace and Howe.

Bernstein, E. 1993 (1899). *The Preconditions of Socialism.* Trans. H. Tudor. Cambridge: Cambridge University Press.

Bernstein, E. 1961 (1909). *Preface to Evolutionary Socialism: A Criticism and Affirmation,* vii–ix. Trans. E. C. Harvey. New York: Schocken Books.

Besomi, D. 2008. "John Wade's Early Endogenous Dynamic Model: 'Commercial Cycle' and Theories of Crises." *European Journal of the History of Economic Thought* 15: 611–39.

Besomi, D. 2010. "The Periodicity of Crises: A Survey of the Literature." *Journal of the History of Economic Thought* 32: 85–132.

Blaug, M. 1982. *A Methodological Appraisal of Marxian Economics.* Amsterdam: North-Holland Publishing Company.

Bober, M. M. 1965. *Karl Marx's Interpretation of History.* New York: Norton.

Böhm-Bawerk, E. von. 1890. *Capital and Interest.* Trans. W. Smart. London: Macmillan.

Bonar, J. 1899. Review of Bernstein, *Evolutionary Socialism. Economic Journal* 9: 551–3.

Bonar, J. 1922. *Philosophy and Political Economy.* London: Allen & Unwin.

Bottigelli, E. 1969. Présentation, traduction et notes. *Karl Marx: Manuscrits de 1844.* Paris: Éditions Sociales.

Boyer, G. R. 1998. "The Historical Background to *The Communist Manifesto.*" *Journal of Economic Perspectives* 12: 151–74.

Boyer, G. R. 2004. "Living Standards, 1860–1939." In R. Floud and P. Johnson, eds. *The Cambridge Economic History of Modern Britain. II: Economic Maturity, 1860–1939,* 280–313. Cambridge: Cambridge University Press.

Breit, M. and Lange, O. 2003 (1934). "The Way to the Socialist Planned Economy." Trans. Jan Toporowski. *History of Economics Review* 37: 51–70.

Brewer, A. 1984. *A Guide to Marx's Capital.* Cambridge: Cambridge University Press.

Brien, A. 1988. *Lenin. The Novel.* London: Paladin Books.

Briggs, A. 1990. *Victorian People. A Reassessment of Persons and Themes.* London: Penguin Books.

Brophy, J. M. 2007. "Recent Publications of the Marx–Engels Gesamtausgabe (MEGA)." *Central European History* 40: 523–37.

Bullock, A. 1993. *Hitler and Stalin: Parallel Lives.* Toronto: McClelland & Stewart.

Buret, E. 1840. *De La Misère des Classes Laborieuses en Angleterre et en France.* Paris: Paulin.

Cannadine, D. 1992. *The Decline and Fall of the British Aristocracy.* London: Pan Macmillan.

Carver, T. 1981. *Engels.* Oxford: Oxford University Press.

Carver, T. 1983. *Marx and Engels: The Intellectual Relationship.* Brighton: Wheatsheaf Books.

Carver, T. 1989. *Friedrich Engels: His Life and Thought.* Basingstoke: Macmillan.

Carver, T. 1996. "Engels and Democracy." In C. J. Arthur, ed. *Engels Today,* 1–28.

Carver, T. 1998. "Re-translating the *Manifesto*: New Histories. New Ideas." In M. Cowley, ed. *The Communist Manifesto: New Interpretations,* 51–62. New York: New York University Press.

Carver, T. 1999. "The Engels–Marx Question: Interpretation, Identity/ies, Partnership, Politics." In M. B. Steger and T. Carver, eds. *Engels after Marx,* 17–36. University Park, PA: The Pennsylvania State University Press.

Chaloner, W. H. and Henderson, W. O. 1971. Introduction. *The Condition of the Working Class in England,* xi–xxxv. Oxford: Basil Blackwell.

Churchlich, N. 1990. *Marxism and Alienation.* London: Associated University Presses.

Claeys, G. 1984. "Engels' *Outlines of a Critique of Political Economy* (1843) and the Origins of the Marxist Critique of Capitalism." *History of Political Economy* 16: 207–32.

Clark, J. B. 1971. Introduction to Karl Rodbertus, *Overproduction and Crises* (1898), 1–18. New York: Burt Franklin.

Clark, R. W. 1989. *Lenin: The Man Behind the Mask.* London & Boston: Faber and Faber.

Cole, G. D. H. 1956. *The Second International 1889–1914.* London: Macmillan.

Cole, G. D. H. 1962. *Socialist Thought: The Forerunners 1789–1850.* London: Macmillan.

Collier, A. 1996. "Engels: Revolutionary Realist?" In C. J. Arthur, ed. *Engels Today*, 29–45.

Collins, H. 1967. "The English Branches of the First International." In A. Briggs and J. Saville, eds. *Essays in Labour History in Memory of G. D. H. Cole*, 242–75. London: Macmillan.

Concheiro, E. 1998. "A Century after His Death: Friedrich Engels and the Concept of Political Parties." *Science and Society 62*: 163–80.

Cooper, T. 1826. *Lectures on the Elements of Political Economy.* Columbia, SC: Doyle E. Sweeny.

Cottier, G. M.-M. 1961. "Une source de K. Marx et de F. Engels: *De la Misère* des Classes *Laborieuses* d'E. Buret." *Du Romantisme au Marxisme*, 115–38. Paris: Alsatia.

Cowling, M. 1967. *1867. Disraeli, Gladstone and Revolution: The Passing of the Second Reform Bill.* Cambridge: Cambridge University Press.

Crafts, N. 2004. "Long-Run Growth." In R. Floud and P. Johnson, eds. *The Cambridge Economic History of Modern Britain II: Economic Maturity, 1860–1939*, 1–24. Cambridge: Cambridge University Press.

Dennehy, A. 1996. "*The Condition of the Working Class in England*: 150 Years On." In C. J. Arthur, ed. *Engels Today*, 95–127.

Dobb, M. 1940. *Political Economy and Capitalism: Some Essays in Economic Tradition.* London: Routledge & Kegan Paul.

Dobb, M. 1969. *Welfare Economics and the Economics of Socialism.* Cambridge: Cambridge University Press.

Dobb, M. 1970a. *Welfare Economics and the Economics of Socialism: Towards a Commonsense Approach.* Cambridge: Cambridge University Press.

Dobb, M. 1970b. Introduction to Karl Marx, *A Contribution to the Critique of Political Economy* (1859), 5–16. Moscow: Progress Publishers.

Dobb, M. 1982. "Marx's Critique of Political Economy." In E. J. Hobsbawm, ed. *The History of Marxism 1. Marxism in Marx's Day*, 79–102. Brighton: Harvester Press.

Dolléans, E. 1953. *Histoire du Mouvement Ouvrier I: 1830–1871.* 5th ed. Paris: Librairie Armand Colin.

Draper, H. 1986. *Karl Marx's Theory of Revolution III: The "Dictatorship of the Proletariat."* New York: Monthly Review Press.

Duncan, G. 1973. *Marx and Mill: Two Views of Social Conflict and Social Harmony.* Cambridge: Cambridge University Press.

Edelstein, M. 2004. "Foreign Investment, Accumulation and Empire, 1860–1914." In R. Floud and P. Johnson, eds. *The Cambridge Economic History of Modern Britain II: Economic Maturity, 1860–1939*, 190–226. Cambridge: Cambridge University Press.

Elliott, C. F. 1967. "Quis Custodiet Sacra? Problems of Marxist Revisionism." *Journal of the History of Ideas 28*: 71–86.

Falkus, M. 1987. "Rodbertus, Johann Karl." In J. Eatwell, M. Milgate, and P. Newman, eds. *The New Palgrave: A Dictionary of Economics 4*: 218–19. London: Macmillan.

Fawcett, H. 1865. *The Economic Position of the British Labourer.* Cambridge & London: Macmillan.

Feinstein, C. H. 1978. "Capital Formation in Great Britain." In P. Matthias and M. M. Postan, eds. *The Cambridge Economic History of Europe VII. The Industrial Economies: Capital, Labour, and Enterprise*, 28–96. Cambridge: Cambridge University Press.

Fernbach, D. 1974. Introduction to *K. Marx. The First International and After. Political Writings*. London: New Left Review.

Finn, M. C. 1993. *After Chartism. Class and Nation in English Radical Politics, 1848–1874*. Cambridge: Cambridge University Press.

Foley, D. K. 1986. *Understanding Capital: Marx's Economic Theory*. Cambridge, MA: Harvard University Press.

Foxwell, H. S. 1887. "The Economic Movement in England." *Quarterly Journal of Economics* 2: 84–103.

Gårdland, T. 1958. *The Life of Knut Wicksell*. Stockholm: Almquist and Wicksell.

Gay, P. 1952. *The Dilemma of Democratic Socialism: Eduard Bernstein's Challenge to Marx*. New York: Columbia University Press.

Gide, C. and Rist, R. 1964 (1915). *A History of Economic Doctrines*. London: George G. Harrap & Co.

Giffen, R. 1904 (1877). "The Liquidations of 1873–76." *Economic Inquiries and Studies 1*: 98–120. London: George Bell and Sons.

Giffen, R. 1904 (1883). "The Progress of the Working Classes in the Last Half Century." *Economic Inquiries and Studies 1*: 382–422. London: George Bell and Sons.

Gladstone, W. 1863. *The Morning Star*, 17 April, pp. 2–6.

Gladstone, W. 1864. *The Times*, 8 April, pp. 5–7.

Gneuss, C. 1962. "The Precursor: Eduard Bernstein." In L. Labedz, ed. *Revisionism: Essays in the History of Marxist Ideas*, 31–40. London: Allen & Unwin.

Gonner, E. C. K. 1899. *The Social Philosophy of Rodbertus*. London: Macmillan.

Goode, P. 1983. "Kautsky, Karl." In T. Bottomore, ed. *A Dictionary of Marxist Thought*, 248–9. Oxford: Blackwell Reference.

Gray, J. 1825. *A Lecture on Human Happiness*. London: Sherwood, Jones.

Hacking, I. 1990. *The Taming of Chance*. Cambridge: Cambridge University Press.

Harding, N. 1983. "Violence." In T. Bottomore, ed. *A Dictionary of Marxist Thought*, 514–15. Oxford: Blackwell Reference.

Harkort, F. 1844. *Bemerkungen über die Hindernisse der Civilisation und Emancipation der untern Klassen*. Elberfeld: J. Baedeker.

Harney, G. J. 1966 (1850). *The Red Republican*, Vol. 1. New York: Barnes & Noble.

Hatton, T. J. 2004. "Unemployment and the Labour Market, 1870–1939." In R. Floud and P. Johnson, eds. *The Cambridge Economic History of Modern Britain II: Economic Maturity, 1860–1939*, 344–73. Cambridge: Cambridge University Press.

Heinrich, M. 1996. "Engels' Edition of the Third Volume of *Capital* and Marx's Original Manuscript." *Science and Society 60*: 452–66.

Henderson, W. O. 1967. *Engels: Selected Writings*. London: Pelican.

Henderson, W. O. 1976. *The Life of Friedrich Engels*. London: Frank Cass.

Henderson, W. O. 1989. *Marx and Engels and the English Workers, and Other Essays*. London: Frank Cass.

Henderson, W. O. and Chaloner, W. H. 1971. Editors' Introduction to Friedrich Engels, *The Condition of the Working Class in England*, xi–xxxv. Oxford: Basil Blackwell.

Herres, J. and Roth, R. 2005. "Karl Marx." In S. Zahlmann and S. Scholz, eds. *Scheitern und Biographie: Die andere Seite moderner Lebensgeschichten*, 53–70. Giessen: Psychosozial-Verlag.

Hicks, J. 1969. *A Theory of Economic History*. Oxford: Clarendon Press.

Himmelfarb, G. 1984. *The Idea of Poverty: England in the Early Industrial World*. New York: Knopf.

Hobsbawm, E. J. 1964. *Labouring Men: Studies in the History of Labour*. London: Weidenfeld and Nicolson.

Hobsbawm, E. J. 1968. *Industry and Empire: An Economic History of Britain since 1750*. London: Weidenfeld and Nicolson.

Hobsbawm, E. J. 1969. Introduction to Friedrich Engels, *The Condition of the Working Class in England*, 7–17. London: Panther.

Hobsbawm, E. J. 1970. "Lenin and the Aristocracy of Labour." *Marxism Today*, July: 207–10.

Hobsbawm, E. J. 1982a. "Marx, Engels and Pre-Marxian Socialism." In E. J. Hobsbawm, ed. *The History of Marxism I: Marx in Marx's Day*, 1–28. Brighton: The Harvester Press.

Hobsbawm, E. J. 1982b. "Marx, Engels and Politics." In E. J. Hobsbawm, ed. *The History of Marxism I: Marxism in Marx's Day*, 226–64. Brighton: The Harvester Press.

Hobsbawm, E. J. 1998. Introduction to *Karl Marx and Friedrich Engels, "The Communist Manifesto: A Modern Edition,"* 3–29. London and New York: Verso.

Hollander, S. 1965. *The Sources of Increased Efficiency: A Study of Du Pont Rayon Plants*. Cambridge MA: M.I.T. Press

Hollander, S. 1973. *The Economics of Adam Smith*. Toronto: University of Toronto Press.

Hollander, S. 1977. "Adam Smith and the Self-Interest Axiom." *Journal of Law and Economics 20*: 133–52.

Hollander, S. 1979. *The Economics of David Ricardo*. Toronto: University of Toronto Press.

Hollander, S. 1980. "The Post-Ricardian Dissension: A Case-Study in Economics and Ideology." *Oxford Economic Papers 32*: 370–410.

Hollander, S. 1991. "On the Endogeneity of the Margin and Related Issues in Ricardian Economics." *Journal of the History of Economic Thought 13*: 159–73.

Hollander, S. 1992. *Classical Economics*. Toronto: University of Toronto Press.

Hollander, S. 1997. *The Economics of Thomas Robert Malthus*, Toronto: University of Toronto Press.

Hollander, S. 1999. "Jeremy Bentham and Adam Smith on the Usury Laws." *European Journal of the History of Economic Thought 6*: 523–51.

Hollander, S. 2005. *Jean-Baptiste Say and the Classical Canon in Economics: The British Connection in French Classicism*. London and New York: Routledge.

Hollander, S. 2008. *The Economics of Karl Marx: Analysis and Application*. Cambridge: Cambridge University Press.

Howard, M. C. and King, J. E. 1985. *The Political Economy of Marx*. London & New York: Longman.

Howard, M. C. and King, J. E. 1989. *A History of Marxian Economics: Volume I, 1883–1929*. Princeton: Princeton University Press.

Howard, M. C. and King, J. E. 1992. "Marx, Jones, Rodbertus and the Theory of Absolute Rent." *Journal of the History of Economic Thought 14*: 70–83.

Howard, M. C. and King, J. E. 2008. "Karl Marx and the Decline of the Market." *Journal of the History of Economic Thought 30*: 217–34.

Hunley, J. D. 1991. *The Life and Thought of Friedrich Engels*. New Haven & London: Yale University Press.

Hunt, T. 2009. *The Frock-Coated Communist: The Revolutionary Life of Friedrich Engels*. London: Allen Lane.

Hutchison, T. W. 1981. *The Politics and Philosophy of Economics: Marxians, Keynesians and Austrians*. Oxford: Blackwell.

International Working Men's Association. Third Annual Report. 1867. MECW *20*: 428–46.

Itoh, M. 1976. "A Study of Marx's Theory of Value." *Science and Society 40*: 307–40.

Jevons, W. S. 1910 (1882). *The State in Relation to Labour*. London: Macmillan.

Johnstone, M. 1983. "Blanquism." In T. Bottomore, ed. *A Dictionary of Marxist Thought*, 49–50. Oxford: Blackwell Reference.

Joll, J. 1974. *The Second International 1889–1914*. London & Boston: Routledge & Kegan Paul.

Jones, E. 1851. *Notes to the People*, Vol. 1. London: J. Pavey.

Kapp, Y. 1976. *Eleanor Marx II: The Crowded Years (1884–1898)*. London: Lawrence and Wishart.

[Kautsky, K.] 1884. "Tongking." *Die Neue Zeit 2*: 156–64.

Kautsky, K. 1899 (1887). "Frederick Engels." *Austrian Labor Almanac 1887*. Trans. M. W. Simmons. In *Frederick Engels: His Life, His Work and His Writings*, 3–32. Chicago: Charles H. Kerr.

Kautsky, K. 1899. *Bernstein und das sozialdemokratische Programm: Eine Antikritik*. Stuttgart: Dietz.

Kautsky, K. 1909. *The Road to Power*. Trans. A. M. Simons. Chicago: S. A. Bloch.

Kautsky, K. 1919 (1918). *The Dictatorship of the Proletariat*. Trans. H. J. Stenning. Manchester: The National Labour Press.

King, J. E. 1983. "Utopian or Scientific? A Reconsideration of the Ricardian Socialists." *History of Political Economy 15*: 345–74.

King, J. E. 2002. "Nimtz's *Marx and Engels: Their Contribution to the Democratic Breakthrough*." *Research in the History of Economic Thought and Methodology 20A*: 217–22. Amsterdam: Elsevier Science.

Kircz, J. and Löwy, M. 1998. "Friedrich Engels – A Critical Centenary Appreciation: Introduction." *Science and Society 62*: 4–12.

Knight, F. H. 1964 (1921). *Risk, Uncertainty and Profit*. New York: A. M. Kelley.

Kolakowski, L. 2005. *Main Currents of Marxism*. New York and London: Norton.

Kowalik, T. 1987. "Kautsky, Karl." In J. Eatwell, M. Milgate, and P. Newman, eds. *The New Palgrave: A Dictionary of Economics 3*: 16–17. London: Macmillan.

Lange, O. 1938. "On the Economic Theory of Socialism." In O. Lange and F. M. Taylor, eds. *On the Economic Theory of Socialism*, 55–143. Minneapolis: University of Minnesota Press.

Lapides, K. 1987. Introduction, *Marx and Engels on the Trade Unions*, ix–x. New York: Praeger.

Laski, H. J. 1967 (1948). Introduction, *The Communist Manifesto*, 3–105. New York: Pantheon Books.

Lenin, V. I. 1960 (1896). "Frederick Engels." *Collected Works 2*: 15–27. Moscow: Progress Publishers.

Lenin, V. I. 1964 (1914). "Dead Chauvinism and Living Socialism." *Collected Works 21*: 94–101. Moscow: Progress Publishers.

Lenin, V. I. 1964 (1915). "The Conference of the R. S. D. L. P. Groups Abroad." *Collected Works 21*: 158–64. Moscow: Progress Publishers.

Lenin, V. I. 1965a (1918). "The Proletarian Revolution and the Renegade Kautsky." *Collected Works 28*: 227–326. Moscow: Progress Publishers.

Lenin, V. I. 1965b (1918). "Prophetic Words." *Collected Works 27*: 494–9. Moscow: Progress Publishers.

Leontief, W. 1966 (1938). *Essays in Economics: Theories and Theorizing*. New York: Oxford University Press.

Levin, M. 1989. *Marx, Engels and Liberal Democracy*. Basingstoke & London: Macmillan.

Levine, N. 1975. *The Tragic Deception: Marx Contra Engels*. Oxford: Clio Books.

Lexis, W. 1895. "The Concluding Volume of Marx's Capital." *Quarterly Journal of Economics* 10: 1–33.

Lichtheim, G. 1964. *Marxism: An Historical and Critical Study*. London: Routledge & Kegan Paul.

List, F. 1841. *Das nationale System der politischen Ökonomie*. Stuttgart & Tübingen: J. G. Cotta.

Lukes, S. 1983. "Democracy." In T. Bottomore, ed. *A Dictionary of Marxist Thought*, 114–15. Oxford: Blackwell Reference.

Lukács, G. 1971 (1921). *History and Class Consciousness: Studies in Marxist Dialectics*. Cambridge MA: M.I.T. Press.

Magee, G. B. 2004. "Manufacturing and Technological Change." In R. Floud and P. Johnson, eds. *The Cambridge Economic History of Modern Britain II: Economic Maturity, 1860–1939*, 74–98. Cambridge: Cambridge University Press.

Maler, H. 1998. "An Apocryphal Testament: 'Socialism, Utopian and Scientific'." *Science and Society* 62: 48–61.

Malthus, T. R. 1820. *Principles of Political Economy, Considered with a View to Their Practical Application*. London: John Murray.

Mandel, E. 1967. *La formation de la pensée économique de Karl Marx: de 1843 à la reduction du "Capital"*. Paris: Librairie François Maspero.

Manicas, P. T. 1999. "Engels' Philosophy of Science." In M. B. Steger and T. Carver, eds. *Engels after Marx*, 55–82. University Park, PA: The Pennsylvania State University Press.

Marcus, S. 1974. *Engels, Manchester and the Working Class*. New York: Random House.

Marshall, A. 1920 (1890). *Principles of Economics*. London: Macmillan.

Matthew, H. C. G. 1985. "Government and Politics 1846–1901: Free Trade, Franchise and Imperialism." In C. Haigh, ed. *The Cambridge Historical Encyclopedia of Great Britain and Ireland*, 255–60. Cambridge: Cambridge University Press.

Mayer, G. 1934. *Friedrich Engels: Eine Biographie*. Erste Band. Haag: Martinus Nijhoff.

Mayer, G. 1969 (1936). *Friedrich Engels: A Biography* [Abridged]. New York: Howard Fertig.

McCulloch, J. R. 1837b. "Causes and Consequences of the Crisis in the American Trade," *Edinburgh Review* 65: 221–38.

McLellan, D. 1973. *Karl Marx: His Life and Thought*. London: Macmillan.

McLellan, D. 1977. *Engels*. Glasgow: Fontana/Collins.

McLellan, D. 1993. Introduction to Friedrich Engels, *The Condition of the Working Class in England*, ix–xx. Oxford: Oxford University Press.

McLellan, D. 1998. Introduction to Karl Marx and Friedrich Engels, *The Communist Manifesto*, vii–xvii. Oxford: Oxford University Press.

McLellan, D. 2007. *Marxism after Marx*. Basingstoke & New York: Palgrave Macmillan.

Meek, R. L. 1971. *Marx and Engels on the Population Bomb*, 2nd ed. New York: The Ramparts Press.

Meek, R. L. 1975. *Studies in the Labor Theory of Value*, 2nd ed. New York & London: Monthly Review Press.

Meek, R. L. 1976. "Is there an 'historical transformation problem'? A Comment." *Economic Journal* 86: 342–7.

Mehring, F. 1902. "Le 'Manifeste Communiste'." *Le Mouvement Socialiste: Revue Hebdomadaire Internationale* 4: 249–57.

Mehring, F. 1935 (1933). *Karl Marx: The Story of His Life*. 2nd ed. New York: Covici, Friede Publishers.

Menger, A. 1962 (1899). *The Right to the Whole Produce of Labour*. Trans. M. E. Tanner. New York: A. M. Kelley.

Miliband, R. 1983. "Dictatorship of the Proletariat." In T. Bottomore, ed. *A Dictionary of Marxist Thought*, 129–31. Oxford: Blackwell Reference.

Mill, J. S. 1963–91 (1828). "The Nature, Origin, and Progress of Rent." *Collected Works 4*: 161–80. Toronto: University of Toronto Press.

Mill, J. S. 1963–91 (1848a). *Principles of Political Economy*. *Collected Works 2–3*. Toronto: University of Toronto Press.

Mill, J. S. 1963–91 (1848b). "England and Ireland." *Collected Works 25*: 1095–1100. Toronto: University of Toronto Press.

Mill, J. S. 1963–91 (1851). "Newman's Political Economy." *Collected Works 5*: 439–62.

Mill, J. S. 1963–91 (1859a). *Thoughts on Parliamentary Reform*. *Collected Works 19*: 311–39. Toronto: University of Toronto Press.

Mill, J. S. 1963–91 (1859b). "Recent Writers on Reform." *Collected Works 19*: 341–70. Toronto: University of Toronto Press.

Mill, J. S. 1963–91 (1861). *Considerations on Representative Government*. *Collected Works 19*: 371–577. Toronto: University of Toronto Press.

Mill, J. S. 1963–91. *The Earlier Letters 1812–1848*. *Collected Works 13*. Toronto: University of Toronto Press.

Mill, J. S. 1963–91. *The Later Letters 1849 to 1873*. *Collected Works 16*. Toronto: University of Toronto Press.

Mises, L. von. 1980 (1950). *Planning for Freedom*. South Holland, IL: Libertarian Press.

Moorhouse, H. F. 1978. "The Marxist Theory of the Labour Aristocracy." *Social History 3*: 61–82.

Morishima, M. and Catephores, G. 1975. "Is there an 'historical transformation problem'?" *Economic Journal 85*: 309–28.

Morishima, M. and Catephores, G. 1976. "The 'historical transformation problem': A Reply" *Economic Journal 86*: 348–52.

Musto, M. 2009. "Marx–Engels–Gesamtausgabe (MEGA^2)." *Review of Radical Political Economics 41*: 265–8.

Nicholas, T. 2004. "Enterprise and Management." In R. Floud and P. Johnson, eds. *The Cambridge Economic History of Modern Britain II: Economic Maturity, 1860–1939*, 227–52. Cambridge: Cambridge University Press.

Nimtz, A. H. 1999. "Marx and Engels – The Unsung Heroes of the Democratic Breakthrough." *Science and Society 63*: 203–31.

Nimtz, A. H. 2000. *Marx and Engels: Their Contribution to the Democratic Breakthrough*. Albany: State University of New York Press.

Oakley, A. 1979. "Aspects of Marx's *Grundrisse* as Intellectual Foundations for a Major Theme of *Capital*." *History of Political Economy 11*: 286–302.

Oakley, A. 1983. *The Making of Marx's Critical Theory: A Bibliographical Analysis*. Boston: Routledge & Kegan Paul.

Oakley, A. 1984. *Marx's Critique of Political Economy: Intellectual Sources and Evolution, 1844 to 1860*. London: Routledge & Kegan Paul.

Oakley, A. 1985. *Marx's Critique of Political Economy: Intellectual Sources and Evolution, 1861 to 1863*. London: Routledge & Kegan Paul.

O'Neill, J. 1996 "Engels Without Dogmatism." In C. J. Arthur, ed. *Engels Today*, 47–66.

Owen, R. 1821. *Report to the County of Lanark, of a Plan for Relieving Public Distress*. Glasgow: Wardlaw and Cunningham.

Padover, S. K. 1979. *The Letters of Karl Marx.* Englewood Cliffs: Prentice-Hall.

Palgrave, R. H. I. 1883. Report of the Fifty-Third Meeting of the British Association for the Advancement of Science, Southport, pp. 608–9.

Perelman, M. 1985. "Marx, Malthus, and the Organic Composition of Capital." *History of Political Economy 17*: 461–90.

Perelman, M. 1987. *Marx's Crises Theory: Scarcity, Labor and Finance.* New York: Praeger.

Perkin, H. 1978. "'The Condescension of Posterity': The Recent Historiography of the English Working Class." *Social Science History 3*: 87–101.

Pokorni, D. 1985. "Karl Marx and General Equilibrium." *History of Political Economy 17*: 109–32.

Pokorni, D. 1993. *Efficiency and Justice in the Industrial World I. The Failure of the Soviet Experiment.* Armonk, NY & London: M. E. Sharpe.

Popper, K. R. 1983 (1945). "Marx's Theory of the State." In D. Miller, ed. *A Pocket Popper,* 326–37. Oxford: Fontana.

Possony, S. T. 1954. Introduction to *The Communist Manifesto.* Chicago: Henry Regnery.

Przeworski, A. 1985. *Capitalism and Social Democracy.* Cambridge: Cambridge University Press.

Quételet, A. 1842 (1835). *A Treatise on Man and the Development of His Faculties.* Edinburgh: Chambers.

Rabinbach, A. 1992. *The Human Motor: Energy, Fatigue, and the Origins of Modernity.* Berkeley: University of California Press.

Riazanov, D. 1973 (1927). *Karl Marx and Friedrich Engels: An Introduction to Their Lives and Work.* New York & London: Monthly Review Press.

Ricardo, D. 1951–73 (1820). *Notes on Malthus's Principles of Political Economy. Works and Correspondence 2.* P. Sraffa, ed. Cambridge: Cambridge University Press.

Ricardo, D. 1951–73 (1821). *Principles of Political Economy. Works and Correspondence 1.* P. Sraffa, ed. Cambridge: Cambridge University Press.

Ricardo, D. 1951–73 (1823). "Absolute and Exchangeable Value." In P. Sraffa, ed. *Works and Correspondence 4,* 359–97. Cambridge: Cambridge University Press.

Rigby, S. H. 1987. *Marxism and History: A Critical Introduction.* New York: St. Martin's Press.

Rigby, S. H. 1992. *Engels and the Formation of Marxism: History, Dialectics and Revolution.* Manchester & New York: Manchester University Press.

Robbins, L. C. (1935). *An Essay on the Nature and Significance of Economic Science.* 2nd ed. London: Macmillan.

Robbins, L. C. 1976. *Political Economy: Past and Present. A Review of Leading Theories of Economic Policy.* London: Macmillan.

Rodbertus-Jagetzow, J. K. 1899 (1837?). *Die Forderungen der arbeitenden Klassen.* In A Wagner, ed. *Schriften von Dr. Carl Rodbertus-Jagetzow,* 195–223. Berlin: Puttkammer und Mühlbrecht.

Rodbertus-Jagetzow, J. K. 1884 (1852). *Das Kapital. Vierter sozialer Brief an von Kirchmann.* Berlin: Puttkamer und Mühlbrecht.

Rodbertus-Jagetzow, J. K. 1868–9. *Zur Erklärung und Abhülfe der heutigen Kreditnoth des Grundbesitzes.* Jena: Fr. Mauke.

Rogerson, W. P. 1984. "A Note on the Incentive of a Monopolist to Increase Fixed Cost as a Barrier to Entry." *Quarterly Journal of Economics 99*: 399–402.

Rosenberg, N. 1974. "Karl Marx and the Economic Role of Science." *Journal of Political Economy 82*: 713–28.

Rostow, W. W. 1948. *British Economy of the Nineteenth Century.* Oxford: Clarendon Press.

Roth, R. 2002. "The Author Marx and His Editor Engels: Different Views on Volume 3 of *Capital*." *Rethinking Marxism: A Journal of Economics, Culture and Society 14*: 59–72.

Roth, R. and Mosely, F. 2002. "Engels as Editor: Guest Editors' Introduction." *International Journal of Political Economy 32*: 3–13.

Rubel, M. 1963. *Oeuvres de Karl Marx: Économie I*. Paris: Gallimard. Bibliothèque de la Pléiade.

Rubel, M. 1968. *Oeuvres de Karl Marx: Économie II*. Paris: Gallimard. Bibliothèque de la Pléiade.

Rubel, M. 1981. "The 'Marx Legend' or Engels the Founder of Marxism." In G. O'Malley and K. Algozin, eds. *Rubel on Karl Marx: Five Essays*, 15–25. Cambridge: Cambridge University Press.

Rubel, M. 1982. *Oeuvres de Karl Marx. Philosophie*. Paris: Gallimard. Bibliothèque de la Pléiade.

Rubel, M. and Manale, M. 1973. *Marx without Myth: A Chronological Study of his Life and Work*. Oxford: Basil Blackwell.

Russell, B. 1968. *Autobiography*. Toronto: Bantam Books.

Ryazanoff [Riazanov], D. 1930 (1922). *The Communist Manifesto of Karl Marx and Friedrich Engels*. London: Martin Lawrence.

Samuelson, P. A. 1971. "Understanding the Marxian Theory of Exploitation: A Summary of the So-Called Transformation Problem." *Journal of Economic Literature 9*: 399–431.

Sanderson, J. 1969. *An Interpretation of the Political Ideas of Marx and Engels*. London: Longmans.

Saul, S. B. 1985. *The Myth of the Great Depression, 1873–1896*. 2nd ed. Basingstoke & London: Macmillan.

Saville, J. 1987. *1848. The British State and the Chartist Movement*. Cambridge: Cambridge University Press.

Saville, J. 1994. *The Consolidation of the Capitalist State, 1800–1850*. London: Pluto Press.

Say, J.-B. 1819. *Notes Explicatives et Critiques to Ricardo, Principes de l'économie politique*. Trans. F. S. Constancio. Paris: J. P. Aïllaud.

Sayers, S. 1996. "Engels and Materialism." In C. J. Arthur, ed. *Engels Today*, 153–72.

Schumpeter, J. A. 1950. *Capitalism, Socialism, and Democracy*. 3rd ed. New York: Harper & Brothers.

Schumpeter, J. A. 1954. *History of Economic Analysis*. New York: Oxford University Press.

Seigel, J. 1978. *Marx's Fate: The Shape of a Life*. Princeton: Princeton University Press.

Service, R. 2000. *Lenin: A Biography*. Cambridge, MA: Harvard University Press.

Shanin, T., ed. 1983. *Late Marx and the Russian Road: Marx and "The Peripheries of Capitalism."* London: Routledge & Kegan Paul.

Shaw, W. H. 1983. "Historical Materialism." In T. Bottomore, ed. *A Dictionary of Marxist Thought*, 206–10. Oxford: Blackwell Reference.

Smith, A. 1976 (1776). *An Inquiry into the Nature and Causes of the Wealth of Nations*. Oxford: Oxford University Press.

Sowell, T. 1980. *Knowledge and Decision*. Princeton: Princeton University Press.

Sowell, T. 1985. *Marxism: Philosophy and Economics*. New York: William Morrow.

Sowell, T. 1987. "Sismondi, Jean Charles Leonard Simonde de." In J. Eatwell, M. Milgate and P. Newman, eds. *The New Palgrave: A Dictionary of Economics 4*: 348–50. London: Macmillan.

Sowell, T. 2006. *On Classical Economics*. New Haven and London: Yale University Press.

Stedman Jones, G. 1982. "Engels and the History of Marxism." In E. J. Hobsbawm, ed. *The History of Marxism 1. Marxism in Marx's Day*, 290–326. Brighton: The Harvester Press.

Stedman Jones, G. 1987. "Engels, Friedrich (1820–1895)." In J. Eatwell, M. Milgate, and P. Newman, eds. *The New Palgrave: A Dictionary of Economics 2*: 144–6. London: Macmillan.

Stedman Jones, G. 2002. Introduction to Karl Marx and Friedrich Engels, *The Communist Manifesto*, 1–87. London: Penguin Books.

Steger, M. B. 1999. "Friedrich Engels and the Origins of German Revisionism: Another Look." In M. B. Steger and T. Carver, eds. *Engels after Marx*, 181–96. University Park, PA: The Pennsylvania State University Press.

Steger, M. B. and Carver, T. 1999. Introduction to M. B. Steger and T. Carver, eds. *Engels after Marx*, 1–16. University Park, PA: The Pennsylvania State University Press.

Steger, M. B. 1997. *The Quest for Evolutionary Socialism: Eduard Bernstein and Social Democracy*. Cambridge: Cambridge University Press.

Stigler, G. 1965 (1959). "The Politics of Political Economists." *Essays in the History of Economics*, 51–65. Chicago & London: The University of Chicago Press.

Strachey, J. 1959. *The End of Empire*. London: Victor Gollancz.

Sweezy, P. M. 1987 "Socialism." In T. Bottomore, ed. *A Dictionary of Marxist Thought*, 444–7. Oxford: Blackwell Reference.

Symons, J. C. 1839. *Arts and Artisans at Home and Abroad*. Edinburgh: W. Tait.

Tabak, M. 2000. "Marx's Theory of Proletarian Dictatorship Revisited." *Science and Society* 64: 333–56.

Thatcher, I. D. 1998. "Past Receptions of *The Communist Manifesto*." In M. Cowling, ed. *The Communist Manifesto: New Interpretations*, 63–74. New York: New York University Press.

Thompson, N. W. 1984. *The People's Science: The Popular Political Economy of Exploitation and Crisis 1816–34*. Cambridge: Cambridge University Press.

Thompson, N. W. 1998. *The Real Rights of Man: Political Economies For the Working Class 1775–1850*. London: Pluto Press.

Thompson, W. 1827. *Labor Rewarded*. London: Hunt and Clarke.

Tuchman, B. W. 1967. *The Proud Tower. A Portrait of the World Before the War: 1890–1914*. New York: Bantam Books.

Tucker, R. C., ed. 1972. *The Marx–Engels Reader*. New York: Norton.

Tudor, H. 1988. Introduction to Henry Tudor, ed. *Marxism and Social Democracy: The Revisionist Debate 1896–1898*, 1–37. Cambridge: Cambridge University Press.

Tudor, H. 1993. Introduction to Henry Tudor, ed. *Bernstein: The Preconditions of Socialism*, xv–xxxvi. Cambridge: Cambridge University Press.

Turner, M. 2004. "Agriculture, 1860–1914." R. Floud and P. Johnson, eds. *The Cambridge Economic History of Modern Britain II: Economic Maturity, 1860–1939*, 133–60. Cambridge: Cambridge University Press.

Viner, J. 1933. "An Unpublished Letter of Ricardo to Matthus." *Journal of Political Economy* 41: 117–20.

Viner, J. 1958 (1927). "Adam Smith and Laissez Faire." *The Long View and the Short*, 213–45. Glencoe, IL: The Free Press.

Vollgraf, C. E. and Jungnickel, J. 2002 (1994). "'Marx in Marx's Words?' On Engels's Edition of the Main Manuscript of Book 3 of Capital." *International Journal of Political Economy* 32: 35–78.

Vygodskii, V. 2002. "Discussion on the Article by Vollgraff and Jungnickel." *International Journal of Political Economy 32*: 79–82.

Wade, J. 1826. *Digest of Facts and Principles, on Banking and Commerce. With a Plan for Preventing Future Re-Actions.* London: Thomas Ward.

Wagner, A. 1879. *Allgemeine oder theoretische Volkswirtschaftslehre.* Erste Theil: *Grundlegung.* In A. Wagner and E. Nasse, *Lehrbuch der Politischen Ökonomie I.* Leipzig and Heidelberg: Winter.

Weeks, J. 1981. *Capital and Exploitation.* Princeton: Princeton University Press.

Wilde, L. 1999. "Engels and the Contradictions of Revolutionary Strategy." In M. B. Steger and T. Carver, eds. *Engels after Marx,* 197–214. University Park, PA: The Pennsylvania State University Press.

Williamson, O. E. 1968. "Wage Rates as a Barrier to Entry: The Pennington Case in Perspective." *Quarterly Journal of Economics 82*: 85–116.

Wood, G. H. 1962 (1909). "Real Wages and the Standard of Comfort since 1850." In E. M. Carus-Wilson, ed. *Essays in Economic History 3,* 132–43. London: Edward Arnold.

Index

Aarons, E., 6
abstraction *see* methodology of Marxian political economy
Adler, V., 275, 359
agriculture
  and American protectionism, 133
  British competitiveness threatened, 133, 147, 149, 273–4
  communist, 63, 69, 139, 141, 149
    autarky, 149, 174, 319
  cooperative, 149
  classes, 197
  and historical Transformation, 119–20
  and land scarcity, 32, 56–7
  low capital composition, 118
  migration to towns, 44, 254
  proletariat, 44, 197, 254, 260
  and real wages, 260
  scientific, 296
  unionization, 254, 321
  see also: rent, Russia
alienation, 68, 93
Alison, A., 35, 37, 38, 73, 76, 79
Alison, W.P., 79
allocation *see* competitive price mechanism
America
  agricultural development, 149
  America 1887 and Britain 1844 compared, 327
  business practice, 290
  and Chinese immigration, 275–6
  constitutional progress, 176, 186–9, 201–2, 208, 213, 217, 222, 354
  growth of proletariat, 269, 327
  industrial concentration, 164
  real-wage decline forecast, 327
  see also: international trade policy

"American Food and the Land Question," 149, 273
Anderson, K., 306
Andler, C., 80, 81
Andréas, B., 61
Anti Corn-Law League, 33, 42–3
Anti-Dühring, 5, 6, 10, 33, 125, 127, 149, 151, 153, 161, 163, 164, 226, 260, 322, 324
  communist organization, 145–8, 157–8, 296
  historical materialism, 300, 329, 333, 337–8
  Preface 1885, 126, 295, 311
Arkwright, Sir R., 39, 43
Arthur, C. J., 304, 306–7
Ashley, Lord, 43, 238
Austria, 39, 211, 214, 219, 277, 359
Austrian economics, 292, 317
Avineri, S., 18

Babbage, C., 285
Bains, E., 73, 79
Bakunin, M., 20, 247
Bank Acts 1818, 1844, 236
Baran, P. A., 124
Barth, P., 330, 341
Bastiat, C. F., 98
Bauer, Bruno, 3, 42
Bauer, Edgar, 2, 3, 4, 42
Beales, H. L., 365, 366
Beamish, R., 10
Bebel, A., 139, 149, 150, 201, 212, 225, 226, 228, 255, 263, 269, 289, 321, 326, 359
behavior
  national character, 195, 216, 272, 315, 336–8, 339
  working-class *embourgeoisement*, 270–1, 278, 315, 338
Berlin, I., 22–3, 294, 295, 359